Social Problems, Law, and Society

Understanding Social Problems: An SSSP Presidential Series

Understanding Social Problems is a textbook series published in collaboration with the Society for the Study of Social Problems, under the direction of the SSSP Editorial and Publications Committee. The anthologies introduce students to the principles for assessing social problems and to exemplary research studies in the field. Articles selected from the society's leading journal, *Social Problems*, are chosen for their coverage, their relevance, and their accessibility to students. Introductions written by each book's editors situate the issues raised by the articles into a broader sociological perspective.

All royalties from this series go to support the SSSP and its activities.

Titles in the Series

Social Problems across the Life Course

Edited by Helena Z. Lopata and
Judith A. Levy

Drugs, Alcohol, and Social Problems

Edited by James D. Orcutt and
David R. Rudy

Health and Health Care as Social Problems

Edited by Peter Conrad and Valerie Leiter

Forthcoming

Violence against Women

Edited by Claire M. Renzetti and
Raquel Bergen

Social Problems, Law, and Society

EDITED BY
A. KATHRYN STOUT
RICHARD A. DELLO BUONO
WILLIAM J. CHAMBLISS

ROWMAN & LITTLEFIELD PUBLISHERS, INC.
Lanham • Boulder • New York • Toronto • Oxford

ROWMAN & LITTLEFIELD PUBLISHERS, INC.

Published in the United States of America
by Rowman & Littlefield Publishers, Inc.
A wholly owned subsidiary of The Rowman & Littlefield Publishing Group, Inc.
4501 Forbes Boulevard, Suite 200, Lanham, Maryland 20706
www.rowmanlittlefield.com

PO Box 317,
Oxford
OX2 9RU, UK

British Library Cataloguing in Publication Information Available

Library of Congress Cataloging-in-Publication Data

Social problems, law, and society / edited by A. Kathryn Stout, Richard A. Dello Buono, William J. Chambliss.
p. cm. — (Society for the Study of Social Problems presidential series)
Includes bibliographical references and index.
ISBN 0-7425-4206-8 (cloth : alk. paper) — ISBN 0-7425-4207-6 (pbk. : alk. paper)
1. Sociological jurisprudence. 2. Social problems. 3. Law—Social apsects—United States. I. Stout, Angela Kathryn. II. Dello Buono, Richard Alan. III. Chambliss, William J., 1956– IV. Series.
K370.S645 2004
340'.115—dc22

2004004369

Printed in the United States of America

∞™ The paper used in this publication meets the minimum requirements of American National Standard for Information Sciences—Permanence of Paper for Printed Library Materials, ANSI/NISO Z39.48-1992.

Contents

Preface

The articles that follow offer readers a substantial exposure to critical studies in the sociology of law, social movements, and social problems. After an exhaustive consideration of all work published since 1953 in the prestigious journal *Social Problems*, we have made the following selection in order to acquaint students with an evolving, critical perspective focused on law and society. Beginning with several defining works and moving forward into some of the most innovative studies published in recent years, this unique anthology presents a developing theoretical trajectory that will continue to spawn advances in the field. Students will be pleasantly surprised at the liveliness and readability of the articles, some of which are purely theoretical while others make important substantive statements by way of empirical investigation. In addition, the editors have provided three additional chapters that offer context and discussion for the collection to help readers digest the significance of the collection as a whole.

This text reader forms part of a larger project known as the Society for the Study of Social Problems (SSSP) Presidential Series that is being published by Rowman & Littlefield as part of an innovative line of academic texts dedicated to understanding social problems. The series serves as testimony to the SSSP's vision of investigating urgent social problems from interdisciplinary perspectives, the ultimate aim of which is to further the pursuit of scholarly activism and enhance its impact on public policy, grassroots organizing, and social awareness.

The idea for the SSSP Presidential Series arose out of extended discussions that focused on the need to help bring the cutting-edge analyses being produced in the journal *Social Problems* directly into course discussions at the undergraduate and graduate academic levels. Clearly, it is there that the process of activist scholarship enjoys one of its primary points of departure, initiating a complex journey from presentation to discussion, from examination to critique, from stimulation to commitment, and from theory to praxis.

For the SSSP, the pursuit of scholarly activism is its distinguishing characteristic as a professional association. Their annual meetings promote an ongoing encounter of academic professionals, social practitioners, and social activists, all from diverse communities and points of view. By sponsoring competitions and awards, support funds and academic scholarships, and structured spaces for discussion where professors, students, practitioners, and activists can all learn from one another, the SSSP continually strives to develop its unique positioning as a professional, scholar-activist community dedicated to the understanding of and engagement with pressing social problems. The SSSP's acclaimed journal *Social Problems* has for over half a century continued to be one of the most widely cited journals specialized in the study of social concerns. In addition, the triannual *Social Problems Forum* (formerly *The SSSP Newsletter*) has since 1953 stimulated more informal and timely discussions of pressing social issues and projects being put forth by the association. By sponsoring the Presidential Series on Understanding Social Problems, the SSSP has now created yet another channel for placing its focused research into active course discussion by scholars.

This series would never have been brought to fruition without the insistent and sustained efforts of several recent SSSP presidents, including Pamela Roby, Robert Perrucci, John Galliher, and especially Joel Best. Former executive editor Dean Birkenkamp of Rowman & Littlefield also deserves special mention for his vision and cooperation with the SSSP in developing this project. The successful realization of the series would also have been impossible to imagine without the support and tireless efforts of the SSSP's administrative officer Michele Smith Koontz and executive officer Tom Hood.

With regard to the present volume, we would like to additionally thank Maggie Anderson who served as the chair of the SSSP Editorial and Publications Committee, as well as the other committee members for their deliberation and recommendations. We also wish to thank Lorraine Coops, publisher relations associate at JSTOR, for her assistance in acquiring the digitalized versions of previously published *Social Problems* articles as well as assistant editor Jessica Gribble and especially Stephen Driver of the editorial staff of Rowman & Littlefield for all of their help and patience in managing production logistics. Teresa Grygiel provided invaluable technical assistance for which we are grateful.

Finally, we would like to dedicate this volume to the memory of two extraordinary women who in so many ways, both within and outside of the SSSP, helped to inspire successive generations of scholar-activists:

Helena Z. Lopata (1925–2003)
1982–83 SSSP president
and
Beth B. Hess (1928–2003)
1997–98 SSSP president

Their contributions to the struggle for equality and social justice will not soon be forgotten.

Part I

ESTABLISHING THE CONTEXT

CHAPTER 1

Critical Perspectives on Law and Society*

A *SOCIAL PROBLEMS* APPROACH

Richard A. Dello Buono

For over half a century, scholars have published their innovative work in the journal *Social Problems*, seeking to develop critical approaches for the sake of greater understanding and in order to transform the political, economic, and social relations that generate them. One area of research that has shown great promise emerged among scholars who chose to focus on the legal order, seeking to integrate the study of social problems with trends that were developing within the fields of deviance, critical criminology, and the sociology of law. The present volume invites readers to share in this tradition by grappling with a selection of key *Social Problems* articles written by notable experts in the field.

In this introductory chapter and in the chapter by Kathryn Stout that follows, we provide a substantive discussion of the theoretical and social context in which the studies reprinted in this book have developed. The articles we have included are written from a diverse set of paradigmatic angles. What ties them together is their commitment to the development of a critical approach. Many emphasize the important relationship between social movements and the state in comprehending specific, selected social problems. By exploring the interstitial area between the sociology of law, social problems, and social movements, these studies trace out a theoretical trajectory that illustrates many of the important contributions made by social constructionists as well as formative statements made by their more conflict-oriented critics. The collection as a whole suggests the need to ultimately move beyond both constructionist and conflict approaches in order to formulate an adequate, critical approach to contemporary studies of social problems, law, and society. The concluding chapter by William Chambliss illustrates some of the challenges facing those working in this area, arguing that a dialectical model can help overcome the weaknesses in existing theories.

* This approach refers to the collective position of various authors who have published critical analyses in the journal *Social Problems*, the official journal of the Society for the Study of Social Problems (SSSP).

Social Problems and the Critical Tradition

> Every time intellectuals have the chance to speak, yet do not speak, they join the forces that train people not to be able to think and imagine and feel in morally and politically adequate ways. When they do not demand that the secrecy that makes elite decisions absolute and unchallengeable be removed, they too are part of the passive conspiracy to kill off public scrutiny. When they do not speak, when they do not demand, when they do not think and feel and act as intellectuals—and so as public individuals—they too contribute to the moral paralysis, the intellectual rigidity, that now grip both leaders and led around the world. C. Wright Mills, *The Causes of World War III* (1958: 151)

The Society for the Study of Social Problems (SSSP), founded in 1951, constituted from its very beginnings a leading voice in the area of critical perspectives on social issues. Born as a breakaway alternative to the American Sociological Association (Dello Buono 1990), the founders of the SSSP sought to "bring sociological research and theorizing closer to pressing human concerns of the day" (Galliher and Galliher 1995: 99). Former SSSP President S. M. Miller, a graduate student at the time he participated in the Association's founding meeting, offers the following testimony:

> The Society for the Study of Social Problems (SSSP) was born in opposition to the prevailing practices and spirit of the American Sociological Society. . . . What I hoped is that the SSSP would be more than an alternative to ASA sociology. That it would develop a different kind of social science—engaged and facing the contradictions of that engagement. (Miller 2001: 144)

Reflecting back on the decades that have transpired since the Association's founding, former SSSP President (1999–2000) and *Social Problems* editor Robert Perrucci declared the following in his memorable Presidential Address:

> SSSP members have, for 50 years, been successful in committing Galileo's most obvious crime, namely, telling the many truths revealed by their research about the social universe. However, I have called upon you to commit Galileo's hidden crime, namely, conveying those truths to the public in popular styles of writing and speaking. This crime has its personal and professional risks. The reward systems of many of our employing organizations may not be responsive to efforts to bring our message to the public in unconventional ways. But there can be enormous personal satisfaction and fulfillment that comes from advocacy in the pursuit of social justice. (Perrucci 2001: 166)

There can be little question that apart from annual meetings, one of the most important expressions of the SSSP's work can be found in its journal *Social Problems.* This scholarly publication began to circulate in 1953 and has since produced a vast literature that has notably influenced the development of contemporary sociology. Numerous, now-classic statements found in *Social Problems* such as Alvin Gouldner's (1962) "The Myth of a Value-Free Sociology" and Howard Becker's (1967) "Whose Side Are We On?" have continually reaffirmed the critical, value-engaged, and progressive orientation of the journal that was established at its inception.

But within the critical community of scholarship being engendered by *Social Problems,* an intensifying theoretical divergence began to take shape. On one side was a developing appreciation for "social definitionist" approaches that explored in various ways the more subjective aspects of social action and interaction. Here the emphasis was placed on understanding the role of symbols and the process through which everyday social meanings are constructed, and particularly with regard to how such definitional meanings affected everyday institutional life. These "definitionist" currents included symbolic interactionism, the labeling theory of deviance, societal reaction theory, phenomenological sociology, ethnomethodology, and social constructionism. These approaches shared both a theoretical and practical concern for the historical construction of particular sets of social meanings or "labels" and the patterned social processes by which such meanings became attached to social actors and their situational behaviors. Particularly influential in the field of social problems was the "social constructionist" approach pioneered by Spector and Kitsuse (1973, 1977). Theorized about how social actors systematically come to define certain social conditions as "problematic," thus offering a subjectivistic, nonconventional explanation of the "natural history" or rise and fall of specific social problems.

Social definitionist perspectives in all of their varieties posed a substantial challenge to the functionalist orthodoxy that previously dominated sociology, and as such gained considerable prominence in SSSP circles and in the journal *Social Problems* (Brekhus, Brekhus, and Galliher 2001). Major "definitionist" figures from the symbolic interactionist and later, social constructionist perspectives such as Herbert Blumer, Kai Erikson, Edwin Lemert, Malcolm Spector, John Kitsuse, Peter Conrad, and Joel Best served either as presidents or vice-presidents of the SSSP, or as editors of *Social Problems.* Articles appearing in the journal such as Stephen Pfohl's "The 'Discovery' of Child Abuse" (1977) and Malcolm Spector and John Kitsuse's (1973b) "Toward a Sociology of Social Problems," just to pick two, proved to be defining moments in articulating what eventually coalesced into the distinctively definitionist sociological approach to social problems that scholars now refer to as "social constructionism."

At the same time, however, many analysts working on a more "objectivistic terrain" in the tradition of structural sociologists such as Robert Merton and others likewise sought to challenge the sociological mainstream and extend their critical structural approaches in new directions. These perspectives primarily took up positions in conflict-oriented sociologies inspired by critical readings of Weber and Marx. Some within this tradition, like former SSSP President (1960–61) Alvin Gouldner, were able to sense that sociology's encounter with Marx would ultimately result in a "Coming Crisis" of the field (Gouldner 1970).

All of this upheaval was felt within studies of deviance, criminology, and the sociology of law where an explosion of critical thinking took hold in the 1960–70s. The style of sociology associated with the complex legacy of Max Weber had been paradigmatic for earlier generations of scholars interested in the studies of law and society. The extraordinary influence of studies such as William Chambliss' *A Sociological Analysis of the Law of Vagrancy* (1964) (reprinted in the present volume) contributed to a more critical reading of Weber and helped spawn a new generation of critical criminology and legal studies in the 1960s that eventually favored more dialectical approaches. In recognition of this tradition, we have included several representative pieces in the present volume so as to show how they formed early arguments concerning the limitations of social "constructionist" approaches and the need for critical theorists to eventually transcend them.

Over the course of several decades, the critical tradition within structural sociology continued to evolve, shaped in part by the changing historical conditions taking place in the late twentieth century. Numerous debates raged among Marxian theorists such as Antonio Gramsci, Louis Althusser, Nicos Poulantzas, Ralph Miliband, and others concerning the nature of the capitalist state in advanced capitalism. Sociologists such as Immanuel Wallerstein began to turn critical attention to the "capitalist world-system," paving the way for others to pursue the impact of increasing globalization upon issues related to law and society. Within the SSSP, the 1992–93 presidency of William Chambliss turned the thematic focus of the Association's annual meeting directly upon the global character of social problems, something which drew into sharp relief the apparent limitations of social constructionism with its roots in a more micro-sociological approach. These globalization themes soon became echoed in *Social Problems* and in the association's newsletter *The SSSP Forum* where submissions that grappled with global themes steadily increased throughout the 1990s.

When David Smith, a prominent scholar in international political economy, assumed the editorship of *Social Problems,* he published a special issue in late 2001 on "Globalization and Social Problems," something that turned out to be the first, post-September 11 issue of the journal (Smith 2001). It now became increasingly clear that at the turn of the century, globalized themes associated with international sex tourism (Wonders and Michalowski 2001), changing labor conditions under global economic restructuring (Parrado and Zenteno 2001; Anderson, Schulman, and Wood 2001), international legal discourses concerning the practice of female mutilation (Boyle, Songora, and Foss 2001), and others had assumed their proper place within social problems studies. By placing the accelerating tendencies of a globalized political economy squarely in the analytical limelight, the study of social problems assumed a much broader perspective than was heretofore the case. Trends in the misconduct of global capital and repression as a tool of state reproduction of global capital now challenged sociologists, criminologists, and others to revisit and rethink their paradigmatic foundations. Issues of civil rights, once seen more narrowly in a national context, would now become increasingly defined by global conventions and new, "universalizing" human rights terminologies. At the same time, the links between legal repression and global affairs would become increasingly apparent and it now seemed obvious that an urgent need existed to reconcile contemporary socio-legal studies to the changing political economy of globalized capitalism.

Even as we publish the present book, the need to adequately reconceptualize the national state in understanding the legal order and the reproduction of the larger political, economic, and social relations of the global political economy has become an increasingly acute challenge. Recent studies, including several in this volume, illustrate the desirability of going beyond mainstream social constructionism in critical studies of law and social problems. In this collection, we seek to build upon constructionist insights while stressing the necessity to reconnect with the larger national and global political economy that form the structural backdrop for state and social movement dynamics associated with prominent social problems.

Taking Social Constructionism beyond Conflict Theory

There is no question that social constructionism transformed the contemporary landscape of sociology, criminology, and legal studies. Many theorists schooled within the social constructionist tradition have alluded to the need for a processual analysis of structured power relations and the dynamics of their social negotiation. But the paradigmatic limits which confront mainstream constructionism in fulfilling this task eventually become apparent, especially when faced with the larger task of adequately conceptualizing the relationship of law, the state, and social problems in an era of rapidly changing, globalized capitalist development.

The present volume seeks to acquaint readers with these theoretical challenges by emphasizing the need to more fully capture the dynamics of social movements as they stand in relation to the state and as they develop within the larger and historically evolving political economy. A critical sociology of law perspective that remains fundamentally sensitive to the larger political economy offers the best means for grasping the interrelationship between the state and social movements as they are mediated through the legal process. While some of the authors published in this collection will attribute the inspiration of their work on law and society to social constructionism, it is also clear that they seek to weave into their work ever more adequate hybrids of critical and power-centered perspectives that can enable them to apply their interpretative insights more critically to the exploitative systems of labor relations, patriarchy, racial and ethnic discrimination, etc.

Since the inception of *Social Problems*, racial inequality has been a major topic of the publication's substantive focus (Brekhus, Brekhus, and Galliher 2001). At the same time, the journal's initial emphasis on crime, delinquency, deviance, mental illness, social science ethics, and poverty eventually shifted toward an increasing concern with gender and social movements (Brekhus, Brekhus, and Galliher 2001). In the second section of this book, we present some empirical studies from *Social Problems* that focus upon changing laws resulting from periods of social conflict fueled by prevailing systems of social stratification within specific periods of U.S. history. The pieces illustrate why problems of social stratification related to class, race, and gender require analyses that go beyond both mainstream constructionist and pluralist conflict approaches to law and society. Critical social problems such as labor rights, the struggle for racial inequality, and equal treatment in and outside of the 20th Century welfare state, and the societal response to hate crimes, together form the backdrop for some innovative analyses of the legal order. Collectively, these chapters illustrate a growing realization of the need to understand the underlying linkages which social class shares with other forms of social stratification such as race and gender, particularly when these dimensions become expressed in highly visible and complex manifestations of social problems.

By the 1990s, social movements had become a major focus of inquiry within the journal *Social Problems* (Brekhus, Brekhus, and Galliher 2001). In essence, social movements are organized expressions of the resistance generated in response to social contradictions and state policies and institutions which attempt to mediate contradictory social forces (Stout 1989: 110–111) At the same time, organized forms of social resistance as a product of such dynamics tend to unfold at uneven rhythms and contain only the potential for unity and effectively coordinated actions. (Stout and Dello Buono 1991: 345). As Kathryn Stout argues more fully in the chapter that follows, the activities of social movements generally create a dilemma for the state in its ongoing reproduction of the political economy. It can suffice to say here that the challenge which social movements pose for the state, and increasingly, to the global organization of capitalist production, constitutes a visible manifestation of the underlying contradictions of the new international order. This in turn means that the study of the legal limits of protest and the regulation of social movement activity can continue to provide critical insights into social change, but only if it transcends the limitations of traditional social movements theory. In the present volume, we have selected three studies that nicely illustrate the pivotal role of social movements in confronting the state with regard to several, high-profile social problems.

As mentioned earlier, the increasing globalization of the late 20th and early 21st Centuries confronts established sociological literature with fundamental challenges. Paradigms long based in a nation-centered set of categories now join the ranks of Eurocentric, ethnocentric, and patriarchal modes of thinking as items earmarked for obsolescence. As Chambliss succinctly puts it:

> State organized crimes, environmental crimes, crimes against humanity, human rights crimes, and the violations of international treaties increasingly must take center stage in criminology. The nation-state focused definition of crime as acts that are a violation of a particular nation's laws will not suffice unless criminology is to be relegated to some arcane field with no relevance to the issues and problems emerging in the "global village." (Chambliss 1995: 9)

This statement has far-reaching implications for the ongoing and future study of law and society. The failure to accomplish what amounts to a paradigmatic shift in our approach to criminology, law, and social problems would be tantamount to abandoning the critical tradition which C. Wright Mills and others had earlier initiated. How else can we make sense of the expressions of legal repression in the wake of the events of September 11, 2001, as embodied in the Patriot Act, the resurrection of military tribunals, or the widely condemned incarceration practices conducted at the U.S. detention facility at Guantanamo Bay, Cuba? Can criminology be critical if it accepts the official ideological "frame" which portrays the devastating events of September 11 as the "cause" of repressive state conduct? We maintain that just as critical innovation in sociological thinking first helped us to understand the imposition of vagrancy laws as an attempt to exert legal control over labor on the part of crisis-ridden feudal states, new and critical interpretations will now be needed to shed light on the affairs of interventionist states in the current drama of global capitalist realignment being played out in the early twenty-first century.

Changing global conditions affect the nature and capacities of national and transnational social movements. Technological developments in electronic networking, first developed by the Pentagon and later utilized by transnational capital in the redesign of production into global commodity chains, have now emerged as a dynamic factor that promotes grassroots organizing by a variety of social movements (see Waterman 1977). The exponential growth of electronic mail, facilitated by fiber optics and wide spectrum channeling of the Internet, has made possible the rise of new and extremely agile forms of global informational networking that continues to create new possibilities for antiglobalization, environmental, women's, and other social activist groups. The simmering praxis of activists engaged in a worldwide struggle to appropriate a modicum of the technological means to communicate and network represents an accelerating transformation of the technology formerly employed almost exclusively by capital in establishing its global hegemony.

Perhaps critical media studies first sensed the importance of this trend by revealing how corporate-controlled media that engage in "framing" and censorship could both accelerate antidemocratic tendencies as well as promote the expansion of alternative flows of information among grassroots organizations being empowered by the explosion of electronic networking. All of this will increasingly affect changing global perceptions of what constitutes social problems such as corporate "misconduct." After all, it wasn't long ago that corporations could reliably rely on the transnational controlled mass media to minimize international awareness of their global profit strategies. At the same time, it is certainly true that social control agents can also use these same technological advances that promote grassroots movement building in order to monitor such activities more easily and without detection.

The fourth section of the present volume includes several articles that in different ways emphasize the need to incorporate global approaches to law and society. They show that crime and state misconduct, state repression and popular resistance, civil rights movements and international solidarity, and even the very notion of national citizenship itself are all processes increasingly being structured by a globalized logic. The imposing manner in which globalization is shaping the development of theoretical analysis makes ever-more explicit an emerging consensus among critical theorists around the need to remain analytically grounded in the larger political economy in their approach to social problems, law, and society.

So as to illustrate some of the theoretical points made earlier, I will now draw this introductory chapter to a close by briefly focusing on a particular contemporary social problem known as "McDonaldization." My goal here is a heuristic one as I seek to convey the "flavor" of the various approaches to social problems, law, and society discussed so far.

"McDonaldization" as a Social Problem[1]: An Illustration

> "Our vision is to dominate the global foodservice marketplace . . ." (McDonald's Corporation Annual Report to the Shareholders 1994: 2).[2]

The concept of "McDonaldization" was popularized by George Ritzer (1993) to refer to the growing global domination of "fast food" principles as they enter all aspects of social life. In Ritzer's neo-Weberian approach, modern life plunges headlong into the gloom and doom of a global domination termed the "iron cage of McDonaldization" as society is increasingly consumed by values of efficiency, calculability, predictability, and impersonality, or in short, increasing rationality (1993: 147). Notwithstanding my critique of the "privatization" of theoretical imagery performed by Ritzer when expounding his "McDonaldization thesis" (Dello Buono 1995), I view this "problem" of McDonaldization as an interesting and useful point of departure to illustrate various approaches to social problems, law, and society.

Orthodox Weberian macrosociological approaches see changing values and technology as manifestations of a large-scale, ideal-typical social development that involves the increasing rationalization of social life. Organizational theorists and economic sociologists within the Weberian mainstream seek to analyze conflicts between social class or status groups on the one hand and a changing technology and human values set on the other, something that in their reified view appears to develop in history independent from the intentions of human actors (Dello Buono 1981). As can be seen in a variety of contemporary applications (e.g., Chandler 1977), conservative interpretations of Weber's perspective have failed to conceptualize the totality of historical social change because of their overall lack of a dialectical approach and have instead yielded an accumulated literature that remains intimately compatible with neoliberal corporate ideology at the expense of a critical sociological approach (Dello Buono 1995: 29).

Consistent with orthodox Weberian approaches, the elements of organized social resistance to "McDonaldization" are only superficially considered in Ritzer's analysis and are essentially explained away, mostly as a futile and "charismatic" resistance that makes its last gasp from within the highly rationalized sectors of modern society. This orthodox Weberian perspective can be contrasted with interactionist and labeling perspectives that critique this approach to the process of increasing rationality, arguing instead for an even more subjectivistic perspective that places the emphasis upon a social "claims-making" process (Spector and Kitsuse 1973; 1977).

For symbolic interactionists, social problems are those things that people come to label "problematic" through a patterned social *process*. Such theorists attempt to understand how it is that people "construct" social problems by defining certain social conditions as such. The interactionist formulation of social problems developed by Spector and Kitsuse (1973; 1977) utilized what they termed a "natural history approach" to analyze social problems emerging through a process seen, generally, as following a common pattern. As mentioned earlier, this "definitionist" style of analysis that has since become known as social constructionism considers that every social problem has a historical trajectory or a kind of "rise and fall" in prominence. The natural history approach suggests that there are several "stages" in which people who are making claims contribute to the evolution of a social problem. It is an approach that essentially views social problems as subjective "claims-making activities" whereby people actively make assertions or claims as to the existence of a problematic condition. Eventually, the social problem can fade away when people cease making claims as to its existence.

Interestingly, this constructionist approach tends to deemphasize and at times completely *ignores* the validity of the claims being made by people, choosing instead to focus upon the patterned social reaction to their claims. Indeed, the actual existence of an objectively present social condition is, technically speaking, *irrelevant.* In other words, what is important is the subjective dimension, i.e., what people *say, think, or believe* is problematic, this rather than anything having to do with actual, underlying material conditions. If people *believe* that such problems exist, that is entirely sufficient to constitute a *real* social problem. In this sense, "witches," "global warming," "demonic possession," "racism," "declining family values," "cigarette smoking," "same-sex relationships," "child hyperactivity," "unsafe sex," "undocumented workers," and "terrorism" are all equally eligible to evolve into the status of social problems, this in accordance with the organized efforts of people who seriously allege them to exist and who advance such claims against an evolving backdrop of official responses to their accusations.

This highly *processual* approach captured the "ebb and flow" character of social problems by showing how they *emerge* in a particular social context and in so doing, managed to attribute significant importance, at least in principle, to organized social movements in the shaping of emergent social problems. While social constructionism undeniably demonstrated the importance of subjective factors in the social creation of "problems," concerns grew that it may be very disempowering to view problems solely through the lens of human subjectivity. Many critics argue that this perspective focuses too heavily on the most superficial aspects of social problems and succeeds only in transforming them into a purely intellectual endeavor. Little effort seemed to be placed on explaining *why* specific problems seem to emerge when they do. Most theorists operating from within nonconstructionist sociological paradigms remained uncomfortable with the definitionist tendency to trivialize the importance of objective social conditions in shaping emerging social problems.

The maturation of subjectively oriented, interactionist currents into social constructionism was nevertheless marked by an increasing emphasis on the power relations that lurk behind the dynamics of social problem "creation." In this process, the more critical theorists operating within this perspective began to break ranks with the more "value-free" attitude of earlier interactionist theorists. Increasing emphasis was instead placed upon pressing social issues and more attention was given to the structural sources of power that permit elites to heavily influence *which* conditions and conflicts are defined as "problems" as opposed to nonproblems. As constructionism gradually expanded its consideration of the more macrosocial factors leading people to consider certain social conditions as "problematic," the critical content of their approach unquestionably deepened. This notwithstanding, a weak conceptualization of the state along with a pervasive tendency to fail to link back up with the larger structures of the political economy constitute major limitations to the constructionist approach to social problems, law, and society.

Returning to the example of McDonaldization, if social constructionists were to focus upon the "natural history" of McDonald's products as a social problem, they might begin by considering the acquisition of a "stigma" by McDonaldization as earlier, Fordist-era labels of thrifty, piping-hot "fast" products, and the "take-out," "drive-in," and "automat" modalities of prepared foods gave way beginning in the 1970s to more problematic labels, e.g., "high-fat, junk food," "nonrecyclable, fast-food container pollution," "chain store sweatshops," "fast-food women," and so on. The "discovery of fast food/junk food" as a social problem based in McDonaldization processes might be analyzed as it emerged from the claims-making efforts of certain key social sectors or communities, such as certain medical specialists, nutritionists, and other dietary experts, or even certain religious communities seeking a return to more traditional and spiritually sound forms of food consumption. By considering the ongoing activities of these communities, along with the official responses to them, constructionists could identify the problematic nature of McDonaldized practices through a patterned series of stages whereby definitional claims that assert various forms of social harm caused by McDonaldized behaviors become socially recognized. Those social constructionist analyses that move the furthest toward linking their study to the overall relations of power shaping this social definitioning process would come closest to achieving a more critical perspective on the problem of McDonaldization.

In contrast to social constructionism, a more structural, dialectical approach would seek to understand the problem of "McDonaldization" as a contradictory historical tendency which inexorably generates resistance, state, and suprastate responses, all of which results in dynamic forces that actively condition the unfolding conduct of capitalist firms such as the McDonald's Corporation itself as well as the anti-McDonald's social movement organizations that oppose it. This kind of approach more generally sees globalizing capital in the light of the social antagonisms that it spawns and which can be found at multiple levels, something which in time generates multiple centers of resistance. Eventually, corporate forces are compelled to respond to this resistance and do so through corporate strategies aimed at disarticulating resistance as insurgent obstacles to profit (Dello Buono 1995). These response strategies, themselves contradictory, can in turn lead to new focal points of resistance. In contrast to mainstream Weberian approaches, a more critical, dialectical understanding of the social problem of McDonaldization must seek to carefully analyze all those social currents that emerge in opposition to capital and the extent to which organized social movements can thwart unilateral attempts to impose a globalized logic of capitalist exploitation upon ever-expanding terrains of everyday life (Dello Buono 1995).

A critical, dialectical approach to law leads us to expect that the legal order plays in various ways a prominent mediating role as state, supranational, and quasi-state authorities seek to contain emerging social conflicts from threatening the larger profit system upon which the global accumulation of capital depends. It is precisely here that the role of social movements in this dialectical interplay becomes essential. To take the particular case of the McDonald's Corporation as an archetypical example, its profit-seeking conduct over a period of decades[3] has led to numerous expressions of organized protest in opposition to the various ecologically contaminating effects of its packaging, harmful dietary and toxic effects of packaging and nutritional content upon consumers, poor-working conditions and anti-union practices on the part of the corporation, impact upon Third-World hunger and global ecological harm caused by destruction of rainforests in order to encourage increased cattle grazing, exploitation of children through mass advertising of nutritionally unhealthy processed food products, and so on. During the 1980s, the "McToxics" campaign emerged in the United States as thousands protested the corporation's packaging policies, focusing upon the styrofoam wrap which by its sheer volume and reticent degradability contributed to serious disposal problems, including ozone depletion and contamination caused by its burning, as well as the consumer health risks caused by direct contact of hot foods with the disposable containers (Dello Buono 1995). While the diverse sectors that came together in this consumer protest movement eventually succeeded in forcing McDonald's to do away with their polystyrene foam packaging in the United States, the globalized nature of the corporation allowed it to shift its package inventory overseas where it continued to *legally* use the harmful materials in its product sales.

Meanwhile, the McDonald's Corporation has found itself repeatedly compelled to respond to dilemmas caused by public concerns in its home country over its conduct. In 1987, for example, McDonald's launched a major advertising campaign designed to neutralize persistent and increasingly well-organized complaints on the part of nutrition and public health groups about the unsuitability of its fast-food products, especially for children who constitute a major share of the fast-food market and who have been a major object of McDonald's advertising. Shortly after their advertising "counteroffensive" was placed into mass circulation, a letter was sent to the McDonald's Corporation in April 1987 from the attorney general offices of the states of Texas, California, and New York. Their joint review concluded that the massive advertising campaign McDonald's launched to convince the public that their food products are nutritious was in fact deceptive, that McDonald's food is not nutritious overall, and that the Corporation was hereby requested to cease and desist their advertising or risk combined legal action by the three states. McDonald's, a corporation where a significant chunk of sales revenues has always been dedicated to advertising (roughly 6 percent in 1993 according to McDonald's Corporation Annual Report) (Dello Buono 1995), needed to rethink how it would confront a growing social movement resistance to its profit-seeking conduct.

As the company regrouped its forces, it turned its attention to Europe where anti-McDonald's forces were steadily in ascent. In England, the McDonald's Corporation decided to launch a two-pronged offensive that would consist of a sustained advertising campaign alongside of a concerted effort to silence its critics. Here, the firm decided to draw anti-McDonald's forces into the legal arena where the well-established structures of pro-business, state mediation could play a decisive role in protecting its realization of profits. In so doing, it chose the strategy of a "SLAPP" or a Strategic Lawsuit Against Public Participation (Canan and Pring 1988). SLAPPs involve the use of civil tort action to stifle political activism and social movement organizing. A legal strategy that gained considerable notoriety toward the latter decades of the 20th Century, SLAPPs are attractive to powerful social actors, particularly corporations, because of their ability to drag opponents (such as activists and organizers of campaigns contrary to the litigant's interests) into a judicial process that can deplete their opponents' resources while usually ensuring that the more sensitive, substantive issues are kept out of the proceedings (Canan and Pring 1988: 516).

The use of a SLAPP strategy by the McDonald's Corporation in the United Kingdom cannot be explained away *solely* as a product of the peculiarities of English libel law that happen to be exceptionally favorable for plaintiffs. Rather, it is an acute expression of the flexibility of globalized capital whereby transnational enterprises are able to analyze existing legal constraints in distinct national settings and selectively wield the corporate power they have derived from earlier accumulated profits in the service of an ever-expanding, profit-maximization logic. Critical criminologists and sociologists of law are well aware of the social-class character of the structures of legal mediation and how it generally presents a "stacked deck" against the activities of less powerful, resistance communities. In a globalized context, the theater of operations has now become expanded to a planetary level where the terrain is mined with variable sets of national legislation but presided over by only an incipient body of international law. In this global chess game, the indication for powerful transnational corporations to initiate a libel dispute in one nation can signify a preference for a labor dispute in another, or a formal complaint sanctioned under a free trade agreement in still another, and so on, all in accordance with global capital's strategic determination of where its interests are best favored by a particular regime of legality.

In this sense, litigation simply constitutes one more corporate tool to use in tandem with the other expressions of its established power via advertising, buyouts, dumping, etc. So while it may lead a fight in the labor courts, corporate power can likewise be deployed in the form of direct actions designed to influence the public and help further stack the deck toward a favorable legal outcome. An example of this was the long-running trade union dispute McDonald's fought in Ontario, Canada, during which McDonald's employed the highly controversial public relations tactic of instructing its employees to lie in the snow in the shape of the letters "NO" (to the trade unions). The use of corporate resources to thwart labor union organizing remains a pervasive response by transnationals to combat extensive trade union organizing taking place under the global banner of "McJobs," referring to highly exploitative, "flexible" labor force arrangements practiced by McDonaldized firms.

When McDonald's finally chose to orchestrate a SLAPP in the United Kingdom in 1990, it involved the filing of a libel suit against two unemployed members of the activist organization London Greenpeace. London Greenpeace shared common origins with Greenpeace UK but has remained autonomous from it since the 1970s, preferring to emphasize its locally organized and unaffiliated character within a larger ecology movement. The lawsuit revolved around McDonald's complaint concerning a fact sheet circulated by London Greenpeace entitled "What's Wrong with McDonald's?" (Dello Buono 1995). Testimony emerging from the lawsuit later showed that McDonald's had hired two separate private investigation firms to infiltrate London Greenpeace during 1989 so as to gather sufficient "intelligence" for identifying five actual individuals that could be named in a libel suit.

In mounting a SLAPP, McDonald's was building upon a well-established record of previous successes. Under English libel law, the burden is placed on the defendants to entirely prove the truthfulness of their statements if they are to avoid potentially costly penalties. In the past, McDonald's had been able to extract public retractions and apologies from its critics, including trade union groups, environmentalists, national newspapers, television networks, and even on the part of royalty itself in an incident involving Prince Philip. In 1990, however, two of five defendants named in the SLAPP refused to retract the statements contained in the London Greenpeace leaflet. The decision to take on McDonald's in the courts amounted to an act of unprecedented bravery by the unemployed activists, particularly since English law does not provide public defenders in libel cases. The two activists therefore had to mount their own defense against a multibillion dollar, corporate adversary. What subsequently unfolded turned out to be the longest trial of any kind in English history (1994–1997) and one of the most widely publicized SLAPPs ever.

The decisive factors shaping the outcome of what became known as the "McLibel case" included the corporation's vast legal expenditures and the challenges presented by the equally impressive coalition of social groups that organized support for the activists named as defendants. An extensive grassroots fund-raising effort on the part of a broad social movement coalition permitted the two McLibel defendants to sustain a comprehensive legal defense, including the introduction of scores of expert witnesses that effectively seemed in the public eye to put McDonald's itself on trial. Before it was over, the movement coalition had even managed to bring their concerns about English Libel law before the European Court of Human Rights.

Initially, the high-priced legal firm representing McDonald's won an important pretrial victory in the "McLibel suit" by beating back the defendants' request for a jury trial. A judge at the Royal Court of Justice upheld the plaintiff's arguments that the case involved scientific arguments far "too complex" for a lay jury to make any sense of and so it was decided that the trial would be heard by a single judge. Legal maneuvers on the part of McDonald's began to falter, however, as they tried to impede large parts of the defendants' evidence from being heard. Although the trial judge did indeed strike out large parts of defense testimony related to rainforest destruction and abusive labor practices employed across the globe on the part of McDonald's, the defense subsequently managed to win a landmark decision from the Court of Appeals that restored all defense testimony back into active consideration. Fortunately for the anti-McDonald's activists, McDonald's further complicated its case by making an important misstep just prior to the opening of the trial by printing 300,000 copies of its own leaflet for distribution at all U.K. outlets, referring to the London Greenpeace defendants as "liars." This afforded the two activists an opportunity to file a libel countersuit, with both sides subsequently agreeing to have both cases heard concurrently.

After a grueling three-year period of litigation, a judgment was handed down that found the two activists guilty of libel because they could not prove to the presiding judge's satisfaction that all of their claims had been scientifically substantiated. However, the judge acknowledged that *some* of their claims seem to be reasonably proven and thus ordered the amount requested by McDonald's to be reduced by one-half, resulting in a £60,000 fine. The defendants announced that they were unable to pay and would in any case refuse to pay compensation of any amount to McDonald's. About this time, press publicity was peaking around the case and the Corporation, now smarting from much unwanted negative attention, decided to drop its financial claim as well as its demands for an injunction against further protests on the part of the defendants.

Sensing that public opinion was now on their side in what appeared as a David versus Goliath confrontation, the activists decided to appeal the libel decision, bringing the case before three judges from the House of Lords. The appeal verdict partially reversed some of the earlier adverse libel ruling whereupon the activists then lodged a complaint against the British Government before the European Court of Human Rights for unfair libel laws and in defense of the right to criticize multinationals in a case that continued into 2003. The activists also sued the London Metropolitan Police for collaborating with private investigators hired by McDonald's during the trial, and in yet another de facto victory, the police opted for an out-of-court settlement of £10,000 payment to the defendants plus all court costs.

A dialectical approach to the complex and revealing litigation history surrounding the McLibel case helps to reveal numerous aspects of the use of global corporate power, the generally pro-business character of judicial processes, the important role played by social movements, the ongoing struggle for symbolic positioning in the court of public opinion, and so on. This kind of approach to the broader problem of McDonaldization can also help us to better grasp the interconnectedness of socially recognized problems such as "high-fat junk food," "McToxics," "McJobs," "McDeforestation," etc., drawing upon the insights of critical sociological approaches to social movements in order to more fully analyze the nature of the larger legal and symbolic struggles that shape the further development of these problems. A more detailed consideration of how social movements theory can be utilized in a critical, dialectical approach to social problems, law, and society will be presented in the next chapter.

Conclusion

Theorists within the social constructionist tradition point to the need for a processual analysis of structured power relations and the dynamics of their social negotiation. But the limits of such conceptions become apparent when confronted with the larger task of developing an adequate conceptualization of the relationship of law, the state, the political economy, and social problems. While their intellectual roots may in part be attributable to critical reflections on social constructionism and its intersection with conflict perspectives, dialectical theorists of law and society must move decisively beyond the limitations of social constructionism and Weberian pluralist/conflict theory. They can do so by redefining the object of inquiry to be the legal process as nestled in the objective, structured processes through which social relations of domination and repression are created, maintained, and continually resisted. Thus, I contend that in focusing more directly on structural relationships, dialectical approaches to law and society can overcome the excessively subjectivistic formulations of social constructionism while also going beyond the bounds of traditional conflict theory in rooting the source of ongoing social confrontations in the contradictions of the larger political economy.

In sum, we argue that a fuller understanding of the relationship between social problems, social movements, and social change in general will require a more integrated and dialectical explanatory framework in which the legal process in all of its relational complexity is accorded its appropriate weight. This volume presents a diverse set of styles and approaches from the influential journal *Social Problems* that seek to move in this direction. By beginning with landmark theoretical statements on law and society and then following with a variety of empirical studies that explore the contradictory dynamics of class, race, and gender in both a national and global context from a wide range of perspectives, it will be shown how social movements and the larger political economy play an important role in shaping state reactions to the challenges presented by contemporary social problems. There is an urgent need to more fully capture the dynamics of social movements as they stand in relation to the state and the political economy in which they emerge and develop as mediated through the legal process. It is to this key issue of incorporating social movements that we now turn in the following chapter.

Notes

1. This discussion draws heavily upon an article (Dello Buono 1995) which first appeared in the *SSSP Forum* (formerly known as the *SSSP Newsletter* and was later elaborated upon in a piece published (in Spanish) in Peru (Dello Buono 1998).

2. In their 1996 Annual Report to the Stockholders, the Corporation clarifies that "Together, the McDonald's System will capitalize on the unique strengths of our brand, while nurturing it with daily care as we move toward our vision of dominating the global foodservice industry," The *Annual*, Oak Brook, IL: McDonald's Corporation, 1996: 1. The Annual Reports to the Stockholders of the McDonald's Corporation are available in their entirety on their website: www.McDonalds.com.

3. According to the McDonald's Corporation 2002 Annual Report, the firm is the world's leading food service organization, generating over US $40 billion in system-wide product sales (roughly half of which were generated outside of the United States) with over 30,000 restaurants in more than 100 countries on six continents.

References

Anderson, Cynthia D., Michael D. Schulman, and Phillip J. Wood. 2001. "Globalization and Uncertainty: The Restructuring of Southern Textiles." *Social Problems* 48, 4: 478–498.

Aurbach, Herbert A. 1976. "SSSP as the Organization of a Social Movement: Comments and Suggestions." *Social Problems* 24, 1: 37–53.

Becker, Howard S. 1967. "Whose Side Are We On." *Social Problems* 14, 3: 239–247.

Blumer, Herbert. 1971. "Social Problems as Collective Behavior." *Social Problems* 18(3): 298–306.

Boyle, Elizabeth Heger, Fortunata Songora, and Gail Foss. 2001. "International Discourse and Local Politics: Anti-Female-Genital-Cutting Laws in Egypt, Tanzania, and the United States." *Social Problems* 48, 4: 524–544.

Brekhus, Keith L. Wayne H. Brekhus, and John Galliher. 2001. "Social Problems in Social Problems: The Theory and Method of Justice." *Social Problems* 48, 1: 137–142.

Canan, Penelope and George W. Pring. 1988. "Strategic Lawsuits against Public Participation." *Social Problems* 35, 5: 506–519.

Chambliss, William J. 1964. "A Sociological Analysis of the Law of Vagrancy." *Social Problems* 12, 1: 67–77.

———. 1995. "Commentary." *SSSP Forum* (formerly *SSSP Newsletter*) 26, 1: 9.

Chandler Jr., Alfred D. 1977. *The Visible Hand: The Managerial Revolution in American Business.* Cambridge, MA: Belknap Press.

Conrad, Peter. 1997. "Public Eyes and Private Genes: Historical Frames, News Constructions, and Social Problems." *Social Problems* 44, 2: 139–154.

Dello Buono, Richard A. 1981. "Markets and Managers: A Critique of Two Points of View." *Contemporary Crises* 5, 4: 403–415.

———. 1990. "From Critique to Constructive Action: Concrete Steps toward a More Progressive SSSP." *The American Sociologist* 21, 4: 337–341.

———. 1995. "Globalization and the New Corporate Censorship: 'McDonaldization' as a Social Problem?" *SSSP Forum* (formerly *SSSP Newsletter*) 26, 2: 28–38.

———. 1998. "La McDonaldización y sus descontentos: entre la racionalidad y la resistencia a la globalización." In José Dávila Cisneros, ed. *Sociología.* Chosica, Peru: UNE-UNC, 503–517.

Galliher, John F., and James M. Galliher. 1995. *Marginality and Dissent in Twentieth-Century American Sociology: The Case of Elizabeth Briant Lee and Alfred McClung Lee.* Albany: State University of New York Press.

Gouldner, Alvin W. 1962. "Anti-Minotaur: The Myth of a Value-Free Sociology" *Social Problems* 9, 3: 199–213.

———. 1970. *The Coming Crisis of American Sociology.* New York: Basic Books.

Miller, S. M. 2001. "Social Problems and Deviance: Some Parallel Issues." *Social Problems* 48, 1: 144–148.

Mills, C. Wright. 1958. *The Causes of World War III.* New York: Ballantine Books.

Parrado, Emilio A. and René M. Zenteno. 2001. "Economic Restructuring, Financial Crises, and Women's Work in Mexico." *Social Problems* 48, 4: 456–477.

Perrucci, Robert. 2001. "Inventing Social Justice: SSSP and the Twenty-First Century." *Social Problems* 48, 2: 159–167.

Pfohl, Steven. 1977. "The 'Discovery' of Child Abuse." *Social Problems* 24, 3: 310–323.

Ritzer, George. 1993. *The McDonaldization of Society: An Investigation into the Changing Character of Contemporary Social Life.* Thousand Oaks, CA: Pine Forge Press.

Smith, David A. 2001. "Editor's Introduction: Globalization and Social Problems." *Social Problems* 48, 4: 429–434.

Spector, Malcolm and John I. Kitsuse. 1973b. "Toward a Sociology of Social Problems: Social Conditions, Value Judgments, and Social Problems." *Social Problems* 20, 4: 407–418.

———. 1977. *Constructing Social Problems.* New York: Gruyter.

Stout, A. Kathryn. 1989. *Sanctuary in the 1980s: The Dialectics of Law and Social Movement Development.* Ann Arbor: University of Michigan Press.

Stout, A. Kathryn. and Richard A. Dello Buono. 1991. "Political Prisoners as an Emergent Contradiction of State Repression: An Introductory Essay." *Humanity and Society* 15, 4: 338–349.

Waterman, Peter. 1977. "Of Women's Places in Globalised Spaces." *SSSP Forum* 28, 3: 6–14.

CHAPTER 2

Law and Social Change

BRINGING SOCIAL MOVEMENTS INTO THE DIALECTIC

A. Kathryn Stout

Introduction

Social problems are the grist of the sociological enterprise. As dynamic objects of inquiry, social problems also have their own timeline within the development of the discipline. Many of the earliest sociologists broadly conceptualized social problems as abrupt or maladaptive changes in the institutional organization of social life that accompanied the transition from agrarian to industrial capitalism (Fitzhugh 1854), from traditional to modern society (Spencer 1889), from *gemeinschaft* to *gesellschaft* (Tönnies 1963), etc.[1] Fast forwarding to the present, we see that the study of social problems continues to include macro level concerns with epochal social changes, such as the challenges involved in moving from relatively autonomous industrial societies to a "postmodern" era and a globalized world order.

Throughout this timeline, we also observe that scaling down the more macrosocial changes to concrete policy reflected in legal issues brings into sharp relief specific problems. Among the specific problems associated with the early periods of industrialization were issues such as the citizenship status of former slaves and immigrants, the rise of "labor monopolies" during the early struggle for industrial unionization, monopolistic "trusts" during the rise of big business, and concerns about the "moral erosion of children" associated with the rise of public schools. Problems that are not new, but are seen as salient issues in the modern era include environmental pollution, hunger and homelessness, equality in education, the control of war, genocide, terrorism, immigration, control of powerful industries, and the role of labor unions and mass movements.

At a very basic level, there are two meanings of the term "social problems" within the sociological timeline. In the first sense, "problematic" refers to those aspects of society and social life that are selected as the focus of exploration, analysis, and theory development within the discipline. Beginning with August Comte in the nineteenth century, the very nature of society, its structure and changing processes are generally "problematic" for sociology. Similarly, bureaucracy, globalization, social structure, institutions, human agency, and the like become targeted for their "problematic" characteristics.

In the second meaning, "problems" refers to sets of social conditions or social issues of concern to some group or groups of people. Groups of social actors identify, analyze and respond to sets of objective conditions as social problems. The contemporary problems of homelessness, alcoholism, crime, racism, and immigration are examples of social conditions that are identified as problems because groups of actors have organized around these issues. Problems of this kind become the subject of many empirical studies which, in turn, both challenge the discipline and aid in the further development of our theories.

Robert Merton (1967) reaffirmed this notion of the two meanings of "social problems" when he distinguished between "manifest" social problems referring to those which ordinary people perceive in a given era regard as problematic and "latent" social problems which are those social conditions seen as problematic only by sociological "experts." Merton's dichotomy was an early statement of the recurring need for sociologists to analyze both the problems identified by groups of people as well as those that are revealed through sociological theory and research.

In this article, social problems are examined from both the perspective of groups that define conditions as problematic and issues that reflect the theoretical and empirical work of sociologists. Also explored is the evolution of approaches to the changing categories of social problems while seeking to identify those aspects that are problematic to the theoretical enterprise itself.

Stephen Pfohl (1994: xi–xii) draws our attention to the important role played by theorists who, through their work as "experts," provide conceptual images that in the act of constructing explanations serve to either justify and rationalize existing social conditions and relations, or, conversely, take critical and sometimes even radical positions by offering new, vastly different images of problems and their solutions. If homelessness in the United States, for example, is attributed to individual, psychological problems or to negative attitudes toward work and conformity, one set of social policy responses is required. These might include polices that deliver social services to the homeless, but would definitely not seek to alter the basic social relations and structure of society. If, on the other hand and as is suggested by critical/radical theorists, homelessness is the result of historical, structural patterns of inequality embedded in the development of U.S. capitalism, then the solutions must involve more fundamental changes to the social order. In this case, theories no longer remain simply abstract discussions but indeed can attain very real consequences for large numbers of people.

The process whereby unemployment or any other social condition becomes defined as a social problem is complex, however, not beyond our ability to comprehend. It is important to understand that social problems represent a process characterized by a dynamic relationship that exists between sets of objective social conditions created by sets of social actors and then also includes other groups of social actors who experience those conditions and are influenced by them. In short, the experiences lived by people and the explanations they develop shape their concerns as well as the concrete actions they undertake with regard to problematic conditions.

In this article, several varieties of theoretical approaches to the study of social problems are examined in order to identify that which is theoretically problematic, i.e., those aspects which still need to be further developed in our theories. Emphasis is placed on the theoretical and empirical contributions put forward from those working in the areas of critical criminology, the sociology of law, as well as those whose research centers on the study of social movements. It will be argued that these approaches substantially contribute to our understanding of the relationship between sociohistoric processes, social structures, institutional policies and practices (including laws), the objective conditions of social problems (e.g., persistence of hunger) and the social relations or group interactions involved in the social problems process.

If we are to better understand the nature of this complex process, we cannot afford to ignore the role of sociology as a discipline, as a career and as an approach to social life. Drawing from C. Wright Mills' (1959) famous treatise, the development of a sociological imagination involves the ability to see the intersection of sociohistoric forces, social issues, personal problems, and individual biographies. Once revealed, this complex relationship draws into question and presents to us for critique, existing social relations, structures, and ideologies that explain and justify normative patterns of behavior. The possible types of understandings or images that result can range from those which tend to accept as normal and desirable the established social order, though allowing for the need for minor reforms or adjustments, to those that develop into overtly and purposively critical, even radical postures toward society.

Following Mills, I agree that it is the role of sociology to be critical, to question the official interpretations of our social realities, and to provide vision which can allow us to act on our knowledge in a way that affects social policies and transforms our lives. Though still the subject of much debate among sociologists, I assert that it is our professional duty to focus our concerns on addressing issues and problems generated by existing social relations in a way that will promote improvements in the conditions of the least powerful groups who are, in a broad sense, the victims of social problems. This position definitely shapes the kind of approach that can be deemed adequate to the study of social problems in general.

Unemployment, for example, is a permanent structural characteristic, albeit not fixed at any particular rate, of a capitalist economy. Under capitalism, a relatively low level of unemployment is viewed as "normal" or "nonproblematic." Capitalist state laws and policies do not attempt to guarantee employment for all citizens, as is the case in other political economies such as socialist societies. The existence of some level of unemployment can therefore be considered inevitable in capitalist societies and will persist until which time that its capitalist social relations are transformed, and the capitalist state that perpetuates such relations has also been transformed in the service of an alternative, noncapitalist political economy

To the extent that most people are not affected by unemployment, they may be more willing to accept the official explanations of the "normal" situation of capitalist unemployment. On the other hand, if increasing numbers of people, including those higher up in the economic strata begin to experience persistent unemployment, and if after years of social policies aimed at correcting the problem prove unsuccessful, it is predictable that some will come to reject the official justifications, that alternative explanations will become formed, countersystemic ideologies will be forged. Instead of continuing to accept unemployment as an inevitable, relatively minor social problem, it becomes seen by some as an indication of major, structural flaws in the basic organization of social relations and the state's management of them. All of this in turn makes it increasingly likely that the types of responses to what is now seen as the "problem" of unemployment will begin to change in a more critical/radical direction. This development of human agency becomes the basis for social movements that begin to engage in conflict with official government agents and politicians over public support for their views. If successful in their battle, social movements can bring about social change in the form of new social policies, intervening laws, and newly prescribed practices that, in turn, can redirect the future development of the political economy/social structure. From a critical perspective, it is therefore of paramount importance to incorporate the study of social movements into our sociology of social problems

The theoretical basis for understanding the role of social movements in this process is found in the development of critical criminology and the sociology of law, which have offered important insights in conceptualizing the sociohistoric processes that underlie social problems. This includes theorizing about the structural nature of political economies, social institutions, social policies, and social conditions as a whole. Largely missing from these approaches, however, has been an explicit consideration of the role of social movements as a part of the larger social dialectic that characterizes the process of social problems. The primary objective of this paper is therefore to establish the necessity for analyzing social problems along with those social movements that play a role in shaping their historical development as they operate within historically situated structures of political economy and in dynamic engagement with the ongoing policies and practices of the state and its legal order.

I begin by briefly reviewing the various theoretical approaches that have developed within critical criminology and the sociology of law. Then, consideration is given to some of the prevailing tendencies within the sociological study of social movements, with an eye toward identifying those currents that demonstrate the greatest theoretical sensitivity to the concerns of critical criminology/legal studies. This exploration concludes by arguing for the need to further develop a dialectical model that incorporates salient aspects of the political economy, the role of the state, the nature and character of social movements, and the dynamic and interactive way in which all of these factors must be considered in their totality if we are to achieve our aim of advancing a critical understanding of social problems.

Approaches to Crime and Deviance

The general social upheaval within existing social institutions in the 1960s and early 1970s, particularly in North America, created a large-scale social context of crisis. One aspect of this crisis involved a tendency for large numbers of "ordinary people" involved in legitimate forms of political protest to be labeled as deviant or criminal. As Pfohl puts it: "The deviant label was brought closer to home" for sociologists (1985: 286). What quickly became clear is that deviants and criminals could no longer be viewed as outsiders, or "those people," given that growing numbers of students, faculty, and otherwise "normal" citizens were being drawn into the numerous social battles being waged.

This conflict-ridden and rapidly changing social reality presented a direct challenge to the functionalist perspective that dominated sociological theorizing in the 1950s and early 1960s, especially in the United States. Steeped in the Durkheimian tradition (Ashley and Orenstein 1998: 134–138), functionalism characterized society as a system of interrelated and interdependent parts that adapt to new stimuli in a way that always maintains the balance or equilibrium of the social system. Among the fundamental assumptions underlying the functionalist perspective is the notion that social norms are based on a consensus, or generalized agreement among the members of society. Deviance, while always present to some extent, represents a departure from normative patterns and at the same time, fulfills certain functions that actually serve to strengthen society. Among these functions are "group boundary maintenance" and social innovations (Stout 1989: 52–58).

When applied to criminology, the task of functionalist theorizing was to identify the characteristics and conditions that separated offenders from nonoffenders or conformists. By isolating these factors, it was assumed that explanations could be developed that explained the distribution of deviance in society (Best and Luckenbill 1982: 5–7). Among the central critiques of the functionalist approach were its tendency to use tautological or circular logic (Pfohl 1994) and its ahistorical nature which contributed to its inability to deal effectively with social conflict and social change (Ritzer 1988: 102).

The structural functionalist tradition was extended deeply into criminology by Robert Merton and the anomie theorists (see, for example, Cohen 1955, 1959; Cloward, 1959). The cultural diversity of U.S. society was seen as giving rise to groups with competing interests and unequal access to social rewards such as status and political power. While ostensibly recognizing the existence of such conflict, little effort was made to develop an analysis of the *source* of these conflicts. Some effort to correct this omission was offered by Lemert (1964) and others who were beginning to branch off from the functionalist paradigm, e.g., locating the source of conflict within divergent subcultural value systems. In most cases, however, these currents still lacked the ability to move beyond the institutional level of social analysis to one that included the political economy as the source of conflict in social relations between groups.

Criminologists working further outside the functionalist paradigm offered radically different approaches to the study of deviance, crime, and law. One example is William Chambliss' now-classic study of the link between the emergence of the Anglo-American laws of vagrancy and historical political economy (1964). As Raymond Michalowski (1985) reminds us, there were two types of perspectives being developed in the emerging paradigm of conflict theory. On the one hand were "functional-conflict theories" that focused on cultural conflict as the source of social deviance. Austin Turk (1968), for example, explored the relationship between criminality and the legal order, but concluded that such conflict ultimately contributes to an overall social harmony and stability.

By comparison, "power-conflict theories" were more influenced by the Weberian tradition in which it was recognized that there are structural differences in the ability to exert power and control over subordinate social groups. Turk's later work (e.g., 1982) suggested that the authority to impose norms and expectations on subordinate groups is won through the political process. No consideration was given, however, to "the various forms of historically-structured power relations as they relate to the political economy," e.g., stratification based on gender, race, and class (Stout 1989: 59). Despite these shortcomings, there can be little doubt that: "the most important innovation and direction in the 1970s was to take seriously the possibility that criminological inquiry could be linked to conflict theory" (Chambliss 1988: 162).

Interactionism and the Societal Reaction Perspective

Among the various criticisms of both the functionalist and the conflict perspectives is the idea that they could not adequately conceptualize the subjective and interpretative aspects of social behavior. The development of the symbolic interactionist approach served to directly address this critique. Interactionism drew upon the Meadian tradition of social psychology in which the objective nature of social reality was rejected in favor of studying the meaningfulness of social interaction as experienced by the individuals involved. Herbert Blumer coined the term "symbolic interactionism," thereby establishing the Chicago School of Interactionism which, in turn, spawned other variants such as the more positivistic version that emerged as the "Iowa School of Interactionism" under Manford Kuhn (Martindale 1981: 384).

The problem with these interactionist approaches was that their resolution of the serious flaws of functionalism resulted in a radical shift toward a social-psychologistic and subjectivistic posture that further complicated the formation of a critical analysis capable of linking back up with the larger relations of political economy. As Larry Reynolds succinctly states:

> Interactionism truly lacks a decent appreciation and adequate understanding of social structure and social organization. All of this is to say that Symbolic Interactionism manifests a marked astructural, or microscopic, bias, and any framework with such a bias is bound to be both ahistorical and noneconomic . . . (and) destined to be profoundly apolitical. (Reynolds 1987: 137)

Certain currents did develop, however, that sought to incorporate the insights from power-conflict theory into interactionist analysis. This kind of synthetic approach made interactionism more critical in the political sense and more amenable to macrosociological analysis overall. A good example of this critical labeling perspective emerged in what became known as the Societal Reaction perspective. According to Pfohl (1994: 360), the initial influence of societal reaction theory began to be felt in three important areas: (1) The critique of official statistics, (2) the definition of what should be considered deviant, and (3) the reflexive nature of the research process. From this overall approach, societal reaction theory could no longer take for granted preconceived definitions of deviance, but instead relied upon definitions used by real people in particular historical contexts.

Theorists operating in this tradition began to see the social meanings of "deviance" and deviant labels as processes heavily conditioned by social power. To the extent that it became utilized in practice, this style of research clearly contributed to deepening the critical understanding of crime, law and deviance. It also helped produce important studies such as Joseph Gusfield's (1963) analysis of the social base of the Women's Christian Temperance Movement (WCTU) as an important exploration in the historical process of deviant category creation.

According to Gusfield's analysis, the WCTU of the early twentieth century was originally made up of mostly rural, Protestant, middle-class women who opposed the drinking habits of the lower class. Following a series of social and economic changes later on in the century, the decline of the traditional petite-bourgeoisie of rural Protestants felt "left behind" as Catholic immigrants (who did not oppose drinking) ascended in status (Wood and Jackson 1982).

In reaction to this perceived threat and mounting frustrations, the WCTU took at the drinking habits of both the lower-class immigrants as well as the rising elements of the "new middle class." By developing a keen sensibility to the changing historical conditions of the North American context, this kind of approach produced important insights into the social process of the defining alcohol consumption as deviant behavior. What makes Gusfield's work so important is not just his historical method of analyzing social deviance but his utilization of a social movements approach. He was essentially popularizing a style of research that was assimilating the interests and concerns of previously autonomous sociological approaches to crime and deviance on the one hand and studies of social movements on the other.

Other theorists also contributed to breaking down these disciplinary walls such as Anthony Platt's (1969) study of the "child-saving movement" which utilized a critical, societal reaction approach to analyze the emergence of the juvenile justice system. Platt provided an in-depth account of the process whereby "concerned" middle-class women worked to organize the state's response to the "problems" of children in poverty around the turn of the century (Stout 1989: 70–71). While working to cultivate an appreciation of structured inequalities in the distribution of social power, the societal reaction perspective ultimately proved incapable of adequately conceptualizing the nature and source of social power. Platt himself later contended that the societal reaction perspective could not advance past a certain point in developing an overall critical approach to deviance and social movements. In a second edition to his work *The Child Savers*, Platt declares that the societal reaction approach:

> [u]nderestimates the significance of structural conditions and depends too much on a subjective critique of the child-saving movement and professional ambitions. By placing the child-saving movement in the context of the political economy of Progressivism, its failures can be understood in new light. . . . The child-saving reforms were part of a larger movement to readjust institutions to conform to the requirements of the emerging system of corporate capitalism. (Platt 1977: xiii–xix)

There is no question that the larger social context surrounding academia was an important influence upon all sociological theorizing, including those working within the interactionist currents of societal reaction. As Pfohl points out:

> The critical perspective did not merely emerge. It exploded against the conflictual social landscape of America and Western Europe during the late 1960s and early 1970s. Although intellectually nurtured by the development of the societal reaction perspective and its efforts to demystify the process by which certain behaviors and people are labeled deviant, the central impetus for critical theorizing was far more concrete. Ivory towers of university scholarship were rapidly transformed into intellectual battlegrounds for discerning the nature of a wide spread and deeply felt political crisis. (Pfohl 1985: 335).

Sociology of Law

The critical perspective was similarly destined to move into the adjacent discipline of the sociology of law. Socio-legal studies are often traced to the mid-19th century with the works of Albert Venn Dicey, Oliver Wendell Holmes Jr., and E. Adamson Hoebel (Vago 2003: 54–55). By the end of the 19th century, a discourse developed around the nature of law and its relationship to society. Important concerns with the relationship between law and society were found in the late 19th Century of Marx and the early 20th Century sociological writings of Durkheim and Weber.

Classical legal theory employed an "insider's perspective" which viewed law as a closed system with its own internal logic. From this view, known as legal formalism, the state and its legal order were seen as neutral, impartial, and mostly decentralized mechanism of regulating society, including the economy. Analogous to the premises employed by the functionalist perspective in sociology, classical legal theorists described the law as necessary and inherently neutral, reflecting a social consensus.

Sharp criticisms of legal formalism were offered by critical thinkers who argued for an "outsiders" perspective on law (Horwitz 1992; Chambliss and Seidman 1971). An outsiders or external perspective views law as the product of socio-historic conditions and forces, including the economy, culture, structured social power, etc. The noted jurist and former Chief Justice Oliver Wendell Holmes can be included among those who launched a critique of legal formalism in the 1930s. Others included Karl Llewellyn who typified what can be described as a critical branch of legal realism.

Horwitz (1992) and others suggest that an additional intellectual influence on the development of the sociology of law came out of the approach referred to as Sociological Jurisprudence that included Roscoe Pound among its foremost advocates. Among the many contributions made by Roscoe Pound was the distinction between the "law in books," and the "law in action" as well as the concept of "legal lag" (Chambliss 1988). Similar to Thorstein Veblen's sociological notion of "cultural lag," "legal lag" refers to the failure of the law to keep pace with social changes, including those related to the transition from agrarian to industrial society.

In the United States, studies of law and society are nominally referred to interchangeably as the sociology of law, socio-legal studies, and legal sociology. All share a primarily academic orientation with slight variations in approaches (Treviño 2001). Elsewhere including Britain, for example, socio-legal studies were more policy oriented than in the United States. The Law and Society Association, based in the United States, was the first North American professional association to bring together "scholars from many fields and countries, interested in the place of law in social, political, economic and cultural life" (www.lawandsociety.org).[2] Those interested in law and society were explicitly concerned with issues involving power, social control, stratification, and the social organization of law (Vago 2003: 340). In her presidential address to the Law and Society Association, Lynn Mather attributes the distinctions between the fields of law and society and that of socio-legal studies to the differences in the relation between law academics and social science, suggesting that competing notions within "the law and society paradigm will become even more apparent as the diversity of law and society scholars increases" (2003).

Clearly, a central theme in law and society theorizing is the analytical and empirical relationship between society, and in particular, the economy and the legal order. From a functionalist perspective, law is one of the primary social institutions that responds to social changes, for example, the introduction of industrial technologies. Legal institutions define the normative system to which social actors respond. From this view, society is as it should be and any problems are indicators that one or more of the social institutions is in need of reform. This is an inherently noncritical perspective and this is why legal realists so emphatically criticized functionalist-oriented theorists for being "apologists" for the existing system (Horwitz 1992). By assuming that scientific inquiry was objective and value-free, functionalist interpretations tended to be reductionist and unable to adequately conceptualize the pervasive role of social conflict and the overarching issues of domination.

In contrast, those operating from a critical or radical perspective gave priority to the analysis of crime and deviance as it reflected the nature of the social order and its relationship to state power, state law, and the legal process. Even though interactionism in the more critical form of societal reaction research became directly concerned with power relations, it still lacked a necessary focus on the structural relationships between law and society. In seeking to transcend the subjectivism of the interactionist and societal reaction approaches, critical theorists of crime began to incorporate a "conflict theory" of political power (e.g., Turk 1968; Cain 1975; Chambliss and Mankoff 1975; Chambliss and Seidman 1971). While critical criminology focuses more directly on the structural relationships between law and society, sociology of law theories went beyond to examine more fully the nature and character of the state in society as it mediates conflicting social groups through the legal order.

Referring to the emergence of a critical/radical criminology beginning in the 1960s, Chambliss asserts that this "new criminology" has its roots in the 1930s class-based criminological analysis that was foreshadowed by the popularity of functionalist approaches in the 1950s (1984: 5). Redeveloped in the 1960s and 1970s, critical criminology extended the 1930s' efforts by focusing on the relationship between criminal behavior and the political, economic, and social forces of specific historical periods.

David Friedrichs suggests that the search for a "new criminology" was a predictable response to the state of criminological theorizing which was suffering from a "crisis of legitimacy" (1980).

The pioneers of the "new critical criminology" called for the inclusion of law and the legal order as central areas of inquiry. This strengthened the basis for the further development of the sociology of law and society. Influenced largely by critical and radical theorizing, this emergent paradigm shared little in common with traditional approaches to the sociology of law as dominated by juridical analysts employing a legalistic framework (Hunt 1978). In seeking to address the dynamics of social control and popular resistance as mediated through the legal process and rooted in the larger political economy in which they operate, the critical criminologists and sociology of law theorists turned first to a critical reading of Weber, and later moved to incorporate Marxist and Neo-Marxist analyses. The entire legal order, including the various agencies of social control, became viewed as part of the forces and relations of production that shape contemporary social existence (Humphries and Greenberg 1981; Piven and Cloward 1971).

Influenced by the logic of Marxist theories, two variants of critical/radical theorizing about law and society emerged (known as *Instrumental Marxism* and *Structural Marxism*). Key principles of Marxist theorizing were utilized to better understand the nature and dynamics of structured power relations and their relationship to law, society, and social change. For Marx, the driving force behind social change is found in class struggles which are the result of inherent contradictions or opposing forces found in the *substructure* of social systems. Class relations such as those of owners and workers in capitalism are inevitably conflictual as each pursues its own interests which are in direct opposition to the interests of the other. The capitalist state reflects and maintains this relationship while mediating the problematics that arise from them.[3]

Focusing on Marx's concept of contradictions, Marxist sociologists are able to conceptualize the dynamic interplay of social structure, social policy, social struggle, and the like. However, the two dominant variants of Marxist influenced theories in criminology and in the sociology of law disagree on a number of key points. Of primary concern for this discussion is the issue of the "relative autonomy" of the state from the ruling class. In other words, is it the state a direct tool of domination by the ruling class as is the case for *Instrumental Marxists,* or is it an arena through which social conflicts are mediated and regulated as suggested by *Structural Marxism.* In *Instrumental Marxism,* the nature and character of the economy is the primary determinant of all other social institutions, relations, conditions, and ideologies. In a capitalist order, the legal process is viewed as a direct tool of the dominant capitalist class. Law, therefore, is seen as a reflection of the interests of the ruling class (capital) and the legal process is a direct tool of class domination (Stout 1989: 93; Beirne and Quinney 1982: 4).

Left out of the overly mechanistic view inherent in the instrumentalist perspective is the dialectical nature of social processes. From this perspective, the structural elements of society are the first and last determinants of the social condition, leaving out the important role played by human agency in this process. It was up to those employing a more *Structural Marxist* analysis to bring back into the mix the dynamic process of social change that included a consideration of the important role played by class and status group struggles.

Structural Marxist interpretations emphasize the interactions between the legal order, the state, and the political economy. The legal order is the primary tool of state power and the state itself is an expression of class struggle in capitalist development. Social conflicts are mediated through the state apparatus, primarily the legal arena where the rules of conflict are predetermined. The nature of the capitalist state is such that is must guarantee the continued accumulation of capital and profit, but it must do so in a way that is influenced by the liberal democratic political process.[4] In this sense, the capitalist state has a dual and conflictual nature that allows, in a theoretical and empirical sense, for legal "victories" by less powerful social groups.

From a structural Marxist interpretation of the legal order, the nature and characteristics of crime "depend upon the nature of the existing contradictions, the conflicts that develop as people respond to the contradictions, and the mechanisms institutionalized for the handling of the conflicts and dilemmas produced by the contradictions" (Chambliss 1988: 301). Of key importance among the contributions of this theoretical approach is its ability to bring the dialectical nature of social processes into clear relief. Though the structural Marxist approach is subject to a number of critiques (see Beirne 1979; Calavita 1983; Cotterrell 1984), it provides a very good basis for understanding the dynamics of law, state power, and social change. What remained missing from this approach, however, was an adequate conceptualization of the important role played by social movements.

Bringing in Social Movements

Predictably, the theoretical trajectory in deviance, crime, and law studies also paralleled studies of social movement studies. The sociological tradition in the study of social movements has revolved around distinct plateaus of analysis, e.g., social psychological, structural, etc., and there has been a persistent trend toward positivistic approaches at the expense of critical theorizing. Anthony Oberschall (1973: 21–22) attributes the lack of discourse between social movement studies and the fields dedicated to law and society, deviance, and crime to the strong influence which Merton had on sociology.

Merton "clearly distinguishes deviant from non-conforming behavior" (Oberschall 1973: 21–22; see also Merton 1957: 355–356). According to Merton, personal motives guide the adaptive deviant's behavior rather than any interest in directly challenging the dominant social norms. By comparison, the nonconformist more consciously seeks to change the existing ideologies and structures of society. Studies of deviance, crime, and law tended to focus on Merton's notion of deviants while social movement studies tended to focus on nonconformists.

It has by now become clear that the sociological approach to social movements can provide critical insights into the nature of contemporary social problems. By operating to some extent "outside" of the institutionalized channels of a given society, social movement participants are uniquely positioned to understand the conditions which become regarded as problematic by some social groups. In the course of their ongoing activities, such movements develop alternative understandings and beliefs which, although branded by the prevailing social meanings of the larger society, often reveal ongoing efforts to redefine social conditions in a way consistent with the movement's cause. This kind of *definitioning* process, if successful, can call into question the "official definitions" put forward by the state and help to reveal the underlying injustices residing in the social structures of the larger society.

In essence, social movements involve groups of people who organize outside of existing social institutions and engage in social action in order to affect some aspect of their social world. Lewis Killian's work on social movements led him to assert that the central factor in defining all such movements rested in its organization of efforts to intervene in the process of social and cultural change (1964). Social movements can involve actions designed to bring about social change or perhaps to resist and reverse social changes that have already taken place. In any case, it is dissatisfaction with existing social, economic, or political conditions that in this view forms the principal impetus for the development of these organizations.

Sharing a common aim of bringing about social change, social movements exhibit a broad range of specific goals. On one end of the continuum are social action organizations seeking relatively minor changes in either public policy or laws governing single issues. At the other end are protest organizations whose aims embody a revolutionary vision for the total reformulation of society (Stout 1994). Various other means of making distinctions between different social movements have been discussed in the literature, considering, for example, whether they are instrumental or expressive in nature. Instrumental movements seek to change the structure of society, as is the case with the Civil Rights Movement while expressive movements focus on changing the character, behavior or lifestyles of individuals such as in the case of the New Age movement. In the latter case, it is by changing people that these movements seek to ultimately change the larger society (Harper and Leicht 2002).

Likewise, the strategies and tactics of protest used by social movements can vary depending on the nature of the perceived injustice or social problem, the politics of the movement members, and the resources available to the movement. While all social movements seek to generate popular support for their cause, the specific strategies they can provide important distinctions. More reformist groups engage in fundraising, congressional lobbying, and lawsuits to influence specific legal reforms. In contrast, others may rely more upon direction action such as the development of community-based service organizations or alternative, countercultural communities. In the case of revolutionary groups, tactical measures can even include mobilization for armed actions in support of military strategies of protest and transformation. These varied approaches can be seen in three movements dedicated to promoting civil rights: the National Association for the Advancement of Colored People (NAACP), Student Nonviolent Coordinating Committee (SNCC), and the Black Panther Party (BPP) (Stout 1994; Dello Buono 1993).

Another dimension that distinguishes between types of social movements relates to their respective political ideologies. Some are associated with conservative, right-wing politics, such as the New Christian Right or "white power" groups. These movements are "reactionary" in that they essentially call for the reversal of some policy, trend, or dramatic social change that has been adopted, often to redress one or another injustice in the past. At the other end of the political spectrum are those movements with a progressive or left-wing ideology. One example of a progressive movement is the loosely knit coalition of groups known as the Global Justice Movement (presented in the popular press as the "antiglobalization" movement). Progressive movements generally seek changes that will promote greater social justice for those who are exploited, oppressed, or excluded within the economic, social, and political sectors of society.

The existence of social movements seeking to bring about social change is itself evident of dissatisfaction with one or another aspect of social organization, state policy and the like. As such, they represent a challenge to the legitimacy of the state by drawing into question its policies and practices. Depending on a number of factors, including the nature of the changes sought by the social movement and its degree of militancy, various state agencies and sectors of the government develop a response to the protests.

In some cases, the state accommodates the movement as happened in the case of the group Mothers Against Drunk Driving (MADD) whose push for more restrictive and punitive drunk driving laws was successful. In other instances such as in the case of the Sanctuary Movement of the 1980s as well as various Peace and Justice groups of the preceding twenty years, the state responded by using surveillance tactics, sometimes infiltrating groups, and ultimately criminalizing key movement members in an attempt to thwart their progress (Stout and Dello Buono 1991).

The nature and extent of social change resulting from this dynamic interplay between social movements and the state can vary considerably. Local efforts to address social problems can result in something as simple but important to the community as the installation of a traffic light or increases in police patrols. Larger-scale struggles for worker safety protections resulted in the creation of the federal-level, Occupational Safety and Hazard Administration (OSHA), although as one notes, this was largely a case of symbolic law (Calavita 1983).

We are able to observe that demands for racial equality in the United States, for example, have produced a series of far-reaching legislative attempts to remedy this structured inequality. To date, however, they have failed to fully remedy the social problems associated with institutionalized racism. Struggles to secure equal treatment for women in the economic and political arenas have had notable successes, but still have not addressed such salient issues as the extremely high rates of domestic and sexual violence against women. Efforts in recent years to secure legal and more generally, human rights protections for immigrants and refugees have experienced serious setbacks as unstable economic conditions and the "war on terrorism" have combined to feed nativistic or nationalistic public sentiments. To all of this, we continue to raise all sorts of analytical questions about the changing social relations and attendant social problems associated with the present period of rapidly increasing globalization. For example, as environmental issues and their respective social movements both become more global in nature, their complexity deepens as does their theater of operations. The post-Seattle coalition of global justice movements that have lined up in opposition to hegemonic "free trade" agreements, the World Trade Organization and unequal global capitalist domination is perhaps the most recent example of an unfolding area in need of serious study.

From this discussion, it can be seen that the dynamic nature of social problems, social movements, law, and social change is as complex as it is exciting. There are numerous sets of local, national, and global actors involved in an unfolding drama that demands the attention of critical analysts. From social movement members to agents of the state, and from the mass media to the court of public opinion, members of existing institutions whose ideologies are compatible or oppositional to those held by the movements are part of a power play between groups struggling to advance their organized agenda. Each set of actors likewise engages in a social definitioning process of the objective conditions in question and seeks to create the appropriate response in the face of claims made by other actors in this process. There is a long-standing tradition in sociology of attempting to develop a theoretical framework that can analyze these complex dynamics.

Early social movement theory tended to be psychological in nature, stressing "irrational" collective behaviors of people who lacked adequate constraint upon their behaviors such as "mobs" and the like. Traditional approaches to social movements are grounded in the early theories of collective behavior. From fads and panics to riots and revolutions, noninstitutional forms of collective behavior are seen as deviant in nature, and temporary, "spontaneous and fickle" in character (Stout 1989; see also Smelser 1962; LeBon 1960; Tarde 1912). Later theorists would focus on the personality characteristics of movement leaders and members as explanatory variables (for example, Cantril 1941; Hoffer 1951; Flacks 1967).

The social psychological paradigm offered an important shift in analysis for social movement theory. Social-structural conditions became seen as influencing psychological predispositions (e.g., values and motives) which, in turn, influence individual nonconformist behaviors (Wood and Jackson 1982: 33). In a subtle way, social movements were becoming "normalized," i.e., participants were no longer viewed as intrinsically deviant or morally deficient as previously seen from the psychological perspective. Instead, the essence of social movement behaviors was reconceptualized as individual adjustments to stressful social conditions (Stout 1989; see also Gusfield 1963; Gurr 1969; Blumer 1978.

As theorizing turned toward a more distinctly sociological analysis, the paradigmatic focus initially leaned toward a Durkheimian approach (Tilly 1978:16). Many social-structural theories tended to "normalize" social movements by suggesting they were the product of normal human reactions to uncomfortable social conditions or an imbalance between societal demands and individual perceptions.

Most traditional theories of social movements, particularly in North America, suffered from the lack of any real dialogue with Marxian theory and the political economy approach. In the final analysis, it was a missed opportunity that left social movement theory, at least prior to the 1960s, heavily steeped in either Durkheimian structural, neo-Durkheimian functionalist, or social-psychological models that drew their inspiration from Weberian action theory and/or Meadian symbolic interactionism. With the turbulent period of the 1960s, a crisis in sociological theory developed, putting establishment sociology on a direct collision course with its own social context (Stout 1989: 19–20).

The growth of protest groups and social movements in the 1960s led to conflict approaches regaining popularity among U.S. sociologists. Within the field of social movement studies, the conflict approach was used to explain the interactions of social movements and the state, or the political process of contention based on an analysis of the resources available to contending groups. The most significant variant of conflict theory and social movement studies was the Resource Mobilization approach which eventually came to dominate social movement studies.

Resource mobilization theorists directly incorporated into their analyses the notion of the relative social power of movements. With a primary concern of explaining the dynamics of social movement development, this approach managed to draw into its focus the relationship between social movements, social change, and structurally situated social relations between groups (Stout 1989; see also, Gamson 1987; McCarthy and Zald 1977). Informed by organizational theory, the resource mobilization perspective was viewed as central to the process of developing social movements and their institutionalized components known as "Social Movement Organizations" (SMOs) (Zald and Ash 1966). The Civil Rights Movement, for example, is a social movement more properly seen as the result of coordinated efforts on the part of various social movement organizations (Dello Buono 1993)

There are a variety of useful analyses offered by the resource mobilization approach. In Oberschall's variant, a rational choice model is added to explain the actions of movement participants and their opponents (1979). Discussions of the dynamics of social movement development focused on the availability of resources for the movement and its opponents. Resources were found to constrain the choices of both participants and authorities, thereby influencing the possible outcomes or resolutions that emerged from the conflict dynamics of social protests (Oberschall 1979: 67; Freeman 1979).

Steven Barkan's comprehensive study of the dynamics of both the Civil Rights and the Anti-Viet Nam War movements utilizes a critical-Weberian approach to the relationship between the legal order and social groups. Barkan focused on the important "impact of legal procedure, and especially criminal prosecutions and trials, on social movements" (1985: 11). Specifically, he explores the various conditions under which the legal system will serve as an effective deterrent to movement development, or conversely, when the legal system will prove to be an invaluable resource, aiding and supporting movement goals (Stout 1989: 37–38).

The relative success or failure of social movements is defined by the movement's ability to grow and develop a broader base of support and additional resources, and its relationship to existing institutions. Institutions may, as was the case with MADD, respond variably to movement demands. On the other end of the spectrum of institutional responses, repressive tactics by governmental agents may also result in movement growth and evolution into full-blown social revolutions (Gamson 1975; Gamson, Fireman, and Rytina 1982). As the sole legitimate entity empowered with the use of force, the state wields the power to harass, criminalize, imprison, and otherwise impose constraints on social movement efforts. Conversely, social movements with the exception of militant revolutionary groups do not have access to the use of force as a resource with which to wage conflict. However, this line of inquiry remains focused on the processes of contention or conflict from an organizational perspective. Implicit in this analysis is the "value-neutral" and pluralist character of the state, except when the state is seen as acting to preserve its own ideological interests (Stout 1989: 50). There is a need to move beyond the political process analysis to one that captures the objective conditions and contradictory forces of the political economy.

Mayer Zald and John McCarthy succinctly frame the concerns of Resource Mobilization theorists in this way:

> [Resource mobilization] . . . emphasizes both the societal support and constraint of social movement phenomena. It examines the variety of resources that must by mobilized, the linkages of social movements to other groups, the dependence of movements upon third parties for success, and the tactics used by authorities to control or incorporate movements. (1979: 1–2)

Some work in the resource mobilization approach addresses directly the structural factors that are seen to contribute to the nature and character of social movement development. Charles Tilly suggests that large-scale structural changes (e.g., urbanization and industrialization) are important not because they create social disorganization, but instead because:

> . . . they strongly affect the number, identity and organizations of the contenders which in turn determine the predominant form and loci of conflict. In the short run, the magnitude of conflict depends on an interaction of the tactics of contenders and the coercive practices of the government. In the longer run, the magnitude of conflict depends on the established means by which contenders can enter and leave the polity, and the frequency with which entries and exits actually occur. (1970: 4)

Rebecca Garner and Mayer Zald conducted comparative analyses that linked the rise and fall of social movements to elements in the social structure (1987). Though focusing on characteristics of capitalism and other political economies, Garner and Zald emphasize the ideological character of state politics. Not fully developed is an analysis of the state as it concretely operates in relation to the political economy.

More recent criticisms of the resource mobilization approach have sought to more fully elaborate upon the microsocial aspects of social movement development. Influenced by earlier efforts to take a cultural approach to social movements, attention was being called to social movement actors, their cognitive processes and communication networks more than to any objective or structural elements. From emotion to rhetoric and the concept of "frames" or ways of presenting claims of injustice and calls to action, this line of inquiry sought to move beyond earlier works influenced by symbolic interactionism and political process theory (Jasper 2003; Gamson 1992).

Perhaps most salient to our discussion is the fact that the resource mobilization approach lacked a coherent analysis of the relationship between social movements and the larger objective conditions of the changing social structure. This approach did offer a significant contribution to a more precise understanding of the internal dynamics and subsequent character of social movements. It could not, however, develop a clear understanding of the character of the state and its institutions against the backdrop of the political economy. What therefore remains generally unclear in the resource mobilization perspective is an analysis of the nature, source, and forms of social conflict. This implies the lack of a critical understanding of the larger social conditions that engender social movements in the first place. When combined with the theoretical offerings of critical criminology and the sociology of law, a more complete picture of the process is revealed.[5]

Conclusion

By focusing on the intersection between social problems, the law, social movements, and social change, we have established a number of key arguments in the preceding discussion. First, an approach that exposes the dynamic character of social problems as sets of objective conditions that simultaneously exist along side of a subjective and multileveled definitional process is highly desirable. Second, viewing the objective conditions that are labeled social problems as outcomes of specific state policies, laws, and practices reveals much about the nature of the historically situated political economy from which they are generated. I maintain that the structured differences in social, economic, and political power between classes and groups in society becomes apparent when analyzing the sociopolitical struggles of those who are seeking to change the objective conditions of society and those who wish to maintain the status quo.

The primary objective of this paper has been to establish the necessity for analyzing social problems along with those social movements that play a role in shaping their historical development as they operate within historically situated structures of political economy and in dynamic engagement with the ongoing policies and practices of the state and its legal order. A review of various theoretical approaches to the study of law, social problems, social movements, and social change reveals the need to develop further an integrated model that incorporates salient aspects of the political economy, the role of the state, and the nature and character of social movements. The study of social problems, law, crime and deviance, and social movements were, to a significant degree, separate intellectual pursuits albeit with some important common threads. Having traced the evolution of sociological thought on this subject, we can sense that divergent literatures in the study of social problems, critical criminology/legal studies, and social movement theory can be usefully brought together to provide a solid basis for further inquiry. In my view, the goal of such an enterprise should be to capture the dialectical relationship between the objective social conditions, sociohistoric forces, social structures, and institutions on the one hand, and the more subjective or interpretive dimension presented by social movements and other social actors.

Social problems are best understood as a dialectical process simultaneously involving an objective set of social conditions, structured social relations, and as the product of an interpretive process in which social actors define their experiences and act upon them. The problematic objective social conditions are created by the state's policies and practices which are themselves tied to, the political economy. In the U.S. capitalist system, these include, but are not limited to problems and conflicts generated by inherent structural contradictions in the political economy. For example, finding ways to legitimize the maintenance of an economic environment that promotes the continued accumulation of capital and pursuit of profit is a perpetual struggle for capitalists. Failure at any point to generate legitimacy exacerbates conflicts between workers and owners, between consumers and suppliers of goods and services, and between other groups that are historically situated in competitive relations based on race, gender, citizenship status, and the like.

At the same time that state policies promote and maintain capitalist social relations, in order to legitimize its actions that support capitalist social relations, it must respond to the rules of a constitutional government and a liberal democratic political process. The identification of social problems and calls for state action from groups who are ill affected by the problems highlights the contradiction that often exists between the reality that state policy favors a system based on structured inequalities and one in which all groups are to be treated as equals.

Theories about the nature and character of society do not emerge from a vacuum, nor can they be purely objective, value-free sets of scientific observations and analyses. As we saw throughout the earlier discussion, there are many factors external to the research process that influence the development of sociological theories. Probably the most significant of these would include the sociohistoric context in which the theorists are operating, the educational experiences or training of the sociologist, and the political agenda and perspective of the sociologist.

All of this suggests certain obstacles still facing critical theorists. For example, the political perspective put forward in the work of professors, administrators, bureaucrats, and researchers affect their "employability." Unpopular, "extreme" points of view which often prove to be convenient labels assigned to critical perspectives can be labeled as undesirable, subversive, and even as a public threat. Sometimes, the political nature of our activities as social scientists, practitioners, advocates and activists is made explicit in our internal, professional dialogue. Other times, and most often when we present our work to the public, the political differences are downplayed and often window dressed to appear as if they are strictly "academic" or scientific debates. In the first instance, I believe that further advances in the development of our critical inquiry require us to once again confront the urgent question posed by the title of an article published in 1967 by Howard Becker in the journal *Social Problems*, namely: "Whose Side Are We On?"

Notes

1. J. Freund states that: "Tönnies formulated and even inaugurated a typology of social relations which no sociologist can henceforth ignore . . . Indeed all the discussion on the opposition between competition and accommodation, conflict and association, cooperation and hostility, fusion and tension, integration and dissolution, solidarity and rivalry, community and revolt, and all other forms of social concord and discord, bring us back directly or indirectly to the work of Tönnies." p. 153 in Freund, J. 1978. "German Sociology in the Time of Max Weber." In *A History of Sociological Analysis*, Eds. T. Bottomore and R. Nisbet. London: Heinemann. See also Giddens 1971.

2. Further discussion of the early influences on and evolution of the sociology of law, including the Law and Society Association, can be found in several articles from the 1998 Symposium on Socio-legal Scholarship published in the *Law and Society Review*, Volume 32, 2. See also several articles on the sociology of law in a global context and in various countries around the world in Volume 32, 2 of the *American Sociologist* published in 2001. British sociology of

law is covered well by Max Travers (2001). David Trubek (1972) offers an excellent discussion of Weber and the sociology of law.

3. This abbreviated discussion of Marxist theory should be supplemented by referring to Balbus (1973, 1977); Beirne (1979); Beirne and Quinney (1982); Chambliss (1989); Cotterrell (1984); Flacks and Turkel (1978).

4. Antonio Gramsci (1971) used the term "hegemony" to represent the dynamic process through which hierarchically structured relations penetrated the consciousness of subjects. Hegemony refers to a sophisticated, integrated form of cultural leadership (ideological domination) exercised by the ruling class (Stout 1989). See also Chambliss (1988: 283) for a more concise and accessible explanation of the concept "hegemony."

5. Though beyond the scope of this paper, social movement theorists have begun work that parallels that in critical criminology and the sociology of law to take into consideration the changing macrolevel sociohistoric processes, e.g., globalization. For example, see Cutler (1999); Robinson (2000); Silbey (1997); Balakrishnan (2003).

References

Ashley, David and David Michael Orenstein. 1998. *Sociological Theory: Classical Statements*, 4th edition. Boston: Allyn & Bacon.

Balakrishnan, Rajagopal. 2003. "International Law and Social Movements: Challenges of Theorizing Resistance." *Colum. J. Transnational L.* 41: 397.

Balbus, Isaac D. 1973. *The Dialectics of Legal Repression*. New York: Sage.

———. 1977. "Commodity Form and Legal Form: An Essay in the Relative Autonomy of the Law." *Law and Society Review* 11: 571–581.

Barkan, Steven E. 1985. *Protestors on Trial: Criminal Justice in the Southern Civil Rights and Vietnam Antiwar Movements*. New Brunswick, NJ: Rutgers University Press.

Becker, Howard S. 1967. "Whose Side Are We On?" *Social Problems* 14, 3: 239–247.

Beirne, Piers. 1979. "Empiricism and the Critique of Marxism on Law and Crime." *Social Problems* 26, 4: 373–385.

Beirne, Piers and Richard Quinney (eds.). 1982. *Marxism and Law*. New York: John Wiley.

Best, Joel and David F. Luckenbill. 1982. *Organizing Deviance*. Englewood Cliffs, NJ: Prentice-Hall.

Blumer, Herbert. 1978. "Social Unrest and Collective Protest" In Norman K. Denizen (ed.), *Studies in Symbolic Interaction* 1: 1–54.

Cain, Maureen. 1975. "Rich Man's Law or Poor Man's Law?" *British Journal of Law & Society* 2, 1: 61–66.

Calavita, Kitty. 1983. "The Demise of the Occupational Safety and Health Administration: A Case Study in Symbolic Action." *Social Problems* 30, 4: 437–448.

Cantril, Hadley. 1941. *The Psychology of Social Movements*. New York: John Wiley.

Chambliss, William J. 1964. "A Sociological Analysis of the Law of Vagrancy." *Social Problems* 12, 1: 45–69

———. 1984. *Criminal Law in Action,* 2nd edition. New York: Wiley & Sons.

———. 1988. *Exploring Criminology*. New York: MacMillan.

———. 1989. "On Trashing Marxist Criminology." *Criminology* 27, 2: 231–238.

Chambliss, William J. and Milton Mankoff (eds). 1975. *Whose Law? What Order?* New York: Wiley & Sons.

Chambliss, William J. and Robert Seidman. 1971. *Law, Order, and Power.* Reading, MA: Wesley.

Cloward, Richard A. 1959. "Illegitimate Means, Anomie, and Deviant Behavior" *American Sociological Review* 24, April: 164–76.

Cohen, Albert J. 1955. *Delinquent Boys: The Culture of the Gang*. New York: Free Press.

———. 1959. "The Study of Social Disorganization and Deviant Behavior." In Robert K. Merton, Leonard Broom and Leonard S. Cottrell (eds.), *Sociology Today*. New York: Basic Books.

Coser, Lewis A. 1977. *Masters of Sociological Thought: Ideas in Historical and Social Context*, 2nd edition. Fort Worth, TX: Harcourt Brace Jovanovich.

Cotterrell, Roger. 1984. *The Sociology of Law: An Introduction*. London: Butterworths.

Cutler, A. Claire. 1999. "Locating 'Authority' in the Global Political Economy." *International Studies Quarterly* 43, 1: 59–82.

Dello Buono, Richard A. 1993. "Black Radicalism." In Michael W. Williams (ed.), *The African-American Encyclopedia*. New York: Marshall Cavendish.

Fitzhugh, George. 1854. *Sociology for the South, or, The Failure of Free Society*. Richmond, VA: A. Morris.

Flacks, Richard. 1967. "The Liberated Generation: An Exploration of the Roots of Student Protest." *The Journal of Social Issues* 23: 52–75.

Flacks, Richard and Gerald Turkel. 1978. "Radical Sociology: The Emergence of Neo-Marxian Perspectives in U.S. Sociology." *Annual Review of Sociology* 4: 193–238.

Freeman, Jo. 1979. "Resource Mobilization and Strategy: A Model for Analyzing Social Movement Organizations." In Mayer N. Zald and John D. McCarthy (eds.), *The Dynamics of Social Movements*. Cambridge, MA: Winthrop.

Friedman, Lawrence M. 1986. "The Law and Society Movement" *Stanford Law Review* 38 763–780.

Friedrichs, David O. 1980. "The Legitimacy Crisis in the U.S.: A Conceptual Analysis." *Social Problems* 27, 5: 540–550.

Freund, J. 1978. "German Sociology in the Time of Max Weber," in T. Bottomore and R. Nisbet, eds., *A History of Sociological Analysis*. London: Heinemann.

Gamson, William A. 1975. *Strategies of Social Protest*. Homewood, IL: Dorsey Press.

———. 1987. "Introduction." In Mayer N. Zald and McCarthy (eds.), *Social Movements in an Organizational Society*. New Brunswick, NJ: Transaction Books.

———. 1992. "The Social Psychology of Collective Action." In Aldon D. Morris and Carol McClung Mueller (eds.), *Frontiers in Social Movement Theory*. New Haven, CT: Yale University Press.

Gamson, William A., Bruce Fireman, and Steven Rytina. 1982. *Encounters with Unjust Authority*. Homewood, IL: Dorsey Press.

Garner, Roberta Ash and Mayer N. Zald. 1987. "The Political Economy of Social Movement Sectors." In Mayer N. Zald and John D. McCarthy (eds.), *Social Movements in Organizational Society*. New Brunswick, NJ: Transaction Books.

Giddens, Anthony. 1971. *Capitalism and Modern Social Theory*. Cambridge, UK: Cambridge University Press.

Gramsci, Antonio. 1971. *Selections from the Prison Notebooks*. New York: International Publishers.

Gurr, Ted Robert. 1969. *Why Men Rebel*. Princeton, NJ: Princeton University Press.

Gusfield, Joseph R. 1963. *Symbolic Crusade: Status Politics and the American Temperance Movement*. Urbana: University of Illinois.

Harper, Charles L. and Kevin T. Leicht. 2002. *Exploring Social Change: America and the World*. Upper Saddle River, NJ: Prentice-Hall.

Hoffer, Eric. 1951. *The True Believer*. New York: Harper and Row.

Horwitz, Morton. 1992. *The Transformation of American Law, 1870–1960: The Crisis of Legal Orthodoxy*. New York: Oxford University Press.

Humphries, Drew and David Greenberg. 1981. "The Dialectics of Crime Control." In David Greenberg (ed.), *Crime and Capitalism*. Palo Alto, CA: Mayfield.

Hunt, Alan. 1978. *The Sociological Movement in Law*. Philadelphia: Temple University Press.

Jasper, James M. 2003. "Social Movement Theory after the Big Paradigms: Towards a Rhetorical Vision of Action." Unpublished. http://www.uga.edu/gwci/Jasper.pdf

Killian, Lewis. 1964. "Social Movements." In Robert E.L. Faris (ed.), *Handbook of Modern Sociology*. Chicago: Rand McNally.

Layish, Michael. 1997. "From the Editor: Some Lessons of Hindsight." *Law & Society Review* 31, 4: 633–636.

LeBon, Gustave. 1960 [1895]. *The Crowd: A Study of the Popular Mind*. New York: Viking.

Lemert, Edwin M. 1964. "Social Structure, Social Control, and Deviation." In Marshall B. Clinard (ed.), *Anomie and Deviant Behavior*. New York: Free Press.

Martindale, Don. 1981. *The Nature and Types of Sociological Theory*, 2nd edition. Boston: Houghton Mifflin.

Mather, Lynn. 2003. "Reflections on the Reach of Law (and Society) Post 9/11: An American Superhero?" *Law and Society Review* 37, 2: 259–276.

McCarthy, John D. and M. N. Zald. 1977. "Resource Mobilization in Social Movements: A Partial Theory." *American Journal of Sociology* 82, 6: 1212–1241.

Merton, Robert. 1957. *Social Theory and Social Structure*. Glencoe, IL: Free Press.

———. 1967. *On Theoretical Sociology*. New York: Free Press.

Michalowski, Raymond J. 1985. *Order, Law and Crime: An Introduction to Criminology*. New York: Random House.

Mills, C. Wright. 1959. *The Sociological Imagination*. New York: Oxford University Press.

Morris, Aldon D. 1984. *The Origins of the Civil Rights Movement: Black Communities Organizing for Change*. New York: Free Press.

Oberschall, Anthony. 1973. *Social Conflict and Social Movements*. Englewood Cliffs, NJ: Prentice-Hall.

———. 1979. "Protracted Conflict." In Mayer N. Zald and John D. McCarthy (eds.), *The Dynamics of Social Movements*. Cambridge, MA: Winthrop.

Pfohl, Stephen J. 1985. *Images of Deviance and Social Control: A Sociological Understanding*. New York: McGraw-Hill.

———. 1994. *Images of Deviance and Social Control: A Sociological Understanding*, 2nd edition. New York: McGraw-Hill.

Piven, Francis Fox and Richard A. Cloward. 1971. *Regulating the Poor: The Function of Public Welfare*. New York: Pantheon.

Platt, Anthony M. 1969. *The Child Savers: The Invention of Delinquency*. Chicago: University of Chicago Press.

———. 1977. *The Child Savers: The Invention of Delinquency*, 2nd edition. Chicago: University of Chicago Press.

Reynolds, Larry T. 1987. *Interactionism: Exposition and Critique*. New York: General Hall.

Ritzer, George. 1988. *Contemporary Sociological Theory*, 2nd edition. New York: Alfred A. Knopf.

Robinson, Ian. 2000. "Neoliberal Restructuring and U.S. Unions: Toward Social Movement Unionism?" *Critical Sociology* 26, 1/2: 109–139.

Silbey, Susan S. 1997. "Let Them Eat Cake: Globalization, Postmodern Colonialism, and the Possibilities of Justice." *Law and Society Review* 31, 2: 207–237.

Skolnick, Jerome. 1966. *Justice without Trial: Law Enforcement in Democratic Society*, 2nd edition. New York: John Wiley & Sons.

Smelser, Neil. 1962. *Theory of Collective Behavior*. New York: Free Press.

Spencer, Herbert. 1989. *Principles of Sociology*. New York: Appleton.

Stout, A. Kathryn. 1989. *Sanctuary in the 1980s: The Dialectics of Law and Social Movement Development*. Ann Arbor, Michigan: UMI.

———. 1994. "Social Action and Protest Organizations." In Susan Auerbach (ed.), *The Encyclopedia of Multiculturalism*. New York: Marshall Cavendish.

Stout, A. Kathryn and Richard A. Dello Buono. 1991. "Political Prisoners as an Emergent Contradiction of State Repression: An Introductory Essay." *Humanity and Society* 15, 4: 338–349.

Tarde, Gabriel. 1912. *Penal Philosophy*. Boston: Little, Brown.

Tilly, Charles. 1970. "The Changing Place of Collective Violence." In Melvin Richter (ed.), *Essays in Social and Political History*. Cambridge, MA: Harvard University Press.

———. 1978. *From Mobilization to Revolution*. Reading, MA: Addison-Wesley.

Tönnies, Ferdinand. 1963 [1957]. *Community and Society.* New York: Harper and Row.

Travers, Max. 2001. "Sociology of Law in Britain." *American Sociologist* 32, 2: 26–40.

Treviño, Javier. 2001. "The Sociology of Law in Global Perspective." *American Sociologist* 32, 2: 5–10.

Trubek, David M. 1972. "Max Weber on Law and the Rise of Capitalism." *Wisconsin Law Review* 72, 3: 720–753.

Turk, Austin. 1968. *Criminality and the Legal Order*. New York: Rand McNally.

———. 1982. *Political Criminality: The Defiance and Defense of Authority*. Beverly Hills, CA: Sage.

Vago, Steven. 2003. *Law and Society,* 7th edition. Upper Saddle River, NJ: Prentice, Hall.

Wood, James L. and Maurice Jackson. 1982. *Social Movements: Development, Participation and Dynamics*. Belmont, CA: Wadsworth.

Zald, Mayer N. and Roberta Ash. 1966. "Social Movement Organizations: Growth, Decay, and Change." *Social Forces* 44: 327–341.

Zald, Mayer N. and John D. McCarthy. 1979. *The Dynamics of Social Movements*. Cambridge, MA: Winthrop.

Part II

CRITICAL VIEWS ON SOCIAL PROBLEMS, CONFLICT, AND LAW: BEYOND CONSTRUCTIONISM

In this first section, some landmark theoretical statements on social problems, law, and society are presented. Together, they help provide a context for understanding the role played by social constructionism as well as some of the limitations associated with it. By giving careful consideration to their arguments, we come away with a better sense of the challenges facing us in advancing a critical perspective on law and society in the twenty-first century.

Steve Woolgar and Dorothy Pawluch's article leads off by providing an extremely useful discussion of the influential role played by social constructionism in social problems theory. By responding to what was a rapid growth of social definitionist approaches, they reveal essential similarities between constructionist approaches to social problems and deviance. In doing so, they raise serious questions concerning what is to be considered "problematic" in constructionist studies, thus helping to reveal the limits of such approaches.

Their notion of "ontological gerrymandering" aims to capture the selective and ultimately arbitrary and thus problematic means by which constructionists call into question the "truth status" of certain social processes associated with "social problems," while at the same time minimizing or ignoring altogether the specter of doubt regarding their own definitionist enterprise. Woolgar and Pawluch give particular emphasis to Stephen Pfohl's (1977) landmark study "The 'Discovery' of Child Abuse," where the problem of child mistreatment is explained by reference to concrete, sociohistorical practices of power, namely, as a creation on the part of a medicalizing coalition of pediatric radiologists, psychiatrists, and other pediatric specialists. The authors argue that Pfohl's attempt to distance himself from the "real" or objective facticity of abusive behavior is characteristic of social constructionists. Yet, they show that this is inconsistent with the way in which he treats the notion of child beating, essentially using "beating" as an objectified point of reference in order to use constructionist analysis as a form of explaining the definitioning process by which it subsequently becomes "discovered" as the pathology "child abuse."

This practice of calling into question the "realness" of selected claims regarding a phenomenon while at the same time taking for granted and then relying upon other pivotal categories, which themselves consist of sociohistorical "reality claims," amounts to the "ontological gerrymandering" practice of social constructionists. Woolgar and Pawluch essentially indict social definitionists for lacking any reliable basis for the erection of conceptual firewalls in the construction of their own discourse. If Woolgar and Pawluch are correct, it would seem that constructionists are compelled to be either opportunistic in the establishment of these objectivistic firewalls or else burn up in the very process of their hot pursuit. But the discussion does not end here.

By way of an invited response to their article, Stephen Pfohl's commentary brilliantly responded to Woolgar and Pawluch's critique with a reflexive and self-critical argument that simultaneously documented his own shifting position in asserting the desirability of moving toward a social deconstructionist perspective. In so doing, Pfohl essentially credits social constructionism for having "opened up the space" for critical reflection upon social problems and deviance in a manner by which the "construction" of sociological knowledge itself could become viewed as "problematic." At the same time, he begins to hint at the inadequacy of these approaches. Pfohl's commentary displays sensitivity to the concerns displayed by more structurally oriented, political-economic approaches and responds by calling for a critical, poststructuralist discourse that is "power reflexive" in orientation, one that as a matter of course turns upon itself as well as the object of its ongoing inquiry.

For Pfohl, the fruits of analysis rest in revelation, not in some explanation steeped in Durkheimian social facticity, and his approach indeed reveals that "power-invested practices" ultimately constitute the process in which social problems become defined and redefined. This short commentary invites others to follow his lead in going beyond the early notions of social constructionism in search of connecting interpretative analysis to the historically circumscribed social relations of power.

By way of contrast, Frances Fox Piven's chapter, excerpted from her SSSP presidential address in 1980, consists of a frontal assault upon the societal reaction perspective. She argues that interactionist logic effectively extinguishes human agency from its analysis, thus eliminating the purposeful aspects of behavior, and this becomes especially apparent in studies of deviance. Rule-breaking behavior in this context becomes looked at in terms of the differential layers of societal reaction to this conduct. This amounts to the loss of human agency, according to Piven, that led the societal reaction school to attempt to construct a theory of "pure domination" in which the presence of force was erased in favor of stigma. Among other characteristics, she notes that social movements of resistance and opposition are largely ignored in favor of less threatening forms of deviance. Interactionist theorists thus dedicate little attention to the causes of rebellious social movements with the result of effectively losing sight of the basic underlying dialectic of domination and resistance.

William Chambliss' chapter is a seminal work in the critical sociology of law. He provides a historical analysis of the vagrancy laws in England and the United States, providing a now-classic illustration of how power and conflict underlie the process of law creation. In many ways, this article broke new ground. Through a careful content analysis of laws on vagrancy, Chambliss was able to determine the population to which they were being addressed and thus discover the historical context that gave rise to these laws. His analysis employed a critical, "bottom-up" view of history, that is, one from the perspective of the lower classes, in place of the more traditional kind of historical approach that privileges the vantage point of kings and presidents. By way of a critical reading of Weber, Chambliss set out to show not only how the vagrancy laws emerged and changed over time but also how they were used as a mechanism for controlling the labor supply. In this way, the article provides an enduring example of how laws posing as moral statements of right and wrong are often designed to reproduce existing political and economic relations. This concern with the relationship of laws enacted upon the labor force marked an incipient turn toward a dialectical, Marxist approach that Chambliss would use in his later work in order to grapple with the central concerns addressed by critical criminology and the sociology of law.

For his part, Austin Turk's chapter sets forth the desirability of a "power approach" to the study of law and society. He stresses the need *not* to take for granted the relationship between law and conflict, but rather to leave it as an issue for empirical inquiry. By viewing law as a set of power assets, rather than some sort of conflict regulator, he sets the stage for a more logically coherent, conflict approach to the sociology of law. Turk's article represented an early call for research that seeks greater understanding into how legal resources are mobilized and controlled. Turk and others with similar views were highly influential on the development of critical criminology.

In the final chapter of this section, Piers Beirne offers an eloquent defense of Marxian theory and seeks to establish that approach as the paradigmatic base for the "new criminology." He constructs a broad critique of those mainstream critics who seek to dismiss Marxian criminology and shows how critical criminology arose as a political response to mainstream sociology and criminology, building off the critical spirit that was engendered by labeling and conflict approaches that sought to demystify the legal order. He is careful to point out, however, that the structural logic developed by Marxist theorists of law did *not* emerge from within any of the critical perspectives of academic sociological thought. Rather, he shows how they arose out of internal debates within Marxism itself, particularly those centered on conceptualizing the nature of the capitalist state. Beirne identifies structural Marxists such as Nicos Poulantzas, Louis Althusser, and others as importance sources of insight that, together with the critical legal theory put forth by commodity exchange theorists such as the Russian Marxist Evgeny Pashukanis, helped shape the emerging Marxist perspective on law and society.

References

Beirne, Piers. 1979. Empiricism and the Critique of Marxism on Law and Crime. *Social Problems* 26, no. 4:373–85.

Chambliss, William J. 1964. A Sociological Analysis of the Law of Vagrancy. *Social Problems* 12, no. 1:67–77.

Pfohl, Stephen. 1985. Towards a Sociological Deconstruction of Social Problems. *Social Problems* 31, no. 3:228–32.

Piven, Frances Fox. 1981. Deviant Behavior and the Remaking of the World. *Social Problems* 28, no. 5:489–508.

Turk, Austin T. 1976. Law as a Weapon in Social Conflict. *Social Problems* 23, no. 3:276–91.

Woolgar, Steve and Dorothy Pawluch. 1985. Ontological Gerrymandering: The Anatomy of Social Problems Explanations. *Social Problems* 32, no. 3:214–27.

CHAPTER 3

Ontological Gerrymandering

THE ANATOMY OF SOCIAL PROBLEMS EXPLANATIONS

Steve Woolgar and Dorothy Pawluch

In this paper we examine a body of recent contributions to the study of social problems which adopt a predominantly "definitional" or "social constructionist" perspective.[1] Our objective is to provide a critical commentary on the character of sociological argument common to this school. We call our approach an "ethnography of argument," where "ethnography" denotes our attempt to take a distanced (or anthropologically strange) view of the activities we observe, and where "argument" is a generic term for activities such as reasoning, explaining, persuading, and understanding. Our approach is thus informed by recent developments in the ethnography of scientific practice (Knorr-Cetina 1981; Latour and Woolgar 1979; Lynch, 1985; Traweek, Forthcoming; for a review of this literature see Knorr-Cetina 1983; Woolgar 1982) which portrays the work of explanation as a practical accomplishment.[2]

We begin by identifying the strategy and explanatory moves characteristic of social problems argument within the definitional perspective. We use the term "ontological gerrymandering" to describe its central strategy. Second, we examine how this strategy is used in programmatic theoretical statements and, then, in empirical work what has followed the definitional approach, particularly Stephen Pfohl's (1977) analysis of child abuse. Third, we show that ontological gerrymandering is at the center of some conceptual problems which have characterized labeling approaches to the study of deviance. We speculate that the conceptual strategies and problems we identify in social problems explanations may be characteristic of all sociological argument which invokes a selective relativism with respect to the phenomena it seeks to explain. In the final section we discuss three distinct ways to understand the significance and implications of the critique we offer.

Structure of Social Problems Argument

The distinctive feature of the social problems arguments we consider here is the departure from traditional conceptualizations of social problems in terms of objective conditions and causes. The definitionalist school instead views social problems in terms of the activity whereby they are *defined* or constructed. Social problems are sociologically *defined* as what people think they are. Spector and Kitsuse (1977: 75) express the theoretical rationale for this approach as follows:

> Our definition of social problems focuses on the process by which members of society define a putative condition as a social problem. Thus we define social problems *as the activities of individuals or groups making assertions of grievances and claims with respect to some putative conditions.* (emphasis in original)

A number of recent articles have analyzed changing definitions of behaviors and conditions, and have attempted to account for these changes in terms of the claims-making activities of the individuals and groups involved. Some authors have been more successful than others in remaining impartial to the truth value of their claims. But in a fundamental sense all these works make claims of their own, the truth value of which is never questioned. It is this common feature of social problems explanations that we analyze here.

There is a remarkable similarity in the explanatory structure of the studies we examined. Each identifies three main features: a phenomenon or putative condition to which claims-making activities have been directed; one or more definitions or claims made about the condition; and the identity of the definers (or claimants). All the case studies exhibit the same two-part format. First, the explanation begins by invoking certain sets of behaviors and conditions, and by presenting a picture of varying responses (definitions and claims) associated with them. Second, each study invokes characteristics of prevailing socio-historical circumstances to account for variations in definitions. More specifically, the studies we examined attempt to situate claims-making activities within socio-historical contexts by reference to social "forces" (Aronson 1982: 484; Markle and Troyer 1979: 611; Nuehring and Markle 1974: 513; Pfohl 1977: 310; Rose 1977: 75), prevalent "world views" (Conrad and Schneider 1980: 27–28), "cultural conceptions" (Conrad and Schneider 1980: 36) and "social structure" (Ball and Lilly 1982: 488; Schneider 1978: 361, 370). The second part of the explanatory format depends on the first. Without achieving a disjunction between the behaviors and conditions, on the one hand, and the responses, on the other, there would be nothing to explain. If there was no variation in response, if particular responses resulted uniquely from particular conditions, there would be no place for the intervention of socio-historical circumstances. Thus, the portrayal of an indeterminate relationship between conditions and responses is a crucial prerequisite for explanation. Partly for this reason, and partly because an analysis of the sociological use of interests as explanans is already available (Woolgar 1981), we concentrate on the first part of the explanatory format in this paper.

The first part of the explanation can itself be broken down into three key moves. First, authors identify certain conditions or behaviors. Second, they identify various definitions (or claims) made about these conditions (or behaviors). Third, the authors stress the variability of the definitions vis-à-vis the constancy of the conditions to which they relate. They imply that since the condition does not vary, variations in the definition of the condition must result from the social circumstances of the definers rather than from the condition itself.

In the simplest version of this explanatory form, the lynch pin is the assumption that the condition itself does not vary. More generally, the explanation depends upon some "objective" statement about the condition and some explanations are based upon assumptions about an "actual change" in the condition. Taking the existence of putative behaviors, conditions, and the character of phenomena (or changes therein) for granted allows the authors to stress the "fact" that the definitions and claims associated with these behaviors and conditions have changed. By virtue of the contrast between the claimed objective state of affairs pertaining to the conditions, and the supposed social contingency of the related definitions, the authors seek to reassert the basic axiom of their analysis: that the fluidity of the definitions reflects that they are fundamentally socio-historical accomplishments.

But how do authors manage to portray statements about conditions and behaviors as objective while relativizing the definitions and claims made about them? The metaphor of *ontological gerrymandering* suggests the central strategy for accomplishing this move. The successful social problems explanation depends on making problematic the truth status of certain states of affairs selected for analysis and explanation, while backgrounding or minimizing the possibility that the same problems apply to assumptions upon which the analysis depends.[3] By means of ontological gerrymandering, proponents of definitional explanation place a boundary between assumptions which are to be understood as (ostensibly) problematic and those which are not.[4] This "boundary work" creates and sustains the differential susceptibility of phenomena to ontological uncertainty. Some areas are portrayed as ripe for ontological doubt and others portrayed as (at least temporarily) immune to doubt.

The Work of Ontological Gerrymandering

We begin with recent theoretical statements of the definitional approach to social problems. Spector and Kitsuse (1977) elaborate the imperative to study definitions of social problems rather than the imputed conditions themselves. To do so, they employ the assumption that in many cases definitions of social problems vary while conditions do not. They note, for example, that during the 1930s the official definition of marijuana included the notion that it was both dangerous and addictive. During the 1960s, however, marijuana was no longer classified as addictive. The authors then make this change in definition speak to a range of investigable sociological questions:

> there is nothing in the nature of marijuana itself to explain this definitional change. *The nature of marijuana remained constant throughout the interval* and, therefore, an explanation of the variation must come from another source. In fact, its "nature" cannot adequately explain either the definition

> of marijuana as an addictive or nonaddictive substance. The explanation of the definition must be sought in the conceptions held by various groups, the notion of addiction they applied, the type of evidence they used to support their views, the political strategies and tactics they used to gain acceptance of their definitions and the support given to them by governmental agencies for institutionalizing those definitions. (Spector and Kitsuse 1977: 43, our emphasis)

Gusfield (1981: 8) similarly makes the assumption that the condition itself is invariant:

> The social construction of social problems implies a historical dimension. The *same* "objective" condition may be defined as a problem in one time period, not in another. (our emphasis)

In the same vein, Conrad and Schneider (1980: 1) introduce their collection of analyses of deviant behavior that has undergone definitional change with the assertion:

> A slow but steady transformation of deviance has taken place in American society. *It has not been a change in behavior as such*, but in how behavior has been defined. Deviant behaviors that were once defined as immoral, sinful, or criminal have been given medical meanings. (our emphasis)

In each case, the key assertion is that the actual character of a substance (marijuana), condition, or behavior remained constant.[5] But in each case the authors fail to acknowledge that their identification of "the nature of marijuana," or their assertion of the constancy of a condition or behavior, can itself be construed as a definitional claim. In naming, identifying or describing conditions, these authors inevitably give definition to the putative behaviors and conditions they discuss. While the claims of the claims makers are depicted as socio-historical constructions (definitions) that require explanation, the claims and the constructive work of the authors remain hidden and are to be taken as given.

The Empirical Literature

The ontological gerrymandering evident in programmatic theoretical statements is sustained in empirical case studies which follow a definitional or labeling approach. In *all* the empirical work we examined, authors assume the existence and (objective) character of underlying conditions around which definitional claims have been made. There is, however, some variation in the extent to which these accounts make *explicit* claims for the actual (or objective) character of putative conditions.

In the more explicit examples, authors describe the actual character of a condition. For example, in Gusfield (1975) the actual number of deaths per year from automobile crashes assumes the role of a given. Some authors fix the constancy of conditions by stating that "the phenomenon itself was not new" (Loseke and Cahill 1984: 296) or that the behavior has been "around for millennia" (Johnson and Hufbauer 1982:

65) or "throughout the ages" (Pfohl 1977: 310). In other examples, authors go beyond assumptions about the existence and character of putative conditions by claiming (actual) changes in the extent to which these conditions exist. Changes in the amount, intensity or distribution of a condition serve as the basis for discussion of claims-making activities. Lidz and Walker (1980: 47–59) fix the pattern of heroin use in the United States during the period of a heroin crisis and conclude (1980: 83) that "there was not really an epidemic increase in heroin use." Their claim that the rate of heroin use did not rise dramatically is used to imply that an explanation for the crisis must be sought elsewhere.

An alternative construction contrasts an (actual) change in conditions with an opposite change in definitional activity. Chauncey (1980: 49–50) describes the creation of a teenage drinking problem when "there (were) no clear indications of a growing problem involving adolescents and alcohol" and where some indicators in fact showed a decline. Spector and Kitsuse (1977: 128) use a similar argument about poverty and the quality of the environment. The implication here is that putative conditions could not possibly explain definitional changes because the evidence shows that the putative situation was improving rather than deteriorating.

On other occasions, authors avoid any *explicit* claim for the objectivity of a condition which is the focus of claims-making activities being discussed. In these cases, the condition is rarely described directly in any detail. Instead, authors name or refer to a substance (Ball and Lilly 1982; Becker 1963; Markle and Troyer 1979; Nuehring and Markle 1974; Troyer and Markle 1983, 1984), physiological process (McCrea 1983; Rothman 1983), or behavior (Aronson 1982; Chauncey 1980; Conrad 1975, 1976; Gusfield 1975, 1981; Morrow 1982; Randall and Short 1983; Rose 1977; Schneider 1978; Spector 1977). It is possible that these authors are leaving implicit their realist assumptions about the condition. Alternatively, they may be trying to avoid any assumption about the ontological status of the condition. Whichever is the case, these authors nonetheless organize their reports of definitions and claims so as to assign, de facto, an objective status to these conditions. The authors appeal to our commonsense knowledge that these conditions have not changed character over time.[6] Thus, they leave implicit the claim that Spector and Kitsuse (1977: 43) make explicit for programmatic purposes: "the nature of marijuana remained constant throughout the interval." The de facto assignation of objective status is also evident in the lack of reference to "putative margarine" (Ball and Lilly 1982), "putative birth" (Rothman 1983), "putative hiring practices" (Randall and Short 1983), or "putative homosexuality" (Spector 1977).

Therefore, variation and considerable ambivalence is associated with the claim that the definition results from the socio-historical circumstances of the definers rather than from the condition itself. Whereas some analysts (Ball and Lilly 1982: 488; Randall and Short 1983: 410; Rose 1977: 75) imply that the definition tells you *more* about the definers than the condition, others (Conrad 1976: 590; Gusfield 1975: 288; Markle and Troyer 1979: 622; Schneider 1978: 361) take the line that definitions tell you about the definers and *not* about the condition.[7]

Certain social problems arguments display an obvious objectivist commitment when they draw upon assumptions about the existence, constancy, or extent of a condition in order to go beyond the relevance of claims-making activities and pronounce upon the warrant for certain claims. Chauncey (1980: 45) argues that the facts about teenage drinking "belie the inflammatory rhetoric." Rose (1977: 78) dismisses the claim that it is impossible to rape an unwilling woman on the grounds that "there is no data to support such contentions." Conrad (1976) explicitly challenges the applicability of a medical model to the putative problem of deviant behavior in children. More subtly, Morrow (1982: 92) argues that the extent of drug addiction, alcoholism, psychiatric disorders, and substandard performance among doctors was *acknowledged* or *recognized*, while the "physician impairment label" attached to this putative behavior is portrayed as a *conceptualization*, *interpretation*. or "*discovery*" (quotation marks in original). Similarly, McCrea (1983: 111) argues that gynecologists "*discovered*" and then *claimed* that menopause was a "deficiency disease" (quotation marks in original), but that feminists are now *exposing* the sexism in women's health care.

Despite these variations, every example of the empirical literature displays a common feature: one category of claims is laid open to ontological uncertainty and then made the target for explanation in terms of the social circumstances which generated them; at the same time, the reader is asked to accept another category of claims on faith. Some of these latter claims, especially those about the extent of, or warrant for, a condition could be avoided. However, for the social problems argument to "work," authors cannot avoid the claim for the existence and/or constancy of at least one relevant condition.

The Example of Child Abuse

In order to examine the work of ontological gerrymandering in detail, we focus on an article that discusses the issue of child abuse (Pfohl 1977). We chose to discuss this work in detail because its clarity of exposition makes it especially easy to discern the explanatory structure common to a large number of similar contributions and because it is sometimes regarded as an exemplar of the definitional approach to social problems.[8] Pfohl deals with changing definitions of child beating in America (see also Parton 1979). Briefly his account is as follows:

Prior to the nineteenth century, child beating was believed necessary for discipline and obedience, and was legitimated by a legal tradition that gave guardians limitless power over their children. Beginning in the nineteenth century, reformers directed attention to the plight of beaten and neglected children but viewed their predicament as part of the larger problem of poverty. The reform movements aimed to save society from future delinquents by taking children out of their corrupt environments and placing them in institutions. In the early twentieth century, the Depression and the perceived failure of institutionalization undermined the philosophy of preventive penology. There was at the same time an increased awareness of children and interest in child welfare. But these developments did not focus attention on the perpetrators of abuse. Child welfare agencies were either unaware of abusive behavior or constrained by a model of casework that focused on psychic disturbances rather than family politics. Physicians who encountered abused children directly were unaware of "abuse" as a diagnosis or unwilling to believe that parents could harm their own children. They were also constrained by the norm of confidentiality between doctor and patient and by reluctance to become involved in a criminal justice process that would both take time and preempt their control over medical practice.

One group of physicians, however, was not subject to these constraints and could benefit from the "discovery." Pediatric radiologists worked constantly with children's x-rays but had no relationship with patients or their families. This low status specialty saw an opportunity for advancement by linking themselves to the problem of abuse. They were supported in their "discovery" by two other marginal specialties, pediatrics and psychiatry. On their own, none of these specialties could overcome the impediments Pfohl identified, but the interests of all three were advanced by a coalition. Together they generated and publicized a medical, as opposed to a legal, label for abuse (the battered child syndrome) that allowed them to benefit from the diagnosis without bringing in extra-medical controls.[9]

Pfohl's analysis embodies the main features of definitional explanations. The condition ("child beating") to which the claims-making activities refer is portrayed as fixed; by contrast, definitions of this (unchanging) condition are portrayed as highly variable—child beating has been variously the prerogative of the parent, part of the larger problem of poverty, a function of the psychopathic impulse of the disturbed parent, and child abuse; finally, these variations in definition are "explained" by reference to socio-historical circumstances.

Pfohl fixes the nature of the condition with comments such as the following: "Despite documentary evidence of child beating through the ages, the 'discovery' of child abuse as deviance and its subsequent criminalization are recent phenomena" (1977: 310). He also fixes the extent of the problem by citing a *Stanford Law Review* article (Eads 1969) in support of his contention that "there has never been any evidence that . . . battering behavior was actually increasing" (1977: 315). In neither case is the nature and adequacy of the evidence discussed. The evidence is neither to be understood as fabricated, nor as the result of claims-making activities. It is to be taken on trust, the objective touchstone for a telling contrast. The structure of this contrast (. . . despite X for a long time, Y is only recent . . .) establishes the problematic of the paper: why did Y not occur before? The existence of X (documentary evidence), it is implied, is sufficient reason for Y (the discovery). Two sentences later, however, Pfohl states that this is not so. The documentary evidence is insufficient; instead "social forces" are necessary for the discovery: "This paper is a study of the organization of social forces which gave rise to the deviant labeling of child beating" (1977: 310). This sentence is important because it instructs the reader how to make sense of what follows. In Smith's (1978) terms, the reader is encouraged to find the rest of the text as an adequate puzzle for the solution given at the outset. It is not the phenomenon itself (child beating) that gives rise to changes in its definition.

Pfohl's article is entitled "The 'Discovery' of Child Abuse." The use of the word discovery in connection with the definitional approach is curious. Discovery refers to the act of disclosing, making known or bringing to light. If the premise argues that social problems are constituted by their definitions, it is inconsistent to talk about them as discoveries.[10] Pfohl manages the tension of his ontological stance toward the phenomenon by placing the word "discovery" in quotation marks. The use of quotation marks suggests to readers that what seems to be a discovery is something other than it appears (Latour and Woolgar 1979: Chapter 2). It is not a discovery but an invention or construction; readers are to understand that in the rendering of discovery, the constructive/definitional work of others has been involved. By highlighting the involvement of definitional work, Pfohl argues that child abuse was not discovered but created by certain medical interests. The use of quotation marks suggests Pfohl is carefully attempting to distance himself from the position that child abuse is a real objective fact. At the same time, Pfohl effectively backgrounds or conceals the constructed character of other key concepts. The boundary between concepts to be taken as problematic and those to remain unquestioned (at least during the course of this analysis) is fashioned by the use of contrast structures. For example, we notice that although there are quotation marks around the word "discovery," there are not quotation marks around the word evidence. For Pfohl, it was evidence that was available, not "evidence."[11] More significantly, the contrast between child beating and child abuse implies the objective character of the former and the evaluative, subjective character of the latter. The former refers to the (actual) behavior in question, while the latter is a label which has only recently been applied to that behavior. The contrast between an unchanging (timeless) objectivity and the merely transient character of the applied label reinforces the notion that child abuse is socially constructed.

The contrast projects child beating as an impartial description of the behavior and child abuse as an evaluative reaction to it. The reader is encouraged not to recognize that the term child beating is also evaluative in the sense that it too involves a particular perception of the putative act. "Child beating" may come across as a less pejorative term than "child abuse," but it is nonetheless a label or a construction. Yet Pfohl's account asks the reader to take for granted the label "child beating" while attention is directed to the constructive work of those who propose the label "child abuse."

Pfohl's implicit claim to remain impartial with respect to the validity of the assertion that child beating represents a case of parental abuse is belied in the structure of his analysis. It reads as an account not so much of how the category "child abuse" came to be applied to child beating but as an explanation for why the category had not been previously applied. This implies some immutable link between child abuse and child beating, and renders the formulation of the label "child abuse" a discovery of that link after all. We previously noted Pfohl's dismissal of the commonsense view that the incidence of child beating increased to such an extent that people finally took notice of it. "The discovery (of abuse) is not attributable to any escalation of abuse itself'" (1977: 315). Here the word discovery is not qualified with quotation marks. This is not merely a "slip" but a foreshadowing of a commitment to the realist view of child abuse. If Pfohl was in fact treating "abuse" simply as a category created to explain child beating, the sentence cited above would be tautological. Pfohl uses "abuse" to denote both the label to be explained and the objective behavior that might, in principle, explain the label. We say "in principle" because in this particular case Pfohl argues there is no evidence to suggest that battering actually increased. Pfohl here takes issue with the idea that child abuse was recognized only because the situation had reached such exaggerated proportions; he does not challenge the realist position that child abuse has always existed and has only recently been recognized. The remainder of the article becomes an explication of why it was recognized for what it was in the 1950s and 1960s rather than before.

In describing previous reactions to child beating Pfohl writes that the reformist movements ". . . failed to differentiate between abuse and poverty and therefore registered no social reaction against beating as a form of deviance" (1977: 312). The use of the word "failed" indicates that Pfohl believes abuse not only existed but could be differentiated from the more general problem of poverty. It is because the reformers did not recognize this distinction that child abuse "as a specific form of deviance" (1977: 315) did not come to light. Only once the "link between poverty and morality began to weaken" (1977: 314) and once the philosophy of preventive penology was undermined, was the backdrop set for the discovery. With respect to the decline of the philosophy of preventive penology, "the lessening of its role removed a significant barrier to concern with abuse as an act of individual victimization" (1977: 314). But other impediments remained, according to Pfohl. There was a lack of organized interest among members of legal and child welfare agencies as well as a number of structural and psychological constraints impinging on members of the medical profession. "*Abused and neglected children* awaited the advocacy of some other organized interests" (1977: 314, our emphasis). Pediatric radiologists, in conjunction with pediatricians and psychiatrists, removed the final blinder and finally uncovered the plight of abused children. The use of such words as barriers, impediments, deterrents, and constraints, reaffirms that Pfohl's article is an account not of the creation of a label but of the slow removal of one barrier after another until the parental abuse of children was finally revealed for what it was.[12]

Social Problems and the Sociology of Deviance

The social problems literature we have examined adopts an analytic perspective characteristic of work in the sociology of deviance.[13] In particular, much work in the definitional approach to social problems has espoused a version of the labeling theory of deviance.[14] It is not surprising, then, that the conceptual problems of the definitional approach to social problems also appear in the labeling theory of deviance. However, labeling theorists have shown rather more interest in the conceptual problems which plague their theoretical perspective.

One important comment on these conceptual problems is Rains' (1975) elegant discussion of the divergent theoretical strains which characterize the labeling perspective. Rains points out that a crucial issue hinges upon deciding how to speak about what reactions to deviance are reactions to. For Lemert (1951), the use of the term "putative" alerts readers to the ambiguity of the correspondence between ascribed and actual deviance, but ultimately leaves the decision about the warrant for the label "deviant" as a matter for empirical investigation; notwithstanding the labeling process, the actual fact of deviance is taken to be an *objective* real life event which exists independently of societal reaction. By contrast, Kitsuse (1962) restores the essential ambiguity of the term "putative" by refusing to engage the issue of actual deviance. In line with one of the central tenets of early ethnomethodology, Kitsuse takes the labeling process as *constitutive* of the phenomenon of deviance; the issue of interest here is the attribution of "deviance" to anyone, regardless of whether they are "deviant." In part due to partial readings of writers like Lemert and Kitsuse, work adopting the labeling perspective has come to exhibit a fusion of the objectivist and constitutive positions. But the combination of two such contrasting positions has not been happy:

> The fledgling position that reactions to deviance might alternately and more properly be conceived of as reactions that constitute deviance has had sufficient theoretical appeal to affect the emergent labeling literature, but has not had sufficient theoretical clarity to withstand the inroads of sociological common-sense. (Rains 1975: 8)

Rains speaks of the tension between these two different ways of conceptualizing deviance. The tension is evident in the compromise position of more recent applications of the labeling perspective: societal reactions to deviance are held to be (mere) imputations and yet are taken to be specifically unwarranted.

In similar vein, Pollner (1974) argues that Becker's (1963) account of labeling theory embodies a confusion between two quite distinctive epistemological models of the labeling process. The first model is the common sense view that deviance inheres in acts of deviance and can exist independently of the community response. The second model is the view that the labeling process is constitutive of deviance; there is no deviance apart from the response of the community. Pollner points out that Becker's espousal of the latter view, and his view that it is a distinctive sociological model of labeling in fact belies Becker's implicit reliance on the first model. For Pollner, the indiscriminate mixing of the two models gives rise to an internally contradictory theoretical formulation.

We thus see that the "tension" identified by Rains appears in Pollner's account as an "internal contradiction" between objectivist and constitutive versions of the labeling process. Both Rains and Pollner are dissatisfied with this state of affairs. For example, Rains concludes that compromise has blunted the strategic advantages of either polar position.

We believe the ontological gerrymandering discussed above is crucial to authors' practical management of the tensions and internal contradictions in the deviance literature. Ontological gerrymandering provides a means whereby authors can "get on with" the argument and remain oblivious to the critical points made almost ten years ago; this boundary work makes it possible to live with tension and contradiction.

There are two important aspects of Rains' own argument to which this point is particularly relevant. First, Rains comments that Kitsuse's use of the term "imputation" makes it possible to describe the process of imputation without regard for warrant. Yet, as she points out, the mere use of the term invites a reading that the imputation is unwarranted. Indeed, Kitsuse (1962: 255) himself anticipates this "misunderstanding" by disavowing any critical intent in his analysis of "imputations."[15] This raises the vexed question as to whether or not it is possible to produce descriptions of phenomena which are indeed impartial with respect to their ontological status.

Secondly, Rains points out that whereas labeling theorists rely on the theoretical principle that all societal reactions might be unwarranted, they in fact describe the labeling process as it applies to particular substantive arenas of social action. In their selection of substantive arenas they display a remarkable affinity for "socially ambiguous subject matters" (1975: 6). Witches are a popular topic because "the deviant act is nonexistent" (Currie 1968: 28). Similarly, mental illness and juvenile delinquency are attractive because they "are so nebulously defined . . . The grounds for deciding whether a person is 'really' mentally ill are, for example, notoriously elusive" (Rains 1975: 7). Here Rains uses an objectivist formulation of the phenomenon to account for its treatment by labeling theorists. She does not say that the chosen subject matters are *taken to be* socially ambiguous. Nor that the grounds for deciding mental illness are *thought to be* notoriously elusive. This is much more than a matter of emphasis. Her construal of these as objective conditions enables her to base her explanation in the actual character of the world. The "fact" that "the grounds for deciding mental illness are notoriously elusive" is made to account for the activities of certain labeling theorists, namely their choice of topics for analysis. If this "fact" was portrayed as less than objective, if for example it was a mere imputation, then its adequacy as a determinant of choice would become problematic. Who, after all, would be persuaded that the activities of labeling theorists are determined by something which *may or may not* have a certain character?

Although it may seem precious to make the point with respect to Rains' own analysis, the appearance of this explanatory maneuver in such a careful and thoughtful essay suggests a further point. Perhaps all attempts at accounting (explaining) depend upon presenting at least some state of affairs as objective. Perhaps there must always be some reliable, dependable, and non-fluid determinant of the phenomenon to be explained. We suggest, then, that the theoretical "tension" identified by Rains and the problem we have identified in the social problems literature are much more than the errors of combining different theoretical traditions. It is an expression of the continual play between objective facts and representations of those facts which characterizes all explanations of this kind. Ontological gerrymandering is one device whereby this all-pervasive tension is practically managed.

Implications

Our attempt to dissect the structure of definitional explanations of social problems is not a call for a return to the study of social problems in the style opposed by the definitionalists. The critique we offer can be understood in three quite different ways.

First, our critique can be understood as a description of what passes for a successful style of explanation of social problems. It could be a kind of procedural manual for the construction of such explanations. If sufficiently accurate, it might provide guidelines for sociologists wishing to emulate the current style of definitional explanation.

Second, however, our critique can be read as a demonstration of serious inconsistencies in the structure of social problems arguments. In particular, proponents fail to live up to the programmatic relativism which they espouse in calling for a purportedly different, definitional perspective. In the course of specific, empirical case studies, the programmatic claims give way to clearly discernible lapses into realism. This reading of our critique might suggest more caution be exercised in attempting empirical studies in the definitional perspective. At best, authors have given insufficient attention to the match between their proclaimed objectives and their explanatory practice.

A third reading of our critique is that the kind of inconsistencies we identify are an inevitable feature both of certain social problems arguments and, more generally, of the same style of sociological argument as it applies to other substantive areas. In this reading, the inconsistencies we identify are unavoidable. They are not mere technical difficulties in social problems arguments, but pervasive features of all attempts to explain social phenomena.

This makes it possible to speculate that the boundary work we have identified is more generally symptomatic of all explanations wherein analysts invoke a selective relativism with respect to phenomena. That is, certain phenomena are highlighted as the legitimate and pertinent objects of study which require explanation while other phenomena, although in principle equally amenable to this treatment, are backgrounded and taken as given. Frequently, it is said of certain aspects of social life that things "could have been different." However, the ensuing explanation is not itself subject to this dictate; the analyst's construction of the "explanation" of this state of affairs is emphatically *not* to be regarded as socially contingent, as a result of current conventions, and as lacking logical necessity. In short, explanatory work has to seem distinctively "asocial." The selective application of relativism is thus crucial both in construing phenomena as "social" (for the purposes of establishing a topic for sociological explanation) and in denying the social character of sociologists' own practices.

Since the inconsistencies we identify are unavoidable features of sociological argument as we know it, a further implication of the third reading of our critique is that we search for forms of argument which go beyond the current impasse between proponents of objectivism and of relativism. Is it possible to establish a form of discourse which is free from the tension engendered by espousals of relativism within the conventions of an objectivist form of presentation? What would an argument free from ontological gerrymandering look like?

As a first step in pursuit of these weighty questions, much more needs to be done to try and understand how inconsistencies are managed in the course of explanation. How and why is it that these inevitable inconsistencies of argument are only selectively used as a means of undermining and faulting explanation? What enables practitioners to draw attention to some inconsistencies while repressing their omnipresence? Our suggestion is that part of the answer to these questions can be obtained by a close examination of the rhetorical strategies which constitute social problems explanation. In this paper we have begun by identifying one set of such strategies as exhibited in the work of sociologists. Further examination of our explanatory practices promises to provide intriguing insights into this fundamental feature of the way we make sense of our world.

Conclusion

In this paper we have tried to re-establish the salience of conceptual problems raised with respect to the labeling perspective for recent work in the definitional study of social problems. Instead of recommending the search for their "solution," or urging greater caution in their negotiation, we suggest that examining the practical management of these problems offers a key to better understanding the fundamentals of social problems explanation. In this paper, we have tried to articulate one central device for managing these problems: the strategy of "ontological gerrymandering." Since many of the conceptual problems raised with respect to the sociology of deviance are more generally applicable to sociological argument as a whole, we anticipate that our analysis of social problems explanation has a significance beyond its particular substantive origins.

Notes

1. Throughout this paper we use the term "definitional" to refer to what has been also called the "labeling," "subjectivist," "constructionist," "constructivist," and "perceptionist" approach to the study of social problems.

2. Although "ethnography" also connotes the attempt to describe phenomena from the inside, as they appear to participants, our use of the term here emphasizes the advantages of not taking for granted those activities of argument in which we ourselves participate.

3. We use the term "backgrounding" in place of the more cumbersome phrase "relegate to the background."

4. Gieryn (1983) has shown how natural scientists engage in "boundary work," the selection and portrayal of various characteristics of science, in order to create a particular public image of the scientific enterprise. Whereas Gieryn discusses scientists' behavior in public settings, here we examine boundary work at the more profound level of textual explanation.

5. The importance of this assertion for the recommended program of analysis can be appreciated by noticing the effect of removing it from each of the above three quotations.

6. In certain cases, this request is made by appeal to our common sense, to what, after all, we "know" to be the case (for example, Spector 1983).

7. An exactly similar ambivalence is evident in discussions of the relation between official statistics and the social reality which they purport to represent (see, for example, Douglas 1967; Hindess 1973).

8. Evidence for the (perceived) centrality of Pfohl's work is admittedly equivocal. Pfohl's (1977) paper does not cite the earlier papers of Spector and Kitsuse. On the other hand, Pfohl (1977: 310) does claim to "synthesize conflict and labeling perspectives." Spector includes Pfohl's (1977) article in a reader which claims to bring together readings that "complement the labeling, value conflict, or social construction perspective on social problems. Constructing social problems " . . . provides the theoretical orientation for these empirical materials" (Spector 1980: vii). One referee of our paper noted that "the Pfohl paper is often given as an example of the kind of work one might do from the definitional stance."

9. Parton's (1979) account of child abuse in Britain similarly argues that another medical specialty, forensic pathology, was able to transcend the structural constraints and promote their

professional interests by recognizing the problem of child abuse. In Britain, according to Parton, forensic pathologists came into contact with the most extreme cases of abuse and were closely allied to the courts and the criminal justice process. They consequently saw themselves as bridging the gap between medicine and law.

10. Similarly, Levine (1978) claims to treat alcoholism simply as a definition, a new paradigm or "*gestalt*" that emerged in American popular and medical thought at the end of the eighteenth century due to a unique set of sociohistorical circumstances. There is an implicit avowal of impartiality with respect to the validity of this perception. Yet he refers repeatedly to addiction as a discovery. Indeed, his article is entitled "The Discovery of Alcoholism" which implies that the physiological processes the word refers to have existed all along and needed only to be rendered visible. The use of the word "discovery" transforms addiction from an assertion made or a conception advanced by certain parties to a phenomenon that these groups propitiously came upon.

11. In our text, of course, we are selecting different terms for qualification; we use quotation marks around different terms to highlight their constructive origins.

12. The structure of argumentation implicit in Pfohl's article is much more obvious in Parton who is much less careful about camouflaging his commitment to the idea that child beating is in fact a case of parental abuse. Parton speaks of his attempt "to understand and explain why the problem of child abuse was recognized in Britain when it was and in the manner in which it was." He states: "This paper argues that we cannot understand these developments simply by trying to catalogue the 'objective' clinical characteristics and dimensions of the problem for these have existed in some form throughout history. If we are to explain why the recognition of the problem emerged when it did and in the manner in which it did, we must analyze the social forces that facilitated, influenced, initiated and reacted to it" (1979: 431). Clearly, then, Parton's study is not an explication of how certain assertions about social problems are made, by whom and with what consequences, but about how certain groups came to recognize or discuss child abuse for what it was.

13. Indeed, many contributors appear unclear as to what distinguishes the fields of deviance and social problems. Some authors (for example, Scott and Douglas 1972: 250; Warren and Johnson 1972: 70) appear to use the terms interchangeably, while others (for example, Mauss 1975: 26) maintain that some social problems are associated with economic and technological changes rather than with supposedly deviant behavior. Merton and Nisbet (1976) use "social problems" as a general rubric which subsumes the phenomena of both deviance (crime, mental illness) and social disorganization (race relations, poverty, sex roles, and so on). Spector and Kitsuse describe contributions to social problems and to deviance as "related bodies of writings" (1977: 63; see also Kitsuse and Spector 1975). Many of the articles (for example, Conrad 1975; Nuehring and Markle 1974; Schneider 1978) collected in a reader on "Social Problems" (Spector 1980) define their subject matter as deviance rather than social problems, even though all but one of them (Gusfield 1975) previously appeared in the journal *Social Problems*.

14. Labeling theorists have been concerned with the labeling of individuals and with the processes and implications of labeling individuals as deviant. Their focus has been on who gets labeled as deviant, by whom, and with what consequences. Analogously, the recent emphasis in social problems has been on what gets labeled as deviant and by whom. Just as deviance and deviants are seen by labeling theorists as constituted through the application of the labels, those adopting the definitional perspective on social problems see social problems as the result of the claims-making activities of individuals and groups. In fact, social problems has a tradition of definitional approaches which predates the emergence of labeling theory by at least thirty years. This tradition can be traced from the work of the value-conflict school in the 1920s and 1930s (Case 1924; Fuller and Myers 1941a, 1941b) and continuing with Becker (1966) and Blumer

(1971). Spector and Kitsuse (1977) point out, however, that the only common feature of these writings is the concern to take to task the functionalist paradigm which dominated the study of social problems. In its place, they offered a diverse range of programs and few followed through on their suggestion that social problems are definitions constructed by members of society.

15. In an exactly similar way, some sociologists of science go to great lengths to profess neutrality and impartiality with respect to the truth status of the scientific knowledge which they are portraying as "socially constructed" knowledge (see, for example, Bloor 1976).

References

Aronson, Naomi. 1982. "Nutrition as a Social Problem: A Case Study of Entrepreneurial Strategy in Science." *Social Problems* 29: 474–87.

Ball, Richard A. and J. Robert Lilly. 1982. "The Menace of Margarine: The Rise and Fall of a Social Problem." *Social Problems* 29: 488–98.

Becker, Howard S. 1963. *Outsiders*. New York: Free Press.

———. 1966. "Introduction." Pp. 1–31 in Howard S. Becker (Ed.), *Social Problems: A Modern Approach*. New York: Wiley.

Bloor, David. 1976. *Knowledge and Social Imagery*. London: Routledge and Kegan Paul.

Blumer, Herbert. 1971. "Social Problems as Collective Behavior." *Social Problems* 18: 298–306.

Case, Clarence. 1924. "What Is a Social Problem?" *Journal of Applied Sociology* 8: 268–73.

Chauncey, Robert L. 1980. "New Careers for Moral Entrepreneurs: Teenage Drinking." *Journal of Drug Issues* 10: 48–70.

Conrad, Peter. 1975. "The Discovery of Hyperkinesis: Notes on the Medicalization of Deviant Behavior." *Social Problems* 23: 512–21.

———. 1976. *Identifying Hyperactive Children: The Medicalization of Deviant Behavior*. Lexington, MA: D. C. Heath.

Conrad, Peter and Joseph W. Schneider. 1980. *Deviance and Medicalization: From Badness to Sickness*. St. Louis, MO: C. V. Mosby.

Currie, Elliott P. 1968. "Crimes without Criminals: Witchcraft and Its Controls in Renaissance Europe." *Law and Society Review* 3: 7–32.

Douglas, Jack D. 1967. *The Social Meaning of Suicide*. Princeton, NJ: Princeton University Press.

Eads, William E. 1969. "Observations on the Establishment of Child Protection Services in California." *Stanford Law Review* 21: 1129–155.

Fuller, Richard C. and Richard R. Myers. 1941a. "The Natural History of a Social Problem." *American Sociological Review* 6: 320–28.

———. 1941b. "Some Aspects of a Theory of Social Problems." *American Sociological Review* 6: 24–32.

Gieryn, Thomas F. 1983. "Boundary-Work and the Demarcation of Science from Non-Science: Strains and Interests in Professional Ideologies of Scientists." *American Sociological Review* 48: 781–95.

Gusfield, Joseph R. 1975. "Categories of Ownership and Responsibility in Social Issues: Alcohol Abuse and Automobile Use." *Journal of Drug Issues* 5: 285–303.

———. 1981. *The Culture of Public Problems*. Chicago: University of Chicago Press.

Hindess, Barry. 1973. *The Use of Official Statistics in Sociology*. London: Macmillan.

Johnson, Michael P. and Karl Hufbauer. 1982. "Sudden Infant Death Syndrome as a Medical Research Problem since 1945." *Social Problems* 30: 65–81.

Kitsuse, John I. 1962. "Societal Reaction to Deviant Behavior." *Social Problems* 9: 247–56.

Kitsuse, John I. And Malcolm Spector. 1975. "Social Problems and Deviance: Some Parallel Issues." *Social Problems* 22: 584–94.

Knorr-Cetina, Karin D. 1981. *The Manufacture of Knowledge: An Essay on the Constructivist and Contextual Nature of Science*. Oxford: Pergamon.

———. 1983. "The Ethnographic Study of Scientific Work: Toward a Constructivist Interpretation of Science." Pp. 115–40 in Karin D. Knorr-Cetina and Michael J. Mulkay (Eds.), *Science Observed: Perspectives on the Social Study of Science*. London: Sage.

Latour, Bruno and Steve Woolgar. 1979. *Laboratory Life: The Social Construction of Scientific Facts*. Beverly Hills, CA: Sage.

Lemert, Edwin M. 1951. *Social Pathology: A Systematic Approach to the Theory of Sociopathic Behavior.* New York: Mcgraw-Hill.

Levine, Harry Gene. 1978. "The Discovery of Addiction." *Journal of Studies on Alcohol* 39: 143–74.

Lidz, Charles W. and Andrew L. Walker. 1980. *Heroin, Deviance and Morality*. Beverly Hills, CA: Sage.

Loseke, Donileen R. and Spencer E. Cahill. 1984. "The Social Construction of Deviance: Experts on Battered Women." *Social Problems* 31: 296–310.

Lynch, M. 1985. *Art and Artifact in Laboratory Science: A Study of Shop Work and Shop Talk in a Research Laboratory*. London: Routledge and Kegan Paul.

Markle, Gerald E. and Ronald J. Troyer. 1979. "Smoke Gets in Your Eyes: Cigarette Smoking as Deviant Behavior." *Social Problems* 26: 611–25.

Mauss, Armand L. 1975. *Social Problems as Social Movements*. Philadelphia: J. B. Lippincott.

McCrea, Frances B. 1983. "The Politics of Menopause: The 'Discovery' of a Deficiency Disease." *Social Problems* 31: 111–23.

Merton, Robert K. and Robert Nisbet. 1976. *Contemporary Social Problems* (3rd Ed.). New York: Harcourt Brace Jovanovich.

Morrow, Carol Klaperman. 1982. "Sick Doctors: The Social Construction of Professional Deviance." *Social Problems* 30: 92–108.

Nuehring, Elaine and Gerald E. Markle. 1974. "Nicotine and Norms: The Re-Emergence of a Deviant Behavior." *Social Problems* 21: 513–26.

Parton, Nigel. 1979. "A Natural History of Child Abuse: A Study in Social Problem Definition." *British Journal of Social Work* 9: 431–51.

Pfohl, Stephen. 1977. "The 'Discovery' of Child Abuse.' *Social Problems* 24: 310–24.

Pollner, Melvin. 1974. "Sociological and Common-Sense Models of the Labelling Process." Pp. 27–40 in Roy Turner (Ed.), *Ethnomethodology*. Harmondsworth, UK: Penguin.

Rains, Prudence. 1975. "Imputations of Deviance: A Retrospective Essay on the Labeling Perspective." *Social Problems* 23: 1–11.

Randall, Donna M. and James F. Short. 1983. "Women in Toxic Work Environments: A Case Study of Social Problem Development." *Social Problems* 30: 410–24.

Rose, Vicki McNickle. 1977. "Rape as a Social Problem: A Byproduct of the Feminist Movement." *Social Problems* 25: 75–89.

Rothman, Barbara Katz. 1983. "Midwives in Transition: The Structure of a Clinical Revolution." *Social Problems* 30: 262–71.

Schneider, Joseph. 1978. "Deviant Drinking as a Disease: Alcoholism as a Social Accomplishment." *Social Problems* 25: 361–72.

Scott, Robert A. and Jack D. Douglas (Eds.). 1972. *Theoretical Perspectives on Deviance*. New York: Basic Books.

Smith, Dorothy E. 1978. "K Is Mentally Ill." *Sociology* 12: 23–53.

Spector, Malcolm. 1977. "Legitimizing Homosexuality." *Society* 14: 52–56.

———. 1980. *Readings in Social Problems.* Lexington, MA: Ginn Custom.

———. 1983. Private Communication. May 7th.

Spector, Malcolm and John I. Kitsuse. 1977. *Constructing Social Problems.* Menlo Park, MA: Cummings.

Traweek, Sharon. Forthcoming. *Uptime, Downtime, Spacetime and Power: An Ethnology of the Particle Physics Community in Japan and the United States.* Princeton, NJ: Princeton University Press.

Troyer, Ronald J. and G. E. Markle. 1983. *Cigarettes—The Battle over Smoking.* New Brunswick, NJ: Rutgers University Press.

———. 1984. "Coffee Drinking: An Emerging Social Problem?" *Social Problems* 31: 403–16.

Warren, Carol A. B. and John M. Johnson. 1972. "A Critique of Labeling Theory from the Phenomenological Perspective." Pp. 69–92 in Robert A. Scott and Jack D. Douglas (Eds.), *Theoretical Perspectives on Deviance.* New York: Basic Books.

Woolgar, Steve. 1981. "Interests and Explanation in the Social Study of Science." *Social Studies of Science* 11: 365–94.

———. 1982. "Laboratory Studies: A Comment on the State of the Art." *Social Studies of Science* 12: 481–98.

Commentary on "Ontological Gerrymandering"*

TOWARDS A SOCIOLOGICAL DECONSTRUCTION OF SOCIAL PROBLEMS

Stephen Pfohl

The "social constructionist" perspective has carved out a conceptual space for a radical reading (and writing) of social problems as nothing but the cultural, political, and material effects of the human struggle for the organization of power in (and as) history. Within this space we are invited to imagine that those "things" we experience, define, and react to as problematic are, in "fact," never independent of the differentiating social practices which produce them. Despite the compelling "common sense" in which they present themselves, as fact-like things, *sui generis*, they are read as "no-things," but differentially impowered and impowering artifacts. This is a thoroughly sociological story. All that is problematic and nonproblematic, and the socially circumscribed boundaries dividing the normatively acceptable from its other, are seen as nothing but power-charged artifactualities, fictive narratives within which people "discover" themselves and the meaning of their place in a history.

Woolgar and Pawluch, in a provocative, insightful, and sympathetic critique, ask two questions of this story. First, how is it that certain of its elements (descriptions of problematic" behaviors or conditions) are occasionally presented as if they were facts and not artifacts? Here the authors interrogate Spector and Kitsuse for positing the "nature of marijuana" as a constant independent of the variable facticity of its problematic social definition. I too am chided for allegedly making an immutable (factual) link between child abuse and child beating. My work is charged with a "selective relativism." This is said to undermine the consistency of my constructionist argument that there "really" was no child abuse prior to its "discovery," and this "discovery" was the effect of a play of power at a particular moment in history. Similar inconsistencies are said to plague the constructionist perspective as a whole.

The second question asked by Woolgar and Pawluch is this: How do constructionists create a story that convinces? How are constructionist explanations made to work? An answer is posed in terms of a rhetorical strategy—ontological gerrymander-

---

*Editor's note: This commentary on the previous chapter authored by Woolgar and Pawluch was published alongside of the original article in Volume 31,(3) of *Social Problems* and is reproduced here in its entirety.

ing—that casts doubt on the ontological status of social problems definitions, while leaving unblemished the "actual" or "objective" nature of the behaviors or conditions to which such definitions refer. An additional feature of this rhetorical device involves "backgrounding" or minimizing the possibility that the constructionist story is no less artifactual than the definitional "truths" it analyzes. Yet, rather than condemning constructionists for these self-sustaining rhetorical practices, Woolgar and Pawluch speculate that such devices are constitutive features of any successful sociological explanation.

Against these arguments, I will take up two positions. The first concerns the issue of "selective relativism." The second deals with whether ontological gerrymandering constitutes a logically necessary feature of sociological explanation. My objective is not so much to defend previous constructionist expositions as to suggest directions for continued movement from within the theoretical space pioneered by this perspective. Woolgar and Pawluch are correct in observing numerous theoretical, methodological, and empirical inconsistencies in certain seminal formulations of the constructionist viewpoint. With this I find no disagreement. What is excluded by the Woolgar and Pawluch critique will be my concern—the possible dissemination of a more radically reflexive version of constructionist theorizing, a version more atuned to thorny epistemological problems, a version we might call a social deconstructionist perspective.

Regarding this issue of selective relativism, Woolgar and Pawluch read the constructionist perspective as "foreshadowing a commitment" to a realist view of problematic social conditions. This is a serious misreading. If this perspective foreshadows anything, it is a "surrealist view" of social conditions. By this, I mean that those "things' which appear as social facts (*sui generis*) are fictive effects of powerful structuring practices by which we repeatedly embody ourselves in a history. This is a loaded sentence. Within it are traces of Marx, Durkheim, and Nietzche.[1] As we read social problems from within the space opened by constructionism, we take leave of a world of facts in order to examine the transformative ritual practices which situate us here and now, at home in a world of artifacts. There is nothing here but the effects of domesticating drama, the timely consequences of our mode of production and reproduction. It fills us up, just as we "discover" our problems within it. And so there appear before us such disturbing matters as child abuse, rape, and the threat of nuclear extermination. But even these "things" strike differently, relative to our power-effective positioning in the "order of things" produced. Thus my minister exorts, "Fear not for that which may appear as if a cloud of nuclear extermination, is in truth the coming of He who has risen. So rejoice." And my brother counsels, "You can't say that's rape. I mean how many times have you been with the same chick and you know she's really hot for it, even if she says she's not?" And the same with child abuse. The "truth" of these matters is effected by the social positioning in which we find ourselves.

I read my 1977 account of the "discovery" of child abuse very differently than Woolgar and Pawluch. In part, this is because my original article contained but faint clues as to its strategic theoretical objectives and epistemological commitments. For this failure to foreground my positions sufficiently, I take responsibility and now attempt to set the record straight, or at least to rewrite the straight record. There were several reasons for not having done this previously, the most obvious being that my thinking about such matters is today more elaborate than in 1977. This implies no simple discontinuity between my position now and then. Discontinuities are rarely so simple. What is written now is made possible by the theoretical space then afforded by the constructionist viewpoint.[2]

In 1977 I was a sociologist immersed in the radically relativist theoretical language of phenomenology and ethnomethodology. To what, however, were the interpretive practices described by these perspectives relative? I was struggling to connect interpretive practice to matter of historically circumscribed power (Pfohl 1981). The article on the "discovery" of child abuse was part of this struggle. From within this text, I view neither variable definitions of "children" or their "beating," nor the fact-like constraints of historical materiality as things independent of the structuring practices by which each is codeterminately produced. This distinguishes my use of the constructionist framework from that ascribed to me by Woolgar and Pawluch. They see my discussion of "documentary evidence" about the beating of children prior to the "discovery" of abuse as itself evidence of "assumptions about the unchanging (objective) character of underlying conditions." In actuality, I had chosen the word "documentary" as reference to the ethnomethodological concept "documentary interpretation" (Garfinkel 1967: 78) to qualify the term "evidence." My intent, although implicit, was to suggest what Woolgar and Pawluch make explicit—that historical evidence of all sorts is itself a social construction.

My point was not that there really was something, which today we call child abuse, and that certain things prevented it from being seen before 1960. Mine was a story, not of things, but of the constructionist effects of a shifting web of powerful social practices that once inhibited and later invited a reading of broken childhood bones and bodies as matters of parental pathology. The difference is important. The aim of my work was not *constructive*—to uncover the true story of child abuse and to show how this truth was obscured at earlier points in history. Rather, it was *deconstructive*—to displace the truth of a dominant story about the humanitarian march of therapeutic interventionism. It was to open a space for wondering why child beating is today most commonly read as a story of determinate pathology rather than, for instance, as the indeterminate effect of a bloody domestic drama—a powerful play of violence behind the closed doors of privatized power—performed by people denied access to a script of public power and embedded in the text of corporate capitalism (or some other hierarchical formation of socially productive practices). This, of course, is another story. In contrast to the charges brought by Woolgar and Pawluch, I do not assume the objective truth of this story any more that I previously assumed that abuse was "really" there before it was discovered.

What I do assume is this—that the material and definitional actualities of child abuse or any "thing" else are bound together in an indeterminate relation that "is" the effect of a transformative displacement of one set of social structuring practices by some other(s). From within this collision or collusion of structuring practices arises a "true" story—the "real facts" of the matter, the self-evidency of "things" and the like. There are not truths aside from this elusive (intertextual) formation (Derrida 1974). This is our present, the here and now in which "things" strike us as problematic and within which we strike back. The truth of things is thus imbedded in a ceaseless repetition of an indeterminant act of differentiation between colliding practices. But so also is truth effected as an act of deference. To make something "truly" present is to make absent something other. "Things" thus become "real" only in a socially differentiated act of silencing. This (categorically) imperial exclusion marks the historical production of "things in themselves." Yet this is exactly what they are not. They are nothing but the cultural, political, and material effects of a human struggle for the organization of power in (and as) history. I am repeating the sentence that began this essay. This is the sentence under which we labor.

> [T]he desire of deconstruction may itself become a desire to reappropriate the text actively through mastery to show the text what it "does not know." And as she deconstructs, all protestations to the contrary, the critic necessarily assumes that she at least, for the time being, means what she says . . . In other words, the critic provisionally forgets that her own text is necessarily all-deconstructed. (Spivak 1974: xxvii)

Provisional forgetfulness weaves itself throughout constructionist accounts of such "things" as the "discovery" of child abuse. In constructing my sociological narrative I metaphorically condensed an analysis of social practices into a discussion of "factors" and "forces." In framing my story in this fashion, I froze an indeterminate conjuncture of dynamic processes into terms that seemingly imply a constancy of "things"—barriers, impediments, obstacles to seeing and the like. Woolgar and Pawluch arrest this play of metaphoric condensation. They seize the act of freezing concepts as evidence for speculating that (temporary) backgrounding is a constitutive feature of explanatory work in general. Here Woolgar and Pawluch seem in agreement with deconstructionist Spivak, when she describes the critic who, by necessity, "provisionally forgets" the socially constructed nature of her "mastery" of "things" within her text.

But what if the provisionality of forgetting becomes a reflexive feature of the practice of theorizing itself? What if it places "under erasure' (Derrida 1974) the possibility that theorizing can ever escape the textual network of powerful social practices into which it asserts itself? To ask such questions is to reach sympathetically beyond the speculative concerns raised by Woolgar and Pawluch. It is to explore the possibility of a deconstructive sociological narrative analytically exploding, rather than objectively explaining, the artifactual nature of problematic social practices. It is to acknowledge that the textual terms of its own analysis are bound, not by the rules of a method that privileges sociology as an objectivity apart from the world of its subject, but by the historical and material rules of concrete social interaction (Ryan 1982). It is to situate sociological theorizing as a practical activity in the production of history. This denies sociology its dream of a positive science. It does not deny the value of reflexive sociological analysis that understands itself as effecting a provisional knowledge, positioned by the power of its relationship to other practices. As a social practice, sociological theorizing collides with other practices, transformatively displacing them in the narrative it weaves. As a "power-reflexive" social practice, a deconstructionist sociology simultaneously displays, if imperfectly, the mode of its own production, its situationally bound strategies of textual construction (Pfohl 1985). This is what distinguishes it from other social practices and from the "ontological gerrymandering" involved with the "normal" practice of social science explanation. A deconstructive sociology is neither positive nor a normal science. It turns analytically upon itself, just as it acts upon its "subject," thus disclosing, not a determinate world of social facts, but an indeterminate production of artifacts, itself included. This is its strategic truth. It opens before us, again and again, the power-invested practices that provisionally affect the things of this world.

> Deconstruction seems to offer a way out of the closure . . . By inaugurating the open-ended indefiniteness of textuality . . . it shows us the lure of the abyss as freedom. The fall into the abyss of deconstruction inspires us with as much pleasure as fear. We are intoxicated with the prospect of never hitting bottom. (Spivak 1974: xxvii)

Here we slide onto thinly provisional ice beyond even the most modest shores of positivism. Even the safe experiential realism of phenomenology is left aside. And yet we find pleasure in what we do. We are freed from all but the mode of production which provides us with a story of ourselves and the world. And this, of course, is everything. Here is a space afforded by the abyss opened by the constructionist intervention, we celebrate a ritual of deconstruction, not as a bottomless trap of "infinite" regress, but as the strategic possibility for a finite reconstruction, again and again, of the social problems presented by the always contestable constellation of structuring practices in which we are engaged. This is the uneasy promise of the constructionist enterprise. As it turns to deconstruction, the power-reflexive matter of its "truth" is before us. In the words of Michel Foucault (1980: 132),

> It's not a matter of emancipating truth from every system of power (which would be a chimera, for truth is already power) but of detaching the power of truth from the forms of hegemony, social, economic and cultural, within which it operates at present.

Notes

1. And Marcel Mauss, and a thoroughly sociological Freud, and a power-reflexive ethnomethodology in relation to Antonio Gramsci and Louis Althusser, and the poststructuralists—Roland Barthes, Julia Kristeva, Michel Foucault, Jacques Derrida, Jean Baudrillard, and Gayatri Chakravorty Spivak—thank you. In these we "find" grounds for an image of society as a contestable text, powerfully inscribed by the differential relations of social, sexual, imperial, and economic production. I drop these names across this page to provide clues about where we might turn, having read ourselves into that space of indeterminacy cut out by the constructionist invention.

2. In this regard, it is unfortunate that a footnote submitted with the original text of my article was eliminated in the process of copyediting. This note was to encourage a reading of that work as an attempt to collate the phenomenological underpinnings of the constructionist method with a structurally oriented political economy of definitional work, the latter presaged by a growing number of Marxist studies of the social formation of legal reality.

References

Derrida, Jacques. 1974. *Of Grammatology*. Translated by Gayatri Chakravorty Spivak. Baltimore, MD: Johns Hopkins University.

Foucault, Michel. 1980. *Power/Knowledge: Selected Interviews and Other Writings, 1972–1977*. Collin Gordon (ed.). New York: Pantheon.

Garfinkel, Harold. 1967. *Studies in Ethnomethodology*. Engelwood Cliffs, NJ: Prentice-Hall.

Pfohl, Stephen. 1977. "The 'Discovery' of Child Abuse." *Social Problems* 24: 310–23.

———. 1981. "An Interview with Stephen J. Pfohl," with Robert Menzies. *Canadian Criminology Forum* 4: 61–72.

———. 1985. *Images of Deviance and Social Control: A Sociological History*. New York: McGraw-Hill.

Ryan, Michael. 1982. *Marxism and Deconstruction: A Critical Articulation*. Baltimore, MD: Johns Hopkins University Press.

Spivak, Gayatri Chakrovorty. 1974. "Translator's Introduction," to Jacques Derrida, *Of Grammatology*. Baltimore, MD: Johns Hopkins University

———. 1981. "Translator's Preface to 'Draupadi' by Makasveta Devi." *Critical Inquiry* 8: 382–83.

CHAPTER 4

Deviant Behavior and the Remaking of the World*

Frances Fox Piven

. . . In order to develop my critique, I first need to locate the ideas of the societal reaction school by retracing some of the main steps in the development of sociological thought on deviance. For a very long time and long before there were sociologists, social thinkers, usually out of an expressed concern for social order, have tried to understand why people sometimes break the rules of their society. The reason for this focus seems evident. Social order depends on the observance of rules. But inherent in the imposition of many rules is the exercise of power, the domination of some people by other people against their will, and the use of the state to enforce that domination. And inherent in the defiance of many rules is not only a threat to social order, but a challenge to the particular pattern of domination on which that social order rests. Domination and challenge, and thus conformity and deviance, are at the center of history. They are expressions of the basic dialectical movements through which societies change, or perhaps fail to change. Grand theories of state and society—because they are about the nature of social order and the nature of challenges to that order—are, however indirectly, statements about that basic dialectic. Grand theories of state and society are, in other words, also theories about the phenomena we have come to call deviance . . .

Societal reaction theory not only offered a new perspective on rule-violating behavior, but it hinted at a new perspective on the very nature of society and history. First, it was argued that social rules have specific political origins under specific historical circumstances, that rulemaking arises out of a political process in which some groups use the state to impose their will on others. It followed that the making and enforcing of social rules was the "formal" cause of deviant behavior. When Becker (1963: 9) resurrected Durkheim's (1938: 70) famous assertion, "What confers this [criminal] character . . . is not the intrinsic quality of a given act but that definition which the collective conscience lends them," he provided a needed antidote to the careless

*Editor's Note: This article consists of excerpts from the author's Presidential Address to the Society for the Study of Social Problems, New York, August 1980, which later appeared in Vol. 28, No. 5 of *Social Problems* in 1981.

assumption made by many sociologists that social rules were self-evident and unproblematic. Moreover, he properly avoided Durkheim's idea that social rules were the product of the "collective conscience," and instead located rule making in processes of political conflict. No doubt many people had always understood that the making and enforcing of social rules were expressions of power in a differentiated and conflict-ridden society; but to all appearances most sociologists had not, for they had promulgated an image of society as a reified consensus from which rules simply emanated. The alternative view offered by the societal reaction school was thus surely to the good. It reminded us of the Hobbesian themes, but without the Hobbesian animus toward ordinary people. There was domination of some people by other people, and there was the state. It directed our attention to politics, and to the role of the state as a coercive force. But this was only the beginning of an exploration of the dynamics of rule making and rule violation which, in the main, the societal reaction school did not then pursue.

It did not pursue such an exploration because it was soon preoccupied with another argument which rapidly became the insignia of the school. This was, of course, the labeling thesis, which asserted that sociologically significant deviant behavior is actually the creation of dominant groups, a result of deviant roles imposed upon people through interaction with social control agencies. True, people sometimes violate the rules, but these behaviors are unimportant, in some variants only haphazardly related to the labeling process. What is important in accounting for deviance are the identities imposed from above. Thus deviance is not the result of a power-hungry or defective human nature and it is not the result of a defective or malintegrated society. It can be understood, in fact, as the result precisely of societal integration. Erikson (1964: 13–15), whose work is widely cited by societal reaction analysts, helped give this idea a certain grandeur by invoking the awesome Durkheimian image of the ritual naming and branding of witless and unlucky creatures as the process through which the community defines norms and their limits, and ensures its own stability . . .

Labeling theory brought total closure to this perspective, for it carried the sociological argument a further step. It argued that sociologically significant deviance did not occur except as it was brought into being by processes of social control. We had thus moved from blaming the human nature of those who broke the rules, to blaming the malintegrated society, to blaming those who named and created the outcasts. The deviant became a hapless victim, and it is perhaps better to be a hapless victim than a vicious or defective human animal.

But this benevolence exacted a high price. What was forfeited was some understanding, however reluctant and incomplete, that even the vicious and defective might be acting with motive and purpose. The societal reaction school bought pity for the deviant by weaving a theory in which the fact of deviance as human action, human action oriented toward some purpose, was extirpated. Only the powerful had a capacity to act purposefully by enacting and enforcing rules. Societal reaction thus defined away the ubiquitous evidence that women and men can resist the rules of their society. No matter how pervasive the historical testimony to this capacity for resistance, evasion and defiance, it has been recast as socialized behavior. The societal reaction school, in short, has woven a theory of pure domination . . . and my argument has several parts.

Sociology and the Obliteration of Human Agency

. . . Writing in the early '50s, Lemert expressed dissatisfaction with the "embarrassingly large number of theories . . . advanced to account for various specific pathologies of human behavior" (1951: 75). This led him to the bold conclusion that no general theory of the "original" causes of what he called "primary" deviation was possible. What was possible was a theory of the "effective" causes of what he called "secondary" deviation. And primary deviance achieves the authentically sociological status of secondary deviance as a consequence of the encounter with societal reaction; for repetitive stigmatizing experiences induce the individual to construct and accept a deviant self-image, and so—as Tannenbaum (1938: 19) had put it earlier—to become what he or she is defined as being. Thus Lemert stated: "From a narrower sociological viewpoint the [primary] deviations are not significant until they are organized subjectively and transformed into active roles and become the criteria for assigning status" (1951: 75). Having set out this initiating idea, he subsequently framed a more general proposition which, as I will suggest later, has implications which go far beyond the more limited relationship of stigma to secondary deviation; he argued that "social control becomes a 'cause' . . . of deviation" (1972: 49).

Here was an interesting idea, one whose possibilities have still only barely been explored. But in the hands of most who have taken up the idea, the results have been more troubling than interesting. One cause of trouble has been the denigration of primary deviation, and thus of the active capacity of men and women to oppose and evade social rules . . . In effect, the societal reaction school pressed the sociological theorem to its logical conclusion: namely, all behavior is a socialized product. Thus Durkheim and Parsons had thought that the values central to a society are embodied and expressed in conforming action. The societal reaction school tells us that these same values, in their opposite aspect, are embodied and expressed in deviant action. And with that, the vocabulary of negative socialization proliferated. Ceremonies of "status degradation" are staged in order to accomplish "identity stripping" and to confer invidious identities so that the person is engulfed by the negative identity, capitulates to it, and introjects it. The deviant is a socialized person who accepts, believes, and feels that one is what one has been defined as being, and goes on to organize life patterns around that stigmatized identity. The socialized careerism of confirmed conformity thus has its analog in the socialized careerism of secondary deviation; each is a socialized product, but an opposite one, of the same societal consensus. There are only two kinds of action, and both are products of social control: one is socialized conformity and the other socialized deviance. From this perspective, the deviant act has no social history, the deviant actor no biography. All springs full-blown from stigma. With this argument, the societal reaction school completed the evolution of a sociological paradigm which made men and women the mere reflection of a reified society and its reified value consensus . . .

I have referred to the obliteration of human agency as the central error in the sociological study of deviance, and especially in the societal reaction variant, and it is time I explained myself. I mean that reflective and purposeful people matter in the patterning of social life, that human actors play some role in molding their own conduct, in choosing to do one thing and not another. Or, as Giddens says, "Social theory must incorporate a treatment of action as rationalized conduct ordered reflexively by human agents" (1976: 8). And because agency matters in the patterning of action, it also must matter in the patterning of society, and of history. To say this is not to dismiss or ignore the situational constraints within which human agents think and act. It is rather to say that action cannot be entirely reduced to or derived from these situational constraints, that structural determinants of one kind or another are only part of an explanation of human conduct.

With these comments, I put myself squarely on one side of a much tortured issue in social thought. The idea of human agency is troubling and elusive with its connotations of an autonomous human essence or soul. It is difficult to incorporate within a sociological discipline straining for acceptance as science—and much influenced in its idea of science by a deterministic model adapted from 19th century natural science. Accordingly, the idea of human agency was more or less eliminated as sociology developed, although not without some wondering and unease along the way (Dawe 1978; Scott 1963). But it was not determinism alone which led to the near-total dismissal of human agency. It was also the simplicity of a sociological determinism which matched a theorem about society as a palpable force with a conception of human nature as totally susceptible to societal influences. Human nature was purged of the diverse passions imagined by Hobbes, and came to be understood by a single dominant need, the need for acceptance by the group. Hence the normative consensus that was society became the internalized norms of the members of society. If that was so, it could not be people who made and remade society, but it was society that made and remade people.

These assumptions no longer seem so satisfactory, so complete in their scope of explanation. There is a growing sense that something is missing, not only in the unilinear and deterministic sociological model, but in other unilinear and deterministic models as well. People do not always act in ways predicted by the normative structures of their society, and they do not always act in ways predicted by other structuralisms either. The idea of human agency is reemerging to worry us once again, dividing not only major theoretical schools, as positivism as a whole is divided from the various "interpretive" sociologies descended from Husserl, but fracturing schools from within, creating only a crack perhaps within the Parsonian tradition but something approaching a chasm within the Marxist tradition.[1] The issue of agency particularly presses itself to the fore when we try to understand not why people do what is expected of them, not why they do what is approved and rewarded, but why they sometimes break the rules, why they defy the expectations of their community, and why they risk the often terrible penalties that such defiance entails. Sometimes people somehow innovate, and sometimes they resist, and if this were not so, then social life would never change.

Innovation and resistance are so much a part of human experience that some basic human capacity, beyond the capacity to mold ourselves for group acceptance, must be at work. One dimension of that capacity may arise from the obvious truth that human animals are driven by other needs, that they aspire to other ends than social acceptance. Dennis Wrong makes this point well:

> What of desire for material and sensual satisfactions? Can we really dispense with the venerable notion of material "interests" and invariably replace it with the blander, more integrative "social values"? And what of striving for power, not necessarily for its own sake—that would be rare and pathological—but as a means by which men are able to impose a normative definition of reality on others? That material interests, sexual drives and the quest for power have often been over-estimated as human motives is no reason to deny their reality. To do so is to suppress one term of the dialectic between conformity and rebellion, social norms and their violation, man and social order, as completely as the other term is suppressed by those who deny the reality of man's "normative orientation" or reduce it to the effect of coercion, rational calculation, or mechanical conditioning. (1961: 191)

Another dimension of human agency may arise from our nature as problem-solving creatures. If we have diverse needs and are problem-solving creatures, then we will sometimes discover ways to act on these diverse needs and risk social rejection. Moreover, human beings appear to invest themselves in problem-solving activities a great deal, and to bring large abilities to bear in that effort. It leads them to develop interpretations or theories of their life situation, of how the world in which they live works, and of how their problems can be solved in the context of such a world.

Over time, of course, such theories come to be incorporated in a body of belief called culture, and these beliefs tell the participants in that culture what is wrong and what is right, what is possible and what is not possible. But while people thus inherit interpretations, they also change the interpretations they inherit, although perhaps in modest ways. They continue to think, to solve problems, to discover purposes and resources for action not revealed by culture.

Human agency also seems to be a variable capacity, nurtured and enlarged in some social contexts, and suppressed or constrained in others. In particular, exposure to social diversity and to social change would seem to enlarge the capacity of people as agents, while a static and homogeneous social world may constrict the human ability to imagine new solutions and purposes, and to act on them. In this sense, the diversity and fluidity of modern societies may cultivate human agency, while traditional societies may repress it. It may also be the case that the body of beliefs that people inherit promotes the invention of new solutions and the discovery of new purposes, as Lane suggests when he argues that market ideology encourages certain aspects of individual autonomy (1978; 1980). Conversely, inherited beliefs may discourage innovation. This cultural difference both reflects and parallels the differences in social experience of people in modern and traditional societies.

Human agency may have other dimensions as well. It may be rooted in innate creative or rebellious capacities, or flow out of some need for autonomous identity. But this sort of speculation is not necessary to my argument. If people have needs other than that for social acceptance, and if they have a capacity to think about their situation in innovative ways, then they are capable of evolving purposes that are not mere reflections of a normative consensus. Rule-violating behavior is the chief expression of that capacity in history. But when the societal reaction school dismissed primary deviance, and made secondary deviance a socialized product, it expunged human agency from history; that was the first large step toward the social construction of a theory of pure domination.

Sociology and the Obliteration of Force

The second step taken by the societal action school in the development of a theory of pure domination was to obliterate force as a mechanism of domination. This may seem ironic, but I will argue that the school was driven by its view of deviance as a socialized product to construct a world without force or terror.

I find this world unrecognizable. It is a world without killing, or maiming, or torture, or banishment, or mind control. Of course, societal reaction analysts do speak of total institutions, but they speak of them mainly in Goffman's framework of depersonalization, identity stripping, ritual degradation, and the introjection of deviant identities. In other words, the societal reaction school, preoccupied with stigma as the crucial source of social control, has expunged the vocabulary of force from the lexicon of social control.

How is it, then, that the societal reaction school came to construct a world in which there is domination but no force?[2] The reason is obvious. The world of societal reaction lacks force because it lacks human agency, the capacity of people to challenge domination. One is only led to acknowledge force if one first acknowledges challenges to those who control the means of force. Those challenges constitute the central contests of history-contests between princes and peasants, priests and communicants, masters and slaves, landlords and tenants, industrialists and workers. I do not know of any significant historical struggles between people and their rulers in which force was not the central expression of domination. Consider the history of labor struggles, especially in the United States. Above all else, this was a history of armies, militia, deputies, and Pinkertons deployed by ruling-class groups to smash strikes. The use of force has not been limited to collective rule violators: force or the threat of force is regularly used against individual deviants as well. The conversion hysterics of the nineteenth century were often locked in combat with physicians who perceived the seemingly intractable symptoms of hysteria as a threat to their incipient claims to professional expertise. Accordingly, physicians prescribed or threatened to prescribe beatings, brandings, cliterectomies, and suffocation until the fits subsided. Or think of the world today, of the murder of tin miners in Bolivia, of blacks in South Africa, of religious rebels in Saudi Arabia, of prostitutes and homosexuals in Iran, of insurgent peasants in Guatemala and El Salvador. These challengers do not mainly confront stigma and the question is not whether they will survive to become secondary deviants, it is whether they will survive at all.

But the societal reaction school does not see force because it has conducted its inventory of conflict at the peripheries of power where the threat to structures of privilege is so minimal as to require no means of social control beyond stigma. The school has an almost obsessive preoccupation with categories of people who do not intend to challenge any rule at all, and who in fact do not. Societal reaction textbooks contain copious references to dwarfs and midgets, but none to food riots, rent riots, relief riots, ghetto riots or revolutions. When we do get to people who intend to challenge rules and do so, it turns out that they are mainly those who spurn traditional sexual, familial, or lifestyle norms. In Spector and Kitsuse (1977), the largest single category of index citations to deviant behavior refers to homosexuality, thus reminding us again of the complaint by Gouldner (1968), Liazos (1972), and others that the societal reaction school had mainly given us fragmented accounts of scattered protests against Puritanism. My argument is not simply that these are, in the larger world of power relations, relatively less important challenges. As a matter of fact, I will later argue that these lesser challenges—these more apolitical forms of individualistic rule violation—do in fact have considerable political significance, and in any case an adequate theory of deviance must be able to explain why people break the particular rules that they do. For now, however, my point is that by concentrating more or less exclusively on these forms of deviance, the societal reaction school has constructed a world in which there are no challenges to the central structures of rules upon which domination depends, and that is why the school does not recognize the existence of the force upon which domination depends.

Instead of force, there is stigma. Now I do not want to discount the role of stigma. In fact, stigma usually accompanies the exercise of force. More than that, it precedes force. The public defamation of rule breakers is a crucial process by which dominant groups reassert the legitimacy of their social ideas and try to discredit the ideas of their challengers. But invidious definitions do not always deter the rule breakers, and surely they are not invariably introjected. People who defy the rules often have ideas justifying their challenges that defamation alone cannot overcome. It is more likely that stigma helps to isolate the rule breakers from potential sources of support and thus prepares the way for the use of force to secure compliance. Thus the challengers are denounced at the centers of state power, condemned everlastingly from the pulpits, excoriated in the press, and diagnosed (usually at a distance) by the psychological professions. Once successfully isolated, it is then that they can more safely be killed on their picket lines, in their places of worship, or on their tenement stoops and squatter holdings; and defamation continues as they are taken forcibly before the ecclesiastical courts, the agencies of criminal justice, or the therapeutic agencies of the state. Still, it is not defamation that is the main weapon. Defamation is merely put to the service of making force efficient . . .

Deviance and the Transformation of Societal Reaction

There is yet another and equally important sense in which the societal reaction perspective is a theory of pure domination. It ignores the effects that those who violate the rules sometimes have on the social arrangements within which they live. The labeling perspective remains fixated on secondary deviance, on the image of the deviant who is engulfed by social control agencies and capitulates to stigma. At most the perspective permits particular people to sometimes succeed in avoiding engulfment, in disavowing stigma. It therefore takes no account of the occasions on which the people who break the rules engulf their rulers, so that elites are the ones made to capitulate.

The deviants of the societal reaction model cannot win political victories for two main reasons inherent in the model. One reason is that they are not trying to win. Indeed, most are not trying to do anything of significance at all. They do not break the rules because they are attempting to accomplish ends, or because they have particular understandings of their world which inform those ends, or because they have particular relational resources which give them the capacity to act. None of this is true for these deviants. They do not act; they merely respond to the reactions of others. Only out of their interaction with the social control agencies do deviant creatures begin to take human form, to acquire purpose and understanding—but then, it is a purpose and understanding provided by the social control agents. Winning and losing, victory and defeat, do not belong in the world of these creatures.

The second reason why the deviants of the societal reaction school cannot change their society is that, even if they had some purpose, even if they wanted to win, they could not. The school says that most people do not have the resources needed to prevail in any contest with the agents of social control. This is what Schur means when he says that the labeling framework implies "a dual focus on the powerless and the powerful. It is the latter's superior resources that largely account for the deviantizing of the former and also their own immunity for deviantizing" (1979: 601).[3] Some people do escape the labeling process, and these are the ones who have what the societal reaction school calls resources, usually the resources to buy or wheedle protection from stigma. But most people are powerless.

The school thinks most people are powerless because it thinks of resources for power as attributes distributed by social rank. Such a definition of power is familiar and simple: people with valued traits (or things) can make others do what they want, and since these traits (and things) are distributed by social class, so is the capacity to exert influence correlated with social class. Much of the time such a definition works fairly well in explaining our experience. But it doesn't explain all of our experience, and it is too static and too narrow a definition to comprehend the dynamics of rule violations and reactions to rule violations. Sometimes people without money and status prevail, and if they prevail they must have power.

Their power, the power of those we call powerless, derives from the patterns of interdependency that characterize all social life, and from the leverage that inheres in interdependent relations. In other words, power itself is interactional. People have power, the ability to make others do what they want, when those others depend upon them. Thus feudal lords have wealth, social standing and force of arms, and peasants have none of these things. Most of the time the lords are the powerful, the peasants are the powerless, and the distributional conception of power is confirmed. But it is not only peasants who need overlords in the feudal system of production; overlords also need peasants. It is not only labor that needs capital in an industrial system of production; capital is not capital without labor. It is not only wives who need husbands; husbands need wives, as doctors need patients, teachers need students. It is not only the poor who need the rich in a society of densely interdependent relations, but the rich also need the poor.

Most of the time these interdependencies do not yield much influence to people on the bottom, and that is because those people obey the rules that ensure their cooperation on sharply unequal terms. They obey the rules out of fear; the force of arms always matters. They also obey the rules because they have reconciled themselves to think that the rules are right, or perhaps because they think there is no hope of another way. But because they are problem-solving creatures, people sometimes develop new interpretations. They come to think the rules that ensure their cooperation on sharply unequal terms are wrong and that change is possible. They may be prompted to these new interpretations by some added encroachment by their rulers, as when feudal duties were increased before the French revolution. Or it may be that changes in the organization of their daily life yield them new solidarities or other capacities for action that did not exist before, as when handicraft workers were brought together in mass production industries where their capacity to exert influence through strikes was enormously enhanced. Or people may be prompted to think that change is possible if elites become weakened or divided, as when a regime is losing a foreign war. Whatever the specific antecedents, some people sometimes break the rules that ensure their cooperation and demand changes in the terms. When they do, they activate their power, the power inherent in the actual dependence of the rulers on the ruled. Peasants withhold their feudal rents and dues; workers withhold their labor; or people everywhere withhold their cooperation in civil life by breaking the rules of civil order. And when this happens, people sometimes, for better or worse, change the world.

Societal reaction theorists can more easily ignore the impact on social life of rule violations because the kinds of rule violations on which they fasten tend to have little impact on dominant groups. Stutterers and alcoholics do not challenge the important interdependent relations of a society. But if we raise our eyes from these narrow categories of deviation, we can see the history of rule breakers who do change the world. Countless instances will do to make the point, and they do not have to be examples of immediate victories to do so. Consider, for example, the tens of thousands of unemployed English weavers who assembled at Peterloo in 1819 to demand political reform. The weavers were peaceful, if in a military mood, but the challenge implied by the very assemblage of these multitudes of working-class people was not likely to be mistaken by elites in the climate of class warfare that prevailed in England. E. P. Thompson, the noted English historian, explains that "in the provinces the very notion of working men attending meetings under the auspices of men of their own rank was, in the minds of the loyalist gentry, synonymous with riot and insubordination" (1963: 679). Accordingly, there was a social reaction: the regular troops joined by the incensed citizen militia of Manchester rode the crowd down, killing some and wounding many. The weavers withdrew in disarray. But as news of Peterloo spread and outrage grew, it was the English ruling class that withdrew, as Thompson points out:

> The enduring influence of Peterloo lay in the sheer horror of the day's events . . . And because of the odium attaching to the event, we may say that in the annals of the "free-born Englishman" the massacre was yet in its way a victory. Even Old Corruption knew, in its heart, that it dare not do this again. Since the moral consensus of the nation outlawed the riding down and sabering of an unarmed crowd, the corollary followed—that the right of public meeting had been gained. (1963: 710)

The weavers at Peterloo who won the political right of assembly were of course only one instance in 19th century English history of recurrent defiance that included poaching and blackmail, arson and machine breaking, riots and strikes, and that ultimately yielded the full range of political rights and some of the economic protections that have become part of the normative structure of England today. One feature of that normative structure is that it curbs the exercise of power, and especially of force, by ruling groups and the state. It restrains and limits societal reactions with an apparatus of legal rights. That normative structure and the protections it affords did not emanate naturally from something called society, and it was surely not merely the creation of a ruling class. It was forged as the ruling class tried to contend with those who broke the rules, and who did so with forethought and purpose . . .

Societal Reactions and the Transformation of Deviance

I have so far emphasized the importance of rule violations as challenges from below, but societal reactions are equally important: they are the other side of the dialectic of domination and resistance. Like the challengers, those who react to challenge also make and remake the world. This is a way of saying that those who break the rules not only make history, but that they do so in ways which reflect history. Rule-violating actions reflect history because they are shaped and constrained by the social context in which they emerge, a social context that is itself partially formed by the cumulative influences of societal reactions over time. These cumulative influences help explain the prevalence of the individualistic forms of deviant behavior that have so preoccupied the societal reaction school.

Forms of deviant action are obviously as diverse as the rules prohibiting them. Revolutionary violence, madness, exotic movements of religious protest, suicide, addiction, theft, and murder are all distinctively different human actions. Some are collective, others individualistic; some are directed against the self, and some against other groups. Which kind of actions people engage in, and which rules they violate, have been of enormous importance in human history. In the dialectic of domination and resistance, it matters greatly whether people go mad or rebel. In this sense, most of the forms of deviant action singled out by the societal reaction school are important.

They are important precisely because their impact is negligible, because somehow people have come to express their human agency in relatively impotent ways.

Why is it that when people act against the rules, it is so often against rules which have little to do with maintaining central structures of domination? That question ought to be of major interest in the study of deviance, but it is not. No sociological perspective systematically examines this question. Indeed, no sociological perspective has even undertaken to compare the forms of rule violation in search of an answer to this question.

One obvious first step in understanding the varieties of deviant action is to examine and compare the different social contexts within which various actions emerge. People act, but they act within specific social conditions inhibiting some actions and enabling others. People are not wholly constrained by social context, but neither can they wholly transcend it.

Societal reactions constitute one crucial determinant of social context. Dominant groups who react to challenges make and remake the world by altering the social conditions within which subsequent rule violations emerge. These changes do not obliterate the capacity of people to defy the rules of their society, but by altering the conditions under which people exercise this capacity, societal reactions generate both new limitations and new possibilities for action. Societal reactions thus help to explain why people come to violate some rules rather than others.

The societal reaction school has been preoccupied with the consequences of the societal reaction process for subsequent rule-violating behavior, but it has mainly focused only on negative socialization and its contribution to the persistence of deviant patterns. To see the full range of ways in which "social control causes deviance," we should look at the full repertoire of societal reactions—not only stigma, but force, propaganda, and institutional innovations of many kinds, including the granting of concessions. We should also examine the full range of outcomes of the societal reaction process. To be sure, the stabilization of deviant action is an important outcome, but so is its interruption. Moreover, in response to societal reactions, people may shift from one form of rule-violating action to another.

Finally, we should try to find out why societal reactions produce these varying effects by examining their impact on the social conditions which make one kind of deviant action possible and another unlikely or impossible. Two dimensions are of obvious importance: the impact of societal reactions on people's social ideas about themselves and the world around them, and the impact on resources for action which are variously yielded by the kinds of social relationships in which people are enmeshed. Thus societal reactions include efforts to undermine the beliefs held by the rule violators, or sometimes to support their beliefs, or to impress new beliefs; and societal reactions, by modifying social relations, diminish or enlarge or alter the opportunities for action available to people.

The impact of societal reactions on deviant action is complex because it is interactive. Rule violators are not simply the passive objects of societal reactions; they are active, responding subjects. They struggle with the implications of competing social beliefs, and they assess the possibilities for action of changing social relations. As their interpretations and relational resources are modified under the impact of societal reactions, they adapt by abandoning or renewing or altering their patterns of rule-violating action. These responses, in turn, produce further responses from dominant groups: they may bring a particular form of societal reaction to an end, or precipitate intensified reactions, or provoke entirely new forms. All of this, once again, produces new consequences for patterns of rule violation. By thus approaching the study of deviant behavior as a dialectic of action and reaction, we may develop an authentically interactive perspective.

One way of explaining the prevalence of the particular forms of deviant action with which the societal reaction school has been preoccupied, and especially the prevalence of such self-destructive forms as alcoholism, drug use or mental illness, is by looking at the cumulative effects of a history of societal reaction on the interpretations and resources that inform the actions of these rule violators. People who deviate in individualistic and self-destructive ways are also problem-solving creatures. They too act with purpose, and their purpose is informed by a particular interpretation of their world, of what is right and what is wrong, and what, if anything, can be done about it. They also have the capacity to discover opportunities for action that are not foretold by the normative consensus. If, then, their exercise of human agency takes convoluted forms, it is because their interpretations and resources lead them in these directions. If they attack themselves instead of their rulers, it is because their interpretations tell them they are themselves to blame, and it is because their options for action constrain them to act only against themselves. To explain individualistic and self-destructive forms of rule violation, we therefore need to explain the ideological and relational influences which inform these types of resistance.

Those influences do not come out of the air. They are incorporated in definite institutions like hospitals, asylums, prisons, and schools. These institutions have a definite history, and a definite dynamic propels that history. In large part it is the history of societal reaction, and the dynamic that propels it is the dynamic of rule violation. Consider as an example the rise in American society of the health system (which has grown to consume 10% of the GNP) and its impact on the forms of rule-violating behavior. Early in this century, American workers, enraged by the rampant crippling and killing in the new industrial system, agitated for improved safety conditions in the factories, mills, and mines. Their agitation was not without effect and, over time, they won modest improvements in safety. But safety measures were costly and were conceded by employers only reluctantly. Continued agitation for better working conditions was, therefore, countered by industry solutions which took the form of concessions such as pensions and medical care, a series of programs that did not eliminate the crippling conditions of the workplace but, instead, medicated or pensioned off the cripples. In time, the very existence of these programs helped to shape the way workers thought about workplace conditions, directing them to reinterpret the problem of safety as a problem in the availability or quality of health care. At the same time, the programs also created new relationships and facilities—doctors, drugs, clinics—to process the people who acted on their problems according to these medical interpretations.

In a broadly similar way, the unemployed and underemployed of our own time struggle to solve their problems through a series of institutionalized societal reactions called "Medicaid" and disability programs—with the bizarre consequence that even the experience of economic need and insecurity is interpreted in terms of a medical ideology, and acted on in terms of medically defined resources; perhaps that is why the disability caseloads have risen to staggering levels. Middle-class women may search for ways of understanding their situation and acting on it; when they do so by way of pervasive medical doctrines and widely available medical treatment, the consequence is that a good many are led to exercise their human agency as prescription drug addicts. In other words, the expansion of the health system, the mental health system, and the disability system can each be viewed as large-scale and cumulative, and as institutionalized societal reactions to a history of rule violations which over time come to channel the human capacity for resistance into the individualistic and self-destructive forms we usually call social deviance, as distinct from political deviance.[4]

But that is not the whole of it. I have not come this far to argue that social control works, albeit in circuitous ways. People continually develop new interpretations to counter received interpretations; they discover new resources for power in the context of efforts at domination; and they do so because they are problem-solving creatures.

Last year at this ceremony, the then-president of the Society described a series of protest movements that emerged in the last decade among just the pariah groups who are most entangled with agencies of social control: the disabled, the aged, paupers, and mental patients, for example. He called these movements "tertiary deviance" (Kitsuse 1980: 9). But inventing a label consistent with the societal reaction lexicon does not make these developments consistent with the societal reaction perspective. It is to John Kitsuse's credit that he described and cheered developments that simply should not have occurred from the perspective of the societal reaction school, given what he himself—in the aftermath of the insurgent '60s and '70s—recognizes as its "oversocialized" conception of deviant behavior (1980: 5).

Kitsuse ought to have gone further in examining the implications of these events for the societal reaction perspective. He should have pressed the question of why the pariahs revolted at all. He refers to the "outrage and anger" of these groups as having been "galvanized by the political ferment of the late '60s"; but since the protests themselves were the ferment, this explanation amounts to saying that protest caused itself. He further says that the civil rights movement inspired other protests; but since the civil rights movement is classified as tertiary deviance, this explanation also amounts to saying that the civil rights movement not only caused itself, but other tertiary movements as well.[5] Even if we pass over the tautology, reference to one protest is never sufficient to account for another. It is true that people are influenced in their evolution of deviant purposes by the examples around them, and that, therefore, people are more likely to protest when others have shown the way; but it is not a simple matter of contagion. People are goaded by example when the example makes sense in terms of their understandings of their own situation and their capacities for action. What is needed to account for the events to which Kitsuse is drawn is an explanation of the capacity of people to resist or challenge rules that goes beyond stigma and secondary deviation. Merely to give this human capacity a different name each time it is exercised—whether before the encounter with stigma or after—is not an explanation. If people can rebel after being labeled, they possess the same capacity before being labeled. Tertiary deviance, in short, raises the same problems of explanation as primary deviance, but under another name.[6]

Why then did the pariahs erupt in movements of political protest? In each of these movements, people not only experienced anger, and not only drew on the example of the civil rights movement, but they drew on capacities for deviance which were yielded by the agencies of social control with which they were enmeshed.

In the background of these protests was the enormous expansion of the agencies of the social welfare state, and the consequent expansion of their clientele, in the period since the Great Depression. These institutional developments can be understood, at least in part, as a series of societal reactions to rule violations in the 1930s and 1960s: the insurgent movements of industrial workers, the unemployed, and the aged in the earlier period; and the insurgent movement of blacks in the postwar period, a movement that ranged from highly politicized crime and riots to the southern civil rights and northern welfare rights protests. Societal reaction took the form of initiating and expanding new systems of social control—old-age security programs, welfare programs, disability programs, health programs, community mental health programs, senior citizen programs, and so forth. But to use the term "social control" does not fully describe this enormous expansion of the welfare state. These institutional societal reactions included new benefits for the stigmatized and the promulgation of a rhetoric of social welfare rights. In part, that rhetoric of rights legitimated the expansion of the control apparatus. It was also, however, a concession to the challenges from below which had helped generate the expansion of the agencies. And it was these institutional developments which also were to yield people new possibilities for defiant action.

The protest movements—among the aged, the disabled, the paupers and the mentally ill—which welled up in the late 1960s reflected new interpretations or reinterpretations which drew upon the rhetoric and practices of the agencies. Each protest meant that people had recast a stigmatized identity as a collective identity, and that they had recast a relationship of subjugation as a relationship founded on rights. Each protest was made possible by the relational resources generated by the institutions. Thus people were able to act together because they were brought together—in the senior citizen centers, in the waiting rooms, and on the welfare lines—by the institutions which presumably controlled them. They were able to act in large numbers because the institutions had created so many of them. They were able to find in these institutions a target vulnerable to their defiance and their demands. In other words, people were able to forge an ideology of rights out of the rhetoric and practices of social control, and they were able to wrest resources for power out of the new relationships created by social control.

I therefore bring this paper to a close with the proposition that each successive effort to impose social control may change the bases for resistance, and may change its forms, but defiance always erupts again. This proposition locates the study of deviant behavior where it belongs—in politics and in history.

I have one afterthought. I cannot help but suspect that many in the societal reaction school never intended to go where they have gone. At least some among the school intended to illuminate the politics underlying the making and enforcing of social rules. When they looked at rule making, they saw a politics of domination, a politics in which some people imposed rules on other people. These rule makers were human actors who, presumably with reflection and purpose, stamped society with their own beliefs and interests, and imposed those beliefs and interests on other people. They also saw the human damage that such imposition could do. What they did not see were the human actors at the other end of rule making who, with reflection and purpose, also try to stamp society with their beliefs and interests by resisting, evading, and defying the rules imposed on them. However inadvertently, the societal reaction school purged the elemental dialectic of resistance from social life. The result was a theory that domination is total, that it works. That theory is wrong.

Notes

1. The issue of agency is in fact central to Marxism, for on the resolution of this issue hangs the question of how history happens—the question of whether, for example, capitalism will collapse as a consequence of the unfolding of economic and technological processes, or collapse only if active revolutionary agents overthrow it. Viewed in this way, the issue of agency has divided Marxists for a very long time, as the different but nevertheless similarly activist positions

of Lenin and Luxemburg were pitted against the increasingly evolutionary positions of other leaders in the Second International. The issue has reemerged in recent years, most dramatically in the debate between the Marxist structuralists who follow Althusser and their Marxist critics. See Thompson (1978); also Gouldner (1980) and Miller (1979) for a more general exposition of this division within Marxist thought. See also Singer (1980) for the argument that all of this is a corruption of the essentially determinist theories of Marx himself. Miller's inquiry into the different theoretical bases for agency is particularly illuminating. He makes the point that Marx was ambiguous, stamping the role he ascribed to human agency with historical necessity by virtue of the rationalism he attributed to human actors.

2. Since the societal reaction school has all but ignored force, it is not surprising to find, as Gouldner (1968) has pointed out, that it has had to ignore those who actually hold power. One knows this at once by the language which is invoked to describe those who make or enforce rules. They are not designated by their monopolization of the means of force, or their control of large-scale economic resources, or their hegemony over religious doctrine. Instead, they are merely "audiences" to outrageous acts, aroused "claims-makers," and indignant "moral entrepreneurs." They oppose children running about unsupervised or they oppose marijuana use, and so they mobilize the child-saving crusades or campaigns to criminalize drugs. To be sure, these mobilizations over questions of everyday morality and family life frequently have more significance for larger patterns of domination than appears on the face. They are often instigated and financed by those at the pinnacles of economic, political, and religious power, or are at least exploited by them as the means to prevent or discredit more fundamental challenges. Yet it is characteristic of the societal reaction literature that these linkages between moral entrepreneurship and the pinnacles are not made, and the genuinely important historical moral crusades, even those contemporaneous with the emergence of the societal reaction school, go unanalyzed. No one in this school analyzed the corporate-sponsored anticommunist mobilization led by McCarthy which blunted the radical perspectives that had gained ground in the Great Depression, especially within an insurgent labor movement. No one analyzed the movement of "massive resistance" led by southern Bourbons to ward off challenges by blacks both to segregation and to the structures of southern economic and political power.

3. Here we are not joining those critics who argue that labeling theory fails because it does not point to the "real" deviance in American society, namely the deviance of ruling-class groups who fix prices, cut welfare grants, and murder Southeast Asians (see, for example, Liazos 1972 and Chambliss, 1976). We also are indignant at such actions. But to call all of this "deviance" is merely to substitute the moral judgments of the sociologists for the understandings of deviance that exist in the society—understandings that, of course, reflect patterns of power.

4. For a similar analysis of the impact of the rise of the public educational system on the transformation of deviant patterns, see Piven and Cloward [1980].

5. Kitsuse defines the civil rights movement as an example of tertiary deviance because he defines blacks as secondary deviants. As he suggests elsewhere in his paper, he tends to take the view that the occupants of any inferior position in a system of social stratification should be understood to be secondary deviants, no matter whether the invidious distinctions are based on age, gender, social class, minority status, immigrant status, or whatever. In effect, this makes the concept of secondary deviance coterminous with the prestige dimension of social stratification, and since virtually everyone in a system of social inequality is inferior to someone else, we have all become secondary deviants. With that leap, the concept of secondary deviation is shorn of any distinctive meaning. Not least, it purges from the term deviant behavior the meaning that it entails the violation of norms; now people are deviant merely as a consequence of occupying a position in a system of social stratification which is inferior to some other position. In just this conceptual blurring of the definition of secondary deviation,

we see how completely the societal reaction school has extinguished human agency from its perspective on deviant behavior.

6. Kitsuse's argument follows Schur (1980). Schur also views the imposition of stigma in "deviance-defining" as essentially part of a system of social stratification, and closely similar, therefore, to other processes through which socially valued statuses are distributed. Schur, like Kitsuse, focuses on the recent mobilization of protests among people labeled deviant. While he goes much further than Kitsuse in his effort to account for the conditions that make protest possible, his explanation is still mainly descriptive, albeit a description couched in language drawn from some of the literature on interest groups and protest movements. Nevertheless, he fails to explain why protest occurred when it occurred among groups that had hitherto been quiescent.

References

Becker, Howard S. 1963. *Outsiders: Studies in the Sociology of Deviance*. New York: Free Press.

Chambliss, William J. 1976. "The State and Criminal Law." Pp. 66–106 in William J. Chambliss and Milton Mankoff (eds.), *Whose Law, What Order?* New York: John Wiley.

Dawe, Alan. 1978. "Theories of Social Action." Pp. 362–417 in Tom Bottomore and Robert Nisbet (eds.), *A History of Sociological Analysis*. New York: Basic Books.

Durkheim, Emile. 1938. *The Rules of Sociological Method*. (Trans. by S. A. Solovay and J. H. Mueller.) Chicago: University of Chicago Press.

———. 1951. *Suicide*. Glencoe, IL.: Free Press

Erikson, Kai. 1964. "Notes on the Sociology of Deviance." Pp. 9–22 in Howard S. Becker (ed.), *The Other Side: Perspectives on Deviance*. New York: Free Press.

Giddens, Anthony. 1976. *New Rules of Sociological Method: A Positive Critique of Interpretive Theories*. New York: Basic Books.

Goode, Erich. 1975. "On Behalf of Labeling Theory." *Social Problems* 22 (June): 570–583.

Gouldner, Alvin W. 1968. "The Sociologist as Partisan." *The American Sociologist* 3 (May): 103–116.

———. 1970. *The Coming Crisis of Western Sociology*. New York: Basic Books.

———. 1980. *The Two Marxisms: Contradictions and Anomalies in the Development of Theory.* New York: Continuum Books, Seabury.

Kitsuse, John. 1962. "Societal Reaction to Deviant Behavior: Problems of Theory and Method." *Social Problems* 9 (Winter): 247–256.

———. 1975. "The 'New Conception of Deviance' and Its Critics." Pp. 273–283 in Walter R. Gove (ed.), *The Labeling of Deviance*. New York: Sage.

———. 1980. "Coming Out All Over: Deviants and the Politics of Social Problems." *Social Problems* 28 (October): 1–13.

Lane, Robert E. 1978. "Autonomy, Felicity, Futility: The Effects of the Market Economy on Political Personality." *The Journal of Politics* 40: 2–24.

———. 1980. "Individualism and the Market Society." Paper presented at the Annual Meeting of the American Political Science Association, Washington, DC, August.

Lemert, Edwin. 1951. *Social Pathology*. New York: McGraw-Hill.

———. 1972. *Human Deviance, Social Problems and Social Control*. Second Edition. Englewood Cliffs, NJ: Prentice-Hall.

———. 1974. "Beyond Mead: The Societal Reaction to Deviance." *Social Problems* 21(April): 457–468.

Liazos, Alexander. 1972. "The Poverty of the Sociology of Deviance: Nuts, Sluts, and Preverts." *Social Problems* 20 (Summer): 103–120.

Mankoff, Milton. 1980. "Societal Reaction and Career Deviance: A Critical Appraisal." Pp. 278–295 in Stuart H. Traub and Craig B. Little (eds.), *Theories of Deviance.* Second Edition. Itasco, IL: F. E. Peacock.

Matza, David. 1964. *Delinquency and Drift.* New York: John Wiley.

———. 1969. *Becoming Deviant.* Englewood Cliffs, NJ: Prentice-Hall.

Miller, James. 1979. *History and Human Existence: From Marx to Merleau-Ponty.* Berkeley: University of California Press.

Parsons, Talcott. 1935. "The Place of Ultimate Values in Sociological Theory." *The International Journal of Ethics* XLV (January): 282–316.

———. 1937. *The Structure of Social Action.* New York: McGraw-Hill.

———. 1951. *The Social System.* Glencoe, IL: Free Press.

Petrunik, Michael. 1980. "The Rise and Fall of 'Labeling Theory': The Construction and Destruction of a Sociological Strawman." *Canadian Journal of Sociology* 5 (3): 213–230.

Piven, Frances Fox and Richard A. Cloward. 1977. *Poor People's Movements: Why They Succeed, How They Fail.* New York: Pantheon.

———. 1980. "Social Policy and the Formation of Political Consciousness." Pp. 117–152 in Maurice Zeitlin (ed.), *Political Power and Social Theory,* Vol. 1. Greenwich, CT: JAI Press.

Rains, Prudence. 1975. "Imputations of Deviance: A Retrospective Essay on the Labeling Perspective." *Social Problems* 23 (October).

Scheff, Thomas J. 1966. *Being Mentally Ill: A Sociological Theory.* Chicago: Aldine.

———. 1980. "The Role of the Mentally Ill and the Dynamics of Mental Disorder: A Research Framework." Pp. 261–277 in Stuart H. Traub and Craig B. Little (eds.), *Theories of Deviance.* Second Edition. Itasco, IL: F. E. Peacock.

Schur, Edwin M. 1979. *Interpreting Deviance.* New York: Harper and Row.

———. 1980. *The Politics of Deviance.* Englewood Cliffs, NJ: Prentice-Hall.

Scott, John Finley. 1963. "The Changing Foundations of the Parsonian Action Scheme." *American Sociological Review* 28 (October): 716–735.

Singer, Peter. 1980. "Dictator Marx?" *New York Review of Books,* September 25, 1980.

Spector, Malcolm and John L. Kitsuse. 1977. *Constructing Social Problems.* Menlo Park, CA: Cummings.

Tannenbaum, Frank. 1938. *Crime and the Community.* Boston: Ginn.

Therborn, Goran. 1976. *Science, Class and Society: On the Formation of Sociology and Historical Materialism.* London: NLB.

Thompson, E. P. 1963. *The Making of the English Working Class.* New York: Vintage Books.

———. 1978. *The Poverty of Theory and Other Essays.* New York: Monthly Review Press.

Wrong, Dennis H. 1961. "The Oversocialized Conception of Man in Modern Sociology." *American Sociological Review* 26 (April): 183–193.

CHAPTER 5

A Sociological Analysis of the Law of Vagrancy

William J. Chambliss

With the outstanding exception of Jerome Hall's (1935) analysis of theft, there has been a severe shortage of sociologically relevant analyses of the relationship between particular laws and the social setting in which these laws emerge, are interpreted, and take form.[1] The paucity of such studies is somewhat surprising in view of widespread agreement that such studies are not only desirable but absolutely essential to the development of a mature sociology of law.[2] A fruitful method of establishing the direction and pattern of this mutual influence is to systematically analyze particular legal categories, to observe the changes which take place in the categories and to explain how these changes are themselves related to and stimulate changes in the society. This paper is an attempt to provide such an analysis of the law of vagrancy in Anglo-American law.

Legal Innovation: The Emergence of the Law of Vagrancy in England

There is general agreement among legal scholars that the first full-fledged vagrancy statute was passed in England in 1349. As is generally the case with legislative innovations, however, this statute was preceded by earlier laws which established a climate favorable to such change. The most significant forerunner to the 1349 vagrancy statute was in 1274 when it was provided:

> Because that abbies and houses of religion have been overcharged and sore grieved, by the resort of great men and other, so that their goods have not been sufficient for themselves, whereby they have been greatly hindered and impoverished, that they cannot maintain themselves, nor such charity as they have been accustomed to do; it is provided, that none shall come to eat or lodge in any house of religion, or any other's foundation than of his own, at the costs of the house, unless he be required by the governor of the house before his coming hither. (3 Ed. 1. c. 1)[3]

Unlike the vagrancy statutes this statute does not intend to curtail the movement of persons from one place to another, but is solely designed to provide the religious houses with some financial relief from the burden of providing food and shelter to travelers. The philosophy that the religious houses were to give alms to the poor and to the sick and feeble was, however, to undergo drastic change in the next fifty years. The result of this changed attitude was the establishment of the first vagrancy statute in 1349 which made it a crime to give alms to any who were unemployed while being of sound mind and body. To wit:

> Because that many valiant beggars, as long as they may live of begging, do refuse to labor, giving themselves to idleness and vice, and sometimes to theft and other abominations; it is ordained, that none, upon pain of imprisonment shall, under the colour of pity or alms, give anything to such which may labour, or presume to favour them towards their desires; so that thereby they may be compelled to labour for their necessary living. (35 Ed. 1. c. 1)

It was further provided by this statute that:

> . . . every man and woman, of what condition he be, free or bond, able in body, and within the age of threescore years, not living in merchandize nor exercising any craft, nor having of his own whereon to live, nor proper land whereon to occupy himself, and not serving any other, if he in convenient service (his estate considered) be required to serve, shall be bounded to serve him which shall him require. . . . And if any refuse, he shall on conviction by two true men, . . . be commited to gaol till he find surety to serve. (35 Ed. 1.c.1)

And if any workman or servant, of what estate or condition he be, retained in any man's service, do depart from the said service without reasonable cause or license, before the term agreed on, he shall have pain of imprisonment (23 Ed. 3).

There was also in this statute the stipulation that the workers should receive a standard wage. In 1351 this statute was strengthened by the stipulation:

> An none shall go out of the town where he dwelled in winter, to serve the summer, if he may serve in the same town. (25 Ed. 3)

By 1360 the punishment for these acts became imprisonment for fifteen days and if they "do not justify themselves by the end of that time, to be sent to gaol till they do" (34 Ed 3).

A change in official policy so drastic as this did not, of course, occur simply as a matter of whim. The vagrancy statutes emerged as a result of changes in other parts of the social structure. The prime mover for this legislative innovation was the Black Death which struck England about 1348. Among the many disastrous consequences this had upon the social structure was the fact that it decimated the labor force. It is estimated that by the time the pestilence had run its course at least 50 percent of the population of England had died from the plague. This decimation of the labor force would necessitate rather drastic innovations in any society but its impact was heightened in England where, at this time, the economy was highly dependent upon a ready supply of cheap labor.

Even before the pestilence, however, the availability of an adequate supply of cheap labor was becoming a problem for the landowners. The crusades and various wars had made money necessary to the lords and, as a result, the lords frequently agreed to sell the serfs their freedom in order to obtain the needed funds. The serfs, for their part, were desirous of obtaining their freedom (by "fair means" or "foul") because the larger towns which were becoming more industrialized during this period could offer the serf greater personal freedom as well as a higher standard of living. This process is nicely summarized by Fredrick Bradshaw:

> By the middle of the 14th century the outward uniformity of the manorial system had become in practice considerably varied . . . for the peasant had begun to drift to the towns and it was unlikely that the old village life in its unpleasant aspects should not be resented. Moreover the constant wars against France and Scotland were fought mainly with mercenaries after Henry III's time and most villages contributed to the new armies. The bolder serfs either joined the armies or fled to the towns, and even in the villages the free men who held by villein tenure were as eager to commute their services as the serfs were to escape. Only the amount of 'free' labor available enabled the lord to work his demense in many places. (Bradshaw 1927: 54)

And he says regarding the effect of the Black Death:

> . . . in 1348 the Black Death reached England and the vast mortality that ensued destroyed that reserve of labour which alone had made the manorial system even nominally possible. (Bradshaw 1927: 54)

The immediate result of these events was of course no surprise: Wages for the "free" man rose considerably and this increased, on the one hand, the landowners problems and, on the other hand, the plight of the unfree tenant. For although wages increased for the personally free laborers, it of course did not necessarily add to the standard of living of the serf; if anything it made his position worse because the landowner would be hard pressed to pay for the personally free labor which he needed and would thus find it more and more difficult to maintain the standard of living for the serf which he had heretofore supplied. Thus the serf had no alternative but flight if he chose to better his position. Furthermore, flight generally meant both freedom and better conditions since the possibility of work in the new weaving industry was great and the chance of being caught small (Bradshaw 1927: 57).

It was under these conditions that we find the first vagrancy statutes emerging. There is little question but that these statutes were designed for one express purpose: to force laborers (whether personally free or unfree) to accept employment at a low wage in order to ensure the landowner an adequate supply of labor at a price he could afford to pay. Caleb Foote concurs with this interpretation when he notes:

> The anti-migratory policy behind vagrancy legislation began as an essential complement of the wage stabilization legislation which accompanied the break-up of feudalism and the depopulation caused by the Black Death. By the Statutes of Labourers in 1349–1351, every able-bodied person without other means of support was required to work for wages fixed at the level preceding the Black Death; it was unlawful to accept more, or to refuse an offer to work, or to flee from one county to another to avoid offers of work or to seek higher wages, or go give alms to able-bodied beggars who refused to work. (Foote 1956: 615)

In short, as Foote says in another place, this was an "attempt to make the vagrancy statutes a substitute for serfdom" (1956: 615). This same conclusion is equally apparent from the wording of the statute where it is stated:

> Because great part of the people, and especially of workmen and servants, later died in pestilence; many seeing the necessity of masters, and great scarcity of servants, will not serve without excessive wages, and some rather willing to beg in idleness than by labour to get their living: it is ordained, that every man and woman, of what condition he be, free or bond, able in body and within the age of threescore years, not living in merchandize, (etc.) be required to serve. (3 Ed.1. c.1) (35 Ed.1. c.1)

The innovation in the law, then, was a direct result of the aforementioned changes which had occurred in the social setting. In this case these changes were located for the most part in the economic institution of the society. The vagrancy laws were designed to alleviate a condition defined by the lawmakers as undesirable. The solution was to attempt to force a reversal, as it were, of a social process which was well under-way; that is, to curtail mobility of laborers in such a way that labor would not become a commodity for which the landowners would have to compete.

Statutory Dormancy: A Legal Vestige

In time, of course, the curtailment of the geographical mobility of laborers was no longer requisite. One might well expect that when the function served by the statute was no longer an important one for the society, the statutes would be eliminated from the law. In fact, this has not occurred. The vagrancy statutes have remained in effect since 1349. Furthermore, as we shall see in some detail later, they were taken over by the colonies and have remained in effect in the United States as well.

The substance of the vagrancy statutes changed very little for some time after the first ones in 1349–1351 although there was a tendency to make punishments harsher than originally. For example, in 1360 it was provided that violators of the statute should be imprisoned for fifteen days (34 Ed. 3), and in 1388, the punishment was to put the offender in the stocks and to keep him there until "he find surety to return to his service" (12 R. 2). That there was still, at this time, the intention of providing the landowner with labor is apparent from the fact that this statute provides:

> . . . and he or she which use to labour at the plough and cart, or other labour and service of husbandry, till they be of the age of 12 years, from thenceforth shall abide at the same labour without being put to any mistery or handicraft: and any covenant of apprenticeship to the contrary shall be void. (12 R. 2)

The next alteration in the statutes occurs in 1495 and is restricted to an increase in punishment. Here it is provided that vagrants shall be "set in stocks, there to remain by the space of three days and three nights, and there to have none other sustenance but bread and water; and after the said three days and nights, to be had out and set at large, and then to be commanded to avoid the town" (11 H. & C. 2).

The tendency to increase the severity of punishment during this period seems to be the result of a general tendency to make finer distinctions in the criminal law. During this period the vagrancy statutes appear to have been fairly inconsequential in either their effect as a control mechanism or as a generally enforced statute.[4] The processes of social change in the culture generally and the trend away from serfdom and into a "free" economy obviated the utility of these statutes. The result was not unexpected. The judiciary did not apply the law and the legislators did not take it upon themselves to change the law. In short, we have here a period of dormancy in which the statute is neither applied nor altered significantly.

A Shift in Focal Concern

Following the squelching of the Peasants' Revolt in 1381, the services of the serfs to the lords ". . . tended to become less and less exacted, although in certain forms they lingered on till the seventeenth century . . . By the sixteenth century few knew that there were any bondmen in England . . . and in 1575 Queen Elizabeth listened to the prayers of almost the last serfs in England . . . and granted them manumission" (Bradshaw 1927: 61).

In view of this change we would expect corresponding changes in the vagrancy laws. Beginning with the lessening of punishment in the statute of 1503 we find these changes. However, instead of remaining dormant (or becoming more so) or being negated altogether, the vagrancy statutes experienced a shift in focal concern. With this shift the statutes served a new and equally important function for the social order of England. The first statute which indicates this change was in 1530. In this statute it was stated:

> If any person, being whole and mighty in body, and able to labour, be taken in begging, or be vagrant and can give no reckoning how he lawfully gets his living; and all other idle persons going about, some of them using divers and subtle crafty and unlawful games and plays, and some of them feigning themselves to have knowledge of . . . crafty sciences shall be punished as provided. (22 H.8.c. 12 1530)

What is most significant about this statute is the shift from an earlier concern with laborers to a concern with criminal activities. To be sure, the stipulation of persons "being whole and mighty in body, and able to labour, be taken in begging, or be vagrant" sounds very much like the concerns of the earlier statutes. Some important differences are apparent however when the rest of the statute includes those who ". . . can give no reckoning how he lawfully gets his living"; "some of them using divers subtil and unlawful games and plays." This is the first statute which specifically focuses upon these kinds of criteria for adjudging someone a vagrant.

It is significant that in this statute the severity of punishment is increased so as to be greater not only than provided by the 1503 statute but the punishment is more severe than that which had been provided by any of the pre-1503 statutes as well. For someone who is merely idle and gives no reckoning of how he makes his living the offender shall be:

> . . . had to the next market town, or other place where they [the constables] shall think most convenient, and there to be tied to the end of a cart naked, and to be beaten with whips throughout the same market town or other place, till his body be bloody by reason of such whipping. (22 H. 8 c. 12)

But, for those who use "divers and subtil crafty and unlawful games and plays," etc., the punishment is "whipping at two days together in manner aforesaid" (22 H. 8. c. 12). For the second offense, such persons are:

> . . . scourged two days, and the third day to be put upon the pillory from nine of the clock till eleven before noon of the same day and to have one of his ears cut off. (22 H. 8. c. 12)

And if he offend the third time "to have like punishment with whipping, standing on the pillory and to have his other ear cut off" (22 H. 8. c. 12).

This statute (1) makes a distinction between types of offenders and applies the more severe punishment to those who are clearly engaged in "criminal" activities, (2) mentions a specific concern with categories of "unlawful" behavior, and (3) applies a type of punishment (cutting off the ear) which is generally reserved for offenders who are defined as likely to be a fairly serious criminal.

Only five years later do we find for the first time that the punishment of death is applied to the crime of vagrancy. We also note a change in terminology in the statute:

> and if any ruffians . . . after having been once apprehended . . . shall wander, loiter, or idle use themselves and play the vagabonds . . . shall be eftfoons not only whipped again, but shall have the gristle of his right ear clean cut off. And if he shall again offend, he shall be committed to gaol till the next sessions; and being there convicted upon indictment, he shall have judgment to suffer pains and execution of death, as a felon, as an enemy of the commonwealth. (27 H. 8. c. 25)

It is significant that the statute now makes persons who repeat the crime of vagrancy a felon. During this period then, the focal concern of the vagrancy statutes becomes a concern for the control of felons and is no longer primarily concerned with the movement of laborers.

These statutory changes were a direct response to changes taking place in England's social structure during this period. We have already pointed out that feudalism was decaying rapidly. Concomitant with the breakup of feudalism was an increased emphasis upon commerce and industry. The commercial emphasis in England at the turn of the sixteenth century is of particular importance in the development of vagrancy laws. With commercialism came considerable traffic bearing valuable items. Where there were 169 important merchants in the middle of the fourteenth century there were three thousand merchants engaged in foreign trade alone at the beginning of the sixteenth century (Hall 1935: 21). England became highly dependent upon commerce for its economic support. Italians conducted a great deal of the commerce of England during this early period and were held in low repute by the populace. As a result, they were subject to attacks by citizens and, more important, were frequently robbed of their goods while transporting them. "The general insecurity of the times made any transportation hazardous. The special risks to which the alien merchant was subjected gave rise to the royal practice of issuing formally executed covenants of safe conduct through the realm" (Hall 1935: 23).

Such a situation not only called for the enforcement of existing laws but also called for the creation of new laws which would facilitate the control of persons preying upon merchants transporting goods. The vagrancy statutes were revived in order to fulfill just such a purpose. Persons who had committed no serious felony but who were suspected of being capable of doing so could be apprehended and incapacitated through the application of vagrancy laws once these laws were refocused so as to include ". . . any ruffians . . . [who] shall wander, loiter, or idle use themselves and play the vagabonds . . ." (27 H. 8. c. 25).

The new focal concern is continued in 1547 and in fact is made more general so as to include:

> Whoever man or woman, being not lame, impotent, or so aged or diseased that he or she cannot work, not having whereon to live, shall be lurking in any house, or loitering or idle wandering by the highway side, or in streets, cities, towns, or villages, not applying themselves to some honest labour, and so continuing for three days; or running away from their work; every such person shall be taken for a vagabond. And . . . upon conviction of two witnesses . . . the same loiterer [shall] be marked with a hot iron in the breast with the letter V, and adjudged him to the person bringing him, to be his slave for two years. . . . (1 Ed. 6. c. 3)

Should the vagabond run away, upon conviction, he was to be branded by a hot iron with the letter S on the forehead and to be thenceforth declared a slave forever. And in 1571 there is modification of the punishment to be inflicted, whereby the offender is to be "branded on the chest with the letter V" (for vagabond). And, if he is convicted the second time, the brand is to be made on the forehead. It is worth noting here that this method of punishment, which first appeared in 1530 and is repeated here with somewhat more force, is also an indication of a change in the type of person to whom the law is intended to apply. For it is likely that nothing so permanent as branding would be applied to someone who was wandering but looking for work, or at worst merely idle and not particularly dangerous per se. On the other hand, it could well be applied to someone who was likely to be engaged in other criminal activities in connection with being "vagrant."

By 1571 in the statute of 14 El. C. 5 the shift in focal concern is fully developed:

> All rogues, vagabonds, and sturdy beggars shall . . . be committed to the common gaol . . . he shall be grievously whipped, and burnt thro' the gristle of the right ear with a hot iron of the compass of an inch about; . . . And

> for the second offense, he shall be adjudged a felon, unless some person will take him for two years in to his service. And for the third offense, he shall be adjudged guilty of felony without benefit of clergy.

And there is included a long list of persons who fall within the statute: "proctors, procurators, idle persons going about using subtil, crafty and unlawful games or plays; and some of them feigning themselves to have knowledge of . . . absurd sciences . . . and all fencers, bearwards, common players in interludes, and minstrels . . . all juglers, pedlars, tinkers, petty chapmen . . . and all counterfeiters of licenses, passports and users of the same." The major significance of this statute is that it includes all the previously defined offenders and adds some more. Significantly, those added are more clearly criminal types, counterfeiters, for example. It is also significant that there is the following qualification of this statute: "Provided also, that this act shall not extend to cookers, or harvest folks, that travel for harvest work, corn or hay."

That the changes in this statute were seen as significant is indicated by the following statement which appears in the statute of 1571:

> And whereas by reason of this act, the common gaols of every shire are like to be greatly pestered with more number of prisoners than heretofore hath been, for that the said vagabonds and other lewd persons before recited shall upon their apprehension be committed to the said gaols; it is enacted . . . (14 Ed. C. 5)

And a provision is made for giving more money for maintaining the gaols. This seems to add credence to the notion that this statute was seen as being significantly more general than those previously.

It is also of importance to note that this is the first time the term "rogue" has been used to refer to persons included in the vagrancy statutes. It seems, a priori, that a "rogue" is a different social type than is a "vagrant" or a "vagabond"; the latter terms implying something more equivalent to the idea of a "tramp" whereas the former (rogue) seems to imply a more disorderly and potentially dangerous person.

The emphasis upon the criminalistic aspect of vagrants continues in Chapter 17 of the same statute:

> Whereas divers licentious persons wander up and down in all parts of the realm, to countenance their wicked behavior; and do continually assemble themselves armed in the highways, and elsewhere in troops, to the great terror of her majesty's true subjects, the impeachment of her laws, and the disturbance of the peace and tranquility of the realm; and whereas many outrages are daily committed by these dissolute persons, and more are likely to ensue if speedy remedy be not provided.

With minor variations (e.g., offering a reward for the capture of a vagrant) the statutes remain essentially of this nature until 1743. In 1743 there was once more an expansion of the types of persons included such that "all persons going about as patent gatherers, or gatherers of alms, under pretense of loss by fire or other casualty; or going about as collectors for prisons, gaols, or hospitals; all persons playing of betting at any unlawful games; and all persons who run away and leave their wives or children . . . all persons wandering abroad, and lodging in alehouses, barns, outhouses, or in the open air, not giving good account of themselves," were types of offenders added to those already included.

By 1743 the vagrancy statutes had apparently been sufficiently reconstructed by the shifts of concern so as to be once more a useful instrument in the creation of social solidarity. This function has apparently continued down to the present day in England and the changes from 1743 to the present have been all in the direction of clarifying or expanding the categories covered but little has been introduced to change either the meaning or the impact of this branch of the law.

We can summarize this shift in focal concern by quoting from the Earl of Halsbury. He has noted that in the vagrancy statutes:

> . . . elaborate provision is made for the relief and incidental control of destitute wayfarers. These latter, however, form but a small portion of the offenders aimed at by what are known as the Vagrancy Laws, . . . many offenders who are in no ordinary sense of the word vagrants, have been brought under the laws relating to vagrancy, and the great number of the offenses coming within the operation of these laws have little or no relation to the subject of poor relief, but are more properly directed towards the prevention of crime, the preservation of good order, and the promotion of social economy. (Earl of Halsbury: 606–607)

Before leaving this section it is perhaps pertinent to make a qualifying remark. We have emphasized throughout this section how the vagrancy statutes underwent a shift in focal concern as the social setting changed. The shift in focal concern is not meant to imply that the later focus of the statutes represents a completely new law. It will be recalled that even in the first vagrancy statute there was reference to those who "do refuse labor, giving themselves to idleness and vice and sometimes to theft and other abominations." Thus the possibility of criminal activities resulting from persons who refuse to labor was recognized even in the earliest statute. The fact remains, however, that the major emphasis in this statute and in the statutes which followed the first one was always upon the "refusal to labor" or "begging." The "criminalistic" aspect of such persons was relatively unimportant. Later, as we have shown, the criminalistic potential becomes of paramount importance. The thread runs back to the earliest statute but the reason for the statutes' existence as well as the focal concern of the statutes is quite different in 1743 than it was in 1349.

Vagrancy Laws in the United States

In general, the vagrancy laws of England, as they stood in the middle eighteenth century, were simply adopted by the states. There were some exceptions to this general trend. For example, Maryland restricted the application of vagrancy laws to "free" Negroes. In addition, for all states the vagrancy laws were even more explicitly concerned with the control of criminals and undesirables than had been the case in England. New

York, for example, explicitly defines prostitutes as being a category of vagrants during this period. These exceptions do not, however, change the general picture significantly and it is quite appropriate to consider the U. S. vagrancy laws as following from England's of the middle eighteenth century with relatively minor changes. The control of criminals and undesirables was the raison de'être of the vagrancy laws in the United States. This is as true today as it was in 1750. As Foote's analysis of the application of vagrancy statutes in the Philadelphia court shows, these laws are presently applied indiscriminately to persons considered a "nuisance." Foote (1956: 613) suggests that ". . . the chief significance of this branch of the criminal law lies in its quantitative impact and administrative usefulness."[5] Thus it appears that in America the trend begun in England in the sixteenth, seventeenth, and eighteenth centuries has been carried to its logical extreme and the laws are now used principally as a mechanism for "clearing the streets" of the derelicts who inhabit the "skid roads" and "Bowerys" of our large urban areas.

Since the 1800s there has been an abundant source of prospects to which the vagrancy laws have been applied. These have been primarily those persons deemed by the police and the courts to be either actively involved in criminal activities or at least peripherally involved. In this context, then, the statutes have changed very little. The functions served by the statutes in England of the late eighteenth century are still being served today in both England and the United States. The locale has changed somewhat and it appears that the present-day application of vagrancy statutes is focused upon the arrest and confinement of the "down-and-outers" who inhabit certain sections of our larger cities but the impact has remained constant. The lack of change in the vagrancy statutes, then, can be seen as a reflection of the society's perception of a continuing need to control some of its "suspicious" or "undesirable" members.[6]

A word of caution is in order lest we leave the impression that this administrative purpose is the sole function of vagrancy laws in the U.S. today. Although it is our contention that this is generally true it is worth remembering that during certain periods of our recent history, and to some extent today, these laws have also been used to control the movement of workers. This was particularly the case during the depression years and California is of course infamous for its use of vagrancy laws to restrict the admission of migrants from other states.[7] The vagrancy statutes, because of their history, still contain germs within them which make such effects possible. Their main purpose, however, is clearly no longer the control of laborers but rather the control of the undesirable, the criminal, and the "nuisance."

Discussion

The foregoing analysis of the vagrancy laws has demonstrated that these laws were a legislative innovation which reflected the socially perceived necessity of providing an abundance of cheap labor to landowners during a period when serfdom was breaking down and when the pool of available labor was depleted. With the eventual breakup of feudalism the need for such laws eventually disappeared and the increased dependence of the economy upon industry and commerce rendered the former use of the vagrancy statutes unnecessary. As a result, for a substantial period the vagrancy statutes were dormant, undergoing only minor changes and, presumably, being applied infrequently. Finally, the vagrancy laws were subjected to considerable alteration through a shift in the focal concern of the statutes. Whereas in their inception the laws focused upon the "idle" and "those refusing to labor" after the turn of the sixteenth century and emphasis came to be upon "rogues," "vagabonds," and others who were suspected of being engaged in criminal activities. During this period, the focus was particularly upon "roadmen" who preyed upon citizens who transported goods from one place to another. The increased importance of commerce to England during this period made it necessary that some protection be given persons engaged in this enterprise and the vagrancy statutes provided one source for such protection by refocusing the acts to be included under these statutes.

Comparing the results of this analysis with the findings of Hall's study of theft we see a good deal of correspondence. Of major importance is the fact that both analyses demonstrate the truth of Hall's assertion that "[t]he functioning of courts is significantly related to concomitant cultural needs, and this applies to the law of procedure as well as to substantive law" (1935: xii).

Our analysis of the vagrancy laws also indicates that when changed social conditions create a perceived need for legal changes that these alterations will be effected through the revision and refocusing of existing statutes. This process was demonstrated in Hall's analysis of theft as well as in our analysis of vagrancy. In the case of vagrancy, the laws were dormant when the focal concern of the laws was shifted so as to provide control over potential criminals. In the case of theft the laws were reinterpreted (interestingly, by the courts and not by the legislature) so as to include persons who were transporting goods for a merchant but who absconded with the contents of the packages transported.

It also seems probable that when the social conditions change and previously useful laws are no longer useful there will be long periods when these laws will remain dormant. It is less likely that they will be officially negated. During this period of dormancy it is the judiciary which has principal responsibility for not applying the statutes. It is possible that one finds statutes being negated only when the judiciary stubbornly applies laws which do not have substantial public support. An example of such laws in contemporary times would be the "Blue Laws." Most states still have laws prohibiting the sale of retail goods on Sunday yet these laws are rarely applied. The laws are very likely to remain but to be dormant unless a recalcitrant judge or a vocal minority of the population insist that the laws be applied. When this happens we can anticipate that the statutes will be negated.[8] Should there arise a perceived need to curtail retail selling under some special circumstances, then it is likely that these laws will undergo a shift in focal concern much like the shift which characterized the vagrancy laws. Lacking such application the laws will simply remain dormant except for rare instances where they will be negated.

This analysis of the vagrancy statutes (and Hall's analysis of theft as well) has demonstrated the importance of "vested interest" groups in the emergence and/or alteration of laws. The vagrancy laws emerged in order to provide the powerful landowners with a ready supply of cheap labor. When this was no longer seen as necessary and particularly when the landowners were no longer dependent upon cheap labor nor were they a powerful interest group in the society the laws became dormant. Finally a new interest group emerged and was seen as being of great importance to the society and the laws were then altered so as to afford some protection to this group. These findings are thus in agreement with Weber's contention that "status groups" determine the content of the law (Rheinstein 1954). The findings are inconsistent, on the other hand, with the perception of the law as simply a reflection of "public opinion" as is sometimes found in the literature (Friedman 1959). We should be cautious in concluding, however, that either of these positions are necessarily correct. The careful analysis of other laws, and especially of laws which do not focus so specifically upon the "criminal," are necessary before this question can be finally answered.

In conclusion, it is hoped that future analyses of changes within the legal structure will be able to benefit from this study by virtue of (1) the data provided and (2) the utilization of a set of concepts (innovation, dormancy, concern, and negation) which have proved useful in the analysis of the vagrancy law. Such analyses should provide us with more substantial grounds for rejecting or accepting as generally valid the description of some of the processes which appear to characterize changes in the legal system.

Notes

1. See also Alfred R. Lindesmith (1959).
2. See, for example, Arnold Rose (1962) and Gilbert Geis (1960).
3. For a more complete listing of most of the statutes dealt with in this report the reader is referred to Richard Burn (1973), *The History of the Poor Laws.* Citations of English statutes should be read as follows: 3 Ed. 1. c. 1. refers to the third act of Edward the first, chapter one, etc.
4. As evidenced for this note the expectation that ". . . the common gaols of every shire are likely to be greatly pestered with more numbers of prisoners than heretofore. . ." when the statutes were changed by the statute of 14 Ed. c. 5 (1571).
5. Also see in this connection, Irwin Deutscher (1955).
6. It is on this point that the vagrancy statutes have been subject to criticism. See, for example, Lacey, Forrest W. (1952), "Vagrancy and Other Crimes of Personal Condition," *Harvard Law Review* 66: 1203.
7. See, for example, *Edwards vs. California* 314 S: 160 (1941).
8. Negation, in this instance, is most likely to come about by the repeal of the statute. More generally, however, negation may occur in several ways including the declaration of a statute as unconstitutional. This latter mechanism has been used even for laws which have been "on the books" for long periods of time. Repeal is probably the most common, although not the only, procedure by which a law is negated.

References

Bradshaw, Fredrick. 1927. *A Social History of England,* 3rd edition. London: W. B. Clive, University Tutorial Press.

Burn, Richard. 1973. *The History of Poor Laws*. New York: August M. Kelly.

Deutscher, Irwin. 1955. "The Petty Offender." *Federal Probation*, XIX, June, 1955.

Earl of Halsbury. 1912. *The Laws of England*. New York: Butterworth & Co., Bell Yard, Temple Bar.

Foote, Caleb. 1956. "Vagrancy-Type Law and Its Administration." *University of Pennsylvania Law Review* 104: 503–650.

Friedman, N. 1959. *Law in a Changing Society*. Berkeley: University of California Press.

Geis, Gilbert L. 1960. "Sociology, Criminology, and Criminal Law." *Social Problems*. 7, 1: 40–47.

Hall, Jerome. 1935. *Theft, Law and Society*. Boston: Little, Brown.

Lacey, Forrest W. "Vagrancy and Other Crimes of Personal Condition." *Harvard Law Review*. 66: 1203.

Lindesmith, Alfred R. 1959. "Federal Law and Drug Addiction." *Social Problems* 7, 1: 48.

Rheinstein, Max. 1954. *Max Weber on Law in Economy and Society*. Cambridge, MA: Harvard University Press.

Rose, Arnold. 1962. "Some Suggestions for Research in the Sociology of Law." *Social Problems* 9, 3: 281–283.

CHAPTER 6

Law as a Weapon in Social Conflict*

Austin T. Turk

. . . Given that law is intimately linked with social diversity and conflict, the most parsimonious explanation of the linkage seems to be that people find they cannot trust strangers. As the scale and complexity of social relatedness increase, so does the diversity of human experiences. The more diverse the experiences people have had, the more diverse their perceptions and evaluations of behavioral and relational alternatives may be. The greater the diversity of perceptions and evaluations, the greater may be the variability in what is perceived as justice in the specific terms of everyday life. (The implied distinction is between "norms in action" versus whatever similarities might be found in terms either of a general belief in justice as an abstract value, or of verbal responses to hypothetical questioning regarding the substantive meanings and relative importance of various normative statements or labels.) Aware that others' ideas of justice may vary from their own, people try—in accord with their own ideas and interests as they understand them to maintain or gain control of, or to contest or evade, the processes by which normative expectations come to be formally articulated and enforced across, rather than only within, the boundaries of culturally homogeneous groups (whether the salient boundaries be those of families, clans, tribes, nations, or other groupings).

The empirical reality of law—apparently well understood in practice if not in theory—seems, then, to be that it is a set of resources for which people contend and with which they are better able to promote their own ideas and interests against others, given the necessity of working out and preserving accommodative relationships with strangers. To say that people seek to gain and use resources to secure their own ideas and interests is, of course, to say that they seek to have and exercise power. While the meaning of power is far from settled, a convenient starting point is to view power as the control of resources, and the exercise of power as their mobilization in an effort to increase the probability of acceptable resolutions of actual or potential conflicts.[1]

*Editor's Note: This essay has been excerpted from the full article published in 1976 under the same title in *Social Problems* 23, 3: 276–291.

Although it helps to recognize that "law is power," a more specific conceptualization of what kinds of resource control are possible is necessary if we are to arrive at a useful understanding of what the general proposition means. I see five kinds of resource control, all represented in the cultural and social structural reality of law. These are (1) control of the means of direct physical violence, i.e., war or police power; (2) control of the production, allocation, and/or use of material resources, i.e., economic power; (3) control of decision-making processes, i.e., political power; (4) control of definitions of and access to knowledge, beliefs, values, i.e., ideological power; and (5) control of human attention and living time, i.e., diversionary power.[2]

(1) Having the law on one's side in a conflict implies that one can rightfully use or call upon others (allies, champions, or the authorities claiming jurisdiction over the area, people, or matters involved) to use violence to support one's claims against others. Modern polities are characterized by the presence and availability of control agencies specializing in the accretion, organization, and use of the means of violence, and asserting the principle that violence is—excepting more and more narrowly defined emergency situations—a resource reserved for official use only. Decisions by authorities, including decisions regarding the respective claims of disputing parties, are accompanied by the implied threat of physical coercion should any of the affected parties refuse to act in accord with such decisions.

(2) People's life chances are affected just as decisively by how much their economic power is enhanced or eroded by law. The invention and elaboration of property and tax laws, in particular, reflect and help implement decisions on (1) what kinds of activities, products, and people should be rewarded more and what kinds less, and (2) how great should be the range between maximum and minimum rewards. "Radicals" seek modifications of law so as to change the criteria for reward, and very often also to reduce the range of rewards; "liberals" seek modifications so as to ensure at least a "decent" minimum in the range of rewards, and may accept—if they do not seek—some reduction in the range; "conservatives" resist modification, but may accept some "decent minimum." Though orderly (usually meaning limited and gradual) economic changes can be facilitated by law, economic decisions once articulated in and supported by law become postulates which further elaborations and even modifications of the law must satisfy. Radical economic changes, therefore, become increasingly difficult to effect by legal means because they require not legal reasoning to satisfy the postulates of a body of law, but rather a new set of postulates and thus a new body of law.

(3) The formulae and procedures of legal decision-making are integral to the workings of politically organized societies. Organizational decisions are in significant ways influenced by and expressed through legal decisions. Most important, the law as culture and as social structure provides the rubric for articulating, interpreting, and implementing organizational norms and decisions. As a substantive and procedural model and as an ultimate support for institutional normative structures, the law contributes—as Selznick (1969) and many others have demonstrated—to private as well as public social ordering, and provides some of the weightiest criteria for assessing proposed changes and resolving internal as well as inter-organizational conflicts. While non-legal factors clearly affect political struggle in general and organizational decision-making in particular, the law—as the most authoritative record of events and as the de-

finitive model, criterion, and arbiter of rightness—is itself a political resource of major importance.

(4) Legal concepts and thought-ways develop in the course of pragmatic efforts by men to comprehend problems of social interaction so as to manage them—including the problematics of dominating the lives of other people. Though not in this regard different from other products of such efforts, law as culture has an especially strong impact upon the frames of reference people use to give meaning to their situations. Those definitions of the real, the true, and the worthy given legal expression or approval are thereby given the support of what is not only one of the most prestigious of cultural structures, but also that structure most directly supported by the apparatus of political control. The reality or value of alternative conceptions can be denied either by simply denying recognition in law, or else more forcefully by explicitly rejecting them in ways ranging from the most extreme forms of suppression to the most subtle forms of rejection in practice conjoined with verbal acceptance or toleration. Censorship by omission or commission is nonetheless censorship. Yet, the greatest importance of law as an ideological resource probably lies not in the facts of deliberate or inadvertent intervention on behalf of some perceptual alternatives versus others, but in the fact that legalism is the cultural bedrock of political order. The very concept of legality is designed to promote adherence to the ground rules of conventional politics (Turk 1972:15–16)—which amount to agreement among contending parties on the supreme value of their common membership in a polity which must be preserved.

(5) Human attention and living-time are finite resources—a trite but profoundly consequential observation. Insofar as the rhetoric and the real workings of law occupy men's attention and time to the exclusion of other phenomena—perhaps of greater import for the probability and quality of life—the law exerts diversionary power. As entrepreneurs of the news, publishing, advertising, and entertainment industries have long known, at least the more reassuring, titillating, or lurid aspects of law can in the name of "human interest" and "information" be presented to capture and hold the public's attention. Nor have the obviously close links between diversionary and ideological power been neglected. Preoccupation with the law, especially in its more attractive and innocuous aspects, not only diverts attention from potentially more dangerous concerns (from the perspective of authorities, de facto including loyal oppositions) but also reinforces the sense of law as an overwhelming, scarcely challengeable reality and criterion of reality.

The conception of law as a set of resources, as power, is methodologically superior to the conception of law as conflict regulator in that the relationship between law and conflict is not assumed, but left open for investigation, and the distinction between legal and non-legal phenomena is grounded in empirical observations rather than normative assumptions. Instead of asking how law regulates conflict, the investigator is encouraged to ask whether law regulates or generates conflict, or in what ways and in what degree the use of legal power does both. Instead of assuming that legal and nonlegal actions and relations are somehow differentiated by criteria of moral legitimacy or functional necessity, the investigator asks whether and how the invocation of such criteria and the introduction of the distinction itself exemplify the control and mobilization of ideological and diversionary resources. Freed from arbitrary ideological and theoretical constraints, the investigator directly confronts the empirical realities that legal power can be used in ways inconsistent as well as consistent with normative criteria of legality, that the empirical relevance of such criteria is decided by the actions rather than the claims of those who wield legal power, and that the law—since it is necessarily promulgated, interpreted, implemented, or enforced by people with specific social and cultural involvements—can never really be neutral vis-à-vis social conflicts.

A particular advantage of the power conception of law is that it facilitates analysis of the processes (as distinct from particular structures) by which normative expectations are given "cross-group" as well as "intra-group" significance—i.e., how they become formally binding upon people who themselves have neither generated such norms nor been socialized as children to accept them. At the most general analytical level, the processes are those—stigmatization and other forms of manipulation—any group uses to achieve some behavioral and relational coherence despite the varying idiosyncrasies of its members. Nonetheless, as one's attention shifts from the most ephemeral and least differentiated forms of group life to more durable and complex social entities, the processes come more sharply into focus as the distinction between legal and non-legal emerges and acquires increasing social and cultural reality. The power conception of law suggests analysis of these processes in the specific empirical terms of how people actually deal with one another, regardless of any conventional understandings or rationales about the existence and significance of particular legal phenomena. Thus, socio-legal research is cast not in terms of the assumed concreteness or meaningfulness of the legal/non-legal distinction, but in terms of the human actions creating the distinction, giving it empirical substance, and altering or erasing it.

Finally, the power conception of law gives socio-legal research a distinctive focus, related to but not confused with the general concerns of the social sciences with social order, conflict, and change. Instead of losing the legal/non-legal distinction in the quest for knowledge useful in conflict management (as in Barkun's case), the distinction itself becomes in two ways the basis for defining research problems. First, the problematic status of the distinction implies the need for historical and anthropological studies to determine the specific conditions where it is introduced (and perhaps to suggest the conditions where it may be transcended) in social life.[3] Second, as the core task of socio-legal research is taken to be that of developing a predictively useful understanding of the control and mobilization of legal resources, the availability of such resources is necessarily presupposed. That is, scientifically meaningful research questions about law and society become possible only when the concept of law is empirically grounded by the differentiation of legal from other cultural and social phenomena in one or more of the following ways: (1) verbal articulation of a set, in some degree a system, of explicit norms; (2) establishment of procedures for making, interpreting, implementing, and changing normative decisions; (3) occupational specialization in knowing the substantive law and in using the established procedures; (4) institution of explicit provisions for the enforcement of substantive and procedural norms, by actual or threatened deprivations; and (5) associated with any or all of the other ways, the display of symbolic trappings designed to emphasize the reality, rightness, and might of law.[4] Rather than some kind of essence, property, or function to be sought in an apparently unlimited variety of cultural and social configuration, "law" thus becomes an empirically specifiable set of objects of scientific attention.

The power conception of law, in sum, offers students of law and society a methodologically tenable definition of the scope of their inquiry that includes it within the social scientific enterprise without reifying, mystifying, or obscuring the legal/non-legal distinction. . . .

Notes

1. "Control" means the availability or accessibility of resources, varying from the extremely limited access of the helpless, through the shared access of competitors or allies, to the exclusive access of the almighty. "Resource" means anything of biological or cultural significance for human welfare. The distinction here between controlling and mobilizing resources is analogous to that which Etzioni (1968: 314–317) makes between "assets" and "power." However, his concept of "power" is much more restricted, or truncated, in that it refers only to mobilization against resistance and excludes much of what is involved in the control and mobilization of symbolic resources. With rather unnecessary inconsistency, he defines "persuasive power" as "exercised through the manipulation of symbols" (358) after suggesting that "the assets from which power is generated are much more scarce than the symbols which are the main base of communication" (335) and arguing that "communication" can be substituted for "power" (336).

2. My conscious indebtedness for terms and ideas used in this effort to sort out the forms and dimensions of power is mainly to Russell (1938), Schermerhorn (1961), and Gamson (1968).

3. This formulation is intended to emphasize that the legal/non-legal distinction is a problematic human invention rather than an inevitable product of some supra-human evolutionary process. Against any emergentist conception of "legal evolution" as an unavoidable and/or irreversible linear progression, the differentiation of legal from non-legal phenomena is simply recognized as an historically specific accomplishment that has occurred, may occur, and may continue.

4. The extent to which sequential or functional relationships may be found among these indicants of the five kinds or dimensions of legal power is an empirical question. Though not directly pertinent, the mediation-courts-punishment-police-counsel cumulative scale order that seems to be emerging from the work of Schwartz and others (Schwartz and Miller 1964; Wimberley 1973; Baxi 1974; Schwartz 1974) suggests that some such relationships may well exist.

References

Aubert, Vilhelm. 1963. "Competition and Dissensus: Two Types of Conflict Resolution." *Journal of Conflict Resolution* 7: 26–42.

Aubert, Vihelm (ed.). 1969. *Sociology of Law*. Baltimore, MD: Penguin Books.

Balbus, Isaac D. 1973. *The Dialectics of Legal Repression: Black Rebels before the American Criminal Courts*. New York: Russell Sage Foundation.

Barkun, Michael. 1968. *Law without Sanctions*. New Haven, CT: Yale University Press.

Baxi, Upendra. 1974. "Comment—Durkheim and Legal Evolution: Some Problems of Disproof." *Law and Society Review* 8 (Summer): 645–651.

Berman, Harold J. 1966. *Justice in the U. S. S. R.: An Interpretation of Soviet Law*. Cambridge, MA: Harvard University Press.

Black, Donald J. 1972. "The Boundaries of Legal Sociology." *Yale Law Journal* 81 (May): 1086–1100.

———. 1973. "The Mobilization of Law." *Journal of Legal Studies* 2 (January): 125–149.

Blaustein, Albert P. and Clarence C. Ferguson, Jr. 1962. *Desegregation and the Law: The Meaning and Effect of the School Segregation Cases.* New York: Vintage Books.

Blumberg, Abraham S. 1967. "The Practice of Law as a Confidence Game: Organizational Cooptation of a Profession," *Law and Society Review* 1 (June): 15–39.

Blumrosen, Alfred W. 1962. "Legal Process and Labor Law: Some Observations on the Relation between Law and Sociology." Pp.185–225 in William M. Evan (ed.), *Law and Sociology.* New York: Free Press.

Caplovitz, David. 1963. *The Poor Pay More,* New York: Free Press.

Carlin, Jerome E., Jan Howard, and Sheldon L. Messinger. 1966. "Civil Justice and the Poor: Issues for Sociological Research." *Law and Society Review* 1 (November): 9–89.

Chambliss, William J. and Robert B. Seidman. 1971. *Law, Order, and Power.* Reading, MA: Addison-Wesley.

Cicourel, Aaron V. 1968. The *Social Organization of Juvenile Justice.* New York: Wiley.

Diamond, Stanley. 1971. "The Rule of Law versus the Order of Custom." Pp. 115–144 in Robert P. Wolff (ed.), *The Rule of Law.* New York: Simon & Schuster.

Epstein, A. L. 1958. *Politics in an Urban African Community.* Manchester, UK: Manchester University Press.

Etzioni, Amitai. 1968. *The Active Society.* New York: Free Press.

Fuller, Lon L. 1964. *The Morality of Law.* New Haven, CT: Yale University Press.

———. 1971. "Human Interaction and the Law." Pp.171–217 in Robert P. Wolff (ed.), *The Rule of Law.* New York: Simon & Schuster.

Galarza, Ernesto. 1970. *Spiders in the House and Workers in the Field.* South Bend, IN: University of Notre Dame Press.

Galliher, John F. 1971. "Explanations of Police Behavior: A Critical Review and Analysis." *Sociological Quarterly* 12 (Summer): 308–318.

Gamson, William A. 1968. *Power and Discontent.* Homewood, IL: Dorsey.

Gibbs, Jack P. 1968. "Definitions of Law and Empirical Questions." *Law and Society Review* 2 (May): 429–446.

Gibbs, James L., Jr. 1963. "The Kpelle Moot: A Therapeutic Model for the Informal Settlement of Disputes." *Africa* 33: 1–11.

Hall, Jerome. 1963. *Comparative Law and Social Theory.* Baton Rogue: Louisiana State University Press.

Hoebel, E. A. 1954. *The Law of Primitive Man.* Cambridge, MA: Harvard University Press.

Lefcourt, Robert (ed.). 1971. *Law against the People.* New York: Vintage Books.

Macaulay, Stewart. 1963. "Non-contractual Relations in Business: A Preliminary Study." *American Sociological Review* 28 (February): 55–67.

Massell, Gregory J. 1968. "Law as an Instrument of Revolutionary Change in a Traditional Milieu: The Case of Soviet Central Asia." *Law and Society Review* 2 (February): 179–228.

May, Henry J. 1955. *The South African Constitution* 3rd Edition. Cape Town: Juta.

McWilliams, Carey. 1942. *Ill Fares the Land: Migrants and Migratory Labor in the United States.* Boston: Little, Brown.

Moore, Howard, Jr. 1971. "Brown v Board of Education: The Court's Relationship to Black liberation." Pp. 55–64 in Robert Lefcourt (ed.), *Law against the People.* New York: Vintage Books.

Nader, Laura (ed.). 1969. *Law in Culture and Society.* Chicago: Aldine.

Nonet, Philippe. 1969. *Administrative Justice: Advocacy and Change in a Government Agency.* New York: Russell Sage Foundation.

Pospisil, Leopold. 1971. *Anthropology of Law: A Comparative Theory.* New York: Harper and Row.

Quinney, Richard. 1974. *Critique of Legal Order.* Boston: Little, Brown.

Russell, Bertrand. 1938. *Power: A New Social Analysis.* London: Allen & Unwin.

Sachs, Albie. 1973. *Justice in South Africa.* Berkeley: University of California Press.

Schermerhorn, Richard A. 1961. *Society and Power.* New York: Random House.

Schwartz, Richard D. 1974. "Legal Evolution and the Durkheim Hypothesis: A Reply to Professor Baxi." *Law and Society Review* 8 (Summer): 653–668.

Schwartz, Richard D. and James C. Miller. 1964. "Legal Evolution and Societal Complexity." *American Journal of Sociology* 70 (September): 159–169.

Schwartz, Richard D. and Jerome H. Skolnick (eds.). 1970. *Society and the Legal Order.* New York: Basic Books.

Selznick, Philip. 1961. "Sociology and Natural Law." *Natural Law Forum* 6: 84–108.

———. 1968. "The Sociology of Law." Pp. 50–59 in David L. Sills (ed.), *International Encyclopedia of the Social Sciences,* Vol. 9. New York: Macmillan and Free Press.

———. 1969. *Law, Society, and Industrial Justice.* New York: Russell Sage Foundation.

Stone, Julius. 1965. *Human Law and Human Justice.* Stanford, CA: Stanford University Press.

Swett, Daniel H. 1969. "Cultural Bias in the American Legal System." *Law and Society Review* 4 (August): 79–110.

Tangri, Beverly S. 1967. *Federal Legislation as an Expression of United States Public Policy toward Agricultural Labor, 1914–1954.* Berkeley: University of California, unpublished Ph.D. dissertation.

tenBroek, Jacobus (ed.). 1966. *The Law of the Poor.* San Francisco: Chandler.

Tumin, Melvin M. and Robert Rotberg. 1957. "Leaders, the Led, and the Law: A Case Study in Social Change." *Public Opinion Quarterly* 21 (Fall): 355–370.

Turk, Austin T. 1969. *Criminality and Legal Order.* Chicago: Rand McNally.

———. 1972. *Legal Sanctioning and Social Control.* Washington DC: U.S. Government Printing Office, DHEW Pub. No. (HSM) 72–9130.

Wimberley, Howard. 1973. "Legal Evolution: One Further Step." *American Journal of Sociology* 79 (July): 78–83.

Wirt, Frederick M. 1970. *Politics of Southern Equality: Law and Social Change in a Mississippi County.* Chicago: Aldine.

Wolff, Robert P. (ed.). 1971. *The Rule of Law.* New York: Simon & Schuster.

Zimring, Franklin and Gordon Hawkins. 1971. "The Legal Threat as an Instrument of Social Change." *Journal of Social Issues* 27 (2): 33–48.

Zinn, Howard. 1971. "The Conspiracy of Law." Pp.15–36 in Robert P. Wolff (ed.), *The Rule of Law.* New York: Simon & Schuster.

CHAPTER 7

Empiricism and the Critique of Marxism on Law and Crime

Piers Beirne

The decade since the intellectual and political unrest of the 1960s has witnessed the emergence of a burgeoning Marxist literature concerned to elaborate a theory of law and crime under capitalist (and occasionally, collectivist) modes of production. Most such work has been accompanied by sectarian, and at times overtly hostile, accounts of the conceptual significance of these objects within Marx's own critique of the categories of bourgeois political economy, and also of the contemporary articulation of the legal system with the various levels and practices constitutive of capitalist social formations. These developments derived a certain urgency from the intuitive notion that the economic, political, and ideological operation of the legal system, and of much of the content of legal doctrine, might somehow explain the surprising longevity of such formations despite their endemic and pervasive contradictions. But intuition hardly satisfies the canons of scientific procedure. In 1975, in his Presidential Address to the Society for the Study of Social Problems, Stanton Wheeler reflected on the import of this literature and pointed out that:

> . . . the emergence of conflict theory and the rediscovery of Marx may perhaps move us in a new direction. . . . It is too early now to judge the fruits of these new conceptions, but it is my strong impression that the achievements have been more rhetorical than anything else, that whatever their value in changing our conception of crime, they have not led to new and fresh empirical inquiry . . . (Wheeler 1976: 527)

It is undeniably true, in the limited sense in which Wheeler intended, that these "new conceptions" have indeed not led to fresh empirical inquiry. However, one of the unintended consequences of Wheeler's advocacy is that the Marxist literature on law and crime has itself been increasingly subjected to empirical scrutiny by non-Marxist sociologists. In the past several years, these latter have mobilized a critical reaction whose goal is the empirical assessment of the conceptual objects specified, loosely, by the "New Criminology," conflict theories and Marxist perspectives on law and crime. But the pursuit of this goal has largely been undertaken in terms of an empiricist logic consonant with formal and mechanical causality. This logic carries with it the unfortunate and ethnocentric maxim that the dialectical method of Marxist analysis is *ab initio* to be ignored by those critics whose task it is to assess Marxist accounts of law and crime.

The initial findings of this critical reaction have, not surprisingly, been far from unanimous in their implications. In their article "Rediscovering Delinquency" Hagan and Leon (1977: 589) have recently argued that the Marxist perspective on law and crime is "1 prone to logical errors, 2 largely unconfirmed, 3 often unconfirmable and 4 possibly quite frequently false." But it is clear from the outset that the deep structure of Hagan and Leon's argument had little substantively to do with delinquency. Far from it, the delinquency legislation associated with a particular society (Canada), during a specific period of time (1857–1952), was used by the authors as a foil to rebut (a) Marxist accounts (e.g., Platt 1969, 1974) of the "same" empirico-temporal data, and (b) the conceptual and objective relationship which Marxists (e.g., Quinney 1975a; Taylor et al. 1973, 1975) are commonly said to hold between class interests and the value component of legal imperatives. The correct interpretation of the relevant data, Hagan and Leon extrapolated, would enable them to evaluate "the emergence of the Marxian perspective and the logic of its premises" (1977: 587). The reader was at once awed by the complexity of this ambitious task, and subsequently dismayed by the woeful disregard for epistemological protocol with which it was completed. Nowhere did the authors precisely identify the nature of their object. This was vaguely and variously described as "a Marxian social historical approach to the study of social evolution" (1977: 587), "this new Marxist perspective on law creation" (1977: 588) and "a Marxian class conflict approach" (1977: 597).

Some commentators (Chiricos and Waldo 1975; Tittle et al. 1978), using very different data and quantitative techniques, seem in general agreement with Hagan and Leon. Others (Cashmore 1978; Jacobs 1978; Jankovic 1978; Lizotte 1978) have concluded that Marxist and conflict perspectives are plausible or have at least been verified by the available evidence. Still further findings range from the skeptical assertion (Brown 1978; Hawkins 1978) that the empirical evidence may have little bearing on these perspectives to the implicit suggestion (Cernkovich 1978) that the very concept of social class ought to be rejected as an explanatory framework for understanding law and crime.

The intention of this paper is neither to vindicate nor to supplement the inadequacies of Marxist perspectives on law and crime. Nor is it to assert that Marxism is impervious to non-Marxist criticism. Rather, it is to argue that the critical reaction to Marxism is intemperate and unwarranted because it has unwittingly conflated its own objects with those generated by concepts in other theoretical structures. More specifically, its instigators have had a tendency both to confuse certain Marxist concepts with concepts internal to conflict and labeling theories, and to ignore the important differences in the theoretical finesse of competing versions of Marxism. This quite probably means that all of the above findings are equally meaningless. Even more seriously, their critique appears incognizant of the epistemological universe from which it derives its own methodology and discourse. Such methodology, I will argue, is akin to what Lakatos (1970) has characterized as dogmatic or naive falsificationism.

Identification of the Object

The refutation or verification of the conceptual objects emanating from any theoretical structure requires, first, that these objects be adequately identified. Proper identification requires a comprehension of their mutual articulation within their theoretical structure, and that they be distinguished from objects which appear similar yet which are contained within other theoretical structures. What of the Marxist analysis of law and crime which emerged in the 1960s—and which is now flourishing, for example, in the Conference on Critical Legal Theory (in Madison), the Birmingham (England) Center for Cultural Studies, and in *Contemporary Crises, Crime and Social Justice*, and *Marxist Perspectives*? Superficially it appears to have been a politically motivated amalgam of certain concepts *already* conceived within the structures of criminology, labeling theory and conflict theory. In outlining what is plausibly the conventional history of this development, Galliher has noted that:

> . . . the popularity of the labeling perspective with its emphasis on societal reaction and created deviance seems to have provided the conditions in the discipline for the swift re-emergence of the conflict orientation once it was triggered by the political milieu. . . . The conflict perspective stressing powerful interest groups' control of the law, police, and courts, in turn created the intellectual basis for the emergence of Marxism in criminology in the 1970's. (Galliher 1978: 253–54)

By this account, then, the Marxist perspective on law and crime was a political response which emerged "in the discipline," "in criminology." Indeed, how could this development have proceeded otherwise? There was no substantive precedent, at least in the USA, for a Marxist analysis of law and crime. Some Marxist writings did exist elsewhere—such as the contributions made by Bonger, Renner, and Gramsci, and numerous works on commodity exchange and criminal law by Pashukanis, Berman, and Krylenko in the USSR in the 1920s.[1] But these remained, and remain, mostly untranslated and therefore effectively unavailable to an English-language audience. Moreover, there was an undercurrent of suspicion that many of these pioneering efforts were closer to European social democracy than to Marxism. And no precedent existed in Marx's own fragmented and unsatisfactory discourse on bourgeois law, even though his illuminating confrontation with Hegel's *Rechtsphilosophie* has periodically afforded some measure of inspiration.

There is, therefore, obvious merit in the observation that the Marxist analysis of law and crime which emerged in the late 1960s had its origins in mainstream sociology and criminology. Strong candidates for the immediate intellectual ancestry of this analysis, as Galliher suggests, are labeling and conflict theories. Nor is this history inconvenienced by the fact that the latter theories gained disciplinary prominence and intellectual respectability in the early 1960s. In that labeling and conflict theories were antiestablishment, cynical, and bent on demystifying the legal order, it is clear that their surface structures were vehicles for carrying a political message not entirely dissimilar to that embraced by Marxism. But if this picture is accurate we are faced with the interesting paradox of a Marxism nurtured in the womb of theoretical structures to which it was, ostensibly, largely opposed. And unless we uncover the genesis of this paradox we could mistakenly be tempted to extract appropriate Marxist concepts from the theoretical structure of which they are only a part, identify them in terms of concepts which are generated in less alien theoretical structures (such as labeling and conflict theories), and attempt to measure the empirical objects specified by the former in terms of the concepts yielded by the latter. It is one thing to argue that the newly acquired institutional position of labeling and conflict theories created a certain elective affinity with Marxism, but it is quite another to argue that they provided sufficient antecedent intellectual conditions for the application of Marxism to law and crime. Unless we recognize that labeling and conflict theories constituted some of the polemical climate but contained few of the intellectual premises for the emergence of Marxism in the USA, then we will be lulled into the complacent notion that Marxism differs from other perspectives not in its theoretical structure but only in that its political purpose is more radical.

Labeling theory—which came in many guises—was seen by its main protagonists as a palliative to a traditional criminology excessively imbued with positivism, correctionalism, and conservatism. For Marxism, the essence of positivism—a term most often used in a derisive rather than any precise epistemological sense[2]—was that it allowed the methods of natural science unproblematically to be transported to the realms of social matter. In effect, this implied that the Kantian dualism of mind and body, of culture and science, could be resolved through the utilitarian guidelines of social engineering. Indeed positivism had first infiltrated American criminology in Chicago, during a period[3] when urban administrators, somewhat unwisely, were restructuring the spatial patterns of the physical environment through the medium of the City Beautiful concept borrowed from the experience of British town planners in the first quarter of the twentieth century. The resultant spirit of pragmatic optimism was soberly transformed by the Depression into one of social realism. However, an abiding legacy of the Depression was the notion that cyclical economic crises, and the social disorganization thereby engendered, could best be counteracted through active intervention by state apparatuses using various pump-priming mechanisms.

Yet positivist criminology was hopelessly unable to account for the new forms of social dissent which mushroomed in the 1960s. For twenty years it had virtually ignored the implications of Sutherland's (1940, 1941, 1949) work on white-collar crime. Sutherland's work neither fostered nor permitted examination of the relationship between legal institutions and social classes, but it did undeniably reveal that crime was more evenly distributed throughout the social structure than criminology admitted. Positivist criminology was not only unable to explain the crimes routinely committed by government and large corporations; it also had no competent explanation of the violence coextensive with civil rights, minority and antiwar movements. Horowitz and Liebowitz (1968), in an influential article, pointed out that the traditional distinction between social problems and the political system was becoming obsolete. Behavior which had previously been perceived and defined as social deviance was now assuming well-defined ideological and organizational contours. Labeling theory, beginning with Becker's noted insight in *Outsiders* that "deviance is not a quality of the act the person commits, but rather a consequence of the application by others of rules and sanctions to an 'offender'" (1963: 9), promised to indicate the manner in which social dissent and traditional forms of deviance were becoming increasingly blurred. What institutional processes enabled certain forms of deviance, and not others, to be designated as deviant?

It is usually the case in the intellectual history of social theory that the dominant paradigms in a discipline are not replaced by other paradigms erected on novel or oppositional sets of epistemological principles. Fundamental epistemological revolutions in social science have been extremely rare. What is more common is that the content of the dominant paradigms is shifted from one focus to another. Works by Becker (1963, 1964), Matza (1964, 1969), and Lemert (1970) roughly defined the limits within which labeling theory would develop largely as a reaction to positivist criminology. The focus of concern shifted from the characteristics of offenders to the social processes whereby an actor was labeled as deviant, stigmatized, and compelled into further deviant behavior. Where positivist criminology saw its pre-given conceptual object as crime defined by statute or common law, labeling theory began by making the very notion of crime subjectively problematic.

Criminologists—or "sociologists of deviance" as the labeling theorists and interactionist called themselves—were now compelled to question the assumptions by which certain interactive meanings became routinized and enshrined with the institutional sanctity of legal authority. What was the social construction of the reality in which society created deviance? How was this reality negotiated? Positivist criminology had emphasized different versions of control theory whose common and basic unit (anthropological man) was subject to social and ecological constraint. Labeling theory, although never successfully challenging the philosophical assumptions of constraint, and conscious of the dangers involved in the classical concept of free will, instead stressed the integrity and rationality of the subjective values of the outsider and the underdog. This entailed the simple methodological injunction that "offender" and "victim" were to be reversed. Where earlier research had tended to concentrate on property crimes and crimes of violence, the new concern was for victimless and often esoteric "crimes." This required that sociologists suspend their personal values in order (empathetically) to understand the value systems under investigation. Where positivist criminology had dissolved the "causes" of crime into a plethora of multicausation and statistical correlations, labeling theory appeared to dissolve all mechanistic notions of causation. But this dissolution was deceptive. What was the form of explanation posited by labeling theory of "secondary deviation" if it was not based on the very mechanistic causation that the labeling theorists detected and despised in positivist criminology? Was not the concept of societal reaction assigned a causative status within labeling theory similar to that assigned, for example, to parental occupation and education in traditional criminology?

Labeling theory left itself open to attack on two fronts. Ethnomethodologists complained that it did not sufficiently explore the processes and meanings of social interaction at the micro level. Marxists complained that labeling theory's focus on the interactive process between rule definers, rule breakers and social audience was not carried through to its implicit conclusion—the mutual interpenetration of polity and economy. What was the nature of the social totality in which these interactive processes occurred? Gouldner concluded that "Becker's school":

> . . . thus views the underdog as someone who is being mismanaged, not as someone who suffers and fights back. Here the deviant is sly but not defiant; he is tricky but not courageous; he sneers but does not accuse; he "makes out" without making a scene. Insofar as this school of theory has a critical edge to it, this is directed at the caretaking institutions who do the mopping-up job, rather than at the master institutions that produce the deviant's suffering. (Gouldner 1970: 107)

Labeling theory graciously gave the deviant a voice, but this voice was unable to articulate the lengthy social distance between "caretaking" institutions and "master" institutions. Nor could it indicate that the social-engineering policies of these institutions did not always occur in *vacuo toto*, that sometimes they were explicable only in the context of the structural relations between social classes. The great bulk of that tradition in American criminology epitomized, in different ways, by Merton's "Social Structure and Anomie" and Cohen's *Delinquent Boys* did, it was true, employ the concept of social class. But it used that concept very differently from the way it is employed by Marxism, as a set of structural relationships mainly constitutive of the social and technical relationships of production and exchange. Instead it tended to assign to "social class" the very imprecise and different meanings also attributed to it during the post-1945 debates—within non-Marxist discourse—on functionalism, social stratification, and convergence theory.

It was conflict theory, drawing on the spirit of Weber, Simmel, Mills and Dahrendorf, that was to supply some of the theoretical vocabulary to fill this lacuna. An impressive body of research (Chambliss 1964; Hall 1952; Roby 1969; Turk 1966, 1969) soon accumulated which indicated that particular pieces of legislation were the result of conflicts of interest. Such conflicts, so the argument continued, were normally resolved according to the wishes of those with power. The conflict theorists were rarely precise in delineating quite in what "power" and "conflict" consisted, how power manifested itself, how conflict was resolved, and why it was resolved at all; but they nevertheless agreed that power and conflict were at the root of social organization. Quinney's seminal *The Social Reality of Crime* is representative of this tendency:

> In any society conflicts between persons, social units, or cultural elements are inevitable, the normal consequences of social life . . . power is the basic characteristic of social organization. (Quinney 1970: 8, 11)

This is, of course, a thematic and crude characterization of the conceptual basis of conflict theory, one that ignores its external relationship with other perspectives such as phenomenology and ethnomethodology, and omits all of its internal subtleties. But it has the modest virtue of demonstrating that a conceptually imprecise conflict theory might unconsciously be identified with an "instrumental" form of Marxism. Conflict theory was generally so vague in its basic assumptions, and so wide-ranging in its scope, that it might easily incorporate (or co-opt) a variety of different perspectives, including Marxism, within the compass of its structure. Jacobs, for example, has asserted that "instead of seeing the law as an impartially administered codification of shared norms, conflict theorists hold that the criminal statutes are created and enforced according to the wishes of those with power" (1978: 515). The rigidity of the causal structure of this argument—whose logical relations are formally almost identical to those held by labeling theory and positivist criminology—is not diminished by the correlative and more complex assertion that "*the more there are differences in economic resources and economic power, the more one can expect that the criminal codes will be administered in a way that pleases monied elites*" (Jacobs 1978: 516). The corollary of this assertion, in turn, often extends the causal chain to the argument that "when sanctions are imposed, the most severe sanctions will be imposed on persons in the lowest social class" (Chambliss and Seidman 1971: 475).

Taken together, these assertions provoke several unanswered questions: Why should such administration please monied elites? What is the relation between the process whereby "elites" become "monied" and the administration of law? How and why are "economic resources" and "economic power" translated into legislative and judicial influence? Why do persons in the "lowest social class" typically receive the most severe sanctions? These questions can perhaps be answered, but they cannot consistently be answered empirically by the insensitive form of historicism which these assertions utilize. Let us assume that conflict theory generally holds both (a) that criminal laws are created and administered in the interests of a ruling class, and (b) that the severity of (legal) sanctions is inversely correlated with the hierarchy of social classes. The problem with these assertions, when taken together, is that the truth of the former might have implications incompatible with the truth of the latter. Indeed a convincing argument can be made that ruling classes have a general interest in promulgating and reproducing the stability of the social order *as a whole*, and that an important way of achieving this is by somehow ensuring that the severity of sanctions *ought* not significantly to be correlated with social class.

The second half of this paper seeks radically to demarcate the causal structure of Marxist propositions on law and crime from the causal structure of labeling and conflict theories, from which Marxism is commonly said to have emerged. The Marxist analyses of law which emerged in the late 1960's did not, it must be stressed, develop from any sector of mainstream sociology. Largely, they arose from earlier concerns within Marxist philosophy and Marxist theories of the capitalist state. The brief discussion which follows argues that the logical structure of Marxism is not causal but relational. As such, much of the empirical evidence directed towards the assessment of Marxist propositions is either grossly misdirected or else inadvertently supports them.

The Object

INSTRUMENTAL MARXIST ACCOUNTS OF LAW AND CRIME

The contemporary empirical assessment of Marxist accounts of law and crime has tended to be based on the false assumption that, as Hagan and Leon (1977: 588, quoting Chambliss 1974: 37) write, law is seen by all Marxists as "first and foremost a reflection of the interests of the governing class." This is not to deny that this position—which may be termed "instrumental Marxism"—has occupied a significant status in the intellectual history of Marxism. But to portray it as representative of even a majority of Marxist theorists today is, however, a flagrant *reductio ad absurdum* of Marxist theory. Instrumental Marxist accounts of law and crime bear less resemblance to current Marxist theory as a whole than to some of the "conspiratorial" premises of conflict theory and some of the apparent structural implications of labeling theory. But the natural affinity between instrumental Marxism and these latter two theories does not allow a critique of Marxism that is based exclusively on instrumentalism.

Instrumental Marxists have tended to derive their *weltanschauung* from an incomplete reading of the *Communist Manifesto's* dictum that "the executive of the modern state is but a committee for managing the common affairs of the whole bourgeoisie" (Marx and Engels 1973: 110). The state and legal system are seen as instruments which can be manipulated, almost at will, by the capitalist class as a whole or, in certain moments, by particular fractions of capital. In this manner several empirical studies (Kolko 1962; Domhoff 1970; Miliband 1969) have sought to prove that the economic power which inheres in the ownership or control of the means of production (industrial, financial, commercial, and land capitals) can typically be transformed into personal political influence on the legislative process. It is argued that this transformation is materialized in such factors as lobbying, campaign financing, intermarriage within the capitalist class, and by straightforward corruption by business of the judiciary and of state and federal legislatures.

In a limited sense instrumental Marxism has performed the useful iconoclastic function of revealing the social fictions promoted by doctrines such as "the rule of law," "equality before the law," and "the separation of powers." But the danger involved in such "demystification,"as Fraser (1976) has ably shown, is that it may achieve little more than a moralistic inversion of the categories already found in legal doctrine. What is good becomes bad, what is right becomes wrong.

> This disguised victory of bourgeois legal theory has already become manifest among radical lawyers in North America whose theoretical radicalism is contained and exhausted in a perception of the law as an elaborate confidence trick . . . The law, in other words . . . is dismissed contemptuously as an elaborate structure of myths, the function of which is to obscure the underlying reality of bitter struggle between social classes. (Fraser 1976: 128)

Instrumental Marxism, in this respect, therefore occupies one end of a continuum with voluntaristic pluralism as its polar opposite, and it is vulnerable to simple empirical refutation. No doubt all of the transformative factors mentioned above do actually occur, but it is most unlikely that they occur with sufficient frequency to enable them to be regarded as the normal path by which economic interests are intercalated with formal political institutions. The capitalist class as a whole cannot be well served by frequent and visible abuses of due process. Instrumental Marxism views the capitalist class a group devoid of internal dissensions and antagonisms, and it ignores the partial autonomy of the legal system and legal doctrine, once developed, relative to other state institutions and relative to the exigencies of particular social classes.

STRUCTURALIST MARXIST ACCOUNTS OF LAW AND CRIME

Structural Marxists have argued that state apparatuses exercise a "relative" autonomy in their relationship with the capitalist class. This means that in its basic struggle with the working class, the capitalist class cannot manipulate state institutions at will. The specific factors which determine the degree of this autonomy have as yet been inadequately theorized, but it is clear in outline that all state apparatuses are subject to the functional constraints of the structural ensemble of social relationships under capitalism. Schematically, the historical sphere within which state apparatuses operate is limited economically (O'Connor 1973), politically (Poulantzas 1973, 1975) and ideologically (Althusser 1971; Genovese 1976). These constraints may, simultaneously, be internal to a state apparatus—in the force of its belief systems, recruitment patterns and organizational stability confronted by the fluid contours of the class struggle(s)—and external. The effect of external constraint is best illustrated by O'Connor's insight that the state incurs two competing social expenses in its quest to guarantee the reproduction of the social formation: costs designed to reproduce the economic mode of production and stimulate the rate of profit, and costs which legitimate the sanctity and harmony of the social order.

The state must, therefore, *routinely* pursue policies which are at variance with the interests or wishes of certain fractions of capital. There are many cases which support this contention: welfare legislation (Anderson 1974) which supports unemployed and nonproductive laborers, rent restriction (Beirne 1977) which inhibits landlords' ability to receive open-market rental incomes, antitrust legislation, zoning ordinances, corporation taxes, and so forth, none of which could be shown to be in the immediate interests of capital. This implies that various state policies, implemented through the medium of the legal form, will necessarily produce empirical cases which conflict with the capitalist class's search for rent, interest, and industrial profit. It may ultimately be partly true that the benevolence of rich men to poor, as Hay (1975: 63) has vividly suggested, is upheld by the sanction of the gallows and the rhetoric of the death sentence. But it is even more true that the capitalist class does not, and cannot typically neutralize opposition or pursue its own interests through the instrumental use of legal sanctions. Balbus (1973), for example, has pointed to the complex factors which mediated such manipulation in black ghetto revolts in Chicago, Detroit, and Los Angeles. Any given court response to collective violence in these cities was likely to be a function of a delicate balance which court authorities are forced to achieve among their compelling and competing interests in order, formal rationality and organizational maintenance.

At least two relevant conclusions can be drawn from the structuralists' contributions. First, the enactment of legislation and the administration of justice are by no means always in the objective interests of the capitalist class, or indeed any class. Marx's own work never posited an a priori causal structure between elements in the "base," e.g., a particular class, and elements in the "superstructure," e.g., law.[4] Overwhelmingly, this structure involved a relational form of analysis whereby particular social relationships between classes are to be understood within the contexts of empirical and historical exigencies. There is, for example, no a priori reason to suspect that dominant economic classes in a given social formation will always be dominant political classes. But the structural variation in the relations between classes is bounded by the limits to which contradictions between classes can survive inherent transformative tendencies. Second, within the boundaries specified by the structural relations, levels and practices of a given social formation, empirical and historical analysis may reveal that some legislation is actually beneficial to one class rather than others. But each case must be examined empirically and on its own merits.[5] What matters, from the structuralist position, is the long-run stability of the social formation, and there is much historical evidence to demonstrate that social formations cannot survive for very long if particular classes within it are able visibly, or even surreptitiously, to manipulate state apparatuses at will.

COMMODITY EXCHANGE AND THE LIMITS OF THE LEGAL FORM

Structuralist Marxists have therefore provided us—and in so doing have soundly defeated instrumental Marxism—with a reasonable explanation of why the content of legislation may not always be in the immediate interests of the capitalist class. But the specific content of legal imperatives does not explain why the overall and long-run interests of the capitalist class are nevertheless embodied in law, why they are embodied in the form of law. Why are these interests not embodied in the form on which they episodically depend, namely, naked coercion? Is the legal system's "relative" autonomy from the class struggle merely another legal fiction, promoted by the capitalist class, which functions to obscure the ultimate causal dependence of law on dominant social classes? If this question is answered affirmatively, then this paper has traveled a circuitous and tortuous route only to discover that the empiricist critique of Marxist theories of law and crime is, paradoxically, correct. The answer, however, appears to be that the legal form itself has an innate quality which represents and perpetuates the dominant mode of production within any social formation.

The importance of this latter point was singularly underlined in the work of the Soviet legal theorist Evgeny Pashukanis (1980).[6] The originality of Pashukanis' theory of law—which was largely contained in his *General Theory of Law and Marxism*—lies in the contraposition of three notions with what Pashukanis took to be the modus operandi of Marx's *Capital.* From Hegel, Pashukanis borrowed the familiar distinction between essence and appearance, and also the notion that the Roman *lex persona* was an insufficient basis for the universality of rights attached to individual agents under capitalist modes of production. And from Pokrovsky, an Old Bolshevik and the leading Russian historian between 1910 and 1932, Pashukanis borrowed the assertion that the development of capitalism must be understood in the context of the historical primacy of mercantile capital.

Pashukanis was first concerned to rebut the view that law is capable of voluntaristic manipulation by dominant social classes. If law is seen simply as a system of relationships which answers to the interests of the dominant class, then how can it be distinguished from all other social relationships which involve regulative norms? If law is seen as a social relationship, and if one asserts that law regulates social relationships, then one must engage the tautology that social relationships regulate themselves.

Clearly, not all rules are legal rules: some rules are customary and traditional, and may be based in moral, aesthetic or utilitarian considerations. The crucial question with which Marxist theory must be concerned is the elucidation of the conditions in which the regulation of social relationships assumes a legal character. Following certain sections of Marx's Hegelian-inspired analysis in Volume I of Capital, Pashukanis argues that the search for the unique social relationship, whose inevitable reflection is the form of law, is to be located in the interaction between commodity owners. The logic of legal concepts corresponds with the logic of the social relationships of commodity exchange, and it is in these relationships—and not in the instrumental demands of domination, submission, or naked power—that the origin of law is to be sought.

Capitalist societies are principally societies of commodity owners. Commodities have a dual and a contradictory character. On the one hand, a commodity is and represents a use value. But commodities necessarily embody different use values because the qualitatively distinct social needs that they fulfill, and the quality and quantity of labor expended in their production, are necessarily different and unequal. On the other hand, a commodity is and represents an exchange value. One commodity may be exchanged for another in a definite ratio. The values encountered in this exchange are expressed by and facilitated through the mediation of another commodity—money—as the form of universal economic equivalent.

The potential for commodity exchange thus assumes that qualitatively distinct commodities enter a formal relationship of equivalence, so that eventually they appear as equal. Commodity exchange obscures a double abstraction in which concrete labor and concrete commodities are equalized *inter se* and are reduced to abstract labor and abstract commodities. This abstraction in turn perpetuates the fetish that commodities themselves, including money, contain living powers: commodities therefore dominate their very producers, human subjects. But the logic of commodity exchange—the basic logic of capitalism—defines and complements the logic of legal fetishism. At the same time that the product of labor is assuming the quality of a commodity, and becoming the bearer of value, the human subject acquires the quality of a juridic subject and becomes the bearer of a right. The constant transfer of rights in the market creates the appearance of an immobile bearer of rights. The concrete rights and obligations established between economic subjects are eventually dissolved into the abstract attributes of the juridic subjects. Concrete political subjects are relegated to abstract political citizens who incorporated egoism, freedom and the supreme value of personality. The capacity to be a subject of rights is finally disassociated from the specific living personality and becomes a purely social attribute. Law is thus the political form for establishing abstract equivalence between isolated economic subjects.[7]

Pashukanis' argument has at least two important implications for the present discussion. First, the range of variation in the context of particular legal norms is circumscribed by the *form* of law, and the form of law is contingent on the dominant modes of production in any social formation. The *content* of legal norms may only vary within these determinate limits. Under the capitalist mode of production, for example, there can be no law which abolishes rent, interest or industrial profit, for that would be to abolish capital itself. But the level of surplus value—or already—produced surplus value in the case of rent extracted by capital will vary according to state policies which are themselves partly conditioned by the relative strengths and weaknesses in the class struggle. Second, law is not an external object whose meaning can be ascertained in isolation from the social relationships of production and exchange. Law both mediates and is mediated by these relationships, and is the political equivalent which lends cohesion to the relationships among atomized economic agents. Thus, to raise questions concerning the equity, or otherwise, of a given law presupposes questions concerning the nature of production and exchange; the former cannot be asked, or measured, without the latter.

Conclusion

One final point is now in order. Currently, many sociologists seem eager to measure the empirical status of law within social structures, but few have bothered to conceptualize the features distinguishing law from other categories of rules. How does law differ from mores, customs, and tradition? Can legal rules sensibly be distinguished from the more mundane rules which social actors routinely use to negotiate everyday life? Is law simply a set of rules whose violation will incur organized sanctions? Or is it a less visible set of ideological injunctions most commensurate with the forms of domination under capitalism, so insidious that our notions of legitimacy and equality are permeated by its intrusiveness? These are important questions, but they can be neither adequately posed nor properly answered within the framework of empiricism. The major contention of the argument here has been that the critical reaction to Marxist accounts of law and crime is at present seriously in error. I have suggested that this reaction has misrepresented its object (the concepts specified by the theoretical structure of Marxism) by confusing it with objects contained within intellectual traditions more familiar than Marxism.

In that it tends to rely on naive falsificationism as its criterion of empirical truth, the critical reaction I have outlined here shares a feature with other varieties of sociological empiricism. The existence of legal controls and legal sanctions "inimicable" to the immediate interests of the capitalist class does not refute or falsify the Marxist perspective. The argument "*this* law is inimicable to the interests of the capitalist class, *therefore* law *in general* does not reflect those interests" is syllogistic unless it is based on the premise that one ought, and one ought to be able, to identify such interests and to distinguish between the immediate and the overall interests of the capitalist class. In order to acquire a modicum of legitimacy for its economic position in production, the capitalist class is best served by a legal system which is constrained to present itself as the embodiment of the universal interest of the social formation rather than of particular interests within it. If these premises themselves are not subjected to empirical scrutiny than no amount of counterfactual examples can falsify or displace the proposition that inimicable legislation does not contradict the overall interests of the capitalist class and that such legislation may actually support that class's interest in long-run stability. Even an overtly empiricist set of propositions must be based on some unspoken theoretical structure, yet unless this structure is explicitly articulated no empirical tests—or vague assertions that Marxism encourages tautologous theorizing—

can displace the proposition that legislation usually but not always reflects the interests of the capitalist class.

Theoretical structures are never rejected on empirical grounds alone. They are either supplemented and modified by new empirical findings, or discarded in favor of theoretical structures which explain more empirical space. But when the goal of the sociological method slides from puzzle solving to testing, when data are put into an artificial nexus with concepts concerning class interests and concepts concerning needs for legitimacy, then the sociological enterprise assumes an insoluble relativism which, as Robert Merton reminded us, is devoid of any central referent beyond an obsession with measurement itself.

Notes

1. The most detailed treatment of the commodity exchange school of law is found in Sharlet (1968). See also the editors' introduction in Beirne and Sharlet, (1924).
2. For excellent analyses of positivism in criminology, see Matza (1964: Chapter 1) and Cohen (1974).
3. Similar developments, it should be noted, were taking place in the sociology of law, or the "science of law" as Pound (1921, 1942) often termed it.
4. I am well aware of the strict limitations inherent in the base/superstructure metaphor, and it is used here primarily for expository purposes.
5. Compare, for example, the abstract and relational logic which underlies Marx's *Capital*, with the illuminating empirical (historical) analyses which Marx provides in his three articles on French politics.
6. The importance of Pashukanis' contribution to a materialist theory of law has only very recently been recovered by Marxists. See Fraser (1976); Arthur (1976, 1978); Balbus (1977); Holloway and Picciotto (1977); Redhead (1978); Beirne and Sharlet, (1924).
7. Since law is based on commodity exchange—or, more precisely, the generalized commodity exchange which is peculiar to capitalist production—the existence of law is therefore both superfluous and practically impossible under communism.

References

Althusser, Louis. 1971. "Ideology and Ideological State Apparatuses," in Louis Althusser, *Lenin and Philosophy and Other Essays*. London: New Left Books.

Anderson, Charles H. 1974. *Toward a New Sociology*. Homewood, IL: Dorsey.

Arthur, Chris. 1976. "Towards a Materialist Theory of Law." *Critique* 7: 31–46.

———. 1978. "Introduction," in Evgeny G. Pashukanis, *Law and Marxism: A General Theory*. London: Ink Links.

Balbus, Isaac D. 1973. *The Dialection of Legal Repression*. New York: Russell Sage Foundation.

———. 1977. "Commodity Form and Legal Form: An Essay on the 'Relative Autonomy' of the Law." *Law and Society* 2: 571–88.

Becker, Howard S. 1963. *Outsiders*. Glencoe, IL: Free Press.

———. 1964. *The Other Side*. Glencoe, IL: Free Press.

Beirne, Piers. 1977. *Fair Rent and Legal Fiction*. London: Macmillan.

Beirne, Piers and Robert Sharlet (eds.). 1924. *Marxism and Soviet Jurisprudence: Selected Writings of Evgeny Pashukanis.* Trans. Peter Maggs. London and New York: Academic Press.

Brown, Robert. 1978. "The New Criminology." Pp. 81–107 in Eugene Kamenka, Robert Brown, and Alice Erh-Soon Tay (eds.), *Law and Society.* New York: St. Martin's Press.

Cashmore, Ernest. 1978. "The Social Organisation of Canadian Immigration Law." *Canadian Journal of Sociology* 3: 409–29.

Cernkovich, Stephen A. 1978. "Conceptual and Empirical Ambiguity in Class-oriented Theories of Crime and Delinquency." *International Journal of Criminology and Penology* 6: 105–20.

Chambliss, William. 1964. "A Sociological Analysis of the Law of Vagrancy." *Social Problems* 12: 67–77.

———. 1974. "The State, the Law and the Definition of Behavior as Criminal or Delinquent." Pp. 7–42 in Daniel Glaser (ed.), *Handbook of Criminology.* Indianapolis, IN: Bobbs-Merrill.

Chambliss, William and Robert Seidman. 1971. *Law, Order, and Power.* Reading, MA: Addison-Wesley.

Chiricos, Theordore G. and Gordon P. Waldo. 1970. "Punishment and Crime: An Examination of Some Empirical Evidence." *Social Problems* 18: 200–17.

———. 1975. "Socioeconomic Status and Criminal Sentencing: An Empirical Assessment of a Conflict Proposition." *American Sociological Review* 40: 753–72.

Cohen, Albert K. 1955. *Delinquent Boys: The Culture of the Gang.* Chicago: Free Press.

Cohen, Stanley. 1974. "Criminology and the Sociology of Deviance in Britain: A Recent History and a Current Report." in Paul Rock and Mary McIntosh (eds.), *Deviance and Social Control.* London: Tavistock.

Domhoff, G. William. 1970. *The Higher Circles.* New York: Random House.

Fraser, Andrew. 1976. "Legal Theory and Legal Practice." *Arena* 44, 45: 123–56.

Galliher, John F. 1978. "The Life and Death of Liberal Criminology." *Contemporary Crises* 2: 345–63.

Genovese, Eugene. 1976. *Roll, Jordan Roll.* New York: Vintage Books.

Gouldner, Alvin W. 1970. *The Coming Crisis of Western Sociology.* New York: Basic Books.

Hagan, John and Jeffrey Leon. 1977. "Rediscovering Delinquency: Social History, Political Ideology and the Sociology of Law." *American Sociological Review* 42: 587–98.

Hall, Jerome. 1952. *Theft, Law and Society.* Indianapolis, IN: Bobbs-Merrill.

Hawkins, Gordon. 1978. "The New Penology." Pp. 108–27 in Eugene Kamenka, Robert Brown, and Alice Erh-Soon Tay (eds.), *Law and Society.* New York: St. Martin's Press.

Hay, Douglas. 1975. "Property, Authority and the Criminal Law." Pp. 17–63 in Douglas Hay et al., *Albion's Fatal Tree.* New York: Pantheon Books.

Holloway, John and Sol Picciotto. 1977. "Capital, Crisis and the State." *Capital and Class* 2: 76–101.

Hopkins, Andrew. 1973. "On the Sociology of the Criminal Law." *Social Problems* 21: 608–19.

Horowitz, Irving L. and M. Liebowitz. 1968. "Social Deviance and Political Marginality." *Social Problems* 15: 280–96.

Jacobs, David. 1978. "Inequality and the Legal Order: An Ecological Test of the Conflict Model." *Social Problems* 25: 515–25.

Jankovic, Ivan. 1978. "Social Class and Criminal Sentencing." *Crime and Social Justice* 10: 9–16.

Kolko, Gabriel. 1962. *Wealth and Power in America.* New York: Praeger.

Lakatos, Imre. 1970. "Falsification and the Methodology of Scientific Research Programmes." in Imre Lakatos and A. Musgrave (eds.), *Criticism and the Growth of Knowledge.* New York: Cambridge University Press.

Lemert, Edwin M. 1970. *Social Action and Legal Change: Revolution within the Juvenile Court.* Chicago: Aldine.

Lizotte, Alan J. 1978. "Extra-legal Factors in Chicago's Criminal Courts: Testing the Conflict Model of Criminal Justice." *Social Problems* 25: 564–80.

Marx, Karl and Friedrich Engels. 1973. "The Communist Manifesto." Pp. 98–137 in Vol. I of *Marx/Engels Selected Works.* Moscow: Progress Publishers.

Matza, David. 1964. *Delinquency and Drift.* New York: Wiley.

———. 1969. *Becoming Deviant.* Englewood Cliffs, NJ: Prentice-Hall.

Merton, Robert K. 1938. "Social Structure and Anomie." *American Sociological Review* 3: 672–82.

Miliband, Ralph. 1969. *The State in Capitalist Society.* New York: Basic Books.

O'Connor, James. 1973. *The Fiscal Crisis of the State.* New York: St. Martin's Press.

Pashukanis, Evgeny Bronislavovich. 1980. *The General Theory of Law and Marxism.* Forthcoming in Piers Beirne and Robert Sharlet (eds.), [1924] *Marxism and Soviet Jurisprudence: Selected Writings of Evgeny Pashukanis.* Translated by Peter Maggs. London and New York: Academic Press.

Platt, Anthony. 1969. *The Child Savers.* Chicago: University of Chicago Press.

———. 1974. "The Triumph of Benevolence: The Origins of the Juvenile Justice System in the United States." Pp. 356–98 in Richard Quinney (ed.), *Criminal Justice in America,* Boston: Little, Brown.

Poulantzas, Nicos. 1973. *Political Power and Social Classes.* London: Sheed and Ward.

———. 1975. *Classes in Contemporary Capitalism.* London: New Left Books.

Quinney, Richard. 1970. *The Social Reality of Crime.* Boston: Little, Brown.

———. 1975a. *Criminology.* Boston: Little, Brown.

———. 1975b. "Crime Control in Capitalist Society: A Critical Philosophy." Pp. 181–212 in Ian Taylor, Paul Walton, and Jock Young (eds.), *Critical Criminology.* London: Routledge and Kegan Paul.

Redhead, Steve. 1978. "The Discrete Charm of Bourgeois Law." *Critique* 9: 113–20.

Roby, Pamela A. 1969. "Politics and Criminal Law: Revision of the New York State Penal Law on Prostitution." *Social Problems* 17: 83–109.

Sharlet, Robert. 1968. *Pashukanis and the Commodity Exchange Theory of Law, 1924–1930: A Study in Soviet Marxist Legal Thought.* Unpublished doctoral dissertation, Indiana University, Boomington.

Sutherland, Edwin H. 1940. "White Collar Criminality." *American Sociological Review* 5: 1–12.

———. 1941. "Crime and Business." *Annals of the American Academy of Political and Social Science* 217: 112–18.

———. 1949. *White Collar Crime.* New York: Dryden Press.

———. 1969. *Criminality and Legal Order.* Chicago: Rand McNally.

Taylor, Ian, Paul Walton, and Jock Young (eds.). 1973. *The New Criminology.* London: Routledge and Kegan Paul.

———. 1975. *Critical Criminology.* London: Routledge and Kegan Paul.

Tittle, Charles R., Wayne J. Villemez, and Douglas A. Smith. 1978. "The Myth of Social Class and Criminality: An Empirical Assessment of the Empirical Evidence." *American Sociological Review* 43: 643–56.

Turk, Austin. 1966. "Conflict and Criminality." *American Sociological Review* 31: 338–52.

Wheeler, Stanton. 1976. "Trends and Problems in the Sociological Study of Crime." *Social Problems* 23: 525–34.

Part III

LAW AND CONFLICTS OF CLASS, RACE, AND GENDER

In this section, we present a selection of empirical studies that explore the contradictory dynamics of class, race, and gender. Holly McCammon's article provides an analysis of the 1935 Wagner Act that established the legal right to strike for U.S. workers. Her study illustrates the usefulness of employing a dialectical approach whereby state policy in a capitalist context is seen as the outcome of an ongoing social class struggle. When confronted with workers' claims to the right to withhold their labor as a means for advancing their interests, the capitalist state experiences a dilemma of how to reproduce the underlying system of class relations while responding to the established political rules of representative democracies. The ongoing contradiction between state activities designed to reproduce capitalist accumulation and the state's continuing efforts to maintain its own legitimacy ultimately establishes the parameters of state conduct and the overall process of law creation and law revision.

In her sociological analysis of the Wagner Act, McCammon considers the role of the Supreme Court, the federal appeals courts, and the National Labor Relations Board (NLRB). She seeks to show how the law specifically sought to control an upsurge in labor actions by establishing the legal guarantee of the right to strike. By enacting the rules governing the right to strike, the state sought to strengthen the collective bargaining process and thus normalize labor relations through a new status quo that could regain a smoothly functioning capital–labor relationship.

McCammon shows that the initial response of the capitalist class to this law was to challenge its constitutionality. After losing a series of high-profile challenges in the courts, capitalists proceeded to mobilize all of their resources for winning new legal restrictions on the right to strike. When a 1938 Supreme Court ruling reiterated the worker's right to strike while simultaneously clarifying that this did not automatically translate into the right to interrupt production, the result was an explicit guarantee of the property rights of capitalist producers—and this resulted in establishing their right to pursue strategies of maintaining production in the face of actual strikes. Additional legal strategies were set into motion, culminating in the Taft-Hartley Act of 1947 that substantially circumscribed the possibilities of labor to lawfully engage in strikes, mostly through the legal designation of many key forms of organized labor activity as "unfair labor practices." McCammon shows how subsequent legal decisions and their effective implementation have been variable in terms of their response to a continuing class struggle, but constant in the manner in which they have regulated labor so as to effectively neutralize any threat that they might pose to the basic social relations of industrial capitalism. This has put workers in a structurally regulated situation that leaves them with little effective power to shape the conditions under which they work.

Next, Steve Valocchi's article attempts to deepen the structural analysis of law by considering the racist nature of state policy formulation and implementation. By focusing on legislation generated during the New Deal period, he shows how "class-centered" and "state-centered" approaches to this important historical period have generally failed to grasp the racial exclusiveness that prevailed. With little attention paid to the racially exclusive organizations of both capital and labor, many analysts have failed to see how New Deal legislation worked to actually ensure continuation of the right to engage in racially discriminatory practices. This is primarily due to a reductionist tradition of evaluating state policies in categories derived from the concerns of industrial production. By according a more central role to race in his analysis, Valocchi reveals the presence of a structured set of discriminatory legal and political processes that have previously thwarted and continue to impede progress toward a more racially equal and hence more democratic society.

In her chapter, Jill Quadagno uses a class-based approach to the welfare state that is enhanced by insights from feminist theory. She seeks to develop a more sociologically complex theory of racial stratification. Her starting point of analysis rests in the well-substantiated notion that the welfare state is a mechanism for actively intervening in the larger society so as to both reproduce as well as modify the existing class, race, and/or gender distributions of wealth and power. She maintains that the way in which the welfare state reproduces existing structures of racial inequality has been amply documented; however, the means by which the welfare state could transform the racial stratification have *not* been adequately identified. Quadagno terms her approach a "power resource" perspective, suggesting that the political arena constitutes the social space whereby structured inequalities gendered by capitalist economics can be addressed. In the area of race relations, she argues that a pervasive racism can be lessened within private spheres if the activities of such institutions are brought into the public sphere. She points out, however, that this can only succeed if the public sphere itself is reconstructed and all such changes presuppose that oppressed racial minorities can prove capable of mustering sufficient political resources.

In the final chapter of this section, Valerie Jenness takes a critical approach to the evolution of the legal category of "hate crimes." She attempts to account for how some people's social status qualifies them for inclusion as victims under the law while others do not. By exploring the broader political process of law formation, she pursues the particular issue of how the content of hate crime law becomes created and institutionalized, and how this revolves around the social definitioning process of exactly who qualifies as victims of hate crimes. Her approach is based on the premise that political and structural variables as typically utilized cannot fully account for the criminalization of hate. She argues that various studies sustain the notion that social movements play a critical role in creating and modifying the symbolic content that defines the social problem of "hate." In so doing, Jenness shows how the established literature has not yet adequately conceptualized the processes by which social movements have shaped the law and lawmaking activities.

In seeking answers, her empirical focus includes U.S. congressional hearings in analyzing what others have referred to as "critical discourse moments." This enables her to track the legislative evolution of state responses to hate. By viewing law as the outcome of cultural production, she wishes to capture the dynamic of social movement-based definitioning activity as it impacts upon the creation of official categories in the legal process. In this way, she demonstrates the need for considering the definitional activities of social movement organizations as they help set the stage for the larger institutional processes of policymaking and law creation.

References

Jenness, Valerie. 1999. Managing Differences and Making Legislation: Social Movements and the Racialization, Sexualization, and Gendering of Federal Hate Crime Law in the U.S., 1985–1998. *Social Problems* 46, no. 4:548–71.

McCammon, Holly J. 1990. Legal Limits on Labor Militancy: U.S. Labor Law and the Right to Strike since the New Deal. *Social Problems* 37, no. 2:206–29.

Quadagno, Jill. 2000. Promoting Civil Rights through the Welfare State: How Medicare Integrated Southern Hospitals. *Social Problems* 47, no. 1:86–89.

Valocchi, Steve. 1994. The Racial Basis of Capitalism and the State, and the Impact of the New Deal on African Americans. *Social Problems* 41, no. 3:347–62.

CHAPTER 8

Legal Limits on Labor Militancy

U.S. LABOR LAW AND THE RIGHT TO STRIKE SINCE THE NEW DEAL

Holly J. McCammon

The U.S. labor historian Irving Bernstein (1969:786) has written that the New Deal period ". . . witnessed a change in American law so profound as to constitute a revolution." The most significant and long-lasting changes in U.S. worker–employer relations came with the New Deal's National Labor Relations (Wagner) Act, passed by Congress in 1935 and affirmed by the Supreme Court in 1937. The act, which provides the legal foundations of present-day labor–employer relations, grants workers a legal right to organize trade unions, to bargain collectively with employers, and to strike. It also established the National Labor Relations Board (NLRB), a federal agency, to act as a formal mediator in industrial disputes.

There is general consensus among scholars that Bernstein's characterization of this restructuring of industrial relations, class conflict, and the state's regulatory role in them is not overstated (e.g., Cox 1960; Montgomery 1979; Brody 1980). What is far less clear is whether the expansion of the state's role and the rights provided to workers have been to the benefit or the detriment of the labor movement. The industrial pluralist school has long held that the New Deal labor policies promised and provided greater power for organized labor in the workplace by granting to workers bargaining arenas in which they could interact with employers on a more equal footing (e.g., Cox 1960; Dunlop 1958; Chamberlain and Kuhn 1986). Others, working within a critical legal studies framework, are quite skeptical of this view (Klare 1978; Stone 1981; Atleson 1983; Tomlins 1985). They argue that the New Deal legislation has not enhanced the power of workers precisely because these developments in the law have constrained and even impeded the ability of workers to organize and to act collectively.

But the consequences of the Wagner Act for workers are better understood through dialectical rather than dualistic reasoning. The Wagner Act did not simply help or hinder the labor movement. Rather, the act and the institution of collective bargaining that emerged from it simultaneously enhanced and diminished the collective capacities of workers (Hurd 1976; Klare 1983). The more interesting and certainly less simple question, then, is how the Wagner Act and its interpretations and applications over time have simultaneously worked in these opposing ways to shape the capacities of workers to organize and act in their common interests.

In this paper I examine the legal regulation of the strike, a collective act that clearly threatens the profit-making potential of capitalist production. The strike is a breakdown in the organization of the economic exchange of labor power for a wage, an exchange that defines capitalist social relations of production. It therefore, arguably, is workers' most powerful form of collective action. Perhaps because of this, there is a rich legislative and legal case history concerning the regulation of the strike that I examine in this analysis.

I argue that the law has empowered workers by granting them the right to strike, but also simultaneously has constrained this right by defining strike action as legitimate—and thus permissible—only in specifically defined circumstances. This "structuring" of collective possibilities clearly has had consequences for the balance of power between capital and labor in the U.S. industrial economy. The argument proceeds in three steps. First, I introduce a theoretical framework to explain how and why class relations and struggles within a capitalist democracy shape state action, and explore within the specific historical context of the post-New Deal years the general form of regulatory policy regarding strike action that emerged out of the Wagner legislation. In the second and third steps of the argument, I demonstrate, through analysis of the law concerning strike activity, that the law's design and its applications have permitted some forms of worker action but have regulated and excluded others. More specifically, the second step in the argument shows how the law has limited the effectiveness of the strike both by allowing employers to hire replacement workers for striking workers and by regulating the ability of unions to picket and to levy union fines. The third step in the argument demonstrates how the law has altered the frequency and the form of strike activity by fostering the exchange of workers' no-strike pledge for an employer's agreement to arbitrate disputes.

Labor Law in a Capitalist Democracy

The potential for conflict is structured into the very nature of the economic and social relationship between workers and employers under capitalism (Przeworski 1985). Their interests, historically, often have not coincided on matters concerning wage, profit, and productivity levels. When industrial disputes arise, labor frequently has utilized the strike to make its demands heard. When states act to resolve such instances of overt conflict, intervention can take a variety of forms, ranging from direct repression to outright accommodation.

In a capitalist democracy such as the United States, struggles among classes in both economic and political arenas shape the nature of state intervention in industrial disputes (Poulantzas 1980 [1978]; Przeworski 1985). Legal policies regarding strike activity are one result of such struggles. In a capitalist economic context, state policies typically will reflect and reproduce unequal class relations (Poulantzas 1980 [1978]; Block 1987; Offe 1974). State policies will generally be designed to structure class struggles and relations in such a way that the organization of capitalist production and the capacity of capital to accumulate profits are not severely threatened over the long term. This is not to suggest that state policies will inevitably serve the interests of capital, only that policies are a product of struggle, and in struggles in a capitalist context, employers and those representing their interests usually secure the advantage.

The formulation, implementation, and enforcement of legal policies concerning strike activity are components of class struggle in which state managers play a prominent role. Struggle in a political realm is shaped and constrained by class forces. But political struggles are also guided by the political "rules of the game," giving politics, to a degree, its own specificity (Block 1987:84). State managers act for reasons not entirely reducible to the interests of groups in civil society. In a representative democracy, politicians must build and retain constituencies. In doing so, they define political platforms to distinguish themselves from the political opposition. Once in power, these managers strive to maintain their political legitimacy and thus their electoral support through forming and implementing "effective" policy.

Thus democratic political and capitalist economic structures ultimately both shape and limit the policies formulated by state managers. Tension in policymaking between the outcome of democratic processes and the demands of capital can and does arise. Policy initiatives designed to enhance state legitimacy can conflict with steps needed to sustain or augment capital accumulation. But the activities of state managers to fulfill what are sometimes referred to as the legitimation and accumulation functions (Poulantzas 1968 [1973]; O'Connor 1973) do not have to be contradictory. I argue, for example, that labor relations law since the New Deal generally has developed to permit those forms of the strike that can be accommodated to capitalist relations of production, i.e., forms that do not threaten or undermine the existence of private property or the ability of capital to generate profits from the ownership and control of property. In contrast, forms of worker action that can or do threaten capitalist production over time have been increasingly excluded from what is legally permissible. Thus, within limits established by the law, workers are empowered to act collectively. In legally providing for and protecting these workers' rights, the state in part establishes for itself the legitimacy necessary to a democratic state.

To support this argument, I explore precisely where the legal boundaries of workers' collective action lie and how these boundaries have developed since the New Deal. These boundaries are the product of ongoing struggles within and among classes and their representatives in the state. The paper therefore attempts not only to delineate these boundaries over time but also to examine the kinds and degrees of constraint imposed on them by class struggle.

State theorists do not agree on the extent to which capitalist productive relations structure state policy. Skocpol (1980:200), for instance, argues that "capitalism in general has no politics, only [extremely flexible] outer limits for the kinds of supports for property ownership and controls of the labor force that it can tolerate." The structuralists and instrumentalists, on the other hand, argue that political actors have far less independence from the imperatives of the economic system or its actors, and are only "relatively autonomous" from capitalist economic relations (Poulantzas 1980 [1978]) or are directly, that is, interpersonally, linked to and guided by the corporate community (Domhoff 1983). Most empirical research on the links between the economy and the polity (e.g., Skocpol 1980; Domhoff 1987; Goldfield 1989) tends to emphasize only the origins of legislative policy, with little or no attention to its historical development—that is, the law's implementation, interpretation, and application over time. Ongoing struggles among classes are continually changing the legal boundaries of legitimate worker action. Where much of the previous research on the state and class struggle has missed this unfolding of class history by focusing only on the law's origin, this study takes a more dynamic approach attending to the ongoing revision and even redefinition of the law's meaning and utilization.

In what follows I deal exclusively with the law itself and with decisions handed down by the Supreme Court, the federal appeals courts, and the NLRB. The interpretation of a law can change rapidly, particularly if the decisions of district and state courts are also taken into account. The legislation of federal law and the interpretation of these laws by the NLRB and their enforcement in the Supreme Court and federal appeals courts, however, are taken to represent national policy in the area of labor relations law. National legal policy is the product of conflicts in society over issues of power and control. The state's construction of the regulations that ultimately appear in the law are often based on "successful" industrial practices already in existence between particular employers and workers. What the law accomplishes then is the institutionalization of the practices and thus very likely their widespread and continued use in industrial relations. Moreover, in that the state legally sanctions a particular practice, it also establishes its capacity to regulate that practice. The specific origin of each particular industrial practice, however, is beyond the scope of this paper. Here I am concerned with the content and development of legal policy.

The Legal Management of Strike Action

In the early 1930s the U.S. economy was in a state of crisis. By 1932 one-quarter of the labor force was without employment and total manufacturing production had dropped by nearly half (U.S. Bureau of the Census 1975). The economic crisis unleashed unprecedented mass protest. Mob lootings, street marches, and rent riots surged as many individuals and families protested and acted on their economic hardships (Piven and Cloward 1979; Jenkins and Brents 1989). The economic turmoil also produced a massive electoral realignment in 1932 that put Roosevelt in the presidency and gave the Democrats a clear majority in both the House and Senate. One of the earliest legislative attempts by the new Democratic administration to rescue the economy was the National Industrial Recovery Act (NIRA), a law providing business leaders with the authority to regulate economic competition. The law also contained a labor provision, Section 7(a), that granted workers a legal right to organize unions and to bargain collectively. The logic behind Section 7(a) was that a strong labor movement would ultimately bring about greater purchasing power among workers, the lack of which was believed to be one of the underlying causes of the Depression (Bernstein 1969). In early 1935, however, the Supreme Court in the *Schecter* case ruled that the NIRA was unconstitutional on the grounds that the law wrongly delegated to the executive branch legislative power to regulate interstate commerce (Cortner 1970).

Although the NIRA was in place only two years, it significantly altered the course of conflict between workers and employers. It ignited a surge of militancy among thousands of industrial workers based upon their belief that now workers indeed had a right to organize unions of their own choosing. Employers at the time viewed the law quite differently. The National Association of Manufacturers (NAM) stated that employers were not obligated to bargain with worker unions, but instead might choose to bargain with individuals or company unions. In fact, the number of company unions soared during this period (Bernstein 1969:39–40), and employer resistance to the organizational and bargaining demands of workers grew. As a result, between 1932 and 1933 the number of strikes doubled while the number of workers participating in strike activity nearly quadrupled, and the figures climbed even higher in 1934 (U.S. Bureau of the Census 1975).

It was in this context that Congress enacted the Wagner Act in 1935, immediately following the Supreme Court's ruling on the NIRA. Section 7(a) of the new law read: "Employees shall have the right to self-organize, to form, join, or assist labor organizations, to bargain collectively through representatives of their own choosing, and to engage in concerted activities, for the purpose of collective bargaining or other mutual aid or protection" (29 U.S.C. Sec. 141–169). Moreover, Section 8(a)(2) stipulated that "the domination or interference with the formation or administration of any labor organization or contribution of financial or other support to it" was a violation of the new law. This provided substantially greater restrictions on the use of company unions. In addition, Wagner offered protection for the right of workers to strike. Section 13 of the Act stated: "Nothing in this Act shall be construed so as to interfere with or impede or diminish in any way the right to strike."

Although the legislators of the Wagner Act had various aims, perhaps their greatest priority was to reduce the high levels of strike activity (Klare 1978; Goldfield 1989). Its first statement read:

> The denial by employers of the rights of employees to organize and the refusal by employers to accept the procedure of collective bargaining lead to strikes and other forms of industrial strife or unrest, which have the intent or the necessary effect of burdening or obstructing commerce. . . . Experience has proved that protection by law of the right of employees to organize and bargain collectively safeguards commerce from injury, impairment, or interruption . . . (Section 1)

Thus one of the key ingredients to economic stabilization coming out of the Wagner Act was an attempt to minimize the number of strikes, not a surprising response to the militant wildcat strikes of 1933 and 1934.

This intent may appear incongruent with the legal protection for strike activity granted in Section 13. It is not. Congress granted the right to strike primarily in order to make collective bargaining work (U.S. Senate, Subcommittee on Labor-Management Relations 1951, cited in Bakke, Kerr, and Anrod 1960:246–48). In effective bargaining, each party must approach the negotiating table with a form of leverage or control over a resource necessary to the interests of the other party. For labor this resource is labor power; their leverage is their ability to withdraw it from production. Thus the right of workers to strike is provided by the law in order to make collective bargaining effective, and the reason to make bargaining effective, as is evident in the wording of the law above, is to stabilize and preserve the basic relationships of production.

But in the immediate aftermath of its enactment, the Wagner Act did not appear at all successful in its goal of reducing worker unrest. The number of strikes in 1937 reached an historic high. A dynamic similar to that following the passage of the NIRA came into play. Workers again viewed the change in law as a clear signal of their right to organize, but their organizational campaigns, led in particular at this time by the CIO, were met by intense, often violent, employer resistance. Workers in the mass production industries (most notably rubber, auto, and steel) responded with spontaneous sitdown strikes, most of which occurred over the issue of union organizing (Bernstein 1969; Edwards 1981; Rubin, Griffin, and Wallace 1983). Employers not only resisted workers in the workplace, but also attempted to fight the Wagner Act and the rulings of the NLRB in the courts. Legal proceedings were brought against the NLRB alleging its use of Wagner to be unconstitutional and injunctions were sought to prevent the Board's "interference" in industrial relations (Gross 1974). As a result, the NLRB spent much of its first years contesting these charges.

Finally, in the 1937 Jones and Laughlin case, the Supreme Court affirmed the constitutionality of the Wagner Act. The court's 5–4 decision in favor of the act was also based on the current "facts of industrial relations" and Roosevelt's strong urging that if the Act was not affirmed the court would be "thwarting the national will" (Gross 1974:225–27). With this important decision Wagner was set in place as law, and the legal proceedings concerning the constitutionality of the board's activities and employers' overt resistance to worker organization in the workplace began to taper. The Jones and Laughlin decision in time directed employers away from attempts to strike down the Board and Wagner, and away from open resistance in the workplace. Instead, they concentrated on lobbying efforts aimed at persuading or pressuring Congress to amend the Wagner Act.

The changes in the labor–capital relationship that Wagner brought about were significant, but its architects were not attempting to fundamentally restructure the U.S. economy (Klare 1978; Montgomery 1979). Wagner's enactment left basic capitalist property relations unaltered. On the other hand, beyond granting new collective rights to workers, Wagner did bring about two important changes in the labor–employer relationship and in these ways altered the terms of class conflict at the point of production. First, the state established legally sanctioned structures—unions and collective bargaining—in which employer–worker disputes would be resolved. Unions and collective bargaining both had existed before the New Deal (Montgomery 1979), but with Wagner they were legally authorized by and thus subject to regulation by the state. These new structures and the rules governing them were to be implemented by the NLRB and enforced by the courts. These two governmental bodies would then define the legitimate form and content of industrial conflict, which, in turn, allowed the state the capacity systematically to shape class conflict.

The terms of conflict were altered significantly in a second way. Workers were given the legal right to participate, through their own representatives, in decision making concerning the workplace. This was, for good reason, perceived by capital as a threat to its right to manage production. For workers, however, the establishment of collective bargaining, something they long had struggled for, truly represented an opportunity to participate. But the system of bargaining implemented in the 1930s was to be managed by the state. Worker participation in this system, as Przeworski (1985) explains, necessarily entails consent to the right of the state to manage the system. Wagner meant not only that the state had established the means by which to manage class conflict, but also that it had established these means so as to acquire the consent of organized workers to them.

The State Manages Strike Effectiveness

REPLACEMENT WORKERS

In the years following the enactment of Wagner, a continuing process of adjustment and definition of the law took place in all branches of government. One area of concern in this process dealt with an employer's response to a strike. In keeping with the recognized sanctity of private property (Klare 1978), legal interpretations of Wagner did not infringe on the right of employers to use strategies to avoid being shut down during a strike. Employers historically have attempted, quite successfully, to continue production during a strike (Herman and Kuhn 1981). They prepare in anticipation of a strike by stockpiling inventories. They shift to or intensify production at other facilities within the company that are not being struck. They subcontract the work with another company, or they continue to operate the plant with either nonunion or replacement personnel. Only on the question of whether employers can hire permanent replacements for striking workers has an elaborated legal case history developed. But even here, the law has helped employers continue operations, not impede them. In what follows, I examine how this happened.

Almost immediately after it ruled the Wagner Act constitutional, the Supreme Court handed down a decision that undermined the potency of the strike. In 1938 the court ruled in the Mackay Radio and Telegraph Co. case that employers had the right to hire permanent replacements to do the work of striking employees. After a strike at the Mackay Radio Company all but five of the striking workers were reinstated by the employer. These five employees, active union members or officers, were told that their jobs were no longer available because the strikebreakers had been hired as permanent replacements. The union filed an unfair labor practice charge with the NLRB against the employer for discriminating against the five employees. Both the board and later, through appeal, the Supreme Court ruled in favor of the strikers that the employees had been discriminated against and unfairly discharged.

The charge and the final ruling, however, overlook a particular statement in the decision that had an important impact for the efficacy of strike activity:

> Nor was it an unfair labor practice to replace the striking employees with others in an effort to carry on the business. Although Section 13 of the act provides, "Nothing in this Act shall be construed so as to interfere with or impede or diminish in any way the right to strike," it does not follow that an employer, guilty of no act denounced by the statute, has lost the right to protect and continue his business by supplying places left vacant by strikers. (Mackay Radio and Telegraph Co. 304 U.S. 345, 346, 1938)

The court in this case clearly discerned the necessary conflict between the legal right of employees to strike and the right of capital to uninterrupted production. In order to resolve the conflict and to relieve employers' fears that Wagner would undermine their right to "carry on the business," the court chose to alter the efficacy of labor's legal right to strike but not the property right of an employer. Although workers have a legal right to strike, they do not have a right to interrupt production.

VOTING RIGHTS

Immediately after the Mackay decision, a dispute came before the NLRB concerning the voting rights of strikers and their replacements in union election proceedings. In *Sartorius* (1938) the board ruled that strikers but not replacements possessed the right to vote in representation elections. But three years later, in Wurlitzer (1941), the board altered its position, holding that both strikers and strikebreakers had voting rights, weakening the position of strikers. This set the stage for a major reworking of the legal grounds underlying voting rights by the Taft-Hartley Act in 1947.

If the Wagner Act was a federal policy giving workers an opportunity to participate in the governance of the workplace, the Labor-Management Relations (Taft-Hartley) Act, a set of amendments to Wagner, was a significant stride in the other direction. The enactment of Taft-Hartley was not an abrupt reversal in the law; the temporary War Labor Disputes Act of 1943 contained elements that would appear in Taft-Hartley; in addition, various employer associations and their "friends in Congress" had been working for its revision since the passage of Wagner (Stryker 1989). Conditions for enacting such legislation were ripe immediately after the Second World War.

With the end of the war the nation was hit hard by a large number of protracted reconversion strikes. Sparked by high levels of inflation, they also were a playing out of the battle between unions and employers over basic issues of workplace control. Workers were practicing "aggressive bargaining," seeking to include issues such as personnel, production, and financial matters that previously had been management prerogative (Brody 1980:178). The protracted General Motors-United Auto Workers strike that began in 1945 is a clear example. The union called upon GM to raise wages without raising prices and demanded that the account books be made available for union scrutiny.

In the years following the Second World War the economy was not in a state of deep crisis as it had been during the 1930s, and the large strikes in key industries alarmed the nation (Millis and Brown 1950). Employer associations, such as the NAM and the Chamber of Commerce, played on these public fears with an intensified media campaign calling for legislation to amend Wagner, to "equalize" the law by restricting "the monopolistic practices of unions and various types of strikes" (Millis and Brown 1950:288). The general shift in public sentiment was manifested in the Congressional elections of 1946 in which the Republicans were able to reclaim majorities in both the House and Senate, and in 1947 the Republican-dominated Congress enacted Taft-Hartley.

The new amendments seriously narrowed the content and structure of the collective bargaining process. Content was narrowed in that secondary boycotts and picketing, closed shops, jurisdictional strikes, recognition strikes where a previously certified union exists, and union organizing among foremen, all became unfair labor practices under Taft-Hartley. The prohibition of secondary activity is particularly interesting because it limits demonstrations of widespread solidarity among workers, e.g., among workers from different firms (see Weiler 1983; Rogers 1984 for elaboration on the fragmenting effects of the law). Taft-Hartley also narrowed the structure of labor relations by defining the only legitimate collective bargaining relationship as that between an employer and an NLRB-certified bargaining unit.

An immediate consequence of Taft-Hartley was to undercut the power of strikers by prohibiting those for whom permanent replacements had been hired from voting in union representation elections. This was accomplished with fifteen words appended to Section 9 of the Wagner Act: "employees on strike who are not entitled to reinstatement shall not be eligible to vote" (29 U.S.C. Sec. 141–187). Labor unions labeled it a "union-busting" device (Benetar 1961). If a decertification election were called during a strike, it was in the interest of the strikebreakers to vote against the union to maintain their jobs. The strikers, with no voting rights, had no opportunity to continue the strike and, perhaps ultimately, to preserve their union. Whereas previous to Taft-Hartley there had been no union decertification proceedings, in 1948 there were 97, 62 of which were successful decertifications (NLRB Annual Reports 1936–49). There is, however, no way to know how many of these resulted from petitions filed by strikebreakers. In the next year the numbers were even higher (132 decertification elections and 82 decertifications).

For 12 years unions that exercised the right to strike did so under these conditions. The Labor-Management Reporting and Disclosure (Landrum-Griffin) Act of 1959 restored strikers' right to vote, but with a qualification: it lasted for only 12 months after the beginning of the strike. In addition, in United Aircraft (1971), the NLRB, by this time controlled by Nixon appointees, ruled that the job rights of replaced workers could be limited. This decision compromised earlier judgments (*Fleetwood Trailer* [1967] and *Laidlaw* [1968]) in which replaced workers were guaranteed reinstatement when and if their jobs opened up again following a strike. In *United Aircraft* the board ruled that it was acceptable for a union to "agree," in an effort to bring a strike to an end, to a time limit on replaced workers' reinstatement rights. In that case it was four and one-half months after the end of the strike.

Landrum-Griffin did reduce the immediate threat of decertification, an ironic consequence because in many other ways the law placed substantial restrictions on unions (Taylor and Witney 1987:584–626). *Landrum-Griffin* was part of a larger offensive against unions during the late 1950s and early 1960s as employers, reacting to the recession in 1957–58, sought to destabilize union power in the workplace (Davis 1986). The seeming benefit of the *Landrum-Griffin* provision that returned voting rights to strikers, however, should be weighed against the fact that the law did not do away with the legal means to weaken the economic impact of the strike. Ultimately this succession of laws and decisions concerning permanent replacements and their voting and job rights continues to give employers, if they desire and are able to take advantage of it, a legal means to render a strike virtually powerless to impede production and, in the extreme case, even to break a union.

Unfortunately, no comprehensive data on the extent to which employers use replacements exists (Estreicher 1987). One study of fifteen employers who continued to operate with replacement workers during strike action supplies some information about their use. Perry, Kramer, and Schneider (1982) find that employers do not always turn to replacement workers, but do so when economic circumstances raise the cost of non-operation. During the early 1960s and again in the early 1970s, employers in their sample, reacting to increased economic competition during periods of low growth, stepped up their efforts to continue operating during a strike. The popular literature suggests that in recent years employers are again increasing their use of strikebreakers to continue production (e.g., Michelson 1978; Business Week 1978; English 1983; Hoerr 1985; Satchell and Golden 1987; Labor Today 1989) Perry and his colleagues conclude that companies remaining in operation during a strike benefit economically by reducing the economic losses that strikers attempt to levy against the firm, and thus it is in the economic interest of employers to continue operations.

It appears that the law provides a legal means for rendering the strike economically less effective, but other factors—the state of the economy and the general tone of labor relations—affect when employers actually use strikebreakers. The law establishes a context in which employers enjoy certain opportunities to promote their interests, and workers confront certain barriers as they attempt to promote theirs.

PICKET LINES AND UNION FINES

Developments in the law have reduced the strike's effectiveness in two additional ways: first, through regulation of the picket line and, second, through regulation of the ability of unions to fine members who return to work during a strike. In both cases the dialectic of the law is again evident. Whereas the issue of permanent replacements resulted in the law's modulation between property rights and the right to strike, the issues of picketing and union fines put individual rights and collective rights in conflict, one originating in the amendments to Wagner found in Taft-Hartley.

A prominent feature of Taft-Hartley is that it attends to individual motivations so as to produce collective consequences that disadvantage organized labor. Section 7 of Taft-Hartley reaffirms workers' right to organize and bargain collectively, but adds the clause, "and shall have the right to refrain from any or all of such activities." This clause in Taft-Hartley recasts workplace conflict in terms of individual rights versus collective rights, restricting the collective rights of organized labor to protect the rights of the individual. This ultimately serves to enhance the position of capital, as can be seen in the regulation of worker picket lines and union fines.

To uphold the sentiment of Section 7 of Taft-Hartley the NLRB has ruled that particular forms of picket line behavior interfere with the rights of individual workers. Specifically, workers have the right to work during a strike, including going to and from work without "restraint or coercion" (Sunset Line and Twine 1948). This wording, however, leaves many questions about picketing unanswered. While a ban on picketing that physically prevents workers from entering and exiting the workplace is unambiguous, the board's interdiction of "mass picketing" in Cory Corp. in 1949 is much less clear. By the terms of this ruling, mass picketing is banned even when it does not obstruct access to the workplace, but the board did not specify how many pickets constitute mass picketing and what degree of coercion might prevent employees from going to work. The lawfulness of picket action is thus left to be determined on a case-by-case basis. Yet the penalties for unlawful picketing are quite serious: unions can face an injunction that prohibits the strike and individual employees may lose their jobs.

The law also restricts the ability of a union to fine a member who decides to return to work during a strike. In 1967 the Supreme Court ruled in Allis-Chalmers that a union has the authority to protect the integrity of the picket line by fining members who cross that line to return to work during a strike. In 1972, however, the Nixon court ruled in Granite State Joint Board that under Taft-Hartley if the member resigns from the union and then returns to work, the union may not fine the worker. The minority opinion of Justice Harry Blackmun disputes both the court's attention to the right of the individual to resign and the court's blindness to the consequences of this action for the collective strength of workers:

> I cannot join the Court's opinion, which seems to me to exalt the formality of resignation over the substance of the various interests and national labor policies that are at stake here. Union activity, by its very nature, is group activity, and is grounded on the notion that strength can be garnered from unity, solidarity, and mutual commitment. This concept is of particular force during a strike, where the individual members of the union draw strength from the commitments of fellow members, and where the activities carried on by the union rest fundamentally on the mutual reliance that inheres in the "pact." (Granite State Joint Board 409 U.S. 213, 1972)

By upholding the individual worker's right to work unpenalized during a strike, the court endorses individual interest while overlooking the collective consequence of the decision.

The *Granite State* case did not deal with the legality of union provisions that restrict members' resignations, either by forbidding resignations during times of strike activity or, more generally, by delaying actual resignation for a period after the letter of resignation has been filed. In 1982, however, in the *Dalmo Victor* case, the NLRB upheld a union's right constitutionally to require a member to wait 30 days after submitting his or her notice before resigning. This ruling was quickly overturned in *Neufeld Porsche-Audi* in 1984, by which time the majority of the board were Reagan appointees. In this case the board stated that such restrictive action by the union abridged the individual's right to resign from union activities at will. In fact, Davis (1986:139) points out that one of the stated policies of the Reagan board was the "repeal of those NLRB provisions which establish collective rights as paramount to individual rights." The dialectic in the application of the law concerning the collective capacities of workers is again apparent in that individual rights are given precedent over collective rights.

THE IMPACT ON STRIKE EFFECTIVENESS

It is difficult to assess whether the regulation of picket lines, the capacity of employers to hire permanent replacements, and the inability of unions to fine members who return to work have genuinely reduced the strike's effectiveness. Studies of the economic effect of recent strikes on business operation or on the marketplace show that strikes do not negatively affect prices, the quantity of goods produced, and even indirect effects on suppliers (Neumann and Reder 1984). A study of strikes in the auto industry (Gunderson and Melino 1987) shows that in the short run a strike may have a negative effect, but that in the long run the impact can be minimal. The fact that the law allows employers to hire strikebreakers, to limit picketing, and to encourage workers to break union ranks and return to work during a strike appears to be important in mediating the impact of the strike.

Whether these developments in the law have reduced the effectiveness of the strike is an important question, but how might that effectiveness be evaluated? One approach is to ask whether striking workers have achieved their stated goals. Today nearly three-quarters of all strikes occur over compensation-related issues (U.S. Bureau of Labor Statistics 1949–80). Those who have examined the relationship between wages and strikes (e.g., Rubin 1986; Ashenfelter, Johnson, and Pencavel 1972) find that throughout this century, workers have usually been able to enhance their material well-being through strike action. On the other hand, if greater collective control in the workplace is the goal of striking workers, the historical record suggests a very different conclusion about the effectiveness of strikes.

Greater control in the workplace might be measured by level of union membership. Although not a perfect measure by any means, unions historically have been the most viable means of organizing resources toward greater collective control over the conditions of work for U.S. workers (Perlman 1928; Przeworski 1985). But research by Rubin, Griffin, and Wallace (1983) shows that strikes have not translated into greater union membership since 1947, the year in which Taft-Hartley was enacted. While only suggestive, the law does appear to reduce the effectiveness of the strike when measured in terms of increased union membership.

These two measures of strike effectiveness—increases in wages and in union membership—show very different results. One suggests that the strike has been consistently successful in raising the wages of organized workers, the other that strikes have become less successful in translating strike action into greater union membership. If the law has indeed had an impact on the strike's effectiveness, these seemingly disparate results indicate the contradictory and dialectical impulses in the law, empowering workers in one manner but constraining their capacity to act collectively in another. There is substantial historical evidence, which I discuss in the next section, that labor law since the New Deal has carefully distinguished between issues that might alter the property relations of capitalism and those that would not, that is, between issues that are zero-sum and non-negotiable and those that are positive-sum and thus more readily negotiable; between issues like workplace control and the wages of labor. These issues are clearly separated in the law as "permissive" and "mandatory," and the capacity of workers to bargain and to strike over each is quite different.

The State Manages the Frequency and Form of the Strike

Today's labor law emphasizes collective bargaining as a peaceful and pluralist means of resolving disputes between workers and capitalists. With the Wagner Act's assurance of labor's right to strike, the integrity of the collective bargaining system is thought to be preserved. I have argued that although workers have the right to strike, the strike in fact may be ineffective in the face of the legal structures that regulate strike activity and allow employers to protect their interests in response to that activity. But beyond these restraints and regulations, labor relations law further shapes collective worker action by directing grievances away from disruptive acts of militancy and into predictable and nondisruptive forms of class conflict. In consequence, both the frequency and the form of the strike have been altered.

THE NO-STRIKE PLEDGE

The labor contract that emerges from the collective bargaining process is a contradictory, but often highly useful document for capital (Edwards 1979; Klare 1983). It makes the worker–employer relationship very predictable; it reduces and sometimes completely eliminates interruptions to production, facilitating long-term business planning for capital. Moreover, the labor contract establishes a set of workplace rules that carry the consent of unionized workers because of the union's role in negotiating the contract. The contract is based on an apparent quid pro quo arrangement: in exchange for labor's no-strike promise, management agrees to arbitrate disputes that cannot be resolved by regular methods. Approximately 95 percent of current labor contracts contain such an agreement (Taylor and Witney 1987:439).

The widespread use of the no-strike pledge can be historically dated to the Second World War. To contribute to the war effort, union leadership (particularly in the CIO) made the no-strike promise in exchange for a "maintenance-of-membership" program established by the National War Labor Board that required all union members to remain members for the duration of the contract (Lichtenstein 1975). Today the no-strike clause is traded for an arbitration agreement. Workers relinquish their legal right to strike in exchange for a guarantee from capital that when grievance disputes over contract violations break down, an outside arbitrator will be called in to settle the disagreement.

Prior to 1957, arbitration as an alternative to direct negotiations between workers and employers was not frequently used (Lynd 1979; U.S. Bureau of the Labor Statistics 1949–56). In 1957 the Supreme Court, applying Taft-Hartley in the *Lincoln Mills* case strengthened the role of arbitration as a means to peaceful settlement of labor–capital disputes. This decision and decisions in the "Steelworkers Trilogy" cases of 1960 (*Warrior and Gulf Navigation, American Manufacturing Co.*, and *Enterprise Wheel and Car Corporation*), which strengthened and expanded the *Lincoln Mills* decision, reflected a political climate of growing opposition to the organizational and disruptive power of labor unions. Opposition to the strength of labor was compounded in 1957 as the economy slowed and employers attempted to reduce labor costs through layoffs, work speedups, and automation (Davis 1986). Such employer endeavors triggered greater worker unrest, most prominently the steel strike of 1959 in which President Eisenhower intervened under provisions in Taft-Hartley. Davis (1986:123) says of the late 1950s and early 1960s: "It is generally forgotten how close American industrial relations came to a raw re-opening of the class war in those years."

The *Lincoln Mills* case was a political response to industrial unrest. The court ruled that if a labor contract stipulates that grievances will be arbitrated and either party refuses, the refusing party can be sued and thus forced to arbitrate under Section 301 of Taft-Hartley. The specific goal of the ruling was to reduce industrial unrest by promoting a federal policy supporting the exchange of a no-strike pledge for an employer's agreement to arbitrate, as evidenced in the court's decision:

> Plainly the agreement to arbitrate grievance disputes is the *quid pro quo* for an agreement not to strike. Viewed in this light, the legislation does more than confer jurisdiction in the federal courts over labor organizations. It expresses a federal policy that federal courts should enforce these agreements on behalf of or against labor organizations and that industrial peace can be best obtained only in that way. (*Lincoln Mills* 353 U.S. 455, 1957)

The judiciary here clearly acted to reduce industrial unrest by establishing a framework in which disagreements could be resolved without disruptive adversarial action, even when disputes between labor and capital had come to an impasse. In doing this, the court importantly altered the nature of class conflict. Requests for arbitrators by employers and unions showed a five-fold increase between the early 1960s and late 1970s (U.S. Federal Mediation and Conciliation Service 1961–1979). Labor disputes henceforward were likely to be channeled into nondisruptive modes of conflict.

VOLUNTARY AND MANDATORY BARGAINING ISSUES

Judicial assumptions of quid pro quo notwithstanding, the contractual exchange of the no-strike pledge for an arbitration agreement is not an equal exchange (Lynd 1979; Stone 1981; Klare 1983). Although workers are legally and absolutely bound to their no-strike pledge, there are a number of issues over which management may refuse to arbitrate or bargain. The law reserves these to capital's discretion as "voluntary" or "permissive," in contrast to "mandatory," bargaining issues. In *Borg-Warner* (1958), the Supreme Court upheld the right of the NLRB to make these distinctions.

When management prohibits permissive issues from appearing on the bargaining table or in arbitration proceedings it is not an unfair labor practice. These issues are considered by law to be "management prerogatives," too close to production concerns to be within the legitimate purview of labor. Permissive issues are those involving investment decisions or anything at the "core of entrepreneurial control" (a term coined in *Fibreboard* 1964), such as decisions about technological innovation, changes in the production process, liquidation of assets, sales and advertising, mergers, and, since the court's decision in *First National Maintenance* in 1981, plant closings. Legal scholars show that the scope of permissive items has been gradually expanding in recent years (Sockell and Delaney 1987). Even if a permissive issue is voluntarily laid on the bargaining table by management, it cannot be negotiated to an impasse, and workers cannot legally strike over such an issue. Mandatory bargaining issues, on the other hand, must be negotiated at the bargaining table if either party so desires, can be bargained to an impasse, and may be legal grounds for a strike. But mandatory issues are restricted to concerns of "wages, hours, and other terms and conditions of employment" (Section 8(d) of Taft-Hartley).

Legal provisions for permissive and mandatory issues can structure conflict between labor and capital to be positive rather than zero-sum. Disputes over wages, for instance (75 percent of strikes today are over compensation-related issues), can be negotiated, and employers can accommodate worker demands without jeopardizing their control of business. Thus the law attempts to structure workplace decision making such that many of its rules are not equally determined by both labor and capital. The law also is designed so that negotiations involving labor deal with issues where employers can agree to worker demands without risking their unilateral control of enterprise.

Moreover, arbitration itself—capital's part of the no-strike bargain—is an unequal proposition for labor. The arbitrator's mediating role in industrial conflict is not neutral in remedying disputes (Stone 1981). The purpose of arbitration is to prevent a breakdown in communication between labor and capital and to preserve the continuity of production. But it is through the disruption of production that labor exerts its power in the workplace. The arbitrator's actions, therefore, work in the interests of capital and to the detriment of the structural capacity of labor to achieve its collective goals. In that the law fortifies and legitimates the arbitration framework, it often works to the detriment of organized labor.

THE WILDCAT STRIKE

The institutionalization of the no-strike-arbitration agreement ultimately transforms the midcontract or wildcat strike into a deviant act in industrial relations (Klare 1983). In the past the wildcat strike fell through the cracks of the collective bargaining edifice, especially so in the Supreme Court's *Fansteel* decision (1939) where sitdown strikes were ruled unprotected activity, thereby leaving workers with no rights to reinstatement. The Wagner Act, however, did provide workers with a legal right to strike, and spontaneous strike action continued to be a legal choice.

Today labor relations law has a very sophisticated mechanism, put into place by the Taft-Hartley amendments, for rendering the wildcat illegal. Section 301 of Taft-Hartley makes a wildcat strike a breach of the labor contract when that contract contains a no-strike clause. When a union is in breach of such a clause, it can be sued by an employer and employees can be punished or discharged. The no-strike clause in the labor contract serves to shift legal discussions of labor disputes from the relatively ill-defined grounds of the rights of labor and capital to the much better-defined, commerce-dominated domain of contracts. It also introduces the assumptions attendant upon contracts, particularly the notion that contracts are voluntary and equal agreements between free and equal negotiants. The labor contract evokes those assumptions in spite of evidence to the contrary: when, in pursuit of a contract, labor relinquishes the right to strike, capital surrenders no equivalent right to not produce, but only agrees to arbitration on disputes deemed legitimate within the legal conception of labor and capital rights.

A number of cases (in addition to those previously discussed, see *American Manufacturing Co., Enterprise Wheel and Car Corp., Lucas Flour Co.,* and *Gateway Coal Co.*) have come before the Supreme Court since *Lincoln Mills* concerning the no-strike clause and the limits on employer actions to prevent a wildcat strike. The Supreme Court's 1960 *Warrior and Gulf Navigation* decision has had far-reaching consequences. This decision expanded that in *Lincoln Mills* by ruling not only that arbitration is a legitimate arena for class negotiations, but that when a labor contract does not explicitly exclude a disputed issue from arbitration, the courts should assume by default that the issue is subject to arbitration. The Supreme Court stated simply that "[d]oubts should be resolved in favor of coverage" (*Warrior and Gulf Navigation Co.* [United Steelworkers of America] v. 363 U.S. 583, 1960). The court, however, carefully excluded "[m]atters which are strictly a function of management." These matters remain the prerogative of capital, are not subject to arbitration, and are not issues over which labor can legally strike.

THE LABOR INJUNCTION

In 1970 another landmark case was decided by the Supreme Court concerning the no-strike pledge. Prior to 1970, an employer or union that failed to arbitrate when so directed by the contract was subject only to litigation at the hands of the other party to the contract (*Sinclair Refining Co.* 1962). In 1970 the Supreme Court ruled in the controversial *Boys Markets* case that the party breaching the contract not only could be sued, but that, in the event that employees struck when the labor contract contained a no-strike clause, a labor injunction could also be issued to block the strike.

The impetus for the decision in *Boys Markets* largely may have come from the growing number of rank and file job actions—often wildcat strikes—during the late 1960s as workers responded to moves by capital to enhance productivity through speedups and changes in work rules (Wallace 1989). In the *Boys Markets* case, workers disagreed with management concerning what was and was not union work and struck in protest. The striking workers were clearly in violation of the no-strike pledge in the labor contract, and the employer sought an injunction to block the strike. The Supreme Court upheld the enforceability of the contract and the validity of a labor injunction to enjoin the strike, stating that:

> the very purpose of arbitration procedures is to provide a mechanism for the expeditious settlement of industrial disputes without resort to strikes, lockouts, or other self-help measures. This basic purpose is obviously largely undercut if there is not immediate, effective remedy for those very tactics that arbitration is designed to obviate. (*Boys Markets* 398 U.S. 249, 1970)

The decision reinstituted an anti-strike weapon that had been outlawed in 1932 by the Federal Anti-Injunction (Norris-LaGuardia) Act. An injunction could now be used for immediate relief from a strike in violation of an arbitration agreement, but the use of the injunction alters the context in which arbitration takes place. If an employer secures an injunction, labor's economic leverage—that is, the strike or even the power that the threat of a strike might mean—is removed, and thus the balance of power can and likely will shift in favor of capital. The status quo is maintained as workers continue to work under the disputed conditions.

Beyond the inequity that the *Boys Markets* decision built into the law, the injunction also tends to be applied unequally. As implied by the Supreme Court's mention of lockouts as well as strikes, unions as well as employers can have recourse to the injunction as an immediate remedy. In fact "reverse *Boys Markets* injunctions" have been sought and won to restrain employer action (Waye 1985; but also Atleson 1985:106–7). No national-level data are available on the number of labor injunctions granted by federal courts, but a number of researchers show that when employers seek labor injunctions they are rarely refused by the courts, that these injunctions are not infrequently granted on weak evidence, and that when unions apply for injunctions against employers they are much more often refused (Aaron and Levin 1951; Aaron 1964; Shatz 1977; Schatzki 1984). Moreover, between 1960 and 1980 the number of injunctions against unions sought by the NLRB was over 25 times the number sought against employers (NLRB 1960–1980).

THE IMPACT FOR THE FREQUENCY AND FORM OF THE STRIKE

Beginning in 1970, the year of *Boys Markets*, until 1978, the U.S. Bureau of Labor Statistics reported the number of strikes terminated by injunction. The first column in Table 1 shows that by the mid-1970s, the peak years of injunction use, around 190 strikes annually were disbanded by injunction, double the number in 1970. This is roughly between 3 and 4 percent of all strikes. If one assumes that these injunctions were used almost exclusively against wildcat strikes—and this is reasonable given the substance of *Boys Markets*—then by the mid-1970s 10 to 12 percent of all wildcat strikes ended by injunction (where the percent is the number of strikes terminated by injunction divided by the number of strikes taking place during the term of a contract; number of all wildcats not shown). *Boys Markets* appears to have had its largest impact in the manufacturing sector where a downward trend in wildcat strike frequency begins between 1969 and 1970 and continues until at least 1980 (see column 3; strike frequency is the number of strikes per million wage and salary earners). This is not, however, the pattern in mining (column 5) where 1978 appears to be the pivotal year, a point to which I will return below.

The extent of the legal right of an employer to use the injunction to block strike action was tested in the *Buffalo Forge* case in 1976. Following the breakdown of negotiations over a labor contract with their employer, office employees struck. Production workers in the same union and in the same company struck in sympathy; their contract, however, contained the no-strike-arbitration agreement. The employer filed for an injunction to halt the production workers' sympathy strike. The case ultimately came before the Supreme Court, which ruled that the arbitration provisions in the production workers' contract did not apply to sympathy strikes because injunctions could be issued only when the dispute over which workers struck was *arbitrable.* The sympathy strike does not fall into this category and cannot be negotiated between union A and employer A because the dispute is between union B and employer A. The court ruled that under these circumstances an injunction could not be issued to block strike action. Otherwise, the *Boys Markets* ruling set legal precedent and strike activity will be enjoined.

The Supreme Court's ruling in *Buffalo Forge* held an implicit message regarding an injunction to halt any form of wildcat strike action, including particularly a sympathy strike: employers should expressly include the sympathy strike in the language of the labor contract's no-strike pledge. Alternatively and perhaps more simply, employers could merely insert provisions in the contract to prohibit sympathy strikes altogether; for instance, that any participation in an "unofficial" strike would result in discharge. Either way, the law again provided employers a means of disabling the strike. It was precisely conflict over this issue that triggered the coal miners' strike in 1977.

Following the developments in *Buffalo Forge* in 1976, it is not difficult to derive the logic that led to the coal miners' strike in 1977, a dispute that drew national attention and involved thousands of organized mine workers. Rank and file members of the United Mineworkers rejected a contract that would have allowed mine owners to prohibit any form of a wildcat strike, including particularly the sympathy strike, a form of action not uncommon in mining. The proposed contract permitted the employer to fire workers who had "picketed or otherwise been actively involved in causing an unauthorized work stoppage or sympathy strike" (cited in Lynd 1978:16). Throughout the 1970s wildcat strikes over health hazards and employer disciplinary policies originating in a single mine and evoking sympathy strikes in other mines had caused problems of "worker instability" in the mining industry (see Table 8.1, columns 4 and 5; Nyden and Nyden 1978). Injunctions under *Boys Markets* had not hindered this practice. Mine owners sought to remedy the problem by prohibiting unofficial strike action in the labor contract. The miners' strike lasted nearly four months, but in the end was broken by the strength of the opposition, and the union's membership accepted the contract that contained stiff penalties for wildcat strike action. Wildcat strikes in the mining industry fell off noticeably after the *Buffalo Forge* ruling in 1976 (see Table 8.1, column 5), but dropped appreciably more with the defeat of the mine workers in 1978.

The events of 1976 to 1978—the ruling in *Buffalo Forge* and the national publicity given to the defeat of the mine workers—greatly reduced the number and frequency of wildcat strikes in the mining industry (Table 8.1, columns 4 and 5). They also noticeably reduced the overall number of wildcat and sympathy strikes. Prior to the ruling in *Buffalo Forge* roughly a third of all strikes took place during the term of a labor contract (Table 8.1, column 6). By 1980 this percentage had fallen by over 60 percent so that only about 13 percent of all strikes were wildcat strikes. Sympathy strikes (almost but not quite a subset of wildcat strikes) have historically been a very small proportion—between 1 and 2 percent—of the total number of strikes (U.S. Bureau of Labor Statistics 1949–80); however, during 1976 and 1980 the percentage of sympathy strikes fell almost 100 percent, particularly dropping off between 1977 and 1978 with the defeat of the miners' union. Interestingly, after 1976, again the

Table 8.1. Number and Frequency of Strikes during Term of Contract (Referred to here as "Wildcats") for All Industries and for Manufacturing and Mining, 1961–1980[a]

Year	*Number of Strikes Terminated by Injunction*	*Number of Wildcat Strikes in MFG*	*Frequency of Wildcat Strikes in MFG*	*Number of Wildcat Strikes in Mining*	*Frequency of Wildcat Strikes in Mining*	*Percent of all Strikes that Are Wildcat Strikes*
1961	—[b]	426	26.1	115	171.1	32.2
1962	—	408	24.2	124	190.8	29.8
1963	—	430	25.3	127	200.0	35.8
1964	—	480	27.8	115	181.4	36.0
1965	—	479	26.5	153	242.1	34.7
1966	—	668	34.8	151	240.8	36.5
1967	—	664	34.1	201	327.9	33.9
1968	—	675	34.1	259	427.4	31.3
1969	—	758	37.6	457	738.3	34.5
1970	96	593	30.6	508	816.7	33.4
1971	118	488	26.3	607	996.7	33.1
1972	155	484	25.4	964	1542.4	39.8
1973	195	402	20.0	1046	1642.2	33.9
1974	210	331	16.6	989	1425.1	26.6
1975	168	217	11.8	1134	1508.0	34.4
1976	169	262	13.8	1385	1777.9	34.5
1977	54	265	13.5	953	1172.2	26.5
1978	41	228	11.1	236	277.3	15.5
1979	—	217	10.3	405	422.8	16.2
1980	—	134	6.6	257	250.2	13.4

Notes:

[a]Operationalizations and data sources by column: (1) Number of strikes terminated by an injunction granted to an employer, AWS MLR; (2) Number of wildcat strikes in manufacturing, AWS; (3) Number of wildcat strikes in manufacturing/million wage and salary earners in manufacturing, AWS HS HLS MLR; (4) Number of wildcat strikes in mining, AWS; (5) Number of wildcat strikes in mining/million wage and salary earners in mining, AWS HS HLS MLR; (6) Number of wildcat strikes/number of all strikes, AWS SA. Abbreviations (all printed in Washington, DC, by the U.S. Government Printing Office): AWS U.S. Bureau of Labor Statistics, *Analysis of Work Stoppages*, various years; HLS U.S. Dept. of Labor, *Handbook of Labor Statistics*, various years; HS U.S. Bureau of the Census, *Historical Statistics of the United States: Colonial Times to 1970, 1975*; MLR U.S. Bureau of Labor Statistics, *Monthly Labor Review*, various years; SA U.S. Bureau of the Census, *Statistical Abstract of the United States*, various years.

[b]Data not available.

year of *Buffalo Forge*, the number of injunctions used against striking workers to end the strike fell off (Table 8.1, column 1), possibly because injunctions had been partially replaced by contract provisions barring unofficial strikes.

In retrospect, these legal developments limiting the wildcat strike are not surprising. The law seeks to suppress the wildcat strike not just because this type of strike has become a breach of the labor contract, but because a wildcat strike is constituted of workers acting on their collective interests and using their most powerful economic weapon: a spontaneous and unpredictable disruption of production. It is action that is not immediately routed into "legitimate" and peaceful channels by management or union leadership. The wildcat strike is a pure and unrestrained demonstration of the structural power of collective worker solidarity.

The suggestion to employers that they prevent wildcat strikes by forbidding them in labor contracts, the ratification of such an agreement with organized miners in 1978, and the entire judicial development of the law that narrowed the "problem" of wildcat strikes to this juncture, contributed to changes in strike action in two ways. First, these developments in the law have contributed at least in some measure to a decline of strike activity in this country. Wallace, Rubin, and Smith (1988) find that the passage of Taft-Hartley and Landrum-Griffin, in particular, served to reduce organizational and wage strikes, respectively. Figure 1 plots annual levels of strike frequency for all strikes and for strikes over wages and over union organizing between 1881 and 1980. The plot of frequencies for all strikes shows that strike occurrence was higher in the years prior to the enactment of Wagner, Taft-Hartley, and the institutionalization of collective bargaining than in later years.[2] The average annual strike frequency between 1881 and 1920 is 132 strikes per million workers. Between 1935 and 1980 the level is 39 percent lower at 80 strikes per million workers; between 1947 and 1980, the period since Taft-Hartley, the figure declines to 73 strikes per million workers annually.

But the critical decline in strike frequency has not occurred for strikes over wages, benefits, hours, and other terms of employment. The level of these strikes has hovered around 40 strikes per million workers annually since the 1940s (see Figure 8.1). Rather, the declines have occurred for strikes concerning issues of workplace control, and this points to the second outcome of developments in the law. The law has contributed to changes not only in the overall frequency of strikes, but also in the form or goal of the strike: strikes are far less likely today to occur over issues concerning workplace control and are far more likely to be about wages and wage-related demands than they were in the 1930s and 1940s.

Following Montgomery (1979:98), control strikes are defined here as strikes concerning "enforcement of work rules, union recognition, discharge of unpopular foremen or retention of popular ones, regulations of layoffs or dismissals, and actions of sympathy with other groups of workers." Unfortunately, pre-1947 data are available for only one component of control strike activity: strikes concerning unionization issues such as recognition, certification, and strengthening of bargaining position (see footnote 2). This subset of control strikes, after being quite high between 1933 and 1947, has continued to decline in frequency since.

It is too simple to see this decline as a result of the empowerment of workers by the Wagner Act and its protections of worker organization and action. Wagner did empower workers in this sense by giving them the legal right to organize unions. But worker organizational power as measured by union density has declined dramatically since the mid-1950s, falling by roughly 40 percent between then and 1980, and the decline continues up to the present (Griffin, McCammon, and Botsko 1990). Moreover, as I have argued, the subsequent interpretation, application, and amendments of the Wagner Act have in many other ways removed from labor's repertoire forms of collective action that could greatly enhance the power of organized workers.

A more encompassing measure of control strikes, including, for example, strikes over union organizing, job security, plant administration issues, and sympathy strikes available after 1946, confirms that the frequency of control strikes has been dropping

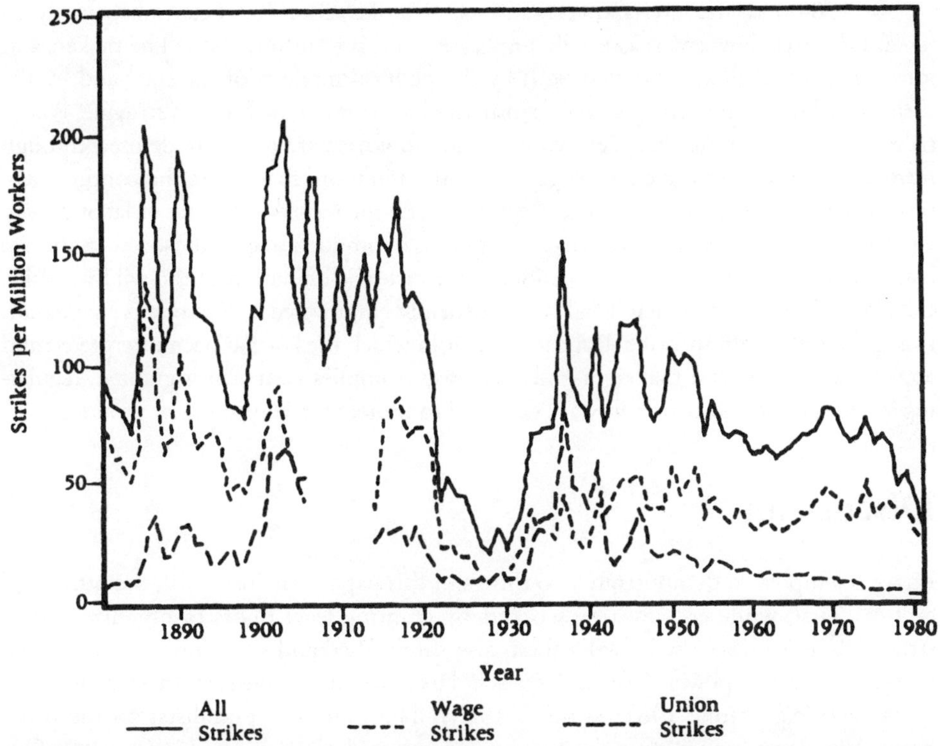

Figure 8.1. Frequency of All Strikes, Strikes over Wages, and Strikes over Union Organizing, 1881–1981[a]

Notes:

[a]Operationalization and data sources: strike frequency = number of strikes/wage and salary earners, AWS ERP HS SA. Abbreviations: (see Table 1) ERP *Economic Report of the President*, various years, Washington, DC, U.S. Government Printing Office.

since Taft-Hartley. Between 1947 and 1980 the frequency of control strikes dropped by nearly 80 percent with a strong downward time trend for the entire period (b = −.80). In the late 1940s there were roughly forty strikes over control-related issues annually for every million workers; by 1980 this figure had fallen to nine. Correspondingly, the percentage of all strikes over control issues fell from nearly 50 percent in 1947 to 20 percent in 1980, while the percentage of strikes over wages and similar matters rose during this period from 46 to 71 percent.[3]

This substantial decline in control strikes can be directly linked to the decline in wildcat strikes. Roughly 85 percent of strikes taking place during a contract (a measure of wildcat strikes; see footnote 1 above) concern issues of workplace control, whereas roughly the same large percentage of strikes occurring between labor contracts are over wages and related issues (U.S. Bureau of Labor Statistics 1970–80). In short, the developments in the law that effectively ban the wildcat strike from U.S. labor–capital relations also nearly completely ban strikes over issues concerning workplace control.

By 1980 both the level and content of U.S. strike action had been substantially altered. Labor relations law is assuredly implicated in this transformation. The makers and interpreters of the law, prompted both by the political interests of the state and by the course of labor–capital struggle, have constructed a narrow arena for class struggle. Potentially disruptive disputes between workers and employers are generally defused through formal legal procedures, such as bargaining and arbitration, that assure the continuity of production. The issues of legitimate dispute, chiefly the terms of the sale of labor power, are closely circumscribed; unavoidable disruptions of production over those few legitimate issues are made as predictable as possible to the virtual elimination of the wildcat strike. U.S. labor law since the New Deal has undeniably empowered U.S. workers by guaranteeing them the right to strike. But the manner in which the law has been interpreted and applied has constrained that right and the power it implies even as it is granted, regulating workers' collective action in ways designed to protect the continuity of production.

Discussion

I have attempted to demonstrate two things in this paper, one historical, the other theoretical. First, while empowering workers by granting legal rights to organize and to strike, labor law since the New Deal has also diminished and substantially constrained workers' collective power. Critical legal scholars and others have seen these constraints in the law (e.g., Stone 1981; Tomlins 1985). The industrial pluralists, on the other hand, have long argued that the law has empowered workers (Leiserson 1959; Cox 1960). In this paper, I have tried to show that the New Deal labor relations policies concerning strike action have not been designed and interpreted either simply to empower or to repress workers. Rather, the Wagner Act, its interpretation, and application have accomplished both—workers are simultaneously strengthened and weakened by the law. This is achieved by an implicit acceptance by the law's custodians that the purpose of the strike is to facilitate bargaining between organized workers and employers but not to interrupt production. In fact, the law's framers clearly realize the harm of interrupted production for capital accumulation and have thus designed and implemented the law such that the right to strike provided in it serves to foster collective bargaining but not the structural power of workers.

This is the historical argument of this paper. But the paper also builds on a theoretical argument about the state in a capitalist democracy. State policymaking is a product of class struggle, struggle taking place in both economic and political arenas. One way in which capitalism—an economic system based on the private ownership and control of property by a few—can coexist with democracy—a political system based on public decision-making about the public welfare—is that the premises of one of those systems are compromised. Since capitalism and democracy have coexisted since the Second World War in relative stability in most of the advanced industrial nations (Therborn 1977), one can ask whether and to what extent one set of principles has been compromised.

This study shows that labor law in the United States promises to workers a set of rights to give them equal power in their negotiations with capital over the conditions of work. The law establishes a set of procedures—the recognition of elected union representatives as partners to capital in collective bargaining and arbitration proceedings, each party's rights of appeal, and labor's right to strike to give teeth to its demands—to rectify a past imbalance of power. But while the law guarantees rights to certain *processes*, it does not guarantee the *substance* of these legal processes. For example, the Wagner Act does not specify that all strikes are legal; it does not specify that workers always have legal recourse to the strike; and it does not specify that an employer's action may never interfere with a strike. To workers' detriment, there is instead a separation in the law between procedure and substance. This has allowed a political space in which adjustments in the law can be made. Time and again, as this paper has shown, the courts, the NLRB, and Congress have adapted the law to the exigencies of capitalist production, and it is these adjustments that have gradually delineated the legal boundaries of collective worker action. Through all of this, the strike has been rendered negotiable, predictable, less effective, and less likely.

Workers can strike, but only over a narrow, legally defined spectrum of issues concerning the conditions of the sale of their labor power and not over issues concerning control of production generally. Restricting strike action to the first set of issues makes conflict between an employer and workers negotiable, often positive sum, but non-threatening to the unilateral control of production by capital. Workers can strike, but some forms of the strike—those typically initiated spontaneously by workers during the term of a labor contract and which are frequently over issues concerning workplace control—have been defined as illegal. In this way, strike action has been made more predictable, allowing employers to plan strategies to avoid the negative economic consequences of a strike if it does occur. Workers can strike, but only under provisions in the law that render the strike less effective. Employers have the right to hire permanent replacements, union picketing is highly regulated, and unions have only limited rights to fine union members who cross picket lines. Workers can strike, but the law tends to channel industrial disputes into nondisruptive modes of behavior such as collective bargaining and arbitration, reducing overall the likelihood of a strike.

The structural power of employers in a capitalist system, as Block (1987) explains, is their capacity to withdraw their investment capital. This capacity constrains state actions. States, materially dependent on a share of the profits generated by capitalist investments, will implement policy to promote a stable climate for business investments. Workers, as full participants in the economy, have structural power as well. They can collectively withdraw their labor power and, thus, should be able to constrain the actions of the state and of capital as well. In the 1930s in this country workers vividly demonstrated this collective capacity, and they won not just a legal right to organize, to bargain, and to strike, but they forced the practical acceptance of these rights by capital. Today, workers have a legal right to strike, but since the enactment of the New Deal legislation, the structural power of the strike has been severely crippled, if not negated, through the practice of U.S. labor relations law. As a result, workers may be left with little real power in the workplace to shape future conditions of work.

Notes

1. A wildcat strike is not precisely the same thing as a strike taking place during the term of a contract (Byrne and King 1986). Wildcats are explicitly those without the support of the national or international union, whereas some strikes during the course of a contract are permitted

by the contract and are thus legitimate in the eyes of the union. Because most contracts contain no-strike clauses, however, most intracontractual strikes are in fact wildcat strikes. Data specifically for wildcats are not available. Operationalizations and data sources are provided in Table 1.

2. Employer repression of worker organization and action that took place during the 1920s, often with the aid of the state, may explain the dramatic drop in strike frequency during this exceptional period (Griffin, Wallace, and Rubin 1986). Data for the number of all strikes are available over this entire period, but data for various types of strikes are not available between 1905 and 1914.

3. Wallace (1989) argues that today only plant administration strikes can be said to represent worker attempts to achieve greater control over the conditions of employment, suggesting that trends in this measure must be examined to discern the current state of control strikes. Plant administration strikes surged during the early 1970s, but sharply tapered off beginning in 1976, the same year as *Buffalo Forge*. Also, the correlation between frequency of plant administration strikes and frequency of wildcat strikes in the mining industry between 1961 and 1980, the years for which data are available, is very high (r = .85). It appears that the surge and decline in these control strikes was largely driven by the circumstances in the mining industry discussed above.

References

Aaron, Benjamin. 1964. "Labor Injunctions in the State Courts-Part II: A Critique." *Virginia Law Review* 50:1147–64.

Aaron, Benjamin and W. Levin. 1951. "Labor Injunctions in Action: A Five-Year Survey in Los Angeles County." *California Law Review* 39:42–67.

Ashenfelter, Orley C., G. E. Johnson, and John H. Pencavel. 1972. "Trade Unions and the Rate of Change of Money Wages in United States Manufacturing Industry." *Review of Economic Studies* 39:27–54.

Atleson, James B. 1983. *Values and Assumptions in American Labor Law*. Amherst, MA: University of Massachusetts Press.

———. 1985. "The Circle of Boys Markets: A Comment Of Judicial Inventiveness." *Industrial Relations Law Journal* 7:88–108.

Bakke, E. Wright, Clark Kerr, and Charles W. Anrod. 1960. *Unions, Management, and the Public*. New York: Harcourt, Brace, and World.

Benetar, David L. 1961. "Voting Rights of Replaced Economic Strikers and of Their Replacements." In *Symposium on the Labor-Management Reporting and Disclosure Act of 1959*, Ed. Ralph Slovenko, 779–84. Baton Rouge, LA: Claitor.

Bernstein, Irving. 1969. *The Turbulent Years: A History Of The American Worker 1933–1941*. Boston: Houghton-Mifflin.

Block, Fred. 1987. *Revising State Theory: Essays in Politics and Postindustrialism*. Philadelphia: Temple University Press.

Brody, David. 1980. *Workers in Industrial America: Essays on 20th Century Struggles*. New York: Oxford University Press.

Business Week. 1978. "Coors Undercuts its Last Big Union." *Business Week* 2544:47–48.

Byrne, Dennis M., and Randall H. King. 1986. "Wildcat Strikes in U.S. Manufacturing, 1960–1977." *Journal of Labor Research* 7:387–401.

Chamberlain, Neil W. and James W. Kuhn. 1986. *Collective Bargaining*. New York: McGraw-Hill.

Cortner, Richard C. 1970. *The Jones and Laughlin Case*. New York: Alfred A. Knopf.

Cox, Archibald. 1960. *Law and the National Labor Policy*. Los Angeles: University of California Press.

Davis, Mike. 1986. *Prisoners of the American Dream*. London: Verso.

Domhoff, G. William. 1983. *Who Rules America Now? A View for The '80s*. New York: Simon & Schuster.

———. 1987. "The Wagner Act and Theories of the State: A New Analysis Based on Class-Segment Theory." *Political Power and Social Theory* 6:159–85.

Dunlop, John T. 1958. *Industrial Relations Systems*. Carbondale: Southern Illinois University Press.

Edwards, P. K. 1981. *Strikes in the United States, 1881–1974*. New York: St. Martin's Press.

Edwards, Richard C. 1979. *Contested Terrain: The Transformation of the Workplace in the 20th Century*. New York: Basic.

English, Carey W. 1983. "Strike No Longer a Scary Word to Companies." *U.S. News & World Report* 95(14):72–73.

Estreicher, Samuel. 1987. "Strikers And Replacements." *Labor Law Journal* 38:287–96.

Goldfield, Michael. 1989. "Worker Insurgency, Radical Organization, and New Deal Labor Legislation." *American Political Science Review* 83:1257–82.

Griffin, Larry J., Holly J. McCammon, and Christopher Botsko. 1990. "The 'Unmaking' of a Movement? The Crisis of U.S. Trade Unions in Comparative Perspective." In *Change In Societal Institutions*, Ed. Maureen Hallinan. New York: Plenum.

Griffin, Larry J., Michael E. Wallace, and Beth A. Rubin. 1986. "Capitalist Resistance to the Organization of Labor before the New Deal: Why? How? Success?" *American Sociological Review* 51:147–67.

Gross, James A. 1974. *The Making of the National Labor Relations Board: A Study in Economics, Politics, and the Law*, vol 1. Albany: State University of New York Press.

Gunderson, Morley and Angelo Melino. 1987. "Estimating Strike Effects in a General Model of Prices and Quantities." *Journal of Labor Economics* 5:1–19.

Herman, E. Edward and Alfred Kuhn. 1981. *Collective Bargaining and Labor Relations*. Englewood Cliffs, NJ: Prentice-Hall.

Hoerr, John. 1985. "A Host of Strikebreakers Is Tipping the Scale against Labor." *Business Week*, July 15, 32.

Hurd, Rick. 1976. "New Deal Labor Policy and the Containment of Radical Union Activity." *Review of Radical Political Economics* 8:32–43.

Jenkins, J. Craig and Barbara G. Brents. 1989. "Social Protest, Hegemonic Competition, and Social Reform: A Political Struggle Interpretation of the Origins of the American Welfare State." *American Sociological Review* 54:891–909.

Klare, Karl E. 1978. "Judicial Deradicalization of the Wagner Act and the Origins of Modern Legal Consciousness, 1937–1941." *Minnesota Law Review* 62:265–339.

———. 1981. "Labor Law as Ideology: Toward a New Historiography of Collective Bargaining Law." *Industrial Relations Law Journal* 4:450–82.

———. 1983. "Labor Law and the Liberal Political Imagination." *Socialist Review* 62:45–71.

———. 1989. "Can There Be Justice in the Supreme Court? The Replacement Worker Ain't Nothing but a Lousy Scab." *Labor Today* 28:15.

Leiserson, William M. 1959. *American Trade Union Democracy*. New York: Columbia University Press.

Lichtenstein, Nelson. 1975. "Defending the No-Strike Pledge: CIO Politics during WWII." *Radical America* 9:49–75.

Lynd, Staughton. 1978. "Labor and the Law: Issues Raised by the Coal Strike." *In These Times*, April, 5–11

———. 1979. "Investment Decisions and the Quid Pro Quo Myth." *Case Western Reserve Law Review* 29:396–427.

Michelson, Peter. 1978. "Coors Beer, the Union Buster." *The Nation*, April 15, 434–36.

Millis, Harry A. and Emily Clark Brown. 1950. *From the Wagner Act to Taft-Hartley: A Study of National Labor Policy and Labor Relations*. Chicago: University of Chicago Press.

Montgomery, David. 1979. *Workers' Control in America: Studies in the History of Work, Technology, and Labor Struggles*. New York: Cambridge University Press.

National Labor Relations Board. *Annual Report (1960–1980)*. Washington, DC: U.S. Government Printing Office.

Neumann, G. and M. Reder. 1984. "Output and Strike Activity in U.S. Manufacturing: How Large Are the Losses?" *Industrial and Labor Relations Review* 37:197–211.

Nyden, Linda and Paul Nyden. 1978. *Showdown in Coal: The Struggle for Rank-and-File Unionism*. Pittsburgh, PA: Miner's Report.

O'Connor, James. 1973. *The Fiscal Crisis of the State*. New York: St. Martin's Press.

Offe, Claus. 1974. "Structural Problems of the Capitalist State." In *German Political Studies*, Ed. Klaus Von Beyme, 31–57. London: Sage.

Perlman, Selig. 1928. *A Theory of the Labor Movement*. New York: Macmillan.

Perry, Charles, Andrew M. Kramer, and Thomas J. Schneider. 1982. Operating during Strikes: Company Experience, NLRB Policies, and Governmental Regulations. *Labor Relations and Public Policy Series* 23. Philadelphia: University of Pennsylvania Press.

Piven, Frances Fox and Richard A. Cloward. 1979. *Poor People's Movements: Why They Succeed, How They Fail*. New York: Vintage.

Poulantzas, Nicos. 1968 [1973]. *Political Power and Social Classes*. London: New Left Books.

———. 1980 [1978]. *State, Power, Socialism*. London: New Left Books.

Przeworski, Adam. 1985. *Capitalism and Social Democracy*. New York: Cambridge University Press.

Rogers, Joel. 1984. "*Divide and Conquer: The Legal Foundations of Postwar U.S. Labor Policy*." Ph.D. dissertation, Princeton University.

Rubin, Beth A. 1986. "Class Struggle American Style: Unions, Strikes and Wages." *American Sociological Review* 51:618–31.

Rubin, Beth A., Larry J. Griffin, and Michael E. Wallace. 1983. "Provided Only that Their Voice Was Strong." *Work and Occupations* 10:325–47.

Satchell, Michael and Sharon F. Golden. 1987. "The Strikers Strike Out." *U.S. News and World Report*, October 26, 41–42.

Schatzki, G. 1984. "Some Observations about the Standards Applied to Labor Injunction Litigation under Section 10(J) And 10(1) of The National Labor Relations Act." *Indiana Law Journal* 59:565–81.

Shatz, S. F. 1977. "Picketing Injunction in California: A Study of the Role of the Courts in Farm Labor Disputes." *Hastings Law Journal* 28:801–75.

Skocpol, Theda. 1980. "Political Response to Capitalist Crisis: Neo-Marxist Theories of the State and the Case of the New Deal." *Politics and Society* 10:155–201.

Sockell, Donna R. and John. T. Delaney. 1987. "The Scope of Bargaining: Who Wins when Fewer Issues Are Mandatory Bargaining Subjects?" *Labor Studies Journal* 11:103–16.

Stone, Katherine. 1981. "The Post-War Paradigm in American Labor Law." *Yale Law Review* 90:1509–80.

Stryker, Robin. 1989. "Limits on the Technocratization of the Law: The Elimination of the National Labor Relations Board's Division of Economic Research." *American Sociological Review* 54:341–58.

Taylor, Benjamin J. and Fred Witney. 1987. *Labor Relations Law*. Englewood Cliffs, NJ: Prentice-Hall.

Therborn, Goran. 1977. "The Rule of Capital and the Rise of Democracy." *New Left Review* 103:3–41.

Tomlins, Christopher L. 1985. *The State and the Unions: Labor Relations, Law, and the Organized Labor Movement in America, 1880–1960*. New York: Cambridge University Press.

U.S. Bureau of Labor Statistics. 1949–80. *Analysis of Work Stoppages*. Washington, DC: U.S. Government Printing Office.

U.S. Bureau of the Census. 1975. *Historical Statistics of the United States: Colonial Times to 1970*. Washington, DC: U.S. Government Printing Office.

U.S. Federal Mediation and Conciliation Service. 1961–79. *Annual Report*. Washington, DC: U.S. Government Printing Office.

Wallace, Michael E. 1989. "Aggressive Economism, Defensive Control: Contours of American Labor Militancy, 1947–1981." *Economic and Industrial Democracy* 10:7–34.

Wallace, Michael, Beth A. Rubin, and Brian T. Smith. 1988. "American Labor Law: Its Impact on Working-Class Militancy, 1901–1980." *Social Science History* 12:1–29.

Waye, J. V. 1985. "'Reverse' Boys Markets Injunctions: The Growing Importance of Section 301 Actions to Restrain Employer Activity." *Employee Relations Law* 11:56–71.

Weiler, Paul. 1983. "Promises to Keep: Securing Workers' Rights to Self-Organization under the NLRA." *Harvard Law Review* 96:1769–1827.

Cases Cited

Allis-Chalmers Manufacturing Co. (NLRB v.), 388 U.S. 175 (1967)

American Manufacturing Co. (United Steelworkers of America v.), 353 U.S. 564 (1960)

Borg-Warner Corp., Wooster Div. (NLRB v.), 356 U.S. 342 (1958)

Boys Market, Inc. v. Retail Clerks, 398 U.S. 235 (1970)

Buffalo Forge v. United Steelworkers of America, 428 U.S. 397 (1976)

Cory Corp., 84 NLRB 110 (1949)

Dalmo Victor, Machinists, Local 1327, 263 NLRB 984 (1982)

Enterprise Wheel and Car Corp. (United Steelworkers of America v.), 363 U.S. 593 (1960)

Fansteel Metallurgical Co., (NLRB v.), 360 U.S. 240 (1939)

Fibreboard Paper Products v. NLRB, 379 U.S. 203 (1964)

First National Maintenance Corp. v. NLRB, 449 U.S. 1079 (1981)

Fleetwood Trailor Co. (NLRB v.), 389 U.S. 375 (1967)

Gateway Coal Co. v. United Mine Workers, 414 U.S. 368 (1974)

Granite State Joint Board, 409 U.S. 213 (1972)

Jones and Laughlin Steel Corp. (NLRB v.), 301 U.S. 1 (1937)

Laidlaw Corp., 171 NLRB 175 (1968)

Lincoln Mills of Alabama (Textile Workers Union of America v.), 353 U.S. 448 (1957)

Lucas Flour Co. (Local 174, Teamsters v.), 369 U.S. 95 (1962)

Mackay Radio and Telegraph Co. (NLRB v.), 304 U.S. 333 (1938)

Neufeld Porsche-Audi, Machinists, Local 1414, 270 NLRB No. 209 (1984)

Sartorius, A. & Co., Inc., 10 NLRB 493 (1938)
Schecter Poultry Corp. v. United States, 295 U.S. 495 (1935)
Sinclair Refining Co. v. Atkinson, 370 U.S. 238 (1962)
Sunset Line and Twine, 79 NLRB 1487 (1948)
United Aircraft Corp., 192 NLRB 62 (1971)
Warrior and Gulf Navigation (United Steelworkers of America v.), 363 U.S. 574 (1960)
Wurlitzer, Rudolph Co., 32 NLRB 163 (1941)

CHAPTER 9

The Racial Basis of Capitalism and the State, and the Impact of the New Deal on African Americans

Steve Valocchi

Sociologists have long been attracted to the Great Depression and the New Deal as historical settings for their research. Whether the subject is social movements, changes in the structure of work and economy, or the increased and changing role of the state, the Depression decade provides one of those pivotal historical moments when previous patterns of social relationships were destroyed, and the conflicts, tensions, and causal processes involved in the creation of important new patterns were starkly revealed. If there is one paradigmatic thread that unites this diverse literature on the 1930s, it is a concern with social class and the state an implicit assumption that class and state structures and relations are at once the constitutive features of American society as well as the features that underwent the most profound changes during this time.[1]

These assumptions are clearly seen in the research on policymaking during the New Deal. Although this research does not agree as to which causal process a class-centered or state-centered process best accounts for the timing and shape of the New Deal social reforms, both theoretical camps agree that the New Deal was the defining moment of American liberalism as it delivered policies and established programs that provided politically guaranteed security to those most vulnerable to the shifting economic winds of the capitalist market (Quadagno 1988a; Weir, Orloff, and Skocpol 1988).

This essay does not dispute this claim. Instead, it tempers this claim and deepens the causal analyses that support this claim by bringing race to the center of the analysis. I argue three points. First, and for the most part downplayed by both class-centered and state-centered perspectives, the creation of the New Deal welfare state was a racially based affair. Many of the programs and policies of the New Deal, while improving the conditions of the poor and the working class, discriminated against African Americans or were implemented in a discriminatory manner. Second, many race-specific policies—policies that were necessary to enable blacks to have effective citizenship status in order to take full advantage of the emerging programs of the welfare state—were not pursued or seen as relevant to the larger liberal agenda. Third, many of the causal dynamics documented by the class-centered and state-centered perspectives do not adequately capture the racial basis of the class interests, party processes and state structures that together delivered a racially exclusive welfare state.

These accounts need to be supplemented or built on a greater appreciation of the role of race, racism, and the changing nature of racial subjugation in the structure and functioning of U.S. capitalism and democracy. In constructing a theory of racial formation, Michael Omi and Howard Winant (1986) argue that, although the concept of race must be seen as an autonomous arena of social relations, it must also be situated historically in the economic and political institutions that give meaning and consequence to these social relations. States, in their view, do more than simply distribute income, goods, and services; they accomplish these activities along racial lines: "they enforce racial (non)discrimination policies . . . [and] organize racial identities" (Omi and Winant 1986: 77).

After a brief summary of the existing accounts of policymaking during the New Deal accounts that are based on the dynamics and organization of capitalism and democracy in the United States I discuss the racial basis of capitalism and democracy as a prelude to reframing the policymaking process of the New Deal.

Existing Paradigms of Policymaking during the New Deal

Recent research in the class-centered explanation of policymaking during the New Deal has argued that the New Deal received much of its urgency from a tidal wave of protest among the unemployed, industrial workers, and the elderly, and at least part of its agenda was motivated by a desire to sop up this discontent (Goldfield 1989; Jenkins and Brents 1989; Piven and Cloward 1971). Also, business elites were actively involved in the policymaking processes of both the social welfare and labor legislation, and these elites fashioned this legislation in accordance with private profit (Quadagno 1984; Domhoff 1990). Finally, this research emphasizes the power of southern planters, as represented in the Democratic party, in putting the brakes on many of the provisions of the New Deal that would nationalize relief programs or undercut segregation and a caste system of labor (Quadagno 1988b).

While accurately portraying the ways in which the class interests of both capital and labor influenced the policymaking process, the class perspective does not seriously consider the ways in which these interests were racially constructed. In other words, it does not examine the policymaking consequences of the racially exclusive organizations of either the working class or the capitalist class; nor does it examine the racial basis of profit making for any other group besides the southern planters.

The research from the state-centered perspective of policymaking during the New Deal locates the reform impulse in the Progressive Era and in the efforts of liberal reformers in Congress and in organizations that had historical ties to that era and contemporary ties to the trade union movement. In this state-centered view, the reformist impulse of these Congressmen and organizations was frustrated not by capitalists nor pushed into the public arena by workers, but was molded by the basic characteristics of U.S. public administration. Characterized by the absence of a state bureaucracy, limited civil service reform, and the dispersion of authority in a federalist political structure, the U.S. state remained institutionally handicapped in its efforts to develop and implement ideologically consistent social policy for broad categories of recipients. This weakness was reinforced by the patronage-based system of benefit distribution by political parties that persisted, despite periodic attacks, well into the post-World War II period. In this context, according to the state-centered view, no administrative structure existed to plan and implement the ideas coming from these "progressive" forces in both the administration and Congress.

While this perspective highlights the ways in which the structure and functioning of the state and parties shaped the reform process, it does not seriously consider the policy consequences of the racial basis of both the state and the party systems. Federalism, party competition, and patronage, to name just a few of the variables seen as important in the state-centered perspective, were built on or operated according to the principle of racial exclusion or subjugation. This principle needs to be recovered and elucidated to understand the racially exclusive nature of the New Deal welfare state.

The Racial Basis of U.S. Capitalism

In a sweeping theoretical and historical analysis of "American exceptionalism,"[2] Michael Goldfield (1990: 89) asserts that the development of American capitalism is closely tied to white supremacy: "The development of a system of white supremacy and the ideology used to justify it originates from and is based on the socioeconomic system." A strict racial classification system and the bondage, slavery, and servitude that accompanied it were constructed by economic elites to satisfy their demand for exploitable labor (cf. Fredrickson 1981). Class theorists, particularly Jill Quadagno (1988b; cf. Domhoff 1990), have also pointed to the economic interests of elites derived from the feudalistic plantation mode of production in the South as preventing the introduction of national pensions. When Depression conditions and working-class protest demanded state action, these same southern planter elites fashioned a system that could be manipulated according to the labor requirements of a plantation economy (Domhoff 1990; Goldfield 1989). In this way, the class power of these elites rested firmly first on slavery and then on the racial subjugation built into the crop lien and debt bondage system of sharecropping (McAdam 1982).

Economic elites in the South, however, were not the only elites whose power rested on racial subjugation. As northern manufacturers resolved their economic differences with planters over the tariff, and as they came to increasingly rely on cheaply produced cotton from the South, these manufacturers joined bankers in implicit support for the southern plantation economy (Domhoff 1972). Their profits were essentially underwritten by the racial subjugation of cotton production (Albion 1939). In addition, there was another, more direct way—a way closer to the homes of northern manufacturers—in which racial subjugation contributed to profit and hence to their economic power. That was the use of racial divisions in their own work force to undercut the organized power of labor and to lower the overall price of that labor.

In the late nineteenth and early twentieth centuries, northern capitalists routinely used the increasing racial and ethnic heterogeneity of the U.S. working class to lower labor costs and pit one worker, one ethnic group, against another. The historical and sociological accounts of workplace organization and conflict, and worker militancy and organization, are replete with the many variations on this dynamic: employers sending labor recruiters to the South to find "lower-priced" black labor to work in the factories of the North; employers using blacks or members of some "other" ethnic group as strike breakers during a labor–management conflict; employers strategically placing members of one ethnic group as foremen or supervisors over members of another ethnic group or organizing the shop floor with a job hierarchy that mirrored the hierarchy of racial and ethnic groups in the larger culture (Asher and Stephenson 1990; Bonacich 1976). Although the form of subjugation differed from that of sharecropping in the South ,and although the victims of this subjugation were European and non-European ethnic groups as well as African Americans,[3] this history reminds us that class relations, class power, and class capacities—all features of a class-centered perspective on policymaking—were built on racial inequality.

As suggested above, the organizations and interests of the working class during this time were also profoundly affected by the racial and ethnic heterogeneity of the working class. Even a cursory examination of labor history in the United States reveals a tendency on the part of labor unions and labor-based political parties to exclude rather than include black workers as well as other non-European ethnic groups.[4] Of course, there have been significant episodes of labor solidarity across these racial and ethnic divisions—the early Populist movement, the organizing efforts by the Knights of Labor in the 1880s and 1890s, the International Workers of the World in the first two decades of the twentieth century, and the Communist Party in the 1930s. Their eventual failure as interracial movements as well as the more numerous examples of racial exclusion and discrimination by white working class organizations attests to the power of race in the class formation process.

Also during the first three decades of the twentieth century, processes of economic mobility, political mobilization, and residential mobility among white European ethnics gradually lessened the divisions and hostilities among the white European ethnics as the members of these different ethnic groups found themselves in the same party or union and living in the same neighborhoods. This same process of assimilation did not take place for African Americans. As a matter of fact, and as we will see with the operation of urban politics in the North before the 1930s, one of the ways in which white ethnics assimilated was by collectively denying equal partnership in the political machines to black urban residents.

What does this review of the racial basis of U.S. capitalism tell us about the dynamics of the welfare state in the New Deal period? First, it sensitizes us to look for race differences in the structure and functioning of many of the programs that expanded the federal government's role in lives of the poor and the working class. Second, the class-centered perspective has argued that organized interests derived from the operation of a capitalist economy exerted both direct and indirect control over the shape of the New Deal reforms. The review suggests that imbedded within the concerns of capitalist class factions about private profit, competitiveness, and labor costs and within the concerns of working class factions and organizations about collective security, adequate wages, and the legal right to organize are racial concerns—the continued right to practice racial discrimination.

The Racial Basis of the State

All state-centered analyses of policymaking find that the decentralized nature of the U.S. state influenced whose interests gained ready access to policymakers during the New Deal, which plans were presented as "workable," and how national-level policymakers were selected (Skocpol and Ikenberry 1983; Weir, Orloff, and Skocpol 1988). Of course, it is impossible to understand the origins of this crucial state structure apart from our legacy of racial slavery and the Constitutional compromises hammered out in the late eighteenth century to preserve this slavery in a republic that officially embraced the ideology of the Enlightenment (Fredrickson 1981). As a matter of fact, the frequently noted southern veto in Congress through control of key committees and the filibuster has its origin in the compromise that gave two-thirds representation to slaves but denied them the right to vote. This feature gave greater representation to "the man who lived among slaves than [to] the man who did not" (Goldfield 1990: 96).

The compromise of states' rights, moreover, became the context within which the franchise was extended to white males while denying this extension to blacks and women. Indeed, as Fredrickson (1981) points out, the rapid extension of the franchise by the end of the Jacksonian period occurred as part of a defense of slavery. The South gave its assent to the franchise extension only because it was an extension to whites only. In that way, it was

> well suited to the maintenance of inter-class solidarity between the planters and non-slaveholders within the South. It could also create a bond between the southern planter elite and the insecure and often Negrophobic lower-class whites who helped make up the rank-and-file of the Democratic Party in the North. (Fredrickson 1981: 155)

The early extension of the franchise to white males within a decentralized state structure not only encouraged an activist and localistic politics, but it also encouraged the creation of another political feature frequently highlighted in state-centered accounts of policymaking. The patronage based nature of party organization—the distribution of public jobs, money, and contracts in exchange for political loyalty—fostered an intense fear of fraud, graft, and inefficiency on the part of the middle class, and thus served as an impediment to the creation of a nationally organized system of social provision until the 1930s (Skowroneck 1982).

The late nineteenth and early twentieth century manifestations of patronage politics—the city machines—were both an impediment to the welfare state as well as a substitute welfare state for those who were loyal, politically connected, and above all, white. As Piven and Cloward (1988: 72–73) note, part of the motivation for the attack on the patronage system by "good government" reformers of the Progressive Era came from "American businessmen [who] needed a widening array of governmental supports without the necessity of dealing with party intermediaries or their voter constituencies." For a while, then, business had it both ways: they could attack the fraud and corruption of the city machines as a way to undercut a national welfare system even as they successfully lobbied to get activities such as utility regulation, licensing, and taxation out of the hands of politicians and into the hands of business and civil service-dominated boards, thus creating a welfare state for the rich (Piven and Cloward 1982).[5] In either case, African Americans were subordinated in or excluded from local politics.

Another feature of the state that shaped social policy during the 1930s was the peculiar nature of the American party system.[6] No understanding of the party system on the eve of the New Deal is complete without an analysis of the Compromise of 1877 which involved the withdrawal of federal troops from the South, or of the System of 1896 which involved the decline of party competition in both the North and the South. Together these changes breathed new life into the Southern Democratic party, enabling it to establish Jim Crow and franchise restrictions on blacks. These changes also transformed the Republican Party into a party of big business that aggressively policed labor militancy at home and sponsored imperialist ventures abroad.

As part of the resolution of the contested 1877 election of President Hayes, the Democratic party agreed to concede the election in return for the withdrawal of federal troops from the South. This compromise occurred along with and reinforced other processes that were reinstitutionalizing racial subjugation at the time: the transformation of the Freedman's Bureau into labor contractors for southern planters (Steinberg 1990); the exclusion of blacks from the opportunities afforded by the 1862 Homestead Act, which gave essentially free land in the West to white citizens but denied that land to blacks; and the pressure exerted on the Republican party by northern business to ease its intervention in the South.

The election of 1896 saw the Democratic Party, invigorated by the Populist movement, launch a national campaign against the Republicans. The result was an unprecedented mobilization of corporate money into the Republican Party, a resounding defeat of the Democratic presidential candidate, and the subsequent decline of party competition throughout the country (Piven and Cloward 1988). The election also set into motion a series of changes in election laws and party procedures that effectively disenfranchised a significant portion of working-class voters in the North and the South.

The structure of political parties may have inhibited the institutional capacity of the state, as state-centered theorists argue, but this is only part of the story. Without effective party competition or popular participation, these parties became dominated by economic elites: industrial and banking elites dominated the Republican Party; planter elites dominated the Democratic Party. To the extent that the Democratic Party was a viable entity in the North in the early twentieth century, it survived in urban areas supported and directed by land developers and real estate businessmen (Bucki 1993; Domhoff 1990). When the New Deal did expand state capacity, it did so in the context of these oligarchical party structures. These oligarchies, moreover, and this gets directly to the point of this brief political history, were based on and owed their power to not only class privilege but race privilege as well.

The Impact of the New Deal on African Americans

Evaluations of the New Deal are usually made using categories provided by industrial society, such as its impact on wages, working hours, commodity prices, labor organization, and urban geography. These categories cannot reveal the full impact of the New Deal on African Americans in general, 56 percent of whom lived in rural areas, nor on African-American workers, 40 percent of whom were engaged in agricultural work (Wolters 1970). These evaluations, moreover, are frequently made with reference to the creation of a narrowly defined welfare state. As suggested above, no analysis of the American welfare state has broadened its object of analysis to include discussions of race-specific or civil rights policy.[7]

Following T. H. Marshall (1950), I argue that the extension of social rights to a citizenry assumes the prior extension of civil and political rights. To the extent that this empirically is not the case, then this gap or disjuncture becomes a factor to be explained in the development of the welfare state.[8] To this end, I not only discuss the major emergency and long-term policy initiatives of the first and second New Deals and assess their impact on African Americans,[9] I also discuss the failed civil rights reforms of the New Deal period.

The Agricultural Adjustment Act (AAA) was intended for the depressed agricultural sector of the economy. All accounts of the impact of the act on blacks agree that it caused grave hardship and was the chief source of downward mobility for blacks in the South (Bloom 1986; Wolters 1970). The provisions to reimburse cotton plantation owners for taking cotton out of production caused many owners to drive black tenant farmers off their lands. The act also ignored the social structure of agriculture in the South in that its reimbursement provisions allowed blatant race discrimination. Many black sharecroppers who should have received reimbursements never received them because these reimbursements were held by the planters as payment for rents, or by store owners as payment for bills, or were never distributed by local officials (Hamilton and Hamilton 1986). What were common discriminatory practices in the South were sanctioned by and institutionalized in national legislation.[10]

The National Industrial Recovery Act (NIRA) was the industrial counterpart of AAA and was designed to limit production, raise wages and prices, and stimulate purchasing power. Contrary to the desires of many businessmen, the codes regulating wages and hours were not made explicitly lower for black workers than they were for white workers. They did, however, establish geographical and occupational classifications, and grandfather clauses which permitted lower wages in the South and in occupations in which blacks were concentrated. In other areas where the blanket code of compliance was enforced and where some blacks worked, employers routinely fired blacks rather than pay them the NRA-prescribed minimum wages (Hamilton and Hamilton 1986). The legislation also allowed higher wages in craft unions which excluded blacks. Black workers in agriculture and domestic services who were not covered in the National Recovery Administration (NRA) codes and hence did not experience wage increases, still had to pay the higher prices for commodities mandated under the NRA (Weiss 1983; Wolters 1970). As in AAA, NIRA took what were common practices in the labor market and enshrined them in national legislation and in the implementation of this legislation. Its effect was to widen the economic gulf between black and white workers.

The Works Progress Administration (WPA), the New Deal program that provided public sector jobs to the unemployed, started as emergency jobs legislation that put people to work at union wages. This emergency legislation met resistance from both southerners who feared its impact on the wage structure of the South and representatives of craft unions who feared its impact on the unions' monopoly over public works contracts. WPA, the successor of this emergency legislation, allowed wages to correspond to the wage scale and practices of local labor markets and this change encouraged discrimination against blacks in both the South and the North (Weiss 1983; Wolters 1970).[11] As a black candidate for Chicago's City Council stated, "Fifty percent of Negroes are out of work. We are the last to get jobs, and we have inadequate relief. Some Negroes who get on WPA are removed for white men" (cited in Drake and Cayton 1945: 354). In addition, WPA administrators in the South allowed the release of black workers from WPA jobs to work the fields at harvest time. Mary White Ovington, a member of the NAACP and a member of Roosevelt's cabinet stated that "[work relief] varies according to the white people chosen to administer it, but always there is discrimination" (cited in Wolters 1970: 208).[12]

The institutionalization of discrimination is perhaps best seen in the New Deal's housing programs. In 1937, President Roosevelt expanded the stock of low-income housing but did so with the proviso that housing projects would remain segregated. The National Housing Act of 1934 which established the Home Owners Loan Corporation expanded mortgage loan guarantees for working and middle-class families but, again, did so in a way that fostered segregation and excluded blacks from equal access to the federally insured mortgage market (Kirby 1980; Trotter 1985). The Underwriting Manual of the Federal Housing Administration (FHA), for example, warned banks that "if a neighborhood is to retain stability, it is necessary that properties shall continue to be occupied by the same social and racial classes" (cited in Judd and Hellinger 1991: 740). In the event that this warning was an insufficient cue to banks to retain segregated housing patterns, FHA administrators advised and sometimes required developers of residential projects to draw up restrictive covenants against nonwhites as a condition of obtaining FHA-insured financing (Judd and Hellinger 1991). Rather than combating a housing segregation that was already under way in many northern cities, the New Deal housing programs consolidated this segregation and contributed to the construction of urban ghettoes (Wye 1972).

The most frequently cited examples of New Deal legislation used to illustrate the liberal impulses of the Democratic Party in the 1930s are the labor legislation (section 7a of the NIRA and the National Labor Relations Act in 1935) and the social security legislation (the Social Security Act of 1935). These acts recognized the working class as an important political and social group whose rights needed protection by the federal government. This official "recognition" ignores the fact that the bulk of the black working class was excluded in the definition of protected groups.

The Social Security Act mandated either federal or state governments to provide insurance-based protection in the event of old age, unemployment, and disability. The legislation excluded household domestics and farm laborers, occupational categories accounting for two-thirds of black employment (Kirby 1980). In the occupations that it did cover, the legislation contained no specific prohibitions against discrimination (Weiss 1983). It also provided a large measure of administrative autonomy to local and state officials, thus allowing them to adjust benefits according to local wage structures and manipulate eligibility standards for moral and economic reasons (Biles 1991; Piven and Cloward 1971).

During the deliberations for the Social Security Act, the National Association for the Advancement of Colored People (NAACP) and the National Urban League (NUL) lobbied that the bill include all workers and be administered at the national level (Hamilton and Hamilton 1992).[13] When the NAACP petitioned the American Association for Old Age Security (AAOAS), a liberal reform organization that had done most of the research for and was a major sponsor of the bill, the NAACP was told that the organization could not address the issue of racial discrimination in the legislation. In a memo from AAOAS President Abraham Epstein to Roy Wilkins, president of the NAACP, Epstein expressed his perplexity with the request: "I am interested first, in social insurance and quite frankly, I do not see how we can solve the Negro problem through social insurance" (Hamilton and Hamilton 1992: 441).

Neither the labor provisions of the NIRA nor the more powerful and durable National Labor Relations Act (NLRA) included an amendment which explicitly outlawed racial discrimination in labor unions. Section 7a of NIRA gave official recognition and encouragement to American Federation of Labor unions that openly discriminated against blacks in access to local unions and, in the unionization that occurred after 7a, employers and employees collaborated to make these unions "lily white" (Wolters 1970: 178). NLRA legalized the closed shop, thus institutionalizing the informal exclusion of thousands of blacks from already existing unions (Hamilton and Hamilton 1986).

During the deliberations on the NLRA, the NAACP and NUL introduced an amendment outlawing racial discrimination. The amendment was successfully fought by both industrialists and the American Federation of Labor (AFL). Clark Foreman, a leader in the fight for the amendment, explained the reasons for the resistance in this way: "The dominating forces were the industrialists and the AFL, both of whom are hostile to Negro labor, the former because they want to keep Negroes as a reserve of cheap labor and the latter because they want to eliminate Negro competitive labor" (Wolters 1970: 170; Sitkoff 1978: 78). Although the more racially egalitarian policies of the fledgling Congress of Industrial Organizations (CIO) encouraged recruitment of blacks to new industrial unions, these policies were not the product of New Deal policy but more the outcome of the "radicalism of many of (the CIO's) organizers' (Sitkoff 1978: 180).

Other than the battle over the antidiscrimination clause in the labor legislation, legislative initiatives dealing directly with race were few and far between. Three initiatives dominated the decade: attempts to make lynching a federal offense, attempts to eliminate the poll tax in southern states, and attempts to eliminate racial segregation in the armed forces (Sitkoff 1978; Weiss 1983). Each attempt was resisted in Congress through filibusters by southern Democrats (Sitkoff 1978). In every instance the Roosevelt administration remained silent during the Congressional proceedings and, despite the intense lobbying by members of both the NAACP and a northern Democratic majority after 1936, the administration would not exercise executive leadership and urge party unity around these pieces of civil rights legislation (Weiss 1983).

This survey of the impact of New Deal programs on African Americans suggests that most of the positive evaluations of this period need to be, at the very least, significantly qualified. Most of these evaluations are done with categories that leave invisible the farm laborers, domestic and service workers, sharecroppers, and tenant farmers, a large number of whom were black. These evaluations implicitly assume that once African Americans participated more fully in industrialized society that they too would qualify for and receive New Deal largesse; they do not consider the legal and extralegal restrictions on blacks' economic and political freedoms that kept many blacks out of or subjugated within the industrializing economy.

The Racial Basis of the State, the New Deal, and African Americans

The commonly accepted explanation in the historical literature for this unequal treatment of African Americans during the New Deal is the entrenched power of the southern wing of the Democratic Party. Self-identified in the South as the party of white supremacy, southern Democrats dominated the committee system of Congress, held all white primaries, dominated the nominating process at national conventions, and were instrumental in the systematic disenfranchisement of the black population in the South after Reconstruction. They were self-conscious in upholding the racial caste system and had the power to do so (Woodward 1974).

This explanation needs to be reframed in terms of the racial basis of the state. First, the pro-South bias in political representation owed its existence to slavery and the Constitutional Compromise which gave white southerners greater voting power. Second, the absence of effective party competition in the South due to both the compromise of 1877 and the system of 1896 gave the southern Democratic Party unchallenged political hegemony,[14] and, as argued, this structure was put into place for racial reasons. Finally, the interests of that hegemonic party were pro-planter due to the tremendous economic importance of the plantation economy for both the South and the North.

Much of the research on the politics of the New Deal gives the impression that northern Democrats in Congress and President Roosevelt would have done much more for blacks without the onerous burden of the southern wing of the party (cf. Sitkoff 1978; Weiss 1983). This research portrays the Roosevelt administration as painfully aware of this political constraint and as having no choice but to sacrifice black interests for working-class interests. As Sitkoff notes, "New Dealers would identify themselves with the black struggle for equality, but not to the detriment of their greater concerns" (Sitkoff 1978: 136; cf. Weiss 1983: 96–119).

Of course, there was little political motivation for Roosevelt or New Dealers in the North to concern themselves with black interests given African Americans' geographical concentration and their inability to vote and hold office in the South.[15] This concentration and powerlessness, however, needs to be placed in the historical and theoretical context developed here. It is itself a function of past racially based state policies and practices that kept blacks in the South after emancipation and that refused to implement promises of land reform and redistribution in the South under the auspices of the Freedman's Bureau (cf. Fredrickson 1981; Steinberg 1990).

In addition, this view that black interests were ignored in national policymaking because they could not vote in the South is based on a narrow and historically inaccurate view of how formally excluded groups have exercised power in the U.S. context: it ignores the coalitional strategies pursued by some powerless groups and the directly disruptive strategies pursued by others (Flacks 1988: 6). As we will see below, blacks during the 1930s exercised varying amounts of power in some cities in the North but they were unable to translate that local power into national power due to the racial biases built into the urban political machines.[16]

The political machines that dominated urban politics in the North during the first four decades of the twentieth century incorporated blacks into party organization in a selective and subordinate fashion (Katznelson 1973; Kilson 1971). Unlike in the South, African Americans in the North had the vote and, by many accounts, used it at a higher rate than other recent migrants to the urban North (Cohen 1990; Grossman 1989). As in the South, however, their participation was regulated by white elites who set up strong organizations to recruit voters, distribute patronage, and maintain power. Seeing the potential advantage of the black vote but viewing this advantage through the "racial attitudes of most of their constituents" (Katznelson 1973: 116), white party bosses constructed parallel or buffer organizations within the black community and distributed patronage selectively to black leaders whom they considered "safe." These organizations were blatantly unrepresentative in that the territorial community procedures for leadership selection were absent. Gerrymandering accomplished this neutralization of territorial political power[17] (Bunche 1973). In addition, the dynamics of patronage acted to select leaders from a different class from those they supposedly represented (Katznelson 1973; Grossman 1989).

These buffer institutions did little to allay racial tensions in the North already strained because of white fears of labor market competition with blacks who were migrating from the South. Before the Depression, Democratic machines in the cities were the province of the white ethnic working class, particularly the Irish. With the black migration, Republicans used the historical connection between blacks and the party of Lincoln to enlist black support and undercut these machines (Grossman 1989). The shift in national power from Republican to Democratic in 1932 proved fortuitous for the Democratic machines. The availability of New Deal largesse after 1932 revived these faltering machines and turned blacks toward the party better able to provide relief and jobs (Patterson 1969; Weiss 1983). Blacks were incorporated into the Democratic Party on terms similar to their position in the Republican Party (Biles 1991).

The local party structures were, in turn, the building blocks of northern Congressmen. These Congressmen took their agendas and depended on support from the party structures. Many New Deal legislators owed their power to the political work of the ward leaders or local party bosses, who in turn owed their power to the judicious distribution of patronage to their white constituents (Erie 1988). Understanding this racial basis of political power for Democrats in the North explains why Roosevelt's landslide victory in 1936 did not "embolden" the northern wing of the party to support a racially progressive platform. Roy Wilkins of the NAACP echoes this conclusion in his observation of a successful filibuster of an antilynching bill in January of 1938: "[there was] a sort of gentleman's agreement between the filibusters and the supporters—most of whom did not want this bill but would have to vote for it if it came up" (quoted in Weiss 1983: 245).

As a matter of fact, Roosevelt's attempts, beginning in 1937, to give the executive branch more power in the budget-making process sparked a revolt by Democratic Congressmen, many of them from the North, who feared losing their control over rewarding local party organizations with New Deal largesse (Sitkoff 1978). When one recognizes the racial subordination built into these local organizations and thus the racial subordination upon which the national power of northern Democrats was built, we see more clearly the ways in which the racial practices of the local party made their way into New Deal politics. We also see the dangers of exaggerating the differences between the northern and southern wings of the Democratic party with regard to racial matters.

The Racial Basis of Capitalism, the New Deal, and African Americans

Although a great deal of debate exists in the social science literature about how much influence capital and labor had in shaping New Deal programs and policies, most historical accounts document the many prominent corporate capitalists and their policy planning organizations that were interested in and had varying degrees of influence on the reforms that went before Congress. The expertise of these individuals and their organizations derived in part from employee welfare schemes they had established in their corporations beginning in 1880, schemes that offered different benefits by race or benefits that varied by occupational category and seniority; they then consciously kept blacks in those occupations or fired blacks before whites (Brandes 1976; Cohen 1990).

Organized labor took little interest in the social policies of the New Deal; the American Federation of Labor was struggling for survival and the fledgling Congress of Industrial Organizations was still a committee of grassroots, dissident or loosely structured locals. The AFL was initially opposed to national social security legislation because it thought the legislation would discourage workers from joining unions (Quadagno 1984); at the same time, it favored the labor legislation because it wanted a national framework to contain the tremendous upsurge in worker militancy between 1933–1935 that was threatening its existence (Goldfield 1989). As I have shown, even the limited influence that the AFL exerted on the New Deal reaffirmed its position vis-à-vis African-American workers. Although these prominent organizations of capital and labor had clear economic interests in many New Deal initiatives and these interests were racially based, the process of policymaking is a much more complicated process than the simple translation of the balance of class forces into public policy. As indicated above and supported by recent research, the state apparatus also plays an important role in determining which of these economic interests are given political voice and how explicitly political interests interact with economic interests to give shape to policy proposals. More accurately, the policymaking process can be portrayed as an interaction between the economic interests embedded in the national party organizations and the political deals hammered out in Congress and the executive branch to, in part, preserve these economic interests (Domhoff 1990).

Although the economic foundation of the Democratic Party rested on the southern planters whose fortunes were basically guaranteed through one-party dominance in southern elections, the fortunes of these planters were, in turn, tied to certain business interests in the North (Domhoff 1990). Beginning in the first decade of the twentieth century and owing to the growing political clout of the urban machines, these interests, particularly real estate, gained control over or entered alliances with the machines (Piven and Cloward 1982). Urban machines also provided the resources for many northern immigrants to establish small businesses and real estate ventures, and thus helped secure an immigrant middle class that voted Democratic and served as a bridge to the immigrant working class in the cities. It was on this economic basis that many of the Democratic machines of the North came to rest.

The different economic interests of North and South were brought together in the policymaking process of the New Deal as both northern and southern Democrats voted together to secure public works projects, urban construction, and agricultural subsidies to planters in the South and ranchers in the South and West (Mollenkopf 1983). As Domhoff notes,

> the old alliance between the Southern planters and the Northern ethnic real estate developers became a pro-spending alliance that used its control of Congress to further its own economic interests against a tight-fisted Republican party based almost entirely in the industrial and bank capital of the internationalist and nationalist segments. (Domhoff 1990: 240)[18]

Symbolic of this alliance and of the need to preserve it under changing social conditions was a 1935 decision by the Democratic Party leadership to increase the number of votes needed to move a bill out of committee. The 1934 Congressional elections delivered a large Democratic victory in the House of Representatives and, as Richard Bolling, a former Representative and observer of Congress, notes, the large influx of Democratic newcomers as well as a handful of Labor and Progressive newcomers "disconcerted the Democratic leadership who worried about the unorthodox views the newcomers might have" (Bolling 1968: 128).

The disagreements over welfare and civil rights legislation that sometimes erupted between the two wings of the party must be placed in that context. These disagreements were clearly of secondary importance to the alliance's common agenda. When northern urban Democrats did voice their disagreement with southern Democrats on welfare or civil rights legislation they did so precisely because these northern Democrats knew that this legislation had no chance of passage. For even as some Democrats were voicing these disagreements to gain support from African-American and urban liberal voters in the North, they were voting with southerners in party caucuses on questions of party leadership and the seniority system, voting in ways that kept race off the political agenda (Bolling 1968; Domhoff 1990).

These northern Democrats from the machines cooperated with the southern Democrats not only because this coalition was the best that they could find to further the agenda of their economic elites. These northern machine Democrats had their own racially based reasons for entering precisely this kind of alliance with their southern friends. The increased migration of African Americans to northern cities was beginning to threaten the established leadership of the machines and thus the tenuous links from the local to national party. Any arrangement that could preserve these links was preferred (Domhoff 1990).

The policymaking process associated with the New Deal reforms reflected the bargains hammered out in this Democratic coalition. In virtually all of these reforms race was kept off the political agenda, and when popular insurgencies of the industrial working class and their subsequent electoral consequences forced a serious discussion of social welfare reform and labor law, the resulting legislation was the outcome of bargaining between blocs of business interests, on the one hand, and between business interests and plantation elites, on the other (Jenkins and Brents 1989; Quadagno 1984). The white working class had little direct input in the policymaking process; African Americans had even less.

Conclusion

By uncovering the racial bases of U.S. capitalism and the democratic state, this paper develops a theoretical and historical framework for a reanalysis of one of the most well-analyzed periods of policymaking in U.S. history—the New Deal. The extant analyses of this period call attention to the interests of capital, the fear generated by the insurgencies and mobilization of the working class, and the articulation of these interests and fears in a particular configuration of party and state structures in accounting for the creation of a national welfare state that was to a large extent employee financed, non-redistributive, and state and locally controlled. These analyses and the perspectives upon which they are constructed do less well in helping us understand the racially exclusive nature of this welfare state and why it was constructed without addressing the basic civil rights of African Americans. To understand this, these perspectives need to be built on a greater appreciation of how race, racism, and the changing nature of racial subjugation affected the organizations and interests of classes, parties, and state structures.

This greater appreciation yields several new insights. First, the key to the South's power in Congress lay in the Constitutional compromises that gave white southerners disproportionate electoral power and in the realigning elections of the late nineteenth century that eliminated party competition and accelerated the political disenfranchisement of blacks in the South. Second, The concentration of blacks in the South and their subsequent disenfranchisement were due to the racially biased policies and practices of the federal government which constrained blacks' geographical mobility and economic opportunities after emancipation. Third, the political machines in the urban North which provided the only vehicle for black political mobilization developed practices that limited the voting power of and patronage for blacks who were beginning to migrate in large numbers to certain northern cities in the early twentieth century. These machines were the building blocks of the northern Democrats who actively supported the New Deal social welfare reforms and were wedded to local business interests in the North and planter interests in the South. The politics of the policymaking process involved protecting not only the economic interests of these elites but their racial interests as well. These insights help us understand how the extension of social rights to the working class was a racially based affair.

These insights also help us understand why our liberal welfare state resists efforts to move in a more social democratic direction. In effect, the welfare state was carefully constructed not only to reinforce market incentives within the working class (Piven and Cloward 1971) but also to do this in a racially unequal manner. This dual dynamic helps account for one of the most frequently noted characteristics of the U.S. welfare state—its bifurcated nature. In one system we provide employment-based, automatic, and generous benefits for a citizenry that is overwhelmingly white and in the other system, we extend meager, means—tested benefits to those who do not work or who work in an uninsured workplace—a group that is disproportionately non-white. Thus any attempt to extend benefits in universalistic directions confronts the resistance of both a profit-oriented capitalist class and a working and middle class that is politically divided by race. The political coalitions necessary to overcome the resistance of business prove doubly difficult to construct, as racial divisions are not only embedded in the structure and functioning of civil society but also in the structure and functioning of the state.

Notes

1. For a sampling of this sociological literature on the New Deal, see Amenta and Carruthers 1988; Domhoff 1990; Goldfield 1989; Jenkins and Brents 1989; Levine 1988; Quadagno 1984; Rubin, Griffin, and Wallace 1983; Skocpol and Ikenberry 1983.

2. The academic literature on American exceptionalism seeks to answer the question of why the United States, unlike all other advanced capitalist nations, had no viable working-class political party.

3. Unlike today, these groups were all viewed as existing along the same racial classification hierarchy. Thus, Italians were seen as one "race" with traits and capacities one notch above blacks.

4. Who initiated this racial antagonism and who ultimately benefited and lost from this antagonism—be it employers or "higher priced" white workers—is not important in this discussion. The important point is that working-class capacities, working-class organizations, and working-class political interests were all affected by the exclusion or subordination of blacks.

5. For an excellent local history that documents this dual dynamic on the part of business in Bridgeport, Connecticut, see Bucki 1993.

6. Both the class-centered and the state-centered accounts stress this system although for different reasons. Quadagno (1988a), in her class-centered analysis, notes the peculiar economic basis of the American South and the ways in which a planter elite turned its economic power into unmediated political power through its control of the Democratic Party. Skocpol and Ikenberry (1983), in their state-centered analysis, also note the power of the Southern-dominated Democratic Party but see this power as stemming from the absence of effective competition from the Republican Party in this region. Neither perspective roots these features of the party system in the dynamics of racial subjugation.

7. Orloff (1993) is beginning this discussion for gender; Quadagno (1992) is beginning this discussion for race.

8. This disjuncture did not go unnoticed in the black community. Black organizations have always fused race with class issues in devising platforms to alleviate poverty (Hamilton and Hamilton 1986).

9. For a sampling of this literature see Biles 1991; Kirby 1980; Sitkoff 1978; Sternsher 1969; Weiss 1983; Wolters 1970.

10. Although AAA negatively affected blacks, it also contributed to the decline of sharecropping, a development that freed blacks from the isolation and terror of the rural South and pushed them to urban areas in both the South and the North (Bloom 1986). This "benefit," however, was neither immediate nor unambiguous. In the short run, at least, it strengthened the hand of the planters by increasing their profits without the need for any labor whatsoever.

11. Although most historians have found that New Deal agencies discriminated against blacks, the WPA experience suggests that the administration did attempt to ease discrimination in public jobs through the use of hiring quotas (Kruman 1975). Despite these efforts, decisions about who to hire and at what level were left to local administrators who excluded blacks from skilled work and from supervisory positions (Wye 1972).

12. There were, of course, areas where relief, both cash and jobs, was administered equally to blacks and whites (Greenberg 1992; Trotter 1985). Even these cases did not result in a bridging of the economic gulf: the more pressing needs of the African-American population meant that this equal treatment meant unequal outcomes.

13. Throughout the New Deal, the NAACP and NUL were most enthusiastic about programs that provided jobs on a national basis rather than ones that provided means-tested cash assistance decided at the local and state levels (Hamilton and Hamilton 1986).

14. The seniority of southern Congressmen due to the unchallenged nature of electoral contests resulted in great influence in Congress: southern Democrats held more than two-thirds of the House chairmanships and about one-half of the Senate chairmanships as late as the 1950s.

15. Eighty percent of blacks lived in the South before 1932. As I will show, however, even northern legislators from areas with large concentrations of blacks did not actively promote a civil rights agenda or an agenda that tried to address discrimination in New Deal programs.

16. Also, this view ignores the experience of another disenfranchised group—women until the 1920s—and the power they exercised in the Progressive Era mainly through protest, voluntary organizations, clubs, and by building alliances with more powerful political constituencies (Skocpol 1992). The inability of blacks to pursue a similar strategy may derive from the profound differences in the situations of these minority groups (Chafe 1977).

17. Election districts in many northern cities were drawn in ways that prevented "the full force of the vote in concentrated Negro population areas" (Bunche 1973: 94; Greenberg 1992: 95).

18. This alliance developed slowly throughout the New Deal and was strongest from 1939–1956. The informal political alliances between these two constituencies that had existed since the Civil War were formalized by Roosevelt's policy innovation of "cooperative federalism"—a strategy that provided federal money but allowed varying degrees of local autonomy in the distribution of that money (Piven and Cloward 1988).

References

Albion, Robert G. 1939. *The Rise of New York Port, 1815–1860.* New York: Scribner's Sons.

Amenta, Edwin, and Bruce G. Carruthers. 1988. "The Formative Years of U.S. Social Spending Policies: Theories of the Welfare State and the American States during the Great Depression." *American Sociological Review* 53: 661–78.

Asher, Robert, and Charles Stephenson. 1990. *Labor Divided: Race and Ethnicity in United States Labor Struggles, 1835–1960.* Albany: State University of New York Press.

Biles, Roger. 1991. *A New Deal for the American People*. DeKalb: Northern Illinois Press.
Bloom, Jack M. 1986. *Class, Race, and the Civil Rights Movement*. Bloomington and Indianapolis: Indiana University Press.
Bolling, Richard. 1968. *Power in the House*. New York: E. P. Dutton and Company.
Bonacich, Edna. 1976. "Advanced Capitalism and Black/White Relations in the United States: A Split Labor Market Interpretation." *American Sociological Review* 41: 34–51.
Brandes, Stuart D. 1976. *American Welfare Capitalism, 1880–1940*. Chicago: University of Chicago Press.
Bucki, Cecelia F. 1993. *The Pursuit of Political Power: Class, Ethnicity, and Municipal Politics in Interwar Bridgeport, 1915–1936*. Ann Arbor, MI: University Microfilms International.
Bunche, Ralph J. 1973. *The Political Status of the Negro in the Age of FDR*. Chicago: University of Chicago Press.
Chafe, William. 1977. *Women and Equality*. New York: Oxford University Press.
Cohen, Lizabeth. 1990. *Making a New Deal: Industrial Workers in Chicago, 1919–1939*. New York: Cambridge University Press.
Domhoff, G. William. 1972. *Fat Cats and Democrats: The Role of the Big Rich in the Party of the Common Man*. Englewood Cliffs, NJ: Prentice-Hall.
———. 1990. *The Power Elite and the State: How Policy Is Made in America*. New York: Aldine de Gruyter.
Drake, St. Clair, and Horace R. Cayton. 1945. *Black Metropolis: A Study of Negro Life in a Northern City*. New York: Harcourt, Brace and Company.
Erie, Steven P. 1988. *Rainbow's End: Irish-Americans and the Dilemmas of Urban Machine Politics, 1840–1985*. Berkeley: University of California Press.
Flacks, Richard. 1988. *Making History: The American Left and the American Mind*. New York: Columbia University Press.
Fredrickson, George. 1981. *White Supremacy: A Comparative Study of American and South African History*. Oxford: Oxford University Press.
Goldfield, Michael. 1989. "Worker Insurgency, Radical Organization, and New Deal Labor Legislation." *American Political Science Review* 83: 1257–1282.
———. 1990. "Class, Race and Politics in the United States: White Supremacy as the Main Explanation for the Peculiarities of American Politics from Colonial Times to the Present." *Research in Political Economy* 12: 83–127.
Greenberg, Cheryl Lynn. 1992. *"Or Does It Explode?" Black Harlem during the Great Depression*. New York: Oxford University Press.
Grossman, James R. 1989. *Land of Hope: Chicago, Black Southerners, and the Great Migration*. Chicago: University of Chicago Press.
Hamilton, Charles, and Dona Cooper Hamilton. 1992. "The Dual Agenda of African American Organizations since the New Deal: Social Welfare Policies and Civil Rights." *Political Science Quarterly* 107: 435–452.
———. 1986. "Social Policies, Civil Rights, and Poverty." Pp. 287–311 in *Fighting Poverty: What Works and What Doesn't*, Sheldon H. Danziger and Daniel H. Weinberg, eds. Cambridge, MA Harvard University Press.
Jenkins, J. Craig, and Barbara G. Brents. 1989. "Social Protest, Hegemonic Competition, and Social Reform: A Political Class Struggle Interpretation of the Origins of the American Welfare State." *American Sociological Review* 54: 891–909.
Judd, Dennis R., and Dan Hellinger. 1991. "Segregation forever?" *The Nation* 253: 740–744.
Katznelson, Ira. 1973. *Black Men, White Cities: Race, Politics, and Migration in the United States, 1900–30, and Britain, 1948–68*. Chicago: University of Chicago Press.

Kilson, Martin. 1971. "Political Change in the Negro Ghetto, 1900–1940's." Pp. 167–192 in *Key Issues in the Afro-American Experience,* Vol. II, Nathan I. Huggins, M. Kilson, and D. M. Fox, eds. New York: Harcourt Brace-Jovanovich.

Kirby, John B. 1980. *Black Americans in the Roosevelt Era: Liberalism and Race.* Knoxville: University of Tennessee Press.

Kruman, Marc W. 1975. "Quotas for Blacks: The PWA and the Black Construction Worker." *Labor History* (Winter): 37–51.

Levine, Rhonda F. 1988. *Class Struggle and the New Deal.* Lawrence: University Press of Kansas.

McAdam, Doug. 1982. *Political Process and the Development of Black Insurgency, 1930–1970.* Chicago: University of Chicago Press.

Marshall, T. H. 1950. *Citizenship and Social Class and Other Essays.* Cambridge, UK: Cambridge University Press.

Mollenkopf, John. 1983. *Contested Cities.* Princeton, NJ: Princeton University Press.

Omi, Michael, and Howard Winant. 1986. *Racial Formation in the United States.* New York and London: Routledge and Kegan Paul.

Orloff, Ann Shola. 1993. "Gender and the Social Rights of Citizenship." *American Sociological Review* 58: 303–328.

Patterson, James T. 1969. *The New Deal and the States: Federalism in Transition.* Princeton, NJ: Princeton University Press.

Piven, Frances Fox, and Richard Cloward. 1971/ *Regulating the Poor: The Functions of Public Welfare.* New York: Vintage Books.

———. 1982. *The New Class War: Reagan's Attack on the Welfare State and Its Consequences.* New York: Pantheon Books.

———. 1988. *Why Americans Don't Vote.* New York: Pantheon Books.

Quadagno, Jill. 1984. "Welfare Capitalism and the Social Security Act of 1935." *American Sociological Review* 50: 632–647.

———. 1988a. *The Transformation of Old Age Security.* Chicago: University of Chicago Press.

———. 1988b. "From Old-age Assistance to Supplemental Security Income: The Political Economy of Relief in the South, 1935–1972." Pp. 235–264 in *The Politics of Social Policy in the United States,* Margaret Weir, Ann S. Orloff, and Theda Skocpol, eds. Princeton, NJ: Princeton University Press.

———. 1992. "Labor Unions and Racial Conflict in the War on Poverty." *American Sociological Review* 57: 616–634.

Rubin, Beth, Larry J. Griffin, and Michael Wallace. 1983. "Provided Only that Their Voice Was Strong: Insurgency and Organization of American Labor from NRA to Taft-Hartley." *Work and Occupations* 10: 325–347.

Sitkoff, Harvard. 1978. *A New Deal for Blacks: The Emergence of Civil Rights as a National Issue.* New York: Oxford University Press.

Skowreneck, Stephen. 1982. *Building a New American State: The Expansion of Administrative Capacities, 1877–1920.* New York: Cambridge University Press.

Skocpol, Theda. 1992. *Protecting Soldiers and Mothers.* Cambridge, MA: Harvard University Press.

Skocpol, Theda, and John Ikenberry. 1983. "The Political Formation of the American Welfare State in Historical and Comparative Perspective." *Comparative Social Research* 6: 87–148.

Steinberg, Stephen. 1990. *The Ethnic Myth: Race Ethnicity and Class in America.* Boston: Beacon Press.

Sternsher, Bernard. 1969. *The Negro in Depression and War: Prelude to Revolution, 1930–1945.* Chicago: Quadrangle Books.

Trotter, Joe William. 1985. *Black Milwaukee: The Making of an Industrial Proletariat, 1915–45*. Chicago: University of Illinois Press.

Weir, Margaret, Ann Shola Orloff, and Theda Skocpol. 1988. *The Politics of Social Policy in the United States*. Princeton, NJ: Princeton University Press.

Weiss, Nancy J. 1983. *Farewell to the Party of Lincoln: Black Politics in the Age of FDR*. Princeton, NJ: Princeton University Press.

Wolters, Raymond. 1970. *Negroes and the Great Depression: The Problem of Economic Recovery*. Westport, CT: Greenwood.

Woodward, C. Vann. 1974. *The Strange Career of Jim Crow*, 3rd rev. ed. New York: Oxford University Press.

Wye, Christopher G. 1972. "The New Deal and the Negro Community: Toward a Broader Conceptualization." *Journal of American History* 59: 621–639.

CHAPTER 10

Promoting Civil Rights through the Welfare State

HOW MEDICARE INTEGRATED SOUTHERN HOSPITALS

Jill Quadagno

The Civil Rights Act of 1964 outlawed segregation in public accommodations, banned discrimination in employment and in public education, and barred the use of federal funds in programs that operated in a discriminatory manner. It coincided with the largest expansion of the welfare state since the New Deal, President Lyndon Johnson's Great Society. The Economic Opportunity Act of 1964 created new programs for community action, job training, and housing for the poor (Naples 1998); amendments to Social Security in 1965 created Medicare, a new program of health insurance for people 65 and older (Marmor 1970); the Housing and Urban Redevelopment Act of 1968 provided federal funds for the construction of twenty-six million new low-income housing units (Massey and Denton 1993).

Between 1964 and 1970, federal expenditures on job training increased from $200 million to $1.4 billion, funding the Job Corps, the Neighborhood Youth Corps, the Manpower Development and Training Act, Jobs in the Business Sector, and the Work Incentive Program. Federal officials could not implement job training programs without enforcing equal employment opportunity, an objective that embroiled them in conflicts with the skilled trade unions over racial discrimination in apprenticeship programs and hiring practices (Pedriana and Stryker 1997). Although the confrontation did lead to integration in jobs involving federal contracts, the effect on private sector employment was minimal (Reskin 1998). Further, the rift fractured the Democratic party by alienating its most loyal constituents and undermined union support for job training programs directed toward the poor (Quadagno 1992; 1994).

Programs intended to increase housing for low-income people also became absorbed in the struggle for racial equality. As federal officials sought to promote open housing in segregated white neighborhoods, communities imposed new zoning regulations and building restrictions designed to exclude the poor, and whites fled to the suburbs (Massey and Denton 1993; Oliver and Shapiro 1995). Over the long-term, federal support for housing subsidies declined and metropolitan areas remained racially segregated (Massey and Denton 1993).

Racial discrimination was as pervasive in the health care system as in other social institutions. Many hospitals maintained "white" and "colored" floors, labeled equipment by race, and reserved a certain number of beds for patients of each race. Throughout the South, black doctors were refused staff privileges and black students were excluded from nurse training programs (Meltsner 1966). Fourteen southern states had constructed entire hospital systems based on the principle of "separate but equal" (Knowles and Prewitt 1969). The problem was not confined to the South. In northern cities, too, many hospitals segregated black patients from white patients and discriminated against black health care workers (Smith 1993).

Yet unlike integration efforts in most institutional spheres, in the health care system, the process proceeded rapidly and smoothly. Within the six-month period between July and December in 1966, nearly every hospital in the country admitted patients regardless of race. Most racially segregated wards were dismantled, and hospitals began granting staff privileges to black physicians. Why did hospitals eliminate racial barriers with minimal resistance? At first glance, the answer seems obvious. Hospitals needed the funds that Medicare would provide and no hospital could receive these funds unless it was in compliance with the Civil Rights Act. Yet, recipients of federal funds for job training and housing also had to comply with civil rights. In these sectors, however, the efforts of federal authorities to gain compliance met with widespread defiance and resistance. Thus, the explanation must be sought at a more complex level of analysis.

In this paper, I draw on insights from power resource and feminist theories of welfare state stratification to develop a theory of racial stratification. I first examine how federal policy tacitly allowed a racially segregated health care system to flourish by defining hospitals as "private" institutions whose institutional rules and regulations were outside state jurisdiction. I then analyze how the first major expansion of the welfare state since the New Deal coincided with a redefinition of the scope of state authority, transforming hospitals from private to public institutions.

The paper demonstrates that the welfare state can be an effective mechanism for reducing racial inequality under certain conditions: 1) if political resources can be mobilized to challenge racially discriminatory practices; 2) if institutions that reproduce systems of oppression are shifted from the private to the public sphere; 3) if the rules and conditions for the distribution of benefits reinforce the objective of promoting racial equality; and 4) if the benefits are provided on a continuous and universal basis so that the state has the capacity to force racially biased institutions to change.

The paper combines original archival research with secondary materials and selective interviews with key informants. The archival research was conducted in the National Archives in College Park, Maryland, and the Library of Congress. The main data sources are the records of agencies within the Department of Health, Education, and Welfare that were responsible for hospital integration from the late 1940s to the late 1960s: the Public Health Service and the Office of the General Counsel (Record Group 235), and the Social Security Administration (Record Group 47). The archival data is supplemented by personal interviews with federal officials and physicians who were involved in the effort to integrate hospitals and who provided information on issues that were not fully elucidated in the archival records.

The Welfare State and Inequality

It is, by now, axiomatic that the welfare state is an "active force in the ordering of social relations" capable of reconstructing patterns of social stratification (Esping-Anderson 1990: 23). Situated within larger structures of power and rule, the welfare state represents an intervention by the state in civil society to alter social and market conditions. It redistributes income and power across divisions of class, gender, and race (Esping-Anderson 1990; O'Connor, Orloff, and Shaver 1999).

CLASS AND GENDER INEQUALITY

The central premise of the class-based theory of the welfare state (termed power resource theory) is that the liberation of workers from oppression proceeded in three stages with first, the granting of civil rights (the right to work without coercion), then, political rights (the right to vote and organize for collective action), and finally, social rights (the right to economic welfare and security) (Marshall 1964). Social rights modify the inequality that is inherent in the system of market distribution and empower workers by shifting the decision making from the private sphere of the market to the public sphere of the state (Esping-Anderson 1990; Korpi 1989). A key component of power resource theory is that the pursuit of social rights flows from the power invested in workers as a numerical majority (Myles 1988).

Most research derived from power resource theory has analyzed variations across nations in the benefits that the welfare state provides to individuals (Janoski and Hicks 1994; Myles 1988). The effect of these benefits for class stratification depends on a set of rules and conditions that determine how claims on the resources of the state are made and what economic, social, and political obligations to the state are, in turn, incurred. Nations that rely on means-tested benefits which are only granted to individuals whose incomes fall below a certain level, can discourage cross-class solidarity and create social divisions of status and class. Nations that promote private sector benefits reinforce, rather than suppress, market-based stratification (Esping-Anderson 1999). Only when nations provide social insurance benefits as an earned right does the welfare state redistribute income and foster equality and class solidarity (Korpi 1989).

The welfare state can also transform systems of gender inequality. Here, the task is not to liberate workers from the whip of the market, but to liberate women from systems of male domination. Like power resource theorists, feminist theorists of the welfare state view social benefits to individuals as a potential vehicle of female liberation. Whether these benefits serve this function depends on the rules and conditions that determine eligibility. For feminist theorists, the fundamental distinction is whether benefits are claimed on the basis of paid work as opposed to benefits based on family status such as marriage or widowhood. Some programs may reward marriage and motherhood, but penalize women who do not make this traditional choice (Abramovitz 1988; Boris and Bardaglio 1983). Others reward paid work, but exclude unpaid labor, reinforcing the gender hierarchy and reproducing the sexual division of labor (Harrington Meyer 1996; Sainsbury 1996). Only benefits that allow women to "form and maintain autonomous households . . . without having to marry to gain access to a breadwinner's income" are liberating (Orloff 1993: 318). They relieve women of the compulsion to enter or stay in a marriage merely because they are economically vulnerable.

The welfare state can also liberate women by creating new institutional arrangements that increase women's access to paid employment and equal pay (Hobson 1990; Lewis 1997). Programs for childcare and elder care, for example, substitute state-provided services for unpaid family labor and are, themselves, a source of employment (Ruggie 1984); the absence of such services promotes housewifery and dependence on a male breadwinner (Orloff 1993). Thus, while benefits may help women in and of themselves, they can also transform gender relations by altering social institutions.

Feminist theorists generally agree that, although the decision rules and guiding ideologies of policies do not always decisively favor women, outcomes are more likely to be equalized if these decisions are not left to individuals within families. By transferring decision making about the distribution of resources from the family to the state, the welfare state brings decisions about women's well-being into the public sphere. The enhancement of social rights can mobilize women politically and expand citizenship in concrete ways. If women garner a greater share of power, they can produce a favorable change in policy arrangements (Naples 1998). They can also extend "women's domestic values into civic and national life" and redefine, in a woman-friendly way, the social problems that the welfare state should solve (Skocpol 1992: 37).

Power resource theorists recognize that the political arena is the site for altering the inequality created by the market. It is in the public sphere that the rule of law can be applied and where inequality can be challenged. However, they take the constitution of the public sphere as a given. Political processes are located in the public sphere; the market is private. What they fail to recognize is that the definition of what is public and what is private is not inherent in the nature of an institution, but is politically negotiated. For feminist theorists, by contrast, the definition of the public sphere is contested terrain and the politicization of civil society is a crucial element in the struggle for women's equality (Fraser 1992; Gordon 1990). The state's ability to intervene in power relationships within the family depends on crossing the boundaries between the private and the public spheres. As long as families, workplaces, educational institutions, or clubs are defined as private, they are treated as sanctuaries "in which the internal relations of members [obey] discrete institutional principles" (Fox-Genovese 1991: 67). Growing state intervention in private institutions has resulted directly from the erosion of the barriers between the public and the private spheres, indeed, undermining the very distinction between public and private. The result has made legal intervention to redress "natural" inequalities such as pregnancy and childbearing possible, as well as the economic inequality of the marketplace.

In summary, then, the welfare state may merely reproduce forms of oppression, but it can also be a vehicle of liberation for workers and for women. It can reduce class and gender inequality by 1) bringing decisions about the distribution of resources into the public sphere; 2) redistributing those resources to individuals in a way that liberates them from systems of oppression; and 3) transforming the institutional arrangements that sustain these forms of oppression. What has still to be determined is whether these theoretical principles also apply to the advancement of racial equality. Although there is now a substantial body of research that demonstrates that the welfare state has been a key institution in the construction and reconstruction of the racial order in American society, the necessary criteria for the welfare state to transform patterns of racial stratification have yet to be specified.

THE WELFARE STATE AND RACIAL INEQUALITY

In the United States, an oppressive racial order was preserved by the peculiar compromise of the national state with a regional political economy in the South that was neither industrialized nor democratic. At the national level, the racial order was maintained by southern Congressmen who gained seniority in Congress because they ran for office unopposed, and who used their control over key congressional committees to ensure that federal authorities could not intervene in local political and economic arrangements. At the local level, the "racial state" was maintained by oppressive racial codes that permeated all southern institutions and its agents in the local legal system and the local welfare system (James 1988). African Americans could neither vote nor run for political office, and their lives were circumscribed by rigid racial segregation. The legal basis of racial segregation derived from *Plessy v. Ferguson*, the 1896 Supreme Court ruling that "separate but equal" facilities were constitutional. At the local level, "separate but equal" institutions were policed by the local "racial state."

The racial order of the South was institutionalized in the structure of the American welfare state from its inception. Under the New Deal, the Social Security Act of 1935 created two programs of social insurance, Unemployment Insurance and Old Age Insurance, which provided social rights to industrial workers, but excluded agricultural workers and domestic servants—three-fifths of all black workers. Instead, at the insistence of southern Democrats, these workers were only eligible for the means-tested benefits, Aid to Dependent Children and Old Age Assistance, which left decisions about eligibility to local authorities (Lieberman 1998; Quadagno 1988). Racial criteria were also used to determine eligibility for benefits and levels of benefits. In southern states, as a matter of practice, black beneficiaries received lower Old Age Assistance benefits than whites because their "standard of living" was lower and they, thus, had less presumed need. In administering unemployment benefits, local Employment Service offices either excluded black workers entirely or offered them the most menial, low-paying jobs. Finally, the New Deal reproduced the racial order through housing policies that permitted "redlining" and restrictive covenants, and provided public funds for the construction of racially segregated projects (Massey and Denton 1993; Oliver and Shapiro 1995; Quadagno 1994). Through these processes, the New Deal welfare state tacitly reproduced existing racial arrangements, organizing and enforcing "the racial politics of everyday life" (Omi and Winant 1994: 83).

The antipoverty programs created by the Economic Opportunity Act of 1964 and other federal initiatives of that decade represented an effort to undo the New Deal legacy by reconstituting racially biased programs or by compensating African Americans with new benefits. Federal job training programs targeted minority youths. Federal housing programs targeted urban ghettos. Community action agencies expanded federal authority in urban racial politics by modifying the old political alignments and permitting the state to claim new powers (Morone 1990). These programs gave many poor people, especially minority women, their first opportunity to participate in politics (Naples 1998). As the welfare state became absorbed in the struggle for racial equality, some programs provoked white backlash that led to cutbacks in funding, while others enhanced equality of opportunity and increased the political resources of racial minorities. Yet, no theoretical principles have been delineated that can explain the role of the welfare state in the restructuring of the racial order.

While race is sometimes included in theoretical formulations of the welfare state, it is often an afterthought, not a core component of the analysis. What Oliver and Shapiro (1995: 3) term the "sedimentation of racial inequality" becomes Esping-Anderson's (1999: 42) framework of an example of "intergenerational risk transmission" which demands "an explicit commitment to egalitarianism, primarily in the form of equal opportunity policies." However, Esping-Anderson fails to develop the concept of "intergenerational risk transmission" and never considers impediments to the implementation of an egalitarian ideal. Feminist theorists do, explicitly, recognize that the distribution of benefits systematically varies by race. Harrington Meyer (1996), for example, shows that black women are only half as likely as white women to receive the spouse benefit under Social Security. Yet, feminist theorists do not specify how the processes that create racial inequality may differ from the processes that create gender inequality. Nor do they theorize the processes that can lead to the transformation of racially biased institutions.

Although theories of class and gender stratification of the welfare state do not directly deal with racial stratification, they delineate principles that can be modified to incorporate the unique factors associated with racial oppression. The first principle is that the redistribution of power depends upon the mobilization of political resources. In power resource theory, workers transfer control from the market to the state by using their numerical majority to gain political power and then, establish social rights. This principle is problematic for feminist theorists since the women's movement mobilized before women had the right to vote, and women's "power resources" have never granted them the same degree of political representation as men (Nelson 1984; Orloff 1993). Instead, women have often relied upon extrainstitutional forms of politics to alter the distribution of resources and transform institutional arrangements (Skocpol 1992; Schmitt and Martin 1999).

The argument that oppressed groups can mobilize political power through their voting rights is even more problematic for understanding processes of racial liberation. Unlike workers whose struggle for social rights followed the struggle for civil and political rights, these struggles occurred simultaneously for African Americans in the U.S. This meant that southern blacks had no "power resources" in the form of the vote. Even when they gained the vote with passage of the Voting Rights Act of 1965, African Americans could never muster a political majority (unlike workers who can capture the state by their sheer numbers). Rather, they had to attempt to transform racial arrangements through the legal system and through extrainstitutional means by using only their vote at the margins of politics, to swing an election outcome. The vote is, thus, a weak form of power for numerical minorities that cannot guarantee any redistribution of power.

The second principle derived from theories of class and gender stratification of the welfare state is that it is in the public sphere that systems of inequality can be challenged. For power resource theorists, the outcome of the struggle for class equality depends on the ability of workers to gain benefits that by-pass the market. These benefits help redistribute power from employers to workers. For feminist theorists, the outcome of the struggle for gender equality depends on the ability of women to gain benefits that by-pass the family. Publicly distributed benefits help to transform power arrangements within the private sphere of the family. In the struggle for racial equality, however, the transferal of resources from the private to the public sphere could not lead to a redistribution of power from white to African Americans because the public sphere was dominated by a local racial state. The local racial state monopolized political resources and protected the racially biased arrangements of the private sphere. Thus, the impediments to racial liberation were not only deeply embedded in the private sector, but sustained and reproduced in the public sector. The task, then, involved two processes: incorporating these private institutions into the public sphere so they could be regulated by the state, and also reconstructing the public sphere. The process of how the racial order was transcended and the public sphere, redefined, is illustrated by the case of hospital integration.

Racial Segregation in the Health Care System

The segregation of the health care system was supported by a federal program that provided funds for hospital construction through the Hill-Burton Hospital Survey and Construction Act of 1946. Under Hill-Burton, federal policy preserved a legacy dictated by the local racial state. Segregated practices were protected by the principle that the hospital was a private institution beyond the regulatory authority of the state.

PRESERVING THE PRIVATE

When World War II ended, the hospital industry pressed for aid that had been deferred by more than a decade of depression and war. The American Hospital Association organized a commission to develop support for a national program of hospitals. The commission recommended a huge program of hospital construction: an additional 195,000 beds at a capital investment of $1.8 billion. Congress found hospital construction attractive, not only because of pressure from the hospital lobby, but also because a federally funded construction program would expand the economy and create employment, a pressing need in all congressional districts in the postwar era. Two hospital construction programs were adopted immediately after the war, one to expand Veteran's Administration hospitals, the other to expand community hospitals (Starr 1982).

In 1945, President Harry Truman proposed a comprehensive health measure that included funds for hospital construction, grants to states for public health services, and a national health insurance program. The only legislation to result from these proposals was the Hill-Burton Hospital Survey and Construction Act of 1946, which provided funds for hospital construction (Poen 1979; Starr 1982). To be eligible for Hill-Burton funds, states had to conduct surveys of their need for health facilities, develop a plan to meet those needs, and maintain a system of licensing to ensure minimum safety and quality standards. Any public or private nonprofit institution that could demonstrate a need for expanded facilities could apply for federal construction funds.

The proposed Hill-Burton Act expanded federal authority over hospitals since it could deny funds to hospitals that did not meet local needs, or that failed to maintain adequate standards. To prevent federal intervention that might have challenged the rights of hospitals to practice racial segregation, southern Congressmen inserted a statute specifying that hospitals were private entities whose operations could only be regulated by the states, not by federal authorities. As Alabama Senator, Lister Hill, who wrote the bill, testified on the Senate floor:

> Who shall practice in the hospitals and the other matters pertaining to the conduct of hospitals, we have sought, in the bill, to leave to the authority and determination of the States, and not have the federal government, through this bill, invade the realm of the operation and maintenance of the hospitals.[1]

As a result, federal officials had no say in how much any hospital would receive and, critically, could not regulate internal hospital policies.[2] Instead, eligibility and regulatory issues would be handled by a state agency designated to run the program (Wing 1978).

Federal statutes did require that institutions receiving Hill-Burton funds sign a nondiscrimination assurance agreeing to provide care to people who were unable to pay and to all persons in their service area regardless of race, creed, or color. However, Section 622, inserted by southern Congressmen, allowed hospitals to use federal funds to construct separate facilities for different "population groups" as long as the segregated facilities were of "equal quality." It also allowed racial segregation within a hospital as long as no patient was denied admission if beds allotted to the "other population group" were available. Thus, care could be organized around the principle of "separate, but equal." Section 622 allowed hospitals to deny staff privileges and jobs based on race to doctors and other health care workers because these employment issues involved "internal" hospital policy, private matters that were outside the jurisdiction of the federal government.

The Hill-Burton program was administered by the Public Health Service (PHS), one of 13 agencies within the Department of Health, Education, and Welfare (HEW), an enormous bureaucracy that, by the 1960s, had authority over 200 programs (Miles 1974). Organizationally, HEW programs were administered through regional and local offices and were, thus, responsive to local political forces. In the Hill-Burton program, all decisions were filtered through the local racial state.

Between 1947 and 1974, the Hill-Burton program disbursed $3.7 billion to the states, contributing 30 percent of the funds for all hospital projects and generating an additional $9.1 billion in local and state matching funds (Starr 1982). Federal funds supported 7,750 hospitals and clinics. At least 98 accepted no black patients; many others contained racially segregated wings and wards with basements and halls reserved for black patients. For example, Alabama used Hill-Burton funds to construct racially segregated or separate facilities in all but two of its 67 counties (Smith 1998). Other southern states engaged in similar practices.

REDEFINING THE PRIVATE SPHERE

Class theorists and feminist theorists both emphasize the significance of electoral resources for transforming systems of domination. In the United States, African Americans in the South had no electoral resources. Instead, they had to rely upon the legal system, a slower and more difficult process for initiating change, and also on extra-institutional forms of politics—protest and demonstration.

The civil rights challenge to health care segregation was initiated in the wake of a landmark 1954 Supreme Court decision that overturned *Plessy v. Ferguson* in education. In *Brown v. Board of Education*, the Supreme Court ruled that the doctrine of "separate but equal" had no place in public education and that segregation deprived the minority group of equal protection of the laws guaranteed by the Fourteenth Amendment. The Brown case raised the question of whether the "separate but equal" provisions of the Hill-Burton program were constitutional. The Court had indicated that its decision applied to areas other than education including public housing, public golf courses, and public auditoriums. The issue, now, was whether federal funds could be used to finance hospital construction program projects that might be of doubtful constitutionality.

Hospitals presented a powerful barrier to civil rights objectives because they were legally defined as private organizations. Their private status insulated them from the legal prohibitions that applied to public entities, including the equal protection provision of the Fourteenth Amendment (Smith 1998). The definition of hospitals as private deprived HEW officials of the authority to intervene in "internal" hospital affairs. All activities within the "range of administration, personnel, maintenance, or operation of the hospital" were outside HEW's jurisdiction.[3] This included such issues as admission policies, room assignments, and the use of the cafeteria.

HEW attorneys debated whether to review Hill-Burton operations in the context of the Supreme Court decision, but concluded that HEW lacked authority to issue new regulations contradicting the laws of Congress that were enacted prior to the decision. Although "separate but equal" facilities might be discriminatory in light of the Brown decision, the present statute allowed HEW to continue funding segregated hospitals as long as the separate facilities were "of like quality."[4] However, HEW refused to evaluate whether segregated hospitals were actually providing similar quality care. As one official explained, "We are not intending to suggest, at this time, that we are required to be concerned with relative quality of segregated services."[5]

HEW attorneys also decided that the federal government had no jurisdiction over internal hospital policy decisions, like admission practices or room assignments, which fell under the category of hospital "operation."[6] These remained private matters. Until it was "definitely established that hospital segregation was unconstitutional, HEW was 'certainly under no statutory mandate to anticipate the outcome of court tests of that issue.'"[7] When hospital administrators inquired about whether HEW policy would change in light of the Brown decision, they were informed that "the propriety of separate hospital facilities for separate racial groups (was) not directly affected by court decisions to date."[8] The school desegregation decision did not relieve HEW of its responsibility to carry out the Hill-Burton statute as written.[9]

Brown v. Board of Education provided a new political resource for civil rights advocates who could now challenge the constitutionality of racial segregation in health care. In 1956, the NAACP filed the first of a dozen lawsuits against hospitals and other health care facilities asking the courts to declare the "separate but equal" provision of the Hill-Burton program unconstitutional and to force hospitals to integrate patient care facilities, student training, and state and local medical societies. Some suits were dismissed. Others made incremental progress. For example, one suit filed in 1959 by the NAACP against the city of Lakeland, Florida, charged that the new Lakeland General Hospital had received Hill-Burton funds to construct an addition to an existing hospital, which had a wing reserved for black patients.[10] Further, when the new wing became overcrowded, the hospital administrator moved all Negro patients from the new building to the old building.[11] Although the District Court dismissed the case for lack of evidence, the hospital attempted to ward off further integration efforts by renovating the old building and admitting patients of both races. The psychiatric and nursery facilities in the new building were also opened to both white and black patients.[12]

Similarly, a suit filed in 1962 against Grady Hospital in Atlanta, Georgia, charged the hospital with racial discrimination in staffing practices, patient admissions, and nursing school admissions.[13] The plaintiffs requested relief in two forms: 1) a declaratory judgment that Section 291(e)(f) of the Hill-Burton Act was unconstitutional and 2) an injunction against the continued operation and assignment of facilities on a segregated basis. In response to the suit, the hospital opened a psychiatric ward for black patients, improved the black maternity ward, and made plans to open a Negro orthopedic ward. The Fulton County Medical Society admitted two black physicians who were recent additions to Grady's visiting staff to active membership.[14]

The lynchpin of the NAACP litigation strategy against the hospitals was to challenge the definition of private that granted them immunity from federal oversight. The major obstacle was to prove that the equal protection provision of the Fourteenth Amendment, which applied to the rules, regulations, and services provided by state and local government, also applied to hospitals. Attorneys for the hospitals argued that there was no such link between the hospitals and the state (Smith 1998). In a suit against two private hospitals in Virginia, the plaintiffs alleged that, even though the hospital had a private board, it was within the scope of civil rights statutes because it was "almost a wholly tax supported institution with tax money coming from the city of Lynchburg and the state of Virginia."[15] The U.S. District Court ruled that the hospitals were not required to integrate their services even though they received federal construction funds. Rather, the judge held that the "funds were given with the understanding that the private facilities might retain private affairs in their own way" (Powell 1963: 340). To ensure that this status was maintained, the hospital board moved to transfer the hospital's assets into a private corporation.[16]

Until 1963, court decisions continued to uphold the principle that the equal protection clause of the Fourteenth Amendment did not apply to private institutions. The case of *Simpkins v. Moses H. Cone Memorial Hospital* finally overturned these claims, not only contesting hospitals' claims of immunity, but also providing the legal underpinning for the Civil Rights Act of 1964. When the hospital applied for a grant from the Hill-Burton program, the plaintiffs asked the Court to declare it unconstitutional to give federal grants to racially discriminatory hospitals. For the first time, the Department of Justice intervened on behalf of the plaintiffs arguing that the government had an obligation to protect its citizens from unconstitutional action made possible by operation of a federal statute. Although the U.S. District Court dismissed the complaint on the grounds that the hospitals were private in character and, therefore, beyond the reach of the Fourteenth Amendment, the plaintiffs appealed the decision.

On March 2, 1963, the Federal Court of Appeals struck down the statute that provided the legal basis for the "separate but equal" clause of Hill-Burton (Powell 1963). Because the hospital received federal funds, it was not a private entity, but an "arm of the state" and thus, was subject to Fourteenth Amendment prohibitions. The Court decision prohibited internal segregation in any facility on the basis of race, creed, or color, banned hospitals or other health care facilities from denying staff privileges on the basis of race, and asserted that all benefits associated with staff privileges must be available without discrimination.[17] Thus, the Simpkins decision now signified that all hospital operations were in the jurisdiction of the public sphere and were subject to regulation by the state, challenging the constitutional basis of the practices and procedures that had guided HEW's funding decisions for 17 years. Litigation proved to be a powerful tool for redefining the rights of African Americans.

Yet, like Brown and other landmark decisions, the Simpkins decision had little immediate impact on southern hospitals because segregationists defied the ruling. Although HEW issued new Hill-Burton regulations that prohibited hospitals from discriminating in admissions, from denying physicians hospital privileges on the basis of race, and from segregating patients by ward or room, HEW had limited authority to force compliance. The major impediment was that these regulations only applied to pending applications, not to hospitals that had received Hill-Burton funds in the past (Wing 1978). Hospitals that violated their nondiscrimination assurances could not be asked to repay federal funds that had been improperly used. The new HEW mandate applied only to hospitals that sought further federal assistance because Hill-Burton disbursed grants for one-time construction projects.[18] HEW's only leverage was to withhold further federal funds for construction of new projects.[19] Thus, the Simpkins decision failed to provide a broad mandate to desegregate.

HEW's inability to enforce its new policy regulations retroactively, and its continuing linkages to the local racial state, meant that the civil rights victory in Simpkins did little to alter existing institutional arrangements. Judicial intervention simply was not sufficient to end racial discrimination and states and local governments continued to defy court orders. The attention of civil rights activists shifted to the federal arena as national support for civil rights broadened.

THE EXPANSION OF POLITICAL RESOURCES

In 1964, African Americans in the South still lacked guaranteed voting rights, but they mobilized other sources of political power. They used a range of tactics from lobbying, to protest, to demonstrations. The lobbying campaign against health care segregation was directed at HEW, the Congress, and officials in the executive branch. The campaign originated from regions where the civil rights movement had extensive grassroots mobilization and numerous well-organized networks of civil rights groups operating to develop strategies and spread collective action (Morris 1986). Catherine Patterson, a member of CORE and the Gadsden Freedom Movement, complained that the new Baptist Memorial Hospital in Gadsden, Alabama, constructed with Hill-Burton funds, reserved just 25 beds for Negro adults and the entrances were labeled "colored" and "white."[20] Mr. Horace Reed, President of the Volusia County Branch of the NAACP in Florida, complained that in the Halifax Hospital "separate wards were being maintained for Negro and white patients, even the most insignificant equipment [was] labeled 'Negro' and 'white,' Negro employees were required to occupy a segregated area in the cafeteria" and employees were assigned duties on the basis of race. A lack of access led to poor care, which not only threatened health, but even life itself. In Charlotte, North Carolina, for example, there was "a tacit agreement between the hospital, city police, and ambulance operators that whenever a Negro citizen was injured, this patient was carried to the inferior all-Negro Good Samaritan Hospital."[21] One night, a Negro male, Mr. Hughie David, age 39, complained of a severe headache. Mr. David had been under treatment by Dr. Richard James, a white physician, who sent him to the emergency room at Charlotte Memorial, the white hospital. Dr. James examined his patient and concluded that he needed immediate hospitalization for subarachnoid hemorrhages. The hospital admissions office told Dr. James that there were no Negro beds available, so Mr. David was sent to Good Samaritan hospital. Dr. James did not have staff privileges at Good Samaritan, which lacked the facilities to perform an angiogram and had no neurosurgeon on staff. Mr. David died the following morning.[22]

Civil rights activists also engaged in protests and demonstrations against health care facilities and organizations of health care professionals. The NAACP joined with the National Medical Association, an organization of black physicians, and picketed white medical societies whose members refused to grant privileges to black doctors or refused to serve black patients. It won a victory in Kentucky when several hospitals responded to picketing by granting staff privileges to black doctors (Jones 1982).

Through these activities, civil rights advocates mobilized a key political resource not usually incorporated in welfare state theories—the weight of public opinion (Burstein 1998). By 1964, civil rights was clearly viewed by the American public as the most important problem facing the nation, and public support for racial integration was high (Schuman, Steeh, Bobo, and Krysan 1997; Burstein 1993). In 1942, 68 percent of whites supported racially segregated schools, 54 percent favored segregated transportation, and 55 percent believed whites should have the first chance at jobs. By 1963, 63 percent supported integrated schooling, 79 percent opposed segregated transportation, and 85 percent believed that African Americans should have as good a chance as whites for jobs (Schuman, Steeh, Bobo, and Krysan 1997). Members of Congress whose political futures depended on responding to public opinion now openly challenged HEW's policy position (and implicitly the policies of the local racial state). As Senator Harrison Williams complained to an HEW official:

> Your description is . . . of an agency following a narrow interpretation of the letter of the law and wholly ignoring the intent of the law. By stating that Hill-Burton does not specifically outlaw segregation once the patient has been admitted into the hospital, you are, in effect, adopting the principle of separate, but equal facilities. Considering that the United States Supreme Court, in a unanimous decision, declared this doctrine unconstitutional, I find it hard to accept your position. I cannot think that a Federal agency must continue to operate, some eight years after the Court's decision, in a manner that perpetuates this principle.[23]

New HEW staff members appointed by the Kennedy administration also opposed current practices. Lisle Carter, the Deputy Assistant Secretary of HEW, angrily asked whether segregated facilities could ever be nondiscriminatory.[24] Hospitals had, after all, provided assurance that "no person in the area would be denied admission to the proposed facilities as patients because of race." Assistant Secretary, James Quigley, also challenged official policy, arguing that it was imperative that HEW reconsider its position in regard to the Hill-Burton program: "Whatever justification there may have been for the original interpretation at the time it was made in the late 1940s, which permitted internal segregation, no such justification exists in 1963." Quigley feared that "if we do not act in this area quickly and effectively, we are going to have pickets outside our door one of these mornings."[25]

The first bill prohibiting federal funding for construction of segregated facilities was proposed in the House in 1957.[26] The bill, which was written by Congressman Adam Clayton Powell, became known as the Powell Amendment. Powell proposed that no funds be provided to any agency that practiced segregation. The measure was defeated by a vote of 123 to 70, as were bills that were introduced in succeeding years.[27] The Simpkins ruling lent the legitimacy of the Courts (and by implication, the Constitution) to the issue. When Congress passed the Civil Rights Act of 1964, the Powell Amendment became Title VI, which prohibited discrimination from any organization that received federal funds (Smith 1998).

In June 1964, HEW made a survey of state statutes that were "inconsistent" with the nondiscrimination assurances in the Hill-Burton program.[28] Eleven southern states had statutes mandating the segregation of white and Negro patients in hospitals and other health care facilities, the provision of separate black and white sanitary facilities and eating places, separate hospital entrances, separate wards within hospitals, and separate training schools for Negro and white nurses. The statutes were enforced through fines or imprisonment.[29] Although these statutes often violated a hospital's nondiscrimination assurance, HEW officials decided they could not intervene unless a court ruled that "the applicable portion of the statute [was] invalid or inoperative." If no court decision existed, then HEW would rely on the opinion of the state attorney general. Thus, despite new civil rights legislation, HEW counsel's opinion could "have little effect on an applicant who may be subject to local enforcement efforts." As an agency with deeply embedded ties to local political structures, HEW lacked the institutional capacity to promote change.[30]

Title VI went into effect in January 1965. It applied to more than 400 federal programs administered by 33 agencies. It was the only title of the Civil Rights Act not delegated to the Courts, but to the federal bureaucracy. Next to the Courts, HEW became the foremost government agent for changing the nation's racial patterns. Now it was HEW's job to implement the law, a task complicated by loopholes inserted into Title VI by southern Congressmen (Rabkin 1980: 310). One loophole prohibited federal officials from taking any sanctions until they demonstrated that compliance could not be secured voluntarily. Other provisions specified that any regulations adopted had to be approved by the president, that unless the proper Congressional committee gave consent, funds to a recipient who ignored the regulations could not be terminated, and that the termination would be limited to the programs where noncompliance was found. Title VI also excluded employment practices that were covered by other titles of the Civil Rights Act and, thus, administered by other federal agencies (Jones 1982).

Implementing Title VI through the Welfare State

HEW had the largest Title VI enforcement office in the federal government. It was responsible for coordinating all compliance investigations in all its programs. Each agency, in turn, was responsible for carrying out day-to-day enforcement activities. Each regional director was assigned a special assistant to help coordinate activities between agencies.[31] This arrangement meant that regional managers and field staff who had previously complied with local practices promoting racial segregation, now became Title VI compliance investigators.

The Public Health Service (PHS) was given responsibility for desegregating 20,000 hospitals, 2,000 nursing homes, and over 1,000 home health agencies through a newly created Office of Equal Health Opportunities (OEHO). OEHO's head was Robert Nash, a career service employee, who was determined to overturn HEW's historic policies. In his view, the passage of Title VI now required a different resolution "in favor of nondiscrimination in the disbursement of benefits."[32] Yet, OEHO had a full-time office staff of only 31 and a field staff of 72, and its only leverage was its ability to investigate complaints and develop community-wide programs to accelerate compliance (Miles 1974). Although Title VI applied to all hospitals that currently received Hill-Burton funds, hospitals that had completed construction projects remained untouchable beyond the enforcement power of federal authorities. Not surprisingly, one year after passage of the Civil Rights Act, virtually no progress had been made in desegregating southern hospitals. Federal authorities now had the legal mandate, but no institutional capacity, to enforce that mandate.

By 1965, health rights advocates had the courts, the law, and the weight of public opinion on their sides. Yet, these gains were insufficient to change hospital practices. By historical accident, the capacity to implement the law came through a new welfare program with the passage of Medicare.

THE EXPANSION OF THE WELFARE STATE

National health insurance was the most prominent aspiration of President Harry Truman's administration. Although the Democrats controlled both houses of Congress from

1939 to 1946, they did not make up a voting majority because southern Democrats voted with conservative Republicans to block most of Truman's major domestic proposals. Truman continued to advocate national health insurance following his 1948 election victory, but his proposal was defeated by the American Medical Association, which labeled it "socialized medicine," and by the southern Democrat/conservative Republican coalition (Poen 1979; Hacker 1998). Health insurance proponents then shifted to an incremental strategy to insure just the aged. Organized labor and officials in the Social Security Administration waged a decade-long campaign, but had to contend with opposition from the conservative coalition. In 1960, Congress passed the Kerr-Mills bill as a way of avoiding Medicare. Kerr-Mills provided funds to the states for medical assistance for the poor, while standards of need and benefits were left to the states (Marmor 1970). Southerners supported the Kerr-Mills program (and then, for the most part, refused to participate in it) because it provided unconditional funds for state-run health programs.

When Lyndon Johnson ascended to the presidency, he made health insurance the highest priority of his Great Society (Starr 1992). In 1965, Congress enacted Medicare, the first new social insurance program since the New Deal (Marmor 1970). Medicare not only paid the hospital and physician costs of elderly individuals, but it also provided the federal government with the institutional capacity to enforce Title VI. As Medicare was implemented, it was inexorably absorbed into the struggle for health care integration. As Congressman Powell (1963: 340) noted, "'How would the elderly Negro fare under the Medicare system which is now being considered in Congress?' If the hospital bars him, if it shunts him into wards with inadequate facilities, and if his doctor cannot practice in the hospital, the elderly Negro will receive little benefit from the Medicare plan." Medicare could not be implemented without confronting the segregated health care system.

MEDICARE AS A VEHICLE OF TITLE VI COMPLIANCE

Medicare would pay the costs of hospital care for the aged (which had more than doubled in the past decade), posthospital extended care, outpatient diagnostic services, and depreciation on hospital assets under rules that were extremely favorable to the hospital industry (Marmor 1970; Starr 1982). Thus, Medicare infused an enormous flow of capital into hospitals, strengthening the position of the industry through millions of dollars annually in federal expenditures.

As the Social Security Administration (SSA) begun certifying hospitals and nursing homes for Medicare eligibility, Medicare was swept into the Title VI compliance efforts. To become eligible for federal funds, hospitals applying for Medicare certification now also had to prove they were not engaging in racial discrimination. Unlike Hill-Burton funds, which were provided for a one-time project, Medicare increased federal regulatory authority by providing a continuous flow of federal dollars and, thus, a continuous enforcement capacity over hospitals. If hospitals refused to comply, they would be ineligible to receive funds from Medicare.

In the fall of 1965, representatives from the SSA met with PHS officials to plan how to determine if hospitals were complying with Title VI. They agreed that the SSA would contribute staff and help formulate rules and procedures to determine whether hospitals were eligible for Medicare funds. The PHS would take responsibility for the large city hospitals and university hospitals. The SSA would assume the more complex task of confronting the local racial state. Its job was to review the smaller hospitals, nursing homes, and home health agencies, especially targeting the 5,500 hospitals and nursing homes in the South.[33] The SSA Regional Offices would then review the compliance reports to see if they were complete and acceptable.

To initiate the process, all hospital administrators received a letter informing them that they could not receive Medicare funds unless they could certify that the hospital did not discriminate in patient admissions, room assignments, or staff assignments.[34] Then, a staff of nearly 500 people was hastily assembled, including several hundred temporarily assigned from other HEW programs, medical students who were on summer internships, and some outside consultants. After a three-week crash training program in civil rights, they were sent to the South to inspect hospitals and review their compliance reports. According to one physician involved in the effort, "The most feared investigators were white southerners. They knew what they were looking for. We were dealing with deceit at all levels. They sniffed it out."[35]

Three characteristics of the SSA helped facilitate the process of Title VI compliance—its organizational capacity, its degree of autonomy, and its policy legacy. The concept of organizational capacity refers to "the extent to which state goals, however determined, can actually be carried out" (Finegold and Skocpol 1995: 52). An organization's capacity to implement policy changes depends on both "the formal and informal procedures, routines, norms, and conventions" embedded in its organizational structure and on its receptiveness to a new policy agenda (Hall and Taylor 1996: 938). Of all agencies within HEW, the SSA was the most organizationally capable of implementing Title VI. It had the field and regional offices already operating to administer the Social Security program and a large staff of managers, assistant managers, and field representatives. It had just issued nineteen million Medicare cards, opened 100 district offices, and hired thousands of people to implement Medicare.

The concept of autonomy refers to "the extent to which the operational goals of public officials are formulated independently from the goals of external actors" (Finegold and Skocpol 1995: 52). The SSA was the only federal agency that was relatively autonomous from both national and local state pressures. All other federal programs that HEW administered were discretionary, meaning that Congress made decisions on how much funding would be provided each year. Social Security, by contrast, was an entitlement program with benefits granted automatically to anyone who met conditions of eligibility. Because of this policy structure, the SSA did not have to respond to demands from particular communities and constituencies. Benefits were not provided through local relief authorities, but went directly to beneficiaries. Not delegating decision-making power to the regions insulated the SSA from local political influence (Lieberman 1998).

Finally, an organization's policy legacy establishes the parameters of options open to it, as well as limiting the direction of future programmatic possibilities (Pierson 1994). Unlike the PHS, the SSA had a policy legacy that was compatible with civil rights objectives. Its historical agenda was to protect the vulnerable, and its clients were the elderly, the widowed, and the disabled. As Commissioner Robert Ball explained:

> From the very foundation of the social security program, our objective has been to provide courteous, efficient service, and equal treatment, under the law, to all claimants. Our training activities have always stressed this. Our legislative proposals . . . have always been prepared with this in mind. The claims manual, itself, represents an exhaustive effort to assure equal treatment of claimants under the law. . . . The whole process of certifying the eligibility of providers of services, including their compliance with Title VI of the Civil Rights Act, is merely an extension of these principles to a new group of beneficiaries.[36]

The SSA's one concern about using Medicare certification to determine Title VI compliance, was that it could damage delicate public relations surrounding the new health care program. As Ball explained:

> The first hard news coming out of implementation of the hospital insurance program would be controversy over whether certain providers of service (discriminate). . . . Not only would these controversies be aired in the public press long before benefits (were paid), they would be aired at the very time we are making every effort to quiet the fears of doctors and others about the Federal Government's involvement in the areas of hospital and medical insurance.[37]

To counter these fears, early in 1966, the SSA embarked on an aggressive public information campaign. Staff distributed booklets explaining Title VI requirements to 10,000 hospitals, 14,000 nursing homes, and 1,000 home health agencies. Officials presented talks to labor groups, institutional provider groups, the insurance industry, religious groups, fraternal organizations, and senior groups. National organizations, like the American Hospital Association and the American Medical Association, were asked to help prepare hospitals to comply with Title VI. The SSA also attempted to reach local opinion makers community by community.[38]

By May 30, 1966, the SSA had a list of all institutions that were in compliance with Title VI.[39] The SSA then developed an action list to identify those hospitals not yet cleared. As Robert Ball declared, "I would like to keep the Public Health Service going during the next week in moving into every area where there is a significant problem and pressing quickly for solutions. Or, if we can no longer expect voluntary compliance, to immediately sue."[40]

THE TRAJECTORY OF HOSPITAL COMPLIANCE

On July 1, 1966, Medicare was put into operation. Some observers argue that the process of certifying Medicare providers "pushed the HEW bureaucracy to the brink of chaos and encouraged expedient actions and compromise" (Wing 1978: 159). According to HEW Undersecretary Wilbur Cohen, however, the signs reading "white" and "colored" were removed from southern hospitals, and "in one day, Medicare . . . broke the back of segregated health services" (Berkowitz 1995: 244). In fact, by July 21, 1966, fewer than 0.5 percent of hospitals were not certified for Medicare eligibility. In the

South, however, 132 counties had no hospitals approved for Medicare, a total of 320 hospitals.[41] Mississippi and Alabama were the slowest to comply.[42]

Compliance was hindered by the difficulty of establishing clear measures of racial integration. For example, inspectors told a hospital in Lynchburg, Virginia, that it could not be certified unless 13 percent of the patients were black. Hospital administrators complained that the quota was too large, given the low percentage of minorities in the service area.[43] Another problem was that eliminating racial barriers did not necessarily lead to integration. Some African Americans feared they would not receive care if they entered a white hospital.[44] In one town in Arkansas, both hospitals were officially desegregated, but patients continued to go to racially separate hospitals. Administrators complained, "Tell us what we are doing wrong and we will make it right." James Lemons, a Negro and an antipoverty official of the program, told federal officials, "Give us some guidelines . . . give us time . . . don't shut off our hospital beds."[45]

The most controversial issue was biracial room occupancy, which represented the most visible symbol of segregation and thus, the greatest threat to the authority of the local racial state. In Alabama, hospitals refused to make biracial room assignments. As a result, only 5 percent of the estimated 18,600 beds met the compliance requirement.[46] In Mississippi, the only threats of violence were triggered by this issue. In Canton, the local hospital administrator received a threatening phone call and was visited by four local Klansmen who told him they planned to bomb the hospital if patients were placed in integrated rooms. At another Mississippi hospital, FBI agents investigated allegations of civil rights violations. When the local HEW manager entered the hospital in Meridian, Mississippi (site of the murder of three civil rights workers), for a minor operation, he shared a room with the head of the local NAACP, an act that was widely criticized by the community. After his release, however, the hospital did make other biracial room assignments. Despite community opposition, the majority of doctors in the state participated willingly in Medicare because they would now be paid for services they had previously performed for free.[47]

If a county had no approved hospital, then Medicare beneficiaries had no health care. In Mount Bayou, Mississippi, for example, the black hospital could not meet the medical requirements for Medicare approval, while the white hospital was having Title VI difficulty.[48] As a result, Medicare beneficiaries had to drive long distances to other hospitals. Further exacerbating the problem was that many insurance companies had canceled their hospital coverage of older people the day Medicare began operating. Beneficiaries who lived in areas where Medicare was not operating thus, had no insurance coverage at all. The dilemma deprived "the most needy citizens of all—the lowest income, least educated, least resourceful, Negro and white alike—of the benefits the law was designed to provide."[49] It also created public relations problems for the SSA. As one staff member explained:

> For a long time, the people of this area have been fed a steady diet of antigovernment propaganda heightened, of course, by their deep fears of the civil rights program, but until now, they have not largely tended to associate social security . . . with all this. Now, I believe there is a very strong feeling that social security has gone over to the enemy.[50]

Some southern hospitals found a way to avoid complying with Title VI and still receive reimbursement from Medicare by billing the government under an "emergency treatment" provision, which was initially allowed.[51] Gradually, this flexibility was eliminated.[52] Others did the "HEW shuffle" during on-site inspections, moving white and black patients into new beds in new rooms and wards for the study team's visit (Nash 1968). By August, 150 problem hospitals remained, encompassing 98 communities, the "hard core" cases that would require time-consuming development.[53] Staff from the OEHO met personally with representatives from these hospitals and informed them that they were now ineligible for Hill-Burton funds and could not be certified for Medicare. One hospital with "white" and "colored" entrances was required to remove the signs and label one "entrance" and the other "exit." Separate waiting areas could not be assigned by race, but labeled "overflow." Local civil rights organizations served as monitors of enforcement activities.

The threat of withholding Medicare funding provided enormous leverage, and by October, only 12 southern hospitals still were not certified.[54] Most hospital authorities quietly signed nondiscrimination assurances, and most hospitals took steps to comply with Title VI. Some wrote to black physicians inviting them to apply for staff privileges. A few hospitals held out longer by rejecting Medicare patients, but the courts took aggressive measures, filing suit against private hospitals that engaged in overt discrimination. In the long run, the financial viability of all hospitals depended on the continuous receipt of this stream of federal funds. Yet, one of the unintended and perverse consequences of the integration of white hospitals was the closing of many small black hospitals in the South (Beardsley 1986).

After OEHO had been operating for 15 months, a separate Office of Civil Rights (OCR) was created within HEW. OCR was given responsibility for supervising all HEW civil rights activities and for handling difficult cases. Responsibility for day-to-day activities remained with the various agencies (Miles 1974). Then, in 1967, OEHO was dissolved entirely and its responsibilities transferred to the newly expanded OCR. Because no new funds were delegated for OCR, it had to compete for funds with other on-going programs, as well as for other activities with high priorities, especially school desegregation.[55] Suffering from a chronic problem of understaffing, OCR failed to review many hospitals after the initial compliance activities were completed. Some hospitals took advantage of lax enforcement efforts to reinstate their discriminatory practices. Although it is important not to overstate the success of the integration effort, noncompliance was confined to a few cases and formal barriers were removed everywhere. By 1985, southern hospitals were the most integrated in the nation (Smith 1998).

Conclusion

The welfare state can transform patterns of class stratification by buffering workers from the insecurity of the market and thus, empowering them to challenge employers over wages and conditions of work. The welfare state can also reconstruct gender relations by providing women with a livelihood that allows them to establish an autonomous household and by offering social services that increase their access to paid work. This case study of hospital integration suggests that, under certain conditions, the welfare state can also reconstruct race relations by intervening in the social institutions that produce and sustain racial inequality. What are those conditions? The evidence indicates that the following four conditions are required. First, racial minorities must garner sufficient political resources to challenge institutionalized patterns of racial discrimination. Since racial minorities cannot, by definition, mobilize voting power through their numerical superiority, they must rely on other forms of political influence that are more transient and episodic. Second, the institutions that maintain the racial order must be incorporated into the public sphere so that they can be subject to the regulatory authority of the state. The redefinition of the public sphere is thus, an inherently political act whose effectiveness in reducing inequality will vary according to its scope. Third, the funds and regulatory apparatus of the welfare state must be directed toward the objective of promoting racial equality. This objective cannot be achieved by simply providing benefits to individuals, but must also involve institutional change. Fourth, the benefits provided through the welfare state must be continuous and universal. If the benefits are not enduring, and if they allow some institutions to "escape" from coverage, then they will promote tokenism and noncompliance.

During the 1960s, the welfare state had an impact that varied across institutional spheres depending on how fully these conditions were met. Civil rights advocates sought to expand equality of opportunity in employment and to end racial discrimination in housing. The law supported these objectives and the welfare state provided funds for job training and housing that might have provided the leverage to implement them. However, these funds were targeted to specific projects or programs and limited in their reach to those few arenas that were incorporated into the public sphere. Most employers, contractors, and homeowners did not receive federal funds. As a result, federal officials were only minimally successful in integrating the labor market and the housing market because jobs and neighborhoods remained in the "private" sphere, outside the regulatory jurisdiction of the state.

In the health care system, by contrast, civil rights advocates mobilized their limited political resources to end racial inequality in access to health care. They litigated to transform the definition of hospitals from private to public institutions; they also engaged in demonstrations and lobbying to alter public opinion and pressure state bureaucrats to promote compliance with civil rights objectives. These efforts only succeeded, however, because they coincided with the implementation of Medicare, a universal program of health insurance for the aged that not only provided benefits to individuals, but also to institutions. Medicare funds proved to be a powerful mechanism to undermine resistance and promote compliance with equal opportunity initiatives because funds were payable to all hospitals and the flow of dollars was continuous.

In the 1960s, the route to equality of health care access was through racial integration. Although the formal barriers to racial equality have been removed, more than three decades later, racial discrepancies in access to care remain. From conception to death, African Americans receive less health care and health outcomes remain profoundly unequal (Rice and Winn 1990; Lado 1994). To a large degree, racial differences in health care access are the result of the failure of the state to eliminate racial barriers in other institutional spheres. Continuing patterns of residential segregation sustain hospital segregation. The most segregated hospitals are those in cities with high levels of residential segregation, especially those in the Northwest and North Central regions of the United States (Smith 1993). Health care segregation is also the result of practices that are not directly discriminatory, but have the same effect as direct racial discrimination. Some health care facilities have moved from African-American and Latino communities to the predominantly white suburbs. Other hospitals have closed or moved emergency rooms and obstetrical care units, the point of entry for the poor. Some have adopted highly restrictive admission policies or engaged in patient dumping, the practice of transferring emergency room patients from private hospitals to local public hospitals (Lado 1994). In many cases, the motivation is to change the patient mix to increase reimbursement from insurers. These tactics, which are designed to limit access for the poor, have a disproportionate impact on African Americans, who are perceived by private facilities as potential revenue losses.

Despite the eradication of direct racial barriers, health outcomes remain profoundly unequal, the result of such complex processes as the rationing of health care according to ability to pay, the provision of inadequate and inferior health care for poor people, and the nation's inability to institute measures to eliminate continuing segregation in other social institutions that have an indirect impact on the provision of health care services. Although the welfare state may be capable of profoundly transforming systems of racial stratification, these unresolved dilemmas illustrate its limitations. Not all forms of inequality can be resolved through benefit programs. Rather, what is required is a more fundamental restructuring of social, economic, and political institutions in the United States.

Notes

1. Research Group 235, Records of the Public Health Division, Office of the General Counsel, HEW, Box 7: Hospital Construction. File: Segregation and Discrimination. Memo to The Secretary from Alanson Willcox, March 4, 1964.
2. RG 235, HEW, Box 7: Hospital Construction. File: Segregation and Discrimination. Memo from Gladys Harrison to Harold Siegel, January 18, 1954.
3. RG 235, HEW, Box 7: Hospital Construction. File: Segregation and Discrimination. Letter from Hubert Eaton to Dr. Boisfeuillet Jones, October 13, 1962; Letter from Boisfeuillet Jones, Special Assistant to the Secretary, to Dr. Hubert Eaton, November 13, 1962.
4. RG 235, HEW, Box 7: Hospital Construction. File: Segregation and Discrimination. Memo from Darrell Lane to Parke Banta, June 10, 1954; Memo: Hospital survey and construction-nondiscrimination requirements under present statute, January 31, 1956.
5. RG 235, HEW, Box 7: Hospital Construction. File: Segregation and Discrimination. Memo from Edward Rourke, October 11, 1961.
6. RG 235, HEW, Box 7: Hospital Construction. File: Segregation and Discrimination. Hospital construction program nondiscrimination-constitutional question, November 16, 1956.
7. RG 235, Records of the Public Health Division, State Files, HEW, Box 2. File: Mississippi, Louisiana. Memo from Gladys Harrison to Edward Rourke, November 16, 1956.

8. RG 235, HEW, Box 7: Hospital Construction. File: Segregation and Discrimination. Memo from Gladys Harrison to Parke Banta, January 31, 1956.

9. RG 235, HEW, Box 7: Hospital Construction. File: Segregation and Discrimination. Memo from Alanson Willcox to Jack Haldeman, February 12, 1963.

10. RG 235, HEW, Box 7: Hospital Construction. File: Segregation and Discrimination. Memo from Office of General Counsel to Carl Harper, Regional Attorney, December 31, 1959.

11. RG 235, HEW, Box 7: Hospital Construction. File: Segregation and Discrimination. Memo from Carl Harper to Edward Rourke, Assistant General Counsel, Office of General Counsel, May 4, 1962.

12. RG 235, HEW, Box 7: Hospital Construction. File: Segregation and Discrimination. Letter from James S. Carr, Deputy Regional Attorney to Edward Burke, Assistant General Counsel to HEW, October 16, 1962.

13. RG 235, HEW, Box 7: Hospital Construction. File: Segregation and Discrimination. "Negroes' Suit Demands Full Grady Hospital Integration." Atlanta Constitution, September 25, 1962, 1.

14. RG 235, HEW, Box 7: Hospital Construction. File: Segregation and Discrimination. Letter from James S. Carr, Deputy Regional Attorney to Edward Burke, Assistant General Counsel to HEW, October 16, 1962.

15. RG 235, HEW, Box 7: Hospital Construction. File: Segregation and Discrimination. Memo to General Counsel to Marion E. Gardner, Wood v. Hogan, Lynchburg General Hospital, June 25, 1962.

16. RG 235, HEW, Box 7: Hospital Construction. File: Segregation and Discrimination. Letter from Virgil A. Wood to Robert F. Kennedy, June 8, 1962.

17. RG 235, HEW, Box 7: Hospital Construction. File: Segregation and Discrimination. Memo from Edward Rourke to Luther Terry, April 6, 1964.

18. RG 235, HEW, Box 7: Hospital Construction. File: Segregation and Discrimination. Letter from Alanson Willcox to Reginald Hawkins, August 20, 1964.

19. RG 235, HEW, Box 7: Hospital Construction. File: Segregation and Discrimination. Memo from Alanson Willcox to Wilbur Cohen, August 14, 1963.

20. RG 235, HEW, Records of the Public Health Division, State Files, Box 1. File: Alabama. Correspondence between Catherine Patterson, Burke Marshall, and Alanson Willcox, October 4, October 23, October 25, 1963.

21. RG 235, HEW, Box 7: Hospital Construction. File: Segregation and Discrimination. Letter from Reginald Hawkins to Alanson Willcox, July 27, 1963.

22. RG 235, HEW, Box 7: Hospital Construction. File: Segregation and Discrimination. Letter from Reginald Hawkins to Alanson Willcox, July 27, 1963.

23. RG 235, HEW, Box 7: Hospital Construction. File: Segregation and Discrimination. Letter from Senator Harrison Williams to Jack Haldeman, February 4, 1963.

24. RG 235, HEW, Box 7: Hospital Construction. File: Segregation and Discrimination. Memo from Lisle Carter to Alanson Wilcox, June 18, 1962.

25. RG 235, HEW, Box 7: Hospital Construction. File: Segregation and Discrimination. Memo from James Quigley to Alanson Wilcox, July 10, 1963.

26. Congressional Record, April 3, 1957, 4480–4482.

27. Congressional Record, April 3, 1957, 4482.

28. RG 235, HEW, Box 7: Hospital Construction. File: Segregation and Discrimination. Memo from Gladys Harrison to Parke Banta, January 31, 1956, Appendix I, State Statutes.

29. RG 235, HEW, Box 7: Hospital Construction. File: Segregation and Discrimination. Conduct required under state statutes which is inconsistent with the nondiscrimination assur-

ances in the Hill-Burton, mental retardation facilities and community mental health centers construction programs, June 26, 1964.

30. RG 235, HEW, Box 7: Hospital Construction. File: Segregation and Discrimination. Conduct required under state statutes which is inconsistent with the nondiscrimination assurances in the Hill-Burton, mental retardation facilities and community mental health centers construction programs, June 26, 1964.

31. RG 47, Records of the Social Security Administration, Office of the Commissioner, Box 300. File: PA 16, Title VI Compliance. Title VI of the Civil Rights Act, December 14, 1965.

32. RG 47, Box 300. File: PA 16, Title VI Compliance. Memo from Robert Nash to James Murray. Medicare and Civil Rights, March 19, 1966.

33. RG 47, Box 300. File: PA 16, Title VI Compliance. Title VI of Civil Rights Act of 1965, 1.

34. RG 47, Box 300. File: PA 16, Title VI Compliance. Hospital Application for Participation; Guidelines for Compliance with title VI.

35. Telephone interview with Dr. Richard Smith, career service officer in the Public Health Service and Special Projects officer, February 17, 1999.

36. RG 47, Box 300. File: PA 16, Title VI Compliance, Commissioner's Bulletin.

37. RG 47, Box 300. File: PA 16, Title VI Compliance, Memo from Robert Ball to the Undersecretary, October 13, 1965.

38. RG 47, Box 300. File: PA 16, Title VI Compliance. Memo from Robert Ball to the Secretary, March 14, 1966.

39. RG 47, Box 300. File: PA 16, Title VI Compliance. Memo from Louis Zawatzky to Jack Futterman, January 18, 1966.

40. RG 47, Box 300. File: PA 16, Title VI Compliance. Note from Robert Ball to Irv Wolkstein, July 2, 1966.

41. RG 47, Box 298. File: PA 16, Hospital Compliance Report. Memo from Roy Swift. Corrected number of Southern counties with no Medicare hospitals, July 25, 1966.

42. RG 47, Box 298. File: PA 16, Hospital Compliance Report. Title VI Compliance Problems.

43. RG 47, Box 300. File: PA 16, Title VI Compliance. Memo from Roy Swift to Robert Ball, May 27, 1966. Observations on Title VI Compliance Efforts.

44. Interview with Dr. Richard Smith.

45. RG 47, Box 298. File: PA 16, Hospital Compliance Report. "Federal Compliance Complaint is Puzzle for Officials of Two Hospitals in Lincoln." Elk Valley Times, June 29, 1966.

46. RG 47, Box 300. File: PA 16, Title VI Compliance. Memo from James Murray to Robert Ball, Medicare and civil rights, February 15, 1966.

47. RG 47, Box 298. File: PA, Title VI Compliance. Letter from Roy Swift to Robert Ball.

48. RG 47, Box 298. File: PA 16, Hospital Compliance Report. Taborian Hospital.

49. RG 47, Box 298. File: PA, Title VI Compliance. Report of Title VI Issues, Natchez, Mississippi, July 15, 1966.

50. RG 47, Box 298. File: PA, Title VI Compliance. Letter from Roy Swift to Robert Ball.

51. RG 47, Box 298. File: PA 16, Hospital Compliance Report. Memo from Peter Libassi to Robert Ball, July 25, 1966.

52. Telephone interview with Robert Ball, former commissioner of Social Security, October 24, 1997.

53. RG 47, Box 298. File: PA 16, Hospital Compliance Report. Memo from Louis Zawatzky to Robert Ball, August 17, 1966.

54. RG 47, Box 298. File: PA 16, Hospital Compliance Report Determination of Inability to Secure Compliance by Voluntary Means, December 30, 1966.

55. RG 47, Box 300. File: PA 16, Title VI Compliance. Organization of PHS Office of Equal Opportunity, January 11, 1966.

References

Abramovitz, Mimi. 1988. *Regulating the Lives of Women*. Boston: South End Press.

Beardsley, E. H. 1986. "Goodbye to Jim Crow: The Desegregation of Southern Hospitals, 1945–1970." *Bulletin of the History of Medicine* 60: 367–386.

Berkowitz, Edward. 1995. *Mr. Social Security: The Life of Wilbur J. Cohen*. Lawrence: University Press of Kansas.

Boris, Eileen, and Peter Bardaglio. 1983. "The Transformation of Patriarchy: The Historic Role of the State." Pp. 71–84 in *Families, Politics, and Public Policy*. Irene Diamond, ed. New York: Longman.

Branch, Taylor. 1988. *Parting the Waters*. New York: Simon & Schuster

Burstein, Paul. 1993. "Explaining State Action and the Expansion of Civil Rights: The Civil Rights Act of 1964." *Research in Political Sociology* 6: 117–137.

———. 1998. "Bringing the Public Back In: Should Sociologists Consider the Impact of Public Opinion on Public Policy?" *Social Forces* 77: 27–62.

Esping-Andersen, Gosta. 1990. *The Three Worlds of Welfare Capitalism*. Princeton, NJ: Princeton University Press.

———. 1999. *Social Foundation of Postindustrial Economies*. New York: Oxford University Press.

Fraser, Nancy. 1992. "Rethinking the Public Sphere: Actually Existing Democracy." Pp. 109–142 in *Habermas and the Public Sphere*. Craig Calhoun, ed. Cambridge, MA: MIT Press.

Finegold, Kenneth, and Theda Skocpol. 1995. State and Party in America's New Deal. Madison: University of Wisconsin Press.

Fox-Genovese, Elizabeth. 1991. *Feminism Without Illusions*. Chapel Hill: University of North Carolina Press.

Goldfield, Michael. 1997. *The Color of Politics*. New York: New Press.

Gordon, Linda. 1990. *Women, the State, and Welfare*. Madison: University of Wisconsin Press.

Hacker, Jacob S. 1998. "The Historical Logic of National Health Insurance: Structure and Sequence in the Development of British, Canadian, and U.S. Medical Policy." *Studies in American Political Development* 12: 57–130.

Hall, Peter, and Rosemary Taylor. 1996. "Political Science and the Three New Institutionalisms." *Political Studies* XLIV: 936–957.

Harrington Meyer, Madonna. 1996. "Making Claims as Workers or Wives: The Distribution of Social Security Benefits." *American Sociological Review* 61: 449–465.

Hobson, Barbara. 1990. "No Exit, No Voice: Women's Economic Dependency and the Welfare State." *Acta Sociologica* 33: 235–250.

James, David R. 1988. "The Transformation of the Southern Racial State: Class and Race Determinants of Local–State Structures." *American Sociological Review* 53: 191–208.

Janoski, Thomas, and Alexander Hicks. 1994. *The Comparative Political Economy of the Welfare State*. Cambridge, UK: Cambridge University Press.

Jones, Augustus. 1982. *Law, Bureaucracy and Politics*. Washington, DC: University Press of America.

Knowles, Louis L., and Kenneth Prewitt. 1969. *Institutional Racism in America*. Englewood Cliffs, NJ: Prentice Hall.

Korpi, Walter. 1989. "Power, Politics and State Autonomy in the Development of Social Citizenship." *American Sociological Review* 54: 309–328.

Lado, M. E. 1994. "Breaking the Barriers of Access to Health Care: A Discussion of the Role of Civil Rights Litigation and the Relationship between Burdens of Proof and the Experience of Denial." *Brooklyn Law Review* 60: 239–273.

Lewis, Jane. 1997. "Gender and Welfare Regimes: Further Thoughts." *Social Politics* 4: 160–177.
Lieberman, Robert C. 1998. *Shifting the Color Line: Race and the American Welfare State.* Cambridge, MA: Harvard University Press.
Maioni, Antonia. 1998. *Parting at the Crossroads.* Princeton, NJ: Princeton University Press.
Marmor, Theodore. 1970. *The Politics of Medicare.* New York: Aldine.
Marshall, T. H. 1964. *Citizenship and Social Class.* Oxford: Oxford University Press.
Massey, Doug, and Nancy Denton. 1993. *American Apartheid.* Cambridge, MA: Harvard University Press.
Meltsner, M. 1966. "Equality and Health." *Pennsylvania Law Review* 115: 22–38.
Miles, Rufus, Jr. 1974. *The Department of Health, Education and Welfare.* New York: Praeger.
Morone, James A. 1990. *The Democratic Wish.* New York: Basic Books.
Morris, Aldon. 1986. *The Origins of the Civil Rights Movement.* New York: Free Press.
Myles, John. 1988. *Old Age in the Welfare State.* Lawrence: University Press of Kansas.
Naples, Nancy A. 1998. *Grassroots Warriors.* New York: Routledge.
Nash, Robert. 1968. "Compliance of Hospitals and Health Agencies with Title VI of the Civil Rights Act." *American Journal of Public Health* 58: 246–251.
National Medical Association. 1963. "Integrationist Battlefront." *Journal of the National Medical Association* 55: 339.
National Urban League. 1965. *Health Care and the Negro Population.* New York: National Urban League.
Nelson, Barbara. 1984. "Women's Poverty and Women's Citizenship: Some Political Consequences of Marginality." *Signs* 10: 209–232.
O'Connor, Julia S., Ann Shola Orloff, and Sheila Shaver. 1999. *States, Labor Markets and Families.* Cambridge, UK: Cambridge University Press.
Oliver, Melvin, and Tom Shapiro. 1995. *Black Wealth/White Wealth.* New York: Routledge.
Omi, Michael, and Howard Winant. 1994. *Racial Formation in the United States.* New York: Routledge.
Orloff, Ann. 1993. "Gender and the Social Rights of Citizenship: The Comparative Analysis of State Policies and Gender Relations." *American Sociological Review* 58: 303–328.
———. 1996. "Gender in the Welfare State." *Annual Review of Sociology* 22: 51–78.
Pedriana, Nicholas, and Robin Stryker. 1997. "Political Culture Wars 1960s Style: Equal Employment Opportunity—Affirmative Action and Philadelphia Plan." *American Journal of Sociology* 103: 633–691.
Pierson, Paul. 1994. *Dismantling the Welfare State.* Cambridge, UK: Cambridge University Press.
Poen, Monty. 1979. *Harry S Truman vs. the Medical Lobby.* Columbus: University of Missouri Press.
Powell, Adam Clayton. 1963. "Hospital Integration and Job Opportunity: Equality Goals for 1963." *Journal of the National Medical Association* July: 338–341.
Quadagno, Jill. 1988. *The Transformation of Old Age Security.* Chicago: University of Chicago Press.
———. 1992. "Social Movements and State Transformation: Labor Unions and Racial Conflict in the War on Poverty." *American Sociological Review* 57: 616–634.
———. 1994. *The Color of Welfare: How Racism Undermined the War on Poverty.* New York: Oxford University Press.
Rabkin, Jeremy. 1980. "Office for Civil Rights." Pp. 304–353 in *The Politics of Regulation.* James Q. Wilson, ed. New York: Basic Books.
Reskin, Barbara. 1998. *The Realities of Affirmative Action in Employment.* Washington, DC: American Sociological Association.

Rice, M. F., and M. Winn. 1990. "Black Health Care in America: A Political Perspective." *Journal of the National Medical Association* 26: 429–436.

Ruggie, Mary. 1984. *The State and Working Women*. Princeton, NJ: Princeton University Press.

Sainsbury, Diane. 1996. *Gender, Equality and Welfare States*. Cambridge, UK: Cambridge University Press.

Schmitt, Fredrika E., and Patricia Yancey Martin. 1999. "Unobtrusive Mobilization by an Institutionalized Rape Crisis Center: 'All We Do Comes from Victims.'" *Gender and Society* 13: 364–384.

Schuman, Howard, Charlotte Steeh, Lawrence Bobo, and Maria Krysan. 1997. *Racial Attitudes in America*. Cambridge, MA: Harvard University Press.

Skocpol, Theda. 1992. *Protecting Soldiers and Mothers*. Cambridge, MA: Harvard University Press.

Smith, David Barton. 1993. "The Racial Integration of Health Facilities." *Journal of Health, Politics and Law* 18: 851–869.

———. 1998. "Addressing Racial Inequities in Health Care: Civil Rights Monitoring and Report Cards." *Journal of Health Politics, Policy and Law* 23: 75–105.

Starr, Paul. 1982. *The Social Transformation of American Medicine*. New York: Basic Books.

Terry, Luther. 1965. "Hospitals and Title VI of the Civil Rights Act." *Hospitals* 39: 34–37.

Wing, Kenneth. 1978. "Title VI and Health Facilities: Forms without Substance." *Hastings Law Journal* 30: 137–190.

CHAPTER 11

Managing Differences and Making Legislation

SOCIAL MOVEMENTS AND THE RACIALIZATION, SEXUALIZATION, AND GENDERING OF FEDERAL HATE CRIME LAW IN THE U.S., 1985–1998

Valerie Jenness

In 1998, three highly publicized cases of homicide involved victims apparently chosen because of a single social characteristic. In March, four young girls were gunned down in a Jonesboro, Arkansas, schoolyard by two of their classmates; the boys now in custody for the killings revealed they sought to shoot girls because girls angered them. In June, James Byrd, a 49-year-old black man in Texas, was beaten and then dragged behind a truck to his death by three white men affiliated with a white supremacist group. Most recently, in Laramie, Wyoming, Matthew Shepard, a young gay man, was pistol-whipped, tied to a fence, and left to die. To various degrees, each of these events provided a platform for public discussion of the meaning of hate crime and the law's responsibility to recognize the difference between "hate crime" and "ordinary crime." This distinction signals that a new category of crime—hate crime—has secured a place in the "social problems marketplace" (Hilgartner and Bosk 1988).

As journalists, activists, politicians, educators, community representatives, and others continue to debate how best to respond to a reported "rising tide of bigotry and bloodshed" (Levin and McDevitt 1993), the law has become the primary institution charged with defining and curbing hate- or bias-motivated violence. Legal reform has been a, if not the, dominant response to bias-motivated violence in the U.S. (Jenness and Grattet 2000). During a congressional debate on hate crime, U.S. Representative Mario Biaggi argued: "The obvious point is that we are dealing with a national problem and we must look to our laws for remedies" (*Congressional Record* 1985:19844). Accordingly, in the early 1980s, state and federal lawmakers throughout the U.S. began responding to what they perceived to be an escalation of intergroup conflict with a novel legal strategy: criminalizing hate-motivated intimidation and violence. As U.S. Representative John Conyers, Jr., now the ranking member of the Judiciary Committee, explained: The enactment of hate crime legislation "will carry to offenders, to victims, and to society at large an important message, that the Nation is committed to battling the violent manifestations of bigotry" (U.S. Congress 1985a:62).

But the question remains, what manifestations of violent conduct and what types of people occupy center stage in Congress's battle against bigotry and why? Since the inception of the term "hate crime," federal legislators have generally agreed that "hate crimes, which can range from threats and vandalism to arson, assault and murder, are intended not just to harm the victim, but to send a message of intimidation to an entire community of people" (U.S. Representative Conyers, cited in *Congressional Record* 1988:11393). Moreover, the general justification for federal legislation has been that harassment and intimidation, assault, and destruction of property assume a particularly dangerous and socially disruptive character when motivated by bigotry (Jacobs and Potter 1998; Jenness and Grattet 2000; Lawrence 1999). In contrast to congressional debates featuring competing definitions of social problems (e.g., paid work, family, and gender [Burstein and Bricher 1997] or welfare reform [Naples 1997]), members of Congress never departed from this basic formulation. There has, however, been considerable controversy over what types of people and what "target groups" (Soule and Earl 1999) should be protected by hate crime legislation. As a result, some victims of discriminatory violence have been recognized as hate crime victims while others have gone unnoticed: people of color, Jews, gays and lesbians, women, and those with disabilities increasingly have been recognized as hate crime victims, while union members, the elderly, children, and police officers have not been recognized by law as victims of hate crime. This differentiation affects the kinds of people protected, and thus the kinds of violence prosecutors can pursue as hate crime.

Distinctions along these lines reflect the statutes that define hate- or bias-motivated violence as "hate crime," distinct from "ordinary crime" (Grattet, Jenness, and Curry 1998; Jenness and Grattet 1996, 2000; Lawrence 1999). That is, the statuses included in the concept of "hate crime" are first and foremost a matter of legal interpretation. Moreover, how some statuses become included in the legal category of hate crime is a function of how law is shaped—a fundamentally political process. With this in mind, this article examines one element of a larger political process by addressing a central question in social problems theory and sociolegal studies: How can we understand and account for the creation, content, and institutionalization of legal meanings, especially those that identify victims associated with a contemporary social problem? To investigate the full range of definitional activities that construct social problems, we need to "expand interest into the construction of people categories" because "constructing people-types is integral to the process of constructing condition-types" (Loseke 1993:207–208).[1] This a particularly useful move with regard to hate crime because, in large part, the people-category (i.e., victims) defines the condition-category (i.e., hate crime).

An accumulating body of work examines the processes of legal reform, criminalization, and legislative campaigns that define crime and thus victims of crime. The literature points to important exogenous factors that first provide the impetus for criminalization and then sustain the process over time, including a diverse array of social actors, interest groups, social movements, political opportunities, structural conditions, and media (for reviews see Galliher and Cross 1983; Grattet, Jenness, and Curry 1998; Hagan 1980; Rafter 1990). Although analysts combine these factors to account for the emergence and content of legal categories, the result is only a partial picture. An exclusive focus on political influences and social structural variables diverts attention away from how legal ideas are assembled, presented, and processed within lawmaking arenas (Arnold 1990:92). In previous work on hate crime law, for example, Jenness and Grattet (1996) used a complete inventory of hate crime statutes in the U.S. and social indicator data to investigate the social forces shaping the passage of hate crime legislation; they concluded that structural and policy determinants do not sufficiently explain the recent criminalization of hate. In light of these findings, they argued that symbolic, social movement, and discursive factors must be considered more fully. Accordingly, in later work Grattet et al. (1998) found evidence that social movement-related factors, especially the presence of social movement organizations (SMOs) and expert networks, provide robust and durable predictors of the criminalization of hate; however, they did not link this finding to specific legislative processes that produce law and determine its content. Exactly how social movement mobilization shapes law and the work of lawmakers remains to be addressed.

Consistent with a growing literature (Arnold 1990; Chock 1991, 1994, 1995; Naples 1997), more analytic attention needs to be devoted to examining how legislative reform in particular and policymaking more generally are organized and unfold as proposals for legal reform are introduced, managed, and accepted or rejected in legislative arenas. In this institutional arena, legislative debates occur, constituency interests are negotiated, and political wills are enacted as key players engage in what Burstein (1991:327) calls "the struggle for the adoption of particular policies" when policymakers sift through alternative proposals (Kingdon 1984). In particular, we need to know how SMOs pursuing legal reform—what Best (1990:14–15) refers to as "outside claimsmakers"—interact with policymakers' interpretive and discursive practices to give meaning to statutes as they develop and stabilize over time.

This article's empirical focus is how hate-motivated violence and efforts to use law to control it were constructed, in both discrete moments and over time, in the U.S. Congress. It is here that decisions about the legal categories and substantive content of federal laws that define hate crime have been made, undone, and remade in visible and consequential ways. From 1985 to the present, Congress has held hearings on hate crimes and hate crime legislation, resulting in the passage of three federal hate crime laws. These hearings, including the reports and debates they inspired, are "critical discourse moments" (Chilton 1987; Gamson 1992:26) that reveal "the logic of congressional action" (Arnold 1990).[2]

Theoretical Concerns

The theoretical motivation for the empirical analysis of these hearings is consistent with two interrelated literatures. First, drawing from social problems theory, this work examines "interpretive processes that constitute what comes to be seen as oppressive, intolerable, or unjust conditions" (Miller and Holstein 1993:4). As with most social conditions constructed as social problems, victims have been rendered apparent in the social problem of hate crimes. In commonsense terms, we routinely label persons who have been unjustly harmed or damaged by forces beyond their control as victims (Holstein and Miller 1990; Loseke 1993; Weed 1995). In the case of hate crime, we can (now) point to racial minorities injured by racially motivated violence, gays and lesbians harmed by violence motivated by homophobia, and women harmed simply because they are female. These types of people define the larger problem of hate crime.

A social constructionist approach to victimization devotes analytic attention to the social processes by which persons become recognizable, known, and understood as victims, as opposed to injured persons (Holstein and Miller 1990; Loseke 1993). This approach to the study of victimization is based on the notion that meaning does not inhere in objects, but is conferred upon them as they are interpreted, organized, and represented through social interaction by socially legitimate collective actors, in this case social movement activists and legislators, engaged what Loseke (1993:207) calls "people production." (Other actors, especially the media, also play roles in the construction of hate crime and hate crime victims. [e.g., Best 1999 on the "Iron Quadrangle"].) Social constructionists are particularly interested in understanding the definitional processes that result in assigning victim status to some individuals and groups, but not to others. Such processes are critical because, once designated, victim status carries with it distinct understandings of the social relations that surround the individual, as well as his/her relationship to a larger social problem. Among other things, the label of victim underscores the individual's status as an injured person harmed by forces beyond his/her control; dramatizes the injured or harmed person's essential innocence; renders her/him worthy of others' concern and assistance; and often results in legal reform designed to address the attendant social problem (Holstein and Miller 1990; Loseke 1993; Weed 1995). This approach departs radically from conventional formulations of victimization and allows us to reconceptualize victimization in terms of interactional, discursive, and institutional practices.

Second, this work pursues one of the most promising lines of sociolegal research: examining how legal categories in general and legal subjects in particular are identified and institutionalized (Sarat and Kearns 1997; Silbey and Sarat 1989). To disentangle the process whereby some individuals and constituencies are rendered worthy of legal recognition and recourse, while others are not, I focus on mesolevel processes of social movement mobilization (Beuchler 1990; Gerhards and Rucht 1992; Klandermans 1992; Staggenborg 1998) as they interface with microprocesses of "categorization work" (Frohman 1997; Holstein 1993; Loseke 1993; Jayyusi 1984) to generate law. In so doing, this article examines law as a cultural production—made, contested, and ultimately institutionalized. To understand this fundamental process as it relates to hate-motivated violence and the creation of hate crime victims as a contemporary "people-category" associated with the social problem of hate crime, my analysis focuses on three provisions—"race, religion, and ethnicity," "sexual orientation," and "gender"—to examine how the people-category of hate crime victim was shaped over time in ways that racialized, sexualized, and gendered the law. Throughout, my focus is on how processes of social movement mobilization, categorization work, domain expansion, differentiation, and institutionalization interrelate.

Federal Hate Crime Law in the U.S.

Following the states' lead, the U.S. Congress passed three laws specifically designed to address bias-motivated violence, and it continues to debate additional legislation, such as the Hate Crimes Prevention Act (S. 1529).[3] In 1990 President Bush signed the Hate

Crimes Statistics Act, requiring the U.S. Attorney General to collect statistical data on "crimes that manifest evidence of prejudice based on race, religion, sexual orientation, or ethnicity, including where appropriate the crimes of murder, non-negligent manslaughter; forcible rape; aggravated assault, simple assault, intimidation; arson; and destruction, damage or vandalism of property" (Public Law 101–275).[4]

In 1994, Congress passed two more hate crime laws. The Violence Against Women Act specifies that "all persons within the United States shall have the right to be free from crimes of violence motivated by gender." As protection of this right, the Act creates a new civil remedy for victims of crimes of violence motivated by gender; in so doing, it affixed the term hate crime to "a crime of violence committed because of gender or on the basis of gender, and due, at least in part, to animus based on the victim's gender" (Public Law 103–322).

Also in 1994, Congress passed the Hate Crimes Sentencing Enhancement Act, which identifies eight predicate crimes—murder; nonnegligent manslaughter; forcible rape; aggravated assault; simple assault; intimidation; arson; and destruction, damage, or vandalism of property—for which judges are allowed to enhance penalties of "not less than three offense levels for offenses that finder of fact at trial determines beyond a reasonable doubt are hate crimes" (Public Law 103–322). For the purposes of this law, hate crime is defined as criminal conduct wherein "the defendant intentionally selected any victim or property as the object of the offense because of the actual or perceived race, color, religion, national origin, ethnicity, gender, disability, or sexual orientation of any person" (Public Law 103–322).

Data and Method of Analysis

DATA

I relied upon "the official record" surrounding federal hate crime bills. Specifically, I examined verbatim transcripts of the hearings, reports, debates, and committee prints addressing the three bills that ultimately became law: The Hate Crimes Statistics Act (HCSA), the Violence Against Women Act (VAWA), and the Hate Crimes Sentencing Enhancement Act (HCSEA).[5] Itemized in Table 11.1, these documents reflect the work of six Congresses as they grappled with these three bills. The official record of this lawmaking consists of 43 documents (22 congressional hearings, 12 congressional reports, seven congressional debates, and two committee prints) totaling 4,140 pages. Combined, these materials reveal the legislative workings and attendant discourse of hundreds of lawmakers and other government officials, as well as activists, victims, representatives from social movement and watchdog organizations, and survivors/victims of bias-motivated crime.

METHOD OF ANALYSIS

After arranging the documents in order to produce a comprehensive empirical record of how federal legislative bodies considered, debated, and accepted/rejected proposals to criminalize bias-motivated violence, I organized the information on each bill/Act around key analytic dimensions, including: 1) the identity of the claimsmakers involved in the law's production (activists, politicians, social movement representatives, victims/survivors of violence, etc.); 2) the types of claims put forth in favor of and in opposition to various legislative proposals; and most importantly, 3) the various ways status characteristics-especially race, religion, ethnicity, sexual orientation, and gender were characterized, described, implicated, and negotiated in the process of making federal hate crime law.

Once these dimensions were coded and tracked over time, from 1985 to 1998, I undertook a comparative case study (Yin 1984). Each legislative hearing, report, and debate was treated as a case, one that ultimately could be combined with and compared to other individual cases. The logic of this approach is that "each individual case study consists of a whole study, in which convergent evidence is sought regarding the facts and conclusions for the case; each case's conclusions are then considered to be information needing replication by other individual cases" (Yin 1984:52). This method of analysis allows for "pattern-matching" through "controlled comparisons" as a primary method of increasing internal validity (Stake 1994; Yin 1984). By comparing individual cases along relevant dimensions, I identified empirical patterns and trends, while theoretical ideas emerged and were continually reformulated via analytic induction (Glaser and Strauss 1967; Strauss and Corbin 1994; Yin 1984).

This method of analysis ultimately allowed me to move beyond empirical investigation toward the theoretical concerns identified earlier. To do so, I first establish a historical context for federal hate crime law; then I offer an analysis of an important element of the substantive character of hate crime: how selected statuses became "target groups" (Soule and Earl 1999), defined and institutionalized in federal law. I focus on this particular feature because it, along with an "intent standard" (Berk, Boyd, and Hamner 1992), distinguishes hate crime law from other bodies of law (Grattet, Jenness, and Curry 1998; Jenness and Grattet 1996, 2000; Lawrence 1999). More importantly, it is this feature of hate crime legislation that is most closely aligned with the theoretical concerns identified earlier. My analysis focuses on how "race, religion, and ethnicity," "sexual orientation," and "gender" were introduced, justified/ denied, and ultimately adopted as key provisions in federal hate crime law. Since each provision represents a policy innovation in its own right, I approach each—and the discourse that surrounds it—as a window through which we can see how law in general and legal subjects in particular are created and given meaning over time, such that injured persons are transformed into legally recognizable victims of "hate crime" and the legal concept hate crime is imbued with racialized, sexualized, and gendered meanings.

Making and Institutionalizing Federal Hate Crime Legislation

THE HISTORICAL CONTEXT

Hate-motivated violence and hate crime legislation, as types of behavior and policy response, respectively, emerged in the latter part of the twentieth century. The so-called "rights movements" of the 1960s and 1970s provided the structural basis and discursive themes necessary to set the stage for reenvisioning violence and hateful expressions directed toward minorities as hate crime (Jenness and Broad 1997; Jenness and Grattet 2000; Maroney 1998). These movements converged to question, and make publicly debatable, issues of "rights" and "harm" as they relate to a variety of constituencies. The civil rights, women's, and gay and lesbian movements "called attention to the personal costs of minority groups' political victimization," while "the victims' rights movement called attention to the political context of personal victimization" (Maroney 1998:579). Combined, these movements instigated public discussions about violence born of bigotry and manifest as discrimination.

In the late 1970s, the civil rights and crime victim movements merged to produce an anti-hate crime movement composed of an array of anti-hate crime organizations (Broad and Jenness 1996; Jenness 1995a, 1995b; Jenness and Broad 1997; Jenness and Grattet 2000). "The extraordinary amount of police, legislative, judicial, scholarly, and community activity around hate crime in such a short period of time—less than two decades—is the result of an emerging social movement against hate crime" (Maroney 1998:568). This movement played a key role in defining victims of hate crime.

The Establishment of "Race, Religion, and Ethnicity" as Core Status Provisions in Hate Crime Law

Prior to the first hate crime Congressional hearings in 1985, many organizations in the anti-hate crime movement mobilized at the state level around bias-motivated violence. Their claims accomplished two things. First, they attracted media attention (Best 1999; Jacobs and Potter 1998; Rovella 1994). Second, they presented examples of bias-motivated crime ensured that the problem achieved "empirical credibility" (Jenness 1995b; Jenness and Broad 1997).[6] In response, several states passed hate crime laws (Grattet, Jenness, and Curry 1998; Jenness and Grattet 1996, 2000; Soule and Earl 1999). Thus, some forms of bias-motivated violence were already deemed criminal activity.

Following these successes at the state level, anti-hate crime SMOs turned their attention to federal law. Most notably, the Anti-Defamation League of B'nai B'rith (ADL) was an innovator in collecting, documenting, and publicizing incidents of hate-motivated violence. Since 1979, the ADL has tracked anti-Semitic violence and published an annual "Audit of Anti-Semitic Incidents." Based on data reported to ADL regional offices, these reports describe various "acts of harassment, threat and assault against individuals, their property and their institutions" (Anti-Defamation League 1990:1). These reports consistently revealed a substantial increase in anti-Semitic vandalism and violence from year to year (Anti-Defamation League 1988). By the mid-1980s, the ADL became a central player in national efforts to enhance the monitoring of bias crimes and the systematic collection of hate crime data. The definition of the problem, its extent, and its worsening trend were largely a result of their efforts. Senator Simon, for example, recognized "the group that has kept the best statistics in this

Table 11.1. Documents Comprising the Official Record for Federal Legislation Related to Hate Crime Law, 1985–1998 (Excluding Pending Legislation)

Bill/Law	*Title*	*Document*	*Legislative Body/Audience/Outlet*	*Congress*	*Date*	*Pages*
HCSA	Hate Crimes Statistics Act	Hearing	Subcommittee on Criminal Justice, House Judiciary Committee	99th	3/21/85	148
HCSA	Crimes Against Religious Practices and Property	Hearing	Subcommittee on Criminal Justice, House Judiciary Committee	99th	5/16/85	52
HCSA	Crimes Against Religious Practices and Property	Hearing	Subcommittee on Criminal Justice, House Judiciary Committee	99th	6/19/85	39
HCSA	Hate Crimes Statistics Act	Report	Committee on the Judiciary	99th	7/18/85	4
HCSA	Hate Crimes Statistics Act	Debate	Congressional Record	99th	7/22/85	7
HCSA	Ethnically Motivated Violence Against Arab-Americans	Hearing	Subcommittee on Criminal Justice, House Judiciary Committee	99th	7/16/86	205
HCSA	Anti-Gay Violence	Hearing	Subcommittee on Criminal Justice, House Judiciary Committee	99th	10/9/86	223
HCSA	Anti-Asian Violence	Hearing	Subcommittee on Civil and Constitutional Rights, House Judiciary Committee	100th	11/10/87	459
HCSA	Hate Crimes Statistics Act	Report	Committee on the Judiciary	100th	4/20/88	13
HCSA	Racially Motivated Violence	Hearing	Subcommittee on Criminal Justice, House Judiciary Committee	100th	5/11/88	111
HCSA	Hate Crimes Statistics Act	Debate	Congressional Record	100th	5/18/88	19
HCSA	Hate Crimes Statistics Act	Hearing	Subcommittee on the Constitution, House Judiciary Committee	100th	6/21/88	287
HCSA	Racially Motivated Violence	Hearing	Subcommittee on Criminal Justice, House Judiciary Committee	100th	7/12/88	73
HCSA	Hate Crimes Statistics Act	Report	Committee on the Judiciary	100th	9/15/88	8
HCSA	Hate Crimes Statistics Act	Report	Committee on the Judiciary	101st	5/1/89	13
HCSA	Hate Crimes Statistics Act	Report	Committee on the Judiciary	101st	6/23/89	10
HCSA	Hate Crimes Statistics Act	Debate	Congressional Record	101st	6/27/89	11
HCSA	Hate Crimes Statistics Act	Debate	Congressional Record	101st	2/8/90	26

continued

Table 11.1. Documents Comprising the Official Record for Federal Legislation Related to Hate Crime Law, 1985–1998 (Excluding Pending Legislation) (*continued*)

Bill/Law	*Title*	*Document*	*Legislative Body/Audience/Outlet*	*Congress*	*Date*	*Pages*
HCSA	Hate Crimes Statistics Act	Debate	Congressional Record	101st	4/3/90	4
HCSA	Hate Crimes Statistics Act	Debate	Congressional Record	101st	4/4/90	1
VAWA	Women and Violence	Hearing	Committee on the Judiciary	101st	6/20/90	112
VAWA	Women and Violence	Hearing	Committee on the Judiciary	101st	8/29/90	82
VAWA	The Violence Against Women Act	Report	Committee on the Judiciary	101st	10/19/90	88
VAWA	Women and Violence	Hearing	Committee on the Judiciary	101st	12/11/90	223
VAWA	Violence Against Women: The Increase of Rape in America	Print	Committee on the Judiciary	102nd	3/21/91	37
VAWA	Violence Against Women: Victims of the System	Hearing	Committee on the Judiciary	102nd	4/9/91	442
VAWA	The Violence Against Women Act	Report	Committee on the Judiciary	102nd	10/29/91	111
VAWA	The Violence Against Women Act	Hearing	Subcommittee on Crime and Criminal Justice House Judiciary Committee	102nd	2/6/92	120
HCSEA	Bias Crime	Hearing	Subcommittee on Crime and Criminal Justice House Judiciary Committee	102nd	5/11/92	184
HCSEA	Hate Crimes Sentencing Enhancement Act	Hearing	Subcommittee on Crime and Criminal Justice House Judiciary Committee	102nd	7/29/92	214
HCSA	Hate Crimes Statistic Act	Hearing	Subcommittee on the Constitution House Judiciary Committee	102nd	8/5/92	139
VAWA	Violence Against Women: A Week in the Life of America	Print	Committee on the Judiciary	102nd	10/1/91	38
HCSEA	Hate Crimes Sentencing Enhancement Act	Report	Committee on the Judiciary	102nd	10/2/91	7
VAWA	Violence Crimes Against Women	Hearing	Committee on the Judiciary	103rd	4/13/93	84
VAWA	The Violence Women Act	Report	Committee on the Judiciary	103rd	9/10/93	111
HCSA	Hate Crimes Sentencing Enhancement Act	Report	Committee on the Judiciary	103rd	9/21/93	7
VAWA	Violence Against Women: Fighting the Fear	Hearing	Committee on the Judiciary	103rd	11/12/93	57

(*continued*)

Table 11.1. Documents Comprising the Official Record for Federal Legislation Related to Hate Crime Law, 1985–1998 (Excluding Pending Legislation) (Continued)

Bill/Law	*Title*	*Document*	*Legislative Body/Audience/Outlet*	*Congress*	*Date*	*Pages*
VAWA	Crimes of Violence Motivated by Gender	Hearing	Subcommittee on Constitutional and Civil Rights, House Judiciary Committee	103rd	11/16/93	129
VAWA	The Violence Women Act	Report	Committee on the Judiciary	103rd	11/20/93	66
HCSA	Hate Crimes Statistics Act	Hearing	Subcommittee on the Constitution, House Judiciary Committee	103rd	6/28/94	58
HCSA	Reauthorization of the Hate Crimes Statistics Act	Hearing	Committee on the Judiciary	104th	03/19/96	110
HCSA	To Reauthorize the Hate Crimes Statistics Act	Report	Committee on the Judiciary	104th	05/13/96	6
HCSA	Hate Crimes Statistics Act	Debate	Congressional Record	104th	06/21/96	2

Totals: 3 bills/laws, 6 Congresses, 22 Congressional Hearings, 12 Congressional Reports, 7 Congressional Debates, 2 Committee Prints, 4140 Pages of Documents whole field is the Anti-Defamation League of B'nai B'rith. They report a rising tide of anti-Semitic activity. It is the only solid statistical evidence we have in the nation" (*Congressional Record* 1990a:1072). Moreover, when law enforcement representatives, especially those from the Bureau of Justice Statistics, opposed the HCSA on the grounds that hate crime data simply could not be collected, Simon responded: "But it does seem to me that if Mr. Schwartz over here with the ADL can collect data on this kind of problem, we ought to be able to do it in the Department of Justice. I think it is an important service that is needed in the nation" (U.S. Congress 1988a:122).

The ADL's Legal Affairs Department also drafted a model hate crime bill to be introduced in state legislatures. The ADL's model legislation contained two parts: the Institutional Vandalism Statute prohibits an individual from vandalizing, defacing, or damaging places of worship, cemeteries, schools, or community centers; while the Intimidation Statute provides enhanced penalties for crimes committed because of the victim's actual or perceived race, color, religion, sexual orientation, or national origin. By the time the U.S. Congress held its first hearing on hate crime on March 21, 1985, almost half the states had adopted a hate crime statute similar to the ADL's model. At this point, the term hate crime referenced a narrowly defined phenomenon. The (early) definition of hate crime, which was restricted to acts involving racial, religious, or ethnic bias, was largely the result of the watchdog groups, especially the ADL. Consistent with the ADL's data collection efforts and model legislation, early federal legislative proposals focused only on "race, religion, and ethnicity" as the core provisions in federal hate crime legislation, thus only people of color, non-Christians, and ethnic minorities were envisioned as target populations.

Introduced in 1985 and supported by "The Coalition on Hate Crimes,"[7] the HCSA was the first piece of federal legislation to bring national attention to the problem of hate-motivated violence, underscore the need for official response, and create a new category of crime to be counted as part of larger federal efforts to keep track of crime. Early in the formulation of this bill, only provisions for race, religion, and ethnicity were included. In the first hearing, Representative Mineta called the HCSA "a piece of legislation that will help protect Americans from the most insidious types of crimes, those that are motivated by a hatred of a person merely because of their race, their religious or their ethnic background" (U.S. Congress 1985b:27).

After hearings on "Crimes Against Religious Practices and Property" in July 1985, the House Committee on the Judiciary urged passage of the HCSA to "collect and publish statistics on crimes motivated by racial, ethnic, and religious prejudice" (U.S. Congress 1985c:1). Although representatives from the Federal Bureau of Investigation (FBI) objected to the bill on the grounds that it was unenforceable, no testimony contested the legitimacy of race, religion, and ethnicity as core provisions in hate crime legislation. Moreover, no additional status provisions were mentioned, much less formally introduced as amendments to the bill. Clearly, this conceptualization of the social problem was devised by outside claimsmakers (i.e., SMOs and their representatives), generally agreed upon by the relevant moral entrepreneurs, and encountered little resistance when it was imported into the federal legislative arena.

Adding "Sexual Orientation" to the List of Status Provisions in Hate Crime Law

Soon, the domain of hate crime law began to expand. Domain expansion occurs when claimsmakers offer new definitions that extend the boundaries of the phenomenon deemed problematic (Best 1990; Jenness 1995a, 1995b). The domain covered by federal hate crime legislation began to expand as new target groups were identified. Specifically, after the HCSA bill was introduced in 1985, but before it passed in 1990, "sexual orientation" was added to its list of status provisions; similarly, the HCSEA included "sexual orientation" as a provision. This addition expanded the domain of protected groups and gave new meaning to the term hate crime by redefining the people-category associated with it.

Similar to the role the ADL played in the initial hearings on hate crime, in subsequent hearings on the HCSA and the HCSEA, the National Gay and Lesbian Task Force (NGLTF) and other gay and lesbian civil rights groups proved crucial in evoking and sustaining the expansion of the law. Joan Weiss, executive director of the National Institute Against Prejudice and Violence, acknowledged the work of the NGLTF: "We have the Anti-Defamation League data; we have the National Gay and Lesbian Task Force data; we have data from a variety of sources and, in fact, as far as we're concerned, the evidence of the existence of the problem is irrefutable" (U.S. Congress 1988b:18).

On October 9, 1986 the Subcommittee on Criminal Justice of the Committee on the Judiciary conducted an oversight hearing on antigay violence (U.S. Congress 1986a). At this hearing, the NGLTF and other gay and lesbian organizations played the central role by testifying on the causes, manifestations, and consequences of antigay and lesbian violence, as well as the public invisibility and epidemic scope of the problem. Kevin Berrill, the director of the NGLTF's Violence Project, was the first to testify and his chief concern was to "recommend official monitoring of antigay incidents and other hate crimes" (U.S. Congress 1986a:4). He said, "Presently there is a bill, H.R. 2455, which has passed the House and is pending in the Senate, that would mandate the collection of statistics on crimes motivated by racial and religious prejudice. We [the NGLTF] urge its passage and ask Congress to enact legislation that would require the collection of data on antigay crimes" (U.S. Congress 1986a:4).

Testimony designed to include sexual orientation in federal hate crime law made frequent comparisons between antigay and lesbian violence and violence based on race, religion, or ethnicity. For example, Berrill compared homosexuals to Jews:

> I would like to point out that many of the witnesses at this hearing will be wearing a pink triangle, which was the badge that identified homosexual inmates of Nazi concentrations camps. Although it is an often overlooked fact, tens of thousands of gay persons were herded into the camps, and, along with Jews, gypsies, and others, were gassed and incinerated. We wear the triangle to remember them and to remind people of the terrible cost. (U.S. Congress 1986a:5)

On behalf of the American Psychological Association, Gregory Herek compared the status of gays to racial, religious, and ethnic minorities: "If we simply make it illegal to discriminate and illegal to be openly hostile, to be openly prejudiced against gay people in the same way we have tried to address prejudice against racial minorities, ethnic minorities, and religious minorities, then that is going to help achieve that climate in which violence is unacceptable" (U.S. Congress 1986a:18–19). A report prepared by the NGLTF and included as part of the official record of the hearing on antigay violence urged Congress to "protect the full range of groups in this country that are subjected to acts of violence because of their status or identity. [By] failing to include provisions for gay and lesbian people in hate crime legislation, lawmakers send a message to the public and to criminals that antigay violence is considered less serious than crimes against other minorities" (U.S. Congress 1986a:55–56). Recommendations such as these rendered violence motivated by homophobia or heterosexism equivalent to violence motivated by racial, religious, or ethnic prejudice. Inside claimsmakers, legislators in this case, heeded these comparisons.

The importance of these claims, as well as the groups that presented them, were continually mentioned by lawmakers. Representative Conyers, for example, explained: "I think it is very important that the proliferation of these groups, along with existing civil rights organizations, is very helpful in formulating remedies" (U.S. Congress 1988b:25). When questioned about the sexual orientation provision by legislators who opposed it, Conyers noted the importance of SMOs and other outside claimsmakers:

> The reason we did not include octogenarians who are assaulted is because there was no testimony that suggested that they ought to be, as awful as the crimes visited upon them are, and the reason we did not account for policemen killed in the line of duty, although police organizations do, is that there was no request that they be separated out from the uniform crime statistics. (*Congressional Record* 1988:11395)

Representative Gekas, who opposed the inclusion of sexual orientation, immediately responded:

> [I]f the only criterion is to have the gay rights organization have its request acceded to by inclusion in that, I say to the Members that the gentleman should join with me now in a motion to recommit, to put this bill back into committee and allow the inclusion in this bill of statistics to be gathered on the incidence of child abuse, of attacks on the elderly, attacks on policemen, and attacks on other groups which might for one reason or another be victims of such type of crime. (*Congressional Record* 1988:11403)

Despite objections like these, however, increasingly widespread acceptance of comparisons between gays and lesbians and racial, religious, and ethnic minorities is evident. Following the hearings on antigay violence, sexual orientation was routinely acknowledged as a basis for hate crime. The first subsequent hearing—a July 10, 1987 hearing devoted to Anti-Asian Violence—contained many references to race, religion, ethnicity, and sexual orientation. For example, Representative Mineta claimed: "We are here today to discuss the experiences of one group, Americans of Asian and Pacific ancestry, a group which remains a target for much violence and abuse. [A]11 such attacks are appalling and destructive. Worse still: Acts of racial, religious, ethnic or sexual intolerance appear to be on the upswing" (U.S. Congress 1987:3). Six months after the hearing on antigay and lesbian violence, the Committee on the Judiciary submitted a report to the Committee of the Whole House that reflected acceptance of sexual orientation as necessary provision in the now-revised bill. Thereafter in the history of federal hate crime legislation, sexual orientation routinely appeared in lists of statuses to be considered for inclusion in law.

The inclusion of sexual orientation did not go uncontested; instead, it "prompted an assault on the bill by conservatives in the House and Senate" (Fernandez 1991:272). Although some objections were based on the grounds that including sexual orientation along with race, religion, and ethnicity would make the data collection effort too broad and expensive, by far the primary objection was that antigay and lesbian violence is more distinct from than similar to violence connected to race, religion, or ethnicity. Therefore, opponents argued, the federal government should not provide gays and lesbians with special, undeserved rights; to do so would render violence against gays and lesbians equivalent to violence against racial, ethnic, and religious minorities in ways that are both undesirable and unjustifiable.

One version of this argument insisted that it is not the federal government's responsibility to protect gays and lesbians from discriminatory violence. For example, Gekas, McCollum, Coble, and Dannemeyer, all of whom supported the race, religion, and ethnicity provisions, dissented from the recommendation to pass the HCSA with the sexual orientation provision:

Normally a federal nexus is essential to justify a federal response. Absent such a nexus, one must be able at the very least to base federal involvement in state matters on the goal of either supporting the common good or promoting state law enforcement. It must be emphasized that crime against any class of persons is obviously reprehensible. However, there is no reason to believe that crime against homosexuals transcends the ability of individual states to respond. There is no evidence of an interstate organization such as the Ku Klux Klan or the Nation focused on homosexuals. There is no mention of homosexual rights in the Constitution. In fact, there appears no convincing evidence that homosexuals are more targeted for crime than groups such as women, the elderly, members of the police or passengers on urban mass transit. Thus, gathering at considerable cost federal statistics on crime against homosexuals is not only unjustified in itself but also unfair vis-à-vis other affinity groups (U.S. Congress 1988a:12).

They concluded: "[I]t is a Federal responsibility to ensure the equal protection of all citizens regardless of their race, religion, or ethnic origin. It is not a Federal obligation to protect citizens in their sexual orientation" (U.S. Congress 1988a: 13).

These protests continued in subsequent congressional debates. Dannemeyer and Helms in particular dissented in congressional hearings immediately leading to passage of the HCSA (*Congressional Record* 1989, 1990a, 1990b). Helms opposed including sexual orientation in the bill and claimed that Congress was being "hoodwinked" into passing the "flagship of the homosexual, lesbian legislative agenda" (*Congressional Record* 1990a:1076):

> [W]here do you think the idea of legislation to require the collection of statistics on so-called hate crimes originated? If this is such a wonderful crime fighting tool, it surely must have originated with a group known for its

> tough stance on crime, right? Wrong. This idea was dreamed up by the National Gay and Lesbian Task Force. That is a matter of record. [I]t is clear that the militant homosexuals have been building up the numbers of complaints-not, let me emphasize, of criminal offenses or charges. They have been building up numbers of complaints—to bolster their case that this type of legislation is necessary. [T]he evidence is clear, Mr. President. Studying hate crimes against homosexuals is a crucial first step toward achieving homosexual rights and legitimacy in American society. This Senator cannot, and will not, be party to any legislation which fuels the homosexual movement. (*Congressional Record* 1990a: 1076)

In response, supporters such as Representative Green, asserted that "the removal of sexual orientation from H.R. 3193 would reinforce the widespread perception that victimization of homosexuals is acceptable" and therefore "sexual orientation should not be separated from other forms of hate violence because perpetrators of racial, religious, and antigay crimes are frequently the same" (*Congressional Record* 1988:11397).

After much heated debate, the term "sexual orientation" was replaced with the phrase "homosexuality or heterosexuality." As a way of appeasing dissenting opinion concerned about "special rights" for gays and lesbians, Representative Miller proposed to amend the bill such that "whether we agree or disagree, whether we support or do not support such antidiscrimination rights, no such rights are created by this bill. I believe with this perfecting amendment, Mr. Chairman, that we have a chance to put this issue to rest and pass what is basically a good bill" (*Congressional Record* 1988:11404). Many of those who previously protested the inclusion of sexual orientation in the bill supported this amendment. Representative Swindall, for example, proclaimed:

> I opposed the bill in the full committee because: First, I thought the term "sexual orientation" is on its face an ambiguity. It could very easily, I believe, be construed to include child molestation. It could be inclusive of a great many things far beyond the scope of what I believe the evidence in the full committee focused on. For that reason, I for one support the change in the wording "sexual orientation" to the more specific language of homosexuality or heterosexuality. I further support the language that states that in no way is this to be construed as to give rights that do not currently exist; specifically, the right to complain of discrimination based on homosexuality. (*Congressional Record* 1988:11405)

The new language proved acceptable. The HCSA became law in 1990 and the sexual orientation provision was not debated in subsequent HCSA oversight hearings (U.S. Congress 1992a, 1994), a reauthorization hearing (U.S. Congress 1996a), or the attendant report on the HCSA (U.S. Congress 1996b). Although the status of gays and lesbians as victims of hate-motivated violence was contested to a greater degree than was the status of racial, ethnic, and religious minorities, it was recognized and institutionalized as a key element of the character of hate crime law.[8] This was accomplished primarily through discursive tactics sustained by social movement representatives as they convinced legislators to write law that represented the interests of their constituency(ies).

Both insider and outsider claimsmakers rendered seemingly disparate and dissimilar phenomena comparable. Legislators and activists alike engaged in categorization work that designated "the people-category" in a way that linked the new innovation (i.e., the sexual orientation provision) with the previously accepted social policy (i.e., the race, religion, and ethnicity provision), this adding new victims (i.e., gays and lesbians) to the list of previously established victims (i.e., racial, ethnic, and religious minorities). The particular grounds for framing these dimensions of social life as comparable varied, but it was generally accomplished in two ways, each of which reveals a particular type of linking as a strategy of persuasion. First, the commonality of accepted provisions was located in a substantive, policy relevant dimension of social life. For example, Representative Studds observed: "The reason that race, religion, ethnicity and sexual orientation are in this bill is that so far as we know, and that is the key phrase, so far as we know, these are the principal categories of such acts of hate. That is what the testimony before the committee revealed" (*Congressional Record* 1988:11406). Similarly, others argued that the various status characteristics—race, religion, ethnicity, and sexual orientation—were comparable because all were ascribed, rather than achieved, social statuses. For example, Representative Bryant observed: "prejudice and hate-motivated crimes were motivated by prejudice toward individuals for being what they innately are" (*Congressional Record* 1988:11405). This view makes ascribed status the grounds for equivalence. In contrast, those contesting the inclusion of the sexual orientation provision argued that "homosexuality" or "gay and lesbian" is not equivalent to "black," "Jew," or "Arab-American" because the former is an achieved status—an "affinity group" according to Representative Dannemeyer (U.S. Congress 1988a:12) or a "lifestyle choice" according to Senators Hatch and Helms (*Congressional Record* 1990a)—while the latter is construed as an innate, apoliticized individual characteristic, something beyond an individual's realm of choice or volition.

The second way comparability is achieved or contested is by referencing the spirit of previously established law, especially civil rights law, and framing certain status characteristics as commensurate with it; the link is between established and innovative law. For example, Victoria Toensing, deputy assistant attorney general, Criminal Division, stated, "[I]t is important to note that the conduct prohibited by this legislation is covered, in part, by existing federal law" (U.S. Congress 1985a:50). In contrast, Representative Dannemeyer objected to the inclusion of crimes motivated by prejudice on the basis of sexual orientation on the grounds that doing so "will adopt as a matter of public policy sexual orientation on a par with what we have traditionally brought within the protected classes of the 1964 Civil Rights Act, namely, race, religion, and ethnicity" (*Congressional Record* 1990b:1425). From his point of view, such a move would "change the basic definition of the 1964 Civil Rights Act to include a new status that would have the dignity of being within the proscription [*sic*] of the Act" (quoted in Fernandez 1991:276). This move would, according to Representative Gekas, ensure "we were wading into dangerous waters when we were attempting to raise the homosexuals to a constitutionally guaranteed or protected class which was not in accord with race, creed, and color, as already articulated in the Civil Rights Act of 1964" (*Congressional Record* 1989:13542). In response, Representative Frank insisted that the integrity of the Civil Rights Act of 1964 would not be harmed:

> I would point out that meets the suggestion that this bill somehow puts homosexuality on the same basis as religion, ethnicity, etceteras. As a factual matter, it never did, and does not, because under our law you may bring an antidiscrimination suit in housing or in employment or in other areas with a Federal contractor if you are discriminated against based on religion, ethnicity, or race. You may not under existing law do that on the basis of homosexuality. (*Congressional Record* 1988:11406)

In the end, discursive moves arguing that expanding the domain of the law was fundamentally consistent with the qualities and characteristics of previously recognized legal subjects or previously legitimated and institutionalized legal terrain proved successful.

Legitimating "Gender" as a Status Provision in Hate Crime Law

Once race, religion, ethnicity, and sexual orientation were inscribed into hate crime law, gender followed. Gender was first mentioned as a legitimate provision in 1986 by Representative Oakar during a hearing on "Ethnically Motivated Violence Against Arab-Americans" (U.S. Congress 1986b); however, it was not until two years later that Congress began to seriously consider gender as a status provision in hate crime legislation; and, it was not until 1994 that gender found a place in federal hate crime law. How this occurred is instructive because it points to a different process through which domain expansion and attendant victim differentiation can occur.

In the early 1990s, the VAWA was an innovative idea. One reporter described it as a "novel approach" to violence against women that was "virtually unthinkable by mainstream politicians just a few years ago" (Rabin 1994:8A). In the first congressional hearing on "Legislation to Reduce the Growing Problem of Violence Against Women" (U.S. Congress 1990a), Senator Joseph Biden, Jr., the bill's chief sponsor, itemized three goals of the VAWA: "The first goal is to try to make streets a little bit safer for women; the second goal is to make their homes a little bit safer; and the third goal is to protect their civil rights" (U.S. Congress 1990a:2, 3, 4). To meet the first and second goals, the VAWA allocated over $1.6 billion for education, rape crisis hotlines, training of justice personnel, victim services (especially shelters for victims of battery), and special units of police and prosecutors to deal with crimes against women. To meet the third goal, Title III of the Act provides a civil remedy for "gender crimes":

> The Congress finds that (1) crimes motivated by the victim's gender constitute bias crimes in violation of the victim's right to be free from discrimination on the basis of gender; (2) current law provides a civil remedy for crimes committed in the workplace, but not for gender crimes committed on the street and in the home; and (3) State and Federal laws do not adequately protect against the bias element of gender crimes, which separates these crimes from acts of random violence, nor do they adequately provide victims the opportunity to vindicate their interests. (U.S. Congress 1990b:23)

In essence, Title III of the Act entitles victims to compensatory and punitive damages through the federal courts for a crime of violence if it is motivated, at least in part, by animus toward the victim's gender. This allowance implicitly acknowledges that some, if not most, violence against women is not gender neutral; instead, it establishes the possibility that violence motivated by gender animus is a proper subject for civil rights action.

Title III of the VAWA positioned select crimes against women as equivalent to acts of violence based on race, ethnicity, national origin, religion, and sexual orientation:

> Title 3, called Civil Rights for Women, would make sexual violence a violation of federal civil rights law. "This is the beginning, middle and end of the legislation," says Biden. In reclassifying rape, wife-beating, and other gender-based felonies as bias crimes, the provision would write into law the view of rape as a socially embedded institution. (*New Republic* 1993:14)

From the point of view of the VAWA and its supporters, the true nature of rape, domestic violence, and other forms of violence against women is akin to a civil rights violation; accordingly, these acts of violence are akin to other forms of hate crime: "The purpose of Title III is to put gender-motivated crimes against women on the same footing as other bias crimes" (Kelly and Long 1992:287).

Testimony presented at multiple hearings on the VAWA (U.S. Congress 1990a, 1990c, 1991a, 1991b, 1992b, 1993a, 1993c, 1993d) and reflected in the associated congressional reports (U.S. Congress 1990b, 1991c, 1992c, 1993b, 1993e) revealed that support for Title III was based less on direct pressure from those engaging in collective action, and more on the previously established logic used to justify the status provisions now taken for granted in the HCSA and the HCSEA. That argument involved seeing hate crimes as acts of discrimination, involving not only victimization of specific individuals, but also of a broader social group the victims represent. At this point in the development of federal hate crime law, this notion was easily extended to women's victimization. Supporters maintained that acts of violence against women were not merely private injuries to unfortunate individuals; instead, some of the most common forms of violence against women, such as rape and domestic violence, are essentially hate crimes—violent sexism—that warrant federal civil rights protection. Senator Biden explained: "One of the things we're trying to do in the Violence Against Women Act is to make it a policy of the country that rapes are hate crimes committed against women, crimes of violence directed disproportionately at one group based on their gender. That is why it makes a civil rights violation" (U.S. Congress 1990a:36). Thus, the rationale underlying Title III was that harassment, intimidation, and assault directed at women assumes a particularly offensive, dangerous, and socially disruptive character when motivated by animus based on gender, analogous to the disruption caused by other hate crimes. That advocates employed this argument and that it was largely uncontested suggests the logic of the argument itself had already achieved legitimacy.

Interestingly, the redefinition of gender violence required to convert acts such as rape into hate crimes did not evoke much debate, especially compared to the magnitude and intensity of the debates over the sexual orientation provision in the HCSA. In sharp contrast to the arguments effectively made to exclude the gender from the HCSA,[9] some hearings on the VAWA (U.S. Congress 1993a, 1993c) featured no oppositional testimony and the remaining hearings, reports, and committee prints related to the VAWA manifest very little evidence of contestation over including the status of "gender" in hate crime.

The minimal resistance to Title III of the VAWA was expressed in a handful of ways, each easily addressed and subsequently dismissed by legislators without the testimony of outside claimsmakers (i.e., representatives from women's organizations). For example, some argued that while it is appropriate to include gender in hate crime laws, it was nonetheless simply not feasible to do so. In particular, some believed that including gender would make the concept of hate crime too cumbersome, if not entirely impossible, since violent crimes against women are so pervasive. Second, some argued that not all acts of violence against women fit the definition of a hate crime because: a) women are frequently acquainted with their attackers while other victims of bias-violence are not, and/or b) statistically speaking, violence against men is as common, if not more common, than violence against women. Third, in light of a report submitted by the U.S. Supreme Court, some suggested that the bill might burden the federal courts unnecessarily. Fourth and finally, concerns about the constitutionality of Title III were expressed (see, for example, U.S. Congress 1992b). These objections were dispelled by demonstrations of the feasibility of collecting data on bias-motivated violence against women, the identification of commonalities between gender-based violence and other forms of (now) recognized hate crime, the creation of a constitutional justification for the civil rights remedy, and the modification of the bill's wording before it became law.'

Notably, objections to the incorporation of gender were not anchored in the types of concerns and expressed with the same logic that dominated testimony and debate about "sexual orientation" in the HCSA hearings. For example, there was no debate about the legitimacy of sex as a status in need of protection and legal consideration, in large part because the legitimacy of "sex" as a line of stratification resulting in discrimination had long since gained legal and extralegal currency. Also, objections were not incessantly expressed or hotly debated. In fact, the testimony and debates that concern the VAWA reveal tacit agreement about the importance of the Act. Indeed, Biden acknowledge the lack of opposition when he said, "I am in the unusual position here of trying to build a case against my own bill because I want the record to reflect—I want it to be an honest record" (U.S. Congress 1990a:107).

Also in contrast to earlier efforts to incorporate sexual orientation into federal hate crime law, outside claimsmakers, in this case SMOs concerned with the status and welfare of women, played a minimal role. The most influential group, the National Victim Center (NVC), is a professional, broad-based, public interest organization more than a direct channel for aggrieved minority groups (i.e., people of color, Jews, gays and lesbians, women, etc. [Broad and Jenness 1996; Jenness and Broad 1997; Weed 1995]). Thus, unlike the HCSA and the HCSEA, the VAWA was formulated within an organization largely removed from the politics of specific constituencies of potential and actual victims. This "top-down" approach to lawmaking, coupled with the fact that a template for hate crime law had already been constructed and legitimated, ensured that the further expansion of "people-category" associated with the social problem of hate crime was not contingent upon the type of categorization work described in the previous section.

Indeed, there is no evidence to suggest that feminist sponsored antiviolence projects were central in the initiation and early formulation of the VAWA (Broad and Jenness

1996; Jenness and Broad 1997); thus, they did not play a crucial role in linking gender to the concept of hate crime. Not until 1993, well after the VAWA had been conceived and a just a year before it became law, did representatives from nationally-known feminist organizations testify in federal hearings on hate crime. Then, Patricia Ireland (president of NOW), Sally Goldfarb (senior staff attorney for NOW's Legal Defense and Education Fund), and Eleanor Smeal (president of the Feminist Majority) offered supportive testimony in hearings held by the Subcommittee on Civil and Constitutional Rights, Committee on the Judiciary (U.S. Congress 1993d:113).

While the support of these groups comes as no surprise given the women movement's historical commitment to combating violence against women, the fact that it emerged fairly late in the history of federal lawmaking around hate crime is instructive. Both state and national feminist civil rights organizations were "notably absent" from original and subsequent discussions of the VAWA (Broad and Jenness 1996; Jenness and Broad 1997). With the exception of a few state coalitions that initiated and sponsored letter-writing and consciousness-raising campaigns, the state and national organizations devoted surprisingly few resources and attendant mobilization to the VAWA until after the Act had received enough support to marshal predictions of its imminent passage: "The VAWA and all that it represents has become an important element in the institutional environment of the organizational field under study [feminist sponsored and sustained anti-violence projects], one that has been externally generated and presented to the organizational field, rather than internally developed and imposed on the larger socio-political environment" (Jenness and Broad 1997:162 [emphasis in the original]). In other words, the inclusion of gender in federal hate crime law was not contingent upon the presence of outside claimsmakers and the accomplishment of the type of categorization work described in the previous section on sexual orientation."

Discussion and Conclusion

Only a little over a decade ago, U.S. Representative Conyers, Jr. proclaimed that "hate crimes motivated by intolerance need to be distinguished from other crimes motivated by other factors" (U.S. Congress 1988b:8). In large part because of the anti-hate crime movement in the U.S. and subsequent lawmaking by legislators, violence motivated by bigotry is now recognized as qualitatively different from other forms of violent conduct, both in legal and extralegal discourse. Hate crime has been distinguished from "normal" crime, primarily because of activist, media, and legislative attention devoted to the perpetrators' motivation, as well as the socially recognizable characteristics of the victims (Best 1999; Jenness and Grattet 2000). As Laurence Tribe, Professor of Constitutional Law at Harvard University, testified "Nothing in the U.S. Constitution prevents the Government from penalizing with added severity those crimes directed against people or their property because of their race, color, religion, national origin, ethnicity, gender or sexual orientation, and nothing in the Constitution requires that this list be infinitely expanded" (U.S. Congress 1992d:7). So what distinctions were made and how were those distinctions made? And what can the process of making these distinctions tell us about social problems and how their attendant victims are constructed?

Since 1985, every U.S. Congress has devoted attention to the task of responding to hate-motivated violence in the United States. This has resulted in hundreds of hours of congressional hearings and debates, as well as three new federal laws. The legislative histories of the three laws that are in place—the Hate Crimes Statistics Act, the Violence Against Women Act, and the Hate Crimes Sentencing Enhancement Act—reveal that the content of federal hate crime law, at least in terms of select status provisions, has been shaped by interrelated processes: social movement mobilization, categorization work by both insider and outsider claimsmakers that is best characterized as "linking" strategies of persuasion, domain expansion that results in differentiation of victims, and institutionalization. Each of these processes is institutionally qualified and temporally bound.

Summarized in Table 11.2, the empirical analysis in this work details how, through the inclusion of status provisions in hate crime law (i.e., "race, religion, and ethnicity," "sexual orientation," and "gender"), the substantive character of federal law was shaped in racialized, sexualized, and gendered ways. Early claims from local, regional, and state SMOs focused on the scope and consequences of race, religion, and ethnicity-based violence. Growing awareness of such violence became grounds for promoting federal hate crime legislation by a limited number of SMOs and their representatives. This activity cemented a trio of statuses—"race, religion, and ethnicity"—as the anchoring provisions of all hate crime law. This occurred without contestation over the legitimacy of these status provisions, which had already been legitimated by other polities (i.e., states).

The character of hate crime law was reshaped when the law's domain expanded to include additional provisions (see Table 11.2). Shortly after federal hate crime law was envisioned, proposals were made by outsider claimsmakers, most notably social movement representatives, to further differentiate hate crime victims by adding "sexual orientation" to the list of provisions in federal hate crime law. Through direct and sustained testimony, SMO representatives were able to bestow empirical credibility upon the violence connected with this provision (i.e., antigay violence). In addition, they successfully engaged in discursive tactics that rendered the meaning of sexual orientation more similar to than dissimilar from the meanings already attached to race, religion, and ethnicity. By successfully engaging in these linking strategies of persuasion, SMOs proved crucial to the expansion of hate crime law to cover sexual orientation. In other words, the

Table 11.2. Social Movement Organization Mobilization and the Adoption of Select Status Provisions in Federal Hate Crime Law, 1985–1998

	Status Provisions			
	Proposed		*Adopted*	
SMO Mobilization	*Early (pre 1990)*	*Late (post 1990)*	*Early (pre 1990)*	*Late (post 1990)*
Yes	Race/Religion/ Ethnicity, Sexual Orientation		Race/Religion/ Ethnicity, Sexual Orientation	
No	Octogenarian, Union Members, Children, Elderly, Police Officers	Gender, Disabilities		Gender Disabilities

addition of sexual orientation was contingent upon the presence and viability of direct, sustained social movement mobilization coupled with particular discursive moves that prove decisive in social problems talk, especially "congressional talk" (Chock 1995). While the domain of hate law expanded to include more injured people, it did so by further differentiating between types of crime victims in the people-category.

In contrast, other provisions initially recommended for inclusion in the law, but not added to the bill prior to its passage, did not attract significant, sustained social movement mobilization in congressional hearings. For example, prior to the passage of the HCSA, some legislators argued: "We believe that the measure does not go far enough and include violence by and against union members" (U.S. Congress 1989:7). Since hearings were not held on this type of bias-motivated violence (see Table 11.1), there was no structural opportunity for representatives from unions to establish the empirical credibility of the problem and engage in the categorization work required to legitimate this provision; as a result, union affiliation was not adopted as a provision in federal hate crime law. As Table 11.2 reveals, this same pattern applies to claims about children, the elderly, and police officers: all were status provisions proposed early in federal lawmaking, but never adopted as core elements of federal hate crime law.

Later in the process of institutionalizing federal hate crime legislation, however, the place and importance of direct social movement mobilization and discursive strategies that link elements of policy, in this case by promoting similarity(ies) over difference(s), declined as institutionalized logics become more pronounced. For comparative purposes, an examination of the legislative history of "gender" as a provision in federal hate crime law reveals that later in the history of federal lawmaking around hate crime, the importance of collective action, as measured through the presence of SMOs at congressional hearings and in congressional debates and reports, declined. Once a corpus of hate crime law was established and select provisions cemented in law, new provisions—in this case, gender—were adopted without direct pressure applied by sustained mobilization from relevant SMOs and their representatives, and despite the fact that it was purposely excluded earlier in the institutional process.

While many federal hearings on violence against women have been held, they were not initiated nor sustained by feminist SMOs. Instead, as lawmakers coalesced around the meaning of hate crime law in previous hearings, established policy pedigrees were institutionalized. This, in turn, shaped the subsequent domain expansion of the law by distinguishing yet another element of the people-category, in this case, gender. This occurred without much fanfare and without relevant SMOs engaging in decisive categorization work, but in light of the fact that gender—like race and religion—was already a standard subject of federal discrimination law. That is, the sense that gender as a legal subject parallels race has been commonplace for over a quarter of a century.

This pattern, particular to the later phase of lawmaking, is further evidenced by the history of the "disability" provision in hate crime law. Although space constraints prohibit a detailed analysis, disability was added to both the reauthorization of the HCSA and the HCSEA. The changing character of the law along these lines occurred despite the fact that federal lawmakers have never held a hearing on violence directed at those with disabilities and no contestation occurred over this provision (see Table 11.1). Moreover, the official records of federal level hate crime lawmaking reveal that representatives from the disabilities movement have yet to even make an appearance and offer testimony related to federal hate crime legislation. Regardless, disabilities, and thus persons with disabilities, have found a home in hate crime legislation, albeit rather late in the institutionalization process (see Table 11.2). Through the inclusion of disabilities in federal hate crime law, another class of hate crime victims was designated, thus the people-category commonly referred to as hate crime victim is even further expanded and, at the same time, differentiated. Here, too, this occurred in light of the fact that disability—like race, religion, and gender—was already a standard subject of federal discrimination law, in large part because of the earlier passage of the Americans with Disabilities Act in 1990.

Taken together, these findings suggest a number of underlying processes that can be hypothesized to operate at a general level and across various campaigns to construct people-categories (Loseke 1993), especially when there is little competition over problem definition (Burstein and Bricher 1997). First, the success of social movement mobilization as it interfaces with lawmaking and translates into law is contingent upon a particular type of categorization work: effective linking strategies of persuasion. Second, social movement mobilization is more crucial to the construction of "people-categories" early in the history of the construction of the "condition-category." That is, early in the natural history of a social problem, mesolevel social movement mobilization interfaces with microlevel processes of categorization work to determine the content of the people-categories. Third, as institutional templates develop, large scale institutional processes eclipse mesolevel social movement-related processes to determine the increasingly expanded and differentiated content of the people-category. In other words, later in the natural history of a social problem, larger processes of institutionalization interface with previously established legal templates to determine the content of people-categories. Finally, this work suggests that an exclusive focus on broad structural imperatives or "moral entrepreneurs" and lobbying activities provides only a limited view of how and why legislators take action, what kinds of crime policy they design, and what types of injuries are recognized by law. To more fully understand this process, it is useful to consider the timing of each of these elements described above as they are enacted in a larger institutional process, with the relationship between discursive practices and the larger institutional environment changing over time.

Obviously, a case study such as this one cannot verify or rigorously falsify these patterns. More studies of the unfolding meanings associated with social problems in general, and legally defined victims in particular, are needed to determine whether different types of law, victims, and social problems show different tendencies over time. A comparison of findings across studies like this one would determine if generalizations about the processes posited here can be supported.

Notes

1. Ibarra and Kitsuse (1993:26) proposed replacing the term "putative condition" with the term "condition-category" as a way to move beyond epistemological debates that address the degree to which social problems theorists engage in "ontological gerrymandering" (Mauss and Jenness 2000; Woolgar and Pawluch 1985). Accordingly, Loseke (1993) uses the term "people-categories" to refer to "putative people" who inhabit those categories.

2. Critical discourse moments are symbolically revealing discrete historical events that stimulate discourse on a particular topic, make an issue especially visible, and create perturbations. They contribute to the production of social problems by publicly defining social conditions as problematic in particular ways and, at the same time, define a repertoire of victims associated with the social problem. I view these discursive moments as a form of practice, a manifestation of the structure of social relations represented in them. Borrowing from Foucault (1979) and, more recently, Ferguson (1984), administrative discourse both expresses and reflects a particular structure of institutions and practices; it both creates and represents the positions of persons and events. In this case, the administrative discourse is legislative, the positions for persons are "hate crime victims," and the events are "hate crimes."

3. Throughout the 1980s and the 1990s most state legislatures passed at least one law designed to deal with bias-motivated violence. For discussions of state hate crime law, see Grattet, Jenness, and Curry (1998); Jacobs and Potter (1998); Jenness and Grattet (1996, 2000); Lawrence (1999); and Soule and Earl (1999). The Hate Crimes Prevention Act (HCPA) "amends the Federal criminal code to set penalties for persons who, whether or not acting under the color of law, willfully cause bodily injury to any person or, through the use of fire, firearm, or explosive device, attempt to cause such injury, because of the actual or perceived: (1) race, color, religion, or national origin of any person; and (2) religion, gender, sexual orientation, or disability of any person, where in connection with the offense, the defendant or the victim travels in interstate or foreign commerce, uses a facility or instrumentality of interstate or foreign commerce, or engages in any activity affecting interstate or foreign commerce, or where the offense is in or affects interstate or foreign commerce" (S. 1529).

4. As discussed later, in 1994, the HCSA was amended to include disability as a protected status.

5. The Hate Crimes Prevention Act of 1998 (S. 1529) is excluded from this analysis as it is currently being debated in the U.S. Senate and has yet to become law.

6. Claims are empirically credible "to the extent that there are events and occurrences that can be pointed to as documentary evidence" (Snow and Benford 1992:140).

7. The Coalition on Hate Crimes was comprised of civil rights, religious, ethnic, and law enforcement groups, as well as a diverse array of professional organizations, including the ADL, the American Bar Association, 30 attorneys general, the National Institute Against Prejudice and Violence, the National Gay and Lesbian Task Force, the American Psychological Association, the American Psychiatric Association, the Center for Democratic Renewal, the American Civil Liberties Union, the American Jewish Congress, People for the American Way, the National Organization of Black Law Enforcement Executives, the U.S. Civil Rights Commission, the Police Executives Research Forum, the Criminal Justice Statistics Administration, the International Association of Police Chiefs, the National Council of Churches, the National Coalition of American Nuns, and the American Arab Anti-Discrimination Committee.

8. Later, when the HCSEA was introduced, debated, and enacted, the provision for sexual orientation went uncontested (see, for example, U.S. Congress 1992a; 1992d), just as the establishment of race, religion, and ethnicity was uncontested throughout the history of the HCSA. More recently, it is going uncontested in the current piece of legislation being debated in the Senate, the Hate Crimes Prevention Act (S. 1529). This is important to note insofar as domain expansion efforts are not always successful: "claimants usually begin their campaigns by typifying problems in especially compelling ways. Domain expansion extends the claims into more controversial territory, often challenging existing arrangements" (Best 1990:85).

9. Prior to passage of the HCSA, the Coalition on Hate Crimes contemplated recommending including gender as a protected status in the HCSA, but eventually decided against it

for a variety of reasons. First, some members of the Coalition believed that the inclusion of gender would delay, if not completely impede, the timely passage of the HCSA. Second, some members of the Coalition argued that including gender would open the door for age, disability, position in a labor dispute, party affiliation, and/or membership in the armed forces provisions. Third, some believed that including gender would make enactment of the HCSA too cumbersome, if not entirely impossible, since violent crimes against women are so pervasive. Fourth, and related, others argued that not all acts of violence against women fit the definition of a hate crime. Fifth, some members of the Coalition argued that expanding the categories of officially recognized hate crimes to include gender would not improve upon current efforts to collect official data on rape and domestic violence. Focusing on feasibility, opponents feared that adding gender as a victim category would simply overwhelm the data collection efforts of law enforcement agencies and human rights organizations that track hate crimes. Related, the large number of crimes against women would overshadow statistics on hate crimes against members of other groups. The failure to include gender in the HCSA, as well as other key pieces of legislation and policy designed to address violence, did not go unrecognized (Jenness 1995a; Jenness and Broad 1994, 1997; Levin 1994).

10. A significant portion of one of the longest hearings on the VAWA was devoted to determining whether Title III of the VAWA is constitutional (U.S. Congress 1992b). Prior to passage, and in light of congressional testimony and debates, the VAWA's wording was altered in three ways. First, several findings were added to the bill to make clear the basis and purposes of the civil rights remedy. Second, the term "overwhelming," as a way of defining the level of animus required to qualify as hate-motivated, was omitted often it was deemed unnecessary and restrictive. Third, language enumerating various crimes was eliminated from the original definition of "gender-motivated" crime to eliminate the negative implication that only these crimes would give rise to a cause of action under Title III. For a review of these changes, as well as the justifications that underlie them, see U.S. Congress (1991a).

11. Ramirez, Soysal, and Shanahan's (1997) research found that nations adopting women's rights later in the adoption period under study, 1890–1990, were less influenced by protracted national struggles and the local social mobilization of women than nations adopting women's rights earlier in the adoption period.

References

Anti-Defamation League. 1988. *Hate Crimes Statutes: A Response to Anti-Semitism, Vandalism and Violent Bigotry*. New York: The Anti-Defamation League of B'nai B'rith.

———. 1990 1989. Audit of Anti-Semitic Incidents. New York: The Anti-Defamation League of B'nai B'rith.

Arnold, R. Douglas. 1990. *The Logic of Congressional Action*. New Haven, Conn.: Yale University Press.

Berk, Richard, Elizabeth A. Boyd, and Karl M. Hamner. 1992. "Thinking more clearly about hate-motivated crimes." In *Hate Crimes: Confronting Violence Against Lesbians and Gay Men*, eds. Gregory Herek and Kevin Berrill, 123–143. Newbury Park, Calif.: Sage Publications.

Best, Joel. 1990. *Threatened Children: Rhetoric and Concern About Child Victims*. Chicago, Ill.: University of Chicago Press.

———. 1999. *Random Violence. How We Talk About New Crimes and New Victims*. Berkeley, Calif.: University of California Press.

Beuchler, Steven M. 1990. *Women's Movements in the United States*. New Brunswick, N.J.: Rutgers University Press.

Broad, Kendal, and Valerie Jenness 1996. "The institutionalizing work of contemporary antiviolence against women campaigns in the U.S.: Mesolevel social movement activism and the production of cultural forms." *Research in Social Movements, Conflicts and Change* 19:75–123.

Burstein, Paul. 1991. "Policy domains: Organization, culture, and policy outcomes." *Annual Review of Sociology* 17:327–350.

Burstein, Paul, and Marie Bricher. 1997. "Problem definition and public policy: Congressional committees confront work, family, and gender, 1945–1990." *Social Forces* 75:135–169.

Chilton, Paul. 1987. "Metaphor, euphemism, and the militarization of language." *Current Research on Peace and Violence* 10:7–19.

Chock, Phyllis Pease. 1991. "'Illegal aliens' and 'opportunity': Myth-making in congressional testimony." *American Ethnologist* 18:279–294.

———. 1994. "Remaking and unmaking 'citizen' in policy-making talk about immigration." *Polar: Political and Legal Anthropology Review* 17:45–55.

———. 1995. "Ambiguity in policy discourse: Congressional talk about immigration." *Policy Sciences* 28:165–184.

Congressional Record. 1985. (July 22):19840–19844.

———. 1988. (May 18):11392–11410.

———. 1989. (June 27):13541–13551.

———. 1990a. (February 8):1067–1092.

———. 1990b. (April 3):1423–1426.

Ferguson, Kathy. 1984. *The Feminist Case against Bureaucracy*. Philadelphia, Pa.: Temple University Press.

Femandez, Joseph. 1991. "Bringing hate crimes into focus." *Harvard Civil Rights-Civil Liberties Law Review* 26:261–292.

Foucault, Michel. 1979. *Discipline and Punish: The Birth of the Prison*. New York: Vintage Books.

Frohman, Lisa. 1997. "Convictability and discordant locales: Reproducing race, class, and gender ideologies in prosecutorial decisionmaking." *Law & Society Review* 31:531–555.

Galliher, John F., and John. R. Cross. 1983. *Morals Legislation without Morality: The Case of Nevada*. New Brunswick, N.J.: Rutgers University Press.

Gamson, William A. 1992. *Talking Politics*. New York: Cambridge University Press.

Gerhards, Jurgen, and Dieter Rucht. 1992. "Mesomobilization: Organizing and framing in two protest campaigns in West Germany." *American Journal of Sociology* 98:555–595.

Glaser, Barry, and Anselm Strauss. 1967. *The Discovery of Grounded Theory*. Chicago, Ill.: Aldine.

Grattet, Ryken, Valerie Jenness, and Theodore Curry. 1998. "The homogenization and differentiation of hate crime law in the United States, 1978–1995: Innovation and diffusion in the criminalization of bigotry." *American Sociological Review* 63:286–307.

Hagan, John. 1980. "The legislation of crime and delinquency: A review of theory, method, and research." *Law & Society Review* 14:603–628.

Hilgartner, Stephen, and Charles Bosk. 1988. "The rise and fall of social problems: A public arenas model." *American Journal of Sociology* 94:53–78.

Holstein, James A. 1993. *Court Ordered Insanity: Interpretive Practice and Involuntary Commitment*. New York: Aldine de Gruyter.

Holstein, James. A., and Gale Miller. 1990. "Rethinking victimization: An interactional approach to victimology." *Symbolic Interaction* 13:103–122.

Ibarra, Peter, and John Kitsuse. 1993. "Vernacular constituents of moral discourse: An interactionist proposal for the study of social problems." In *Constructionist Controversies: Issues in*

Social Problems Theory, eds. Gale Miller and James A. Holstein, 22–54. New York: Aldine de Grutyer.

Jacobs, James, and Kimberly Potter. 1998. *Hate Crimes: Criminal Law and Identity Politics.* New York: Oxford University Press.

Jayyusi, Lena. 1984. *Categorization and the Moral Order.* Boston, Mass.: Routledge & Kegan Paul.

Jenness, Valerie. 1995a. "Hate crimes in the United States: The transformation of injured persons into victims and the extension of victim status to multiple constituencies." In *Images and Issues: Typifying Contemporary Social Problems*, ed. Joel Best, 213–237. New York: Aldine de Gruyter.

———. 1995b. "Social movement growth, domain expansion, and framing processes: The gay/lesbian movement and violence against gays and lesbians as a social problem." *Social Problems* 47:145–170.

Jenness, Valerie, and Kendal Broad. 1994. "Anti-violence activism and the (in)visibility of gender in the gay/lesbian movement and the women's movement." *Gender & Society* 8:402–423.

———. 1997. *Hate Crimes: New Social Movements and the Politics of Violence.* Hawthorne, N.Y.: Aldine de Gruyter.

Jenness, Valerie, and Ryken Grattet. 1996. "The criminalization of hate: A comparison of structural and polity influences on the passage of 'bias-crime' legislation in the U.S." *Sociological Perspectives* 39:129–154.

———. 2000. *Building the Hate Crime Policy Domain: From Social Movement Concept to Law Enforcement Practice.* New York: Russell Sage Foundation.

Kelly, Andrea Ines, and Elisa Long. 1992. "Violence against women: Proposed legislation." *Texas Journal of Women and the Law* 1:285–290.

Kingdon, John. 1984. *Agendas, Alternatives, and Public Policies.* Boston, Mass.: Little, Brown.

Klandermans, Bert. 1992. "The social construction of protest and multiorganizational fields." In *Frontiers in Social Movement Theory*, eds. Aldon Morris and Carol McClurg Mueller, 77–103. New Haven, Conn.: Yale University Press.

Lawrence, Frederick M. 1999. *Punishing Hate: Bias Crimes under American Law.* Cambridge, Mass.: Harvard University Press.

Levin, Brian. 1994. "Violence against women: Is it a hate crime?" *Klanwatch Intelligence Report* June:4–7.

Levin, Jack, and Jack McDevitt. 1993. *Hate Crimes: The Rising Tide of Bigotry and Bloodshed.* New York: Plenum Press.

Loseke, Donileen R. 1993. "Constructing conditions, people, morality, and emotion: Expanding the agenda of constructionism." In *Constructionist Controversies: Issues in Social Problems Theory*, eds. Gale Miller and James A. Holstein, 207–216. New York: Aldine de Grutyer.

Maroney, Terry A. 1998. "The struggle against hate crime: Movement at a crossroad." *New York University Law Review* 73:564–620.

Mauss, Armand, and Valerie Jenness. 2000. "Social problems." In *The Encyclopedia of Sociology*, eds. Edgar Borgatta and Marie Borgatta. N.Y.: MacMillan.

Miller, Gale, and James A. Holstein (eds.). 1993. *Constructionist Controversies: Issues in Social Problems Theory.* Hawthorne, New York: Aldine de Gruyter.

Naples, Nancy. 1997. "The 'new consensus' on the gendered 'social contract': The 1987–1988 U.S. Congressional Hearings on Welfare Reform." *Signs: Journal of Women in Culture and Society* 22:907–945.

New Republic. 1993. "Caught in the act." (July 12):13–16.

Rabin, Roni. 1994. "Anti-crime bill gives women new weapon against gender offenses." *The Detroit News* (August 5):8A.

Rafter, Nicole H. 1990. "The social construction of crime and crime control." *Journal of Research on Crime and Delinquency* 27:376–389.

Ramirez, Francisco, Yasemin Soysal, and Suzanne Shanahan. 1997. "The changing logic of political citizenship: Cross-national acquisition of women's suffrage rights, 1890 to 1990." *American Sociological Review* 62:735–745.

Rovella, David E. 1994. "Attack on hate crime is enhanced." *National Law Journal* (August 29):A1.

Sarat, Austin, and Thomas R. Kearns. 1997. "Editorial introduction." In *The Rhetoric of Law*, eds. Austin Sarat and Thomas Kearns, 1–27. Ann Arbor: University of Michigan Press.

Silbey, Susan, and Austin Sarat. 1989. "Dispute processing in law and legal scholarship: From institutional critique to a reconsideration of the juridical subject." *Denver Law Review* 66:437–498.

Snow, David A., and Robert D. Benford. 1992. "Master frames and cycles of protest." In *Frontiers in Social Movement Theory*, eds. Aldon C. Morris and Carol McClurg Mueller, 133–155. New Haven, Conn.: Yale University Press.

Soule, Sarah, and Jennifer Earl. 1999. "'All men are created equal': The differential protection of minority groups in hate crime legislation." Paper presented at the annual meeting of the American Sociological Association in Chicago, Illinois. (August)

Staggenborg, Suzanne. 1998. "Social movement communities and cycles of protest: The emergence and maintenance of a local women's movement." *Social Problems* 45:180–204.

Stake, Robert E. 1994. "Case studies." In *Handbook of Qualitative Research*, ed. Norman Denzin, 273–285. Thousand Oaks, Calif.: Sage.

Strauss, Anselm, and Juliet Corbin. 1994. "Grounded theory methodology: An overview." In *Handbook of Qualitative Research*, ed. Norman Denzin, 273–285. Thousand Oaks, Calif.: Sage.

U.S. Congress. 1985a. "Crimes against religious practices and property." Washington, D.C.: U.S. Government Printing Office.

———. 1985b. "Hate crimes statistics act." Washington, D.C.: U.S. Government Printing Office.

———. 1985c. "Hate Crimes Statistics Act." Washington, D.C.: U.S. Government Printing Office.

———. 1986a. "Anti-gay violence." Washington, D.C.: U.S. Government Printing Office.

———. 1986b. "Ethnically motivated violence against Arab Americans." Washington, D.C.: U.S.

———. 1987. "Anti-Asian violence." Washington, D.C.: U.S. Government Printing Office.

———. 1988a. "Hate Crimes Statistics Act." Washington, D.C.: U.S. Government Printing Office.

———. 1988b. "Racially motivated violence." Washington, D.C.: U.S. Government Printing Office.

———. 1989. "Hate Crimes Statistics Act." Washington, D.C.: U.S. Government Printing Office.

———. 1990a. Women and violence, Pt. 1." Washington, D.C.: U.S. Government Printing Office.

———. 1990b. "The Violence Against Women Act of 1990." Washington, D.C.: U.S. Government.

———. 1990c. "Women and violence, Pt. 2." Washington, D.C.: U.S. Government Printing Office.

———. 1991a. "Violence against the women: Victims of the system." Washington, D.C.: U.S. Government Printing Office.

———. 1991b. "The Violence Against Women Act of 1991." Washington, D.C.: U.S. Government Printing Office.

———. 1992a. "Hate Crimes Statistics Act." Washington, D.C.: U.S. Government Printing Office.

———. 1992b. "Violence against the women: Victims of the system." Washington, D.C.: U.S. Government Printing Office.

———. 1992c. "Violence against the women: Victims of the system." Washington, D.C.: U.S. Government Printing Office.

———. 1992d. "Hate Crimes Sentencing Enhancement Act of 1992." Washington, D.C.: U.S. Government Printing Office.

———. 1993a. "Violent crimes against women." Washington, D.C.: U.S. Government Printing Office.

———. 1993b. "The Violent Against Women Act of 1993." Washington, D.C.: U.S. Government Printing Office.

———. 1993c. "Violence against women: Righting the fear." Washington, D.C.: U.S. Government Printing Office.

———. 1993d. "Crimes of violence motivated by gender." Washington, D.C.: U.S. Government Printing Office.

———. 1993e. "Violent Against Women Act of 1993." Washington, D.C.: U.S. Government Printing Office.

———. 1994. "Hate Crimes Statistics Act." Washington, D.C.: U.S. Government Printing Office.

———. 1996a. "Reauthorization of the Hate Crimes Statistics Act." Washington, D.C.: U.S. Government Printing Office.

———. 1996b. "To reauthorize the Hate Crimes Statistics Act." Washington, D.C.: U.S. Government Printing Office.

Weed, Frank. 1995. *Certainty of Justice: Reform in the Crime Victim Movement.* New York: Aldine.

Woolgar, Steve, and Dorothy Pawluch. 1985. "Ontological gerrymandering." *Social Problems* 32:214–227.

Yin, Robert. 1984. *Case Study Research: Design and Methods.* Newbury Park, Calif.: Sage.

Statute Citations

Public Law 101–275
Public Law 103–322

Part IV

SOCIAL MOVEMENTS, DILEMMAS, AND STATE RESOLUTIONS

This section extends consideration to the important role played by social movements as they impinge upon the state as well as the kinds of ways in which the state responds. In his chapter, Lawrence Neuman explicitly seeks to link social movements to state policymaking and law creation. His dialectical approach is rooted in state transformation theory that seeks to weave insights from social constructionism into a historical analysis of state conduct and policy creation. By employing a critical reading of constructionism, he seeks to accord significant weight to objective, sociohistorical conditions and to consider how such conditions shape people's social construction of meanings. He incorporates resource mobilization theory into his analysis by employing concepts such as "political opportunity structures," this in order to enhance state transformation theory by ultimately focusing upon the three-way intersection of public discourse, political mobilization, and state conduct.

Neuman's empirical focus is placed upon the "trust problem," that is, the political problem of corporate monopolies during the period of the latter two decades of the nineteenth century up through World War I. The analysis consists of showing how social movements form "frames" or packages of political interpretations concerning certain social issues. He shows how the progressive movement, riding on the crest of a structural transformation taking place in the U.S. political economy, helped create a frame for shaping public views regarding the "illegitimacy" of monopolistic firms. Neuman argues that the creation of a dilemma for the state developed through a complex, political interplay of public understandings of the "trust problem," eventually leading to a state response in the form of antitrust legislation.

Kitty Calavita's chapter explores the legal processes that have developed in the United States over recent decades with respect to anti-immigrant legislation. Her study involves the infusion of a "symbolic politics" approach into a broader political economy analysis. She seeks to explain the particular kind of anti-immigrant sentiments that became linked with the notion of defining immigrants as a "tax burden." Her study shows that this linkage culminated with Proposition 187 in the state of California, which sought to ban undocumented immigrants from access to basic public services.

The starting point of her analysis rests in the "crisis of Fordism" that spread throughout the United States and elsewhere toward the latter decades of the twentieth century. The rise of "balanced-budget" conservatism and neoliberal economic policies in general provided the shifting ideological setting for symbolic declarations of public political sentiment among large sectors of U.S. voters. By citing a well-established literature that shows how nativist social movements in the United States tend to surge at times of economic instability and crisis, she illustrates a dynamic that becomes particularly exacerbated during periods of major immigrant influx.

According to Calavita, attempts by U.S. federal and state authorities to "regain control of the border" resurged during the 1970s when opinion polls showed a large majority of the public in favor of restricting immigration. Although a rapidly expanding scholarly debate remains largely inconclusive as to whether large-scale immigration was actually a fiscal burden or instead constituted a national economic asset, public opinion was overwhelmingly swayed toward the idea that recent immigrants were a drain on public services and the taxpayers who fund them. The transformation of these sentiments into symbolic law is part of a social definitioning process in which political activity sets out to assign blame for existing social problems. Its symbolic nature arises from the collective sentiment that is created, giving large sectors of the public a sense of "sending a message," particularly since many understand that their votes, even if successful, will be tempered by decision making that would take place elsewhere. Calavita's approach makes an important contribution toward establishing the role of symbolic law within changing political and economic circumstances. She argues for the need to integrally understand how changing material conditions provides the basis for shifting public attitudes as they become expressed in symbolic political activity.

Sherry Cable and Michael Benson's chapter examines the rise of ecological social movements from a structural perspective, emphasizing the failures of state regulatory policies and the expansion of corporate environmental crime as the legal backdrop for movement emergence. Their analysis suggests that public perceptions of the pro-corporate bias of the state result in innovative grassroots organizing, including local strategies of environmental "crime prevention." By using a natural history approach to the emergence of environmentalist social movements, the authors show how the challenge mounted to existing laws and their enforcement calls the state's legitimacy into question, something that in turn can result in the state targeting the movement for social control. This is particularly likely in the case of the environmental movement since the state has a hard time exerting its regulatory controls over corporate offenders, given the established due process accorded to them and the immense resources at their disposal that can be utilized to mount a legal defense.

Cable and Benson demonstrate that the power that can be mobilized by grassroots community movements concerned about the environment must be understood against the backdrop of the existing legal framework and ongoing conduct of the state. They argue that U.S. legal culture with respect to environmental misconduct has swung increasingly toward a posture of "total justice," that is, that normative expectations for justice have given rise to expectations for compensation against liabilities incurred. This repeats a trend experienced earlier in the case of labor, civil rights, and product liability issues. It is precisely this evolving legal culture that in turn helps to stimulate social movement activity in favor of environmental social justice. The risk of experiencing state repression may in turn encourage the movement to impose their own informal sanctions against offenders, utilizing boycotts, pickets, and the mass media in building public awareness of the alleged crimes being committed. Cable and Benson's study implies that the prevailing structural trends of the larger economy remain a key factor for explaining the extent to which economic development concerns will overshadow environmental concerns, and thus, to what extent corporate wrongdoers will feel emboldened to defend their practices and challenge state attempts at environmental regulation.

References

Cable, Sherry, and Michael Benson. 1993. Acting Locally: Environmental Injustice and the Emergence of Grass-Roots Environmental Organizations. *Social Problems* 40, no. 4:464–77.

Calavita, Kitty. 1996. The New Politics of Immigration: A Balanced-Budget Conservatism and the Symbolism of Proposition 187. *Social Problems* 43, no. 3:284–305.

Neuman, W. Lawrence. 1998. Negotiated Meanings and State Transformation: The Trust Issue in the Progressive Era. *Social Problems* 45, no. 3:315–35.

CHAPTER 12

Negotiated Meanings and State Transformation

THE TRUST ISSUE IN THE PROGRESSIVE ERA

W. Lawrence Neuman

In the 1890s Americans feared trusts and saw them as powerful, aberrant invaders that spread instability and corruption. The "trust problem" was how to legally restrain—if not eliminate—them. From the late 1880s through World War I, the problem occupied the center of public discourse. Hans Thorelli (1955:342) noted, "By 1900 the trust problem was one of the two or three items at the head of the nation's agenda." In 1900 the trust was a dying—if not dead—form of business organization, but people used "trust" interchangeably with "monopoly" as terms for the modern corporation. By 1915 the problem had been transformed. Americans accepted the corporation as a normal feature of a modern economy. The politically volatile problem had been defused and absorbed into a framework of anti-trust law, economic theory, and administrative regulation, with government officials protecting the public interest.

In retrospect, the trust problem was the question of how to accommodate and legitimate the new corporate organization and relations. Corporations restructured the organizational forms and behaviors of economic actors, altered property relations, and shifted markets from a local or regional to a national level (Berk 1994; Campbell and Lindberg 1990; Fligstein 1990; Roy 1997; Sklar 1988). As the large corporation appeared in advanced industrial economies, a distinct relationship emerged between the corporation and the state in each (Freyer 1992; Keller 1990). "Nowhere did large enterprise take root so readily or flourish so luxuriantly as in the turn-of-the-century United States. And in no other country was there so strong a political, legal and regulatory response" (Keller 1990:23). Antitrust was a distinctly American response to industrial expansion (Dobbin 1993; Galambos and Pratt 1988:57): "Ironically . . . in America, the evolution of antitrust law had the unintended consequence of accelerating the development of large-scale corporations . . ."(Hollingsworth 1991:40).

While historians offer competing interpretations for the rise of big business, antitrust, and other Progressive Era reforms, "political sociologists" theories seek to understand how public issues become institutionalized as state policy. In particular, state transformation theory links historical accounts of policy creation to general state theory. It holds that movements influence state policy innovations in a dialectical process that includes a cultural dimension: "[T]ransformation occurs in the context of negotiations over cultural symbols that legitimate the structural change" (Quadagno 1992:618–619). Indeed, "altering cultural codings is one of the most powerful ways a social movement actually brings about change" (Swidler 1995:33). Thus, a key contribution of the theory is to argue that politically mobilized groups advance new meanings in public discourse as a strategic way to shape policy and its institutionalization.

My goal is to refine state transformation theory and apply it to the trust problem. The theory has a distinct, yet underspecified cultural dimension. Most theories of the state are materialist but include vague notions of ideology or Gramscian hegemony. They have not yet incorporated the "constructionist turn" in the social problems, social movements, and symbolic politics literatures. I draw on ideas in these literatures to specify "negotiated culture" in state transformation theory. My analysis builds on the historically oriented critics' understanding of the corporation's ascendance and its relationship to the state which rejects the corporation's triumph as being an inevitable, "natural" outcome of efficient markets and technologically driven "rational" behavior (Berk 1994; Campbell and Lindberg 1991; Fligstein 1990; Roy 1997). Influenced by the new institutionalism (DiMaggio and Powell 1991), they say that such explanations divert attention from the framework of social institutions, state structures, and contingent political processes that constituted new forms of property, facilitated market expansion, and were essential for the rise and expansion of the modern corporation.

"Negotiated culture" links an interpretative frame, organizational forms to advance the frame, and the state apparatus. It weds resource mobilization to constructionist approaches in the movement literature and extends them to include countermovements and elite mobilization. The general culture is a broad resource full of symbolic meanings, while "negotiated culture" refers to a dynamic processes in which political actors strategically select from existing meanings and construct new meanings (Pedrina and Stryker 1997:639).

Constructionist Approaches

My goal is to infuse ideas from three literatures into state transformation theory to enrich it, even if the ideas are not yet fully integrated across the separate literatures. A constructionist perspective emphasizes the symbolic-cultural meanings of controversies or decisions and places them in historical context. Despite its microlevel origins, constructionism is compatible with mid-range theorizing (Layder 1993) and the new sociology of knowledge. It understands that "historical eras differ not only in what people think, but what is thinkable" and looks at "how ideas become plausible to those who hold them" (Swidler and Arditi 1994:314, 321). The core idea of constructionism is that people continuously construct meanings, and once created, the meanings shape subsequent beliefs and behavior. It urges one to look at issues in public discourse as social creations with a capacity to mold public understanding of a situation, and hence affect public actions.

Constructionism suggests that contending political actors create meanings and try to defeat those who offer rival meanings.[2] The contest's outcome is uncertain, but shaped by a mix of cultural and organizational resources. Meanings that emerge victorious become a decisive cultural-legal resource that will shape subsequent discourse and suppress alternative policies (see Scheppele 1994:395).

SOCIAL PROBLEMS

Applied to social problems,[3] constructionism emphasizes how socially created definitions propel issues from the unnoticed background into the prominent foreground of public discourse and, once there, have an impact as profound as objective conditions. By contrast, objectivists focus on the material conditions around which people become mobilized and document such conditions. A strong reading of the constructionist paradigm (Spector and Kituse 1977) exclusively focuses on the rhetoric and strategies of the definition; objective conditions are irrelevant because all views are socially constructed. A "contextual" or weak reading (Best 1989, 1993) is more fruitful. It says one must situate public perceptions in a sociohistorical context; observers need to make independent assumptions about objective conditions in which people socially construct definitions (Best 1989:246–48).

I want to incorporate three constructionist ideas about social problems into state transformation theory: claimsmaking, problem ownership, and assigning responsibility. Creating a social problem is a claimsmaking activity in which actors assert and promote definitions of situations (Spector and Kituse 1977:73). Claims specify victims, identify associated evils, and link problems to core cultural beliefs and values. Analysts focus on the claimsmaking process instead of the claimsmakers social backgrounds (Spector and Kituse 1977:82). Problems have a natural history or career that includes antecedents to claimsmaking. Spector and Kituse (1977:140–154) divide claimsmaking into stages: attempts to assert the existence of a condition and define it as offensive; responses by official organizations; and finally claimsmakers rejecting official responses and creating new, parallel institutions. Claimsmakers typify: they characterize and illustrate a view on a problem using concrete examples; in doing so they emphasize some aspects of the problem, focus on certain causes, and advocate particular solutions (Best 1989:xxi). They use dramatic presentations and examples to make their view of a problem appear "real" to a broad audience, instill moral outrage with detailed anecdotes of victims or offenders, and provide authenticity with quantitative information on counts, trends, or increases (real or exaggerated).

A contest for problem ownership or control over problem definition is central in social problem processes (Gusfield 1981:10–12). Winning ownership is a major ideological victory. It helps to attract new resources (time, funds) as more people accept the definition. With broader support, activists can forge new alliances and unlock resources. Simultaneously, their opponents' definitions lose authority and are neutralized (Emirbayer and Goodwin 1994:1440). Ownership fosters "presumptive rights" and confers a privileged position toward a problem (Cobb and Elder 1983:182–184). These rights legitimize and reinforce owners' claims relative to those of opponents. Claimsmakers can use their credentials and expertise to gain ownership and presumptive rights (Edelman 1988:20). For example, the medical community has presumptive rights over health problems, and police have such rights over crime issues.

Advocates declare they have unique or expert knowledge, sponsor public forums to investigate the problem (as they define it), and establish formal organizations or specialized publications to secure ownership of a problem: "To have authoritative knowledge is to have an institution, group or person in which to settle disputes and establish truth" (Swidler and Arditi 1994:311). By establishing a formal organization and "official" publications, advocates promote the appearance of being "moderate" or "reasonable." This helps them build alliances and secure additional resources. Opponents who must rely on direct action tactics and who lack official status or formal organizations find themselves at a strategic disadvantage.

A critical claim is assigning responsibility for a problem (Gusfield 1981:13–16). One form, causal responsibility, asks, Why did the problem occur? It also attaches motives (blame) that exonerates or condemns specific actors (Spector and Kituse 1977:91–92). Thus, actors assigned naive, noble, or pure motives can avoid responsibility for negative acts, while those with tainted or abhorrent motives are denounced for identical acts. A condition declared to be normal, natural, or something about which nothing needs or can be done is removed from moral responsibility or blame (Gusfield 1981:32–36, 47–50). A second form, political responsibility, asks the question, Who will fix it? Claimsmakers may assume responsibility themselves, leave it to the "natural" market, or assign it to a third party.

SOCIAL MOVEMENTS

Resource mobilization theory dominates the social movement literature, but here, too, constructionism has had an impact (Buechler 1993). I want to incorporate two constructionist ideas, movement frame and movement culture, and two resource mobilization ideas, political opportunity structures and professionalization.

Social movements advance a frame or "schemata of interpretation" which "allows its user to locate, perceive, identify, and label a seemingly infinite number of concrete occurrences" (Goffman 1974:21). Movement frames "are ways of organizing thinking about political issues . . . their usefulness [rests] in increasing understanding and their economy and inclusiveness in providing a coherent explanation of a diverse set of facts" (Gamson 1992:71). Movements create, sustain, and extend a frames boundaries (Snow et al. 1986). Snow and Benford (1988:5) remark, "Movements themselves are engaging in meaning-work . . . in the struggle over the production of ideas and meanings." A frame that resonates with the dominant cultural beliefs is more potent and spreads more quickly; this is its "narrative fidelity" or "ideational centrality" (Snow and Benford 1992:141), yet, a frame aligned with dominant cultural beliefs may have its radicalism inhibited (Tarrow 1992). Likewise, control of the frame is critical. Competing social movement organizations (SMOs) can "steal" elements from another's frame (Tarrow 1992). This has two implications. The frame may disperse, becoming a broad cultural shift that attracts many adherents. Alternatively, its unique claims may be depleted by competitors, undercutting it as a distinct, coherent vision.

A frame cannot persist at the level of abstract ideas; it needs a social foundation. A movement culture sustains interpretative schemes or frames (Gamson 1992;

Goodywn 1976; Klandermans 1984; Klandermans and Oegema 1987; McAdam 1982). New beliefs in a frame appear early in the micromobilization process, as new social identities emerge in informal groups: "Long before a controversy develops into an open conflict and challengers enter the scene, public discourse has created various sectors within a society, each with its own opinions and position. . ." (Klandermans 1992:96–97). A movement culture includes the social practices, values, and traditions that sustain symbols, rituals, institutions, and social relations consistent with the frame. It supports a web of friendships, moral beliefs, and neighborhood or community solidarity. Over time, movement members embrace frame values, amplify the frame, and connect it to other cultural institutions and beliefs. A movement culture links agency to structure, personal identity to political practice, and organization to action.

A movement frame is a type of cognitive resource (see Williams 1995:125). A political opportunity structure (POS) is a resource that creates an "opening" for change. A POS develops when the balance of power between elites and challengers shifts, cleavages develop among elites, established political institutions weaken, electoral patterns become unstable, or potential coalition partners appear. It includes action by self-interested state managers who try to expand their power and advance their political beliefs (Amenta and Zylan 1991). Protest movements start and grow in cycles, waves, or clusters that correspond to POS openings (Tarrow 1994). Movement waves trigger a "wave of reform" when a wide range of policies is created or undergoes significant change (Tarrow 1994). This occurs in a situation of "constitutive politics" (Berk 1994:11) or "nonnormal" conditions when the field of battle is altered; it affects all sides and stimulates frame innovation. Thus, frame innovation is linked to temporal cycles of protest and reform. Radical ideas may gain acceptance during extraordinary "breaks" in existing beliefs, in periods of social unrest, and when a crisis intensifies ideological polarization (Swidler 1995:34). Snow and Benford (1992:142) observe, "The cyclical pattern to movement frames, framing activity and the resultant ideational webs that some movements spin . . . can be crucial to the emergence and course of a cycle of protest."

SMOs vary by professionalization. Some SMOs develop a professional staff and formal organization. They become less likely to pursue direct-action tactics and are oriented more toward institutionalized channels of influence (e.g., lobbying). A formal organization and full-time staff facilitates persistence, coalition-building, and a focus on organizational maintenance (Staggenborg 1991). A SMO selects an organizational form from among the available "organizational repertoire" in which "certain models are privileged by the existing distribution of power, status and wealth . . ." or creates new forms (Clemens 1993:771). Moreover, the formal organization "is rarely a neutral tool . . . because formal organizations shape the world view and actions of their members, and because they limit the form of subsequent organization" (Conell and Voss 1990:266). Since a SMO operates in a multiorganizational field, coalition formation polarizes into movement supporters and opponents (Everett 1992; Klandermans 1992). Alliance formation initiates a "conflict system" with bipolar interpretations and definitions. This constrains a frame's uniqueness, as SMOs compromise and reduce differences to maintain coalition ties. Resources from external actors may deradicalize demands by creating dependency relationships (Pichardo 1988) or by bringing a frame into conformity with dominant cultural beliefs. SMO professionalization highlights the constraints that operate on the definition of social problems and the creation of new frames.

SYMBOLIC POLITICS AND AGENDA SETTING

Lastly, I draw on the political science literature for two constructionist ideas, symbolic politics and agenda setting. Symbolic politics is not trivial politics, or a "mere" contest of symbols; language and symbol usage shape political events and behavior (Edelman 1977, 1988). Symbols influence how people understand events and shape perceptions; they reinforce values and evoke nonanalytic cultural responses (Green 1987:2). Claimsmaking, problem definition, and frame creation are highly symbolic activities, and actors use meanings in ways that mask complexity, contradiction, and reversal (Edelman 1988:16–17). "A policy's name allows us to ignore inconsistencies and ambiguities; the name reassures us that there is agreement on the dominant ideology. . ." (Handler and Hansenfeld 1991:41). For example, elite actors often try to derail opponents by creating new names for or redefining a policy (Cobb and Elder 1983:126–27). The heart of politics is persuasion, and rhetorical techniques are tools of persuasion, so actors engaged in claimsmaking use rhetoric strategically. "The function of rhetoric is not to provide acceptable proofs, but to induce decisions and judgments, to move the relevant facts to some action or disposition . . ." (McGee and Lyne 1987:391).

Policy innovation is constrained by what reaches the public agenda. What reaches the agenda largely depends on the balance of power among organized groups and on an issue's symbolic potency. Policy innovations rarely appear in isolation; they arrive in a "policy image" (i.e., a package of information and symbolic, emotive appeals). A policy image includes causal stories or anecdotes and is an idea parallel to typification (social problems literature) and frame (movements literature). Once the image reaches an agenda, it may become institutionalized into law or policy, shaping subsequent policy and agendas (Carmines and Stimson 1989).

The mass media deserve special attention. The media serve gatekeeping and issue amplification roles; they rarely initiate arousal but select issues from among those advanced for the agenda before public agitation spreads (Baumgartner and Jones 1993:247; Beckett 1994; Cobb and Elder 1983:143). "The media can bring claims to public attention, but that does not insure that people will attend to them" (Best 1990:187). Once on the agenda, an issue must attention (McFarland 1991; Peters and Hogwood 1985) and repel threats to dislodge it since arenas of public discourse have a limited "carrying capacity" (Hilgartner and Bosk 1988). Issues can be derailed or displaced by a more urgent problem (e.g., war or foreign invasion), by a purely symbolic solution to problems, or by a shift in the venue from open public discourse to a less visible realm.[4] In the latter case, advocates may rhetorically transform a disputed moral claim about ultimate goals into an instrumental technical-administrative issue (Best 1990; Edelman 1977; Gusfield 1981). Once moved into a technical-expert realm, an issue gets absorbed into a mode of discourse the public defines as "objective" or "neutral." This subverts some claims and elevates others. As the rules of claimsmaking shift, actors who lack access to official-legitimate technical knowledge (e.g., science, law) are disarmed and immobilized (see Cobb and Elder 1983:45; Gusfield 1981; Stryker 1990).

STATE TRANSFORMATION THEORY MODIFIED

We need to integrate the ideas outlined above into state transformation theory. The theory's central question is, How do movements transform state structures? (Quadagno 1992:618). It emphasizes historical contingency, and unlike other theories of the state, does not assign causal priority to pluralist interest groups, state capacity, ruling-class domination, or mass-turmoil factors. It asks, How do movements pressure for new laws or a new agency, alter the selection of personnel, affect agency autonomy, or force the adoption of new policies, especially in "critical" historical periods? The theory links the creation and struggles over social meaning to institutionalized state power and policy in a three-way interaction between a) public discourse, b) mobilized political forces, and c) state actors and institutions.

The processes depicted in state transformation theory incorporate various constructionist concepts. Thus, during periods of qualitative political change (POS), mobilized actors (claimsmakers) create new meanings (movement frames, policy images) with specific features (typification, causal, and political responsibility). Contending actors try to control interpretations of key events, define the terms of public discourse (problem ownership and presumptive rights) and advance their ideas in forums of public awareness and decision making (agenda setting). This contest constrains the creation of new state agencies and policies because cultural meanings shape popular understanding and attention. The new frame emerges through an iterative process as actors test new strategies and respond to a succession of new conditions, competing actors, and evolution in the movement's organizational structure.

A group's success or failure in changing public policy depends on more than its ideas. Success depends on its capacity to create a mutually reinforcing combination of ideas and organizational practices (movement culture) and to deploy them strategically. Crucial to success is a group's capacity to mobilize resources (including professionalization), make organizational innovations, and form alliances. Such processes apply to groups beyond traditional challenger or protest movements and include elite movements, (i.e., organized action by classes or groups with control over legitimate institutional resources).

An ability to innovate and quickly respond is pivotal because popular attention, agendas, and policy shift in "short bursts of dramatic change" parallel to waves of protest: "Mass political involvement and issue discourse are episodic and discrete" (Carmines and Stimson 1989:136) with significant agenda building or policy change concentrated "during periods of general heightened public attention" (Baumgartner and Jones 1993:20). Movements that have political success and institutionalize their interpretation in such critical periods have long-term effects on policy in what has been called "path dependency" (Pedrina and Stryker 1997).

THE TRUST PROBLEM

The "trust problem" was at the center of the political agenda from the 1880s to World War I. Attention crested between the Democratic party defeat of 1896 that realigned party politics for three decades and passage of the Clayton Act (1914). Concern accelerated in the context of a realigning election, nationalist–imperialistic expansion, intense class conflict, the rise of the Progressive and Socialist parties, and America's first large-scale wave of corporate mergers.

The claimsmaking literature reminds us that the intense debate over the trust did not spring automatically from "objective conditions"; nor was it a simple reflection of the backgrounds or class interests of leading social actors; nor was it the unambiguous result of competition among a plurality of interest groups. Although objective conditions alone did not generate a rethinking of the trust problem, they were critical to it. America's first great merger wave, combined with a soaring stock market and the collapse of railroad investments, reconfigured the industrial sector (Lamoreaux 1985; Nelson 1959; Roy 1997). Capitalists formed monopolies in the sugar, tobacco, whiskey, meat packing, and cash register industries: "From 1895 to 1904, 157 holding companies absorbed more than 1,800 existing firms. The great majority of these new corporations—the "big businesses" of the early twentieth century—controlled 40 percent or more of the market . . ." (Keller 1990:24). For example, U.S. Steel Corporation consolidated 148 firms in 1901, capitalized at 1.4 billion. A year later, International Harvester was incorporated with control over 95 percent of the farm implement industry, that in 1890 had contained over 900 independent firms. Critics increasingly saw the Sherman Antitrust Act as ineffective in addressing the trust problem due to restrictive court rulings.

Objective conditions had changed profoundly, but people felt and reacted to the conditions through the language, symbols, and interpretative frames available to them. As a contest emerged among actors for alternative ways to think about the trust (i.e., the large corporation), claimsmakers tried to control discourse by redefining terms and embedding them in frames linked to potent cultural values. Different groups accepted diverse meanings of symbolic terms (e.g., democracy, competition [Thimm 1976:63]).

"From the passage of the Sherman Act in 1890 to the onset of the First World War," Galambos and Pratt (1988:57) remark, "debate over the trusts (the label trusts continued to be applied during these years to all large corporations, generally with negative connotations) and arguments about the efficacy of antitrust were significant issues in electoral politics." The problem evoked intense emotion and reappeared in party platforms, political speeches, protest movement pamphlets, and intellectual debates. In his first annual message to Congress in 1901, Theodore Roosevelt said, "Many of those who have made it their vocation to denounce the great industrial combinations, although with technical inaccuracy, known as 'trust,' appeal especially to hatred and fear" (in Hofstadter 1963:142).

The trust had been an explosive issue from 1887 to 1890, but interest waned after the Sherman Antitrust Act passed (1890) and populism was defeated (1892).[5] Concern reemerged after the 1893 to 1896 depression, the violent nationwide Pullman Railroad Strike (1894), the 1896 election and dramatic merger wave (Bringhurst 1979;

Hoffman 1970; Kloppenberg 1986; Link and McCormick 1983, McGeer 1986; Noble 1970; Zunz 1990). Renewed interest in the problem grew after 1896. Between 1891 and 1895, the *New York Times* published an average of 40 articles per year on trusts and antimonopoly concerns. During the first six months of 1899, the *Times Index* listed 245 articles and 17 editorials on the problem. Attention grew in Congress as well. In the five years following the vague Sherman Antitrust Act, an average of fourteen antimonopoly bills was introduced per session; this dropped to eight with the 54th Congress (1895–1897). However, the number then grew in each succeeding session from eleven bills in the 55th Congress (1897–1899), to twenty-three bills and eight resolutions in the 56th Congress (1899–1901) to thirty-nine pieces of legislation in the 57th Congress (1901–1903 [Thorelli 1955; Leinwand 1962]). As the issue resurfaced, observers borrowed symbols and rhetoric from classical liberal and populist ideologies in political language and law. In the debates during the 1896–1902 merger movement, the symbol and reality of the trust remained blurred (McCraw 1974:182).

EARLY DEBATES

Politicians, intellectuals, and business leaders debated the problem in publications and national conferences. The Chicago Civic Federation (precursor to the National Civic Federation) and the U.S. Industrial Commission sponsored conferences in 1899 and 1900. At the same time, small business owners and farmers formed local "antitrust leagues." Numerous academic works appeared, including Clark's *Control of Trusts* (1901), Rossignol's *Monopolies Past and Present* (1901), and Jenks' *The Trust Problem* (1900 [Thorelli 1955:311–343]). Such works reflected popular concern: "Of no small importance . . . the difference between the mainstream professional thought and the trend of popular opinion was becoming increasingly narrow" (Thorelli 1955:329).

Contemporaries first framed the problem in moral terms. In 1899 the president of the Indiana State Board of Commerce stated, "It is clear that there is both good and evil in the present trust scheme" (Chicago Civic Federation 1973:55). Political and intellectual leaders viewed trusts as part of economic progress and industrial expansion; trusts resulted from the same market forces that had produced great wealth and efficiency. At the 1899 Chicago Conference on Trusts (Chicago Civic Federation 1973:67–68), Azel Hatch remarked, "They are a natural evolution in industrial progress. . . ." Yet, trusts also disrupted markets and spread corruption, social misery, immoral business practices and political radicalism. Observers struggled to understand such contradictory effects. The dilemma became how to retain the economic benefits but contain the negative impacts:

> They [trusts] seek to justify their operations on the plausible ground that they improve the quality and increase the quantity of manufactured goods, reduce the prices to the consumer, save money, time and labor to the customer, and add to the aggregate wealth and prosperity of the country . . . [But] At the expense of the producer of the raw materials, whose products are forced upon the market at ruinous prices; . . . of discharged employees and laborers, whose places are filled by fewer hands or improved machinery,

> whose wages cease, whose families must starve or steal or join the great army of tramps and paupers . . . of the toil and enterprise of every honest competitor, who is driven out of business . . . of the entire public, which is sooner or later left no choice but to submit to the exaction as the triumphant monopoly may dictate. (Chicago Civic Federation 1973:46)

Claimsmakers offered competing interpretations. Populists saw the corporation as the evil monopolistic trust and sought its abolition. Economic conservatives defended it by referring to the virtues of individualism and natural market forces and advocated a laissez faire policy. Social Gospel adherents thought the industrial corporation inescapable but sought to harmonize it with a desire for social stability and reduced social misery; they advocated limited, positive government action in the public interest. Socialists accepted the large corporation as inevitable and demanded its nationalization: "We socialists rejoice that the trust has come to show you that the logical sequence of the ownership and control of what is now known as private property . . . will be organized into trusts until there will be one trust" (Chicago Civic Federation 1973:321). The position of the corporation was "up for grabs"; it was unsettled ideologically, politically, and economically.

By the end of the nineteenth century, it was not clear whether the large corporation would be a permanent feature of the economy. Few could see just how dramatically the economy was being restructured, comprehend the full impact of the new business organization, or recognize that they were in the midst of a shift in the "social structure of accumulation" American capitalism (McDonough 1994). Looking back, many saw the corporation evolving out of individual firm behavior that conformed to "natural" market forces (Berk 1994). Natural laws were "a way of thinking, strongly embedded in the late-nineteenth-century American mind . . ." (Sklar 1988:10). Change brought "corresponding trends in social thought" and new "forms of thought" had to be constructed (Sklar 1988:11, 15).

THE PROGRESSIVE FRAME

Progressivism was a conceptual innovation. It offered a new frame at a critical juncture, accompanied by a new movement organization. Progressives reframed the trust problem by shifting the parameters of debate from individualism (laissez-faire policy) versus paternalism (direct government involvement), to conservatism (protect the status quo) versus radicalism (unrest and spreading socialism). Academics who elaborated the developing progressive frame were aware of the German activist state and the large socialist movement in Europe (Wunderlin 1992:102). A Progressive leader, Richard Ely, feared a battle between capital and labor, with ideological polarization and violent unrest. He created "middle ground" by painting conservatism in pejorative terms; instead of representing virtuous individualism, tradition and natural law, it was an outmoded political economy. Its antithesis, radicalism, would destroy the market system, private property and individual freedom. Ely's alternative included both the market and positive government (Green 1987:36–42). "Progressive" entered the political vocabulary, "not as a value-free analytic tool but as a political weapon developed within a political context . . . a new critical perspective on corporate power" (Green 1987:37).

Progressivism as a movement took several forms. Beginning in the upper midwest, the movement's regional origins differed from those of the radical populists, but it drew on agrarian populism. As an electoral alternative, it gained visibility with Robert LaFollette's break with the Republican Party machine and his election as the first Progressive governor in 1900. His success was followed by Progressive victories in Iowa, Minnesota, Missouri, North Dakota, and Kansas (Caine 1974; Ekirch 1974:107–123; Green 1987:54–85). Progressivism encompassed a range of issues (e.g., municipal reform, labor conditions, food safety, social welfare, conservation, and electoral reform). It fostered a movement culture and spanned academic thought and developments in art, literature, and philosophy (Crunden 1984; Ekirch 1974:1933; Kloppenberg 1986). It was a public consciousness that portrayed America at the threshold of a new stage in social and technological evolution (Glassberg 1987).

The Progressive frame emerged in a context in which new media forms undermined traditional politics (Clemens 1997) and a "new journalism" that exposed corruption, abuse of power, and the impact of rapid industrialization, creating a sense of crisis: "making people conscious of uncomfortable truths that earlier nineteenth-century conditions had obscured: that society's diverse producer groups did not exist in harmony . . . private interests posed a danger to the public's interests. The crisis brought on by the recognition of these two problems extended from the onset of the depression in 1893 until 1908 . . ." (McCormick 1981:257). Sparked by new technology, rising living standards, and aroused popular interest, "muckraking journalism" was a mass media innovation. *McClure's*, *Harper's*, and *Cosmopolitan* were established, followed by other magazines and books as capitalists, politicians, and intellectuals intensely debated the trust problem (Chalmers 1964; Filler 1976).

The new corporations lacked legitimation. Muckraking journalists typified them as illegitimate, linking them to discredited trusts and corrupt practices. Social Darwinist and laissez-faire individualist ideologies were ill-suited for justifying new, large-scale bureaucratic organizations and the new type of economic system in which they dominated (Thimm 1976).

DISTINGUISHING "GOOD" AND "BAD" TRUSTS AS A SOLUTION

As the frame evolved, leading actors claimed that the problem was a contradiction between the economic benefits and social costs of the large corporation. Attempting to gain ownership over the issue, President Theodore Roosevelt borrowed an idea Charles Schwab had offered at a 1901 symposium on the trust—assign the benefits to some firms and the costs to others, using a moral dichotomy of good and bad trusts. Immoral individuals operated "bad trusts," using unethical, corrupt means; they cheated consumers, mistreated workers, and misused their new wealth. Led by upstanding, ethical entrepreneurs and managers, "good trusts" inevitably emerged from natural economic laws and technical requirements. Such people did not corrupt others with their wealth; they were responsible owners earning fair profits by efficient production and administration. Roosevelt held "only those combinations that engaged in unfair restraint of trade or competition should be subject to prosecution" (Ekirch 1974:132). Isolating the small minority of "bad" trusts sheltered other corporations from criticism.

Roosevelt's moral resolution had narrative fidelity and identified causal responsibility (some owners were immoral), but it did not settle political responsibility (who would solve the problem). A mechanism was needed to distinguish "good" from "bad" trusts, something existing laws failed to do since legal standards were ambiguous and the courts unpredictable. In 1903 Roosevelt created the Bureau of Corporations in the new Department of Commerce and Labor to uphold "fair" standards of competition and publicize (or "shame") trusts that operated "unfairly." A "neutral" agency with limited powers, the Bureau governed competition by slowly converting local, implicit business norms into uniform national commercial rules. It monitored firm behavior, codified norms and restored stability by informing old and new entrants alike of the "rules of the game." In the same year he established the Antitrust Division in the Justice Department. It was assigned enforcement powers to contain political corruption by the trusts and punish serious antitrust law violators. It was a visible symbol for populist politicians who criticized lax Sherman Act enforcement.

THE DISTINCTION FAILS

Roosevelt's framing the problem in political–moral terms failed to address deeper structural and political–legal issues. The ascendance of the corporation had divided the capitalist class and signaled the rise of a new class segment (Roy 1990). Entrenched class segments in finance and manufacturing fused in the 1875 to 1895 period, but a new cleavage materialized. After railroad stocks collapsed in the 1893 to 1896 Depression and Wall Street expanded in 1898–1904, the trusts evolved into corporate holding companies. The capitalist class split into two segments, "the entrepreneurial segment and the corporate class segment" (Roy 1991:149). The structural issue was how to bridge the intraclass division and assimilate the new segment into a reconstituted, unified class.

By 1900, both segments mobilized politically. The entrepreneurial segment continued its local activism, supporting political parties, participating in trade organizations and forming new organizations (National Anti-Monopoly League, National Association of Manufacturers). The corporate segment grew more self-conscious and mobilized into formal organizations that had a regional or national focus (New York Reform Club, American Asiatic Association, National Civil Service League, National Civic Federation, American Association for Labor Legislation [Sklar 1988:23–25]). The strategic organizational innovation of a national organization, like the National Civic Federation (NCF), that included business, academic, and labor leaders in a more professional structure, influenced the search for a frame that could redefine and provide a new understanding of the problem.

The NCF and similar organizations were movement organizations. Some analysts categorize political actors with access to institutional power as being nonmovements. Yet, a political movement is a proactive, goal-oriented collectivity that develops through social networks, builds organizations, and elaborates a frame around shared goals. Early professionalized advocacy organizations were organizational innovations formed by the politically mobilized members of an emerging dominant class sector searching for strategies and an ideological framework to articulate, defend, and justify their social position. The class position of movement members ensured abundant resources, including a capacity to hire technical-expert knowledge workers, create formal organizations, and co-opt critics.

Roosevelt's state-mediated resolution mended the intraclass cleavage temporarily. Some corporate actors allied with established wealth and power. They recognized broader, shared class interests. Other mavericks were unwilling or unable to compromise around common, class-based interests. Many capitalists continued to mobilize against unions and distrusted the rapidly growing new corporations. Smaller capitalists saw the problem as how to formalize the existing normative standards and punish its violators. Rising corporate leaders, on the other hand, wanted to consolidate their gains and stabilize market conditions (Kolko 1963:23). Roosevelt's resolution promised market stability and reasserted political legitimacy under the aegis of expanding state administrative capacity.

In this era, business conduct was governed little by law or administrative bureaucracy. Patronage politics and a case law-based judicial system were dominant (Freyer 1979; Skowronek 1982). The business community relied on normative standards that had evolved over the years into stable, local environments. Implicit business ethics and norms kept competitive relationships civil. Rapid industrial expansion and ascending corporate organizations disrupted existing local or regional norms. Established business owners saw the aggressive, competitive tactics and technical advantages of corporations as "unfair" or "immoral." The old populist frame condemned the trust in moral terms, but capitalists rejected its radical egalitarianism and agrarian ideals. The alternative of classical liberalism with its free, open competition and laissez-faire policy provided little solace.

Despite attempts to resolve the issue and restore legitimacy, popular anger over monopoly, corruption, industrial strife, and workplace injuries grew. Legitimacy eroded as people saw the state as ineffective or controlled by "the interests": "By 1905 a political explosion of some sort was likely, due to the accumulated frustrations people felt about government's failure to deal with the problems of industrialism" (McCormick 1986:349). In popular language and symbolically, the trust problem persisted.

REASONABLE RESTRAINTS FRAME

Faced with a growing legitimacy crisis, mobilized actors sought a new frame for the problem, one that endorsed the large corporation and placed its operation in a comprehensive set of state regulations. They incorporated broad cultural themes (technological progress and international competitiveness) to justify the large corporation (McCormick 1986:345).

> Concentration and cooperation in industry in order to secure efficiency are a world-wide movement. The United States cannot resist it. If we isolate ourselves and insist upon the subdivision of industry . . . we shall be defeated in the world's markets. We cannot adopt an economic system less efficient than our great competitors, Germany, England, France and

> Austria. Either we must modify our present obsolete laws regarding concentration and cooperation . . . or else fall behind in the race for the world's markets. (Van Hise 1973:277)

They also built on new thinking in economics, especially marginal utility theory. It asserted that the corporation arose naturally from market operations and blamed economic disruptions on uncontrolled overproduction and pricing practices (Sklar 1988:71). This shift in causal responsibility implied a shift in political responsibility.

As they elaborated the frame, actors drew on changes in legal thinking, especially the law on restraint of trade. Common law interpretations had prevailed until 1897. There was no separate federal law on restraint of trade prior to the Sherman Act, although many states had antitrust laws. Common law only outlawed unreasonable restraints of interstate trade, such as direct acts to restrict goods and services that raised prices to very high levels or prevented new competitors from entering a market. A new phase in legal thinking, the "Harlan construction" (named for Justice John Marshall Harlan), developed from the Trans-Missouri decision (1897). It departed from common law jurisprudence by establishing a small-producer version of "natural liberty" holding all combinations or contracts that restricted interstate trade to be illegal; there were no "reasonable" restraints.

Judicial rulings in the Harlan phase had accentuated uncertainty. The Court's rulings deviated from both common law and the executive branch's position. Rulings effectively polarized policy choices between a return to the pure competitive market and a statist reconstruction of the economy as corporate capitalism. No trusts were dismantled in this stage because of executive branch inaction. The Sherman Act prohibited restraints of trade due to great market power; it did not outlaw corporations per se. Legal debates over the Sherman Act refocused the problem; they shielded the corporate organizational form while attacking specific corporate behaviors. During the Harlan construction, the Court reinterpreted the Sherman Act as outlawing many behaviors, or restraints of trade, that arose directly from interstate trade carried out by corporations that had substantial market power.

REGULATION AS A NEW SOLUTION

Central to Roosevelt's second resolution was removing the trust issue from partisan politics and the judiciary, and placing it in technically oriented federal agencies. He advocated a statist "policy image" or package of federal licensing, "reasonable" trade restraints, and more intense federal regulation. The NCF cautiously joined Roosevelt's renewed offer to end the problem (Sklar 1988:219). A 1907 national conference with 492 delegates from state and federal government, business associations, academia, and organized labor debated the trust issue and moved toward a permanent resolution: "The real significance of these early conferences was not in the visible results, but in the changing consciousness of the participants" (Weinstein 1968:29–30).

The 1908 Hepburn Bill consolidated the second attempted solution. The bill protected corporate expansion under extensive federal regulation, restored the Sherman Act's common law interpretation to allow "reasonable" restraints of trade, instituted federal registration of large corporations and unions, and expanded publicity to control corporate behavior.

REGULATION FAILS

Opposition led by smaller manufacturers defeated the Hepburn Bill. In the end, the corporate segment accommodated to a vocal, organized group of small and medium-sized capitalists and withdrew support from a state-led reorganization of the economy (Sklar 1988:264–65). During this period, leftist Progressives, in a loose alliance with populists and radicals, criticized the large corporation, and business lobbying continued to expand. A wave of well-publicized scandals in 1905 to 1908 highlighted business-government corruption (McCormick 1986; Schneirov 1994:208). Public leaders, like Louis Brandeis, attacked concentrated economic power as undermining democracy's very foundation (Brandeis 1934; McCraw 1984; Urofsky 1971). Prompted by rising media criticism, the 1907–1908 financial panic (Johnson 1961), the Hepburn Bill's defeat, and Taft's election (1908), the trust problem again rose to the top of the political agenda. Yet, its parameters had been narrowed. The central issue that remained was the degree and form of state regulation.

CORPORATE LIBERAL FRAME

The Hepburn Bill defeat opened another opportunity to redefine the problem. By 1909, the Progressive movement had split into a corporate-nationalist Roosevelt wing and a liberal-populist LaFollette wing. As LaFollette lost support and the liberal-populist Progressive frame weakened, other issues arose to mobilize corporate leaders.

> Around 1908 a qualitative shift in outlook occurred among large numbers of these men of authority, a shift roughly comparable to one during the mid-eighties. Once again, irritants became anxieties, a context of threat replaced isolated reactions, and responses acquired that cumulative self-accelerating character which created an increasing urgent movement to discipline an unruly society. (Wiebe 1967:208–209)

Responding to the rising sense of public crisis, the NCF the leading organization to articulate the interests of the corporate sector, turned to state-level organizing. It grew from 1,500 to 5,000 members between 1907 and 1912 by focusing on two issues: a permanent resolution to the issue of the trust, and a response to the spread of socialist ideas. These issues unified most capitalists and mended the reopened rift. The NCF a well-organized "elite movement organization," was generating a "movement culture" of concerned leaders to forge a new frame and emerging into an institutional form for forging broad intraclass unity (see Mintz 1995).The NCF established class solidarity by identifying and combating a common enemy, socialism. The pattern of a common class threat triggering short-term intraclass unity and political mobilization is repeated at other times in U.S. history (Akard 1992; Domhoff 1996).

The NCF redefined the trust problem within an emerging new frame, Corporate Liberalism. The frame evolved slowly over more than a decade of debate in legal and academic circles: "This process occurs piecemeal, competing models of industrial order did not occur to politicians, managers, farmers, or state-builders in comprehensive or programmatic detail" (Berk 1994:12). Within the Corporate Liberal frame, leaders advocated seeing the corporation, not as a legal fiction created by the state, but as a "natural" or organic body with rights prior to the state. The frame diffused a classical liberal understanding of property and the market, defining them as presocial or "natural." The ideas about private property and the market became central to how the emerging frame legitimated the corporation and restricted the state to policing only its intentionally harmful behavior. As Roy (1997:44) notes, such a public–private division and "economic and political categories are not natural and inevitable," but were created through political struggle.

Legal and political events also shaped the evolving frame. After years of slow expansion, the Bureau of Corporations stabilized as a vehicle for guiding wayward corporations. President Taft rejected a state-led reorganization of the economy around large corporations, and he instead expanded the Antitrust Division, returning to a traditional approach. Antitrust enforcement grew after 1908; the federal courts decided 90 antitrust cases between 1909 and 1914.

The Supreme Court announced the "rule of reason" doctrine in the Standard Oil and American Tobacco cases of 1911. An antitrust case against the oil trust began in 1906 when Standard Oil controlled 90 percent of national oil refining capacity and used aggressive tactics to achieve dominance. The Court said that the firm had violated the law, but ruled that it took into consideration the "nature and character" of the firm's behavior. The reasonableness of firm behavior was also considered in the tobacco trust case (American Tobacco 1911). The rule of reason doctrine returned to common law principles and gave the courts flexibility in interpreting the Sherman Act. The Act outlawed "unreasonable" restraints of trade, but permitted "reasonable" restraints. These were distinguished by an active intent at restraint and the Court's view of the "public interest." The doctrine advanced beyond the good/bad trust dichotomy and shifted authority to the courts: "Unfortunately, the Court's opinion was murky. . . . This ambiguity has never been explicitly resolved" (Posner 1976:27). It created room for politically motivated considerations (Thompson and Brady 1964:52).

Progressive and corporate leaders supported the Rule of Reason doctrine and a stronger Bureau of Corporations (Sklar 1988:86–189). As Sklar notes (1988:173) "in its Rule of Reason decisions in 1911, the Supreme Court laid the juridical basis for what may be called the corporate-liberal solution to the trust question." The doctrine brought a small but critical crop of antitrust cases: the DuPont group of explosive manufacturers was split into three parts; the Eastman Kodak company was found to have monopolized photographic apparatuses and supplies; and the glucose and farm machinery monopolies were prosecuted (Neale 1970:100). Antitrust Division appropriations grew from 1910 to 1914 and its unspent surplus declined (Toppin 1955):

> Despite antitrust activism and few mergers, the trust problem did not disappear. . . . [F]rom the Civil Federation's trust conference in October 1907 to the debates over the Hepburn Bill in early 1908, a consensus forming since the turn of the century had crystallized and come to encompass a cross section of capital, union labor and farm groups, as well as influential circles of intellectuals, professionals and political leaders. The common outlook favored (1) the legalization of reasonable restraints of trade; (2) effective federal regulation of interstate commerce . . . ; (3) the establishment of some federal administrative agency. . . . (Sklar 1988:282)

Two issues yet to be settled were the role of organized labor and the degree of state intervention, specifically the federal licensing of corporations.[6]

The trust problem was at the forefront of the 1912 three-way Presidential election. Each party's platform offered to revise antitrust policy, reflecting the three Progressive Era frames. Taft favored limited state action in a judicial response that would discipline the "bad" trusts who threatened market competition. Renewing ideas from the Hepburn Bill, Roosevelt advocated a strong state role to shape a corporate economy that would permit firms to engage in reasonable "restraints of trade" under close state guidance. Wilson offered an accommodative position, expand regulation to dampen public agitation, and address the capitalist class cleavage. His regulatory commission was designed "to maximize harmony, minimize friction . . . [the commission] contributed decisively to the winding down of a generation-long warfare, not only between the people and the interests, but between different types of capitalists" (McCraw 1974:189). His Corporate Liberal solution removed the issue from public debate into a weak administrative bureaucracy that some powerful interests could influence.

EXPANDED REGULATION AS A SOLUTION

Congressional hearings on the problem increased after 1910 and, following the 1912 Presidential election, two new laws recast antitrust policy. The Clayton Act extended the Sherman Act by specifying monopolistic and illegal corporate behaviors. The Federal Trade Commission Act established an independent regulatory commission that superseded the Bureau of Corporations and regulated competition: "The ideas embodied in the Federal Trade Commission Act represented a triumph of the agitation and education done by the NCF over the previous seven years" (Weinstein 1968:89).

The Clayton and FTC Acts defused trust problem agitation, limited judicial power, and narrowed the range of legal business behaviors, in the process, they restricted competition and stabilized business conditions. A goal of the corporate sector had been to "civilize" competition, and it was the major outcome of antitrust reform (Bittlingmayer 1996; Brownlee 1974). Antitrust, as Wiebe (1958:683) observed, "contained potentially the exact solution big industrialists sought." It defused antibusiness agitation and legitimated the corporation within an administrative–legal framework that avoided direct control over corporations.

In 1912 Woodrow Wilson stated, "I am for big business, and I am against the trust" (Kolko 1963:209). This redefinition of the problem concealed a contradiction, accommodating both the trust (large corporation) and a symbol of its antithesis: "The antitrust laws, however loaded with political symbolism . . . did not fundamentally alter the nation's new brand of corporate capitalism. . . . Curiously, antitrust measures actually helped legitimize the role of the large corporation" (Galambos and Pratt 1988:60, 62).

The unruly populist thrust of antitrust had been absorbed into legal–technical regulatory administration by 1915 (Skowronek 1982:248–74). The corporation and antitrust were no longer contradictory. The menacing problem had been transformed into a new frame; one negotiated in struggles in which an organized movement of corporate leaders was a key actor (Lustig 1982; Sklar 1988:174, fn. 191; Weinstein 1968). Corporate liberals succeeded in transforming the trust problem, even if their understanding of their "economic interests were at best ambiguous, fixed only dialogically through the progress of forging alliances and identifying adversaries . . ." (Berk:1994:170).

> It is immensely difficult to attempt to present a reasonably well-balanced summary view of the general climate of socio-economic thinking and intellectual opinion in which antitrust policy was conceived. . . . One of the reasons why it is almost impossible to present an integrated picture of this body of thought . . . is that its component parts are almost all borrowed goods (Thorelli 1955:565).

With popular agitation quelled, new meanings could be solidified, and new laws, agencies and corporate strategies ensued. This was not inevitable; political actors with cultural and organization resources and who forged strategic alliances made it happen.

Conclusion

State transformation theory explains how the "policy innovation" of antitrust, or corporate liberal economic regulation, grew out of the "trust problem" that had once signified antipathy toward the corporation. Movement organizations negotiated key terms and interpretative schemes. Movement success occurred when the continuously negotiated cultural meanings intersected with organizational innovations and a political opening. This analysis suggests three areas for refining state transformation theory.

First, new cultural meanings (e.g., claims, movement frames) are negotiated in a fluid, dialectic process marked by confusion and shifting coalitions of multiple actors across decades. Claimsmakers borrow, experiment with, and change vocabulary as they search for new frames in an ongoing contest to gain control over definitions, terms, and symbols (Green 1987:58). Also, the trust problem did not follow Spector and Kituse's (1977) four-stage natural history model. Competing groups, including state actors, asserted claims many times in several forms with multiple definitions. Claimsmaking is an ongoing, nonlinear process of constructing meaning that gets enmeshed with other issues on multiple "fronts" (academics, law, partisan politics, and government legislation). Competing groups and state managers are neither homogenous nor unified but negotiate definitions in shifting coalitions.

Second, organizational innovations accompany new meanings. Actors elaborate and promote meanings in contests that involve new forms of organization. Movements are not limited to challengers in subordinate classes but can include mobilized members of dominant class segments. As the organizational repertoire expands (Clemens 1993, 1997), new types of "political interest" organizations (e.g., NCF), new modes of discourse (high-profile national conferences, formal lobbying, use of mail questionnaires), and new media (muckraking in magazines, newspapers, and books) appear. Successfully advancing a definition depends on having access to organizational resources (including a "professional" mode of operation) and a capacity to change. The social and political structures grow out of a duality of cultural schemes and actual resources (Sewell 1992).

Lastly, the consequences of claimsmaking and problem redefinition go far beyond a movement's attempt to persuade "the public." A victorious problem definition leaves visible public debate, where it is disputed, to become wrapped in technical vocabulary and buried in an administrative bureaucracy (McCormick 1986:278–279; Sklar 1988:90). Once made part of law and a state agency, it becomes a "policy legacy" that shapes subsequent academic scholarship and legal–administrative policy (Pedriana and Stryker 1997; Skocpol 1985; Stryker 1990). The impact of newly constructed meanings persist long after the contest over claims ends, as they get absorbed into scientific-technical discourse (Stryker 1990).

A "transposability of schemes" occurs when actors apply a frame or interpretative scheme developed in one setting to a larger context (Sewell 1992). An example of this is when ideas and interpretative schemes that political actors strategically developed in public contests diffuse into the discourse of scientific or professional communities. Ideas negotiated to win political battles are transposed into the basic assumptions and categories of "neutral" legal–administrative policy debate.

The contest among actors who advocate competing social constructs of a problem is a critical component in the process of institutional change. At stake in the trust problem was the line between public and private, the idea of "natural" corporate rights and the meaning of property. Cultural meanings and institutions created in Progressive Era struggles have become the basis of systemic thinking about antitrust and the corporation. The meanings and institutions developed over eighty years ago continue into the present.

Institutional change and negotiated cultural meaning are codependent. Significant institutional change does not occur without the construction of new meaning in academic thought, legal and policy deliberation, and public discourse. "Individuals, groups and organizations struggle to change . . . they produce new truths, new models by which to understand themselves and their societies" (Friedland and Alford 1991:254). State transformation theory suggests that the institutional change that supported and sustained the rise of the modern corporation did not develop only as a result of new "objective" conditions; it required the parallel development and diffusion of new conceptual categories and understandings. Institutional change is an interactive, contingent process.

Political actors develop new conceptual categories through struggles with opposing actors who offer alternative interpretative schemes. If advocates of alternative schemes had been successful, an alternative path of institutional development would have been launched. I do not wish to suggest that once institutionalized, the core meanings around a policy become so rigidly fixed in place that they permanently lock out all alternatives. In fact, policy discourse often retains residues of the initial struggle, albeit in a latent form. These alternative understandings can be reactivated or triggered in a later political opening when core meanings get renegotiated. Yet, the reappearance of a past alternative meaning in a new and different context is not the same; its salience and significance has been irreversibly altered after a different understanding is institutionalized.

Notes

1. For overviews of Progressivism, see Abrams (1964), Crunden (1984), Ekirch (1974), Hofstadter (1955), McCraw (1974), and McCormick (1981, 1986). Berman (1990:813) has a useful summary.

2. Green (1987:14) argues that when social researchers ignore language as a political symbol and use the categories of political discourse uncritically, their ability to analyze historical phenomenon is seriously constrained. Also see Dobbin (1993) on a cultural approach to public policy.

3. For examples see Beckett (1994), Best (1990), Gusfield (1981), Handler and Hansenfeld (1991), or Rittenhouse (1991). Best (1989) lists other examples.

4. A related issue is media fragmentation. Competing media channels connect to diverse communities of discourse, how people interpret a problem develops from an interaction between events and understandings in a specific discourse community (see Jacobs 1996).

5. Historians and legal scholars offer several accounts of the intent and meanings of the Sherman Act (see Grandy 1993; Letwin 1965; Posner 1976).

6. Judicial interpretation transformed the Sherman Act into a major antilabor statute. Labor leaders believed that the Clayton Act would assist them and called it their "Magna Carta" because it exempted labor organizations. Support for the Clayton Act came from pro-labor districts (McDonagh 1992). Corporate leaders did not fear the labor exemption, and events in the 1920s proved them correct (Murray 1959; Taft 1964:243–244).

References

Abrams, Richard M. 1964. *Conservatism in a Progressive Era.* Cambridge, Massachusetts: Harvard University Press.

Akard, Patrick J. 1992. "Corporate mobilization and political power." *American Sociological Review* 57:597–615.

Amenta, Edwin, and Yvonne Zylan. 1991. "It happened here." *American Sociological Review* 56:250–265.

Baumgartner, Frank, and Bryan Jones. 1993. *Agendas and Instability in American Politics.* Chicago: University of Chicago Press.

Beckett, Katherine. 1994. "Setting the public agenda." *Social Problems* 41:425–447.

Berk, Gerald. 1994. *Alternative Tracks: The Constitution of American Industrial Order, 1865–1917*. Baltimore, Maryland: Johns Hopkins University Press.

Berman, David R. 1990. "State legislators and their constituents." *Social Science Quarterly* 71:812–823.

Best, Joel, ed. 1989. *Images of Issues: Typifying Contemporary Social Problems* New York: Aldine de Gruyter.

———. 1990. *Threatened Children*. Chicago: University of Chicago Press.

———. 1993. "But seriously folks." In *Reconsidering Social Constructionism*, eds. James A. Holstein and Gale Miller, 129–149. New York: Aldine de Gruyter.

Bittlingmayer, George. 1996. "Antitrust and business activity." *Business History Review* 70:363–401.

Brandeis, Louis Dembitz. 1934. *The Curse of Bigness*, ed. Osmond Fraenkel. New York: Viking.

Bringhurst, Bruce. 1979. *Antitrust and the Oil Monopoly*. Westport, Connecticut: Greenwood Press.

Brownlee, W. Elliot. 1974. *Dynamics of Ascent: A History of the American Economy*. New York: Knopf.

Buechler, Steven M. 1993. "Beyond resource mobilization?" *Sociological Quarterly* 34:217–235.

Caine, Stanley P. 1974. "*The origins of Progressivism.*" In *The Progressive Era*, ed. Lewis L. Gould, 11–34. Syracuse, New York: Syracuse University Press.

Campbell, John L., and Leon Lindberg. 1990. "Property rights and the organization of economic activity by the state." *American Sociological Review* 55:648–668.

———. 1991. "The state and the organization of economic activity." In *Governance of the American Economy*, eds. John Campbell, J. Rogers Hollingsworth, and Leon Lindberg, 356–395. New York: Cambridge University Press.

Carmines, Edward G., and James A. Stimson. 1989. *Issue Evolution*. Princeton, New Jersey: Princeton University Press.

Chalmers, David M. 1964. *The Social and Political Ideas of the Muckrackers*. New York: Citadel Press.

Chicago Civic Federation. 1973. *Chicago Conference on Trusts*. New York: Arno Press.

Clemens, Elisabeth S. 1993. "Organization repertoires and institutional change." *American Journal of Sociology* 98:755–798.

———. 1997. *The People's Lobby: Organizational Innovation and the Rise of Interest Group Politics in the United States, 1890–1925*. Chicago: University of Chicago Press.

Cobb, Roger W., and Charles D. Elder. 1983. *Participation in American Politics*. (2nd ed.) Baltimore, Maryland: Johns Hopkins University Press.

Conell, Carol, and Kim Voss. 1990. "Formal organization and the fate of social movements." *American Sociological Review* 55:255–269.

Crunden, Robert M. 1984. *Ministers of Reform*. Urbana: University of Illinois Press.

DiMaggio, Paul J., and Walter W. Powell. 1991. "Introduction." In *The New Institutionalism in Organizational Analysis*, eds. Walter W. Powell and Paul J. DiMaggio, 1–38. Chicago: University of Chicago Press.

Dobbin, Frank R. 1993. "The social construction of the Great Depression." *Theory and Society* 22:1–56.

Domhoff, G. William. 1996. *State Autonomy or Class Dominance?* New York: Aldine De Gruyter.

Edelman, Murray. 1977. *Political Language*. New York: Academic Press.

———. 1988. *Constructing the Public Spectacle*. Chicago: University of Chicago Press.

Ekirch, Arthur A., Jr. 1974. *Progressivism in America*. New York: New Viewpoints.

Emirbayer, Mustafa, and Jeff Goodwin. 1994. "Network analysis, culture and the problem of agency." *American Journal of Sociology* 99:1411–1454.

Everett, Kevin D. 1992. "Professionalization and protest." *Social Forces* 70:957–977.

Filler, Louis. 1976. *The Muckrakers.* University Park: Pennsylvania State University Press.

Fligstein, Neil. 1990. *The Transformation of Corporate Control.* Cambridge, Massachusetts: Harvard University Press.

Freyer, Tony Allan. 1979. *Forums of Order.* Greenwich, Connecticut: JAI Press.

———. 1992. *Regulating Big Business.* New York: Cambridge University Press.

Friedland, Roger, and Robert R. Alford. 1991. "Bringing society back in." In *The New Institutional in Organizational Analysis,* eds. Walter W. Powell and Paul J. DiMaggio, 232–266. Chicago: University of Chicago Press.

Galambos, Louis, and Joseph Pratt. 1988. *The Rise of the Corporate Commonwealth.* New York: Basic Books.

Gamson, William A. 1992. "The social psychology of collective action." In *Frontiers in Social Movement Theory,* eds. Aldon Morris and Carol M. Mueller, 53–76. New Haven, Connecticut: Yale University Press.

Glassberg, David. 1987. "History and the public." *Journal of American History* 73:957–980.

Goffman, Erving. 1974. *Frame Analysis: An Essay on the Organization of Experience.* New York: Harper and Row.

Goodwyn, Lawrence. 1976. *Democratic Promise.* New York: Oxford University Press.

Grandy, Christopher. 1993. "Original intent and the Sherman Antitrust Act." *Journal of Economic History* 53:359–376.

Green, David. 1987. *Shaping Political Consciousness.* Ithaca, New York: Cornell University Press.

Gusfield, Joseph R. 1981. *The Culture of Public Problems.* Chicago: University of Chicago Press.

Handler, Joel F., and Yeheskel Hansenfeld. 1991. *The Moral Construction of Poverty.* Newbury Park, California: Sage.

Hilgartner, Stephen, and Charles L. Bosk. 1988. "The rise and fall of social problems." *American Journal of Sociology* 94:53–78.

Hoffman, Charles. 1970. *The Depression of the Nineties.* Westport, Connecticut: Greenwood.

Hofstadter, Richard. 1955. *The Age of Reform.* New York: Random House.

———. 1963. *The Progressive Movement, 1900–1915.* Englewood Cliffs, New Jersey: Prentice Hall.

Hollingsworth, J. Rogers. 1991. "The logic of coordinating American manufacturing sectors." In *Governance of the American Economy,* eds. John Campbell, J. Rogers Hollingsworth, and Leon Lindberg, 35–73. New York: Cambridge University Press.

Jacobs, Ronald N. 1996. "Civil society and crisis." *American Journal of Sociology* 101:1238–1272.

Johnson, Arthur M. 1961. "Antitrust policy in transition, 1908." *Mississippi Valley Historical Review* 48:415–434.

Keller, Morton. 1990. *Regulating a New Economy.* Cambridge, Massachusetts: Harvard University Press.

Klandermans, Bert. 1984. "Mobilization and participation." *American Sociological Review* 49:583–600.

———. 1992. "The Social construction of protest and multi-organizational fields." In *Frontiers in Social Movement Theory,* eds. Aldon Morris and Carol M. Mueller, 77–103. New Haven, Connecticut: Yale University Press.

Klandermans, Bert, and Dirk Oegema. 1987. "Potentials, networks, motivations, and barriers." *American Sociological Review* 52:519–531.

Kloppenberg, James T. 1986. *Uncertain Victory.* New York: Oxford University Press.

Kolko, Gabriel. 1963. *The Triumph of Conservatism.* Glencoe, Illinois: Free Press.

Lamoreaux, Naomi R. 1985. *The Great Merger Movement in American Business, 1895–1904.* New York: Cambridge University Press.

Layder, Derek. 1993. *New Strategies in Social Research*. Cambridge, Massachusetts: Polity Press.

Leinwand, Gerald. 1962. "*History of the U.S. Federal Bureau of Corporations*." Ph.D. dissertation. (New York University)

Letwin, William. 1965. *Law and Economic Policy in America*. New York: Random House.

Link, Arthur S., and Richard L. McCormick. 1983. *Progressivism*. Arlington Heights, Illinois: Harlan Davidson.

Lustig, R. Jeffrey. 1982. *Corporate Liberalism*. Berkeley: University of California Press.

McAdam, Doug. 1982. *Political Process and the Development of Black Insurgency, 1930–1970*. Chicago: University of Chicago Press.

McCormick, Richard L. 1981. "The discovery that business corrupts politics." *American Historical Review* 86:247–274.

———. 1986. *The Party Period and Public Policy*. New York: Oxford University Press.

McCraw, Thomas K. 1974. "The progressive legacy." In *The Progressive Era*, ed. Lewis Gould, 181–201. Syracuse, New York: Syracuse University Press.

———. 1984. *Prophets of Regulation*. Cambridge, Massachusetts: Harvard University Press.

McDonagh, Eileen L. 1992. "Electoral bases of policy innovation in the Progressive Era." *Journal of Policy History* 4:162–187.

McDonough, Terrence. 1994. "Social structures of accumulation, contingent history, and stages of capitalism." In *Social Structures of Accumulation*, eds.David Kotz, Terrence McDonough, and Michael Reich, 101–132. New York: Cambridge University Press.

McFarland, Andrew S. 1991. "Interest groups and political time." *British Journal of Political Science* 21:257–284.

McGee, Michael C., and John R. Lyne. 1987. "What are nice folks like you doing in a place like this?" In *The Rhetoric of the Human Sciences*, eds. John S. Nelson, Allan Megill, and Donald McCloskey, 381–406. Madison: University of Wisconsin Press.

McGeer, Michael E. 1986. *The Decline of Popular Politics*. New York: Oxford University Press.

Mintz, Beth. 1995. "Business participation in health care policy reform." *Social Problems* 42:408–428.

Murray, Robert K. 1959. "Public opinion, labor and the Clayton Act." *Historian* 21:255–270.

Neale, A.D. 1970. *Antitrust Laws of the United States*. (2nd ed.) New York: Cambridge University Press.

Nelson, Ralph L. 1959. *Merger Movements in American Industry, 1895–1956*. Princeton, New Jersey: Princeton University Press.

Noble, David W. 1970. *The Progressive Mind, 1890–1917*. Chicago: Rand McNally.

Pedrina, Nicholas, and Robin Stryker. 1997. "Political culture wars 1960s style: Equal opportunity employment-affirmative action and the Philadelphia Plan." *American Journal of Sociology* 103:633–691.

Peters, B. Guy, and Brian W. Hogwood. 1985. "In search of the issue attention cycle." *Journal of Politics* 47:238–253.

Pichardo, Nelson A. 1988. "Resource mobilization." *Sociological Quarterly* 29:97–110.

Posner, Richard A. 1976. *Antitrust Law: An Economic Perspective*. Chicago: University of Chicago Press.

Quadagno, Jill. 1992. "Social movements and state transformation." *American Sociological Review* 57:616–634.

Rittenhouse, C. Amanda. 1991. "The emergence of premenstrual syndrome as a social problem." *Social Problems* 38:412–425.

Roy, William G. 1990. "Functional and historical logics in explaining the rise of the American industrial corporation." *Comparative Social Research* 12:19–44.

———. 1991. "The organization of the corporate class segment of the U.S. capitalist class at the turn of the century." In *Bringing Class Back In*, eds. Scott McNall, Rhonda Levine, and Rick Fantasia, 139–163. Boulder, Colorado: Westview.

———. 1997. *Socializing Capital: The Rise of the Large Industrial Corporation in America*. Princeton, New Jersey: Princeton University Press.

Scheppele, Kim Lane. 1994. "Legal theory and social theory." *Annual Review of Sociology* 20:383–406.

Schneirov, Matthew. 1994. *The Dream of a New Social Order*. New York: Columbia University Press.

Sewell, William H., Jr. 1992. "A theory of structure." *American Journal of Sociology* 98:1–29.

Sklar, Martin J. 1988. *The Corporate Reconstruction of American Capitalism 1890–1916*. New York: Cambridge University Press.

Skocpol, Theda. 1985. "Bringing the state back in." In *Bringing the State Back In*, eds. Peter Evans, Dietrich Rueschemeyer, and Theda Skocpol, 3–43. New York: Cambridge University Press.

Skowronek, Stephen. 1982. *Building the New American State*. New York: Cambridge University Press.

Snow, David A., and Robert D. Benford. 1988. "Master frames and cycles of protest." Paper presented at the "Workshop on Frontiers in Social Movement Theory," Ann Arbor, Michigan. (June)

———. 1992. "Master frames and cycles of protest." In *Frontiers in Social Movement Theory*, eds. Aldon Morris and Carol M. Mueller, 133–55. New Haven, Connecticut: Yale University Press.

Snow, David A., E. Burke Rochford, Jr., Steven K. Worden, and Robert D. Benford. 1986. "Frame alignment processes, micromobilization, and movement participation." *American Sociological Review* 51:464–481.

Spector, Malcolm, and John I. Kituse. 1977. Constructing Social Problems. Menlo Park, California: Cummings.

Staggenborg, Suzanne. 1991. *The Pro-Choice Movement*. New York: Oxford University Press.

Stryker, Robin. 1990. "Science, class and the welfare state." *American Journal of Sociology* 96:684–726.

Swidler, Ann. 1995. "Cultural power and social movements." In *Social Movements and Culture*, eds. Hank Johnson and Bert Klandermans, 24–40. Minneapolis: University of Minnesota Press.

Swidler, Ann, and Jorge Arditi. 1994. "A new sociology of knowledge." *Annual Review of Sociology* 20:305–329.

Taft, Philip. 1964. *Organized Labor in American History*. New York: Harper and Row.

Tarrow, Sidney. 1992. "Mentalities, political cultures and collective action frames." In *Frontiers in Social Movement Theory*, eds. Aldon Morris and Carol M. Mueller, 174–202. New Haven, Connecticut: Yale University Press.

———. 1994. *Power in Movement*. New York: Cambridge University Press.

Thimm, Alfred L. 1976. *Business Ideologies in the Reform-Progressive Era, 1880–1914*. Tuscaloosa: University of Alabama Press.

Thompson, George C., and Geald Brady. 1964. *Antitrust Fundamentals*. Belmont, California: Wadsworth.

Thorelli, Hans B. 1955. *The Federal Antitrust Policy*. Baltimore, Maryland: Johns Hopkins University Press.

Toppin, Edgar A. 1955. "A study of the defense and defenders of big business, 1880–1900." Ph.D. dissertation. (Northwestern University)

Urofsky, Melvin I. 1971. *A Mind of One Piece: Brandeis and American Reform.* New York: Scribner.

Van Hise, Charles R. 1973. *Concentration and Control.* New York: Arno Press.

Weinstein, James. 1968. *The Corporate Ideal and the Liberal State, 1900–1918.* Boston, Massachusetts: Beacon.

Wiebe, Robert H. 1958. "Business disunity and the Progressive movement, 1901–1914." *Mississippi Valley Historical Review* 44:664–685.

———. 1967. *The Search for Order, 1877–1920.* New York: Hill and Wang.

Williams, Rhys H. 1995. "Constructing the public good." *Social Problems* 42:124–144.

Wunderlin, Clarence E., Jr. 1992. *Visions of a New Industrial Order.* New York: Columbia University Press.

Zunz, Oliver. 1990. *Making America Corporate, 1870–1920.* Chicago: University of Chicago Press.

CHAPTER 13

The New Politics of Immigration

"BALANCED-BUDGET CONSERVATISM" AND THE SYMBOLISM OF PROPOSITION 187

Kitty Calavita

Introduction

As the twentieth century comes to a close, developed countries around the world are increasing efforts to control immigration (see Cornelius, Martin, and Hollifield 1994). While international trade agreements undo barriers to the free movement of capital and goods in the name of unfettered economic exchange, immigration rhetoric is increasingly restrictionist. So pervasive is this new restrictionism that, in the United States at least, immigration is one of the few public policy issues in this contentious period on which most political leaders agree, with President Clinton and Newt Gingrich both calling for greater control of the borders (Boremeier 1995; Lacey 1995; Shogren and Healy 1995).

The new restrictionism is manifest in California in a series of anti-immigrant policy proposals at the state level. One of the most extreme is Proposition 187, which was passed by a landslide in November 1994. Among its major provisions, Proposition 187 would bar undocumented immigrants from attending public schools and receiving nonemergency health care, and it would require school and health clinic personnel to report to the authorities those they suspect are undocumented.

In this paper, I attempt to make sense of the new nativism as reflected in Proposition 187. But my focus is not simply on the question, "Why has there been a resurgence of nativism in the United States?" A long tradition of research has established that anti-immigrant sentiments often surface during economic downturns or social transformations such as the United States has been undergoing for the last two decades (Higham 1955; Cornelius 1982; Espenshade and Calhoun 1993). Instead, I explore two related, but somewhat more complex, questions. First, why is this latest round of nativism focused almost single-mindedly on immigrants as a tax burden, a focus that is unusual, if not unique in the history of U.S. nativism? In other words, it is the historically specific theme of the nativism underlying Proposition 187 that is of interest here.

I explain this immigrants-as-a-fiscal-burden focus by linking it to transformations in the late twentieth-century political economy. Specifically, I trace what has been called the "crisis of Fordism" that is reflected in workers' stagnant wages and increasing insecurity, and the dismantling of the welfare state (Piore and Sabel 1984; Lipietz 1985, 1987; Sayer and Walker 1992; Harrison and Bluestone 1982, 1988; Piven and Cloward 1993). I then argue that the targeting of immigrants and other marginalized groups as a fiscal drain is one symptom of the "balanced-budget conservatism" associated with this political–economic transformation (Plotkin and Scheuerman 1994).

Second, I explore how this balanced-budget conservatism and the socioeconomic malaise in which it is grounded are embodied in Proposition 187. Here I argue that Proposition 187 is less a straightforward policy directive than it is a symbolic statement of fear, anger, and frustration emanating from the economic uncertainty that drives balanced-budget conservatism. One exit poll of California voters found that those who voted for Proposition 187 did so above all to "send a message." Elaborating on Edelman (1964, 1977), I argue that Proposition 187 represents a new kind of symbolic politics in which voters use the ballot to "express discontents" (Edelman 1964:3), *fully cognizant of that purely symbolic function.*

The paper thus brings together two sets of literature to explain this latest instance of restrictionist lawmaking. First, I draw from the substantial body of literature documenting the "crisis of Fordism" in the late twentieth century, the decline in workers' standard of living, increases in job insecurity, and the retrenchment of the welfare state (Harvey 1982; Bowles, Gordon, and Weisskopf 1984; Lipietz 1987; Block 1987; Harrison and Bluestone 1988; Kolko 1988; Sayer and Walker 1992; Phillips 1993; Plotkin and Scheuerman 1994). These developments, and the balanced-budget conservatism to which they give rise, are critical to understanding Proposition 187 and the hostility to immigrants it represents.

In addition, however, I draw from the literature on symbolic politics (Gusfield 1963; Edelman 1964, 1977; Citrin, Reingold, and Green 1990; Calavita 1983, 1990; Engel 1987). In bringing together these two literatures, I argue that Proposition 187 is neither simply an instrumental response to economic conditions, nor a purely symbolic measure meant only to declare the cultural or political dominance of the majority. Rather, it can best be understood as a particular type of symbolic statement, the content of which and the motivation for which are grounded in prevailing economic conditions.

In a recent analysis of anti-immigrant sentiment in the United States, Espenshade and Calhoun (1993) contrast a "labor market competition" hypothesis and a "symbolic politics" hypothesis as if they were mutually exclusive explanations for hostility toward immigrants: Immigrants are perceived as an economic threat; alternatively, the hostility toward immigrants is symbolic of a cultural identity crisis. Instead, this analysis of Proposition 187 suggests that to grasp the complexities of the new nativism we must integrate an understanding of underlying material conditions with an appreciation for the symbolic dimensions of political activity.

One more clarification is in order. While Proposition 187 is a California initiative, this is not a regional analysis of nativism, nor do I pretend to answer the question "Why specifically California?" Other states with a large influx of immigrants such as Texas, Florida, and New York have not (yet) undertaken similar initiatives; this probably has less to do with voters' potential receptivity to such a measure than to the idiosyncrasies of local politics and the related distinctive nature of immigration to those states (particularly Florida and New York, where settled immigrant communities have substantial political clout). As we will see, the systemic forces to which I link Proposition 187 and the new nativism are national and international in nature. Indeed, survey data and opinion polls that I will discuss suggest there is widespread support for a federal law along the lines of Proposition 187, and several other states are now pursuing similar initiatives. While there are no doubt specific factors peculiar to California that contributed to the creation of this state initiative in 1994 (which I will mention briefly), the thrust of this paper is not on such microlevel regional analysis. Instead, I focus on the systemic factors that contribute to the initiative's widespread appeal, both in California and, according to surveys, across the country.

In the next section I provide a brief historical introduction to U.S. nativism. This selective review of three periods—the 1870s to the 1890s; 1900 to World War I; and World War I and its aftermath—suggests that while certain general themes (most notably, the implication of immigrant racial inferiority) recur throughout the history of nativism, the focal points shift with the political–economic landscape and corresponding ideological imperatives.

Nativism in Industrial America: A Thematic Review

Since at least the mid-1800s, each wave of new immigration to the United States has been accompanied by anti-immigrant backlashes and demands for restriction (see Calavita 1984; Higham 1955). The contemporary period is no different in this respect, although the illegal nature of much of the new immigration may add to the sense of powerlessness and lack of control that intensifies the new nativism.[1] What is unique about the contemporary backlash, however, is the almost single-minded focus on the fiscal burden of illegal immigration, with related policy efforts concentrated on barring immigrants from receiving social services.

It has often been observed that anti-immigrant backlashes intensify during economic downturns, perceived threats to national security, and social transformations (Higham 1955; Corelius 1982; Espenshade and Calhoun 1993). However, far less attention has been paid to the fact that the content or central themes of nativism vary as well, corresponding to shifting ideological and political needs and their structural underpinnings. If immigrants serve as scapegoats for social crises, it stands to reason that the specific content of anti-immigrant nativism will shift to encompass the prevailing malaise. A few examples will illustrate such shifts historically and serve as a contrast for the "tax-burden" focus of contemporary nativism.

IMMIGRANT AS STRIKEBREAKER, 1870–1890

Twenty-five million immigrants entered the United States in the last four decades of the nineteenth century, and the majority joined the industrial workforce. The advantages of this massive influx of immigrant workers, most of whom were from Europe, did not go unappreciated. Andrew Carnegie (1886:34–35) called immigration "a golden stream which flows into the country each year" and valued each adult immigrant at $1,500. A business journal echoed Carnegie's appreciation:

> Men, like cows, are expensive to raise and a gift of either should be gladly received. And a man can be put to more valuable use than a cow. (*New York Journal of Commerce* 1892:2)

The U.S. Industrial Commission (U.S. Congress, House Industrial Commission 1901:313–314) lauded the combined effect of mechanization and massive influxes of immigrant labor:

> The fact that machinery and the division of labor opens a place for the unskilled immigrants makes it possible not only to get the advantages of machinery, but also to get the advantages of cheap labor.

When U.S. workers complained to Congress that employers were using the recent immigrants to break their fledgling strikes and reduce wages, Congressional debates focused on the inferiority of the "new immigrants" who, unlike earlier immigrants from northern Europe, were "slaves," "paupers," "serfs," and "lowest beings." It was thus the alleged inferiority of the new immigrants not the new industrial order with its heightened levels of labor strife that was the problem:

> Large numbers of degraded, ignorant, brutal Italian and Hungarian laborers. . . . This is the class of persons, this is the species of immigration with which this [Congress] seeks to deal . . . (*Congressional Record* 1884:5349).

U.S. historian Frederick Jackson Turner similarly blamed the arrival of large numbers of inferior "new immigrants" from southern and eastern Europe for "counteracting the upward tendency of wages" and leading to "the sweatshop system" (quoted in Gossett 1973:292), as did many other leading historians, sociologists, and anthropologists of the day (see also Higham 1955). As Gossett (1973) points out, anti-immigrant sentiment developed along two main tracks organized labor's concerns over wage reductions and job displacement, and "race-thinkers'" preoccupation with racial purity often making for unusual political alliances between those who were diametrically opposed on other issues.

But the issues of race and labor displacement were not mutually exclusive. As Gossett points out:

> We find the racist argument in anti-immigrant agitation not merely among the defenders of the status quo, but also among men who were to become famous for their concern for the welfare of the masses (1973:292).

More important here, the alleged racial inferiority of immigrants became the explanation for depressed wages, labor strife, and the emerging "sweatshop system."

IMMIGRANT AS SOCIALIST AND ANARCHIST, 1900–WORLD WAR I

By 1900, not only were new immigrants declared inferior by virtue of their "acceptance" of substandard wages, but they were now spotted for "un-American" militancy. As one social scientist had warned,

> When [the immigrant] is out of work . . . he looks about and asks his fellow-citizens, sullenly, if not menacingly, what they are going to do about it. He has brought with him, too, what is called "the labor problem" probably the most un-American of all problems. (Godkin 1887:173)

A leading business journal (quoted in *Public Opinion* 1886:355) even proclaimed that immigrants' propensity to radicalism was biological: "Anarchism is a blood disease."

Industrialists in this progressive period relied on notions of immigrant inferiority to explain away class conflict in what they had declared a classless society. The rise of the Industrial Workers of the World (IWW) was attributed to a "foreign invasion of the anarchists and socialists, criminals and outcasts from other nations" (*Bulletin of the National Association of Wool Manufacturers* 1912:142). Miners' strikes in 1902 were the product of

> [t]ens of thousands of the anthracite miners [who] are Poles, Hungarians, Slavs, and other foreigners, who cannot spell a word of English. (quoted in Wiebe 1962:191)

The massive Lawrence Textile Strike in 1912 was similarly dismissed: All the troublemakers were "Italians and other foreign-born operatives" (Wiebe 1962:191). By 1911, the Dillingham Immigration Commission called for "selective" immigration measures that would weed out the defective immigrants (U.S. Congress, Senate Immigration Commission 1911).

WORLD WAR I AND "HYPHENATED-AMERICANS"

During World War I, English classes for immigrants were jointly sponsored by government and industry and focused on the development of patriotism and political conservatism. Henry Ford's English School was widely recognized as a pioneer in these "Americanization" efforts. The first words taught in Ford's school were "I am a good American."[2] By 1917, thirty-two government agencies and dozens of leading industrialists were involved in Americanization work. In the climate of fear in the immediate postwar period, some states enacted laws making attendance at Americanization classes compulsory for recent immigrants.

The National Americanization Committee defined its goals:

> The combating of anti-American propaganda . . . and the stamping out of sedition . . . The elimination of causes of disorder, unrest, and disloyalty which make fruitful soil for un-American propagandists and disloyal agitators. . . . The creation of an understanding and love for America. (quoted in Hill 1919:630)

Americanization was an attempt to reform the allegedly inferior southern and eastern European without restricting the supply of labor, but as race theories became more explicit, such efforts were increasingly regarded as irrelevant. The depiction of the immigrant as a radical and genetically inferior that had been used during the early 1900s to explain away industrial unrest was now the focus of arguments favoring immigration restriction. Pointing to the potential for disloyalty among genetically inferior "hyphenated Americans," the *Saturday Evening Post* urged restrictions, asking, "Why . . . try to make Americans out of those who will always be Americanski?" (paraphrased in Higham 1955:262). The Russian Revolution of 1917 was regularly referred to by members of Congress who warned, "Practically all the IWW and Bolsheviki [in America] are foreigners" (U.S. Congress, House Committee on Immigration and Naturalization 1919:270). And

> We should formulate and . . . enforce a genuine 100 percent American immigration law. . . . The incoming flood remains dangerously alien. (*Congressional Record* 1921:4550)

Lothrop Stoddard, author of *The Rising Tide of Color and Revolt Against Civilization: The Menace of Under-Man* (1922), and noted eugenicist Harry Laughlin, testified at the House hearings on immigration restriction in 1920. The House immigration committee thereafter appointed Laughlin its "expert eugenics agent" (U.S. Congress, House Committee on Immigration and Naturalization 1920). John Trevor, self-appointed expert on the "biological propensity of Jews toward radicalism," testified to the Senate immigration committee the following year (U.S. Congress, Senate Committee on Immigration 1921:293–300). Subsequently, Trevor attended all hearings and informal meetings of the House committee, even helping draft reports. These Congressional discussions of immigration revealed strong racist overtones. In 1924, Laughlin presented a report to Congress in which he used Army IQ data to argue that southern and eastern Europeans were feeble-minded and of inferior racial stock. When the House committee reported their new quota bill that year, they attached a report by Trevor in which he urged that America's racial makeup must be preserved.

The racism and fear of socialism and anarchism that pervaded this debate were similar in many respects to that of the previous period. However, as World War I gave way to the postwar red scare, immigrants were feared above all as disloyal and "un-American." In 1921, Congress passed the Emergency Quota Law (which was extended in 1924) to limit the number of immigrants from southern and eastern Europe, with the explanation that they were "abnormally twisted," "unassimilable," and "filthy un-American" (U.S. Congress 1920:10).

The pattern is repeated throughout the history of U.S. immigration. At moments of social, political, or economic crisis, nativism tends to increase as recent immigrants are singled out as the cause of the crisis. More to the point here, as the crises shift over time, so too do the depictions of immigrants and the prevailing themes of nativism. Since the historical record suggests that during times of crisis recent immigrants are often blamed, it makes sense that as the nature of the crisis changes, so too does the specific content of nativism.

THE RESURGENCE OF U.S. NATIVISM AND PROPOSITION 187

The last three decades have witnessed rapid increases in legal immigration, illegal immigration, and refugee flows to the United States. By 1994, 8.7 percent of the U.S. population or 22.6 million people were foreign-born. While that percentage is smaller than earlier in the century, the absolute numbers are unprecedented. The Census Bureau now estimates that approximately 4 million of the foreign-born reside in the United States illegally (*Los Angeles Times* 1995:A20).

Illegal immigration to the United States gained momentum with the termination of the Bracero Program in 1964. For more than 20 years, the Bracero Program had brought Mexican farm workers to work the fields of the southwestern United States on close to 5 million Bracero contracts. By the time the Bracero Program ended, a relationship of symbiosis between Mexican immigrants and U.S. employers had become well-entrenched, facilitated and nurtured by more than 50 years of U.S. policymaking (see Calavita 1992).[3] With the end of the program, the employment of Mexican labor went underground as the guest workers of one era became the illegal immigrants of the next.

Apprehensions of illegal immigrants by the U.S. Immigration and Naturalization Service (INS) went from about 23,000 in 1960 to 345,000 in 1970, and by 1978, the number of annual apprehensions had risen to more than 1 million (Congressional Research Service 1980; U.S. Immigration and Naturalization Service 1978:19). INS apprehensions are, of course, not a definitive measure of undocumented immigration. Not all undocumented border crossers are ascertained, some are apprehended more than once, some "undocumented" immigrants enter legally and overstay their visas, and some variation in apprehension rates is the result of shifts in border patrol policies or INS resources. However, there is little disagreement among experts that the dramatic increases in apprehensions in this period reflect a substantial increase in the undocumented flow (Bean, Vernez, and Keely 1989; Cornelius, Martin, and Hollifield 1994; Fix 1991; Martin 1994).

The first signs of contemporary restrictionism can be traced to the early 1970s when Representative Peter Rodino held hearings around the country on the topic of illegal immigration. The result was a five-volume Congressional document outlining the dangers of uncontrolled immigration and the contribution of illegal aliens to unemployment and wage reductions (U.S. Congress, House Committee on the Judiciary 1971–1972). In 1979, President Carter appointed the Select Commission on Immigration and Refugee Policy (SCIRP) to make recommendations for reforms that would "regain control of the border." By the time SCIRP recommended employer sanctions that would make it illegal to knowingly employ unauthorized immigrants, the vast majority of the U.S. public favored such a restrictionist approach (Gallup 1980). After three attempts, the Immigration Reform and Control Act (IRCA) was passed in 1986, with employer sanctions as its political centerpiece.[4]

For a variety of reasons (see Calavita 1990, 1995), employer sanctions did not significantly reduce undocumented immigration (Bean, Edmonston, and Passel 1990; Fix 1991; Crane et al. 1990; U.S. Department of Labor 1991), and restrictionist sentiment continued unabated.[5] A *New York Times* poll in 1986 showed that 50 percent of respondents in a nationwide survey wanted immigration (both legal and undocumented) reduced. In 1988, a *Los Angeles Times* national poll found that 64 percent of respondents were convinced that immigrants cost more in social services and unemployment insurance than they contribute in tax revenues (cited in Citrin, Reingold, and Green 1990:1136). A 1993 survey of 1,031 southern Californians found that 87 percent believed illegal immigration to be a very serious or somewhat serious problem; one of the most frequently cited concerns was that undocumented immigrants are a burden on taxpayers (Espenshade and Calhoun 1993).

Scholarly attention also turned to the costs and benefits of the continued flow of immigrants. Without exception, these studies have focused on the tax revenues contributed by immigrants versus the cost of the social services they consume. For example, Parker and Rea (1993) estimate that the annual net cost of federal and local public services for illegal immigrants in San Diego County is $244.3 million and extrapolate that the net cost for California is $5 billion. Stewart, Gascoigne, and Bannister (1992) put the net cost for Los Angeles County at $807.6 million. Huddle (1993) concludes that immigrants (both legal and undocumented immigrants) cost the federal government $42.5 billion more than they contribute in taxes annually, with the cost in California at $18 billion.

Other studies have found that the cost of immigration to California is far less than previously imagined, and that at the national level there is a net fiscal gain (Passel and Edmonston 1994; Clark and Passel 1993; Fix and Passel 1994; Bornemeier 1994; Eisenstadt and Thorup 1994). An Urban Institute study (Clark and Passel 1993) reports that legal and undocumented immigrants in California contribute $12 billion a year more in taxes than they consume in services, with the national figure at $28.7 billion. The authors of this latter study argue that Huddle (1993) overestimated undocumented immigration, using a figure that is 50 percent higher than INS estimates, ignored immigrants' Social Security contributions, and exaggerated the participation rate of immigrants in costly social services (cited in McDonnell 1994). Further, as Clark and Passel (1993) point out, none of these studies includes in its calculations the indirect benefits of immigration, for example the economic contribution of cheap immigrant labor that subsidizes many important industries, such as California agribusiness (see, for example, Arax 1994).

The point here is not to make a case for or against the fiscal/economic contribution of immigrants a task that is clearly beyond the scope of this paper. Rather, it is to point out 1) that the scholarly literature on the costs/benefits of immigration is now almost exclusively focused on fiscal impacts and 2) that there is substantial disagreement among the experts on the nature and size of those impacts. A Rand report (Vernez and McCarthy 1995) has recently compared these studies, finds that their disparate results have to do with radically different assumptions, and concludes that the data particularly relating to the numbers of undocumented immigrants are inadequate to resolve the debate. What is important to this analysis is the substantial gap between the speculative and contradictory nature of these findings and the unwavering convictions of most Americans.

A majority of the U.S. public now supports the enactment of new restrictionist measures and favor politicians who use this issue as a calling card (Klein 1993; Decker

1994; Gibbs 1994). By early 1993, more than 20 restrictionist bills had been placed before the California legislature, and several provisions, including one that bars the undocumented from receiving drivers' licenses, have been passed (Bailey and Morain 1993).

Proposition 187, known as the Save Our State (SOS) initiative, is among the most extreme of restrictionist measures to gain favor. The initiative, which went directly to California voters through a referendum in November 1994, would bar undocumented immigrant children from attending public schools (and require school administrators to request documentation from "suspect" children), and would withhold from the undocumented all nonemergency medical care including prenatal care and inoculations. Despite the apparent unconstitutionality of the former[6] and the potentially dangerous public health consequences of the latter, Proposition 187 won by a wide margin 59 percent to 41 percent (Decker 1994; Nalik and Feldman 1994; Gibbs 1994).

All of the major provisions of Proposition 187 have been put on hold by the courts while numerous constitutional challenges are resolved. Nonetheless, the measure has already had a significant impact, legitimating hostility and discrimination and causing widespread fear in the immigrant community. According to a report in the *Christian Science Monitor* (Munoz 1994:19),

> [A]lready a fifth grade teacher in one California school district has assigned her students to report their own immigration status and that of their parents. And a school security guard in Atherton, California, the day after the election, told two American-born Latinas, "We don't have to let Mexicans in here anymore."

Other reports of discrimination include a McDonald's worker who insisted on seeing immigration documents before serving a customer; a pharmacist who refused to fill a prescription for someone they "suspected" was undocumented; a customer at a restaurant who asked the cook for his green card, adding "It's a citizen's duty to kick out illegals"; and a hotel owner who called the police when a U.S. citizen would not show immigration documents when registering for a room (Munoz 1994:19). Pregnant women are reportedly afraid to seek prenatal care for fear of deportation. In at least one case, the death of a child has been linked to such fear, when the parents of a severely ill eight-year-old postponed seeing a doctor (Romney and Marquis 1994; Romney and Brazil 1994; Martinez 1994).

Despite such damaging consequences even in the absence of enforcement, and despite the substantial legal challenges already posed, there is some impetus to seek a federal version of Proposition 187. Immediately after the election, California Governor Wilson called on Congress to pass a federal variant of the proposition (Brownstein 1994). The U.S. Commission on Immigration Reform, a bipartisan federal commission established by Congress in 1990, has proposed substantial cuts in the benefits received by the undocumented but stopped short of recommending their exclusion from public schools. While undocumented immigrants are already ineligible for most forms of public assistance, the commission recommended withholding all remaining assistance except emergency medical care, echoing one of the major provisions of Proposition 187.[7] A *Time* magazine poll of 800 adult Americans in September 1994 reveals that 55 percent favor "a proposal to stop providing government health benefits and public education to illegal immigrants and their children" (Gibbs 1994:47). A sponsor of Proposition 187 reports that "[o]rganizers in Florida, Washington, New York, and Texas are already calling us" asking advice on how to get similar measures passed in their states (Wood 1994:2).

In an effort to explain these developments, the next section traces the contours of the economic transformation under way in the United States, with a focus on the increased economic insecurity of American workers. Given the long-standing tendency to scapegoat immigrants in times of economic hardship or anxiety, the recent upsurge in nativism is perhaps not surprising. What is unusual is the focus of this round of nativism on immigrants' consumption of social services and the perceived burden on taxpayers.[8] There had been periodic concerns in the late nineteenth century over the immigration of "paupers" and immigrants who became "public charges" (Calavita 1984:68–95). In the depression of the 1930s, Mexicans in the United States were subjected to a racist campaign focusing in part on their burden on relief agencies, which resulted in several hundred thousand Mexican immigrants being "repatriated" (Gamio 1971; Hoffman 1974; Lopez 1981; Reisler 1976; Cockcroft 1986). But, the perception that immigrants in general are a drain on taxpayers and must be excluded from basic social services has never before been the dominant theme of nativist sentiment. In the following section, I argue that this theme derives from a particular set of material conditions and related ideological developments, in particular the rise of "balanced-budget conservatism" (Plotkin and Scheuerman 1994).

Economic Transformation and Balanced-Budget Conservatism

The U.S. economy and that of many other advanced capitalist nations has undergone a radical and rapid transformation in the last 20 years. By the early 1980s, a substantial literature began pointing to the decline in profitability of U.S. corporations and the "deindustrialization" of America following the economic boom of the postwar decades. Some (Harrison and Bluestone 1982, 1988; Piven and Cloward 1993; Plotkin and Scheuerman 1994) highlight the role of foreign competition in this profit squeeze on U.S. corporations that had enjoyed a virtual global monopoly after the destruction of World War II. Others (Harvey 1982; Lipietz 1985, 1987; Piore and Sabel 1984; Sayer and Walker 1992) place a greater emphasis on a broad "crisis of Fordism" that affects many advanced capitalist economies. These latter scholars point out that from World War II to the mid-1970s, most advanced capitalist countries operated on the "Fordist" principles of mass production of standardized products for mass consumption, with internal job ladders and vertically integrated sectors, supplemented by a government system of income maintenance and social security. As Lipietz (1985) explains, Fordism was predicated on a connection between profit rates, wages, and social security. By the 1970s, according to this interpretation, line-balancing problems (resulting in shortages and gluts in production inputs), labor resistance, corporate taxation policies, and a generally rigid structure of production, jeopardized profitability and the system began to unravel.[9] Whatever its precise causes, the average rate of profit of nonfinancial U.S. corporations plummeted from 10 percent in 1965 to little more than 5 percent by the late 1970s (Harrison and Bluestone 1988).

One response to this profitability crisis was to cut labor costs. The corporate strategy almost across the board was to reduce production costs and boost profitability by eliminating jobs, exporting many of them to developing countries, thereby reaping the rewards not only of reduced labor costs offshore but also of an insecure domestic workforce wary of unions and afraid to make demands. According to a Brookings Institution researcher, 4 million manufacturing jobs were lost between 1978 and 1982 alone (Harris 1984). By 1986, industrial employment had fallen 17 percent in textiles, 30 percent in primary metals, and 40 percent in steel (Plotkin and Scheuerman 1994). By 1987, there were actually fewer workers in manufacturing in the United States than there had been in 1966 (Bluestone and Bluestone 1992). In the 1990s, the process continues as General Motors plans to do away with 70,000 more jobs and close 12 plants (Plotkin and Scheuerman 1994). Unemployment statistics reveal the overall trend. The official average U.S. unemployment rate for 1950–1959 was 4.5 percent; in 1960–1969, it was 4.8 percent; in 1970–1979, it rose to 6.2 percent; and, in 1980–1988, the average unemployment rate was almost double the 1950s' figure, at 8.4 percent (Plotkin and Scheuerman 1994).

The effect on wages is clear-cut. Between 1946 and 1973, real wages averaged a yearly increase of 1.84 percent in constant dollars, such that by the 1960s millions of U.S. blue-collar workers could purchase a home, buy a car, and send their children to a public university. Beginning in 1973, real average annual wages began to drop for the first time since the 1930s, and by 1990 they had fallen 19 percent. A study prepared for the Congressional Joint Economic Committee estimated that close to 60 percent of the workers added to the U.S. labor force between 1979 and 1984 earned less than $7,000 per year (cited in *Los Angeles Times* 1987:IV-3). A Commerce Department study reveals that in 1992, 18 percent of full-time workers in the United States earned $13,000 or less (the comparable figure for 1979 was 12 percent) (Rosenblatt 1994). In the early 1990s, fourteen million full-time workers comprising one-fifth of the workforce did not earn enough to keep above the official poverty level (Plotkin and Scheuerman 1994; Kolko 1988).

A central cost-cutting measure in this period of restructuring is to employ workers for specific tasks or periods of demand, letting them go when the demand has subsided. Approximately 30 percent of the U.S. workforce is now comprised of such "contingent" workers doing part-time work or on short-term contracts, who thereby accrue no seniority and enjoy few benefits (Ingwerson 1993). In 1982, approximately 25 percent of new jobs were for part-time or temporary work; a decade later, fully half of all new jobs were for such contingent work (Kilborn 1993). In dramatic contrast to the internal labor markets of the Fordist period, more and more work is subcontracted out or performed by "temps" employed for the duration of specific tasks. Between 1970 and 1984, the numbers of people working for agencies that provide temporary help increased at double the rate of the GNP (Harrison and Bluestone 1988). Elsewhere I have argued that this increase in contingent work and the downward pressure on wages is consistent with continued high levels of undocumented immigration. A large supply of "contingent" that is, illegal immigrant workers may be well-suited to the restructured economy of the late twentieth century with its proliferation of low wage, contingent work. As a former Secretary of Labor once said, undocumented immigrants "work scared and hard" (Marshall 1978:169).

In addition to these direct cuts in labor costs, the profitability crisis elicited a reduced commitment to entitlement programs and a gradual dismantling of the welfare state. As Lipietz (1985:109) puts it, "[B]etween 1974 and 1983 . . . all the major capitalist countries . . . adopted 'austerity' policies designed to make the workers pay for the crisis." Piven and Cloward argue that employers and the state see income-maintenance programs in this new economic climate as detrimental to labor discipline. Thus, certain protections of the welfare state have been eliminated "to compel workers generally to sell labor on whatever terms the market offers" (Piven and Cloward 1993:345).

The retrenchment of the welfare state of course saves money at a time of fiscal crisis. Feldstein (1985) estimates that social programs by the mid-1980s cost $300 billion a year compared to $19 billion two decades earlier, and now comprise one-half of all nondefense federal spending. But, this money-saving measure is, according to Piven and Cloward (1993:348), integrally related to the new economic austerity and efforts to increase profitability through cutting labor costs:

> [T]he peaking of the welfare explosion in the early 1970s coincided with a growing crisis in the economy, and with the mounting of a campaign by business to solve its problems of profitability by forcing workers to take less.

I will show that the dismantling of entitlement and social service programs has been facilitated by the ideology of balanced-budget conservatism that itself is at least partly the product of widespread economic insecurity and frustration.

The "financialization" of the economy (Phillips 1994) is another response to the profitability crisis, compounding the effects of deindustrialization and the falling standard of living for U.S. workers. When manufacturing experienced a profit squeeze, U.S. corporations and other investors sought more lucrative opportunities for profit in financial transactions, draining investment from the already faltering industrial sector. This financialization of the economy, in which speculators and investors call the shots, has led to a disconnection between economic growth and worker well-being (*Business Week* 1985; Harrison and Bluestone 1988).

The takeoff in mergers, acquisitions, and hostile takeovers in the 1980s was part of this financialization of the economy and provided an important link to increased economic uncertainty for workers. With the economy increasingly driven by the logic of stockholder gains, corporations were gobbled up at an unprecedented rate. In 1984, these mergers, acquisitions, and buyouts consumed more than $140 billion. Not only did this siphon capital from investment in productive activity, but it meant that labor costs had to be cut further to pay for the massive corporate debts incurred, amounting to $1.8 trillion by 1988 (*Business Week* 1988).

As Phillips (1994) explains,

> For the first time in modem U.S. history, stock prices decoupled from the real economy, enabling the Dow-Jones industrial average to keep setting records even as employees' real wages kept declining.

In 1993, the U.S. economy grew 3 percent, while household median income declined 1 percent. This disconnection helps explain the current "jobless economic recovery," and is one reason for the increasing polarization of wealth in the United States.

These economic transformations and dislocations are no secret, receiving mention both in President Clinton's first economic speech to Congress and in the mainstream media. The widely read book by political analyst and columnist Kevin Phillips, titled *Boiling Point* (1993), brought to center stage these economic dislocations and the anger of the declining middle class. But as Plotkin and Scheuerman (1994) explain it, public outrage is concentrated on the ballooning federal deficit and rising taxes.

Tracing the roots of this "deficit mania," Plotkin and Scheuerman note that since the New Deal, Washington has stimulated the economy with government funds. They point out that President Reagan was particularly adept at spending beyond his means, despite his rhetoric of fiscal conservatism:

> By piling huge tax cuts on top of even larger military spending increases, and continuing to apply such increases even after the economy entered recovery, Washington self-consciously and drastically built up the deficit to mountainous heights. . . . In this climate of growing budget and financial uncertainty, the more tangible problems of stagnant wages, job insecurity, and rising personal debt had a massive new symbolic target: the dizzying federal debt. . . . Here was a uniquely understandable, singular motive force behind the nation's economic troubles. . . . U.S. politicians have talked about little else since at least the mid-1980s (Plotkin and Scheuerman 1994:16).

But, political expedience and sound economics have prevented Congress from abruptly removing hundreds of billions of dollars in government spending from the economy to reduce the deficit. The result is simultaneously an ideological assault on the public sector ("The deficit has become the central ideological prop in the long-term conservative attack on the public sector" [Plotkin and Scheuerman 1994:20]), and frustration among taxpayers whose attention is focused on the inability of government to balance the budget. This "deficit mania" and disdain for a government that is unable to balance its books, are the source of what Plotkin and Scheuerman call "balanced-budget conservatism." Among its symptoms are an entrenched antigovernment ideology, suspicion of government spending, resistance to taxes, and a subtle semantic shift from "citizen" to "taxpayer" as the central unit of civic life.

This balanced-budget conservatism serves as a target for the frustration and anger of those facing economic uncertainty, deflects responsibility from the private sector's cost-cutting, and facilitates the austerity measures of the government as it dismantles the safety net. Lee Atwater, at the time the chief of Republican strategizing, implies that this balanced-budget conservatism was deliberately constructed, or at least self-consciously exploited:

> In the 1980 campaign, we were able to make the establishment, insofar as it is bad, the government. In other words, big government was the enemy, not big business. If people think the problem is that taxes are too high, and government interferes too much, then we are doing our job. (quoted in Plotkin and Scheuerman 1994:32)

Block (1987) argues that federal budget accounting is archaic, collapsing as it does capital expenditures and current spending (something that, he points out, private households and corporations do not do in their own accounting). The result is a far higher budget "deficit" than would be the case if capital expenditures were calculated separately and federal assets were factored in. But, Block argues, the "balanced-budget ideology" resulting from an inflated deficit is useful to those who would reduce government spending on social programs. Block (1987:137) paraphrases David Stockman, Reagan's budget director: "As David Stockman has acknowledged, the original Reagan tax cuts were a Trojan horse designed to facilitate the cutting of civilian programs by creating a huge shortfall of revenues." The disdain for the public sector that is a hallmark of balanced-budget conservatism not only tempers opposition to the cutbacks, but celebrates them.

Balanced-budget conservatism is thus an ideological response to certain underlying material conditions and the ability of those who would limit social welfare spending to capitalize on those conditions. Whether or not the federal deficit is out of control (some, like Block, argue it is not), is not the key issue here. The perception that it is drives antigovernment sentiment, contempt for the public sector, and hostility toward the poor. Neither does a balanced state budget seem to temper this "deficit mania." Thirty-seven states including California now require a "balanced" budget (the definition of which turns out to be quite malleable),[10] but there is no indication that states with such requirements experience reduced levels of balanced-budget conservatism.

It was in this political–economic context that Proposition 187 was fashioned, and enjoyed almost instant popularity with California voters. No doubt, there are specific reasons why the initiative was developed in California and enjoyed such popular support there, even beyond the fact that California receives a disproportionate number of legal and illegal immigrants. For one thing, Californians have confronted a strong and lingering recession and defense cutbacks that enhance the effects of the more general economic restructuring, as well as high-visibility social crises such as the 1992 Los Angeles riot. Second, ballot-box initiatives are an important ingredient of the policymaking process in California, often leading to stunning victories of policies that might not otherwise make it through the legislature. The landslide victory of Prop. 13 in 1978, which froze property taxes and might be seen as a first sign of the preoccupation with reduced government spending and lower taxes, is exemplary. Finally, Governor Wilson put all of his political weight behind this initiative some have argued as a way to revive his lagging popularity in California and launch his bid for the White House (Brownstein 1994; Ostrow and Fulwood 1994; Scheer 1994). Whatever Wilson's motives, his aggressive campaigning for Proposition 187 no doubt contributed to its high profile.[11] But, the easy receptivity of voters to such nativist rhetoric is by no means idiosyncratic to California, as indicated by several national surveys and polls, as well as a flurry of proposals to replicate Proposition 187 at the federal and state levels.

With the deficit seemingly out of control, increased economic uncertainty for all but the most affluent, and the safety net shrinking, frustrated and anxious voters are predisposed to place the blame on excessive government spending and the poor who are seen as the major cause of such spending. Immigrants are one among several targets consistent with this balanced-budget ideology and the scapegoating of the marginalized "other" that it spawns. The backlash against affirmative action, a growing rejection of "multiculturalism," and the political appeal of welfare reform and its targeting of teenage mothers, probably share the same ideological space.[12] Plotkin and Scheuerman (1994:32) describe such marginalization and scapegoating:

> [B]alanced-budget conservatism elevates protecting taxpayer interests to the highest priority of government, [and] stigmatizes poorer, property-less people as somehow less than fully citizens.

Those who are not even citizens indeed, are not legal residents are the ideal target of blame, more undeserving even than the traditional "undeserving poor." At a time when the welfare state is being dismantled in the name of cutting government spending, and economic uncertainty is on the rise even for the previously secure middle class, this scapegoating of immigrants as the cause of the crisis found a ready audience among the white middle class who disproportionately make up the electorate. Indeed, previously unpopular Pete Wilson increased his ratings many times over with his vocal support of Proposition 187, and was swept into office for a second term.

It might be argued, of course, that the reason for the historically specific theme of this balanced-budget nativism is straightforward: Since the vast social expenditures of the welfare state are a relatively new phenomenon, the expense of providing benefits associated with the welfare state could not have been a prevailing concern earlier in the century. There is something to this straightforward explanation for the fiscal theme of the current nativism, and to the extent that it highlights the shifts in nativism as underlying social conditions change, it underscores my point. However, several issues should be kept in mind. First, much of the discussion in California and across the country centers on outlays for public education a social expenditure predating the modern welfare state by half a century. Second, there were periodic concerns for the fiscal impact of immigrants in the last century, but they never dominated the discourse on immigration. Finally, it should not be forgotten that as recently as 1986 when IRCA was passed, the primary issue regarding illegal immigration was its alleged effect on depressing wages and displacing U.S. workers (hence, the employer sanctions centerpiece of that reform). Immigrants' consumption of costly social services was rarely mentioned in the SCIRP report of 1980, nor in the several years of debates leading up to IRCA in 1986.

The vast expenditures of the welfare state alone cannot explain the current fiscal nativism. This fiscal theme, as expressed in Proposition 187, is rooted not just in the reality of social welfare expenditures; more important, it is grounded in underlying material conditions (increased economic insecurity and the dismantling of the welfare state) and related ideological accounts of those conditions (balanced-budget conservatism).

Proposition 187 as Symbolic Law

While Proposition 187 is thus an expression of nativism in response to increased economic insecurity and the balanced-budget conservatism onto which that insecurity is deflected, its relationship to those economic and ideological conditions is not straightforward. I argue that Proposition 187 was not simply a policy statement designed to limit undocumented immigration or reduce state spending; instead, it was a political statement, supported primarily to send a symbolic message. The content of that message is closely related to the balanced-budget ideology, with its dual hostilities toward immigrants and government.

An important research tradition has documented the symbolic dimension of political action. Gusfield's (1963) groundbreaking work examines the U.S. temperance movement as a symbol of Anglo-Saxon, Protestant cultural dominance at a time of industrialization, urbanization, and immigration. Citrin, Reingold, and Green (1990) similarly consider the symbolic politics of those who oppose voting rights for non-English speakers, bilingual education, and affirmative action, as a reinforcement of their own identity. In 1986, California voters passed by a 2–1 margin a ballot initiative (Proposition 63) that added an amendment to the state constitution declaring English the official language of the state; since then, Arizona, Colorado, and Florida have passed similar initiatives, as have numerous municipalities (Gurwitt 1988; Citrin, Reingold, and Green 1990). Citrin, Reingold, and Green (1990:1149) discuss the symbolic dimensions of these efforts, focusing on language as "a powerful symbol of national identity." Similarly, Engel (1984:580) discusses the rising opposition to "litigiousness" by those who suffer personal injury in a rural county in Illinois in the 1970s as a "ceremony of regret," or "one aspect of a symbolic effort by members of the community to preserve a sense of meaning and coherence in the face of social changes . . .

The following analysis shares more with Edelman's (1964, 1977) work on symbolic action. Unlike Gusfield (1963), Citrin, Reingold, and Green (1990), and Engel (1987), who focus primarily on law or legal movements as symbolic statements of cultural dominance, identity, or meaning, Edelman points to the symbolic role of political action in the assignment of blame or responsibility for a variety of social problems.

According to Edelman (1977), all political language and public policies have a symbolic component in the sense that they derive from and evoke a set of political beliefs about responsibility and blame.

For example,

> A reference in an authoritative public statement or in a social security law to "training programs" for the unemployed is a metonymic evocation of a larger structure of beliefs that . . . workers are unemployed because they lack necessary skills, that jobs are available for those trained to take them. (Edelman 1977:16)

Clearly, Proposition 187 was symbolic in this way. It reconfirmed to a predisposed electorate that illegal immigrants overburden government services and contribute to the fiscal crisis. Thus, as the welfare state is dismantled, the cutbacks are blamed on illegal immigrants who have stretched the system beyond capacity. As one letter writer to the *San Diego UnionTribune* (1995:B9) put it, pointing out that "[o]ur national debt is approaching $5 trillion" and urging implementation of Proposition 187:

> [T]here is a plan to cut projected Medicaid spending by $182 billion during the next seven years. In other words, we should provide free medical care and education to illegal immigrants while the government curtails medical aid for our own citizens?

This symbolic component of Proposition 187 both derives from the balanced-budget ideology and buttresses it, with disdain for the public sector increasing as its major clients are targeted as undeserving.[13]

Edelman has used the concept of symbolic politics in another way as well, to refer to political action that has little impact on objective conditions, but serves the purpose of placating the public. For example,

> If the regulatory process is examined in terms of a divergence between political and legal promises on one hand and resource allocations on the other, the largely symbolic character of the entire process becomes apparent. (Edelman 1964:23)

According to Edelman (1964:3), the electoral process itself acts as a "condensation symbol" in that elections "give people a chance to express discontents and enthusiasms, to enjoy a sense of involvement" even though this participation is largely ritualistic, as most decisions of significance are made elsewhere.

According to evidence provided by exit surveys and opinion polls, Proposition 187 did indeed allow people to "express [their] discontents." In fact, this seems to have been its primary appeal. According to a *Los Angeles Times* exit poll (*Los Angeles Times* 1994a:A22), 78 percent of those who voted for the measure did so because "it sends a message that needs to be sent." The responses, "it will force the federal government to face the issue" (51 percent) and "it will stop immigrants from using state services" (34 percent) placed a distant second and third, respectively, as reasons for affirmative votes (only 2 percent voted for the initiative to "throw kids out of school").

Another poll, taken less than a month before the election, found that those committed to voting for Proposition 187 (59 percent) would vote for it regardless of any potentially negative impacts. When asked, "Do the following arguments make you more or less likely to vote for Proposition 187?" the modal response to arguments against the measure was "no effect." Presented with the argument that "denying illegal immigrants prenatal care and immunization against communicable diseases could create a public health hazard," 42 percent responded that this would have no effect on their vote, compared to only 33 percent who said it would make them less likely to vote for the measure (Feldman 1994:A22).

Voters had been encouraged by initiative sponsors to treat it as a symbolic statement. In the final weeks before the election, media coverage of the proposition was intense, and much of the coverage addressing the potential negative public health consequences, for example, and revealing dissent from a number of national Republican leaders was potentially damaging to the campaign. Proposition sponsors responded by characterizing the initiative as purely symbolic, as a "way to send a message" and register one's anger over uncontrolled illegal immigration. Governor Wilson repeatedly urged voters to support Proposition 187 to send a message of anger and frustration to Washington over its inability to control immigration a federal responsibility and to demand that the state be compensated financially for Washington's failures.

Hesitant voters were told not to worry about any potential negative consequences of the initiative, because it was not likely to be enforced. Initiative coauthor, Harold Ezell (former Western Regional Commissioner of the Immigration and Naturalization Service) even declared that it was "ridiculous" to imagine that Proposition 187 would actually remove 300,000 children from school as opponents charged, since its constitutionality would be immediately challenged (National Public Radio, October 19, 1994). Instead, he said, the measure was meant to

> send a message that even the White House will understand. . . . Proposition 187 is not enough, but it tells the federal government that California has had enough and we're not going to take it anymore. (Ezell 1994:M5)

Much as Edelman might have predicted, then, Proposition 187 was symbolic in that it allowed people to "express discontents." But the enactment of Proposition 187 introduces a political phenomenon not addressed by Edelman, and perhaps signals a new development in symbolic politics. Edelman (1964) had argued that the symbolic function of elections works only so long as the electorate believes it is doing something instrumental in other words, only so long as they do not recognize the purely symbolic function. In order for elections to serve their symbolic function of appeasement, Edelman reasoned, voters must harbor the illusion that their actions will have consequences. But, in the case of Proposition 187, California voters enacted a measure they knew to be purely symbolic; indeed its symbolic dimension was extolled by voters and sponsors alike as its primary virtue. Without imagining that their votes would actually have consequences, and feeling disenfranchised and angry, approximately half of the eligible population did not vote at all; a substantial majority of the other half opted to send a message that they intended primarily as a way to express their anger.

As we have seen, the content of that message both draws from pervasive myths of responsibility and blame, and reinforces them. Thus, not only is the immigrant scapegoating implicit in Proposition 187 a symptom of balanced-budget conservatism as outlined above, but the message it sends legitimates the backlash. Whether or not Proposition 187 is ever officially implemented, its symbolic impact has already been substantial.

Conclusion

The passage of Proposition 187 signals a renewed nativism, the intensity of which has not been seen since the beginning of the century. Given the historical pattern, it is not surprising perhaps that nativism is on the rise in this period of wrenching economic change, capital flight, declining wages, and heightened insecurity. Less predictable is the relentless focus on the burden of immigrants on taxpayers and their consumption of costly social services.

In attempting to explain this fiscal focus of contemporary nativism, I draw from the literature on the crisis of Fordism (Sayer and Walker 1992; Lipietz 1985, 1987; Piore and Sabel 1984), deindustrialization and its effects on workers (Harrison and Bluestone 1982, 1988; Block 1987), and the dismantling of the welfare state (Piven and Cloward 1993). Most important, I borrow the concept of "balanced-budget conservatism" from Plotkin and Scheuerman (1994) to describe the deflection of attention away from these economic transformations and its concentration instead on government spending and the budget deficit as the source of economic and social malaise. The symptoms of this balanced-budget conservatism are an ideological attack on the public sector, disdain for government spending, taxpayer revolts, and hostility both toward the poor who are perceived to be undeserving parasites on hardworking taxpayers, and toward the government, which is seen as fiscally irresponsible. In this ideological and fiscal context, profligate government spending and the "undeserving poor" on whom tax dollars are spent not economic transformations and corporate decision making are the primary targets of responsibility for Americans' declining standard of living.

Proposition 187 fits well into this scenario. As the fiscal crisis and balanced-budget conservatism advance, hostility is directed at illegal immigrants the most undeserving of the poor who are spotted as the cause of runaway government spending and insatiable social service needs. Thus, not only is the recent rise of nativism in the United States linked to prevailing economic transformations and rising insecurities, but the fiscal theme of that nativism can be explained as a symptom of the balanced-budget conservatism that is the dominant ideological account of the economic and social crisis.

In addition to explaining this immigrants-as-fiscal-burden focus, I have argued that Proposition 187 is primarily symbolic, in at least two senses. First, following Edelman (1977), I demonstrate that the initiative evokes a belief system in which illegal immigrants are the scourge of efforts to control spending and in this climate of balanced-budget conservatism thus responsible for all that ails us. As economic insecurity and anger intensify with the continued globalization of the economy and the displacement of domestic labor, Proposition 187 simultaneously channels that anger into anti-immigrant nativism and legitimates the backlash. Whether or not any of its provisions are ever implemented, this symbolic aspect of Proposition 187 has already had, and will continue to have, serious consequences for the immigrant community (and for those "suspected" of being immigrant).

Proposition 187 was symbolic in another way as well. If we are to take California voters at their word, their support for Proposition 187 represented primarily a registration of anger rather than a reasoned effort at instrumental policymaking. As Edelman (1964:3) has put it, the election thus served symbolically as a way to "express discontents." But, in contrast to the electorate of 30 years ago described by Edelman, these voters were fully aware of the purely symbolic nature of the initiative, and indeed self-consciously used the ballot as a way to send a message. With regard to Proposition 187, these voters will probably prove right about their political impotence and symbolic power: Most of the major provisions of the initiative are likely to remain inoperative, at least for the immediate future, blocked by the courts as unconstitutional and/or in violation of federal law, but the symbolic impact of the proposition remains intact.

While immigration is an increasingly visible political issue, and the resurgence of nativism is an important component of this new politics of immigration, relatively few studies have explored these developments (for exceptions, see Cornelius, Martin, and Hollifield 1994; Citrin, Reingold, and Green 1990; Espenshade and Calhoun 1993). While some of this work has examined the connections between the rising restrictionist sentiment and ongoing economic transformations (e.g., Cornelius, Martin, and Hollifield

1994), none has discussed the unique fiscal emphasis of this new nativism. Nor have any studies explored the ways in which material conditions, ideological developments, and symbolic politics interact to produce specific expressions of this nativism. The present study begins to fill this gap. It is hoped that future research will continue this endeavor, perhaps focusing on more regional analyses of the new politics of immigration, or exploring the interconnections between this aspect of the prevailing balanced-budget ideology and other political developments such as the backlash against affirmative action and the popularity of "welfare reform" that may share the same ideological space.

Notes

1. Much nineteenth-century immigration was by definition "undocumented' (but not illegal) since before 1875 there were no federal restrictions on immigration and no official system of documentation and control.

2. Ford's classes were technically voluntary and by invitation. The 'invitation' read: "You are expected to attend the Ford English School. You must learn to read, write, and speak English. This school was established for your benefit, and you should be glad of this opportunity. . . . There is no cxcusc for your rcmaining away from school. Come to the 3rd floor on the Woodward Avenue side, after you ring out. COME TODAY" (quoted in Hill 1919:638; emphasis in original).

3. In the early years of the program, the Immigration and Naturalization Service often favored undocumented Mexican farm workers already in the United States over imported workers for Bracero status, encouraging the flow of illegal immigrants. Furthermore, substantial numbers of Braceros "skipped," leaving their employers before their contracts were up, seeking better wages and working conditions as undocumented "free agents." Finally, with the large influx of Braceros often came friends or family members who added to the illegal immigrant population. In 1954, Immigration Commissioner Joseph Swing launched "Operation Wetback," deporting thousands of undocumented Mexican workers and their families, and promising growers an abundant supply of Braceros if they refused to hire the undocumented. For the duration of the Bracero Program, illegal immigration never reached its pre-Operation Wetback levels (see Calavita 1992; Craig 1971).

4. IRCA's Special Agricultural Worker program, and its amnesty provision, enabled the law to clear the hurdle of special interests and advocacy groups most notably western agriculture and immigrant advocates, respectively. However, it was growing restrictionist sentiment that provided the original political impetus for the reform, which was first designed as an employer sanctions law, and popular support for employer sanctions continued to be the primary political motor driving IRCA (Montwieler 1987; Calavita 1989, 1990). Ironically, it was the legalization provisions that had the most significant impact.

5. While there were decreases in border apprehensions for two years after IRCA was passed, subsequent research indicates this was primarily due to the effect of legalizing close to three million previously undocumented immigrants through IRCA's two legalization provisions (Crane et al. 1990; Bean, Verez, and Keely 1989; Fix 1991).

6. In *Plyler vs. Doe* (1982), the U.S. Supreme Court declared that the Texas policy of allowing school districts to bar undocumented children from public schools violated the equal protection clause of the Fourteenth Amendment.

7. One GOP welfare reform package being considered by Congress would deny legally resident immigrants AFDC payments, Supplemental Security Income, Medicaid, aid for the elderly and disabled, and food stamps (Owen 1995).

8. There are obviously a wide range of issues involved in the immigration debate. As the Executive Summary of the U.S. Commission on Immigration Reform (1994) makes clear, U.S. citizens are concerned, for example, about competition with immigrants for housing and jobs, as well as being ambivalent about a host of "multicultural" issues. I do not intend here to oversimplify this multifaceted debate, but rather to examine the dominant theme of contemporary U.S. nativism as expressed in Proposition 187.

9. Block (1987) argues against both the foreign competition thesis and the broader crisis of Fordism interpretation of declining profits, arguing instead that the declines are the essentially self-inflicted result of U.S. capitalists' failure to concentrate on the production of high value-added goods and to make the investments in human capital such as education and training necessary to this more complex production process.

10. Although California is required by its Constitution to balance its budget every year, according to the nonpartisan Citizens Budget Commission, California now holds the dubious distinction of having the highest proportion of short-term borrowing activity relative to its budget of any state in the nation (quoted in Skelton 1995:A3). In 1994, California borrowed $7 billion to help cover expenses for two years, but its books are "balanced" by creative accounting schemes.

11. One reviewer has suggested that the regional nature of Republican politics may have something to do with the absence of such initiatives in New York. For example, a number of prominent Republican institutions located on the East Coast are favorable toward immigration (most notably, the *Wall Street Journal*, which is consistently pro-immigration). As this reviewer points out, "There are some intervening political variables between the growth of an immigrant population, cuts in social welfare expenditures, and the political outcome . . . in California." One of these variables no doubt was Governor Wilson's unflagging focus on this issue and his highly visible support for the initiative.

12. From this perspective, it may not be coincidental that Governor Wilson chose to focus on five key issues in his ill-fated presidential campaign: illegal immigration, affirmative action, government spending, welfare, and crime (Lesher 1995).

13. A *Los Angeles Times* exit poll is consistent with this interpretation of the political symbolism of Proposition 187 and the widespread appeal of the balanced-budget ideology it expresses. According to this poll (*Los Angeles Times* 1994b), a majority of respondents voted for Proposition 187 regardless of gender, household income, level of education, or "immigration status" (number of generations in the U.S.). Political ideology (liberal, moderate, conservative) was the most important factor distinguishing the electorate on this issue with only 26 percent of self-identified "liberals" voting for the initiative and 78 percent of "conservatives" favoring it. Ethnicity/race was also a distinguishing factor, with 63 percent of whites, 47 percent of Blacks, 23 percent of Latinos, and 47 percent of Asians favoring the measure. Given the targeting of racial minorities implicit in much balanced-budget conservatism, and the racial undertones of the Proposition 187 campaign, it should not be surprising that the measure won a majority only among white voters (whites comprised 81 percent of all voters). What is perhaps more surprising is the significant numbers of ethnic minorities (including Latinos) who favored the initiative.

References

Arax, Mark. 1994. "Raisin farmers hit by shortage of workers." *Los Angeles Times*, September 27:A3.

Bailey, Eric, and Dan Morain. 1993. "Anti-immigration bills flood legislature." *Los Angeles Times*, May 3:A3.

Bean, Frank D., Barry Edmonston, and Jeffrey S. Passel. 1990. *Undocumented Migration to the United States: IRCA and the Experience of the 1980s*. Santa Monica, Calif.: Rand Corporation.

Bean, Frank D., Georges Vernez, and Charles B. Keely. 1989. *Opening and Closing the Doors: Evaluating Immigration Reform and Control*. Santa Monica, Calif.: Rand Corporation.

Block, Fred. 1987. *Revising State Theory: Essays in Politics and Postindustrialism*. Philadelphia: Temple University Press.

Bluestone, Barry, and Irving Bluestone. 1992. *Negotiating the Future: A Labor Perspective on American Business*. New York: Basic Books.

Boremeier, James. 1994. "U.S. study fuels debate on illegal immigrants' impact." *Los Angeles Times*, September 15:A1, A26.

———. 1995. "Clinton moves to curb illegal immigration." *Los Angeles Times*, February 8:A3.

Bowles, Samuel, David M. Gordon, and Thomas E. Weisskopf, 1984. *Beyond the Wasteland*. New York: Anchor Books.

Brownstein, Ronald. 1994. "Wilson proposes U.S. version of Prop. 187." *Los Angeles Times*, November 19:A1.

Bulletin of the National Association of Wool Manufacturers. 1912. No title.

Business Week. 1985. "The casino society." September 16:78–90.

———. 1988. "Learning to live with leverage." November 7:138.

Calavita, Kitty. 1983. "The demise of the Occupational Safety and Health Administration: A case study in symbolic action." *Social Problems* 30:437–448.

———. 1984. *U.S. Immigration Law and the Control of Labor, 1820–1924*. London: Academic Press.

———. 1989. "The contradictions of immigration lawmaking: The Immigration Reform and Control Act of 1986." *Law and Policy* 11:17–47.

———. 1990. "Employer sanctions violations: Toward a dialectical model of white-collar crime." *Law and Society Review* 24:1041–1069.

———. 1992. *Inside the State: The Bracero Program, Immigration and the INS*. New York: Routledge, Chapman and Hall.

Carnegie, Andrew. 1886. *Triumphant Democracy, or Fifty Years' March of the Republic*. New York: Charles Scribner's Sons.

Citrin, Jack, Beth Reingold, and Donald P. Green. 1990. "American identity and the politics of ethnic change." *The Journal of Politics* 52:1124–1154.

Clark, Rebecca L., and Jeffrey S. Passel. 1993. "How much do immigrants pay in taxes?" Program for Research on Immigration Policy Paper PRIP-UI-26. Washington, D.C.: The Urban Institute.

Cockcroft, James D. 1986. *Outlaws in the Promised Land: Mexican Immigrant Workers and America's Future*. New York: Grove Press.

Congressional Record. 1884. 48th Congress, 1st Session.

———. 1921. 66th Congress, 3rd Session.

Congressional Research Service. 1980. "History of the Immigration and Naturalization Service. A report prepared for the use of The Select Commission on Immigration and Refugee Policy." Washington, D.C.: U.S. Government Printing Office.

Cornelius, Wayne A. 1982. "America in the era of limits: Nativist reactions to the 'New' Immigration." *Research Report Series* 3. La Jolla: Center for U.S.-Mexican Studies, University of California, San Diego.

Cornelius, Wayne A., Philip L. Martin, and James F. Hollifield (eds.). 1994. *Controlling Immigration: A Global Perspective*. Stanford, Calif.: Stanford University Press.

Craig, Richard B. 1971. *The Bracero Program: Interest Groups and Foreign Policy*. Austin: University of Texas Press.

Crane, Keith, Beth Asch, Joanna Zorn Heilbrunn, and Danielle C. Cullinane. 1990. *The Effect of Employer Sanctions on the Flow of Undocumented Immigrants to the United States*. Lanham, Md.: University Press of America.

Decker, Cathleen. 1994. "Voters back service cuts for illegal immigrants." *Los Angeles Times*, May 29:A1.

Edelman, Murray. 1964. *The Symbolic Uses of Politics*. Chicago: University of Illinois Press.

———. 1977. *Political Language: Words that Succeed and Policies that Fail*. New York: Academic Press.

Eisenstadt, Todd A., and Cathryn L. Thorup. 1994. "Caring capacity versus carrying capacity: Community responses to Mexican immigration in San Diego's North County." *Monograph Series* 39. La Jolla: Center for U.S.-Mexican Studies, University of California, San Diego.

Engel, David M. 1984. "The oven bird's song: Insiders, outsiders, and personal injuries in an American community." *Law and Society Review* 18:551–582.

Espenshade, Thomas J., and Charles A. Calhoun. 1993. "An analysis of public opinion toward undocumented immigration." *Population Research and Policy Review* 12:189–224.

Ezell, Harold W. 1994. "Enough is more than enough." *Los Angeles Times*, October 23:M5.

Feldman, Paul. 1994. "Anti-illegal immigration Prop. 187 keeps 2-to-1 edge." *Los Angeles Times*, October 15:A1.

Feldstein, Martin. 1985. "The Social Security explosion." *Public Interest* 81:94–106.

Fix, Michael. 1991. *The Paper Curtain: Employer Sanctions' Implementation, Impact, and Reform*. Washington, D.C.: The Urban Institute Press.

Fix, Michael, and Jeffrey S. Passel. 1994. "Who's on the dole? It's not illegal immigrants." *Los Angeles Times*, August 3:B7.

Gallup, George. 1980. "Most U.S. citizens favor a hard line toward illegal aliens." *San Diego Union*, November 30:A22.

Gamio, Manuel. 1971. *Mexican Immigration to the United States*. New York: Dover Publications.

Gibbs, Nancy. 1994. "Keep out, you tired, you poor . . ." *Time*, October 3:46–47.

Godkin, E.L. 1887. "Some political and social aspects of the tariff." *New Princeton Review* 3:173.

Gossett, Thomas F. 1973. *Race: The History of an Idea in America*. New York: Schocken Books.

Gurwitt, Robert. 1988. "English-only campaign is spreading." *Governing* 1:67–68.

Gusfield, Joseph R. 1963. *Symbolic Crusade: Status Politics and the American Temperance Movement*. Urbana: University of Illinois Press.

Harris, Candee S. 1984. "The magnitude of job loss from plant closings and the generation of replacement jobs: Some recent evidence." *Annals of the American Academy of Political and Social Science* 475.

Harrison, Bennett, and Barry Bluestone. 1982. *The Deindustrialization of America*. New York: Basic Books.

———. 1988. *The Great U-Turn: Corporate Restructuring and the Polarizing of America*. New York: Basic Books.

Harvey, David. 1982. *The Limits to Capital*. Oxford: Basil Blackwell.

Higham, John. 1955. *Strangers in the Land: Patterns of American Nativism, 1860–1925*. New Brunswick, N.J.: Rutgers University Press.

Hill, Herbert C. 1919. "The Americanization movement." *American Journal of Sociology* 24:609–642.

Hoffman, Abraham. 1974. *Unwanted Mexican Americans in the Great Depression: Repatriation Pressures, 1929–1939*. Tucson: University of Arizona Press.

Huddle, Donald. 1993. *The Costs of Immigration*. Washington, D.C.: Carrying Capacity Network.

Ingwerson, Marshall. 1993. "Workers brave new job frontiers." *Christian Science Monitor*, March 24:9, 12.
Kilbor, Peter T. 1993. "New jobs lack the old security in time of 'disposable workers.'" *New York Times*, March 15: Al, A6.
Kolko, Joyce. 1988. *Restructuring the World Economy*. New York: Pantheon.
Lacey, Marc. 1995. "New task force targets illegal immigration." *Los Angeles Times*, March 16:A3.
Lesher, Dave. 1995. "Wilson kicks off presidential campaign." *Los Angeles Times*, August 29:A1, A18–19.
Lipietz, Alain. 1985. *The Enchanted World: Inflation, Credit and the World Crisis*. London: Verso.
———. 1987. *Mirages and Miracles: The Global Crisis of Fordism*. London: Verso.
Lopez, Gerald P. 1981. "Undocumented Mexican immigration: In search of a just immigration law and policy." *UCLA Law Review* 28:615–714.
Los Angeles Times. 1987. "Minimum wage hike's real payoff." May 12, Part IV:3.
———. 1994a. "The *Times* Poll: Why they voted." November 9:A22.
———. 1994b. "*Times* Poll: A look at the electorate." November 1 l:A5.
———. 1995. "In U.S., 1 in 11 foreign-born, census finds." August 29:A20.
Marshall, Ray. 1978. "Economic factors influencing the international migration of workers." In *Views Across the Border*, ed. Stanley Ross, 163–180. Albuquerque: University of New Mexico Press.
Martin, Philip L. 1994. "The United States: Benign neglect toward immigration." In *Controlling Immigration: A Global Perspective*, eds. Wayne Cornelius et al., 83–99. Stanford, Calif.: Stanford University Press.
Martinez, Ruben. 1994. "Perspective on Prop. 187: The nightmare is coming true." *Los Angeles Times*, November 28:B7.
McDonnell, Patrick J. 1994. "Immigrant study cites fiscal gain." *Los Angeles Times*, February 23:B4.
Montwieler, Nancy Humel. 1987. *The Immigration Reform Law of 1986*. Washington, D.C.: Bureau of National Affairs.
Munoz, Cecilia. 1994. "Harassment in the wake of Proposition 187." *Christian Science Monitor*, December 27:19.
Nalik, John, and Paul Feldman. 1994. "Santa Ana schools condemn immigration measure." *Los Angeles Times*, September 24:A21.
New York Journal of Commerce. 1892. No title. December 13:2.
Ostrow, Ronald J., and Fulwood, Sam. 1994. "Wilson helped foster illegal influx, Reno says." *Los Angeles Times*, September 30:A3, A32.
Owen, Kelly. 1995. "Immigrants and welfare." *Los Angeles Times*, March 22:A5.
Parker, Richard A., and Louis M. Rea. 1993. "Illegal immigration in San Diego County: An analysis of the costs and revenues." A report to the California Senate. San Diego: State of California Senate, Special Committee on Border Issues.
Passel Jeffrey S., and Barry Edmonston. 1994. "Immigration and race: Recent trends in immigration to the United States." In *Immigration and Ethnicity: The Integration of America's Newest Arrivals*, eds. Barry Edmonston and Jeffrey S. Passel, Chapter 2. Washington, D.C.: Urban Institute Press.
Phillips, Kevin. 1993. *Boiling Point: Democrats, Republicans, and the Decline of Middle-Class Prosperity*. New York: Harper Perennial.
———. 1994. *Arrogant Capital: Washington, Wall Street, and the Frustration of American Politics*. Boston: Little, Brown.
Piore, Michael, and Charles Sabel. 1984. *The Second Industrial Divide*. New York: Basic Books.
Piven, Frances Fox, and Richard A. Cloward. 1993. *Regulating the Poor: The Functions of Public Welfare*. New York: Vintage Books.

Plotkin, Sidney, and William E. Scheuerman. 1994. *Private Interest, Public Spending: Balanced-Budget Conservatism and the Fiscal Crisis.* Boston: South End Press.

Public Opinion. 1886. No title. Volume 1:355.

Reisler, Mark. 1976. *By the Sweat of their Brow: Mexican Immigrant Labor in the United States, 1900–1940.* Westport, Conn.: Greenwood Press.

Romney, Lee, and Jeff Brazil. 1994. "Boy whose parents feared deportation had leukemia." *Los Angeles Times*, November 24:A3.

Romney, Lee, and Julie Marquis. 1994. "Youth dies as medical treatment is delayed." *Los Angeles Times*, November 23:A3.

Rosenblatt, Robert A. 1994. "Survey finds sharp rise in working poor." *Los Angeles Times*, March 31:D1.

San Diego Union Tribune. 1995. "Many illegals would not enter U.S. if all aid was denied." Letter to the Editor, September 1:B9.

Sayer, Andrew, and Richard Walker. 1992. *The New Social Economy: Reworking the Division of Labor.* Cambridge, Mass.: Blackwell.

Scheer, Robert. 1994. "Prop. 187: Stick it to the kids." *Los Angeles Times*, October 13:B7.

Shogren, Elizabeth, and Melissa Healy. 1995. "Gingrich backs Wilson on illegal immigrant costs." *Los Angeles Times*, February 9:A1.

Skelton, George. 1995. "A matter of dollars and sense." *Los Angeles Times*, August 14:A3.

Stewart, William F., Mark Gascoigne, and R. Wayne Bannister. 1992. "Impact of undocumented persons and other immigrants on costs, revenues and services in Los Angeles County." A report prepared for Los Angeles County Board of Supervisors. November 6.

U.S. Commission on Immigration Reform. 1994. *U.S. Immigration Policy. Restoring Credibility.* A Report to Congress, Executive Summary. Washington, D.C.

U.S. Congress. 1901. House Industrial Commission. *Reports of the Industrial Commission.* House Document #184. Volumes 14, 15.

———. 1911. Senate Immigration Commission. *Immigration Commission Report.* Senate Document No. 747.

———. 1919. House Committee on Immigration and Naturalization. "Prohibition of immigration and the problem of immigration." Hearing before the Committee on Immigration and Naturalization.

———. 1920. House Report #1 109.

———. 1921. "Emergency immigration legislation." Senate Subcommittee on Immigration. Hearing before the Committee on Immigration.

———. 1971. "Illegal aliens." House Committee on the Judiciary. Hearings before the Subcommittee on Immigration, Refugees, and International Law of the House Committee on the Judiciary.

———. 1971–1972. "Illegal aliens." House Committee on the Judiciary. Subcommittee on Immigration,Citizenship, and International Law. Hearings before the Subcommittee. Parts 1–5.

U.S. Department of Labor. 1991. "Employer sanctions and U.S. labor markets: Second report." Bureau of International Labor Affairs. Washington, D.C.: U.S. Government Printing Office.

Vernez, Georges, and Kevin McCarthy. 1995. "The fiscal costs of immigration: Analytical and policy issues." Center for Research on Immigration Policy. Report DRU-958-1 IF.

Wiebe, Robert H. 1962. *Businessmen and Reform: A Study of the Progressive Movement.* Cambridge, Mass.: Harvard University Press.

Wood, Daniel B. 1994. "California's immigration revolt." *Christian Science Monitor*, November 10:1–2.

CHAPTER 14

Acting Locally

ENVIRONMENTAL INJUSTICE AND THE EMERGENCE OF GRASSROOTS ENVIRONMENTAL ORGANIZATIONS

Sherry Cable and Michael L. Benson

The legitimacy of the state ultimately rests on whether those subject to its authority believe it is just. The notion of meting out to individuals and groups what they deserve—no more and no less—is the core of the concept of justice (Friedman 1975:17). If the legal system consistently produces results that violate fundamental beliefs about justice, the state's claim to authority is weakened. When perceptions of injustice become pervasive, the state is confronted with challenges to its authority.

Perceptions of environmental injustice arise when citizens come to believe that the state is failing to protect their lives and property from environmental pollution and that pollution costs are being unfairly imposed upon them. We argue that the perception of environmental injustice is rising and, that as a consequence, a new form of social control has developed—the community-based grassroots environmental organization. These groups challenge the distribution of the costs of local environmental pollution and demand better protection of their lives and property.

Emerging in the 1980s, community-based grassroots environmental organizations represent a new trend within the larger environmental movement (Brown and Mikkelsen 1990; Commoner 1987; Goldman 1991; Hamilton 1985; Morrison 1986). Unlike well-known lobbying organizations such as the Sierra Club and the Natural Resources Defense Council, these grassroots organizations focus specifically on local environmental problems and are less concerned with national environmental policy. They form in opposition to the problem of pollution caused by local businesses. Smaller in size than national groups, they tend to draw their members from lower educational and status groups. Currently, between 6,000 and 10,000 such groups are estimated to operate in the United States alone (Edelstein 1988; Freudenberg 1984; Goldman 1991).

Local environmental activists typically do not demand new environmental laws; rather, they press for the enforcement of laws already on the books. Environmental activists do not seek environmental reform but environmental justice. The groups emerge when traditional state-based regulatory mechanisms fail to control what are perceived as the illegal and harmful acts of local polluters. As with community-based crime prevention groups such as Neighborhood Watch, grassroots environmental groups form when people come to believe that traditional social control mechanisms do not work. Both groups represent citizen-initiated responses to perceived failures of the state to prevent crime and protect community well-being. In the case of grassroots environmental groups, the crimes at issue are often committed by corporate entities and hence can be treated as corporate crimes.

An examination of the evolution of grassroots environmental organizations and the obstacles they confront in pursuing justice sheds light on an important development in the environmental movement, while illustrating the inherent tensions faced by liberal democracies in balancing economic growth with democratic decision making. Our analysis explores links between the environmental movement, the evolution of legal culture, and growing concern over white-collar and corporate crime (Cullen, Maakestad, and Cavender 1987; Katz 1980). In this paper, we draw on theories of the state and on the criminal justice literature to suggest a new analytical framework for viewing the state's environmental regulatory activities and the emergence of grassroots environmental organizations. Our framework can be summarized in three assertions.[1]

First, environmental pollution resulting from a corporation's violations of environmental law constitutes corporate environmental crime. The environmental regulatory process often fails to protect citizens from corporate environmental crimes because of the inherent contradictions of the liberal democratic state.

Second, as a consequence of that failure, grassroots environmental organizations emerge as informal control systems to apply pressure on the regulatory process. These organizations bear resemblances to, yet are distinctly different from, community crime prevention organizations.

Third, grassroots environmental organizations exhibit patterns in the way they are formed and in the strategies used to exert influence on enforcement processes. We identify four stages in the life cycle of such groups.

The Failure of Environmental Regulation

In the 1970s, the federal government passed more than 30 major pieces of legislation dealing with the environment (Miller 1991). Administrative structures were established to carry out environmental policies threatening corporate violators with penalties and other sanctions that would reduce corporate profits. The impact and effectiveness of national environmental regulation is a matter of debate.

Some critics contend that laws passed in the 1970s during the zenith of the environmental movement are weak and seldom enforced, and that corporate production processes have continued to pollute with relative impunity (Brown 1979, 1988; Commoner 1987; Goldman 1991; Lash 1984). In contrast, other analysts contend that environmental regulations have had such a substantial impact on business activity that the productivity and international competitiveness of U.S. business has been threatened (see Tucker 1982; Weidenbaum 1986).

While the debate over the impact of national environmental legislation on business activity and the environment is important, it has neglected local dimensions of the environmental problem. To local communities, national and global environmental quality are less important than local environmental quality. Community residents pay greater attention to local conditions—air and water quality, and exposure to toxic chemicals—which impinge on their everyday lives. When corporate production processes result in serious pollution over an extended period, a sense of injustice is frequently provoked among local citizens, who perceive that formal regulatory and control processes are not working. From residents' perspective, local polluters are committing criminal acts with impunity. This perception, we contend, is correct. Regardless of the effectiveness of environmental regulation at the national level, the environmental regulatory process often fails at the local level and results in contaminated communities.

The increase in community exposure to environmental toxic hazards has been called "the plague of our time" (Edelstein 1988:1) and "a new species of trouble" (Erikson 1991:11). Brown exposes the slow poisoning of the U.S. population by toxic wastes (1979) and tracks a "toxic cloud" of air pollutants across the country (1988). The Office of Technology Assessment estimates that there are about 600,000 contaminated sites in the United States. About 888 sites have been either designated or proposed as priority cleanup sites on the Environmental Protection Agency's (EPA) Superfund list. Another 19,000 sites are under review. Using a database compiled from government and nonprofit organizations' statistics on environmental and public health, Goldman states:

> Across the United States, an average of four industrial accidents a day spill toxic chemicals into the environment. Factory mishaps release 370 thousand tons of toxins into the air each year. Industrial plants routinely discharge another 7 million tons of toxic chemicals into the air and water, and dump another 500 million tons of hazardous wastes into the ground. (1991:4)

Although environmental regulation successes at the national level can be documented, it is clear that at the local level the environmental regulatory process often fails to control corporate violations of environmental laws. Why are environmental laws so often poorly enforced by the federal government? To answer that question, we must examine corporate environmental crime and place it in the context of the contradictory roles of the state in relation to corporations and the public.

Corporate Crime and the Contradictory Roles of the State

The definition of corporate crime, like that of its conceptual ancestor, white-collar crime, is notoriously controversial. Disagreement centers largely on whether the concept should be defined narrowly, to include only acts punishable under criminal law, or more broadly, to include acts punishable under civil or administrative law as well (Cullen, Maakestad, and Cavender 1987). Following Braithwaite (1982), we broadly define corporate crime as conduct undertaken by a corporation or individuals acting on its behalf that is proscribed and punishable by law (see also Clinard 1983). As Braithwaite notes:

> To exclude civil violations from consideration of corporate crime is an arbitrary obfuscation because of the frequent provision in law for both civil and criminal prosecution of the same corporate conduct. In considerable measure, the power of corporations is manifested in the fact that their wrongs are so frequently punished only civilly. (1982:1466)

Braithwaite's point is relevant to corporate environmental crimes. That the criminal law is only rarely used against corporate environmental violators testifies more to the power of corporations to shape legislation and enforcement than to the harmfulness of their behavior.

Because it is difficult to prove guilt beyond a reasonable doubt in a corporate setting, regulators and prosecutors often opt for civil sanctions which require a lower burden of proof. Or, they may simply seek an injunction against the corporation to enjoin it against further violations of law. The matter may be settled with a consent decree, "a compromise between two parties in a civil suit, the exact terms of which are fixed by negotiation between the parties and formalized by the signature of a judge" (Mokhiber 1988:8). Civil injunction against corporate violators is the course most frequently used by federal regulators (Mokhiber 1988).

That federal and state regulators often pursue civil rather than criminal remedies is understandable. The control of corporate crime raises difficult policy issues. Indeed, many have argued that the control of crimes committed by businesses requires different measures than those used to control other forms of crime (Clinard and Yeager 1980:299). From the perspective of public policy, it must be recognized that corporations generally commit offenses that are incidental to and in the furtherance of legitimate business objectives. Harsh enforcement measures, no matter how well intended, may have deleterious effects on innocent parties (Bardach and Kagan 1982; Diver 1979). If criminal penalties disrupt business operations, employees can lose their jobs. The spillover effects of criminal sanctions can harm investors, consumers, and the local community (Moore 1987).

Nevertheless, the widespread use of civil injunctions for corporate crimes carries with it potential negative consequences for society. Unlike criminal penalties, civil injunctions do not stigmatize offenders. They lack the punitive and deterrent effects of criminal sanctions, making corporate environmental crimes less costly for corporations and hence more likely to occur.

Traditionally, the different measures used to control corporate crime have included an array of civil and administrative proceedings and sanctions, with the criminal law used primarily as a last resort. In responding to corporate environmental crimes, regulatory officials and prosecutors as representatives of the state have a wide range of available legal remedies and considerable discretion in their selection. With choices available in the types of sanction, the regulatory process becomes politicized. Corporate environmental crimes, in this sense, are constructed and controlled by the state. Thus, an understanding of the role of the state is necessary to comprehend the relationships among corporate environmental crimes, regulatory processes' failure to control them, and the emergence of an informal means of control—grassroots environmental organizations.

The state is charged with the potentially conflicting tasks of facilitating corporations' economic objectives and providing for the public welfare. This dilemma arises from the inherent contradictions between liberal and democratic principles which underlie public discourse and attitudes about government in democratic market-based societies (Bowles and Gintis 1987; Habermas 1975; Krauss 1989; O'Conner 1973; Offe 1972; Wolfe 1977). Liberal ideology demands that the state promote capital accumulation. At the same time, the state must maintain its legitimacy through popular support. According to democratic ideology, individuals participate in government so that decisions which affect the majority are made by the majority. Herein lies the contradiction: economic decisions that have consequences for the public are made without, and sometimes in spite of, public input. Such a course is consistent with liberal ideology, but in clear violation of democratic ideology. As Krauss states:

> The state must in one and the same moment achieve two conflicting aims: it must maintain the conditions for profitable capital accumulation and economic growth while legitimating its own power by appealing to the principle of democracy. (1989:230)

Tensions from the contradictions between liberal ideology and democratic ideology periodically generate crises for the state. The crises affect either the state's accumulation function, in which corporations demand state intervention to promote economic growth policies, or the state's legitimacy function, in which the public demands reforms. Historically, the state has tended to resolve these crises by following a two-pronged strategy. It alternately placates the public through democratic but symbolic reform while continuing to pursue policies promoting capital accumulation (Wolfe 1977).

The contradictory roles of the state are clearly manifested in the federal government's actions on environmental issues. To foster capital accumulation and increase economic growth, policies are promoted which limit corporate liability for environmental damages. Such policies permit corporations to externalize the environmentally damaging costs of production. The externalized costs are then borne by the public, who must pay either in the form of a polluted environment or in the taxes necessary to clean it up. Thus, the state fulfills its function of facilitating capital accumulation and ensuring economic growth.

But fulfilling the accumulation function eventually creates conditions which jeopardize the state's legitimacy. Economic development is inevitably and irrevocably tied to the environment. As economic growth increases to sustain capital accumulation, it also increases resource depletion and pollution. By facilitating the externalization of these environmental costs which cause environmental problems for the public, the state fails to provide for the public welfare. At the local level, the externalization of production costs translates into visible pollution.

Citizens then must deal with contaminated communities, such as Love Canal, Three Mile Island, and Woburn, Massachusetts (Brown 1979; Brown and Mikkelsen

1990; Levine 1982; Walsh 1981, 1988). In dealing with the state's cleanup efforts, citizens come to see in a direct and immediate way that the state favors corporate growth to their disadvantage. A sense of environmental injustice arises from these experiences. In response, citizens frequently pursue an alternative method of social control—an informal system embodied in grassroots environmental organizations.

Crime Prevention and Environmental Organizations as Informal Control Systems

Ordinary people form grassroots organizations when they band together to prevent some kind of harm or to protect themselves. Community-based crime prevention groups are well-known examples of this type of organization. As with community crime prevention organizations, community-based grassroots environmental groups arise when formal, state systems of control are perceived as inadequate. To begin our analysis of grassroots environmental groups' role in controlling corporate environmental crimes, we draw upon the well-developed literature on community crime prevention organizations.

Community crime prevention organizations represent "collective attempts to prevent crime and disorder in a geographically defined residential area, for example, a block or neighborhood" (Rosenbaum 1988:347). They developed in response to the increase in crime rates during the 1960s and 1970s. Citizens, politicians, and law enforcement experts recognized that the criminal justice system had a limited capacity to prevent crime (Rosenbaum 1988). Despite the mobility and communication facilities of patrol cars and radios, the police cannot be everywhere at once. Three national commissions recommended expanding ordinary citizens' role in the war on crime through the use of community crime prevention organizations.

The purpose of these organizations is to increase social interaction among residents to stimulate a sense of community and to strengthen informal social controls in the neighborhood. Community groups can do little to prevent crime without the support of law enforcement agencies, adequate funding, and technical assistance. Consequently, many analysts believe that formal and informal means of crime reduction are complementary strategies that work best together (Lewis, Grant, and Rosenbaum 1988; Yin 1986).

Community crime prevention organizations and grassroots environmental organizations are both community-based, voluntary organizations; most members are middle-class, middle-aged, married homeowners (Rosenbaum 1988; Van Liere and Dunlap 1980). Both types of organization emerged as informal social control systems because of citizens' dissatisfaction with the formal system's failure to protect them. When citizens felt the police were either unable or unwilling to protect them, they formed crime prevention groups to put pressure on local police departments for better service. Grassroots environmental organizations also develop when citizens perceive a threatening situation as beyond the state's control.

The story of one of the first grassroots environmental groups is now well known (Levine 1982). In August 1978, New York state health officials announced the "grave and imminent peril" posed to the residents of a suburban working-class community by the chemical landfill later known as Love Canal. Eventually, residents learned that between 1940 and 1952, Hooker Chemicals Corporation had dumped more than 21,000 tons of chemical wastes into an abandoned canal. In 1952, the corporation closed the dump site, covered it with a clay cap, and sold it to the city of Niagara Falls for one dollar. Officials built an elementary school and playground on the site which became the center of a working-class community.

Soon after the school opened, residents whose homes bordered the schoolyard complained to the city about strong odors, rocks that exploded when dropped, and skin irritations on the feet of children who played barefoot near the school. Their concerns were either ignored completely or treated with short-term remedial measures and dismissed by city and state officials.

Complaints increased in the 1960s and 1970s as more disturbing signs of trouble appeared. Homeowners complained of a black oily substance oozing through their basement walls. Chemical odors were stronger than ever, puddles of rainwater took days to evaporate, and backyard vegetation withered and died. The city of Niagara Falls hired a consulting company whose report documented widespread contamination and recommended that the city clean up the landfill site. But city officials, comparing the large price tag of the cleanup plan to their meager city budget, did not. Citizens who felt the government had not properly protected them, formed a grassroots group in 1978 to pressure state and federal governments to clean up the toxic site and buy out homeowners.

With the 1978 pronouncement by New York state health officials that Love Canal posed a danger to the public, the nature of the environmental movement changed significantly. During the 1980s, grassroots environmental organizations emerged in thousands of communities in the United States. Freudenberg has documented case studies of such organizations in Hardeman County, Tennessee; Pine Ridge, South Dakota; Staten Island, New York; Rutherford, New Jersey; Warren County, North Carolina; and Lincoln County, Oregon (1984). Other studies document contaminated communities and grassroots environmental organizations at Three Mile Island (Walsh 1981, 1988); Legler, New Jersey (Edelstein 1988); Woburn, Massachusetts (Brown and Mikkelsen 1990); South Brunswick, New Jersey (Krauss 1989); Centralia, Pennsylvania (Kroll-Smith and Couch 1990); and Middlesboro, Kentucky (Cable 1992).

Despite similarities between groups focused on crime and those concerned about the environment, differences profoundly affect their relative chances for survival and success.

First, community crime prevention organizations mobilize to oppose street crimes. Most perpetrators are lower-class adolescent males with no formal power in the community. They commit crimes of burglary, vandalism, etc., in a spontaneous, opportunistic fashion. The harmfulness of their behavior is immediately apparent, and specific individual victims can be identified. Thus, the main problem confronting the police and community groups is to identify and deal with the offenders.

In contrast, grassroots environmental groups mobilize to oppose corporate crimes. The perpetrators are corporations, politically powerful legal entities that make important economic contributions to the community. Corporate environmental offenses are not spontaneous. Rather, they are carefully considered and undertaken on the basis of a rational, culturally acceptable cost-benefit analysis. Unlike street crimes, substantial dispute can occur over whether an illegal act has actually taken place. Nor are the harmful consequences of the act immediately apparent. Demonstrating the causal effects of carcinogens, teratogens, and mutagens is difficult.

A second important distinction between community crime prevention and grassroots environmental groups is in their relationships to authority. Although both types arise in response to a perceived failure in official control mechanisms, their relationships to officials vary. With few exceptions, community crime prevention organizations work in conjunction with authorities such as the police. Indeed, to improve police–community relations, the police may even initiate the development of such groups. Other officials, such as a mayor or local representative, may also publicly endorse the community group's activities.

Grassroots environmental groups, in contrast, typically challenge authorities. They question not only the effectiveness of enforcement authorities, but also their integrity and motives, contending that politicians and regulatory officials have "sold out" to corporate interests at the expense of public safety.

The third dimension on which the two types of groups differ is strategy. Differences in the offenders/offenses opposed and the group's relationship to authority have direct implications for the strategies adopted. Community crime prevention groups try to change offenders' behavior either by reducing opportunities for crime in neighborhoods or by raising the likelihood of apprehension. For example, group members may try to improve the physical environment by demanding better street lighting, or they may educate residents about changing their lifestyles to reduce their risk of victimization. They typically work closely with the police, even though many express great dissatisfaction with police effectiveness. The essence of these crime prevention strategies is to modify potential victims' own behaviors and situations to reduce the number and attractiveness of criminal opportunities. Residents hope of fenders will choose to commit their offenses elsewhere.

By contrast, victims of corporate environmental crimes can do little to modify their behavior or situation to reduce their risk. They can have virtually no effect on the corporate offender's opportunities for committing an offense. Rather than changing their own behavior to avoid victimization, environmental group members must change the behavior of a corporate entity that is protected and aided by the state. Thus, grassroots environmental groups must concentrate on changing offender behavior by raising the costs of the offense. The goal is to get the offender to stop the offensive behavior but not necessarily to go somewhere else.

Grassroots environmental organizations typically pursue two broad, interrelated strategies to raise the costs of corporate environmental crimes. The first is to prod authorities to enforce existing environmental laws. Group members write letters to regulators, demand that government agencies uphold citizens' right to public hearings on the issue, attend and sometimes formally intervene in public hearings, and stage demonstrations at agency or state offices. They undertake such actions in the hope that in the long run it will be more cost-effective for the corporation to protect the environment than to pollute it.

This strategy has distinct advantages. Since corporations commit their offenses in a deliberate and rational manner, they are more likely to be sensitive to official sanctions than are street offenders. In addition, unlike street offenses, the perpetrator often is known and easily identified. Increasing the sanction risk for a specific offender is easier than the more expensive undertaking of raising the threat of sanctions for all offenders, which must be done with street crimes.

But there are drawbacks to this strategy. By challenging officials to enforce existing laws, grassroots organizations raise difficult legitimacy issues for the state. As they expose the contradictory nature of the state's functions, the groups themselves risk becoming the targets of formal social control efforts by the state (see Piven and Cloward 1979; Marx 1979; McAdam 1982). Additionally, official sanctions can be difficult to impose because of due process requirements and because corporate offenders have the resources to construct complicated and time-consuming legal defenses.

The second strategy used by grassroots environmental organizations is to impose their own informal sanctions. The groups hold press conferences denouncing corporations; picket company offices; and invite media attention through rallies, marches, and protests in order to publicize the environmental injustice and convince others of its injustice.

Stages in the Life Cycle of Grassroots Environmental Organizations

We identify four phases in the process of a community's recognizing the commission of a corporate crime to its initiation of actions through a grassroots environmental organization. We separate and rank these phases for analytical purposes recognizing that, in particular cases, the order of the phases may not follow this sequence and that some phases may occur almost simultaneously. Our intention is to begin to identify the complex processes involved in grassroots environmental organizations' emergence and activities as they pertain to the social control of corporate environmental crimes.

Phase 1: The perception that a corporate crime has occurred. In this phase, residents come to see and define themselves as victims of a corporate environmental crime. We distinguish between an environmental problem and a corporate environmental crime. An environmental problem exists when the balance of nature in an ecosystem has been disrupted. A corporate environmental crime occurs when that disruption results from a corporation engaging in illegal production processes. Thus, while the perception of an environmental problem involves the violation of ecological laws, the perception of a corporate environmental crime involves the violation of regulatory laws.[2]

For example, Yellow Creek valley residents in southeastern Kentucky had long recognized an environmental problem. The creek has been polluted by waste from the Middlesboro Tanning Company since the 1890s, causing fish kills, a stinging stench, and black foamy water. For decades, individuals complained to corporate and city officials through letters, telephone calls, and occasional petitions. But their efforts failed. Some individuals were bought off with job offers at the tannery. Others became frustrated with the intransigence of the political system and turned their attention elsewhere.

National policies regarding water quality began with the passage in 1970 of the federal National Environmental Protection Act and were clarified in the 1972 passage of the federal Water Pollution Control Act. After environmental laws and a federal regulatory process promising protection from environmental hazards were established, residents came to perceive the pollution of Yellow Creek as a corporate crime.

Phase 2: Individual appeals to state/regulatory processes. In the second phase, citizens make individual appeals to the state through the regulatory process. Appeals typically take the form of requests that the agency apply existing laws to force the corporation to cease its violations and ameliorate the environmental problem. Citizens expect that regulatory agencies will force corporate compliance.

The Three Mile Island (TMI) nuclear power plant suffered a partial meltdown in a reactor in 1978. The accident was at first perceived as a critical environmental problem which residents expected the utility company and the regulatory agency to handle effectively. When the utility company announced its intention to restart the undamaged reactor and operate it as it cleaned up the destroyed reactor, many residents appealed to the Nuclear Regulatory Commission (NRC) to forbid the restart. They were concerned by the prospect of the reactor being operated by the same corporation that appeared responsible for the accident. They also feared the consequences of operating a nuclear reactor only a few yards away from the destroyed reactor—which was essentially a massive, highly radioactive waste dump.

At a public meeting, an NRC commissioner told residents that the agency would hold meetings on the issue within a few days but that public input would not be solicited. Angry citizens and damaging evidence against the corporation discovered by the presidential commission studying the accident pressured the Pennsylvania governor to request that the NRC delay the restart until official investigations were completed and public hearings held. Under criticism for its previous lack of effective regulation, the NRC was not in a position to refuse the governor. Hearings which permitted input from citizens were set.

Phase 3: The perception of environmental injustice. In this phase, citizens become disillusioned with the state and its seemingly inadequate, often incompetent responses and believe that the regulatory process has failed them. A growing sense of environmental injustice leads to pressure on the state for more adequate action. In some cases, individual citizens independently pressure the regulatory process, through telephone calls, letters, and civil damage suits. But more and more frequently, citizens seek environmental justice through a collective effort. Trusting neither the corporation nor the state to protect their interests, concerned residents band together to form grassroots environmental organizations. These organizations are established as informal social control systems to police corporate environmental crimes. Through them, citizens demand reform and put collective pressure on the state by threatening its legitimacy.

Yellow Creek citizens' letters and calls to various officials proved of no use. Frustrated at the continued, flagrant violation of environmental laws and buoyed by the national environmental movement which lent credibility to environmental grievances, valley residents established Yellow Creek Concerned Citizens in 1980 and began a collective effort to clean up the creek.

Members first pressured the city of Middlesboro to control the tannery's waste in order to comply with federal water quality standards. When the city council failed to respond to the group's collective complaints, members threatened to sue the EPA for failure to enforce its own standards.

Phase 4: The outcome of increased democratic pressure. The fourth phase concerns the outcome of the legitimacy crisis generated by democratic pressures. If the grassroots environmental organization is successful in applying democratic pressure on the state, the state resolves the legitimacy crisis by enforcing environmental standards. On the other hand, if the group does not bring enough pressure to bear on the state, the corporation's infractions continue and environmental problems persist.

The intransigence of the EPA led the Yellow Creek group to file suit against the agency in 1983. This action stimulated the EPA to submit the case to the U.S. Justice Department for consideration of prosecution. In 1984, the Justice Department filed a civil action against the city of Middlesboro, alleging violations of the Clean Water Act. The suit was settled in January 1986 with the signing of a consent decree negotiated by the EPA, the city, the tannery, and the grassroots group. Violations continue but at a slower pace and Yellow Creek is significantly cleaner today than it was ten years ago. The settlement with the city provided a health fund and helped creekside residents pay for a water system to replace their contaminated wells.

At Three Mile Island, grassroots environmental organizations pressured the NRC to conduct formal hearings on the restart issue. Testimony in these hearings revealed that the accident was due primarily to mismanagement by the utility company and resulted in a federal criminal indictment in November 1983 of the utility company on 11 charges of falsifying safety records at the destroyed reactor. In a plea bargaining arrangement, the convicted corporation agreed to pay $45,000 in fines and $1 million to an emergency planning fund. In May 1985, the NRC commissioners voted to permit the restart. But commercial nuclear power generation had been closely examined and changes were made in control room design, in operator training procedures, and in a number of regulations (see Walsh 1988).

For reasons that are generally straightforward, grassroots environmental organizations are more likely to successfully gain environmental reforms than are individuals. Collective efforts are more effective because more people are involved, which puts greater pressure on the state to adhere to democratic principles. Thus, environmental justice is most likely to occur when the public demands it. This involves a bottom-up rather than a top-down fight. The bottom-up combat is carried out by grassroots groups, protecting their own communities.

More precise explanations for the successes and failures of organized groups in pressing the state to enforce environmental standards will require further investigation. Contemporary empirical analyses of many types of social movement organizations suggest that success is a result of a complex set of factors, such as the political vulnerability of the state; the economic and social power of the target; media involvement; the nature and extent of social networks; and the availability of such resources as money, equipment, and organizing skills (Cable, Walsh, and Warland 1988; Jenkins 1983; Killian 1984; McCarthy and Zald 1977; Morris 1981; Oberschall 1973; Snow, Zurcher, and Ekland-Olsen 1980; Tilly 1978, 1979; Walsh 1981; Walsh and Warland 1983).

But one point is clear: if collective democratic pressures for environmental reform in a community are successful, the state resolves the legitimacy crisis by enforcing environmental standards only in that particular case. Victory by one grassroots environmental organization does not generalize to others or to the entire social system. The state can accommodate isolated challenges to its authority made by individual contaminated communities, placating the community with environmental reform without endangering its accumulation function. Thus, it is unlikely that significant structural change in the state that would adequately protect the environment can occur without a coordinated, nationwide coalition of grassroots environmental organizations.

Grassroots Environmentalism, Justice, and the Social Control of Corporations

Our analysis concentrates on the emergence of grassroots groups in the environmental movement. We have provided a preliminary sketch of the processes by which such groups develop and posited a relationship between their development and the contradictory roles of the state in a liberal democracy. In this concluding section, we extend our analysis by placing grassroots environmentalism in the broader historical context of the evolution of a legal culture in the United States.

Legal culture refers to the attitudes, ideas, opinions and values about the law held by people in a society (Friedman 1985:31). According to Friedman (1985), U.S. legal culture has been evolving toward a new norm, that of total justice. This norm encompasses two broad principles: *a general expectation of justice* and *a general expectation of recompense for loss and injuries.* People have come to expect fair and just treatment in their disputes with large organizations, whether public or private. They recognize their rights to due process and fair play. They have a general expectation of recompense if they suffer harm, whether intentional or not, at the hands of others, particularly corporations. The evolution of these expectations can be traced through the legal history of workmen's compensation, product liability, due process, and civil rights laws.

Advances in science and technology and gradual improvement in the standard of living in the United States underlie the emerging norm of total justice. As the population of the United States has become more economically secure, it has become less willing to accept business misconduct for the sake of economic prosperity. Scientific and technological advances make life seem more predictable and more controllable. The pain and suffering caused by industrial accidents, poisonous food, dangerous cars, and environmental pollution are no longer accepted as unavoidable aspects of life. Rather, these and other business-induced harms are seen as preventable. This new view of harm has led to greater regulation of business activity.

As part of the trend toward total justice, the idea of defining corporate misconduct as criminal has become more acceptable. The law of corporate criminal liability is evolving and being extended in new directions by courts and prosecutors (Cullen, Maakestad, and Cavender 1987:101–144). At this point, however, the number of corporations and corporate executives charged with crimes each year remains quite small. If that number grows sufficiently, the state may face a legitimacy crisis that will require greater democratic input and may result in greater corporate liability for environmental pollution. The pressure will most likely be initiated by grassroots environmental organizations.

We suggest that the emerging norm of total justice plays a crucial role in both the genesis of grassroots environmental groups and the outcome of their activities. The norm of total justice stimulates the development of such groups by providing them with a new perspective on corporate environmental harm. It can be used as a frame for interpreting various pollution problems as grievances attributable to corporate wrongdoing, prompting citizens to question why business is allowed to avoid obeying the law.

The total justice norm also affects the outcome of grassroots environmentalism through its influence on the courts. Courts have become more willing to hold corporations accountable for the harm they impose on others, even if the harm was not intentional (Friedman 1985). This new legal culture creates a favorable context within which environmental groups may pursue their claims for environmental justice. In their dealings with citizen groups, corporations now must consider the possibility of losing in court.

But these developments must be interpreted cautiously. Grassroots environmental organizations are growing in number and perhaps in strength. Nevertheless, it seems unlikely that they will soon push the state into a legitimacy crisis which would be resolved in the favor of citizens over corporations. As corporations gain experience with grassroots groups, they will undoubtedly become more adept at managing environmental conflicts and more effectively challenge the scientific evidence on which claims of environmental injustice often are based. They will become more skillful at framing issues so that communities feel forced to choose between jobs and health, or between jobs and scenery, rather than exploring how it may be possible to have both. It is safe to assume that corporations will not simply acquiesce to attempts to limit their profitability by externalizing the costs of production. They will fight back.

If Friedman's analysis of the historical forces behind the emerging norm of total justice is correct, then economic development is a key factor. A stagnant or slowly growing economy will make it easier for corporations to pit worker against worker and to assert the primacy of economic development over environmental concerns. An expanding economy, however, is a double-edged sword. On the one hand, a rise in the standard of living provides a motive for people to demand stronger control of corporate environmental crime. As Friedman argues, when people feel their livelihoods are secure, they can focus on improving the quality of life and on demanding justice. On the other hand, economic growth is a leading cause of many of the very environmental conditions that grassroots environmental groups find so outrageous and unjust. It is not clear that prosperity which is environmentally sound and nonpolluting is possible. Hence, continued conflict seems inevitable.

We cannot definitively predict how the conflict between environmental justice and economic development will work out. In all likelihood, the conflict will be resolved, if at all, only slowly and in a very piecemeal fashion. Grassroots environmental groups will continue to demand justice, winning some battles and losing others. Because grassroots groups deal with local environmental problems, even their successes probably will have limited effects on national and even regional environmental quality.

Notes

1. We have limited our focus in this analysis to those environmental crimes committed by corporations under the regulation of the Environmental Protection Agency (EPA). The military, through the federal Department of Energy and Department of Defense, is estimated by some to be the largest generator of hazardous wastes in the United States (Erlich and Birks 1990; Renner 1991; Shulman 1992). But the EPA's powers to enforce environmental laws in the military are critically limited. In the past, the U.S. Justice Department has prevented EPA's efforts to sue other federal agencies, to impose cleanup procedures without the target agency's consent, and, even, to fine them (Renner 1991). Citizens' organizations sometimes emerge in opposition to environmental problems created by federal agencies but, given the state's relationship to them, the processes of grievance perception and mobilization are likely to be significantly different from groups opposed to corporate environmental crimes.

2. Another possible scenario is the expectation of environmental problems if a proposed facility is constructed. Researchers have documented cases in which an industry or waste facility such as a landfill have been proposed for a community and residents oppose it on the grounds that environmental problems are likely to result. Grassroots environmental organizations may or may not be formed, but the emergence and mobilization processes of groups opposing a proposed facility are likely to differ significantly from those of groups opposing an existing facility. Such circumstances raise important research questions but are beyond the scope of the present paper.

References

Bardach, Eugene, and Robert A. Kagan. 1982. *Going by the Book.* Philadelphia: Temple University Press.

Bowles, Samuel, and Herbert Gintis. 1987. *Democracy and Capitalism: Property, Community, and the Contradictions of Modern Social Thought.* New York: Basic Books.

Braithwaite, John. 1982. "Enforced self-regulation: A new strategy for corporate crime control." *Michigan Law Review* 80:1466–1507.

Brown, Michael H. 1979. *Laying Waste: The Poisoning of America by Toxic Chemicals.* New York: Pantheon.

———. 1988. *The Toxic Cloud: The Poisoning of America's Air.* New York: Harper & Row.

Brown, Phil, and Edwin J. Mikkelsen. 1990. *No Safe Place: Toxic Waste, Leukemia, and Community Action.* Berkeley: University of California Press.

Cable, Sherry. 1992. "Women's social movement involvement: The role of structural availability in recruitment and participation processes." *Sociological Quarterly* 33:35–50.

Cable, Sherry, Edward J. Walsh, and Rex H. Warland. 1988. "Differential paths to political activism: Comparisons of four mobilization processes after the Three Mile Island accident." *Social Forces* 66:951–969.

Clinard, Marshall. 1983. *Corporate Crime and Ethics: The Role of Middle Management.* Beverly Hills, Calif.: Sage.

Clinard, Marshall, and Peter C. Yeager. 1980. *Corporate Crime.* New York: Free Press.

Commoner, Barry. 1987. "A reporter at large: The environment." *The New Yorker* 15 June.

Cullen, Francis, William J. Maakestad, and Gray Cavender. 1987. *Corporate Crime Under Attack: The Ford Pinto Case and Beyond.* Cincinnati, Ohio: Anderson.

Diver, Colin. 1979. "The assessment and mitigation of civil money penalties: Federal administrative agencies." *Columbia Law Review* 79:1935–1502.

Edelstein, Michael R. 1988. *Contaminated Communities: The Social and Psychological Impacts of Residential Toxic Exposure*. Boulder, Colo.: Westview.

Erikson, Kai. 1991. "A new species of trouble." In *Communities At Risk: Collective Responses to Technological Hazards*, ed. Stephen R. Couch and J. Stephen Kroll-Smith, 11–29. New York: Peter Lang.

Erlich, Anne H., and John W. Birks, eds. 1990. *Hidden Dangers: Environmental Consequences of Preparing for War*. San Francisco: Sierra Club.

Freudenberg, Nicholas. 1984. *Not in Our Backyards! Community Action for Health and the Environment*. New York: Monthly Review Press.

Friedman, Lawrence M. 1975. *The Legal System*. New York: Russell Sage Foundation.

———. 1985. *Total Justice*. Boston: Beacon Press.

Goldman, Benjamin A. 1991. *The Truth About Where You Live*. New York: Random House.

Habermas, Jurgen. 1975. *Legitimation Crisis*. Boston: Beacon Press.

Hamilton, Lawrence C. 1985. "Who cares about water pollution? Opinions in a small town crisis." *Sociological Inquiry* 55:170–181.

Jenkins, J. Craig. 1983. "Resource mobilization theory and the study of social movements." *Annual Review of Sociology* 9:527–553.

Katz, Jack. 1980. "The social movement against white-collar crime." *Criminology Review Yearbook* 2:161–184.

Killian, Lewis. 1984. "Organization, rationality and spontaneity in the civil rights movement." *American Sociological Review* 49:770–783.

Krauss, Celene. 1989. "Community struggles and the shaping of democratic consciousness." *Sociological Forum* 4:227–239.

Kroll-Smith, J. Stephen, and Stephen Robert Couch. 1990. *The Real Disaster Is above Ground: A Mine Fire and Social Conflict*. Lexington: University Press of Kentucky.

Lash, Jonathan. 1984. *A Season of Spoils: The Reagan Administration's Attack on the Environment*. New York: Pantheon.

Levine, Adeline G. 1982. *Love Canal: Science, Politics, and People*. Lexington, Mass.: D.C. Heath.

Lewis, Dan A., Jane A. Grant, and Dennis P. Rosenbaum. 1988. *The Social Construction of Reform: Community Organizations and Crime Prevention*. New Brunswick, N.J.: Transaction.

Marx, Gary T. 1979. "External efforts to damage or facilitate social movements: Some patterns, explanations, outcomes, and complications." In *The Dynamics of Social Movements*, ed. Mayer N. Zald and John D. McCarthy, 94–125. Cambridge, Mass.: Winthrop.

McAdam, Doug. 1982. *Political Process and the Development of Black Insurgency, 1930–1970*. Chicago: University of Chicago Press.

McCarthy, John D., and Mayer N. Zald. 1977. "Resource mobilization and social movements: A partial theory." *American Journal of Sociology* 82:1212–1241.

Miller, G. Tyler, Jr. 1991. *Environmental Science: Sustaining the Earth*. Belmont, Calif.: Wadsworth.

Mokhiber, Russell. 1988. *Corporate Crime and Violence: Big Business Power and the Abuse of the Public Trust*. San Francisco: Sierra Club Books.

Moore, Charles A. 1987. "Taming the corporate giant? Some cautionary remarks on the deterrability of corporate crime." *Crime & Delinquency* 33:379–402.

Morris, Aldon. 1981. "Black southern student sit-in movement: An analysis of internal organization." *American Sociological Review* 46:744–767.

Morrison, Denton, and Riley Dunlap. 1986. "Environmentalism and elitism: A conceptual and empirical analysis." *Environmental Management* 10:581–589.

Oberschall, Anthony. 1973. *Social Conflict and Social Movements.* New York: Prentice-Hall.

O'Conner, James. 1973. *The Fiscal Crisis of the State.* New York: St. Martin's Press.

Offe, Claus. 1972. "Political authority and class structures: An analysis of the late capitalist societies." *International Journal of Sociology* 2:73–105.

Piven, Frances Fox, and Richard A. Cloward. 1979. *Poor People's Movements: Why They Succeed, How They Fail.* New York: Vintage.

Renner, Michael. 1991. "Assessing the military's war on the environment." In *State of the World,* ed. Lester R. Brown, 132–152. New York: W.W. Norton.

Rosenbaum, Dennis P. 1988. "Community crime prevention: A review and synthesis of the literature." *Justice Quarterly* 5:323–395.

Shulman, Seth. 1992. *The Threat at Home: Confronting the Toxic Legacy of the U.S. Military.* Boston: Beacon Press.

Snow, David A., Louis A. Zurcher, Jr., and Sheldon Ekland-Olsen. 1980. "Social networks and social movements: A microstructural approach to differential recruitment." *American Sociological Review* 45:787–801.

Sutherland, Edwin. 1983. *White-Collar Crime: The Uncut Version.* New Haven, Conn.: Yale University Press.

Tilly, Charles. 1978. *From Mobilization to Revolution.* New York: Addison-Wesley.

———. 1979. "Repertoires of contention in America and Britain, 1750–1830." In *The Dynamics of Social Movements,* ed. Mayer Zald and John McCarthy, 126–155. Cambridge, Mass.:Winthrop.

Tucker, William. 1982. *Progress and Privilege: America in the Age of Environmentalism.* New York: Anchor Press/Doubleday.

Van Liere, Kent D., and Riley E. Dunlap. 1980. "The social bases of environmental concern: A review of hypotheses, explanations, and empirical evidence." *Public Opinion Quarterly* 44:181–197.

Walsh, Edward. 1981. "Resource mobilization and citizen protest in communities around Three Mile Island." *Social Problems* 26:1–21.

———. 1988. *Democracy in the Shadows: Citizen Mobilization in the Wake of the Accident at Three Mile Island.* Westport, Conn.: Greenwood Press.

Walsh, Edward J., and Rex H. Warland. 1983. "Social movement involvement in the wake of a nuclear accident: Activists and free riders in the TMI area." *American Sociological Review* 48:764–780.

Weidenbaum, Murray L. 1986. *Business, Government, and the Public,* 3rd ed. Englewood Cliffs, N.J.: Prentice-Hall.

Wolfe, Alan. 1977. *The Limits of Legitimacy: Political Contradictions of Contemporary Capitalism.* New York: Free Press.

Yin, Robert K. 1986. "Community crime prevention: A synthesis of eleven evaluations." In *Community Crime Prevention: Does It Work?* ed. Dennis P. Rosenbaum, 294–308. Beverly Hills, Calif.: Sage.

Part V

PROBLEMS OF GLOBALIZATION AND HUMAN RIGHTS

This section presents studies that more directly address some of the new kinds of challenges being presented by trends of increasing globalization. Evelyn Glenn's article discusses the historical and sociolegal construction of citizenship in the United States, with particular emphasis upon its gendered and racially structured content. She analyzes the meaning of citizenships as the product of an ongoing political struggle around several key questions: Who are the full members of the larger nation? What are their rights and duties? How fully are they able to practice citizenship in the course of their everyday lives?

Glenn's arguments makes explicit the connection between the evolving legal order and it role in accommodating to the changing political economy, thereby showing how the gender and racial boundaries of citizenship were enlarged through major political struggles for enfranchisement. At the same time, reactionary nativist movements provide a persistent political barrier to full citizenship and that struggle continues to carry on up to the present. She characterizes this process as one framed in political and legal struggles over federal verses states' rights, in struggles for "social citizenship" via a social contract, in the struggle to construct a social welfare state, and more recently, in the struggle to maintain social entitlements won earlier in the face of neoliberal attacks on the welfare state.

By focusing upon the new challenges posed by increasing globalization, Glenn explores the question of how useful the struggles for full citizenship can be as part of a larger strategy for social justice. She contemplates the rise of transnational migrant communities, the growing numbers of people with multiple citizenship, an increasing multiculturalism and growth of racial/ethnic diversity, and the steady growth of an international body of international laws that establishes basic human rights. With the diminishing power of national states that grows out of the expanding power of transnational capital, some currents of political strategy have devoted their efforts toward protest, seeking the reform of supranational organizations such as the World Trade Organization (WTO). As Glenn argues, some communities such as indigenous peoples seek self-determination rather than assimilation, and therefore choose to appeal directly to international human rights bodies so as to avoid according greater legitimacy to their occupiers. National states, she argues, continue to be the primary institutional means by which international legal norms are implemented. This leads her to conclude that social struggles must continue both at national and supranational levels in order to resist the widening social hierarchies of race and gender being fueled by the globalization of capital.

Gregory Maney's chapter considers critical issues of transnational mobilization in social movement activity by way of a case study of the Irish civil rights movement (1967–1972) in British-occupied Northern Ireland. Maney seeks to extend the reach of the social movement literature that typically focuses upon structural, organizational, cultural, and ideological factors. His goal is to explore the impact that transnational alliances have upon social movements seeking far-reaching social change.

His empirical examination of the impact made by the international alliance that supported the minority Irish-Catholic community's struggle for full civil rights in Protestant-dominated Northern Ireland reveals that a series of negative dynamics resulted for the movement. He identifies the problem of "issue overlap" between organizations that joined the international coalition in supporting the civil rights movements and shows how the maintenance of this alliance was complicated as a result.

Transnational support of the movement was based in a variety of conflicting political visions ranging from anti-imperialist, antiracist, and anticolonial ideologies to more conservative, Irish-Catholic nationalist visions whose partisans resented the application of left-wing frames to the "Irish problem." In addition, organizational weaknesses emerged due to chronic infighting between various groups within the coalition. Cultural factors included widespread Irish rejection of countercultural elements within the coalition that were ascendant during the period of the late 1960s. Also important was the ideological struggle between those who sought reform toward full citizenship for the Catholic nationalist minority in areas such as housing and employment versus those sectors of the movement who sought to advance the cause of revolutionary socialism and full independence from Great Britain.

When the infamous massacre known as "Bloody Sunday" occurred in January 1972, the civil rights movement quickly collapsed in the wake of an upsurge of armed Irish Republican Army actions aimed at the British and Unionist authorities in power. Maney shows that the short-lived successes of the Irish civil rights movement were reversed on account of various factors that typically face domestic social movement coalitions. He argues that the problems experienced by the movement were exacerbated still further by the effect of international alliances that pushed domestic partners into greater direct conflict than would have otherwise been the case. Maney concludes that international alliances do not necessarily constitute a clear asset for social movements. Rather, such networks can elevate tensions within a movement, provoke organizational disputes and competition for scarce resources, and intensify ideological differences that can diminish overall popular support. In the end, the net liabilities of transnational mobilization networks may outweigh the opportunities it once offered if ongoing attempts at consensus building cannot be sustained.

In his chapter, James Ron builds off Marxian theorists such as Isaac Balbus, Weberian theorists such as Anthony Giddens, and others from the organizational and policing literatures in order to characterize the contradictory practice of state repression. With a case-study focus on the brutal Israeli suppression of the Palestinian population living in the occupied territories, Ron shows how both savagery and restraint can be exercised in an organized fashion by a militarized state. His analysis carries with it implications well beyond the case of occupied Palestine, suggesting that the dynamics of repression are often far more complex than many critical theorists have previously acknowledged. At the same time, he identifies important variables that can help us conceptualize the residual margin of protection that may often enable oppressed peoples to sustain their resistance.

Raymond Michalowski and Ronald Kramer's chapter discusses the impact that globalization has upon the regulation of corporate criminal conduct. They first approach the issue by suggesting the need to adequately redefine corporate misconduct in a transnational setting. Then they proceed to analyze the growth of a global legal order that is attempting to define and ultimately control transnational corporate wrongdoing. In selecting instances of corporate conduct that include exploitative labor practices, environmental contamination, and activities resulting in harm to consumers, the authors focus on those instances that occur in the "space" between existing national laws, that is, activities considered criminal in the home territory of the transnational corporation (TNC) but noncriminal in the territory where the harm occurs. This analysis demonstrates how powerful TNCs can pressure host nations in order to create hospitable conditions for their investment activities, including weakening or rolling back legislation that regulates corporate activity, as well as promoting lax enforcement of existing laws. As they extend their consideration to the United Nations codes on corporate conduct and consumer protection, they illustrate how global developments challenge critical criminologists to go well beyond existing nation-based conceptualizations of corporate crime. As such, the study of corporate transgressions must include all those transnational activities that violate either national laws or evolving international standards.

References

Glenn, Evelyn Nakano. 2000. Citizenship and Inequality: Historical and Global Perspectives. *Social Problems* 47, no.1:1–20.

Maney, Gregory M. 2000. Transnational Mobilization and Civil Rights in Northern Ireland. *Social Problems* 47, no. 2:153–79.

Michalowski, Raymond J., and Ronald C. Kramer. 2004. The Space between Laws Revisited: Corporate Crime in a Transnational Context. Revised version of article originally published in 1987: The Space between Laws: The Problem of Corporate Crime in a Transnational Context. *Social Problems* 34, no. 1:34–53.

Ron, James. 2004. Exploring the Organizational Dilemmas of Coercive State Conduct: Israel's Repression of the Palestinian Uprising. Revised version of article originally published in 2000: Savage Restraints: Israel, Palestine and the Dialectics of Legal Repression. *Social Problems* 47, no. 4:445–72.

CHAPTER 15

Citizenship and Inequality*

HISTORICAL AND GLOBAL PERSPECTIVES

Evelyn Nakano Glenn

Citizenship is a concept that has not had much currency in American sociology, in contrast to the considerable focus on citizenship in British sociology, especially in relation to the modern welfare state (e.g., Marshall 1964; Titmus 1958, Turner 1986). Among those of us who have historically been excluded from full membership in American society, there are good grounds for being leery of the proclaimed ideal of universal citizenship.

Within the political left, suspicion of the concept of liberal citizenship comes directly from Marx, who pointed out that democratic rights were narrow and partial. Citizens voted only every few years and in between had little political voice. More importantly, he pointed out that democratic rights did not affect economic inequality and, in many ways, helped legitimate it. Thus, democratic citizenship was a bourgeois concept that obscured economic and class division beneath a veneer of equality (Giddens 1996:66; Turner 1993:3).

More recently, feminists have critiqued the "ideal citizen" in liberal theory as essentially masculine (e.g., Pateman 1988, 1989; Okin 1979; Young 1989). According to Pateman (1989), liberal thought is premised on a public–private split, with public defined as the realm of politics, rights, and generality, while activities of daily maintenance, emotion, and specificity are relegated to the private realm. Since women were encapsulated within the private sphere, citizenship was defined essentially in opposition to womanhood.

And that is not all. Historians and legal scholars of race have pointed out that the liberal citizen is also racialized (e.g., Roediger 1991; Haney Lopez 1996; Forbath 1996). Since the early republic, the idea of whiteness has been closely tied to notions of independence and self-control necessary to republican government. This conception grew in concert with the conquest and colonization of non-Western societies by Europeans and

*Editor's note: This article is an edited version of Evelyn Glenn's Presidential Address delivered on August 6, 1999 at the Annual Meeting of the Society for the Study of Social Problems and later published in revised form in *Social Problems* 47, 1: 1–20.

Anglo-Americans. The removal of Native Americans, incorporation of Mexicans in the Southwest, and the takeovers of the Philippines and Puerto Rico, were justified on the grounds that nonwhite peoples were dependent and lacked the capacity for self-governance (Horsman 1981).

Yet, despite the bourgeois, masculinist, and white trappings of American citizenship, the very groups that have been excluded have often been among the most eloquent proponents of the ideal of citizenship. Movements for social justice found the universalistic and egalitarian language of liberal citizenship the most effective rhetorical device to make their claims. It was in this language that blacks called for abolition of slavery, women for suffrage, and workers for the right to form unions. For this reason, as Ruth Lister (1997) has pointed out, it is important not to abandon the "emancipatory potential" of universal citizenship.

Historical Debates about Citizenship in the United States

Before going into issues of globalization, I want to provide a historical context by identifying several recurring themes in the history of American debates over citizenship. I will focus, particularly, on how race and gender figured historically in constructions of and contentions over citizenship. I will then examine whether, and in what ways, contemporary forces of globalization challenge race and gender inequalities in citizenship. I believe that to grapple with contemporary issues of citizenship posed by globalization, we need to first understand recurring themes and issues that have long lain at the heart of contention over citizenship.

The concept of citizenship is, of course, historically and culturally specific. The modern, Western notion of citizenship emerged out of the political and intellectual revolutions of the seventeenth and eighteenth centuries, which overthrew the old feudal orders. The earlier concept of society organized as a hierarchy of status, expressed by differential legal and customary rights, was replaced by the idea of a political order established through social contract. Social contract implied free and equal status among those who were party to it. Equality of citizenship did not, of course, rule out economic and other forms of inequality. Moreover, and importantly, equality among citizens rested on the inequality of others living within the boundaries of the community who were defined as noncitizens. The relationship between equality of citizens and inequality of noncitizens had both rhetorical and material dimensions.

Rhetorically, the "citizen" was defined and, therefore, gained meaning through its contrast with the oppositional concept of the "noncitizen" as one who lacked the essential qualities needed to exercise citizenship. Materially, the autonomy and freedom of the citizen were made possible by labor (often involuntary) of nonautonomous wives, slaves, children, servants, and employees.[1]

At its most general level, citizenship refers to full membership in the community in which one lives (Marshall 1964; Hall and Held 1989). A specifically sociological conception of citizenship as membership is offered by Turner (1993:2), who defines it as "a set of practices [judicial, political, economic, and cultural] which define a person as a 'competent' member of society. . . ." Focusing on social practice takes us beyond a juridical or state conception of citizenship. It points to citizenship as a fluid and decentered complex that is continually transformed through political struggle.

Membership entails drawing distinctions and boundaries for who is included and who is not. Inclusion as a member, in turn, implies certain rights in, and reciprocal obligations toward, the community. Formal rights are not enough, however; they are only paper claims unless they can be enacted through actual practice. Three leading elements in the construction of citizenship, then, are membership, rights and duties, and conditions necessary for practice.

These three elements formed the major themes that have run through debates, contestation, and struggles over American citizenship since the beginning. First, membership: who is included or recognized as a full member of the imagined community (Anderson 1983), and on what basis? Second, what does membership mean in terms of content; that is, what reciprocal rights and duties do citizens have? Third, what are the conditions necessary for citizens to practice citizenship, to actually realize their rights and carry out their responsibilities as citizens?

Membership

Regarding membership, there are two major strains of American thought regarding the boundaries of the community. One tradition is that of civic citizenship, a definition based on shared political institutions and values in which membership is open to all those who reside in a territory. The second is an ethnocultural definition based on common heritage and culture, in which membership is limited to those who share in that heritage through blood descent (Smith 1989; Kettner 1978).[3]

Because of its professed belief in equality and natural rights (epitomized by the Declaration of Independence), the United States would seem to fit the civic model. However, since its beginnings, the U.S. has followed both civic and ethnocultural models. The popular self-image of the nation, expressed as early as the 1780s, was of the United States as a refuge of freedom for those fleeing tyranny. This concept, later elaborated in historical narratives and sociological accounts of America as a nation of immigrants, blatantly omitted Native Americans, who were already here, Mexicans, who were incorporated through territorial expansion, and Blacks, who were forcibly transported. This exclusionary self-image was reflected at the formal level in the founding document of the American polity, the U.S. Constitution. The authors of the Constitution, in proclaiming a government by and for "we the people," clearly did not intend to include everyone residing within the boundaries of the U.S. as part of "the people." The Constitution explicitly named three groups: Indians, who were identified as members of separate nations, and "others," namely slaves; and finally, "the people": only the latter were full members of the U.S. community (Ringer 1983).

Interestingly, the Constitution was silent as to who was a citizen and what rights and privileges they enjoyed. It left to each state the authority to determine qualifications for citizenship and citizens rights, e.g., suffrage requirements, qualifications for sitting on juries, etc. Individuals were, first, citizens of the states in which they resided and only secondarily, through their citizenship in the state, citizens of the United States. The concept of national citizenship was, therefore, quite weak.

However, the Constitution did direct Congress to establish a uniform law with respect to naturalization. Accordingly, Congress passed a Naturalization Act in 1790, which shaped citizenship policy for the next 170 years. It limited the right to become naturalized citizens to "free white persons." The act was amended in 1870 to add blacks, but the term "free white persons" was retained. As Ian Haney Lopez (1996) has documented, immigrants deemed to be nonwhite (Hawaiians, Syrians, Asian Indians), but not black or African, were barred from naturalization. The largest such category was immigrants from China, Japan, and other parts of Asia, who were deemed by the courts to be "aliens ineligible for citizenship." This exclusion remained in force until 1953.

Gender was another boundary. Even though women were not specifically mentioned in the Constitution, it was understood that they were members of a dependent class and, by nature, lacked the capacity to exercise full citizenship. As Linda Kerber (1980) has shown, the founders defined a special role for women as "republican mothers," whose contributions were not to fight or vote, but to care for the home and raise future citizens.[4] Under the common law doctrine of coverture, the legal identity of married women was subsumed by that of their husbands, who represented their wives' interests in the political realm. Women were, thereby, "virtual citizens" rather than "direct citizens." For women, then, the marriage contract superseded the social contract (Gunderson 1987). Well into the twentieth century, women's citizenship status remained tied to their husband's status. Thus, an alien woman gained citizenship upon marrying a male citizen (though not if she was racially disqualified), and a native-born woman lost her citizenship if she married an alien (until the Cable Act was passed in 1922). Still, women who married aliens who were "ineligible by race for naturalization" forfeited their citizenship until this provision was rescinded in 1931 (Smith 1989:277).

It was black Americans, both before and after the Civil War, who were the most consistent advocates of universal citizenship. Hence, it is fitting that the Civil Rights Act of 1865 and the Fourteenth Amendment, ratified in 1867 to ensure the rights of freed people, greatly expanded citizenship for everyone. Section 1 of the Fourteenth Amendment stated that "All persons born or naturalized in the United States and subject to the jurisdiction thereof, are citizens of the United States and of the State wherein they reside. No State shall make or enforce any law which shall abridge the privileges or immunities of citizens of the United States; nor shall any State deprive any person of life, liberty, or property, without due process of law; nor deny to any person within its jurisdiction, the equal protection of the law."

In these brief sentences, the Fourteenth Amendment established three important principles for the first time: the principle of national citizenship, the concept of the federal state as the protector and guarantor of national citizenship rights, and the principle of birthright citizenship. These principles expanded citizenship for others besides blacks. To cite one personal example, my grandfather, who came to this country in 1894, was ineligible to become a naturalized citizen because he was not white, but his daughter, my mother, automatically became a citizen as soon as she was born. Birthright citizenship was tremendously important for second- and third-generation Japanese Americans and other Asian Americans who otherwise would have remained perpetual aliens, as is now the case with immigrant minorities in some European countries. Foner (1998) was on the mark when he said that the black American struggle to expand the boundaries of freedom to include themselves, succeeded in changing the boundaries of freedom for everyone.

The battle was not won, once and for all, in 1867. Instead, the nation continued to vacillate between the principle of the federal government having a duty to protect citizens' rights and states' rights. By the end of the Reconstruction period in the 1870s, the slide back toward states' rights accelerated as all branches of the federal government withdrew from protecting black rights and allowed southern states to impose white supremacist regimes (Foner 1988).

In the landmark 1896 *Plessy v. Ferguson* decision, the Supreme Court legitimized segregation based on the principle of "separate but equal." This and other court decisions gutted the concept of national citizenship and carved out vast areas of life, employment, housing, transportation, and public accommodations as essentially private activity that was not protected by the Constitution (Woodward 1974). It was not until the second civil rights revolution of the 1950s and 1960s, that the federal courts and Congress returned to the principles of national citizenship and a strong federal obligation to protect civil rights.

The 1990s have again seen the pendulum shifting away from national citizenship and federal protections, and toward states' rights. In 1999, the conservative majority on the Supreme Court issued three decisions shielding states from suits for violating Federal law. In one ominous case, *Alden v. Maine*, the court held that states could not be sued in their own courts by state employees for violating the Fair Labor Standards Act (in this case failing to pay overtime wages). Since, in a 1996 decision (*Seneca tribe v. Florida*), the court ruled that such suits could not be brought into federal courts either, state employees were left with no legal recourse. Only the federal government can bring suit, but the U.S. Department of Labor is only equipped to bring a token number of suits on behalf of the nation's 4.7 million state workers (Greenhouse 1999). This law threatens to cripple enforcement of federal civil rights laws, such as the Americans with Disabilities Act. The retreat of federal protection after three decades of federal activism on behalf of civil rights has disturbing parallels to the withdrawal of federal protection of black rights after Reconstruction, and is a sobering reminder that gains in citizenship rights can be rolled back.[5]

The 1990s have also seen the resurgence of nativism, which has always been a strong ideological current that periodically peaks during periods of economic downturn, social unrest, or unease about rapid change. The rise of nativist sentiment after World War I led to the passage of the 1924 Immigration Act, which severely reduced entry from Eastern and Southern Europe and banned entry from Asia. The liberal 1965 Immigration Act, which removed many restrictions and opened the doors to Asian immigration, seemed to signal a renunciation of the nativist heritage. The 1990s decade, however, has seen renewed efforts to reassert a narrow ethnocultural definition of Americanism. These include calls (some successful) to restrict access at U.S. borders

(Rodriguez 1996); to make English the "official language" (Diamond 1996); to scuttle bilingual education (Crawford 1992); to deny welfare to immigrants (Chang 1994); and even to amend the Constitution to do away with birthright citizenship for children of so-called undocumented immigrants (Perea 1997).

Meanings of Rights and Responsibilities

Just as with the question of membership, there has not been a single understanding of rights and duties. American ideas on rights and duties have been shaped by two different political languages (Smith 1989). One, termed liberalism by scholars, grew out of Locke and other enlightenment thinkers. In this strain of thought, embodied in the Declaration of Independence, citizens are individual rights bearers. Governments were established to secure individual rights so as to allow each person to pursue private as well as public happiness. The public good was not an ideal to be pursued by government, but was to be the outcome of individuals pursuing their own individual interest. The other language was that of republicanism, which saw the citizen as one who actively participated in public life. This line of thought reached back to ancient Greece and Rome where republicanism held that man reached his highest fulfillment by setting aside self-interest to pursue the common good. In contrast to liberalism, republicanism emphasizes practice and focuses on achieving institutions and practices that make collective self-government possible.[6]

There has been continuing tension and alternation between these two strains of thought, particularly around the question of whether political participation is essential to, or peripheral to, citizenship. In the nineteenth century, when many groups were excluded from participation, the vote was a mark of standing; its lack was a stigma, a badge of inferiority, hence, the passion with which those denied the right fought for inclusion. Three great movements—for universal white manhood suffrage, for Black emancipation, and for women's suffrage—resulted in successive extensions of the vote to nonpropertied white men, black men, and women, between 1800 and 1920 (Roediger 1991; Foner 1990; DuBois 1978). According to Judith Shklar (1991), once the vote became broadly available, it ceased to be a mark of status. Judging by participation rates, voting is no longer an emblem of citizenship. One measure of the decline in the significance of the vote has been the precipitous drop in persons voting. In 1890, fully 80% of those who were eligible, voted. By 1924, four years after the extension of suffrage to women, participation had fallen to less than half of those registered, and it has been declining ever since.

In many European countries, there is a status of being a denizen, in which one has the same rights as citizens in terms of protection from arbitrary treatment, but not the vote or the right to hold political office (Yuval-Davis 1997). Citizenship, which includes enfranchisement, has higher or different standards, such as genealogy or ethnocultural characteristics. At the same time, actual exercise of the franchise is encouraged or expected through automatic or compulsory registration (Schuck 1998).[7] In the U.S., participation is discouraged by not making registration easy. Requiring reregistration every time one moves is only one example of the obstacles placed upon a highly mobile population. While Americans today would object if the right to vote was taken away, the majority don't seem to feel it necessary to exercise the vote. The U.S. obviously has the capacity to make registration automatic or convenient, but has not made major efforts to do so. Needless to say, it is in the interest of big capital and its minions that most people don't participate politically.

Conditions for Practice

This leads to the third main theme, the actual practice of citizenship and the question of what material and social conditions are necessary for people to actually exercise their rights and participate in the polity. The short answer to this question for most of American history has been that a citizen must be independent—that is, able to act autonomously. In the liberal tradition, which emphasizes individual rights, independence is what enables each of us to make choices in the free market and to pursue our own interests. In the republican tradition, independence is also important because it enables us to act for the common good, rather than out of our immediate material needs, while central to both political traditions. Independence took on additional weight during the revolutionary period as advocates of separation sought to justify breaking from England and to replace the concept of subjectship with that of voluntary citizenship (Gunderson 1987; Kettner 1978). Voluntary citizenship implied political independence.

Independence has remained essential, but its meaning has undergone drastic transformation since the founding of the nation. In the eighteenth century, independence meant owning property so that one was not dependent on another for one's livelihood. In the colonial period and for some three decades after the revolution, states had property requirements for voting; those without property, women, servants, apprentices, hirelings, and paupers were considered to be dependent and, therefore, not qualified to participate in governance (Smith 1989).

In the nineteenth century, as industrialization proceeded apace and wage work became common even for skilled artisans and white collar men, the meaning of independence changed to make it more consistent with the actual situation of most white men. It came to mean, not ownership of productive property, but nothing more than ownership of one's own labor and the capacity to sell it for remuneration (Fraser and Gordon 1994). This formulation rendered almost all white men "independent," while rendering slaves and women, who did not have complete freedom to sell their labor, "dependent." It was on the basis of the independence of white working men that the movement for white Universal Manhood Suffrage was mobilized (Roediger 1991). By the 1830s, all states had repealed property requirements for suffrage for white men, while simultaneously barring women and Blacks (Litwak 1961).

By the late 19th century, capitalist industrialization had widened the economic gap between the top owners of productive resources and the rest, making more apparent the contradiction between economic inequality and political democracy. Rising levels of poverty, despite the expansion in overall wealth, raised the question of whether low-income, unemployment, and/or lack of access to health care and other services, diminished citizenship rights for a large portion of the populace. Growing economic inequality also raised the issue of whether some nonmarket mechanism was needed to mitigate the harshness of inequities created by the market.

One response during the years between World War I and World War II was rising sentiment for the idea of what T. H. Marshall called "social citizenship." In Marshall's words (Marshall 1964:78), social citizenship involves "the right to a modicum of economic security and to share in the full social heritage and to live the life of a civilized being, according to the standards prevailing in the society." Economic and social unrest after World War I spurred European states to institute programs to ensure some level of economic security and take collective responsibility for "dependents"—the aged, children, the disabled, and others unable to work. Most Western European states instituted some form of unemployment benefits, limited old age insurance, national insurance and children's allowances. After World War II, they established more thorough-going welfare, including broad entitlements to health care, old age pensions, child allowances, etc. (Pederson 1992; Salisbury 1996). The significance of the "redistributive" mechanisms of the Welfare State, according to Marshall, was that they enabled working class people to exercise their civil and political rights. In Marshall's vision, social citizenship was important, not only for its own sake, but because it "filled out" what Marx considered the hollow rights of liberal citizenship.

Compared to Western Europe, the concept of social citizenship has been relatively weak in the U.S. Welfare state researchers have pointed out that, although 1930s New Deal programs such as social security and unemployment insurance greatly increased economic security, they continued a pattern of a two-tiered system of social citizenship from the 1890s (Nelson 1990; Skocpol 1992; Fraser and Gordon 1993; Gordon 1994). The upper tier consisted of "entitlements" based on employment or military service, e.g., unemployment benefits, old-age insurance, and disability payments, which were relatively generous and did not require means-testing. The lower tier consisted of various forms of "welfare," such as Aid to Dependent Children (changed to Aid to Families of Dependent Children—AFDC—in 1962), which were relatively stingy and entailed means testing and surveillance by the state. White men, as a class, have drawn disproportionately on first-tier rights by virtue of their records of regular and well-paid employment. White women, more often, had to rely on welfare, which is considered charity, a response to dependence, rather than a just return for contributions. Latino and African-American men were generally excluded from employment-based benefits because of their concentration in agriculture, day jobs, and other excluded occupations; Latina and African-American women, in turn, have often been denied even second-tier benefits (Oliver and Shapiro 1995; Mink 1994). Moreover, in contrast to the situation in most European countries, there has been little sense of collective responsibility for the care of dependents. Thus, raising children is not recognized as a contribution to the society and, therefore, as a citizenship responsibility that warrants entitlements such as parental allowances and retirement credit, which are common in Europe (Glenn 2000; Sainsbury 1996).

As with the other issues of citizenship, the 1980s and 1990s has seen a neo-conservative turn with a concerted effort to roll back even attenuated social citizenship rights. Government funding of social services has been vilified for draining money from hardworking citizens to support loafers and government bureaucrats who exert onerous control over people's lives.

After years of attacks on black and other single mothers "dependent" on welfare, Congress passed the Personal Responsibility and Work Opportunity Act in 1996, which dismantled AFDC and replaced it with grants to the states that limited eligibility for federal benefits for a lifetime maximum of five years. The aim was, as Representative Richard Armey put it, that the poor return to the natural safety nets—family, friends, churches, and charities. States instituted stringent work requirements and limited total lifetime benefits. By limiting total years that they can stay on welfare, proponents argued the new regulations would wean single mothers from unhealthy dependence on the state. In contrast to an overly indulgent government, the market is expected to exert a moral force, disciplining them and forcing them to be "independent" (Roberts 1997; Boris 1998).

In Europe, the language of citizenship has enjoyed a revival within the Left as a rubric to mobilize opposition to the trimming away of welfare state entitlements, such as health care, education, retirement, and child benefits (Yuval Davis 1997). In the U.S., we lack a tradition of social citizenship on which to build a defense of social provision. (In fact, the term is never used.) If we can't appeal to social citizenship, then we need to articulate a notion of citizenship that resonates with American rights language to counter the Right and neoliberal hijacking of citizenship to mean only freedom in the market and responsibility to earn. Thus, we must ask: if people have a responsibility to earn, then, don't they also have a corresponding right to earn?—i.e., to have a job and to earn enough to support themselves at a level that allows them, in Marshall's (1964:78) words, "to participate fully in the cultural life of the society and to live the life of a civilized being according to the standards prevailing in the society."

The Era of Globalization: Challenges to Citizenship

Keeping this history of race and gender within the boundaries, meanings, and practice of citizenship, I turn to the issue of globalization and its implications for citizenship as a realm for creating and challenging race, gender, and class inequalities. I ask, in light of the foregoing history, what are the effects of economic globalization and its concomitants—international and national economic restructuring, transnational flows of goods, capital, people and ideas, and the partial dispersion of sovereignty away from nation states—on historic race/gender class inequalities in citizenship? Does economic globalization and its associated social and cultural shifts create new forms of race, gender, and class inequality? And, given what seems to be the partial dismantling of nation state sovereignty, is citizenship still a useful rubric for organizing for social justice?

We are all familiar with the trappings of globalization: world markets, unfettered capital movement, international mass media, air travel, and electronic communications, all of which involve instantaneous transmission of money, labor, goods, and ideas. For my purposes, I use the term globalization to refer to the creation of a global economy characterized by rapid and unregulated flows of capital across and between states and regions (Mittleman 1997). These flows are restructuring patterns of investment, labor deployment, production, and consumption and, thereby, having enormous impacts on lives and relationships. Anthony Giddens (1996) describes globalization as transforming time and space, so as to greatly expand "action at a distance." Others speak of "deterritorialization" or "denationalization of territories"—a world in which identities and cultures are no longer tied to particular geographic locations (Basch et al. 1994; Sassen 1996a); or even of a "borderless world" in which nation states no longer effectively regulate their boundaries (Ohmae 1999).

In an important sense, of course, we have long lived in a global world, and transnational activity and ties have existed for a long time, so not everything we associate with contemporary globalization is new. As a recent article in the *New York Times* (Kristof 1999) points out, the proportion of total U.S. capital that goes into foreign investment, and the proportion of transnational immigrants, were both higher at the end of the nineteenth century than they are today. (For example, in 1900, 14% of the U.S. population was foreign born, compared to 8% today.) Still, as Portes et al. (1999) point out, earlier transnational economic activity and travel took place only on an occasional basis or, if more regular, involved only a small elite group. What has changed, therefore, is that transnational movement, exchange, and communication have become routine and regular, with masses of people engaged in regular and sustained contact across national borders. This critical mass has been made possible by certain technological prerequisites: air transport, long-distance telephones, facsimile communication, and electronic mail. These technological developments have also accelerated the speed of movement. With electronic transfer, capital sweeps in instantaneously and sweeps out just as quickly, leading to great volatility and frequent financial crises. Similarly, with movement of people, large international cities such as London, Tokyo, and New York have hundreds of jumbo jets per day flying in and out carrying thousands of "foreign" travelers. Mass air travel has also increased the range in sources and destinations for migrants; migration takes place not just between adjacent territories or between colonizer countries and their former colonies, as in earlier times. Thus, countries such as Germany, Italy, and Japan, that used to see themselves as homogeneous—made up of people of one blood—have become multicultural, with Asians, Africans, and Middle Easterners being part of the mix (Kymlicka 1995; Lutz, 1997).

There are many citizenship issues raised by the economic, political, social, and cultural transformations brought about by economic globalization; I would like, here, to focus on three that are particularly relevant to questions of race and gender equality and inequality. In what follows, I remain focused on the U.S., but include European and other comparative examples to highlight both differences and convergences.

Transnationalism: Possibilities and Inequities in Multiple Citizenships

The first issue is the growing phenomenon of transnationalism (Glick Schiller et al. 1992). Increasingly, massive migration has created a situation in which a significant portion of people retain ties in, and navigate between, multiple communities and nations, complicating the notion of citizenship as membership in the community in which one lives. Transnational ties are not a new phenomenon. Many Mexicans migrated for seasonal work to the United States and participated in temporary or return migration, retaining families and ties in their villages of origin. Early Chinese male immigrants residing in the U.S. thought of themselves as sojourners, maintained ties and identities in their communities of origin, and lived in Chinatowns, which were early transnational communities. In the current global economy, however, the number and range of transnational communities has multiplied, including large transnational communities of Latin and Central American, and Caribbean migrants.

In Roberts et al.'s (1999) definition, transnational migrant communities "are groupings of immigrants who participate on a routine basis in a field of relationships, practices, and norms that include both places of origin and places of destination." Portes et al. (1999) emphasize transnational entrepreneurial activity in which migrants maintain ties and shuttle between countries, "importing" goods, food, music, and cultural events from the home country to their coethnics in transnational communities abroad and/or taking back electronic and other first-world consumer goods to their home communities. Transnational entrepreneurial activity is a reaction to the strictures and limitations imposed on migrants in their places of destination (e.g., relegation to low-level service jobs) and the opportunities opened up by globalization. Additionally, migrant communities engage in transnational political and cultural activities, such as raising money for candidates in home elections, helping to rebuild institutions in their communities of origin, and sponsoring visiting dance, music, cultural groups, and sports teams.

Transnational economic and political involvement has been encouraged by legal changes that make dual or even multiple official citizenships accessible to more people. In the last decade, major labor exporting countries, such as Mexico and the Philippines, have been promoting transnational ties as opposed to permanent relocation. "Governments of sending nations have started to perceive their expatriate communities as a source of investments, entrepreneurial initiatives, markets for home country companies and even political representation abroad" (Portes 1999:467). Continuing ties also ensure continuing remittances, a significant source of foreign currency (Parrenas 1998). The Mexican government, under the administration of Salinas de Gortari, set up a Program for Mexican Communities Abroad (PCME) within the foreign ministry to promote arts, culture, and business ties (Roberts et al. 1999:251). Governments interested in promoting transnational ties have encouraged dual citizenship by not denaturalizing nationals who take up other citizenships, but by conferring their citizenship on children of nationals born abroad, by allowing those who had renounced their citizenship earlier, to renaturalize, and by allowing dual citizens to vote (Schuck 1998).

Traditionally, the U.S. has taken the position that one can have allegiance to only one country. However, it has held different standards for birthright and naturalized citizens. It has required immigrants wishing to naturalize to "renounce and abjure, absolutely and entirely, all allegiance and fidelity to any" other state. But it has not required renunciation by those holding dual citizenship by birth or descent (Schuck

1998:151). Immigration scholars have begun addressing the philosophical, legal, and practical issues of dual citizenship, which they agree is becoming more common (Pickus 1998). The U.S. is joining other major labor-receiving countries, such as Canada, in viewing dual citizens as useful sources of capital for investment and for providing entry into foreign business networks. This may account for why the U.S. government no longer requires applicants for naturalization to prove they have been denaturalized by their countries of origin and no longer denaturalizes citizens who become citizens of other countries (Schuck 1998).

Transnationality—maintaining dual or even multiple citizenships—is a strategy that individuals can use to maximize economic and social benefits. This "tool," however, is not equally available to all. Nation states differentially enforce borders and regulate membership to favor certain economic interests. Such differential treatment introduces new forms of transnational class, race, and gender inequality.

Aihwa Ong (1999) describes how Chinese entrepreneurs adapt to the new flexible capital accumulation regime through deployment of what she calls flexible citizenship. Hong Kong and Taiwan entrepreneurs can maximize economic opportunities by locating companies and investing in Asia, while simultaneously gaining political security and Western education for their children by establishing residence in Australia, the U.S., or Canada. Male heads of family firms who leave wives and children in the U.S. while shuttling back and forth to Asia are referred to as "astronauts." Wives who are left in charge of overseeing the children's acquisition of cultural capital call themselves "widows." Sometimes children—so called "parachute kids"—are left to manage on their own in a suburban home bought by the family. Overseas education for children is highly valued because it provides an entrée into markets as sons are expected to expand family business interests in the country of residence after graduation. For this class of entrepreneurs, nation-state borders are freely open and continually crossable.[8]

Compare this with the situation of Filipina women who migrate to fill the demand for domestic workers in Europe, North America, Southeast Asia, and the Middle East (Chang 1997; Parrenas 1998). Their situation in Canada is particularly relevant because by worldwide standards, Canada stands high on quality of life and protection of human rights. Nonetheless, under the Live-In Caregiver Programme, foreign domestic workers are subject to indentured servitude. They are compelled by law to live in the homes of their employers for a minimum of two years out of a period of three years. They are legally classified as temporary workers and subject to deportation upon termination of their contracts (Bakan and Stasiulis 1994; Stasiulis and Bakan 1997). These women have typically left behind children and families to whom they send remittances in the Philippines. They are transnational, but they don't have rights or mobility in either place.

Similar inequities are found in differential policies in Western European countries toward Southern and Eastern European (presumptively white) immigrants, for whom citizenship is easily attainable, versus policies toward immigrants from former colonies (presumptively dark individuals), for whom citizenship is difficult to get (Lutz 1997:99). These examples illustrate that national borders are still significant and policed in ways that construct ethnocultural and racial hierarchies.

Differences Within: Questions of National Identity and Group Rights

Increasing racial and cultural differences within nation states raises a second set of issues. With global movement of people, all developed countries are experiencing crises of national identity—what I have spoken about as membership—who belongs and on what grounds? The mixture of cultures within national borders is reanimating debates about whether membership should be based on ethnocultural criteria (e.g., ability to speak the dominant language) or civic criteria (working and paying taxes).

As my historical review shows, the U.S., as a white settler country composed of European immigrants, indigenous peoples, and a variety of nonwhite minorities, has long wrestled with these questions.[9] The dominant framework for understanding integration of immigrants has been assimilationism, in which (predominately European) immigrants became "American" by giving up their original languages and adopting dominant Anglo-American political and cultural values. During more progressive time periods, Asians, Latinos, and other racialized immigrants were also seen as "Americanizable," albeit more slowly than white immigrants—perhaps taking several generations. During less progressive times, these groups were considered unassimilable, incapable of being full citizens.

What has changed dramatically is the predominance of "nonwhites" in contemporary migrant flows. This is fueling what has been seen as a crisis of American identity. Much has been made of the U.S. Census Bureau's projection that "nonwhites"—blacks, Latinos and Asians—will outnumber European Americans within a few decades. Equally significant is the above-mentioned growth of transnational communities within the U.S. Their presence challenges the ethnocultural concept of American citizenship and the ideal of assimilation.

Portes et al. (1999) note that in the new global economy, migrants to the U.S. may have less impetus to adapt to assimilating into American society than immigrants assimilated in the past. Finding their mobility in the U.S. occupational and social structure limited, many migrants find it advantageous to maintain language and cultural ties that enable them to engage in transnational entrepreneurial activity. This may actually be a more attainable way to achieve economic and social mobility in a racially stratified society, than learning to speak standard English, for example.

Transnational migrants are also much less interested in attaining citizenship than earlier immigrants. Whereas 67% of legal immigrants applied for naturalization in 1946, by the early 1990s, only 37% did so (Soysal 1994: 27). This decline in naturalization reflects the declining significance of citizenship for establishing rights and responsibilities. A growing body of administrative rulings and court cases affirms noncitizen residents'—even undocumented immigrants—inclusion in basic civil rights, such as freedom of speech and due process, and in social entitlements such as education, social security, and Medicare. Noncitizens continue to be excluded from direct political participation, notably the right to vote, and from military service, two remaining markers of full citizenship; otherwise the distinction between citizen and noncitizen has become attenuated.[10]

The United States is not alone in confronting a situation in which a significant portion of the population consists of communities that want to reside permanently, but without making formal allegiance to the country, and to be allowed to make a living, get education for their children, and enjoy democratic freedom without assimilating into the dominant culture. After World War II, labor shortages led Western European countries to relax restrictions in order to receive immigrant workers, mostly from the Mediterranean regions, but also from former colonies in Asia, Latin America, Africa, and the Middle East. Labor migrants were considered "guestworkers," temporary residents admitted to meet labor demands. They were expected to leave when labor demands subsided and accordingly were deemed foreigners and excluded from basic rights. However, contrary to expectation, foreign workers stayed and became a permanent part of the population. By the mid-1990s, an estimated 15 million "foreigners" were residing in Europe without formal citizenship status, constituting from 2–18% of the labor forces in host countries (Soysal 1994:17–24).

Unlike settler countries such as the United States and Australia, which have birthright citizenship, European countries do not grant citizenship on the basis of *jus soli*. Children of immigrants born in the host country must go through naturalization processes that involve waiting periods of five to twelve years. However, in response to the increasing permanence of foreign worker populations, some countries with restrictive lineage-based rules liberalized their laws in the 1990s to make citizenship easier or automatic for second- or third-generation persons born in the country. For example, in Germany, the 1990 Foreigners Law made naturalization of immigrant children born in the country or living there for eight years virtually automatic. A reform of the nationality law in 1999 provides dual citizenship for persons born of foreign parents beginning January 1, 2000, and allows foreigners who have resided in Germany for eight years to apply for naturalization (*Migration News* 1999).[12]

Whether the easing of naturalization will vastly stimulate the taking of citizenship is doubtful. Surveys of eligible immigrants indicate low interest in taking on citizenship, only 6% in one 1986 German Ministry of Labor and Social Affairs survey. Annual rates of naturalization in nine European countries in the 1990s averaged only around 1.9% of the foreign population annually (Soysal 1994:25–27).

As in the U.S., civil and social rights are being decoupled from formal citizenship. Soysal's survey of the policies of nine European countries with regard to various categories of noncitizens (guestworkers, applicants for amnesty, permanent residents, migrants from former colonies) found increasing inclusion of noncitizen residents in such rights as family reunification, freedom of jobs and occupations, access to social service programs, and even voting in local elections (Soysal 1994:119–135). On paper, the United States has been on the inclusionary end of the spectrum in terms of allowing immigrants, even undocumented ones, into the full range of civil rights and social provision available to citizens. Yet the relative stinginess of U.S. social provision, compared to European countries, means that noncitizens in the U.S. lack the conditions necessary to fully realize their rights.

So far, I have talked about individual rights and responsibilities that fall within conventional notions of liberal political theory. The existence of heterogeneous communities within the boundaries of the nation poses additional questions of collective identity, group culture, and minority rights. One problem, from the point of view of liberal political theory, is that minority and multicultural rights are, by definition, collective, rather than individual rights. Some theorists have been studying multiculturalism in a variety of societies and are thinking through new ideas about group rights. For example, Will Kymlicka (1995) identifies three kinds of group rights that need to be articulated: representation rights for disadvantaged groups; rights to self-government and autonomy; and multicultural rights—the right to maintain distinct languages, religions, and family patterns without giving up the right to full membership in the larger nation.

Multicultural and group rights have been the focus of transnational immigrant and minority group organizing. Most of these organizations, such as the Council of Associations of Immigrants in Europe are regional in scope. Interestingly, one of the most effective worldwide movements for group rights has been among, not migrants, but indigenous peoples displaced by both settlers and migrants. This is an example of how transnational air travel and electronic communication has opened up new opportunities for excluded and disadvantaged groups to organize more effectively on their own behalf. Native Americans and Native Hawaiians have joined with the Maoris of New Zealand, Australian Aboriginal people, and other indigenous groups in the struggle for land and self-determination. They seek to resist, on the one hand, being transformed into just another domestic minority, and on the other hand, cultural and social absorption. They are using the world stage to call for recognition of their double status as citizens in the nation state and as members of autonomous peoples (Stasiulis and Yuval-Davis 1995).

Rights that Transcend Nation States: The Role of Nation States vs. Supranational Entities

A third set of issues raised by globalization is whether the nation is any longer the relevant entity for grounding rights and responsibilities. Certainly, nation-states are less able to closely regulate capital flows today than in the past when the processing of assets took time. With instantaneous electronic transfers, things happen so quickly that state mechanisms can't keep up. Similarly, with movement of people, when the volume of flow was smaller and more contained, countries had greater control over who came in and out. Japan long prided itself on its homogeneity and maintained that homogeneity through policing of entry and surveillance of residents. But today, more than one hundred 747s land in Tokyo every day, bringing in thousands of people carrying various types of visas. Officials complain that Chinese racketeers have taken over the vice and sex industries, importing thousands of Southeast Asian women on tourist visas, who then melt into the vice district.

Does this mean that nation-states are no longer relevant in terms of regulating membership and protecting rights? The answer is complicated. Nation-states are indeed losing power in relation to global capital, but, since it is in the interest of capitalists to influence population and capital flows in accordance with their interests, national-states still play an important, albeit selective, role in regulating borders. Saskia Sassen (1996b:9) observes that, at the current moment, there is a consensus among states to lift border controls for the flow of capital, information, and services, but "when it comes to immigrants and refugees . . . we see the national state claiming all of its old splendor and asserting its sovereign right to control its borders. . . ."

However, in other areas Sassen (1996a) notes that sovereignty, formerly the domain of the national state, has been partly "unbundled" and "redistributed" to other entities including supranational organizations, international conventions, and private international legal regimes. This redistribution has occurred in the area of rights. As noted above, although still subject to entry restrictions, once in the country, immigrants in Western countries are increasingly accorded the same basic civil and social rights as citizens. The extension of rights to noncitizens has been grounded in appeals to universalistic personal rights, by-passing references to national or territorial-based rights (Jacobson 1996). For Soysal (1994), this shift to a personal rights framework, signals a new "postnational" model in which rights are no longer tied to sovereign nations.

The personal rights framework is one that is formalized and legitimated by what Sassen (1996a:89) calls "an emergent international human rights regime." Soysal (1994) describes an extensive array of transnational covenants, conventions, treaties, and legal instruments that define and guarantee human rights of a variety of groups, including immigrants and refugees. Many of the covenants, including the International Covenant on Civil and Political Rights and the International Covenant on Economic, Social, and Cultural Rights derive from the Universal Declaration of Human Rights adopted by the United Nations in 1948. There are also regional instruments and mechanisms, most notably the European Convention on Human Rights, the provisions of which have been incorporated into the domestic law of many member nations.

Several scholars (e.g., Turner 1993b; Soysal 1994; Jacobson 1996) argue that the above developments represent a shift from a nation-based (and therefore citizenship-based) notion of rights to a more individual-based notion of universal rights. Turner (1995b) suggests that a nation/citizenship-based concept of rights is inadequate to meet the needs of transnational migrants and indigenous peoples who do not wish to be incorporated at the cost of loss of language and culture. It also does not address the growing interconnectedness of economies and the development of global cultures. He favors a human rights approach, which he argues appears to be more universal (articulated by many nations through the UN charter); more contemporary (not tied to the nation state); and more progressive (not related to management of people by a state).

Yet, the nation state remains the primary vehicle in the actual enforcement of these new universalistically defined rights. As Soysal (1994) notes, the international conventions on human rights (and, it might be added, environmental, labor, gender, and refugee rights) often lack specificity and are not binding. Activists trying to stop the global trafficking in women, who spoke at the Berkshire Conference on Women's History in June 1999, pointed out that, even when international tribunals and courts take up a case, they can only make advisory rulings. There is no enforcement mechanism or ability to order payment of fines or reparations.

Paradoxically, then, the realization of human rights still depends on the nation state's enforcement. The European Convention on Human Rights is effective, in part, because the provisions have been incorporated into the domestic laws of many member nations. The United States has been slow to ratify or adopt international standards in its laws. However, in attempting to deal with cases involving undocumented immigrants since the 1970s, U.S. courts have increasingly referred to human rights codes (Jacobson 1996).

With regard to capital flow and monetary policies, regulatory power has been devolved onto supranational entities, such as the International Monetary Fund (IMF), the World Bank, and the World Trade Organization (WTO). These entities controlled by the capitalists in richer nations, dictate economic and social policy to poorer nation states. They have forced former eastern bloc and third-world countries to undertake so-called "structural adjustment" thereby increasing access to their economies by global capital. These mandated policies include privatization, reduction of state expenditures, and cutting of social services and welfare for the poor, all as conditions for being allowed into the new global economy. The burden of adjustment, thus, falls disproportionately on the poor and women (Cornia, Jolly, and Stewart 1987; Sparr 1994).

The great economic leverage held by these economic supranational bodies has made them the target of activists attempting to get transnational human, environmental, health, safety, and labor issues addressed. They note that these bodies have extensive standards on economic and monetary issues and provisions to impose economic sanctions for violations of economic regulations. Human rights activists would like to see similar standards and mechanisms in place for human rights. Countries, such as Thailand, have been forced to make major concessions in the economic realm through structural adjustment programs in order to receive loans, investments, and other economic benefits. However, Thailand also has been "allowed" to have a thriving slave trade, including the sale of daughters for money or consumer goods, such as refrigerators and televisions (Bales 1999).

In many cases, one suspects there is a tradeoff: the IMF and the World Bank force third-world countries to swallow the bitter pill of economic restructuring, in exchange for which, these same countries are allowed to maintain oppressive "patriarchal" practices in the name of tradition and religion. Governments of many countries that have been integrated into the global economy are controlled by religious fundamentalists who impose laws and practices that subject women to physical and psychological constraint, abuse, and even death at the hands of male family members and religious authorities.

Resistance to the far-reaching power of WTO culminated in one of the largest mass protests in recent U.S. history in late 1999, as WTO directors and representatives met in Seattle to discuss various trade and investment matters. Thousands of activists, ranging from American isolationists to organized labor, from environmentalists to public interest groups converged and staged protests that delayed the start of the meeting. The atmosphere contributed to the eventual collapse of the talks, as third-world representatives refused to accept provisions limiting their autonomy (Verhovek and Greenhouse 1999; Egan 1999).

Conclusions

In summary, in the first part of this presentation, I examined the race and gendered definitions and contestation of boundaries, meanings, and conditions of citizenship in the United States. These contestations reveal the way in which citizenship has both created inequality and been a vehicle for struggles to achieve greater equality. I then examined three kinds of challenges to citizenship posed by economic globalization: the rise of transnationalism, in which a significant portion of the population maintains routine and daily ties and commitments in countries of origin and in countries of residence, sometimes including dual or multiple official citizenships; the increasing diversity of cultural communities within the boundaries of nation states, which has given rise to problems of how difference can be accommodated within a larger solidarity; and human rights issues that transcend the boundaries of nation states and membership in those states.

I return to questions posed earlier: Is citizenship still relevant and useful? Are the themes of membership, rights, responsibilities, and conditions still relevant? I would argue with Turner (1995b), that in the short run, we need to maintain a dual stance, one that recognizes the legitimacy of both traditional notions of rights associated with membership in a community (citizenship rights) and universal rights not tied to membership in particular nation states (personal or human rights). For many situations and groups, rights claims need to deploy both types. Highly marginalized groups, such as indigenous peoples, stateless persons, and sexual minorities must still call on the nation states in which they reside to guarantee and implement civil, political, and social rights and responsibilities. At the same time, the basis for these claims needs to be detached from status in the nation-state and framed in terms of more universalistic notions of individual and group rights.

Relatively neglected by much of the recent literature on postnational citizenship is the issue of political participation and responsibility for governing. Rights talk continues to take central stage and focus has been on opening access to civil and social rights for all; however, as Soysal's survey on noncitizen rights found, voting in national elections was still reserved for citizens. What does it mean to democratic governance when larger and larger portions of a society do not even vote, either out of indifference or because they are disfranchised?

Simultaneously, the new global economy is contributing to new forms of race, class, and gender inequality by widening economic disparities, displacing people from land which provided self sufficiency, and eroding accustomed ways of life that can't be addressed in a strictly domestic context. Struggles for economic justice and human rights, thus, need to be moved to the transnational level. The same technological developments which have allowed multinational corporations and transnational financial institutions to increase their reach and mobility, can be used by migrants, refugees, women, labor unions, AIDs sufferers, and organizations representing marginalized communities to create transnational ties and organize for social change across borders.

Notes:

1. I say "equality," though I mean "a state of less inequality.' Complete equality has never been attained.

2. For the classical origins of these ideas in Greek and Roman thought, see Pocock 1995.

3. Brubaker (1996) points out these two definitions of nationhood-territorial/political vs. personal/ethnocultural are two independent understandings that have generally been associated with differing regions and countries. In relatively culturally homogeneous territories, there may not exist tension between the two conceptions. However, in the U.S., as well as in other territorial units with ethnoculturally intermixed communities (as in much of Central and Eastern Europe), the two models are not easily reconciled.

4. In a recent book, Kerber 1998, extensively analyzes court cases to argue that women's citizenship rights and duties have been differently defined than men's citizenship rights and duties.

5. Though there doesn't seem to be a necessary connection, in fact, periods when there has been a strong activist federal government have been associated with civic definitions of citizenship and protection of minority rights, while periods when there has been federal deferral to states' rights have been associated with ethnocultural Americanism and support for slavery, segregation, and discrimination against despised minorities. This is a problem for us on the Left. Often, our proffered solution to problems of inequality is to call for more democratic participation, particularly at the local level. However, American history shows that democratic participation has not been salutary for minority rights. For example, initiative petitions that allowed ordinary citizens to write and pass laws directly were instituted by states during the Progressive Era as democratic reforms to clean up politics. However, initiative measures have most often been used to restrict minority rights and repeal civil rights protections. Instances from my home state, California, include Proposition 13, passed by voters in 1963, to repeal the Rumford Fair Housing Law; Proposition 209, in 1997, to ban affirmative action programs by state agencies; and Proposition 287 to deny social services to undocumented immigrants in 1998. This raises a big challenge: how do we reconcile democratic participation and protection of minority rights?

6. Smith notes that the two theories have, in some sense, complementary strengths and weaknesses in dealing with the issue of equality in the face of difference. The virtue of the liberal formulation is its universalism and rooting in the notion of natural rights, which can be deployed to claim rights for every human being irrespective of differences in status, gender, race, and ability. The main shortcoming is that rights are defined negatively. All citizens are accorded the right to pursue happiness, but whether all have the means or capacity to do so is not a matter for concern. The strong point of the republican formulation is that it addresses the need for a collective orientation that transcends individual interest. The main shortcoming is that the notion of a common good often assumes a socially homogenous community.

7. In some non-European countries, voting is compulsory, e.g., Egypt and Australia (Yuval-Davis 1997).

8. Canada seeks to draw these transnationals by granting permanent residency to anyone investing $300,000 in Canada. In order to attract Pacific Rim capital, U.S. immigration laws were amended in 1990 to create an "investor" category allowing the granting of green cards in return for $1 million investments that result in ten jobs (Ong 1999:130).

9. See Stasiulis and Yuval-Davis (1995) for a comparative study of settler societies.

10. Of course, these distinctions are subject to being reinstituted, as illustrated by the passage of Proposition 207 by the California electorate to deny welfare benefits to undocumented immigrants.

11. Although recruitment of foreign labor ceased in most of Western Europe by 1974, the population of foreigners continued to grow due to family reunification and birth of children (Soysal 1994).

12. However, not all countries liberalized their law: France enacted tighter rules to make citizenship of French-born children of immigrants less automatic (Soysal 1994:26).

References

Anderson, Benedict. 1983. *Imagined Communities: Reflections on the Origins and Spread of Nationalism*. London: Verso.

Bakan, Abigail B., and Daiva Stasiulis. 1994. "Foreign domestic worker policy in Canada and the social boundaries of citizenship." *Science and Society* 58, 1:7–33.

Bales, Kevin. 1999. *Disposable People: New Slavery in the Global Economy*. Berkeley: University of California Press.

Basch, Linda, Nina Glick Schiller, and Cristina Blanc-Szanton. 1994. *Nations Unbound: Transnational Projects, Postcolonial Predicaments, and Deterritorialized Nation-States*. New York: Gordon and Breach.

Boris, Eileen. 1998. "When work is slavery." *Social Justice* 25, 1:18–44.

Brubaker, Rogers. 1996. *Nationalism Reframed: Nationhood and the National Question in the New Europe*. Cambridge, UK: Cambridge University Press.

Chang, Grace. 1994. "Undocumented latinas: The new 'employable mothers.'" In *Mothering: Ideology, Experience and Agency*, eds. Evelyn Glenn, Grace Chang, and Linda Forcey, 259–286. New York: Routledge.

———. 1997. "The global trade in Filipina workers." In *Dragon Ladies: Asian American Feminists Breathe Fire*, ed. Sonia Shah, 132–152. Boston: South End Press.

Cornia, Giovanni A. 1987. *Adjustment with a Human Face*, eds. Richard Jolly, and Frances Stewart. Oxford: Clarendon Press.

Crawford, James. 1992. *Hold Your Tongue: Bilingualism and the Politics of English Only*. Reading, MA: Addison-Wesley.

Diamond, Sara. 1996. "Right-wing politics and the anti-immigration cause." *Social Justice* 23, 3:154–168.

DuBois, Ellen Carol. 1978. *Feminism and Suffrage*. Ithaca, NY: Cornell University Press.

Egan, Timothy. 1999. "New World disorder; free trade takes on free speech." *New York Times* December 5, Week in Review.

Foner, Eric. 1988. *Reconstruction: America's Unfinished Revolution*. New York: Harper and Row.

———. 1990. "From slavery to citizenship: Blacks and the right to vote." In *Voting and the Spirit of American Democracy*, ed. Donald W. Rogers. Urbana and Chicago: University of Illinois Press.

———. 1998. *The Story of American Freedom*. New York: Norton.

Forbath, William. 1996. "Race, class and citizenship." Unpublished paper.

Fraser, Nancy, and Linda Gordon. 1993. "Contract versus charity: Why is there no social citizenship in the United States?" *Socialist Review* 212, 3:45–68.

———. 1994. "A genealogy of dependence: Tracing a keyword of the U.S. welfare state." *Signs* 19, 2:309–336.

Giddens, Anthony. 1996. "T. H. Marshall, the state and democracy." In *Citizenship Today: The Contemporary Relevance of T. H. Marshall*, eds. Martin Bulmer and Anthony M. Rees, 65–80. London: UCL Press.

Glenn, Evelyn. 2000. "Creating a caring society." *Contemporary Sociology* 29, 1 (forthcoming).

Glick Shiller, Nina, Linda Basch, and Cristina Blanc-Szanton. 1992. "Transnationalism: A new analytic framework for understanding migration." In *Toward a Transnational Perspective on Migration: Race, Class, Ethnicity, and Nationalism Reconsidered*, eds. Nina Glick Schiller, Linda Basch, and Cristina Blanc-Szanton, 25–52. Annals of the New York Academy of Sciences v. 645.

Gordon, Linda. 1994. *Pitied, But Not Entitled: Single Women and the History of Welfare*. New York: Free Press.

Greenhouse, Linda. 1999. "The justices decide who's in charge." *New York Times*, June 27, 1, 4, Week in Review.

Gunderson, Joan R. 1987. "Independence, citizenship, and the American Revolution." *Signs* 13, 1:59–77.

Hall, Stuart, and David Held. 1989. "Citizens and citizenship." In *New Times*, eds. Stuart Hall and Jacques Martin, 173–188. London: Lawrence and Wishart.

Haney Lopez, Ian F. 1996. *White by Law: The Legal Construction of Race*. New York: New York University Press.

Horsman, Reginald. 1981. *Race and Manifest Destiny*. Cambridge, MA: Harvard University Press.

Jacobson, David. 1996. *Rights across Borders: Immigration and the Decline of Citizenship*. Baltimore, MD: Johns Hopkins University Press.

Kerber, Linda. 1980. *Women of the Republic: Intellect and Ideology in Revolutionary America*. Chapel Hill: University of North Carolina Press.

———. 1998. *No Constitutional Right to Be Ladies*. New York: Hill and Wang.

Kettner, James. 1978. *The Development of American Citizenship, 1608–1870*. Chapel Hill: University of North Carolina Press.

Kristof, Nicholas D. 1999. "At this rate, we'll be global in another hundred years." *New York Times* May 23, Week in Review.

Kymlicka, Will. 1995. *Multicultural Citizenship: A Liberal Theory of Minority Rights*. Oxford: Clarendon Press.

Lister, Ruth. 1997. "Citizenship: Toward a Feminist Synthesis." *Feminist Review* 57, Autumn: 28–48.

Litwak, Leon F. 1961. *North of Slavery: The Negro in the Free States, 1790-1860*. Chicago: University of Chicago Press.

Lutz, Helma. 1997. "The limits of European-ness: Immigrant women in fortress Europe." *Feminist Review*, 57:93–111.

Marshall, T. H. 1964. *Class, Citizenship, and Social Development*. Garden City, NY: Doubleday.

Migration News. 1999. "Germany: Option Model Approved," 6, 6, June, http://migration.ucdavis.edu.

Mink, Gwendolyn. 1994. *The Wages of Motherhood: Inequality in the Welfare State, 1917–1942*. Ithaca, NY: Cornell University Press.

Mittleman, James. 1997. "The dynamics of globalization." In *Globalization: Critical Reflections*, ed. James Mittleman, 1–19. Boulder, CO: Lynne Rienner.

Nelson, Barbara. 1990. "The origins of the two-channel welfare state: Workman's Compensation and Mother's Aid." In *Women, the State and Welfare*, ed. Linda Gordon, 123–151. Madison: University of Wisconsin Press.

Ohmae, Ken'ichi. 1999. *The Borderless World: Power and Strategy in the Interlinked Economy*, rev. ed. New York: HarperBusiness.

Okin, Susan. 1979. *Women in Western Political Thought*. Princeton, NJ: Princeton University Press.

Oliver, Melvin L., and Thomas M. Shapiro. 1995. *Black Wealth/White Wealth: A New Perspective on Racial Inequality*. New York: Routledge.

Ong, Aihwa. 1999. *Flexible Citizenship: The Cultural Logic of Transnationality*. Durham, NC: Duke University Press.

Parrenas, Rhacel. 1998. *The Global Servants: Filipina Servants in Rome and Los Angeles*. Ph. D. dissertation, University of California, Berkeley.

Pateman, Carole. 1988. *The Sexual Contract*. Cambridge, UK: Polity Press.

———. 1989. *The Disorder of Women*. Stanford: Stanford University Press.

Pedersen, Susan. 1993. *Family, Dependence, and the Origins of The Welfare State: Britain and France, 1914–1945*. Cambridge, MA: Cambridge University Press.

Perea, Juan F. 1997. "'Am I an American or not?' Reflections on citizenship, Americanization, and race." In *Immigration and Citizenship in the Twenty-first Century*, ed. Noah M. J. Pickus, 49–76. Lanham, MD: Rowman & Littlefield.

Pickus, Noah M. J. 1998. "Introduction." In *Immigration and Citizenship in the Twenty-First Century*, ed. Noah M. J. Pickus, xvii-xxxiii. Lanham, MD: Rowman & Littlefield.

Pocock, J. G. A. 1995. "The ideal of citizenship since classical times." In *Theorizing Citizenship*, ed. Ronald Beiner, 29–52. Albany: State University of New York Press.

Portes, Alejandro. 1999. "Conclusion: Toward a new world-the origins and effects of transnational activities." *Ethnic and Racial Studies* 22, 2:463–477.

Portes, Alejandro, Luis F. Guarnizo, and Patricia Landolt. 1999. "Introduction: Pitfalls and promise of an emergent research field. " *Ethnic and Racial Studies* 22, 2:217–237.

Ringer, Benjamin B. 1983. *We the People and Others: Duality and America's Treatment of Its Racial Minorities*. New York: Tavistock.

Roberts, Bryan R., Reanne Frank, and Fernando Lozano-Ascensio. 1999. "Transnational migrant communities and Mexican migration in the U.S." *Ethnic and Racial Studies* 22, 2:238–266.

Roberts, Dorothy. 1997. *Killing the Black Body: Race, Reproduction, and the Meaning of Liberty*. New York: Pantheon.

Rodriguez, Nestor. 1996. "The battle for the border: Notes on autonomous migration, transnational communities, and the state." *Social Justice* 23, 3:21–37.

Roediger, David. 1991. *The Wages of Whiteness: Race and the Making of the American Working Class*. London: Verso.

Sainsbury, Diane. 1996. *Gender, Equality and Welfare States*. Cambridge, UK: Cambridge University Press.

Sassen, Saskia. 1996a. *Losing Control? Sovereignty in an Age of Globalization*. New York: Columbia University Press.

———. 1996b. "Beyond sovereignty: Immigration policy making today." *Social Justice* 23, 3:9–20.

Schuck, Peter. 1998. "Plural citizenships." In *Immigration and Citizenship in the Twenty-First Century*, ed. Noah M. J. Pickus, 149–191. Lanham, MD: Rowman & Littlefield.

Shklar, Judith. 1991. *American Citizenship: The Quest for Inclusion*. Cambridge, MA: Harvard University Press.

Skocpol, Theda. 1992. *Protecting Soldiers and Mothers: The Origins of Social Policy in the United States*. Cambridge, MA: Harvard University Press.

Smith, Rogers M. 1989. "'One United People': Second-class female citizenship and the American quest for community." *Yale Journal of Law and the Humanities* 1:229–293.

Soysal, Yasemin Nuhoglu. 1994. *Limits of Citizenship: Migrants and Postnational Membership in Europe*. Chicago: University of Chicago Press.

Sparr, Pamela (ed.). 1994. *Mortgaging Women's Lives: Feminist Critiques of Structural Adjustment*. London: Zed.

Stasiulis, Daiva, and Abigail B. Bakan. 1997. "Negotiating citizenship: The case of foreign domestic workers in Canada." *Feminist Review* 57, Autumn: 112–139.

Stasiulis, Daiva, and Nira Yuval-Davis. 1995. "Introduction: Beyond dichotomies-gender, race, ethnicity, and class in settler societies." In *Unsettling Settler Societies: Articulations of Gender, Race, Ethnicity, and Class*, eds. Daiva Stasiulis and Nira Yuval-Davis, 38. London: Sage.

Titmus, Richard. 1958. *Essays on "the Welfare State."* London: Allen & Unwin.

Turner, Brian S. 1986. *Citizenship and Capitalism: The Debate over Reformism.* London: Allen & Unwin.

Turner, Brian S. 1993a. "Contemporary problems in the theory of citizenship." In *Citizenship and Social Theory*, ed. Brian S. Turner, 1–19. London: Sage.

———. 1993b. "Outline of a theory of human rights." In *Citizenship and Social Theory*, ed. Brian S. Turner, 162–190. London: Sage.

Verhovek, Sam Howe, and Steven Greenhouse. 1999. "Seattle is under curfew after disruptions." *New York Times* December 1.

Woodward, C. Van, ed. 1974. *The Strange Career of Jim Crow*, 3rd rev. New York: Oxford University Press.

Young, Iris Marion. 1989. "Polity and group difference: A critique of the ideal of universal citizenship." *Ethics* 99, 2:250–274.

Yuval-Davis, Nira. 1997. "Women, citizenship and difference." *Feminist Review* 57, Autumn: 4–27.

CHAPTER 16

Transnational Mobilization and Civil Rights in Northern Ireland

Gregory M. Maney

While certainly existing prior to World War II, transnational issue networks have flourished in the postwar era as major advances in communication, transportation, and information technologies have increased the scope, frequency, and intensity of interactions across borders. I define transnational issue networks as coalitions of nongovernmental and/or governmental organizations based in more than one society, engaging in, with some degree of cross-societal communication and exchange, activities to promote a common explicit objective on an issue of mutual concern.[1] These networks have formed around issues such as arms proliferation, human rights standards, democratization, development, environmental protection, labor relations, and the statuses of women, indigenous peoples, and ethnic minorities.

Research, to date, has emphasized the positive contributions of transnational issue networks to domestic protest capacities and to campaigns that successfully alter institutional policies at the national and international levels (Keohane and Nye 1977; Meyer and Marullo 1992; Pagnucco and McCarthy 1992; Sikkink 1993; Pagnucco and Atwood 1994; Risse-Kappen 1995; Smith 1995; Coy 1997; Schulz 1998; Hrycak 1999; Rothman and Oliver 1999). While clearly establishing the importance of transnational issue networks, this literature has largely overlooked the possible negative consequences of international involvement for "domestic" protest, conflict, and social change. Are there instances where external intervention diminishes the resources and organizational capacities available to a network for mobilization, reduces levels of cooperation among participating organizations, and diverts attention away from generating pressure on behalf of common objectives?

To explore how mobilizing upon an issue in more than one society impacts the ability of an issue network to effectively pursue its goals, I examined international activities in support of the civil rights movement in Northern Ireland (1967–1972). From its inception in 1920, the state of Northern Ireland has witnessed conflict between the mostly Protestant majority of the population supporting a political union with Great Britain and the largely Catholic minority seeking the reunification of Northern Ireland with the other twenty-six counties of the island of Ireland. A deep desire to ensure the retention of British links coupled with a recalcitrant, irredentist opposition produced political and economic institutions largely controlled by, and favoring, the Protestant unionist majority. The civil rights movement in Northern Ireland, together with its support abroad, effectively challenged the second-class citizenship status of the Catholic nationalist minority without raising the issue of partition.[2] The network demanded fundamental changes in housing allocation, the electoral system, and policing. Ensuing policy changes resulted in a violent backlash from the hardline "loyalist" segment of the unionist population. The backlash, in turn, led to the renewal of an armed republican campaign for Irish reunification. As the civil rights movement began to decline, many promised reforms remained unimplemented or were reversed. Ironically, the transnational network supporting civil rights demands brought Northern Ireland as close to, and as far away from, the nonviolent institutionalization of political dissent as it has ever come. Understanding the roles played by external actors, therefore, promises lessons regarding transnational dimensions of domestic protest, conflict, and social change.

Because researchers have only recently begun to conceptualize barriers to successful cooperation across borders, I draw upon both national-level and transnational-level studies to, both identify and develop a series of concepts explaining the negative dynamics that can emerge within transnational issue networks. I, then, apply these concepts to the Northern Ireland case. A number of ideas drawn upon here, such as structures of political opportunity and resource competition, have their roots in analyses of social movements taking place during the 1960s and 1970s. While developed in reference to more recent instances of organizational interaction, other concepts, such as the strength of personal ties and frame alignment processes, still identified important sources of tension within a case study occurring roughly three decades ago.

While external organizations initially assisted the civil rights movement in Northern Ireland, their involvement eventually weakened the movement's ability to achieve its demands. Outside participation, not only exacerbated problems frequently encountered by domestic coalitions, it also introduced new barriers to interorganizational cooperation. In particular, heightened protest internationally contributed in a number of ways to reduced cooperation, increased feuding, and distractions within the issue network. These findings suggest that, contrary to expectations based on political process theory, transnational mobilization[3] not only can facilitate, but also can hinder, the effective pursuit of social change.

Theory Obstacles to Effective Transnational Mobilization

Research on social movement organizations operating within the context of the nation-state has identified four types of factors shaping coalition dynamics: structural, organizational, cultural, and ideological.[4] Although empirically intertwined, analytically, it is useful to distinguish among them. In the sections that follow, I discuss how mobilizing across borders during a period of heightened protest, internationally affects each set of factors. The literature's emphasis upon building coalitions often necessitates the introduction of factors conducive to cooperation prior to discussion of converse factors that impede cooperation across borders. In addition, because the case study involves ethnic issues, I devote considerable attention to the impact of transnational migration upon network dynamics.

STRUCTURAL FACTORS

Structures of Political Opportunity. Exceptional political opportunities or threats facilitate coalition formation (Staggenborg 1986; Hathaway and Meyer 1993[5]). Conversely, the passing of such opportunities or threats hastens their demise as organizations pursue other issues and form new alliances where they perceive greater opportunities or threats (Jenkins 1987; Meyer and Immig 1993; Meyer and Whittier 1994). While undertheorized, instances of this phenomenon can also be observed on an international level. When the Dominican Revolutionary Party lost control of the presidency in 1986, the transnational network demanding voting rights for Dominicans abroad waned until a resurgence in the 1990s (Perez-Godoy 1999).

Issue Network Overlap. Because of their national or local levels of analyses, past research on coalitions has not identified problems associated with issue network overlap. Concepts like "families of social movements" (della Porta and Rucht 1995) and "social movement spillover" (Meyer and Whittier 1994) capture the tendency of social movement organizations using similar collective action frames to work together on multiple issues. As a result, local and national-level networks formed around different issues often have overlapping memberships (i.e., share organizations in common). For instance, Gerhards and Rucht (1992) find that two coalitions of West German organizations—one protesting against a visit by U.S. President Ronald Reagan, and the other protesting an annual meeting of the International Monetary Fund and World Bank—had roughly one-third of their organizational memberships in common. While similarities between collective action frames increase the likelihood of organizations cooperating with one another, considerable differences between these frames make cooperation more difficult (Benford 1993). As a result, little overlap tends to occur between networks of domestic organizations with contrasting messages regarding domestic social stratification. Five Groups upholding the distributive status quo in one domestic issue arena are not likely to support redistribution in others, particularly during periods of heightened polarization where widespread unrest threatens to undermine the existing social order in its entirety.

Transnational issue networks, however, are more likely to bring together organizations that fall on opposite sides of major social cleavages and ideological divisions within the societies where they are based. Groups that deny structural inequalities in a domestic context may more readily acknowledge them in other societies where their own status, conduct, and identities are not directly in question. Furthermore, selective emphasis by a national mainstream media or state, upon the grievances of subordinated social groupings in hostile states, may prompt action by organizations opposing efforts to address similar grievances at home or in allied states (Lee and Craig 1992;

Carragee 1996). For example, in 1973, the American Federation of Labor-Congress of Industrial Organizations (AFL-CIO) assisted a U.S. government-backed military coup against a democratically elected socialist regime in Chile (Sims 1991). Less than a decade later, the Federation supported the Solidarity movement in Communist Poland—a regime opposed by the U.S. government and negatively portrayed in the American media. In so doing, the AFL-CIO joined with organizations they had previously opposed on Chile, such as the World Council of Churches.

The tendency for mobilization across borders to bring together foes on other issues frequently leads to tensions within transnational issue networks. Using the same example, objections by leftist American and Western European nongovernmental organizations (INGOs) to international human rights activities based on Cold-War politics (Cortright 1993; Kleidman 1993) ensured tensions with AFL-CIO "cold warriors" belonging to the pro-Solidarity network. Other issues also divided the network, such as Palestinian–Israeli relations (Abraham, et al. 1988).

Transnational migration offers another source of antagonisms associated with issue network overlap. Ethnic groups that are structurally subordinated through inward or outward migration flows, may come to form part of a structurally dominant group. In the case of emigration, transnational issue networks supporting the mobilization of a subjugated ethnic group back home, will probably include, not only diaspora-based organizations, but organizations representing marginalized ethnic groups within the society or societies where the diaspora constitutes part of an ethnic/racial elite. Given the likelihood of movements among subordinated ethnic groups emerging during periods of heightened protest internationally, antagonisms frequently erupt within transnational networks addressing ethnic claims as parallels are drawn between the status and grievances of the ethnic group supported abroad and ethnic groups excluded at home.

ORGANIZATIONAL FACTORS

Even in the absence of negative consequences emerging from issue network overlap, poorly organized transnational issue networks may not be able to take advantage of precipitous structures of political opportunity internationally. Underdeveloped and uneven organizational capacities, weak ties between members of different organizations, and resource competition among organizations participating in the network—all present barriers to effective cooperation across borders. I now discuss each of these factors in turn.

Organizational Capacities. On a national level, researchers have found that an underdeveloped organizational field militates against successful "mesomobilization"[6] (Gerhards and Rucht 1992). Recent studies of transnational networks have reached similar conclusions. The general absence and overall weakness of nongovernmental organizations in Mexico and Guatemala during the 1970s, and the poorest, rural regions in post-war El Salvador hindered transnational mobilization on human rights and rural development issues, respectively (Keck and Sikkink 1998; Flint 1999). A study of two separate indigenous rights campaigns found that strong, indigenous, grassroots organizational capacities contributed to more balanced interaction and effective cooperation across borders (Maney 1999). Conversely, weak local capacities resulted in unilateral influence and decision making by INGOs resulting in a less successful campaign to protect indigenous rights.

The specific patterns of both transnational migration and a given international cycle of protest affect the organizational capacities of transnational networks addressing ethnic issues. Large, long-standing, and ongoing emigration flows tend to produce sizable and well-established diaspora-based organizations (Hrycak 1999). Conversely, low levels of emigration, resulting from immigration controls or improved conditions in the homeland, can hinder organizing. The location of migrant populations also impacts their ability to participate in transnational issue networks. Ethnic enclaves in major urban areas achieve an ecological concentration conducive to organizing (Topp 1997). More dispersed and rural patterns of emigration render the opposite effect as lower levels of interaction and a smaller local resource base constrain capacity building. In addition, since heightened levels of protest entail the formation and utilization of organizational capacities, it follows that organizations in societies most caught up in the wave of international protest will, *ceteris paribus*, be most central to network activities, while those in societies escaping turmoil will play only minor roles.

Strength of Ties. Since Granovetter's (1985) influential work, a large body of research has emphasized the importance of strong personal ties for effective interorganizational cooperation (e.g., della Porta 1988; Opp and Gern 1993; Evans 1995). These relationships are characterized by a high degree of familiarity, informality, and reciprocity that facilitate communication, cooperation, and planning among the individuals involved. Frequent interaction generates the trust, sense of group identity, and commitment characteristic of relations between actors with strong personal ties (Powell 1990; Carley 1991). Studies of transnational networks have reached similar conclusions (Sikkink 1993; Smith 1995; Keck and Sikkink 1998). It follows, then, that organizations with weak ties between their members will operate less effectively.

The international patterns of both migration and protest affect the strength of ties within a transnational ethnic network. Migrant populations that retain strong individual and organizational ties across borders are more likely to effectively assist movements originating in their homelands as seen, for instance, in diaspora support for the antifascist movement in Italy and independence rebellions in Ireland (Topp 1997; Hanagan 1998). A failure to maintain contacts, on the other hand, makes close cross-societal communication and exchange more difficult. Moreover, strong cross-societal ties are likely to emerge among individuals and groups adopting the collective action frame, collective identity, and forms of contention characteristic of an international protest cycle. For instance, close friendships arose between members of the American New Left and the German New Left it inspired (McAdam and Rucht 1993). Conversely, individuals and organizations from societies with lower levels of protest will, *ceteris paribus*, have weaker ties.

Resource Competition. Organizational imperatives may override strong personal ties existing between individuals affiliated with different groups. Research in the resource mobilization tradition has identified problems associated with competition for resources among organizations advancing the same or similar causes (Zald and McCarthy 1980).

Concerns about organizational maintenance can lead to either attempted "takeovers" of a coalition or, in contrast, to minimal contributions to its efforts. Both actions produce tensions (Staggenborg 1986; Hathaway and Meyer 1993:5). In a study of human rights groups mainly targeting the United Nations, Smith (1995) notes competition among transnational social movement organizations with similar constituencies. Similarly, Flint (1999) finds that differential access to resources provided by sister cities created conflict among domestic agrarian organizations seeking rural development in El Salvador.

CULTURAL FACTORS

The existence of political opportunities and strong organizational capacities still does not guarantee the emergence of a successful issue network. An emotive impetus must be present to compel organizations not only to act, but act in concert with each other. The relevance of cultural factors, therefore, must be carefully considered. Just as a homogeneous membership increases the durability of networks, a heterogeneous membership can render domestic coalitions highly tenuous (Carley 1991; McPherson, Popielarz, and Drobnic 1992). Differences in collective identities can produce fear and mistrust, inhibiting the development of strong personal ties (Rose 1995; Diaz-Veizades and Chang 1996; Kriesberg 1998). Fear and mistrust are especially likely when identities are constructed in opposition to one or more of the identities or characteristics of other coalition members. Other cultural differences, such as linguistic barriers and styles of presentation, can impede effective communication-preventing consensus, creating misunderstandings, and excluding participants unfamiliar with the modus operandi established within the coalition.

By increasing heterogeneity, transnational issue networks face greater obstacles to positive, sustained interaction. Smith (1994:424–425) finds that even individual organizations experience this challenge: "One major difficulty for transnational social movement organizations is that of integrating culturally diverse and geographically dispersed memberships."

During peaks in protest internationally, a high level of issue network overlap further increases the degree of heterogeneity. As people from markedly different backgrounds interact, the social and cultural distance between them can overwhelm the unity produced by broad agreement on the issue at hand. Diaspora organizations with strong personal ties in the homeland can narrow the cultural gap existing within transnational issue networks. Cultural proximity between those of common ancestry, however, should, by no means, be taken for granted. Ethnic identities and practices are negotiated within, and articulated with, the context of the host country. The fragmented and multifaceted nature of these identities offers opportunities for selective and contrasting emphases upon group conceptions (Ruane and Todd 1996). Even when ethnic identities and practices have been constructed on a mutual and transnational basis, a failure to sustain close, cross-societal ties, over time, can eventually result in divergence. What once faithfully reproduced a collective identity in the homeland, in the course of a generation, may come to be viewed as a fossilized, romantic fantasy. During peaks in international protest, new cultural forms—often linked with protest diffuse rapidly across borders (Brand 1990; McAdam and Rucht 1993; Melucci 1995). When these forms challenge the traditional basis for international solidarity, tensions may surface between those motivated by old versus new ways of thinking and acting.

IDEOLOGICAL FACTORS

Another component of culture—ideology—also plays an important role in coalition dynamics. While the development of a collective action frame that all network members can draw upon is commonly seen as a prerequisite for effective mobilization (Gerhards and Rucht 1992), organizations can disagree to the point where a consensus cannot be reached (Meyer and Kleidman 1991). Such disagreements often reflect different sets of beliefs regarding the underlying social problem, the solution to the problem, and the symbolic-emotive basis for appealing for action (Benford 1993). Furthermore, different analyses of a social problem produce markedly divergent agendas. While some organizations link a host of topics to one common core cause, to those not sharing such an analysis, the issues are unrelated. Consequently, efforts to introduce issues beyond those around which the coalition formed, can create disputes among groups espousing contrasting ideologies.

Exporting and Amplifying Ideological Divisions. The participation of external organizations can exacerbate ideological differences within issue networks. In the case of transnational ethnic networks, Diaspora groups amplify antagonisms, not only by introducing new beliefs, but also by replicating and reinforcing existing ideological divisions in the homeland (Poros 1999). During peaks in international protest, the expanded scope of insurgency and similarity in forms of contention foster the sense that domestic mobilization represents part of a common international struggle transforming the world (Keck and Sikkink 1998). As external organizations intervene on behalf of those with similar beliefs, tensions previously confined to one society are 'exported' to other societies. Moreover, by adding fuel to the fire of existing arguments, organizations in others lands amplify domestic disagreements. As the dissonance reaches a crescendo, the reverberations can shatter the thin cohesion that had previously held a coalition together.

Method

To illustrate the assertions made above, I examined the transnational network of organizations supporting civil rights demands made in Northern Ireland between 1967 and 1972. Because of its timing during the later half of the 1960s, the case offers an excellent opportunity to gain insights on the relationship between international cycles of protest and transnational issue network dynamics. Moreover, with nearly three decades passing, a considerable amount of data on interorganizational relationships within the network has become available. A number of historical accounts, memoirs, and biographies covering the civil rights period in Northern Ireland provide rich sources of relevant information (e.g., Devlin 1969; Arthur 1974; Feeney 1974; Farrell 1976, 1988; McCluskey 1989; Purdie 1990; ODochartaigh 1994; Wilson 1995). I also examined ephemera deposited at the Political Collection of the Linen Hall Library in Belfast, the Hibernica Collection at the Queen's University of Belfast Main Library, and the Public Records Office of Northern Ireland. Research consisted of locating and reading correspondence, minutes, internal memos, publications, and public notices produced by groups described in historical accounts and by those identified as playing key roles in the network.

In addition, during the 1998–1999 academic year, I conducted semistructured interviews with individuals holding leadership positions within the network (Appendix I). Informants were asked to identify organizations, both inside and outside of Northern Ireland, supporting civil rights demands, the degree and forms of cooperation across borders, the contributions of external organizations to civil rights contention, and sources of tension within the network.

From the interviews and archival searches, I created files listing all organizations known to have participated in civil rights contention, their activities, and their relationships with one another. The data set offers insights into the composition, exchanges, and dynamics of the transnational network supporting civil rights demands in Northern Ireland.[7]

Structural Factors

The transnational network supporting civil rights demands in Northern Ireland emerged during a peak in protest internationally and declined rapidly, thereafter, because of the closing of political opportunities and the negative consequences of issue network overlap.

Timing of the Network and Levels of International Participation. The civil rights movement in Northern Ireland emerged as a mass movement at the very peak of protest internationally.[8] The first mass marches were held in Northern Ireland in 1968—one of the most contentious years of the century. As a result, conditions were ripe for the establishment of a vibrant transnational network supportive of civil rights demands in Northern Ireland. Just as some in Northern Ireland protested for an end to the Vietnam War, nuclear disarmament, and the abolition of apartheid, others outside the six counties supported demands for social justice in Northern Ireland (ODochartaigh 1994; Coulter 1988; Farrell 1988; Dooley 1998). For those educated and inspired by events of the day in their own societies and beyond, the civil rights movement in Northern Ireland constituted part of an international struggle to break the chains of oppression and liberate ordinary people from injustice and domination.

To gain an idea of the approximate level of international involvement, I compiled a data file listing all governmental and nongovernmental organizations inside and outside of Northern Ireland known to have supported civil rights demands between 1967 and 1972.[9] The Northern Ireland Civil Rights Association Archive at the Linen Hall Library's Political Collection (herein referred to as LHPC) served as a particularly rich source of information. Table 1 presents three rough measures of involvement. Each suc-

Table 16.1. Geographic Distribution of Organizations Supporting Civil Rights Demands in Northern Ireland, 1967–1972

	Measure 1 All Organizations in Data Set		*Measure 2 Counting Branches as Single Organizations*[b]		*Measure 3 Orgs. and Branches with >1 Recorded Activities*[c]	
Location	*N*	*% of Network*	*N*	*% of Network*	*N*	*% of Network*
Northern Ireland	57	22	101	26	31	49
Great Britain[a]	82	31	128	33	13	21
Republic of Ireland	53	20	67	17	10	16
United States	35	13	60	15	9	14
Belgium/France/Italy Netherlands/W. Germany	12	5	13	3	0	0
Australia/Canada New Zealand	10	4	12	3	0	0
Bulgaria/E. Germany/ Hungary/Poland/USSR	7	3	7	2	0	0
Finland/Iceland/Sweden	4	2	4	1	0	0
Uganda	1	0	1	0	0	0
Subtotals						
Inside Northern Ireland	57	22	101	26	31	49
Outside Northern Ireland	204	78	292	74	32	49
Total	261	100	393	100	63	100

Notes:
Totals not summing to zero due to rounding error.
[a]See note 9.
[b]See note 10.
[c]See note 11.

cessive measure controls for additional factors that might exaggerate the level of international participation. The first measure includes all organizations known to have supported civil rights demands in Northern Ireland. Using this measure, external groups accounted for over 78 percent of all supportive organizations.[10] Second, in an effort to account for variations in organizational structure across societies, chapters/branches of groups were treated as the unit of analysis.[11] Because the Northern Ireland Civil Rights Association served as an umbrella group for organizations working on civil rights, as well as aggressive efforts by the People's Democracy to organize beyond their student base, Northern Ireland had the most centralized organizational field within the network. Nonetheless, chapters based outside the six counties represented nearly three-quarters of all those participating in the network. Third, to control for the possibility of external groups providing only "one-off" assistance or existing on paper only, I pared down the list to include only those organizations and branches where sources offered two or more concrete instances of activities supporting civil rights demands in Northern Ireland. [12] Given the relative scarcity of research and the greater geographic dispersion of archival materials on the activities of organizations located outside of Northern Ireland, one would expect the external share of the network to drop considerably. While more sustained activity occurred within Northern Ireland than in any other single society, the third measure still indicates that there were roughly as many active organizations outside of Northern Ireland as inside.

Insufficient data exist to estimate the relative level of network activity in different societies. In all likelihood, groups in Northern Ireland held more collective public events involving, on average, larger numbers of people than their external counterparts in the network. Nonetheless, Table 1 makes it clear that a large number of organizations outside of Northern Ireland actively supported the movement—supplying information, money, publicity, and political pressure on behalf of the cause. With regard to financial assistance, the main umbrella organization in Northern Ireland, the Northern Ireland Civil Rights Association (NICRA), writes (1978:25):

> The Office and the staff were financed by American dollars which poured into NICRA after the August [1969] violence and by the "widows' mites" gathered in Northern Ireland. As the only readily identifiable anti-unionist organisation from a distance of 3,000 miles, the American support groups had little bother in collecting the much-needed cash.

NICRA depended heavily upon international financial support to fund its activities. As Table 2 shows, large sums came from not only the United States, but a number of other societies as well.

Closing Opportunities, Cyclical Downturn, and Network Decline. Just as increasing political opportunities in Northern Ireland and beyond facilitated the emergence of the transnational network supporting civil rights demands in Northern Ireland, the closing of these opportunities contributed to its decline. By late 1969, a combination of repression and policy concessions raised the likely costs and lowered the likely benefits of further civil rights agitation in Northern Ireland. Escalating violence against demonstrators and the broader Catholic community by the Northern Ireland state and loyalist vigilantes produced a split within the republican movement.[13] In 1970, the majority of republicans opted to effectively exit from the civil rights movement and support an armed campaign for the reunification of Ireland conducted under the newly constituted Provisional Sinn Fein and the Provisional Irish Republican Army.[14] With concessions to key civil rights demands and increasing violence at demonstrations, several leading figures within the civil rights movement formed the Social and Democratic Labour Party (SDLP) in early 1970. The SDLP largely abandoned street politics in favor of pursuing change through legislative arenas. The further intensification of repression sealed the network's demise. On January 30, 1972—commonly known as Bloody Sunday—thirteen civilians were shot to death by British Army paratroopers during a civil rights march against internment. Most observers agree that the civil rights movement ended at this point (NICRA 1978; Devlin-McAliskey 1988; Farrell 1988).[15] In the words of one activist: "things shifted—it was war."

The changed political conditions in Northern Ireland also contributed to tensions and exits beyond its borders. From the network's inception, many external support groups saw the key issue as the reunification of Ireland, not equal rights as British citizens for the Catholic nationalist minority in Northern Ireland. After rioting broke out in Northern Ireland in April of 1969, antagonisms intensified between those wanting to continue the nonviolent pursuit of civil rights demands and those favoring armed insurrection to end the partition of Ireland. The official history of the Northern Ireland Civil Rights Association states: "In America, Australia, and Britain, support groups became divided and confused about what was happening . . ." (NICRA 1978:19–20; LHPC). Much to the annoyance of activists in Northern Ireland who deliberately downplayed Irish nationalist imagery and demands, external organizations increasingly openly advocated reunification. During a parade in New Zealand led by a car adorned with a massive Irish tricolor flag, NICRA Treasurer Ann Hope "had difficulty explaining that I wasn't part of the armed struggle; that the struggle had shifted" (interview with the author). Organizations focusing mainly upon civil rights demands declined rapidly. By the end of 1970, the two largest American organizations supporting the civil rights movement in Northern Ireland no longer existed, as the bulk of their members joined groups supporting armed republicanism.[16]

The shifting of political opportunities in societies beyond Northern Ireland's borders also contributed to the network's decline. The election of a Conservative Party government in Great Britain in 1970, coupled with the increasing threat to sovereignty posed by armed republicanism, hampered the efforts of Labour backbenchers to pressure the British government to intervene in Northern Ireland on behalf of civil rights demands. As a NICRA flier ("NICRA's DEMANDS" nd; LHPC) states:

> The record of the British people has been good in responding to appeals for help. Their Parliament has been much slower to act except under pressure from an informed and aware public opinion. . . . However, the return of the Tories to power, coupled with right-wing Unionist pressure, soon thwarted and ultimately ground the reform program to a halt.

As political opportunities for effective protest faded, the international coalition of organizations supporting civil rights demands in Northern Ireland quickly unraveled. These findings demonstrate the usefulness of structures of political opportunity as a tool for understanding the dynamics prevailing in transnational issue networks.

Table 16.2. Sources of NICRA Revenue for 1972 by Location of Donor

Location	*Amount (£)*	*% of Revenue*
Australia	711.65	4.8
Great Britain	735.00	5.0
New Zealand	704.37	4.8
Northern Ireland	4,744.87	32.1
Republic of Ireland	1,646.85	11.1
United States of America	6,232.92	42.1
Subtotals		
Inside Northern Ireland	4,744.87	32.1
Outside Northern Ireland	10,030.79	67.9
Total	14,775.66	100.0

Source: Account worksheets in the Northern Ireland Civil Rights Association Archive, Linen Hall Library Political Collection.

Issue Network Overlap. Negative dynamics had already emerged prior to the closing of political opportunities, undermining the network's ability to weather the proverbial storm. A number of disagreements arose over issues pertaining to policies and practices outside of Northern Ireland. For example, while most American organizations could agree upon the goal of equal citizenship status for the Catholic nationalist minority in Northern Ireland, disagreements over civil rights for African Americans and U.S. military intervention in Vietnam ensured bitter disputes.[17] Figure 1 illustrates how mobilization of civil rights in Northern Ireland brought together organizations in the United States who, otherwise, had not attempted to cooperate with one another. A portion of groups active in the U.S. civil rights and peace movements also supported civil rights demands in Northern Ireland. These included the Black Panther Party, Communist Party USA, International Socialist Organization, Southern Christian Leadership Conference, Students for a Democratic Society, and Young Socialists of America. However, Irish-American organizations involved in the network (signified by the bold ellipse) such as the American Congress for Irish Freedom (ACIF), the Ancient Order of Hibernians (AOH), and Clann na Gael-opposed the U.S. civil rights movement and supported the war in Vietnam.

Like the American public as a whole, Irish Americans were deeply divided over issues of racial equality and U.S. military intervention in Vietnam. To articulate and attract support, the National Association for Irish Justice (NAIJ)—an umbrella organization with a young, diverse, and mostly progressive membership—compared the plight of Catholics in Northern Ireland to the struggles of African Americans and the Vietnamese people (interview with Ann Hope). In contrast, in older, working-class, urban areas, such as South Boston, a racially informed ethnonationalist identity forged over a century of competition for group advancement and preservation fueled opposition to both the U.S. civil rights and peace movements (Allen 1994; Ignatiev 1995).[18] As a result, organizations drawing their support, primarily, from the more conservative segments of Irish America, vehemently objected to the NAIJ's extension of civil rights and anti-imperialist frames to "the Irish issue."

Not surprisingly, relations between organizations belonging to opposing networks on other issues became acrimonious. During a St. Patrick's Day parade in New York City, AOH parade officials admonished the NAIJ after the band they brought from Ardoyne in North Belfast played the U.S. civil rights anthem "We Shall Overcome" (interview with Edwina Stewart). At a rally in Los Angeles, scuffles broke out between Young Socialists and other audience members wearing the colors of the Irish flag after a skit where a youth gagged with an American flag was forced to take the pledge of allegiance (Arthur 1974). Rather than cooperating in the name of a common cause, each side spent considerable time, money, and effort trying to discredit one another. ACIF Chair, James Heaney, described the NAIJ as communist agitators using Irish issues to promote their own subversive agenda. The NAIJ responded by calling Heaney and the ACIF "reactionary bigots who were blinded to the social realities of Ireland by their hazy, romantic nationalism" (Wilson 1995:38). Both lost supporters as a consequence. By late 1969, eighteen Irish-American organizations forming the Irish Action Committee refused to take part in NAIJ-sponsored events because of its leftist orientation and association with the Black Panther Party (McCluskey 1989). The concept of issue network overlap assisted greatly in the identification of domestic issues that produced intense antagonisms between American organizations participating in the network.

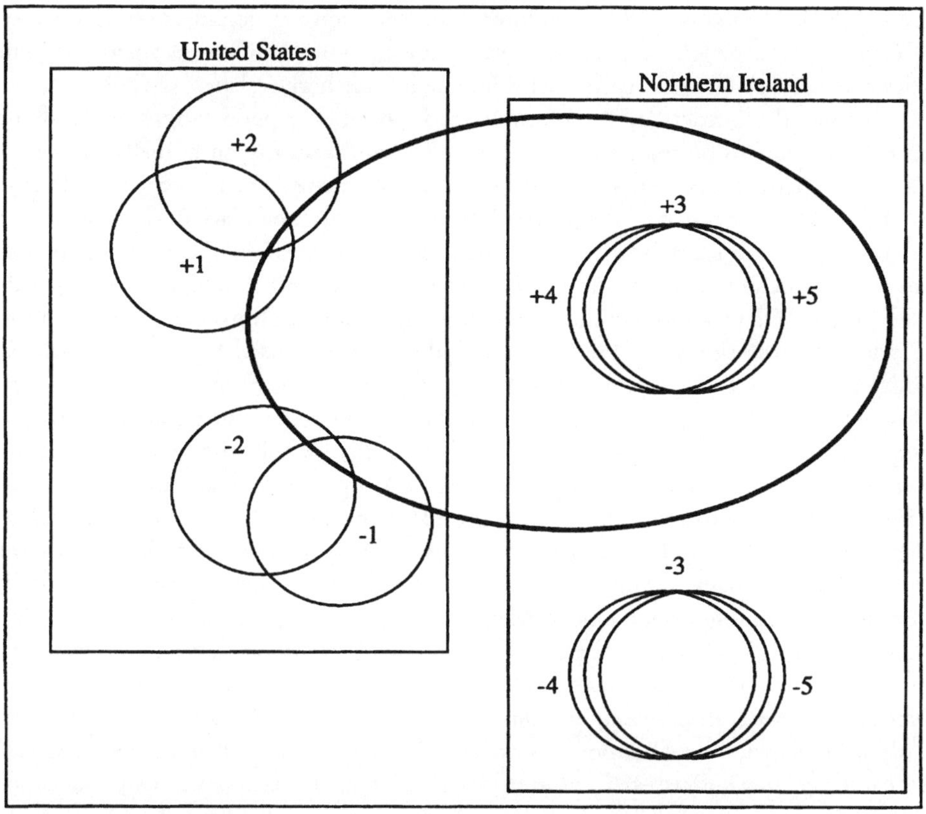

United States
+1/−1 = Organizations supporting/opposing the U.S. civil rights movement
+2/−2 = Organizations opposing/supporting the Vietnam War

Northern Ireland
+3/−3 = Organizations supporting/opposing housing reforms
+4/−4 = Organizations supporting/opposing policing reforms
+5/−5 = Organizations supporting/opposing electoral reforms

Figure 16.1. Issue Network Overlap, U.S.–Northern Ireland Nexus

ORGANIZATIONAL FACTORS

Insufficient Organizational Capacities. Even at the height of political opportunities in Northern Ireland and internationally, network activity remained low in a number of societies with large populations of Irish ancestry, such as Australia, Canada, and New Zealand.[19] Two factors contributed to sparse and belated organized support in these societies: their specific patterns of Irish immigration and the absence of widespread protest. When compared to the Republic of Ireland, Britain, and the United States, the sizes of the populations of persons of Irish ancestry in these three societies were smaller, both numerically and as a proportion of the population as a whole (Akenson 1993). The mostly rural locations of persons of Irish descent in Australia and New Zealand limited the kind of close, daily, mass interaction conducive to organization. In the case of Canada, most people of Irish ancestry were Protestant, reducing sympathy for the grievances of the Catholic nationalist minority in Northern Ireland.

Beyond the borders of Northern Ireland, societies experiencing high levels of protest were, *ceteris paribus*, more likely to have significant organizational representation in the network. New Left student organizations formed the ideological and organizational basis for much of the protest internationally taking place during the period of civil rights mobilization in Northern Ireland (Ross 1988). As Table 1 suggests that among continental Western European societies, the one with the highest level of student protest (France) also had the largest number of organizations participating in the network. Five of the seven French groups identified espoused ideologies associated with the New Left (i.e., Maoist, Trotskyist, Guevarist, etc.). Even in countries where diaspora-based groups played an important role in sustained mobilization, a significant percentage of the support groups had New Left affiliations. In the United States, the Republic of Ireland, and Great Britain, New Left organizations accounted for 21%, 23%, and 14% of the total number of groups involved in the network.[20] Together, these findings suggest that both the patterns of Irish diaspora and the patterns of protest internationally, significantly impacted the geographic distribution of the level, duration, and timing of network activity.

Weak Ties. While cross-societal variations in organizational capacities help to explain the international distribution of activity in support of civil rights demands in Northern Ireland, these variations do not explain why relationships across borders within the network were harmonious or fractious. The strength of ties among individuals and organizations assists us in understanding these dynamics. Transnational cooperation was highest among organizations with strong ties between members, while cross-societal disputes emerged more often among groups with weak or nonexistent ties. For instance, long-standing, frequent, and cordial interaction took place between members of key groups in Britain and Northern Ireland. Two key figures in the network—NICRA Executive member, Betty Sinclair, in Northern Ireland and Connolly Association leader, Desmond Greaves, in England—were associates of many years (interview with Anthony Coughlan). Moreover, Irish émigrés belonging to the Connolly Association in London, upon returning to the Republic of Ireland and Northern Ireland in the early 1960s, helped plant the seeds for what later became the civil rights movement (Feeney 1974). These ties contributed to well-designed, parallel efforts to pressure the British government to intervene on behalf of civil rights demands. By the mid-1960s, the Campaign for Social Justice (Northern Ireland), the Connolly Association (Great Britain), Gerry Fitt (Republican Labour Party MP from West Belfast), and British trade unionists began to pressure the British government to address questions of injustices in Northern Ireland. Activities such as distributing fact sheets, holding conferences, conducting long marches and town meetings, visiting Members of Parliament (MPs), and issuing press releases, brought these issues to the attention of both the British media and politicians. By the summer of 1965, British Labour party backbenchers formed the Campaign for Democracy in Ulster (CDU). In defiance of a longstanding convention, the CDU raised issues of injustices in Northern Ireland in parliament. Frequent correspondence, telephone calls, conferences, and informal get-togethers involving these various groups, resulted in the formulation of common demands and arguments to justify them. In tandem, they raised the awareness and concern of the British cabinet to the point where it had pressured the Northern Ireland government to make reforms even prior to the highly publicized police assaults on civil rights marchers in (London) Derry on October 5, 1968.[21]

On the other hand, where interorganizational ties were weak and unbalanced, cooperation seldom occurred. Of the societies with high levels of mobilization, organizations in the United States had the least familiarity with their counterparts in Northern Ireland. U.S. government immigration restrictions, coupled with improving economic conditions in both parts of Ireland, resulted in decreased levels of Irish emigration to the United States during the 1950s and 1960s. Akenson (1973:242) explains the consequences: "The lack of sustained interest in Ulster among Irish-Americans actually is not so surprising, for most are now two generations away from direct experience of Irish life, and as a group those of Irish descent are securely assimilated into the American establishment." Moreover, contacts between those who managed to recently immigrate to the United States and Irish-American organizations were few and far between (Hanagan 1998). As a result, transatlantic communication and coordination of activities was poor. One republican civil rights activist in London (Derry) only found out through the newspapers about a sit-in at the British Embassy in Philadelphia by a member of a republican support group in the United States (interview with Fionnbarra ODochartaigh). Not surprisingly, misunderstandings abounded. NICRA Secretary, Ann Hope, remembers becoming "indignant" when, at a rally in New York City, Mayor Mario Biaggi claimed, erroneously, that Catholic children in Northern Ireland had to steal bread to survive (interview with Ann Hope). Whereas members of the CDU in Great Britain were well versed in facts on discrimination in Northern Ireland supplied by the Campaign for Social Justice (CSJ), American groups rarely read CSJ materials, including publications that they funded like the *Plain Truth* (interview with Patricia and Conn McCluskey).[22]

Organizational Competition. In addition to weak ties, competition for resources among member organizations contributed to a lack of cooperation within the network. Unlike some transnational issue networks where competition occurs among organizations based in different societies, the focus upon social change in Northern Ireland resulted in competition primarily taking place between groups located in the same society. While external support groups competed with each other for recognition as the voice of the movement in their society, organizations in Northern Ireland argued over whom should receive the spoils of external fund-raising. In the process, rival transnational blocs of organizations formed. During a "unity" conference held in New York in late 1969, repeated assertions by the National Association for Irish Justice that it officially represented the Northern Ireland Civil Rights Association in the United States angered delegates from other organizations. After hearing from American friends who were "very aggrieved" by NAIJ's claims, Campaign for Social Justice leader, Conn McCluskey, raised the matter before NICRA's Executive Committee, resulting in further controversy among groups in Northern Ireland (McCluskey 1989:133–134).

Fear of a coalition being taken over by one of its members is a commonly cited symptom of resource competition (Staggenborg 1986). In March of 1969, four "moderate" members of NICRA's Executive Committee resigned in protest of the growing influence of the People's Democracy (PD). The dissidents stated: "We have been taken over by people preaching the most extreme form of revolutionary socialism, the sort of politics that have been causing trouble in France, Germany, Japan, and many other parts of the world" (Betty Sinclair, quoted in Arthur 1974:61). Even PD member, Bernadette Devlin (1969:147), recognized that "the PD influx into the Civil Rights Association (CRA) was seen by existing members as a sinister takeover plot."

Fears of a take-over were magnified by cross-societal contact within the network. In early December of 1969, two CSJ members, along with a third member of the NICRA Executive Committee, made a bid to establish themselves as the guardians of the movement. The attempted takeover received encouragement and support from the Chair of the American Congress for Irish Freedom, James Heaney. In justifying their actions, the dissidents stated that People's Democracy delegates to the NAIJ conference in New York "may have antagonised thousands of moderate Irish-Americans" by visiting with members of the Black Panther Party (Arthur 1974:75). In noting these international connections, CSJ leader, Patricia McCluskey, states:

> There was this feeling of being used for an agenda beyond civil rights. You had to watch your corner. We just wanted to make sure that people had their fair share. (interview with the author)

The rest of the Executive Committee rebuked the insurgents. In their newsletter, *Free Citizen* (No. 6; LHPC), the PD responded by accusing their opponents of self-interested behavior:

> Dr. McCloskey's main concern with NAIJ is that it is destroying his exclusive and private monopoly of money and support for the North in America, which he has been exercising through the right-wing ACIF. They asked McCloskey to try and raise a stink about who was being sent to the conference from Northern Ireland.

While the PD's allegation regarding the motives behind the attempted takeover may lack merit, their admonition reveals the tensions that existed regarding the distribution of financial resources generated by external support groups.

CULTURAL FACTORS

Counterculture Backlash. A common ancestry among the majority of persons in the network supporting civil rights demands in Northern Ireland did not eliminate cultural differences. Along with the rise in international protest, came the cross-societal diffusion and appropriation of ideas and practices emphasizing sexual liberation, individual expression, the questioning of authority, and a rejection of materialism. The uneven adoption of these counterhegemonic materials produced clashes among network members, both within and across, societies. For example, the New Left student group based out of Queen's University Belfast, People's Democracy, criticized the government of the

Republic of Ireland for, among other things, censoring the arts and banning contraception. The introduction of these issues into the context of the civil rights movement received a largely hostile response from network members located in the 95 percent Catholic Republic. Despite the prominence of New Left student groups and the cultural trends sweeping the world in the 1960s, Akenson (1973:153) asserts that not much had changed in the twenty-six counties:

> In contrast to the fluctuation in morals and values characteristic of most Western nations in the twentieth century, the southern Irish moral schema remains a rock of stability and, judging from the approval with which most Catholic Irishmen greeted Pope Paul's condemnation of artificial methods of birth control, the average layman accepts both the moral rigor and the conservatism with alacrity.

A PD-sponsored march from Newry, in the north, to Dublin, in the south, in early April of 1969, brought these cultural differences to a head. Rather than demonstrating cross-border unity, the march exposed divisions. At the border, PD member Cyril Toman presented police with copies of two books banned in the Republic—J. P. Donleavy's, *The Ginger Man*, and Edna O'Brien's, *The Girl with Green Eyes*. Toman's actions angered students from the Republic, including one organizer of the march, John Feeney. Feeney thought the PD had agreed to refrain from discussing either censorship or birth control (Arthur 1974).

Upon arrival in Dublin, the march proceeded from the General Post Office to the Department of Justice, where protesters burned copies of two pieces of repressive legislation—one from Northern Ireland and the other from the Republic of Ireland. Members of two New Left student organizations—the Dublin branch of Young Socialists and the University College Dublin-based Students for Democratic Action—felt that PD criticisms of the laws of the twenty-six counties were adventuresome and unwarranted. Consequently, despite pleas from PD members, 800 of the estimated 3,000 marchers broke away and held a protest at the British Embassy in Merrion Square. The dispute carried over to Merrion Square where, according to *The Sunday News* (04/13/69; LHPC): "The stone throwing, name calling confrontation between rival Northern and Southern demonstrators outside the British Embassy in Dublin brought the affair down to the level of back street schoolboy war." Later that evening after the march, a fight broke out between a member of Students for Democratic Action and Toman's brother (Coulter 1988).

That those disagreeing were roughly the same age, held the same occupation (students), and embraced New Left ideologies, suggest a clash between old and new sensibilities or expectations regarding appropriate behavior. Perhaps because of the monolithic prominence of a conservative Catholic Church, the more liberal views and practices of the youth countercultures emerging in many societies did not manifest themselves to the same degree in the Republic of Ireland. Conversely, significant Protestant advocacy of contraception, coupled with the desire to attract greater Protestant unionist support, contributed to a willingness among many young Catholic civil rights activists in Northern Ireland to challenge sexually conservative policies in the Republic.

While different levels of counterculture appropriation among students in the Republic of Ireland and Northern Ireland created tensions, countercultural affinities among students in the United States and Northern Ireland reinforced the generation gap existing among U.S. supporters. After Devlin's tour in Chicago, a September 4, 1969 *Chicago Tribune* editorial remarked: "Instead of aligning herself with the Irish Catholic establishment, she appeared on stages with the barefoot blue-jean brigades. Whatever her personal appeal, Miss Devlin has shown herself to be more antiestablishment than pro-Irish." In this way, heightened cultural polarization contributed, not only to tensions within the network, but also to negative publicity for the cause.

Conflicting Identities. Differences in collective identities held by Irish Americans and Catholic nationalists in Northern Ireland also led support groups to withhold valuable assistance to civil rights organizations in Northern Ireland. While linked by common ancestry, the different structural positions of Catholic nationalists as an ethnic minority in Northern Ireland, on the one hand, and of Irish Americans as part of a racial majority in the United States on the other, contributed to markedly divergent levels of identification with African Americans.[23] Events bringing together network members from Northern Ireland and the United States threw the spotlight on these contrasting identities. During her speaking tour in August of 1969, Northern Ireland civil rights activist, Bernadette Devlin McAliskey (1988:87), readily related to ethnic minorities in the United States:

> I was not very long there until, like water, I found my level. "My people"—the people who knew about oppression, discrimination, prejudice, poverty, and the frustration and despair that they produce—were not Irish Americans. They were Puerto Rican, Chicano. And those who were supposed to be "my people," the Irish Americans who knew about English misrule and the Famine and support the civil rights movement at home, and knew that Partition and England were the cause of the problem, looked and sounded to me like Orangemen. They said exactly the same things about blacks that the loyalists said about us at home.

Devlin was not alone in this regard. Most of the civil rights activists I interviewed in Northern Ireland expressed a deep identification with the plight of African Americans. In his book, *Ulster's White Negroes*, Fionnbarra ODochartaigh (1994:14), a co-organizer of the first civil rights march in Derry/Londonderry, states a sentiment shared by many:

> Many of us looked to the civil rights struggles in America for our inspiration. We compared ourselves to the poor blacks of the U.S. ghettos and those suffering under the cruel system of apartheid in racist South Africa. Indeed we viewed ourselves as Ulster's white Negroes—a repressed and forgotten dispossessed tribe captured within a bigoted partitionist statelet that no Irish elector had cast a vote to create.

These contrasting identities triggered a series of battles. In Detroit, Devlin refused to speak until African Americans were let into the event. During her speech, members of the audience heckled her when she advocated black civil rights. Devlin responded by having the person employed to sing John McCormack songs, sing instead, the U.S. civil rights anthem, "We Shall Overcome" (Devlin McAliskey 1988). A number of Irish-American dignitaries seated in the front row, including Catholic clergy, refused to stand for the song when Devlin called upon them to do so. Irish-American groups in the area had been prepared to present her a $1 million check. After the event, they sent the money to the Irish Red Cross instead. Devlin received similar receptions throughout the tour. Hundreds of Irish Americans cancelled checks donated prior to hearing Devlin speak (McCluskey 1989). In Boston, audience members again heckled her, chanting: "Niggers out of Boston, Brits out of Belfast" (Devlin McAliskey 1988).

Other activists experienced similar difficulties. During a 1969 speaking tour in the United States, audience members in New York walked out in protest after Austin Currie (from Northern Ireland) and Conor Cruise O'Brien (from the Republic of Ireland) drew parallels between the civil rights struggles in the United States and Northern Ireland (Dooley 1998).

A gap existed between the nationalist identity that Irish activists had previously tapped into, to generate diaspora support, on the one hand, and the identity emerging from recent social movements throughout the world, on the other. For many Irish Americans, their ethnic identity articulated the cause of Irish independence with the revolutionary republican tradition in the U.S. (Hanagan 1998). The transnational Irish nationalism sown by John Devoy and Michael Collins early in the century remained steadfast within the Irish diaspora. When organizations in Northern Ireland deliberately avoided discussion of constitutional issues and stressed international solidarity among the oppressed, it did not play well with traditional Irish nationalists. In turn, organizations in Northern Ireland viewed Irish Americans as "more republican than for civil rights" (interview with Patricia and Conn McCluskey). An Irish émigré in America, Brigid Makowski, suggested that a NICRA banner be included in a St. Patrick's Day parade in Philadelphia. According to Dooley (1998:79), "the motion was finally adopted, but with the provision that the banner clearly state that Clann-na-Gael was supporting civil rights in Ireland, not black civil rights in the U.S." Ironically, the republicanism that traditionally served as cultural glue now ripped the transnational network apart. Consequently, Northern Ireland activists often deliberately avoided contact with Irish American organizations. Conn McCluskey asserts that, "We were afraid they would harm our social justice cause and present a wrong view of our campaign to the British people" (interview with the author).

IDEOLOGICAL FACTORS

Exporting and Amplifying Divisions. Differences in political analyses strained relationships among network participants. Interactions across borders deepened ideological disputes. For example, leading civil rights figures in Northern Ireland, like Nationalist MPs, Austin Currie and John Hume, advocated sticking to questions of promoting equal citizenship for the Catholic nationalist minority. Those who sought to promote full employment and housing, on demand, for both Catholics and Protestants alike, however, viewed this position as creating "an equality of want" (People's Democracy,

February/March 1971, "Editorial," *Northern Star* 3:2). For the founder of the Derry Unemployed Action Committee, Eamonn Melaugh, the civil rights movement was about ending "poverty and homelessness; asking for a standard of living for everybody compatible with the rest of the United Kingdom and the twentieth century" (interview with the author).

The debate over promoting social versus economic equality soon devolved into name-calling. The People's Democracy labeled the proponents of the social equality perspective as "Green Tories" and puppets of the Dublin (Republic of Ireland) government (NLR 1969:15–16; McCluskey 1989:86).[24] At a rally in Strabane in July of 1969, Eamonn McCann, along with Devlin, chastised Currie and other speakers for not addressing unemployment in both communities. The attacks were strongly rebuked by John Hume, among others (Arthur 1974). Soon the debate spread beyond Northern Ireland. In the same month's edition of the *Irish-American Reporter*, Heaney responded by asserting that PD member, Kevin Boyle, represented only (Arthur 1974:75) "a very small minority of what really are 'Red Tories.'" Similarly, the ACIF leader described another prominent PD personality, Michael Farrell, as a "Red Fascist" (Wilson 1988:31). Heaney privately encouraged Conn McCluskey and other "moderates" to take over the NICRA Executive and purge the PD. On the other side of the political fence, Trotskyist groups in Great Britain and the United States encouraged their fellow travelers in Northern Ireland to continue efforts to transform the civil rights campaign into a working-class movement (interview with Eamonn McCann). In this way, external moral support turned up the volume of the debate on issues that most deeply divided network members in Northern Ireland.[25]

Conclusion

The transnational network of organizations supporting civil rights demands in Northern Ireland faced a number of challenges that typically confront domestic coalitions. The closing of political opportunities, an underdeveloped organizational field, weak ties across organizations, resource competition, divergent cultural practices, contrasting identities, and conflicting ideologies all served to discourage cooperation. Because of the characteristics of Irish immigration and mobilization during a period of heightened protest internationally, the involvement of organizations outside of Northern Ireland exacerbated most of the problems found on a national level. Societies lacking large urban populations of Irish Catholic ancestry and high levels of protest, generally, did not possess organizational fields sufficiently developed to play important roles throughout the duration of the network. Low levels of communication all but guaranteed weak ties between groups in Northern Ireland and the United States. Increased heterogeneity resulting from the participation of groups from other societies (even those as close as the Republic of Ireland) intensified culture clashes and identity conflicts within the network. Cross-societal communication served to pull external organizations into an ideological dispute among groups in Northern Ireland. In the process, disagreements previously confined to Northern Ireland were taken up by groups in the United States and Great Britain. The internationalization of the split, in turn, underscored the differences between organizations in Northern Ireland.

In addition to exacerbating problems encountered by domestic coalitions, the network experienced difficulties that a coalition of groups in Northern Ireland, alone, probably would not have faced. The network brought together organizations in the United States that, otherwise, probably would not have attempted to cooperate because of diametrically opposed positions on domestic issues, such as civil rights for African Americans and U.S. military intervention in Vietnam. Rather than alleviating these tensions, events involving activists from Northern Ireland deepened hostilities by bringing ideologically disparate U.S. support groups into direct contact with one another.

How representative are the findings of this case study? One could argue that transnational networks focusing upon issues other than ethnic claims may be based less on ethnic identities and more on the shared values of their members. Hrycak's (1999) finding that diaspora groups have actively participated in transnational networks working on women's issues in the former Soviet Union, however, suggests that this proposition cannot be assumed.

As seen in the case examined here, the contrasting practices, identities, and ideologies of diaspora and non-diaspora-based organizations increase the likelihood of antagonisms. Moreover, even in networks consisting primarily of those holding shared values, studies cited in the theory section reveal that these networks often experience the same kinds of difficulties in building and sustaining effective cooperation across borders as ethnic issues networks encounter. Disputes over other issues, increased resource competition, greater cultural misunderstandings, and the amplification of ideological disputes have affected not only transnational networks addressing ethnic issues, but those focusing upon human rights practices, democratization, and rural development as well.

Since the period of the case study, the mass commercialization of other technological innovations such as satellite communications feeds, cable television, the fax, and the Internet has occurred. These changes have coincided with a rapid expansion in the number of organizations working together across borders on political issues. While technological and organizational advances have reduced some impediments to transnational cooperation, they have deepened others. For instance, electronic mail has provided organizations with Internet access the ability to forge strong interpersonal ties even in the absence of frequent face-to-face contact. On the other hand, electronic mailing lists with international memberships have served as venues for heated arguments reflecting cultural differences, conflicting identities, and incongruent ideologies. In this way, e-lists efficiently export and amplify disputes within a transnational issue network. Similarly, the widening and deepening of the transnational organizational field have alleviated certain obstacles, while compounding others. An increasing number of international nongovernmental organizations have devoted their resources to building local organizational capacities in third-world countries (Burkey 1993; Sikkink 1993). While making transnational cooperation more feasible, the strengthening of the international organizational field may have intensified interorganizational competition for resources (Flint 1999). While beyond the scope of this paper, the multiple and contradictory implications of recent technological and organizational advances are worthy of research. Nonetheless, the studies of transnational issue networks operating in the 1980s and

1990s reviewed above suggest that several of the obstacles to transnational cooperation identified in the case study persist in the present.

Consequently, the findings presented here have theoretical implications for transnational issue networks more generally. First, the potentially harmful effects of transnational mobilization during peaks in international cycles of protest must qualify the assumption of political process theory that the introduction of influential allies and support groups constitutes an unproblematic, political opportunity for social movements (Tarrow 1998). While external organizations can exert pressure on behalf of demands for social change, they can also contribute to tensions that reduce levels of resources, organizational capacities, and interorganizational cooperation.

Second, because of the expanded spatial scope of mobilization, theories of coalition dynamics developed in relation to national-level or local cases, alone, cannot adequately explain the negative interorganizational dynamics that can emerge within transnational issue networks. Additional concepts and modifications to existing ones are required. The concept of issue network overlap elucidates how the compositions of issue networks vary substantially depending upon whether mobilization is taking place at the national or transnational levels. The concepts of exporting and amplifying ideological divisions emphasize how cross-societal interaction within an issue network worsens sources of tension existing at the national levels.

Third, understanding an international cycle of protest, in general, as well as in its specific manifestations, requires closer attention to variations across societies in structures of political opportunity, in mobilization structures, and in the appropriation of protest ideas. In contrast to other societies with high levels of network activity, heightened racial polarization in the United States stimulated additional support for the civil rights movement in Northern Ireland, but also resulted in network members spending a great deal of their time, money, and effort battling each other. Due to the particular contours of Irish diaspora and international protest, low organizational capacities existed within Australia, Canada, and New Zealand, limiting the roles played in the network by groups in these societies. The conservatism of the Republic of Ireland meant that countercultural ideas and practices were not as readily adopted as in Northern Ireland, leading to clashes during events requiring cross-border cooperation. These differences, in context, greatly impacted whether and how political mobilization occurred.

While the case study suggests the promise of an approach to understanding the dynamics of transnational issue networks, further research is needed to substantiate the claims made here. Studies comparing different types of issue networks or networks working on the same issue, but experiencing contrasting levels of cooperation and success in achieving their objectives would shed light on the general significance of the factors identified as shaping coalition dynamics. Research examining the relative number, size, composition, and dynamics of transnational issue networks operating in different political contexts, including "the doldrums" (Rupp and Taylor 1987)—where overall levels of insurgency are relatively low—would enable a more thorough evaluation of the relationship between network dynamics and international cycles of protest. Other case studies involving Ireland provide excellent opportunities to increase our understanding of this relationship. Transnational networks addressing Irish issues are, by no means, recent phenomena, nor are interorganizational antagonisms arising within them (Dooley 1998).[26]

In pointing out ways that transnational mobilization exacerbates and creates disputes among organizations working on behalf of a common objective, the question arises as to whether networks pursuing social change in their own society are better off without external assistance. My answer is that it depends. If external actors provide benefits (i.e., additional resources, organizational capacities, and opportunities to pressure targeted actors) greater than those they take away from the issue network, then the answer is yes. If not, then the answer must be no. A number of case studies cited above indicate that external intervention can facilitate policy changes by institutional actors on the national and international levels. While negative cases have received little attention in the literature, my own research on indigenous rights networks provides at least one instance where the participation of international nongovernmental organizations did not result in a successful campaign to protect indigenous land tenure, cultural recognition, or political autonomy (Maney 1999). In fact, in a number of instances, interventions by outside organizations were counterproductive.

In the case of the transnational network advancing civil rights demands in Northern Ireland, external governmental and nongovernmental organizations provided substantial additional resources, organizational capacities, and political opportunities for the movement as evidenced by the positive contributions of British organizations discussed above. In this sense, the network benefited from transnational mobilization. Nonetheless, tensions limited the realization of the potential benefits of international involvement. For instance, Irish-American organizations would have contributed far greater sums to civil rights activists in Northern Ireland were it not for the friction caused by disputes over other issues, weak transatlantic ties, resource competition, culture clashes, contrasting identities, and conflicting ideologies. When the structure of political opportunities within Northern Ireland and beyond its borders shifted against the network, the added strains created by transnational mobilization hastened the network's decline, thereby weakening its ability to generate pressure on behalf of civil rights demands.

Can transnational issue networks avoid the myriad of obstacles to interorganizational cooperation presented by transnational mobilization? The perception of political opportunities at both the national and international levels serves as an incentive for organizations to join together and seize the moment before it passes. Ongoing vulnerabilities or receptivity of targeted actors to network demands, as reflected in successful campaigns, demonstrate the efficacy of coalition building. Once certain demands are met, however, a network must have the ability to develop a consensus regarding remaining or new demands, as well as a strategy to achieve them. The network examined here could not reach such a consensus, resulting in mass exits from the network and deep splits among those remaining.

Preexisting organizational capacities in all societies, and especially where the targeted actor is based, are conducive to the reciprocal exchange of information and other forms of assistance. Similarly, strong and balanced ties within and across borders prior to launching a network campaign provide the familiarity and trust essential to conducting well-coordinated and highly strategic activities. Findings, here, that organizations with strong cross-border ties worked better together support conclusions reached in other studies (e.g., Perez-Godoy 1997; Keck and Sikkink 1998). Although they run the risk of exporting divisions and cross-wiring, the utilization of technologies enabling frequent communication, as well as international conferences and meetings, provide opportunities for the development of personal bonds (Smith 1995; Keck and Sikkink 1998). In terms of networks with substantial diaspora participation, large and ongoing migrations of affluent individuals from similar backgrounds who maintain regular contact with actors in the homeland facilitate external organizational capacities as well as strong ties across borders.

Transnational issue networks with members sharing a common culture (including ideology) are less likely to suffer from the disputes that often plague their more diverse counterparts. Regardless of membership composition, frequent, ongoing interactions assist in the development of shared understandings. "Global" mass communications and the development of international political institutions, promote the emergence of international norms and identities that can serve as a basis for unity (Kriesberg 1997). With shared understandings, networks can construct master frames that integrate, or conveniently downplay, differences in beliefs (Gerhards and Rucht 1992; Rothman and Oliver 1999). Master frames that, using Snow and Benford's (1992) terminology, resonate widely and deeply with international public opinion galvanize network participants while placing symbolic pressure upon targeted actors. With thc cxccption of the United States, where a civil rights movement had deeply divided public opinion, the civil rights frame initially deployed by organizations in Northern Ireland, largely achieved these purposes. The increasing deployment of revolutionary socialist and Irish nationalist frames from 1969 onward, on the other hand, did not. Where strong ties and commonly adhered to master frames do not exist, networks are best served by avoiding situations where members with contrasting cultures are brought into close contact with one another. After 1969, Northern Ireland civil rights activists exercised far more discretion in selecting American groups to assist in organizing speaking tours in the United States (interview with Ivan Cooper). That participants in transnational issue networks have learned from negative experiences bodes well for future cooperation across borders.

Notes

1. I use the concept of issue networks instead of social movements for three reasons. First, as generally defined, social movements are limited to nongovernmental organizations. Yet, often, contention over issues involves alliances of public and private organizations (Fisher 1993; Sikkink 1993; Smith 1995). Second, social movements often include organizations active on related, but different issues. Consequently, the term is too broad for an analysis of relationships among organizations pursuing explicit objectives on a single issue. Third, describing organized opposition to a set of demands for social change using the language of social movements requires reference to "countermovements." Given the difficulties often involved in ascertaining which side mobilized first, the use of such terminology may incorrectly specify the relationship between political adversaries. The concept of issue networks avoids all three pitfalls. Moreover, given the paper's focus upon coalitions, I prefer using a concept emphasizing the characteristics and interactions of a set of actors.

2. Under the Government of Ireland Act passed by British parliament in 1920 and through force of arms, the Protestant population in the North of Ireland established a state. The ongoing union of six of the thirty-two counties of Ireland with Great Britain was formally agreed to in the Treaty ending the Anglo-Irish War in 1921. The remaining twenty-six counties were given dominion status and, by 1937, had declared their collective status as a sovereign, independent republic.

3. As defined here, transnational mobilization entails collective action in more than one society by one or more organizations belonging to a transnational issue network. Using this definition, transnational mobilization need not necessarily entail collective action involving actors from more than one society as long as actors in more than one society are engaging in collective action with the purpose of achieving a common explicit objective on an issue of mutual concern.

4. For the purposes of this article, ideology entails a formal set of beliefs about how the social world does and should operate. As such, ideology represents a facet of culture-pervasive ways of thinking, speaking, and behaving manifested in every day life. Ideologies may reinforce culture, challenge it, or leave it unquestioned. The categorical separation of culture and ideology as factors in coalition dynamics, therefore, is not done for heuristic reasons, but rather, in deference to the convention in the coalition-building literature to discuss some cultural factors like identities without discussing ideology (and vice versa).

5. While less frequent, such incongruities can occur within the context of domestic politics. See Balser's (1997) discussion of Earth First!

6. Gerhards and Rucht (1992:558) conceptualize mesomobilization as "the process that enabled the bloc recruitment of groups and organizations." The process involves the coordination and integration of micromobilization groups by bridging organizations.

7. Given that social movements in the United States initiated the international wave of protest in the 1960s, the fact that American groups were involved in a disproportionate number of disputes arising within the network conforms to theoretical expectations. As a result, the majority (but certainly not all) of the examples of obstacles to sustaining effective transnational coalitions will make reference to U.S. organizations.

8. A number of organizations were active on the same issues years before a mass movement emerged. As far back as 1962, the Connolly Association launched a series of civil rights marches in Britain to highlight the injustices faced by Catholic nationalists in Northern Ireland. Other organizations laying the groundwork for the movement included the Campaign for Social Justice, the Campaign for Democracy in Ulster, the Communist Party, the Derry Unemployed Action Committee, the Derry Housing Action Committee, the Derry Labour Party, the Homeless Citizens' League, Movement for Colonial Freedom, the National Council for Civil Liberties, Wolfe Tone Societies, and Young Socialists.

9. Although most of the groups participating in the network were nongovernmental organizations, a few governmental organizations were involved. These included a caucus of members of British parliament known as the Campaign for Democracy in Ulster, the cabinet and certain agencies of the government of the Republic of Ireland, and the foreign affairs ministry of the Ugandan government.

10. While the large number of British organizations partly reflects the grassroots mobilization of local trade union branches, it is also partly a methodological artifact. One document, "The Irish Question: Challenge to Democratic Britain," discovered in the Hibernica collection at Queen's University Belfast, provided a detailed list of all organizations attending a conference in Britain sponsored by the Connolly Association. Comparable materials were not found for any other society except Northern Ireland. Excluding groups whose activities are only known through the document, forty-two British organizations were identified as supporting civil rights demands

in Northern Ireland between 1967 and 1972. This is slightly over one-half of the figure arrived at when information from the document is included. Nonetheless, even when taking this into account, groups outside of Northern Ireland still accounted for almost three quarters of the total number of organizations in the network.

11. The terms "branch" and "chapter" are used interchangeably. Organizations without known branches are treated as having one branch. To avoid double counting in cases where the only known chapter is actually the entire group, organizations with one known chapter are treated as having one chapter. Only chapters based inside of the society in question are counted. Youth groups are treated as separate organizations, while university branches are considered chapters.

12. Instances of assistance include donating money to civil rights organizations in Northern Ireland, holding and attending protest events, publicizing campaigns by producing newsletters and pamphlets, and lobbying politicians. Mention of an organization or chapter by two or more interview subjects is treated as being equivalent to two or more activities recorded.

13. "Republicans" generally support the reunification of Ireland, if necessary, through force of arms and without the consent of the unionist population in Northern Ireland.

14. While deliberately maintaining a low profile, Republicans, including the leadership of Sinn Fein and the Irish Republican Army, played key roles in launching the civil rights movement. This support reflected disillusionment with traditional military tactics after the failed IRA Border Campaign of the 1950s, as well as the growing popularity of the idea that agitation on basic social and economic issues would reconnect the republican movement with its grassroots constituency. See, for instance, Feeney (1974) and Adams (1988).

15. NICRA survived through the late 1970s, in large part, because of the efforts of its office staff.

16. Small rumps of the American Congress for Irish Freedom and the National Association for Irish Justice continued on as the National Council of Irish Americans and the National Association for Irish Freedom, respectively.

17. I believe questions of civil rights for any communal group to be the same issue in principle. However, the differing compositions of networks formed around the rights of different communal groups suggest that, in practice, civil rights for different groups are separate issues. Issues network overlap can be problematic precisely because of the possibility of various constructions of an issue (such as civil rights) among participants in the network under investigation

18. A white identity pervades the Irish diaspora, not just in the United States. See Akenson (1973:274).

19. The relatively high levels of funding supplied by groups in Australia and New Zealand to NICRA in 1972 reflect their increasing involvement in the later years of the network when overall participation was in decline.

20. Cold War politics and the transnational network of communists involved in the civil rights network explain activity in a number of Warsaw Pact countries (interview with Edwina Stewart). The long-standing concern of Nordic countries about human rights violations contributed to activity in Finland, Iceland, and Sweden. The Ugandan government used information supplied by NICRA to deflect criticism of its own human rights practices in the United Nations (ibid.).

21. Prior to the (London) Derry march, British Prime Minister, Harold Wilson, met with the Prime Minister of Northern Ireland, Terence O'Neill, on August 5, 1966 and January 12, 1967. On both occasions, Wilson urged O'Neill to implement reforms of the types advocated by the CSJ and CDU. The main arguments used by the British Labour government for intervening in Northern Ireland affairs were virtually identical to those used by these groups. See Wilson (1971) and Callaghan (1973).

22. Transatlantic ties remained strongest among Irish Americans with traditional republican sympathies (Hanagan 1998). Like their counterparts in Northern Ireland, these individuals either eschewed the civil rights movement as a distraction from the goal of reunification, or abandoned the network in early 1970 to support the armed struggle.

23. While many with large populations of Irish ancestry in other societies also identified themselves with racial majorities, the absence of large-scale civil rights movements meant that race was less of a polarizing issue than in the United States during the time period in question.

24. To his credit, Melaugh was not involved in any of the mudslinging pertaining to this issue.

25. Other divisive issues included whether 1) to engage in events likely to result in loyalist violence; 2) to use force in self-defense; 3) to demand an end to partition; and 4) to pursue the reform of the Northern Ireland parliament.

26. At first glance, it does appear that transnational issue networks addressing Irish issues have primarily emerged during periods of heightened protest internationally. At least some of these networks experienced tensions similar to those endured by the network examined here. For instance, for a discussion of disputes over slavery in the transnational issue network supporting Daniel O'Connell's movement for Catholic emancipation in Ireland, see Dooley (1998).

References

Abraham, Nabeel, Janice Terry, Cheryl Rubenberg, Lisa Hajjar, and Hilary Shadroui. 1988. "Interational human rights organizations and the Palestine question." *Middle East Report* 18:12–20.

Adams, Gerry. 1988. "A Republican in the civil rights campaign." In *Twenty Years On*, Michael Farrell, ed. Dingle: Brandon Books.

Akenson, Donald H. 1973. *United States and Ireland.* Cambridge, MA: Harvard University Press.

———. 1993. *The Irish Diaspora: A Primer.* Toronto: PD Meany Company.

Allen, Theodore W. 1994. *The Invention of the White Race.* New York: Verso.

Arthur, Paul 1974. *The People's Democracy, 1968–1973.* Belfast: Blackstaff Press.

Balser, Deborah B. 1997. "The impact of environmental factors on factionalism and schism in social movement organizations." *Social Forces* 76:199–228.

Benford, Robert D. 1993. "Frame disputes within the nuclear disarmament movement." *Social Forces* 71:677–701.

Brand, Karl W. 1990. "Cyclical aspects of new social movements: Waves of cultural criticism and mobilization cycles of new middle-class radicalism." In *Challenging the Political Order: New Social and Political Movements in Western Democracies,* Russell J. Dalton and Manfred Kuechler, eds. New York: Oxford University Press.

Burkey, Stan. 1993. *People First: A Guide to Self-reliant Participatory Rural Development.* London: Zed Books.

Callaghan, James. 1973. *A House Divided: The Dilemma of Northern Ireland.* London: Collins.

Carley, Kathleen 1991. "A theory of group stability." *American Sociological Review* 56: 331–354.

Carragee, Kevin. 1996. "Defining foreign social movements." *Peace-Review* 8:35–40.

Cortright, David 1993. *Peace Works: The Citizens' Role in Ending the Cold War.* Boulder, CO: Westview.

Coulter, Carol. 1988. "A view from the south." In *Twenty Years On*, Michael Farrell, ed. Dingle: Brandon Books.

Coy, Patrick 1997. "Cooperative accompaniment and peace brigades international in Sri Lanka." In *Transnational Social Movements and Global Politics: Solidarity beyond the State.* Jackie Smith, Charles Chatfield, and Ron Pagnucco, eds., 81–100. Syracuse, NY: Syracuse University Press.

della Porta, Donatella 1988. "Recruitment processes in clandestine political organizations." *International Social Movement Research* 1:155–169.

della Porta, Donatella and Dieter Rucht. 1995. "Left-Libertarian movements in context: A comparison of Italy and West Germany, 1965–1990." In *The Politics of Social Protest: Comparative Perspectives on States and Social Movements.* J. Craig Jenkins and Bert Klandermans, eds., 229–272. Minneapolis: University of Minnesota Press.

Devlin (McAliskey), Bernadette. 1969. *The Price of My Soul.* London: Pan Books.

———. 1988. "A peasant in the halls of the great." In *Twenty Years On.* Michael Farrell, ed. Dingle: Brandon Books.

Diaz-Veizades, Jeannette and Edward T. Chang 1996. "Building cross-cultural coalitions: A case-study of the Black-Korean alliance and the Latino-Black roundtable." *Ethnic and Racial Studies* 19:680–700.

Dooley, Brian. 1998. *Black and Green: Civil Rights Struggles in Northern Ireland and Black America.* London: Pluto.

Evans, Peter B. 1995. *Embedded Autonomy: States and Industrial Transformation.* Princeton, NJ: Princeton University Press.

Farrell, Michael 1976. *Northern Ireland: The Orange State.* London: Pluto.

———. 1988. "Introduction." In *Twenty Years On.* Michael Farrell, ed. Dingle: Brandon Books.

Feeney, Vincent E. 1974. "The civil rights movement in Northern Ireland." *Eire* 9:30–40.

Fisher, Julie. 1993. *The Road from Rio: Sustainable Development and the Non-governmental Movement in the Third World.* Westport, CT: Praeger.

Flint, Adam. 1999. "The limits of 'globalization from below': Salvadoran social movements in the neo-Liberal transition." Paper presented at the 1999 American Sociological Association Annual Conference "Transitions in World Society: At Century's End" (Aug. 6–10, 1999), Chicago, IL.

Gerhards, Jurgen and Dieter Rucht. 1992. "Mesomobilization: Organizing and framing in two protest campaigns in West Germany." *American Journal of Sociology* 3:555–595.

Granovetter, Mark. 1985. "Economic action and social structure: The problem of embeddedness." *American Journal of Sociology* 91:481–510.

Hanagan, Michael. 1998. "Irish transnational social movements: Deterritorialized migrants and the state system: The last one hundred and fifty years." *Mobilization* 3:107–126.

Hathaway, Will and David S. Meyer. 1993.5 "Competition and cooperation in social movement coalitions: Lobbying for peace in the 1980s." *Berkeley Journal of Sociology* 38:157–183.

Hrycak, Alexandra. 1999. "Transnational social movement organizations and the formation of the post-Soviet women's movement: Grass-roots mobilization from above." Paper presented at the 1999 American Sociological Association Annual Conference, "Transitions in World Society: At Century's End" (Aug. 6–10, 1999), Chicago, IL.

Ignatiev, Noel 1995. *How the Irish Became White.* New York: Routledge.

Jenkins, J. Craig. 1987. "Interpreting the stormy 1960s: Three theories in search of a political age." *Research in Political Sociology* 3:269–303.

Keck, Margaret and Kathryn Sikkink. 1998. *Activists Beyond Borders: Advocacy Networks in International Politics.* Ithaca, NY: Cornell University Press.

Keohane, Robert 0. and Joseph S. Nye. 1977. *Power and Interdependence: World Politics in Transition.* Boston: Little Brown.

Kleidman, Robert. 1993. *Organizing for Peace: Neutrality, the Test Ban, and the Freeze.* Syracuse, NY: Syracuse University Press.

Kriesberg, Louis. 1998. *Constructive Conflicts: From Escalation to Resolution*. New York: Rowman & Littlefield.

Lee, Junghi and Robert L. Craig. 1992. "News as an ideological framework: Comparing U.S. newspapers' coverage of labor strikes in South Korea and Poland." *Discourse and Society* 3:341–363.

Maney, Gregory M. 1999. "Rival transnational networks and indigenous rights: The San Bias Kuna and Brazilian Amazonian Yanomami." Unpublished paper.

McAdam, Doug and Dieter Rucht. 1993. "The cross-national diffusion of movement ideas." *The Annals of the American Academy of Political and Social Science* 528:56–74.

McCluskey, Conn. 1989. *Up Off Their Knees: A Commentary on the Civil Rights Movement in Northern Ireland*. Galway: Conn McCluskey.

McPherson, J. Miller, Pamela Popielarz, and Sonja Drobnic. 1992. "Social networks and organizational dynamics." *American Sociological Review* 57:153–170.

Melucci, Alberto. 1995. "The global planet and the internal planet: New frontiers for collective action and individual transformation." In *Cultural Politics and Social Movements*, Marcy Darnovsky, Barbara Epstein, and Richard Flacks, eds., 287–298. Philadelphia, PA: Temple University Press.

Meyer, David S. and Douglas R. Imig. 1993. "Political opportunity and the rise and decline of interest group sectors." *Social Science Journal* 30:253–270.

Meyer, David S. and Rob Kleidman. 1991. "The nuclear freeze movement in the United States." *International Social Movement Research* 3:231–261.

Meyer, David S. and Sam Marullo. 1992. "International change from below: Activism and the end of the Cold War." *Sociological Practice Review* 3:189–202.

Meyer, David S. and Nancy Whittier. 1993. "Social movement spillover." *Social Problems* 41:277–298.

New Left Review. 1968. "People's Democracy: A discussion on strategy." *New Left Review* 55:1–27.

Northern Ireland Civil Rights Association. 1978. *"We Shall Overcome": The History of The Struggle for Civil Rights in Northern Ireland 1968–1978*. Belfast: NICRA.

ODochartaigh, Fionnbarra. 1994. *Ulster's White Negroes: From Civil Rights to Insurrection*. San Francisco: AK Press.

Opp, Karl-Dieter and Christiane Gern, eds. 1993. "Dissident groups, personal networks, and spontaneous cooperation: The East German Revolution of 1989." *American Sociological Review* 58:659–680.

Pagnucco, Ron and David Atwood. 1994. "Global strategies for justice and peace." *Peace Review* 6:411–418.

Pagnucco, Ron and John D. McCarthy. 1992. "The Proliferation of non-violent direct action under repressive regimes: The emergence, structure and strategy of SERPAJ." In *Religion and Politics in Comparative Perspective*, Bronislaw Misztal and Anson Shupe, eds., 125–147. Westport, CT: Praeger.

Perez-Godoy, S. Mara. 1999. "The theoretical components of transnational social movements: Expanding the scope of the political process model." Unpublished paper. University of Chicago.

Poros, Maritsa V. 1999. "The formation and evolution of transnational networks: The case of Asian Indian migration to New York." Paper presented at the 1999 American Sociological Association Annual Conference, "Transitions in World Society: At Century's End" (Aug. 6–10, 1999), Chicago, IL.

Powell, W. W. 1990. "Neither market nor hierarchy: Network forms of organization." In *Research in Organizational Behavior*, Barry M. Staw and Larry L. Cummings, eds. Greenwich, CT: JAI Press.

Purdie, Bob. 1990. *Politics in the Streets: The Origins of the Civil Rights Movement in Northern Ireland*. Belfast: Blackstaff Press.

Risse-Kappen, Thomas. 1995. "Bringing Transnational Relations Back." In *Non-State Actors, Domestic Structures, and International Institutions.* New York: Cambridge University Press.

Rose, Fred R. 1995. "Bridge builders in inter-class coalitions." Paper presented at the 1995 American Sociological Association Annual Conference.

Ross, George. 1988. "Editor's introduction to 1968–back to the future." *Socialist Review* 18:93–98.

Rothman, Franklin D. and Pamela E. Oliver 1997. "From local to global: The anti-dam movement in Southern Brazil, 1979–1992." *Mobilization* 4:41–58.

Ruane, Joseph and Jennifer Todd. 1996. *The Dynamics of Conflict in Northern Ireland: Power, Conflict, and Emancipation.* Cambridge, MA: Cambridge University Press.

Rupp, Leila J. and Verta Taylor. 1987. *Survival in the Doldrums: The American Women's Rights Movement, 1945 to the 1960s.* New York: Oxford University Press.

Schulz, Markus S. 1998. "Collective action across borders: Opportunity structures, network capacities, and communicative praxis in the age of advanced globalization." *Sociological Perspectives* 41:587–616.

Sikkink, Kathryn. 1993. "Human rights, principled issue-networks, and sovereignty in Latin America." *International Organization* 47:411–441.

Sims, Beth. 1991. *Workers of the World Undermined.* Boston: South End Press.

Smith, Jackie. 1994. "Organizing global action." *Peace Review* 6:419–425.

———. 1995. "Transnational political processes and the human rights movement." *Research in Social Movements, Conflict and Change* 18:185–219.

Staggenborg, Suzanne. 1986. "Coalition work in the pro-choice movement: Organizational and environmental opportunities and obstacles." *Social Problems* 33:374–390.

Tarrow, Sidney. 1998. *Power in Movement: Social Movements and Contentious Politics,* 2nd ed. New York: Cambridge University Press.

Topp, Michael Miller. 1997. "The transnationalism of the Italian-American left: The Lawrence Strike of 1912 and the Italian Chamber of Labor of New York City." *Journal of American Ethnic History* 17:39–63.

Wilson, Andrew J. 1995. *Irish America and the Ulster Conflict: 1968–1995.* Washington, DC: Catholic University of America Press.

Wilson, Harold. 1971. *The Labour Government, 1964–1970: A Personal Record.* London: Weidenfeld and Nicolson.

Zald, Mayer N. and John D. McCarthy. 1980. "Social movement industries: Competition and cooperation among movement organizations." *Research in Social Movements, Conflict and Change* 3:1–20.

Appendix: Persons Interviewed, Organizational Affiliation, and Position Held between 1967 and 1972

Ivan Cooper, Chair of the Derry Citizens Action Committee, Stormont MP, and founding member of the Social Democratic and Labour Party; Anthony Coughlan, Secretary of the Dublin branch of the Wolfe Tone Society and writer for its bulletin *Tuarisc and the United Irishman*; James Doherty, Chair of the Irish Nationalist Party and Treasurer of the Derry Citizens Action Committee; Bobby Heatley, Executive committee member of the Connolly Association, Chair of the subcommittee of Ireland of the Movement for Colonial Freedom, and member of the Belfast chapter of the Northern Ireland Civil Rights Association; Ann Hope, Member of the Belfast chapter of the Wolfe Tone Society and Treasurer of the Northern Ireland Civil Rights Association; Eamonn McCann, Member of numerous organizations including the Irish Workers Group, the Derry Labour Party, Derry Housing Action Committee, and the Derry Unemployed Action Committee; Editor of the *Irish Militant*; Executive committee member of the Northern Ireland Labour Party, and NILP representative to the Derry Citizens Defence Committee; Conn McCluskey, Cofounder and leader of the Campaign for Social Justice, Executive committee member of the Northern Ireland Civil Rights Association; Patricia McCluskey, Cofounder and leader of the Campaign for Social Justice, Executive committee member of the Northern Ireland Civil Rights Association; Inez McCormack, Member of the People's Democracy and Newtownabbey Labour Party; Kevin McCorry, Chair of the Trinity College Dublin Republican Club, member of the Belfast Central Citizens Defence Committee, and paid organizer for the Northern Ireland Civil Rights Association; Eamonn Melaugh, Founder of the Derry Unemployed Action Committee, Secretary of the Derry Housing Action Committee, Executive committee member of the Derry Citizens Action Committee; Fionnbarra ODochartaigh, Education Officer and Honorary Secretary of the Derry Unemployed Action Committee and the Derry Citizens Action Committee; Honorary Secretary of the Derry Housing Action Committee, the James Connolly Club, and the Young Republican Volunteer Association; Executive Treasurer of the Republican Clubs; Editor of the newsletters *Reality and Spearhead*; Edwina Stewart, Secretary of the Northern Ireland Civil Rights Association and Executive committee member of the Communist Party of Ireland.

CHAPTER 17

Exploring the Organizational Dilemmas of Coercive State Conduct*

ISRAEL'S REPRESSION OF THE PALESTINIAN UPRISING

James Ron

Introduction

When faced with broadly popular protest movements, the state's coercive apparatus is torn by contradictory desires. On the one hand, security forces hope to end the protests through swift and brutal repression, making short and efficient work of the job. On the other hand, however, senior politicians, as well as commanders of police and military forces, also crave the appearance of legitimacy, requiring them to respect—at least to a limited extent—the rule of law. Drawing on the work of Isaac Balbus (1973), I argue that these opposing imperatives generate a "dialectic of legal repression" that shapes and constrains state behavior. Security forces negotiate this dialectic by creating hidden and deviant operating codes that promote repression while avoiding blatant legal violations. These maneuvers fundamentally distort, but do not entirely by-pass, regular law enforcement procedures.

My arguments rely on forty-five semistructured interviews with former Israeli military personnel who tired to repress the first Palestinian uprising, or *Intifada,* in 1988–1989.[1] Their accounts reveal profound ambiguities within the Israeli state apparatus. On the one hand, the military made a concerted effort to project an image of due process and legality during its repressive actions. At the same time, however, soldiers devised an array of hidden methods to induce Palestinian suffering without triggering excessive external criticism. Together, this package of legal appearance and clandestine practices amounted to an ambiguous policy, one that I term "savage restraint."

Sources of Restraint

Israel occupied the West Bank and Gaza during the 1967 Arab–Israeli war, applying Israeli military rule to the Palestinian inhabitants, and patrolling the region with soldiers,

*Editor's note: This is a revised version of article originally published in 2000: "Savage Restraints: Israel, Palestine and the Dialectics of Legal Repression," *Social Problems* 47, 4:445–472.

police, and paramilitary Border Police contingents. In December 1987, Palestinians revolted against Israeli rule, launching a series of protests termed an *Intifada,* or "shaking off," by observers. During the uprising's six years, Israeli spokesmen highlighted their forces' use of police-style methods to suppress the Palestinian challenge (Straschnov 1994; Yahav 1993; Zamir 1989). Keen to present an appearance of law enforcement against Palestinian criminals, Israeli spokesmen noted that the military was imprisoning law breakers, conducting trials, and convicting suspects on the basis of evidence. By relying on criminal justice measures rather than combat forces, Israel was demonstrating considerable restraint. Israel's critics, conversely, argued that security forces were systematically deviating from their own law enforcement standards, engaging in false arrests, sham trials, excessive force, torture, systematic beatings, prolonged curfews, and collective punishments. Israel, its critics said, was abusing Palestinian legal rights on a massive scale through the use of arbitrary and brutal methods (Al-Haq 1989; Amnesty International 1988, 1991, 1994; B'Tselem 1989, 1991; Middle East Watch 1991, 1993, 1994).

Although the debate polarized into bitterly opposed camps, both interpretations contained kernels of truth. Israeli forces did conduct a police operation of sorts in the West Bank and Gaza, limiting the use of lethal force by Israel's powerful war machine. Although the figure of 204 slain Palestinians was high for a good-faith policing effort, it was lower than what might have been had Israel unleashed a full-scale assault. At the same time, there is little doubt that Palestinians suffered tremendously. This article's task is to include both these "truths" in one explanatory model.

The Dialectics of Legal Repression

Balbus (1973) coined the term "dialectics of legal repression" in his classic study of contradictions within the U.S. criminal justice system during race riots. One the one hand, Balbus noted, states are keen to maintain order, monopolize the means of force, and rapidly subdue physical challenges. When rebellions erupt, therefore, the security forces feel compelled to react decisively. At the same time, however, state representatives are also concerned to preserve their long-term legitimacy, rhetorically embedding their actions in notions of due process and legal rationality. The repression imperative, in other words, works at cross purposes with the legality, or legitimacy, imperative. This contradiction, according to Balbus, sets "definitive constraints on the ability of political elites to dispense efficiently with collective violence" (1973:3). Ironically, he notes, "The very effort of the sovereign to preserve its life is subject to rules which dictate the manner in which this effort may be accomplished" (1973:235).

Mass insurrections are sites of acute contradiction since pressures for greater repression coincide with greater public oversight. During the U.S. race riots, for example, this push-and-pull dynamic produced a coercive style in which official violence was "often brutal and led to considerable destruction of life," but did *not* include the "wholesale slaughter of riot participants" (Balbus 1973:234). Although rank-and-file policemen deviated from the principles of criminal justice—using methods far more brutal than anything their superiors dared admit—they did not jettison them altogether. Senior officials attempted to fend off criticism by emphasizing their commitment to law enforcement, highlighting their use of "courts," "prosecution," and "evidence." Rank-and-file police deviance, coupled with high-level lip service, was the state's way of negotiating the dialectic.

Would this dialectical process apply to nondemocratic instances such as Israel's military rule over the West Bank and Gaza? Many believe that legal sensitivities exist only in democracies, but some scholars have suggested that concern for public appearances exists even in nonliberal contexts such as the post-Stalinist Soviet Union, where notions of "socialist legality" were vital. Soviet security organs went to "extraordinary lengths . . . to pretend . . . that the rules [were] being followed" (Lieven 1999:164). Other instances include Serbia (Ron 2003) and South Africa (Cawthra 1997:45). These nonliberal regimes still craved the appearance of legality, with important results: protestors were not regularly gunned down en masse in public view, and the principles of criminal justice were not jettisoned altogether. Instead, repression was organized in more indirect and subtle ways.

Theoretical Explanations for State Restraint

What promotes this concern with legal appearances? The literature suggests four possibilities, including the interests of capital, civil society, and international human rights activists. Balbus adopted a Marxist perspective, arguing that restraint comes from capitalists eager to ensure that states remain predictable and routinized. Although this argument is intriguing, it seems not to have played a key role in the Israeli case. I found that Weberian studies focusing on state–society relations were more useful in this respect. These note that while modern states have deep roots in civil society, thereby enhancing their control, embeddedness also requires subtler social control techniques. For Giddens, this reflects the simultaneous expansion of the scope of state power as well as a contraction of its intensity (1987:15); for Mann, it signals the replacement of weak despotic rule by a deeper and more comprehensive infrastructural method of control (1993:60). Infrastructural rulers, Mann explains, cannot "brazenly kill or expropriate their [internal] enemies" without exciting opposition" (1984:190). In this he recalls Foucault's (1979) discussion of the transition from traditional punishment to modern discipline. Although punishment is spectacular and intimidating, it excites popular revulsion and protest. Discipline, on the other hand, is a more insidious and less perceptible form of power.

Whereas the Weberians emphasize domestic civil society, others highlight the role of international human rights discourse and activities (Risse et al. 1999). Some speak of an emerging international "human rights regime" (Howard and Donnelly 1986; Forsythe 1985), while others emphasize transnational activist networks (Keck and Sikkink 1998). Most of these studies suggest that within limits, international human rights norms serve as a check on state violence, especially in states such as Israel, which rely heavily on international flows of aid and trade.

Israeli Infrastructural Power

There is little doubt that by the 1980s, Israel's infrastructural power in the West Bank and Gaza was substantial. Over 200,000 Jews had settled in the region, new roads linked the region to Israel's urban heartland, water, electricity and telephones lines were joined to those of Israel proper, and some 150,000 Palestinians commuted to work within Israel each day. Israeli civilian ministries such as health, transportation, communications, and education extended their reach into the West Bank and Gaza, incorporating the region as an integral but subordinate part of the country (Abed 1988; Arnon 1997; Aronson 1990; Benvinisti 1984, 1989; Gazit 1995; Lustick 1988, 1993a; Semyonov and Lewin-Epstein 1987; Shehadeh 1989). Militarily, Israel's dominance was uncontested as Palestinian armed revolts had by 1971 ended in total defeat. When the Palestinian uprising did eventually emerge, therefore, its tactics were those of civil protest, not armed insurgency (Beitler 1995). Although Israel never proclaimed so officially, the West Bank and Gaza were, for all intents and purposes, encapsulated ghettos within a broader Israeli control system (Benvinisti 1984, Ron 2003).

Israel's infrastructural power in the West Bank and Gaza prompted both Palestinian and Israeli civil society to place some constraints on the military's behavior. Palestinian groups such as Al-Haq, the Palestine Human Rights Information Center (PHRIC), and the Jerusalem Media and Communication Center (JMCC) were active and relatively well-funded, developing connections to the international media and organizations. In addition, traditional Palestinian elites such as village headmen (*mukhtars*) and "notables" maintained contact with Israeli military governors, protesting abuses by Israeli troops. As one former commander noted, "I always heard what my soldiers did, eventually, from the Arabs themselves. Their leaders came to me, to the civil administration, and they complained. It always comes out in the end, you can't hide anything."[2] Although combat officers were often unconcerned by Palestinian complaints, the army's civil administration, charged with maintaining reasonable relations with Palestinians, along with the legal division, lobbied for some restraint.

In addition, Palestinian human rights groups maintained regular (if often conflictual) communications with their Israeli counterparts. B'Tselem, a top Israeli watchdog group, was established in 1988, developing ties to established Palestinian groups. Although Palestinian activists had their own international channels, they also funneled information to Israeli activists who lobbied journalists and global human rights groups such as Human Rights Watch, Amnesty International and the Lawyers Committee for Human Rights. This roundabout route was often necessary given successful efforts by Israeli officials to undermine Palestinian claims. Although Palestinians frequently felt they were exploited by paternalistic Israeli and international human rights activists, the links survived, serving as an important source of restraint

Organizational Decoupling within the Security Forces

Israeli concerns for the image of legalism and restraint in West Bank/Gaza was expressed chiefly through rules limiting lethal force. In response, senior officers, political leaders and coercive personnel circumvented the rules, intensified existing procedures, and devised new methods of coercion. This "creative" response to rules would not surprise organizational theorists, who recognize both the importance of rules as well as their only partial real effect. Meyer and Rowan (1991), for example, term the gap between rules and practices "organizational decoupling." According to them, decoupling helps "maintain standardized, legitimating, formal structures while [organizational] activities vary in response to practical considerations" (1991:58). Decoupled organizations promote auras of rule conformity for public consumption, but practically engage in rule deviation to get the work done. Ethnographies are particularly good at describing the realities of "decoupling." Bourdieu's work, for example, demonstrates that "[E]ven in the universe par excellence of rules and regulations, playing with the rule is part and parcel of the rule of the game" (Bourdieu and Wacquant 1992:18). In Bourdieu's formulation, rules provide both starting points and boundary lines for permissible action, but do not dictate action. Actors respond to rules by "inventing within limits" rather than wholeheartedly conforming to prepared scripts (Bourdieu 1993:96). Organizational and workplace ethnographies yield similar findings (Bryant 1974; Burawoy 1979; Gouldner 1954; Ermann and Lundman 1996; Roy 1955). Inventions, evasions, deviations and distortions, however, are different than outright rule rejection, since deviance clusters *around* existing rules rather than by-passing them altogether. As Manning notes for police work, formal rules are the "nexus" around which police act, even when the rules themselves are broken (1977:297).

Policing scholars are highly attuned to decoupling, referring to police "discretion" and to "situational variations" in the application of force (Manning 1977, 1980; Marx 1972, 1980; Punch 1985). Although the state orchestrates the overall application of violence, it is administered in specific contexts by individual agents of social control with substantial latitude (Bittner 1970). This may be especially true at the lowest ranks, since as Cohen (1985:165) suggests, the "actual exercise of power at the lower levels of the system is anarchic and unpredictable." Senior officers and political leaders may also promote deviation by turning a blind eye or promoting tacit understandings.

Scholars working in the literature on policing also suggest that situational variations stem from resource insufficiencies, lack of fit between practical needs and formal guidelines, or the difficulties involved in policing "efficiently" while sticking to the rules (Punch 1985). Police decoupling is facilitated by the spatial dispersal of police, who operate in small, disconnected groups not easily overseen by central administrators. At the same time, however, police are embedded in dense webs of rules and expectations, since their monopoly over legitimate violence cuts to the heart of state-society relations (Bittner 1970).

Police decoupling ultimately produces clandestine "operating codes" that both draw on and deviate from the rules (Della Porta and Reiter 1998:22). Law enforcement personnel develop "imaginative ways of surmounting [legal] obstacles" (Marx 1980), the details of which they often keep within cliques that are "horizontal," encompassing similarly ranked individuals, or "vertical," stretching from senior to junior ranks (Manning 1977:188–189). While some see operating codes as "corruption," others view them as efforts to promote broader organizational goals through informal means. In this case, the use of operating codes are one of the "countless ways in which people try to get their jobs done, frequently with the intention of promoting organizational ends, but which deviate from the normal rules and regulations" (Punch

1985:11). In this sense, police departments resemble other organizations where rules complicate efforts to efficiently accomplish work tasks. As Burawoy (1979:72) notes, workers often "organize their relations and activities in opposition to management" in order to accomplish the tasks management itself assigns.

I shall now set out to sketch an analytical framework for investigating Israeli coercive practices. Israel's security apparatus was faced with conflicting pressures promoting both greater repression and greater restraint. With the West Bank/Gaza under firm Israeli infrastructural control, Israeli security forces faced constraints from civil society and international human rights observers. Police and organizational scholars would expect senior officers, political leaders, and rank-and-file soldiers to respond by decoupling their activities from general rules, creating clandestine operating codes, and forming horizontal or vertical cliques. With the encouragement of vertical cliques, low-ranking troops would break some rules, but would distort others. Evidence gathered from interviews with Israeli veterans suggests that these kinds of activities were indeed implemented.

ISRAELI OPEN-FIRE RULES

Police-like "rules of engagement" in the West Bank/Gaza effectively transformed Israeli security forces from war fighters into policemen. In combat arenas such as southern Lebanon, Israeli soldiers were permitted to open fire freely, but in the West Bank and Gaza, regulations were quite different. There, they could open fire only as method of last resort for self-defense, or to apprehend "dangerous suspects." In the first case, lethal force was appropriate only if Palestinians first opened fire on Israeli troops or attacked them with knives, axes, or chains, while in the second, soldiers were obliged to first warn suspects before shooting (Middle East Watch 1993:42–60). These restraints were one of the key ways in which Israel expressed its commitment to legalism and policing in the West Bank and Gaza. Furthermore, soldiers were permitted to use nonlethal force such as truncheons, gun butts, or their fists only when overcoming resistance to arrest (Middle East Watch 1994:38). Physical abuse past the point of arrest, in theory, was illegal. In addition, soldiers were to respect Palestinian dignity and to avoid cruel or humiliating activities. These reasonable, police-like rules were ostensibly enforced by the army's Internal Affairs unit, a subordinate of the Judge Advocate General's office.

For both practical and political reasons, however, Internal Affairs investigators resolved to focus their efforts only on instances of lethal force. Practically, one investigator explained, "There were so many incidents every day [in 1988], we had no way of checking everything. We just didn't have the manpower. We needed to devise a way of reducing the caseload, so we decided to investigate only when there was a death. We just couldn't investigate the other stuff."[3] Politically, government officials concluded that too many deaths would provoke civil society and international protest. Nonlethal injuries, however, if done with apparent respect for legality, might be more readily excused. Indeed, Internal Affairs investigated 170 cases of lethal force between December 1987 and September 1988, slightly less than the 204 Palestinians slain during that time (Al-Haq 1989:53). Crucially, however, thousands of nonlethal incidents went unquestioned, signaling to soldiers they were free to decouple their practical activities from the formal rules.

The Dialectic in Action

I find it useful to focus on four clandestine operating codes, including distorted incarceration procedures, extrajudicial beatings, torture, and the "shortened procedure" for apprehending suspects. My line of argument suggests these did not occur *in spite of* military regulations, but were instead developed *because* of them. Restraints on lethality functioned as double-edged swords, imposing limits beyond which violence could not go, while generating incentives for nonlethal methods of repression. The military's rules, in other words, were both constraining and enabling.

OPERATING CODE #1: DISTORTED INCARCERATION PRACTICES

Incarceration had been a key Israeli control mechanism ever since the beginning of the occupation. Suspects were detained by Israeli soldiers, held in pretrial detention centers, interrogated by military police or the *Shabak,* Israel's domestic intelligence service, and then sent on to military court (Hajjar forthcoming; Middle East Watch 1994). After conviction by trial or plea bargain, most served time in military prison. Although the system was never a paragon of justice, the military made a special effort to distort the process during the first years of the uprising through false arrests and abusive detention conditions.

Israel resorted to mass detentions because they were a nonlethal method of neutralizing *Intifada* activists. In addition, incarceration helped project "police-like" images of law enforcement and due process to significant audiences. Instead of sending tanks and combat troops to crush demonstrations with naked military force, Israel's soldiers-turned-policemen were using the tools of criminal justice to restore law and order. Yet had Israeli soldiers followed the letter of the law, detention would not have been a cost-effective way of satisfying Israel's repressive needs. Soldiers therefore distorted the system without jettisoning it entirely, reflecting the tensions generated by the dialectic of legal repression.

Trumped-up charges: Soldiers found it exhausting to try and identify those Palestinians actually involved in protest activities. Although soldiers did arrest real suspects, they typically did so during targeted nighttime raids led by Palestinian informants working for the *Shabak.* During routine street patrols, rank-and-file soldiers responded to protests by grabbing young male Palestinians at random, hauling them off to base, and charging them with spurious offenses. This they could do because under the military occupation rules, soldiers were given broad powers of arrest. As a result of this deviant operating code, the Palestinian prison population mushroomed dramatically, transforming detention into a central communal experience. Thus while incarceration was conceived as a "police-like" alternative to lethal force, serving in theory as a constraint, troops clandestinely distorted the procedure to enhance Palestinians' punitive experience.

The numbers were impressive. The average Palestinian prisoner population hovered at 5,000 before the uprising, but topped 14,000 by 1989. Over 1,000 of every 100,000 Palestinians were in prison, transforming the West Bank/Gaza into one of the most heavily imprisoned societies worldwide.[4] In 1990, the rate was 110 in Israel proper, 426 in the U.S., 120 in Northern Ireland, 240 in South Africa, and less than 100 in Western Europe as a whole (Middle East Watch 1991:1). The Soviet Union's incarceration rate in the 1950s was 1,423 (Christie 1994:33). Palestinian incarceration rates, in other words, were closer to the Gulag than to Northern Ireland.

The rank and file used false charges to ease their own burden, but in the process, they generated negative externalities for other parts of the military apparatus. Although some Palestinian protestors were certainly locked up, the mass detentions on false charges created a legitimation problem for officers and Israeli politicians concerned with projecting a "law and order" image to external audiences. As we shall see below, officers elsewhere in the army felt that mass incarceration threatened to undermine the army's reputation as a lawful occupier.

Poor conditions of detention: A second penal system distortion was the quasi-intentional creation of poor detention conditions by rank-and-file soldiers, as well as mid-ranking detention officers. During their first weeks after imprisonment, prisoners were held in overcrowded and filthy holding facilities within West Bank/Gaza military bases. Miriam, a former administrative officer responsible for tracking the holding facility population in 1988, acknowledged that conditions could be difficult in the facilities "since we didn't always have a suitable place to keep them [the prisoners]."[5]

If there had been no distortion of the penal process, detention officers might have responded to mass overcrowding by insisting on adequate facilities, or ordering the release of excess prisoners, especially those accused of minor offenses. Instead, they decoupled their activities from the rules, housing detainees in metal shipping containers unfit for human habitation. These became oven-like in summer and freezer-like in winter, causing substantial suffering. The decoupling was not so profound, however, as to prompt officers to simply kill excess prisoners, or to allow prisoners to suffer irreparable injury. The military sought to project a plausible aura of legality, limiting decoupling to painful detention conditions rather than murder.

Physical violence in prison: A third distortion was the use of physical violence against prisoners by lower-ranking troops. Once forwarded to central prisons from temporary holding facilities, prisoners were regularly abused by guards who respected the ban on lethal violence, but used nonlethal beatings as a form of clandestine punishment. Itai, a reservist serving in the Gaza Beach Camp facility, recalled that

> their way of behavior, the soldiers there [in the prison], it was barbaric. You could see it in the way everyone who would go through the place would give people blows, a blow here, a blow there. The group who was supposed to take the guys to the court in Gaza were issued with truncheons. On the way to the court, they would try their truncheons out on someone and it was . . . it was something really terrible. . . .
>
> Every night, they would bring in new people. . . . like trash in trash carts. They would pile them up inside the trucks, throw them . . . on the road, lift them up in a line—they are tied, of course—and then start to make them

> march. . . . On the way, what they go through on the way. . . . They get beaten up there, really badly beaten up. I don't even know how to describe those beatings.[6]

Similar stories emerged from interviews and published Israeli reports.[7] As was true for detention conditions, the decoupling in this case was not as extreme as it might have been. Soldiers did not kill or irreparably injure most prisoners, but they did use substantial violence to induce suffering.

Overall, the incarceration system illustrates the way in which different military ranks balanced restraint with repression. On the one hand, commanders promoted arrests as proof of their commitment to policing, emphasizing their choice of detention over gunfire. On the other hand, troops at all levels distorted the detention process to deepen Palestinian suffering, including spurious charges, painful detention conditions, and beatings. The criminal justice mechanism of imprisonment, in other words, was refashioned into a weapon of restrained anti-Palestinian violence. Organizational decoupling was substantial enough to generate pain, but limited enough to remain within nonlethal boundaries.

OPERATING CODE #2: EXTRAJUDICIAL BEATINGS

Extrajudicial punishment sessions in which soldiers used truncheons to beat Palestinians were common during the first year of the uprising (Al-Haq 1989; Amnesty International 1988; Schiff and Ya'ari 1989; Friedman 1990). Although these sessions were formally illegal, they had been devised by senior Israeli officers as a distortion of existing regulations permitting soldiers to use force when detaining suspects resisting arrest. Top commanders authorized lower-ranking officers to stretch the regulations, tacitly permitting the use of truncheons well beyond the point of arrest. The beating policy originated within the senior ranks of the Israeli defense ministry, but gradually spiraled out of control as rank-and-file soldiers took charge, interpreting the policy as they saw fit. This clandestine operating code, in other words, was initiated by the "vertical cliques" discussed by Manning (1977), but was then elaborated upon by multiple lower-ranking "horizontal cliques." As was true for detentions, however, decoupling was not so profound as to permit lethality. Thus while thousands were savagely clubbed, only three died as a result of beating-related injuries during the *Intifada's* first ten months (Al-Haq 1989:12).

Senior officers initiated the clubbing for both practical and political reasons. Practically speaking, senior officers saw beating as an effective tactic for combating Palestinian rebelliousness. Prisons were unable to satisfy the army's repressive needs on their own, as detention camps could not be built quickly enough to satisfy demand. According to former Col. Eytan, "There just wasn't enough room in the jails for all the people we arrested."[8] At the lower ranks, beatings were an efficient alternative to the more time-consuming arrest effort, which were resented because they were exhausting. As former Private Efraim explained, soldiers were often reluctant to arrest stone throwers because of the time and bother involved. Suspects had to be forcibly dragged back to base through Palestinian neighborhoods, and then multiple legal forms had to be filled out.[9] For the rank-and-file, the on-the-spot-clubbing were a quick and easy way of expressing their anger and punishing Palestinians.

Politically, senior officers liked beatings because they were a nonlethal method of punishing rebellious Palestinians. According to former Col. Avi, most debates within the military command during late 1987 and early 1988 focused on how to keep the number of Palestinian deaths down while still ensuring that protestors suffered physical punishment.[10] At the very top of a de facto "vertical clique," the defense minister at that time, Yitzhak Rabin, explained in September 1988 that "our purpose is to increase the number of [wounded] among those who take part in violent activities but not to kill them" (Al-Haq 1989:19). Beatings were useful because they complied with the nonlethality principle while magnifying Palestinian pain.[11] The reliance on police-style truncheons, as Manning (1977) might have anticipated, were also helpful because they projected an appearance of "policing," rather than war. "When you're with a club," Col. Avi explained, "it's like the police. Police all over the world have clubs; it's like a legitimation of sorts." The beatings quickly spiraled out of control, however, eventually transforming the truncheons into a public relations liability. But initially, it seemed as if baton-wielding paratroopers might project images of restrained, police-like legality, rather than savage, combat-like violence.

The beating policy remained clandestine in that top officers in the "vertical clique" never put their orders down on paper. Instead, they issued vague instructions speaking of the need to "come into contact with the enemy" and to "use force" against "rioters." These exhortations provided lower-ranking officers and soldiers with the incentive to interpret policy as they saw fit. One Central Command order issued in January 1988, for example, ordered soldiers simply to "to beat rioters,"[12] but few officers could say, precisely and unambiguously, what that meant. For some, the beating should end as soon as legitimate suspects were apprehended and subdued, but for others, the order was an invitation to engage in prolonged physical punishment sessions. As a result, different troopers devised varying interpretations. Former Col. Yiftach said the orders were to "hit in order to punish. Whoever throws a stone, if you catch him, he can't throw stones anymore."[13] Efraim, the former private, claimed, "We used to just beat anyone we wanted . . . If anyone ran from us . . . we grabbed him and beat him." Often, the beating ended right there, but in other cases, it continued, as soldiers crowded around to vent their frustrations. According to two Israeli military affairs correspondents,

> [T]here were countless instances in which young Arabs were dragged behind walls or deserted buildings and systematically beaten all but senseless . . . No sooner had the order gone out than word of excesses, unjustified beatings, even sheer sadism echoed back from the field . . . before long reports flowed in of soldiers thrashing people in their own homes just for the hell of it. Proof that whole families fell victim to the truncheons was readily observed in the hospitals, where women, children and the elderly were brought in for treatment. (Schiff and Ya'ari 1989:150–151)

One interpretation of the policy was devised by Col. Eytan, stationed in Nablus in the northern West Bank. Eytan obtained from the *Shabak* a list of suspected protest leaders in two villages, Hawara and Beita, and sent paratrooper platoons to raid them on January 19 and 20, 1998. After seizing a dozen suspects from each, the soldiers took their victims to nearby fields and methodically broke their arms and legs. According to former Private Amir, one of the troopers involved, soldiers were instructed to hit kneecaps, so as to ensure that the leg broke.[14] Former Lieutenant Dan recalled that Colonel Eytan had given them strict orders not to cause lethal harm, and that he therefore began the beatings himself to show his men how to avoid hitting the victims' stomach or face.[15] The Hawara and Beita beatings illustrate both the twin imperatives of restraint and savagery, as well as the limits to permissible decoupling. Soldiers deliberately broke the limbs of two-dozen Palestinians, but did so carefully, so as to avoid killing their victims. Colonel Eytan, for his part, maintained that the operation was in strict accordance with general Israeli policy, saying he only did what his officers wanted him to do, but were afraid to put in writing.

Overall, the 1988 beating policy was devised by what Manning (1977) would term a clandestine vertical clique in the state coercive apparatus. Initiated and encouraged by senior officials in the Israeli ministry of defense, it stretched down to the lowest levels of the Israeli control system. Seeking a low-cost, nonlethal and "police-like" method of repression, they issued the rank-and-file with vague instructions to beat rioters which were then further distorted by small, dispersed patrols, akin to Manning's horizontal policing cliques. The policy was a decoupled package of deviations within deviations. In its origins, it emerged from efforts at rule distortion by senior officials evading rules governing the use of force against suspects resisting arrest. That distortion was then elaborated upon and further distorted by horizontal cliques in the field. This decoupling within decoupling did not produce lethality, however, and troops were careful to keep their beatings within bounds.

OPERATING CODE #3: TORTURE AND THE LEGITIMATION OF MILITARY JUSTICE

A third clandestine operating code was the use of torture during interrogations, affecting as many as 5,000 persons per annum between 1988–1992 (B'Tselem 1992a:10; Middle East Watch 1994). Although the practice was not new, it was used to a far greater extent after the *Intifada* began. Just prior to the uprising, interestingly, a government commission concluded that *Shabak* interrogators had violated Israeli law by systematically torturing Palestinian detainees and then lying about it to military judges (Landau 1987). The commission drew up guidelines for "moderate physical pressure" to be used in clearly specified instances against certain classes of suspects (Middle East Watch 1994). As in the beating case, those classified orders were distortions of permissible interrogation methods, and were likely to have been illegal in and of themselves. As had been true for the clubbing, however, the original deviant code was distorted by lower-ranking interrogators, leading to the multiple decouplings observed above. Although the torture was aimed in part at punishing Palestinians and extracting information, its primary function in the case of small-time Palestinian offenders was to legitimate mass detentions by extracting forced confessions.

Evidence of torture based on Palestinian testimony is widespread (Middle East Watch 1994). I gained access to a former Israeli military policeman, however, who told me of torture sessions he participated in during 1988 in the al-Fara'a military prison. Omri, a former military policeman, said that most of his victims were young males suspected of minor offenses.[16] The interrogators' goal was to extract information and to obtain a signed confession to secure a conviction in military court. When prisoners wouldn't respond to questions, Omri began to hit suspects with "a club, foot, anything . . . beatings like I can't describe. Just beating and beating . . . We hit them everywhere—head, face, mouth, arms, balls." As evidence of limits to decoupling, however, Omri received clear instructions to "try and not kill them." Although many had "broken arms, legs, and teeth," none of his victims died. When "you couldn't hit them any more without killing them," and the detainees still did not supply the desired answers, the interrogators poured an astringent liquid on the open wounds. The prisoners then "screamed and screamed. Screams like I've never heard before." Although Omri's story was the most vivid perpetrator testimony I encountered, veterans such as Itai, who guarded an interrogation wing in Gaza City, supplied supporting accounts. When interrogators came to the prison, he said, there were "screams which until today, when I sleep at night, I hear them inside my ears all the time . . . horrible screams" (B'Tselem 1991:127).

This "operating code" (Manning 1977) was produced by military efforts to cloak the mass incarceration project in an aura of legitimacy, much as Balbus (1973) observed in the case of the U.S. criminal justice system in the 1960s. With thousands of prisoners pouring into the prisons, legal affairs officers needed to properly process them through speedy batch trials. Military regulations, after all, required that suspects be tried or released (Hajjar 1999, forthcoming), and the mass incarceration effort would have seemed blatantly illegitimate if prisoners were never taken to trial.[17] Evidence of the legal division's insistence on maintaining appearances can be seen in remarkable rates of conviction produced by Israel's military courts. Some 100,000 Palestinians were arrested between 1988 and July 1993,[18] 83,321 of whom were tried in military courts. Of these, only 2,731 were acquitted.[19] Despite the tendency toward fraudulent charges discussed above, in other words, some 80 percent were charged and of those 97 percent were convicted. By convicting most suspects in hasty trials, the military's legal division projected a legitimate image to itself and others.

Torture was integral to this process because convictions required evidence that was all but impossible to obtain any other way. Palestinian witnesses rarely cooperated with Israeli interrogators voluntarily; indeed, it was rare for Israeli investigators to enter Palestinian neighborhoods without heavily armed escort. Given the difficulties in gathering evidence, military prosecutors relied on confessions extracted by force through torture. Orlee, a former military prosecutor, explained that she and her colleagues wanted open-and-shut cases. She spoke highly of one Israeli interrogator known by Palestinians as particularly abusive. "He would really do nice files," she recalled, and would "very much tie up loose ends."[20] The desire for "nice files" led to pressure for detailed confessions, which translated into more coercive interrogations.

Torture, in other words, was a hidden and decoupled operating code devised by interrogators to satisfy military prosecutors, who themselves were eager to legitimize mass incarcerations through conviction in military court. As Human Rights Watch alleged, "the extraction of confessions under duress, and the acceptance into evidence of such confessions by the military courts, form the backbone of Israel's military justice system . . . Because a defendant's signed statement is almost sufficient to convict . . . interrogators have strong incentives to obtain such a statement" (Middle East Watch 1994:2). Efforts to project legitimate images into the public sphere generated illegitimate methods within the interrogation division.

More broadly speaking, torture assumed a central role because of cumulative and increasingly desperate efforts to manage Balbus' (1973) dialectics of legal repression. Police-like regulations prevented soldiers from shooting large numbers of protesting Palestinians, prompting officers to search for nonlethal alternatives, including mass incarcerations. The rising prison population, however, threatened the army's lawful image, since it seemed to verge on the indiscriminate. Military prosecutors sought to manage this by convicting the bulk of prisoners in military tribunals, thereby proving both the prisoners' guilt and the army's adherence to legal principles. Since Palestinians refused to cooperate with Israeli interrogators, however, confessions were most easily obtained through torture. Torture was thus produced by multiple contradictions within the dialectic of legal repression. The dialectic could not be fully resolved, but Israeli soldiers did not stop trying.

OPERATING CODE #4: THE RANK AND FILE'S "SHORTENED PROCEDURE"

Police work, as noted above, is often conducted in dispersed locales with little centralized control, creating incentives for clique formation (Bittner 1970; Punch 1985). As we saw in the case of beatings, the dispersal of Israeli patrols had similar consequences. Small groups moved about Palestinian neighborhoods, devising their own methods of harassment. Shimon, for example, suspected that some of his colleagues engaged in unauthorized violence while on patrol, and then hid the details from others.[21] Efraim, the former private, said his own horizontal clique defined itself in opposition to the senior army brass. "There was an unwritten set of regulations that had no connection to the official procedures," he said. "Tight little social groups did stuff that no one else would know about. The sergeants preferred these [groups] because they were more effective. Senior officers were aware of the informal regime. Field commanders said their ability to monitor all of their far-flung men was limited. Even Col. Avi, who said he was well informed, acknowledged, "there could be tens of incidents I don't know about." Other officers recalled keeping an eye on specific soldiers whom they felt were liable to wreak havoc if unobserved.

One particularly instructive example of clique formation and situational decoupling is the "shortened procedure" used by troops to apprehend Palestinian suspects. During attempted arrests Palestinians often managed to escape and while troopers occasionally gave chase, it was easier to try and gun the fleeing suspect down. The soldiers were hot, tired, and burdened with heavy equipment, and the notion of running after fleet-footed Palestinians through unfriendly neighborhoods was unattractive.

Legally speaking, however, the use of lethal force in such instances was a complex affair. The responsible officer had to first determine the fleeing suspect was indeed suspected of "hostile terrorist activity," and was only then allowed to initiate three successive actions: a shouted warning, "Stop, or I'll shoot"; a warning shot to the air; and then a series of single-spaced shots carefully aimed towards the suspect's legs.

When faithfully enacted, this was a time-consuming process. Suspects often managed to escape, and many troops hoped to find alternatives. They were unwilling to simply gun suspects down without warning, however, as such blatant decoupling could be legally risky. Instead, many used the "shortened procedure" in which all three stages were performed simultaneously, preserving the regulation's outward form. Former Infantry Lieutenant Aviad explained, "What I and others would do is order one soldier to yell, 'stop or I'll shoot!' I would order a second soldier to fire in the air, if we even bothered with that. Then I would take the best shot in the patrol and tell him to shoot towards the suspect . . . all three would do what they were supposed to do at the same time. That way no one could say that he didn't hear a warning shout or didn't see a shot fired in the air."[22] Human rights organizations suspect that hundreds of Palestinians may have been wounded or killed as a result (Middle East Watch 1993).

This procedure demonstrates the response of horizontal cliques (Manning 1977) to the dialectic of legal repression. Small groups felt the existing rules were too difficult and time-consuming, preventing them from getting the job of arrest done. Like Burawoy's (1979) workers who violated management's rules to promote capital's overall agenda, rank-and-file soldiers took it upon themselves to break the army's rules to further its broader repressive interests. Realizing overly blatant violations were risky, however, soldiers did not decouple their actions entirely from the rules. Instead, they collapsed the apprehension procedure's three stages into one simultaneous effort, hoping this might protect them from subsequent inquiries. As Balbus (1973) and Meyer and Rowan (1991) might have expected, the soldiers' hidden operating code (Manning 1977) was crafted so that it broke the rules while appearing to remain within the bounds of the "legal."

Conveying Limits to Deviation

How were messages regarding the limits of permissible decoupling conveyed to rank-and-file soldiers? Actual practices of coercion were located at the center of a series of concentric circles, the innermost ring of which was inhabited by low-ranking soldiers. The outermost circles were populated by legal norms and regulations, legal affairs officers, senior commanders, and public relations representatives. These were chiefly concerned with presenting sanitized images of legality to external observers. Between the two were intermediary rings staffed by mid-ranking officers, low-ranking Internal Affairs investigators, and military prosecutors. These mid-range circles functioned as transmission belts conveying the concerns, norms, and regulations of the broader regulatory environment to the street-level soldiers. It was this middle circle that effectively disciplined the soldiers' behavior, imposing broad limits within which troopers had discretion. Some of those boundaries, such as the ban on mass killings, were so deeply entrenched so as to provoke little comment. Others, such as those regulating the precise modalities of physical beatings, were more hotly debated.

On occasion, the informal code was revealed by high-publicity court martials provoked by particularly blatant rule violations. These cases highlighted organizational decoupling, triggering public outcry. Crank and Langworthy label such events "legitimacy crises" (1992:345), suggesting they are managed by ritualistic acts of degradation and purification that falsely signal fundamental reform. These include firing senior commanders, creating elaborate "review boards," writing new training manuals, and elaborating new guidelines.

In a few isolated occasions, the army conducted high profile trials of soldiers who beat Palestinians to death. These events trial functioned as a marker, reminding soldiers where the limits of decoupling lay (Meyer and Rowan 1991). The vertical clique (Manning 1977) led by top defense ministry officials encouraged extrajudicial beatings but frowned on beating deaths, since they threatened to disrupt the army's image. For the most part, the vertical clique had its way, keeping the horizontal cliques within nonlethal boundaries. Of the 204 Palestinians slain by Israeli forces between December 9, 1987 and November 24, 1988, only three died of beatings, even though thousands, if not tens of thousands, were similarly assaulted (Al-Haq 1989:12).

DECOUPLING TO WHAT EXTENT?

These figures suggest decoupling was not as radical as it might have seemed to many observers. For critics of the Israeli military, the sheer magnitude of soldierly discretion suggested that West Bank/Gaza repression was chaotic and unstructured. Soldiers routinely violated the rules, fashioned their own operating codes, and preyed upon Palestinians as they pleased. As one critical veteran recounted,

> . . . every battalion works out its own set of norms . . . Every battalion commander is the sovereign of the area [under his command.] Every company commander is the *mukhtar* [traditional headman] of a village or two, and every soldier manning a roadblock is a little god. He decides what to do: who will be allowed through and who won't be. Try to understand that every person there has considerable leeway when it comes to making decisions.
>
> The best description I can find for what's going on there is total chaos. . . . There are simply no [rules] governing the implementation of orders, behavioral norms, and methods of punishment. (cited in Al-Haq 1988:20)

Army units rotated frequently, and each new horizontal cliques devise its own methods. A set of checkpoints surrounding a village might change hands four or five times a day, generating constant changes in villagers' lives. Viewed from up close, therefore, it seemed that military decoupling was profound.

This stress on profound decoupling is deceptive, however, in that it focuses chiefly on soldierly invention rather than on *limits* to invention. Viewed from a distance, the extent of military decoupling seems less profound. Troopers devised unique punishments for Palestinians they encountered in the field but dared not go too far, lest they trigger an investigation. Indeed, the limits to deviation were so deeply ingrained that they regularly escaped attention. Like the taken-for-granted "scripts" discussed by new institutionalists, the limits assumed a preconscious quality (DiMaggio and Powell 1991:22). As a result, most criticism of Israeli repression focused on the leeway soldiers had *within* given boundaries, rather than taking note of the boundaries themselves. While many discussed the discretion soldiers had in beating Palestinians, few noted that the assaults seldom ended in death. Critics focused on the autonomy soldiers enjoyed *within* taken-for-granted rules, not on the rules themselves.

Palestinian suffering, therefore, should not be measured in deaths. While Israeli troopers shot dead "only" 204 Palestinians during the first and most powerful ten months of the uprising, they injured over 20,000 and imprisoned some 30,0000 (Al-Haq 1989:12–14). Palestinian pain during 1988, in other words, should be measured in arrests, beatings, and humiliations, not in killings. Although restrictions to lethal force kept soldiers from machine gunning protestors at will, senior officers and rank-and-file troops devised alternative methods of punishment.

Concluding Remarks

During the Palestinian uprising, Israeli troops used substantial violence to suppress Palestinian resistance to military occupation. At the same time, however, soldiers sought to maintain an aura of legality, limiting much of their violence to nonlethal, police-like methods, distorted though they were. Political and military elites knew the mission was to suppress the rebellion as quickly as possible while simultaneously limiting Palestinian fatalities. This contradictory agenda, termed by Balbus (1973) the "dialectics of legal repression," prompted Israeli leaders and their troops to develop innovative methods of nonlethal punishment which promoted Palestinian suffering while avoiding overly blatant violations of formal procedure. Israeli army regulations governing the use of force were thus both constraining *and* enabling, limiting the intensity of violence while permitting nonlethal distortion and elaboration.

Theoretically, I made use of Michael Mann (1984, 1993), who argued that state moderation has emerged historically from increasing links between states and the societies they govern. As states sink deeper roots into society, they amass an "infrastructural" type of power that affords them greater control over more aspects of daily social life, but forces them to reduce their reliance on "despotic" methods. As Giddens (1987) argued, all-powerful state domination typically promotes policing, not war. I identified the international human rights movement as a further source of restraint (Keck and Sikkink 1998; Risse et al. 1999). Israeli infrastructural power was high in the West Bank and Gaza, where the Israeli state had sunk deep infrastructural roots since the 1967 occupation, hoping to ensure long-term Jewish rule. This, paradoxically, came to serve as a source of restraint: once Israeli domination was fully consolidated, Palestinian and Israeli civil society began to act as partial impediments to despotism, much as Mann and Giddens might have anticipated.

Although my study focused on Israel and the occupied West Bank and Gaza, the approach has broader applications. For example, the notion of infrastructural power can help explain patterns of South African state violence during the 1970s and 1980s, when the battle between security forces and anti-apartheid rebels was particularly intense. Whereas apartheid forces exercised some basic restraints in South Africa itself, they waged destructive wars against the African National Congress (ANC) and its allies in Angola and Mozambique. Similarly, the violence of South African-sponsored paramilitaries in the Bantustans was more despotic than the violence wielded by state security forces in South Africa proper. This was particularly marked in KwaZulu Natal, where apartheid agents bolstered the Inkatha paramilitary in its assaults on ANC supporters. South Africa made no effort to wield infrastructural power in Angola, Mozambique, or KwaZulu, and was thus less exposed to the concomitant restraints identified by Mann and Giddens. In South Africa proper, on the other hand, security forces were obliged to work through and around domestic legal guidelines, pushing them to use some of techniques employed by Israeli forces in the occupied West Bank and Gaza.

The notion of infrastructural power can also help explain Serbia's transition from police-style repression in Kosovo during 1989–1997 to full-scale ethnic cleansing in 1998–1999 (Judah 2000; Ron 2003). During the first period, Serbian control over the restive Albanian-majority province was militarily uncontested, as Kosovar Albanians largely chose to pursue nonviolent methods of resistance. Serbian administrative centralization, coupled with Kosovar nonviolent resistance, ensured high levels of Serbian infrastructural power in the province. Once Kosovar rebels launched an armed uprising against Serbian rule in early 1998, however, Serbian styles of violence shifted dramatically, moving to a more despotic regime of coercion. Serbia, as Giddens (1987) would have expected, had moved from brutal "policing" to "war." Crucial in this respect was Serbia's loss of control over significant portions of Kosovar territory, amounting at times to as much as 40% of the province. The less infrastructural power Serbia exercised in Kosovo, the more it came to rely on ethnic cleansing and mass killings. As was true for Angola, Mozambique, and KwaZulu, a less powerful regime of state domination promoted the use of despotic methods.

In an effort to explain actual patterns of Israeli coercion, I drew inspiration from the work of ethnographers, who speak to the tension between rules and practice (Bourdieu 1993; Burawoy 1979); police scholars, who analyze "corruption" and police discretion (Bittner 1970; Manning 1977; Punch 1985); and new institutionalists, who examine the phenomenon of organizational decoupling (Meyer and Rowan 1991; Powell and DiMaggio 1991). Their insights helped demonstrate that coercive forces in zones of high infrastructural power do not passively accept constraints imposed by the surrounding organizational environment. Rather, they seek out new ways of causing pain while remaining in loose compliance with formal procedure, devising clandestine procedures composed of rule distortion and circumvention. At the same time, however, security forces rhetorically commit themselves to the principles of legal rationality. Although some deviations are initiated at the bottom rungs of the coercive apparatus ("horizontal cliques"), many informal operating codes are also devised by "vertical cliques" at the very top of the political and military echelons.

In stressing that Israeli policies were both harsh and restrained, I highlighted the ambiguous nature of political repression in zones of high infrastructural power. While security forces certainly do deviate from lawful policing rules, they are also loathe to bypass them altogether, affording oppressed groups an important however slim margin of protection from state terror. Although human rights abuses still abound, these limits present protestors and political activists with crucial opportunities for survival, mobilization and resistance. More often than not, the dialectical character of social control has been overlooked by governmental critics and human rights activists, distorting their analysis of both resistance and repression.

Notes

1. The Palestinian uprising began in December 1987, and continued, with varying degrees of intensity, until 1993. For information on the origin and conduct of the uprising, see Lustick 1993b; McDowal 1989; Nasser and Heacock 1990; Peretz 1991; Schiff and Ya'ari 1989; Shalev 1991.
2. Col. Avi, interview by author, Tel Aviv, 27 June 1994.
3. Former Lieutenant Arik, telephone interview by author, Jerusalem, winter 1993.
4. This figure excludes the Palestinian population living in Jerusalem. The West Bank and Gaza had approximately 1.5 million Palestinian residents in 1989.
5. Miriam, interview by author, Jerusalem, winter 1993.
6. Quote from B'Tselem (1991: 128–129). I interviewed Itai in northern Israel, 12 July 1994, where he made similar claims.
7. See also Shavit 1991.
8. Former Col. Eytan, interview by author, Israeli West Bank settlement, 22 June 1994.
9. Efraim, interview by author, Tel Aviv, fall 1992 and 27 June 1994.
10. Former Col. Avi, interview by author, Tel Aviv, 27 June 1994.
11. Other attempts at finding less-than-lethal options include resort to tear gas, plastic and rubber coated bullets, and gravel-spewing cannon.
12. The order was included in the Central Command directive Noam Halichot, dated January 1988. A copy was shown to me by Col. Avi during our interview.
13. Former Col. Yiftach, interview by author, Tel Aviv, 11 July 1994.
14. Amir, interview by author, Tel Aviv, 11 July 1994.
15. Lieutenant Dan, interview by author, Jerusalem suburb, 13 July 1994.
16. Omri, interview by author, June 1993. See more details of the interview in Middle East Watch (1994): 305–309.
17. International law limited the use of detention without trial, and human rights activists protested its use.
18. Israeli military spokesperson Captain Avital Margalit, author telephone interview, 10 July 1993.
19. Letter to Human Rights Watch from Lieutenant Colonel Moshe Fogel, Israeli military spokesperson's office, 24 February 1994.
20. Orlee, author interview, Tel Aviv, July 1994.
21. Shimon, author interview, Jerusalem, 26 July 1994.
22. Lieutenant Aviad, interview by author, Jerusalem, June 1992. See also Middle East Watch (1993): 168–169.

References

Abed, George T. (ed). 1988. *The Palestinian Economy: Studies in Development under Prolonged Occupation.* London: Routledge.

Al-Haq. 1989. *Punishing a Nation: Human Rights Violations during the Palestinian Uprising, December 1987–1988.* Ramallah: Al-Haq.

Amnesty International. 1988. *Israel and the Occupied Territories: Excessive Force-Beatings to Maintain Law and Order*. London: Amnesty International.

———. 1991. *Israel and the Occupied Territories: The Military Justice System in the Occupied Territories—Detention, Interrogation and Trial Procedures.* London: Amnesty International.

———. 1994. *Israel and the Occupied Territories: Torture and Ill-Treatment of Political Detainees.* London: Amnesty International.

Arnon, Arie et al. 1997. *The Palestinian Economy: Between Imposed Integration and Voluntary Separation.* Leiden, The Netherlands: Brill.

Aronson, Geoffrey. 1990. *Israel, Palestinians, and the Intifada: Creating Facts on the West Bank.* London: Kegan Paul International.

Balbus, Isaac D. 1973. *The Dialectics of Legal Repression.* New York: Russell Sage Foundation.

Beitler, Ruth Margolies. 1995. "The Intifada: Palestinian Adaptation to Israeli Counterinsurgency Tactics." *Terrorism and Political Violence* 7: 49–73.

Benvinisti, Eyal. 1989. *Legal Dualism: The Absorption of the Occupied Territories into Israel.* Jerusalem: West Bank Data Project.

Benvinisti, Meron. 1984. *The West Bank Data Project: A Survey of Israel's Policies.* Washington, DC: American Enterprise Institute for Public Policy Research

Bittner, Egon. 1970. *The Functions of the Police in Modern Society.* Chevy Chase, MD: National Institute of Mental Health.

Bourdieu, Pierre and Loic Wacquant. 1992. *Invitation to Reflexive Sociology.* Chicago: University of Chicago Press.

———. 1993. *Outline of a Theory of Practice.* New York: Cambridge University Press.

Bryant, Clifton D. (ed.). 1974. *Deviant Behavior: Occupational and Organizational Bases.* Chicago: Rand McNally.

B'Tselem. 1989. *Annual Report 1989: Violations of Human Rights in the Territories.* Jerusalem: B'Tselem.

———. 1991. *The Interrogation of Palestinians during the Intifada: Ill-Treatment, "Moderate Physical Pressure", or Torture?* Jerusalem: B'Tselem.

Burawoy, Micahel. 1979. *Manufacturing Consent.* Chicago: University of Chicago Press.

Cawthra, Gavin. 1994. *Policing South Africa: The Sap and the Transition from Apartheid.* London: Zed Books.

Christie, Nils. 1994. *Crime Control as Industry.* London: Routledge.

Cohen, Stanley. 1985. *Visions of Social Control.* New York: Polity Press.

Crank, John P. and Robert Langworthy. 1992. "An Institutional Perspective on Policing." *Journal of Criminal Law and Criminology* 83(2): 338–363.

Della Porta, Donatella and Herbert Reiter. 1996. "Social Movements and the State: Thoughts on the Policing of Protest." In *Comparative Perspectives on Social Movements.* Edited by Doug McAdam, John D. McCarthy, and Mayer N. Zald. New York: Cambridge University Press.

———. 1998. *Policing Protest: The Control of Mass Demonstrations in Western Democracies.* Minneapolis: University of Minnesota Press.

DiMaggio, Paul J. and Walter W. Powell. 1991. "Introduction." 1–40 in *The New Institutionalism in Organizational Analysis.* Edited by Walter W. Powell and Paul J. DiMaggio. Chicago: Chicago University Press.

Ermann, M. David and Richard J. Lundman (eds.). 1996. *Corporate and Governmental Deviance: Problems of Organizational Behavior in Contemporary Society.* New York: Oxford University Press.

Feagin, Joe R. and Harlan Hahn. 1973. *Ghetto Revolts: The Politics of Violence in American Cities.* New York: MacMillan.

Foucault, Michel. 1979. *Discipline and Punish: The Birth of the Prison.* New York: Vintage.

Friedman, Thomas L. 1990. *From Beirut to Jerusalem.* New York: Anchor Books.

Gazit, Shlomo. 1995. *The Carrot and the Stick: Israel's Policy in Judea and Samaria, 1967–1968.* Washington, DC: B'nai B'rith Books.

Giddens, Anthony. 1987. *The Nation State and Violence.* Berkeley: University of California Press.

Gouldner, Alvin W. 1954. *Patterns of Industrial Bureaucracy.* New York: Free Press.

Hajjar, Lisa. 1999. "Cause Lawyering in Transnational Perspective: National Conflict and Human Rights in Israel-Palestine." *Law and Society Review* 37 (3): 473–504

———. Forthcoming. *Authority, Resistance, and the Law: A Study of the Israeli Military Court System in the West Bank and Gaza.* Berkeley: University of California Press.

Judah, Tim. 2000. *Kosovo: War and Revenge.* New Haven, CT: Yale University Press.

Keck, Margaret E. and Kathryn Sikkink. 1998. *Activists beyond Borders.* Ithaca, NY: Cornell University Press.

Landau, Moshe. 1987. *Report of the Commission of Inquiry in the Matter of Interrogation Methods of the General Security Services regarding Hostile Terrorist Activity, First Part.* Jerusalem: State of Israel.

Lawyers Committee for Human Rights. 1993. *A Continuing Cause for Concern: The Military Justice System of the Israeli-Occupied Territories.* New York: Lawyers Committee for Human Rights.

Lieven, Anatol. 1999. *Chechnya: Tombstone of Russian Power.* New Haven, CT: Yale University Press.

Lustick, Ian S. 1988. *For the Land and for the Lord: Jewish Fundamentalism in Israel.* New York: Council on Foreign Relations.

———. 1993a. *Unsettled States, Disputed Lands: Britain and Ireland, France and Algeria, Israel and the West Bank-Gaza.* Ithaca, NY: Cornell University Press.

———. 1993b. "Writing the Intifada: Collective Action in the Occupied Territories." *World Politics* 45: 560–94.

Mann, Michael. 1984. "The Autonomous Power of the State: Its Origins, Mechanisms, and Results." *Archives Europeanes de Sociologie* 25: 185–213.

———. 1993. *Sources of Social Power, Vol. 2: The Rise of Classes and Nation-States, 1760–1914.* New York: Cambridge University Press.

Manning, Peter K. 1977. *Police Work: The Social Organization of Policing.* Cambridge, MA: MIT Press.

———. 1980. *The Narc's Game.* Cambridge, MA: MIT Press.

Marx, Gary T. 1972. "Civil Disorders and Agents of Social Control." In *Muckraking Sociology.* Edited by Gary T. Marx. New Brunswick, N.J.: Transaction Books.

———. 1980. "The New Police Undercover Work." *Urban Life and Culture* 8: 399–446.

Middle East Watch. 1991. *Prison Conditions in Israel and the Occupied Territories.* New York: Human Rights Watch.

———. 1993. *License to Kill: Israeli Undercover Operations against "Wanted" and Masked Palestinians.* New York: Human Rights Watch.

———. 1994. *Torture and Ill-Treatment: Israel's Interrogation of Palestinians from the Occupied Territories.* New York: Human Rights Watch.

McDowal, David. 1989. *Palestine and Israel: The Uprising and Beyond.* Berkeley: University of California Press.

Meyer, John W. and Brian Rowan. 1991. "Institutionalized Organizations: Formal Structure as Myth and Ceremony." In *The New Institutionalism in Organizational Analysis.* Edited by Walter W. Powell and Paul J. DiMaggio. Chicago: University of Chicago Press.

Nasser, Jamal R. and Roger Heacock. 1990. *Intifada: Palestine at the Crossroads.* New York: Praeger.

Peretz, Don. 1991. *Intifada.* Boulder, CO: Westview Press.

Powell, Walter W. and Paul J. DiMaggio. 1991. *The New Institutionalism in Organizational Analysis.* Chicago: Chicago University Press.

Punch, Maurice. 1985. *Conduct Unbecoming: The Social Construction of Police Deviance and Control.* London: Tavistock.

Risse, Thomas, Stephen C. Ropp, and Kathryn Sikkink (eds.). 1999. *The Power of Human Rights: International Norms and Domestic Change.* New York: Cambridge University Press.

Ron, James. 2003. *Frontiers and Ghettos: The Institutional Underpinning of State Violence in Bosnia and Palestine.* Berkeley: University of California Press.

Roy, Donald. 1955. "Efficiency and the 'Fix': Informal Intergroup Relations in a Piece-Work Shop." *American Journal of Sociology* 60: 255–266.

Schiff, Zeev and Ehud Ya'ari. 1989. *Intifada.* New York: Simon & Schuster.

Semyonov, Moshe and Noah Lewin-Epstein. 1987. *Hewers of Wood and Drawers of Water: Noncitizen Arabs in the Israeli Labor Market.* Ithaca, NY: ILR Press.

Shalev, Aryeh. 1991. *Intifada: Causes and Effects.* Boulder, CO: Westview Press.

Shavit, Ari. 1991. "On Gaza Beach." *New York Review of Books* 38: 3–6. (July 18).

Shehadeh, Raja. 1989. *Occupier's Law: Israel and the West Bank.* Washington, DC: Institute for Palestine Studies.

State of Israel. Ministry of Foreign Affairs. 1990. *Israel's Measures in the Territories and Human Rights.* New York: Israeli Consulate.

Straschnov, Amnon. 1994. *Justice Under Fire: The Military Legal System During the Intifada.* Tel Aviv: Yediot Aharanot.

Tilly, Charles. 1978. *From Mobilization to Revolution.* Reading, MA: Addison-Welsley.

Yahav, David. 1993. *Israel, the "Intifada" and the Rule of Law.* Jerusalem: Israel Ministry of Defense Publications.

Zamir, Yitzhak. 1989. "Human Rights and Security of the State." *Mishpatim* 19 (1): 17–19.

CHAPTER 18

The Space between Laws Revisited*

CORPORATE CRIME IN A TRANSNATIONAL CONTEXT

Raymond J. Michalowski and Ronald C. Kramer

The Problem

Transnational corporations (TNCs)[1] engage in a wide variety of socially injurious actions (Barnet and Muller 1974; Simon and Eitzen 1986). These harmful corporate acts raise a number of important sociological questions. One central set of questions concerns the conceptualization of these corporate harms for purposes of criminological research. Some have argued that the concept of crime only refers to criminal convictions and violations of criminal law (Shapiro 1983; Tappan 1947). Others have proposed that the traditional definition of crime be expanded to include violations of civil and regulatory law, as well as violations of specific criminal statutes (Blum-West and Carter 1983; Clinard and Yeager 1980; Schrager and Short 1978; Sutherland 1940, 1961). Still others claim that state definitions are too restrictive and unduly influenced by corporate power, and therefore, should be abandoned in favor of broader social definitions of crime based on concepts such as human rights (Michalowski 1985; Schwendinger and Schwendinger 1970; Tift and Sullivan 1980).

The increasing global reach of modern transnational corporations aggravates the difficulties of arriving at a satisfactory conception of corporate crime. TNCs at times engage in practices which, while they would be illegal in their home nations, are legal in a number of host nations. The ability of TNCs to significantly influence the legal climate in host countries further renders the particular laws of these nations an inadequate basis for the study of corporate crime.

The purpose of this paper is to contribute to the resolution of this conceptual dilemma. The first step, following Blum-West and Carter (1983), is to separate the study of the organization and causation of socially injurious corporate actions from a consideration of the sociopolitical definition of these acts. This distinction creates two "research domains" (Blum-West and Carter 1983:552) or "paradigms" (Kramer 1985:472). In the first paradigm, the objective is to explain (and eventually control) the harmful corporate

*Editors' note: This is a revised version of an article earlier published in *Social Problems* 34(1):34–53.

actions of TNCs. The definitional paradigm is concerned with understanding the historical and political–economic development of laws and control practices concerning harmful corporate behavior. This corporate criminalization process has been studied almost exclusively at the level of the nation state. We intend to show, however, that the spread of TNCs requires that we broaden this focus in two ways: by examining the social construction of political labels in the international arena as exemplified by the development of United Nations codes of conduct for TNCs, and by incorporating what we term "analogous social injuries" within the scope of corporate crime research.

TNCs and the Relocation of Corporate Hazards

From the late 1960s onward, direct foreign investment by TNCs has expanded dramatically (United Nations 1978:36). In the twenty years from 1960 to 1980, the revenues of TNCs grew tenfold—from $199 billion to $2,155 billion—with U.S.-based corporations accounting for 50 percent of this growth (Cavanaugh and Clairmonte 1983:17). By 1983, the worldwide profits of TNCs had reached a record high of $130 billion (*Multinational Monitor* 1984:11). This internationalization of corporate activity necessitates an expansion of corporate crime research beyond its dominant focus on offenses by corporations in their home countries.[2] While, on a dollar basis, foreign investment in developed nations exceeds that in developing nations (Hamilton 1983:3; United Nations 1978:40; U.S. Department of Commerce 1984:8), it is transnational investments in developing nations that pose the greatest likelihood of injurious corporate activity, and which raise the most perplexing problems for the definition and study of corporate crime. There are several reasons for this.

First, the most significant change in patterns of foreign investment since the Second World War has been the increased location of TNC industrial facilities in developing nations (United Nations 1978: 40–41). Three-fourths of all U.S. companies with sales over $100 million had manufacturing facilities in other countries by 1975 (United Nations 1978:222). By 1977, developing nations had surpassed developed ones in dollar value as locations for manufacturing by U.S. industries (U.S. Department of Commerce 1981:159). Reimportation of overseas assembly by U.S. companies increased fivefold between 1969 and 1983, and in the textiles and electronics industries more than half of all sales by U.S. corporations are assembled abroad (Grunwald and Flamm 1985:12–13). As TNCs export their industrial operations to developing nations, many of the hazards of industrial production and the associated possibilities for corporate crime are relocated from developed to developing countries. Moreover, as the fatal poisoning of over 2,000 residents of Bhopal, India, dramatized (Hazarka 1984:1) the settlement patterns, population density, and limited disaster preparedness of developing nations means that, when problems do occur, the human and environmental costs are likely to be greater than those resulting from similar incidents in developed countries.

Second, the growth in consumer exports to the Third World, as well as the increased local production of consumer goods by TNCs in developing nations, has generated significant consumer safety issues. Differences in marketing practices of TNCs in home versus host nations, variations in the provision of information by TNCs regarding product hazards, and variations in cultural practices regarding product usage has led to unnecessary injury, illness, and death for Third-World consumers of TNC products (Mattelart 1983).

Finally, in comparison to developed nations, developing ones frequently have fewer legal controls over workplace, environmental, and consumer hazards of industrial production (Braithwaite 1984; Castleman 1975; Dewar 1978; Vieira 1985). Therefore, the potential for corporations to behave in socially injurious ways in developing nations is greater. For these reasons the growing internationalization of business points to developing nations as a significant emerging arena for injurious corporate activity. *(Authors' note: The impetus toward the internationalization of corporate business described above expanded dramatically since this articles was first published in 1987.)*

TNCs and Corporate Deviance in the Global South

In recent years corporate injuries to workers, physical environments, and consumers in the developing nations have revealed significant problems with respect to the control of corporate activity in these countries. We will explore each of these arenas, with particular attention to injurious actions that arise in the space between legal systems-actions which were prohibited in home nations, but permissible in the host countries where they occurred.

Working Conditions. According to the International Labor Organization (1985:55), industrial employees of TNCs in the developing nations "suffer from more safety and health problems than similar workers in the developed countries." While in some cases TNC manufacturing operations provide better working conditions than locally-owned factories (Blake 1980; International Labor Organization 1985:44), it is the comparison between TNC operations in home and host countries, rather than between TNCs and local conditions, that raises the most perplexing questions for the study of injurious corporate activities.

In a number of instances, occupational safety and other working conditions in TNC operations have been found to fall below those mandated by law in more developed countries. The exposure of workers in electronics assembly plants to levels of carcinogens and other toxic materials beyond those allowed in the United States, for instance, has been one of the consequences of the exportation of this "clean" industry (LaDou 1984). In the more obviously "dirty" industries such as asbestos and chemical production, foreign workers in U.S. subsidiaries have been knowingly exposed to toxic levels that were illegal in the United States. In 1972 for instance, Amatax, a Pennsylvania asbestos yarn mill, moved its entire production facility to Mexico to take advantage of the fact that Mexico had no laws regulating exposure of workers to asbestos fibers. Similarly, in 1974 Raybestos-Manhattan acquired 47 percent of the stock in a Venezuelan asbestos plant in order to take advantage of Venezuelan law which allows higher levels of airborne asbestos fibers than does the Occupational Safety and Health Administration (OSHA) in the United States (Castleman 1979). In a similar case,

Arasco, the only U.S. producer of arsenic, moved its entire operation to Mexico when OSHA lowered the U.S. limit for exposure to airborne arsenic from 500 to 4 micrograms per cubic meter of air (Mattelart 1983:102). In the electronics industry, Third, World workers in U.S. subsidiaries have been found to suffer eye strain and eye failure due to constant peering into microscopes without the benefit of rest breaks on company time required by law in the United States (Fuentes and Ehrenreich 1983:6).

Industrial operations by some TNCs in developing host countries have used wage and employment practices prohibited in their more-developed home nations. In some cases, work is contracted out to home workers at piece rates which require a level of effort comparable to nineteenth-century garment sweatshops. These contract workers enjoy no benefits in terms of holidays, health insurance, sick leave, or pensions—all of which are legally protected worker rights in more developed nations (Fernandez-Kelly 1983:118). Likewise, the practice of using extended "probationary" periods during which workers (often women) are paid a lower wage rate and then "laid off" just prior to completing this period would be illegal under U.S. labor law (Fuentes and Ehrenreich 1983:9–10). As Fernandez-Kelly (1983:114) found in the "maquiladora" factories of the Mexican border, a variation on this theme is to bring prospective workers in for a "test" during which they spend a day or more sewing garments for no pay in the hopes of possible employment. Ong (1983:431) suggested that employers also deliberately keep workers on "temporary status" for prolonged periods to minimize the risks of unionization. This strategy makes it easy to fire workers who organize or join unions.

Environmental Pollution. In some instances TNCs have located and/or relocated high-pollution industries in less-developed countries in order to escape the pollution control costs imposed by environmental protection laws in their home nation. Blake and Walters (1976:159) have suggested that TNCs "will be very sensitive to disparities among various [national] pollution control standards which affect production costs and competitiveness in international trade" as a means of expanding or protecting profit margins. This sensitivity reflects the fact that pollution control costs in the United States are higher than in most other countries (Pearson and Pryor 1978:170). Robert Strauss (1978:451), President Carter's chief trade negotiator, warned in 1978 of a developing "pattern of flight" as U.S. companies are drawn to developing nations with less costly pollution control laws. Castleman (1978:3) similarly noted that "hazard export is emerging as a driving force in new plant investment in many hazardous and polluting industries." In some cases entire industries involving highly toxic substances such as asbestos, arsenic, mercury, and benzidene dyes have been exported to rapidly developing nations such as Korea, Mexico, Brazil, India, and Ireland (Leonard and Duerksen 1981:55). Even computer and electronics assembly, once thought to be "clean" industries, often expose the environments of developing nations to a wide range of toxic substances that are more closely regulated in the United States (Cultural Survival 1981; *Dollars and Sense* 1984:6).

There has been some disagreement over whether pollution control costs actually play a significant role in location decisions (Flamm 1985:77–78; Randall 1977:v). However, the debate over the relative importance of pollution regulations for location decisions speaks only to the question of corporate motivation, not the consequences of corporate behavior. Even if they are not actively seeking "pollution havens," in many developing nations TNCs remain legally free to expose the water, air, soil, and bodies of workers to hazardous substances at rates higher than those allowed in their home countries (Vieira 1985).

In addition to the problem of pollutants produced by TNCs operating in host countries, hazardous waste produced in developed countries has begun to find its way into developing nations. Some TNCs have sought to avoid the costs of mandated controls on hazardous waste storage in their home nation by transporting wastes to countries which have few or no legal controls on hazardous waste disposal (Centre on Transnational Corporations 1985:59–60). In these cases, the TNCs involved are clearly acting to circumvent laws in their home nations rather than simply being passive beneficiaries of the difference in laws between home and host nations.

Consumer Safety. According to the UN Centre on Transnational Corporations (1985:58), "the one issue that has generated the greatest emotion and controversy in the 1980s regarding transnational corporations . . . is the exportation of products deemed to be harmful to health and the environment." Several cases in recent years have dramatized the kinds of hazards consumers in developing nations face when TNCs circumvent product regulations in their home nations.

The export of children's sleepwear treated with the carcinogenic flame retardant Tris, after the sale of such sleepwear was banned in the United States, was one of the first cases of knowingly exported consumer hazards to receive widespread attention (*New York Times* 1978:26). In the late 1970s, A.A. Robbins company arranged (with the help of United States Agency for International Development) for the distribution of the Dalkon Shield intrauterine device in a number of developing countries. This overseas market was sought after Robbins already knew that the Shield was responsible for 20,000 cases of serious uterine infection, that it had resulted in several thousand hysterectomies among its users in the United States, and that the product would soon be banned at home (Dowie and Johnston 1976; Mintz 1985). In another case, Parke-Davis, a U.S. pharmaceutical company, successfully promoted the drug chloramphenicol on a nonprescription basis in thirty-nine nations but provided no information concerning its dangerous and sometimes fatal side effects—even though the drug was banned in the United States and Japan (Mattelart 1983:100–101).

In addition to the hazards posed by consumer goods, it is estimated that annually 375,000 people in the developing world are poisoned—10,000 of them fatally—through the misuse of industrial and agricultural chemicals exported from developed nations. There is evidence that much of this poisoning results from the failure of TNCs to provide adequate information on the hazards of their chemical exports, and from their active attempts to find markets for chemicals banned at home (Bull 1982; Weir and Schapiro 1981). In one such instance, paraquat was successfully promoted for use as a marijuana defoliant in Latin America after it was banned for that purpose in the United States (del Olmo 1986).

Most of the injurious corporate actions described above were not prosecutable as crimes or regulatory violations in the nations where they occurred. Yet to omit them from the study of corporate crime on this basis does little to help us understand either the organization and causation of injurious actions by TNCs, nor does it call our attention to the definitional process by which these actions have been rendered legal in host nations. This is particularly important because, as we argue below, the special capacity of TNCs to influence regulatory climates in host nations is itself a crucial factor in keeping injurious actions by TNCs from being defined and prosecuted as crimes.

TNCs and Regulatory Climates

TNCs can influence the regulatory climates of developing host nations in indirect and direct ways. The logic of development in the free-market world necessitates that developing nations create hospitable environments for foreign investment. Simply by holding the economic keys to development, TNCs indirectly limit the political willingness of many nations in the global South to establish strict controls over potential or actual corporate harms. At times, TNCs have also exerted pressure in more direct ways to forestall legislation contrary to their interests, and in some cases to subvert political movements or leaders deemed inhospitable to these interests.

Indirect Influences. Free-market nations that have followed a capitalist model of development based on foreign investment find their potentials for economic growth closely linked to their ability to attract TNCs. Domestic elites in developing nations frequently find that general economic improvement and political stability in their countries, as well as their own economic and political success, depend upon creating hospitable environments for investment by foreign TNCs. The deepening need for inflows of foreign investment in developing nations, and the pressures this places on domestic policy, have been extensively examined by a number of dependency theorists.[3] The specific regulatory adaptations that have been made to attract TNCs have been examined in less detail. However, there is some evidence that the existence of a profitable double-standard which allows TNCs in host countries to do what they are prohibited from doing in their home nations is related to the desire of host nations to attract foreign investment by creating regulatory climates hospitable to the interests of TNCs. Controls over the rights of workers to organize for improved wage and working conditions is a good example of how TNCs become the passive beneficiaries of policies designed to attract them.

Labor costs represent one of the most significant factors in the location of manufacturing plants (Burns 1984). For instance, assembly line workers in the United States often earn per hour what assembly workers in developing nations earn per day (Fuentes and Ehrenreich 1983:5). The desire to take advantage of significant differentials in national wage rates has been the primary stimulus for the location of TNC production facilities in developing nations (Grunwald and Flamm 1985:3–9). Leaders in some developing nations have used limitations on worker rights as a strategy to convince foreign companies that, if they do invest, they will enjoy continued benefits from lower labor costs. The belief that this will attract foreign investment has received a degree of confirmation from investment practices of TNCs.[4]

For instance, investment in Thailand by the U.S. semiconductor industry did not reach significant levels until 1977, the year following the installment of a military junta that ended a period of democratic government characterized by strikes and other movements for increased popular control over the economy. Similarly, foreign direct investment in semiconductor assembly in the Philippines entered a period of significant growth beginning in 1972, the year Marcos declared martial law (Grunwald and Flamm 1985:77). In 1982, Marcos continued his efforts to create a profitable climate for these TNCs by issuing a decree banning all strikes in the semiconductor industry as being against the "national interest" (O'Connor and Wong 1983).

Another strategy used in developing nations to attract foreign investment at the expense of labor rights protected by law in developed nations is the creation of economic free zones (EFZs). In some cases these zones are little more than labor camps "where trade unions, strikes and freedom of movement are severely limited, if not forbidden" (Fuentes and Eherenrich 1983:5). For example, advertisements for Caribbean Assemblies, a set of EFZs in Haiti and the Dominican Republic, promise foreign companies a "large, urbanized, low-cost labour pool" and "strict anti-strike and labour regulation laws" (Matellart 1983:106). A promotional document by the South Korea government offers this description of its EFZ: The zone has the characteristics of a reserved territory in which the application of laws or relevant regulations is partially or totally suppressed or attenuated. . . . It is an industrial territory in which a series of fiscal and legal privileges are offered to firms of foreign capital (Medawar 1979:62). Promotional materials such as these make it abundantly clear that limitations on the rights of workers are part of the bait that EFZs offer to foreign companies in some developing nations.

Lim (1983:14) has argued that locating TNC industrial facilities in developing countries is beneficial to workers in nations where unemployment and poverty are widespread, even if the rights of these workers are minimal. This perspective is manifest in the June 6, 1980 issue of *Fortune* magazine which asks, "Even though the people working on Castle and Cooke's banana plantations in Central America earn far less than the U.S. minimum wage, would they be better off if the company decided to move elsewhere?" However, the economic conditions that TNCs "improve" cannot be analyzed in isolation from the economic domination by foreign business interests that characterizes the history of many developing host nations. Moreover, while the factory work provided by TNCs may improve the incomes of some workers, the dependent development it represents generally results in a distorted economy, a split labor market, and exploitation of women who are the primary laborers in these factories (Amin 1974; Frank 1975; Nash 1979; Wallerstein 1979).

Direct Influences. In addition to benefiting indirectly from restrictive labor climates, TNCs have at times actively used their economic power in developing nations to limit the rights of workers to organize into unions to protect and promote their interests. In some case, TNCs have used the threat of the runaway shop to discipline workers. For instance, when the Malaysian government indicated in 1983 that it might permit the formation of a union for electronics workers, U.S. electronics firms in Malaysia indicated that, should this happen, they would consider moving their plants elsewhere. Subsequently, the Malaysian government shelved its plans for the union. In a similar case, Control Data Corporation closed a Korean production facility in response to attempts by workers to unionize (O'Connor and Wong 1983). Such threats or actual incidents of capital flight can have a chilling effect on both labor activism and governmental support for labor rights in nations dependent on foreign investment.

Besides attempts to influence specific policies, some TNCs have used their economic and political power to alter the flow of broader political developments in host nations. In some cases, TNCs have contributed to the elimination of progressive or socialist governments in favor of conservative ones. Activities of this sort are often based on clandestine contacts between TNCs and governments in home or host nations. As a result, relatively little is known about their scope or frequency. However, cases such as ITT's contributions to the overthrow of Salvador Allende in Chile, the participation of United Fruit, International Railways of Central America, and Electric Bond and Share in bringing about the downfall of the progressive leader, Jacobs Arbenz, in Guatemala in 1954, and the financial support provided by some U.S. corporations to the Nicaraguan contras in their efforts to overthrow the socialist government there, indicate that TNCs are not above using their power to alter the flow of political events in developing nations (Bonner 1983; Jensen 1973; Kenworthy 1973; LaFeber 1984; Langley 1985:142–43).

Overall, the combined effects of economic pressures to create a favorable climate for foreign investment, and support by transnational corporate capital for governments or political parties hospitable to their interests, can create a set of structural/legal conditions which allow TNCs in host countries to do what would be illegal in their country of origin. We are not suggesting that all TNCs have taken full advantage of these favorable structural/legal climates, or that all actively engage in efforts to create these climates. We are suggesting that researchers must always be sensitive to the political influences of TNCs on the political climates and legal frameworks of host countries. Accordingly, the laws governing corporate behavior in these nations are a poor starting place for setting the scope of inquiry into corporate offenses in a transnational context.

The UN Code as International Politics

Multinational business is now international politics. Multinational companies are increasingly being forced to operate in a framework determined, not just by the laws of supply and demand, but also by a proliferating set of intergovernmental arrangements specifically targeted at them (Robinson 1983:3). Recognizing that the political power of TNC's is truly transnational and hegemonic, and that independent national action is limited, many developing countries have come to believe that the only way they can confront and control TNCs is through the creation of international standards. The two most far-reaching attempts to establish worldwide standards for TNCs have been undertaken by the United Nations with the Draft Codes of Conduct on Transnational Corporations and the Guidelines for Consumer Protection. The development of these codes is a unique and highly relevant empirical case for a theoretical examination of the political definition of harmful corporate actions.

The code development process has brought into sharp focus the fundamental differences of perspectives and interests between developed and developing nations, and between free-market and centrally planned economies. Charles Lindblom (1977:ix) succinctly characterized these differences when he wrote: "Aside from the difference between despotic and libertarian government, the greatest distinction between one government and another is in the degree to which market replaces government or government replaces market." The formation of the draft codes for consumer protection and transnational corporate behavior at the United Nations represents an attempt to replace markets with politics. Through the political mechanisms of the United Nations, less developed nations are seeking to implement rules governing the market relations between TNCs, and the citizens and governments of the nations in which they operate.

Historical Background. The politicalization of international business regulation has its roots in the Cold War. As capitalist and communist nations struggled to gain client states in the global South, developing nations obtained a degree of leverage over their industrialized suitors (Robinson 1983). The developing nations, many of them recently enfranchised, made claims concerning the harmful practices of TNCs and called for a New Economic Order and some form of binding control over TNCs. Throughout the 1970s, the United Nations led the crusade for a comprehensive, legally binding international code of conduct for TNCs. This crusade was led by the developing "non-aligned" nations known as the Group of 77, international trade unions, and some small, developed nations, such as the Scandinavian states (Hamilton 1983). In response to a 1974 report, "The Impact of Multinational Corporations on Development and International Relations" the United Nations Economic and Social Council (ECOSOC) created a Commission and Centre on Transnational Corporations. The Commission was charged with the job of drawing up a set of recommendations which could become the basis for a Code of Conduct dealing with TNCs.

The Commission on Transnational Corporations Met Annually from 1975 into the 1980s

However, the economic downturn associated with the 1974 oil crisis and the corresponding increased need of the developing nations for foreign investment tempered the Commission's work (Robinson 1983). Additionally, several other international groups issued separate guidelines for TNCs. In 1976, the Organisation for Economic Co-operation and Development (OECD) established its Guidelines for Multinational Enterprises, and, one year later, the International Labor Organization (ILO) approved the Declaration of Principles Concerning Multinational Enterprises and Social Policy. In 1980, the United Nations Conference on Trade and Development (UNCTAD) promulgated the Set of Multilaterally Agreed Equitable Principles and Rules for the Control of Restrictive Business Practices, and the World Health Organization's (WHO) International Code of Marketing of Breast Milk Substitutes was passed by the General Assembly in May of 1981.

The ILO, UNCTAD, and WHO guidelines were all sectoral codes developed in response to particular problems. The OECD guidelines were a preemptive Western strike calculated to "sensitize firms to their social, economic, and political responsibilities and, to make the rest of the world aware, and in particular the LDCs negotiating a UN code of conduct for transnational corporations, that the West is not prepared to see excessive constraints imposed on their major creators of wealth" (Robinson

1983:7). Despite the passage of these international guidelines, or perhaps because of them, the UN code of conduct for transnationals remained in draft form.

(Authors' note: The impetus behind the creation of a general and binding Code of Conduct for all transnationals lost much of its political momentum with the unraveling of the Communist bloc in the late 1980s. The "new world order" that ensued was a far cry from the New Economic Order sought by the Group of 77 that had originally spearheaded the Code of Conduct for Transnationals. Freed from the need to mollify potential clients in global South as part of their struggle with the Soviet Union, OECD nations began to pursue a new strategy for global business relations—neo-liberalism. A central tenet of the neo-liberal strategy is that market forces, not political ones, should determine the operations of the global capitalist economy, including the behaviors of the TNCs that are its primary engines of growth. In this environment the Code languished and the Centre on Transnational Corporations ceased to be a visible presence in the United Nations. Meanwhile, the political-economic battleground between developed and developing nations shifted to the General Agreement on Trade and Tariffs, and later to its successor, the highly controversial World Trade Organization.)

Conclusion: Emergent Definitions and the Study of Corporate Crime

Despite the apparent triumph of neoliberal ideology and practices, the struggle to create a Code of Conduct on Transnational Corporations as well as the other more limited codes that were passed during that period, was not inconsequential. It helped create both a worldwide language and set of general principles against which the conduct of TNCs can be measured. This returns us to our central argument that the laws of nation-states represent theoretically problematic frameworks for the study of corporate harm.

In 1980s some criminologists responded to challenge of deriving behavioral standards independent of law by employing various concepts of "human rights" in constructing alternative definitions of crime (Schwendinger and Schwendinger 1970; Tift and Sullivan 1980). These "human rights" definitions of crime have, in turn, been criticized for the potential that researchers who utilize them are substituting their personal moral concerns for those contained in law. Shapiro (1983:307) argues that corporate crime research that extends beyond the boundaries of what is illegal is inevitably flawed because it is suffused with the "moral agenda" of the observer. John Braithwaite (1985:18) suggests that "those who choose to study violations of 'politically defined human rights,' or some other imaginative definition of deviance, will deserve to be ignored for indulging their personal moralities in a social science that has no relevance for those who do not share that morality."

The most common rejoinder to criticisms of this type is that relying upon law to define the boundaries of criminological inquiry is no less suffused with moral choice than is choosing definitions based on concepts of human rights. While this observation may be accurate, it provides no particular guidance regarding why we should choose one particular framework for defining the parameters of study over another. We suggest that the first step is to replace the positivist concept of "bias free" research with the critical theory concept of reflexivity. Within a positivist conception of social science bias is a preference for one set of social outcomes over another that should be avoided in favor of a value-free science in which the researcher holds no preferences with respect to the world in view. Within this framework social scientists who reveal preferences for some social agendas over others are suspected of allowing commitment to compromise reason (Habermas 1974:264). In contrast to positivist notions of value-free science, critical reflexivity is a mode of analysis that recognizes the existence of moral preferences in ourselves and others, and demands that we analyze the nature and construction of those preferences so that they contribute to rather than detract from our ability to achieve purposeful understanding. We suggest this approach offers a theoretically grounded way to expand the study of corporate crime beyond the limits of the law while incorporating a positive commitment to the reduction of social injuries by corporate actors.

Critical reflexivity according to Habermas (1973:15) develops when we examine what he terms taken-for-granted "validity claims" and "redeem or dismiss them on the basis of arguments." Law is a socially and historically legitimated authority system. The validity claims implicit in laws have been established through the historical interplay of economic and political forces. If law is used to define the scope of corporate crime studies, the possibilities for a critical understanding of social injuries by TNCs is negated by the unanalyzed history of power relations imbedded in the laws that govern them. Moreover, alternative discourses which problematize the validity claims of established laws are also omitted from inquiry, sealing researchers inside the boundaries of existing law. We can avoid this epistemological straightjacket through a consciously critical use of less restricted discourses that question the validity claim that law is a nonproblematic starting point for the study of crime.

Where injurious actions by TNCs violate existing national laws there is little conceptual difficulty in placing them within the purview of corporate crime studies. However, only by moving beyond national laws can we begin to study transgressions that arise in the space between national legal systems. The study of injurious actions by global corporations requires a conception of transgression developed through discourse at the same level, and which is capable of adapting to changing forms of injurious corporate action. With this in mind we offer the following expanded framework for the study of corporate crime in a global context: *Corporate transgressions by TNCs comprise any action in pursuit of corporate goals which violates national laws, international codes developed within the UN, bi- or multilateral treaties, or which results in social injury analogous in severity and source to that caused by corporate violations of law or international codes.*

We have substituted the term "transgressions" for "crime" because it avoids the semantic and theoretical problem that arises when corporate actions that are not specifically prohibited under law are labeled as crime, while retaining the sense of wrongfulness associated with "crime." The more radical component of our definition is the inclusion of injuries that are analogous in severity and source to acts which violate national laws, treaties, or international conventions, but which do not presently violate any positive law. We have three reasons for doing this.

First, doing so is an honest statement of our preferences for the reduction of avoidable, injurious actions committed by TNCs against humans and/or the environment, whether or not they fall under legal control.

Second, this inclusion advances both the behavioral and the definitional research domains in the study of corporate wrongdoing.[5] New forms of injurious corporate actions can emerge more swiftly than laws or standards aimed at controlling them, as demonstrated by cases such as Nestlé's marketing of breast milk substitutes (Chetley 1979), or the spread of genetic engineering beyond the reach of existing national laws (Schneider 1986a, 1986b). Including analogous forms of corporate injuries under the umbrella of corporate crime studies authorizes researchers to study behaviors which are not (yet) prohibited, but whose origins and consequences may be identical to those which are prohibited by law.

Finally, comparative analyses of the processes whereby some corporate injuries are socially and politically constructed as illegal while others are defined as the unavoidable consequences of necessary economic practices is central to any mature inquiry into the meaning to corporate behavior. Excluding injurious activities from study because they have not been politically defined as transgressive closes off this crucial area of inquiry, and renders criminologists of corporate crime blind to all injuries except those the state authorizes them to see.

Notes

1. There is an ideological distinction and a political debate over whether the term "transnational corporation" or the designation "multinational corporation" should be used to name the modern world-company. The term trans/national implies an entity with an existence above and beyond the states in which it operates, while "multinational" suggests only a business with operations in more than one country. We use the term "transnational" here for two reasons. First, we agree with the theory that the corporations in question have an existence that transcends the nation-state. Second, the designation "transnational corporations" or "TNCs" is consistent with the majority of the United Nations documents regarding business across borders.

2. For example, see Clinard (1946); Clinard and Yeager (1980); Coleman (1980), Conklin (1977); Denzin (1977); and Edelhertz (1970); Farberman (1975); Geis (1967); Hartung (1950); Leonard and Weber (1970); Shapiro (1984); Sutherland (1940, 1961); Vaughn (1983).

3. See, in particular, Amin (1974); Chase-Dunn (1978); Frank (1975); Sunkle (1973); and Wallerstein (1979).

4. From the point of view of TNCs there are limits to the attractiveness of strict controls over labor rights. Regimes that are so repressive as to loose legitimacy can incite significant popular unrest. If the regime is not able to control this opposition, the resulting political instability can negate the benefits of a strong antilabor government (International Labour Organization 1985:62–63). The 1986 ouster of Marcos, a strong antilabor dictator, from the Philippines is a case in point.

5. For elaborated discussions of analogous social injury see Kramer (1985) and Michalowski (1985).

References

Amin, Samir. 1974. *Accumulation on a World Scale.* New York: Monthly Review Press.

Barnet, Richard J. and Ronald E. Muller. 1974. *Global Reach: The Power of the Multinational Corporations.* New York: Simon & Schuster.

Blake, David H. and Robert S. Walters. 1976. *The Politics of Global Economic Relations.* Englewood Cliffs, NJ: Prentice Hall.

Blake, Michael. 1980. *A Case Study on Women in Industry.* Bangkok: Asian and Pacific Centre for Women and Development.

Blum-West, Steve and Timothy J. Carter. 1983. "Bringing white-collar crime back in: an examination of crimes and torts." *Social Problems* 30:545–54.

Bonner, Raymond. 1983. "U.S. ties to anti-Sandinistas are reported to be extensive." *New York Times* April 3:A1.

Braithwaite, John. 1984. *Corporate Crime in the Pharmaceutical Industry.* London: Routledge and Kegan Paul.

———. 1985. "White collar crime." *Annual Review of Sociology* 11:1–25.

Bull, David. 1982. *A Growing Problem: Pesticides and the Third World Poor.* Oxford: Oxfam.

Burns, James J. 1984. "International siting priorities for a high technology firm." *Industrial Development* 153:11.

Castleman, Barry. 1975. "The flight of hazardous industries to unregulating countries." Report issued by the Maryland Public Interest Group.

———. 1978. "How we export dangerous industries." *Business and Society Review* 27:7–14.

———. 1979. "The export of hazardous factories to developing nations." *International Journal of Health Services* 9:569–606.

Cavanaugh, John and Fredrick F. Clairmonte. 1983. "From corporations to conglomerates." *Multinational Monitor* 4 (January): 16, 20.

Centre on Transnational Corporations. 1985. *Environmental Aspects of the Activities of Transnational Corporations: A Survey.* New York: Centre on Transnational Corporations.

Chase-Dunn, Christopher K. 1978. "Core-periphery relations: the effects of core competition." Pp.159–76 in Barbara H. Kaplan (ed.), *Social Change in the Capitalist World Economy.* Beverly Hills, CA: Sage.

Chetley, A. 1979. *The Baby Killer Scandal.* London: War on Want.

Clinard, Marshall B. 1946. "The black market." *American Sociological Review* 11:250–70.

Clinard, Marshall B. and Peter Yeager. 1980. *Corporate Crime.* New York: Free Press.

Coleman, James W. 1983. *The Criminal Elite: The Sociology of White Collar Crime.* New York: St. Martin's Press.

Conklin, John. 1977. *Illegal but Not Criminal: Business Crime in America.* Englewood Cliffs, NJ: Prentice Hall.

Cultural Survival. 1982. "Poisons in the Third World." *Cultural Survival* 6 (Winter): 3–10

del Olmo, Rosa. 1986. "Aerobiologia y drogas." Paper presented at the Fourth Annual Latin American Conference of Critical Criminology, Havana.

Denzin, Norman K. 1977. "Notes on the criminogenic hypothesis: A case study of the liquor industry." *American Sociological Review* 42:905–20.

Dewar, Helen. 1978. "Study cites firms flight to Third World to avoid safeguards." *Washington Post,* June 30:A2.

Dollars and Sense. 1984. "High tech and health." *Dollars and Sense* 99 (September):6–7.

Dowie, Mark and Tracy Johnston. 1976. "A case of corporate malpractice." *Mother Jones* 2 (November):36–50

Edelhertz, Herbert. 1970. *The Nature, Impact and Prosecution of White Collar Crime.* Washington, DC: National Institute of Law Enforcement and Criminal Justice.

Farberman, Harvey. 1975. "A criminogenic market structure: The automobile industry." *Sociological Quarterly* 16:438–57.

Fernandez-Kelly, Maria. 1983. *For We Are Sold, I and My People.* Albany: State University of New York Press.

Flamm, Kenneth. 1985. "The semiconductor industry." Pp. 38–138 in Joseph Grunwald and Kenneth Flamm (eds.), *The Global Factory.* Washington, DC: Brookings Institution.

Fortune. 1980. "The corporation haters." *Fortune* 101 (June, 16):126–36.

Frank, Andre Gunder. 1975. *On Capitalist Underdevelopment.* London: Oxford University Press.

Fuentes, Annette and Barbara Ehrenreich. 1983. "The new factory girls." *Multinational Monitor* 4 (August):5–10.

Geis, Gilbert. 1967. "The heavy electrical equipment antitrust cases of 1961." In Marshall B. Clinard and Richard Quinney (eds.), *Criminal Behavior Systems.* New York: Holt, Rinehart and Winston.

Grunwald, Joseph and Kenneth Flamm. 1985. *The Global Factory.* Washington, DC: Brookings Institution.

Habermas, Jürgen. 1973. *Legitimation Crisis.* Boston: Beacon Press.

———. 1974. *Theory and Practice.* London: Heinemann.

Hamilton, Geoffrey. 1983. "International codes of conduct for multinationals." *Multinational Business* 12 (Summer):1–10.

Hartung, Frank E. 1950. "White collar offenses in the wholesale meat industry." *American Journal of Sociology* 56:22–34.

Hazarka, Sanjoy. 1984. "Gas leak in India said to kill 410." *New York Times* December 4:A1.

International Labour Organization. 1985. *Women Workers in Multinational Enterprises in Developing Countries.* Geneva: International Labour Office.

Jensen, Michael.1973. "Allende target of proposals." *New York Times* June 22:A1.

Kenworthy, E.W 1973. "Senate group finds ITT and U.S. at fault on Chile." *New York Times* June 22:A1.

Kramer, Ronald C. 1985. "Defining the concept of crime: A humanistic perspective." *Journal of Sociology and Social Welfare* 12:469–87.

LaDou, James. 1984. "The not-so-clean business of making chips." *Technology Review* 87:23–36.

LaFeber, Walter. 1984. *Inevitable Revolutions: The United States in Central America.* New York: Norton.

Langley, Lester P. 1985. *Central America: The Real Stakes.* New York: Crown.

Leonard, H. Jeffrey and Christopher J. Duerksen. 1981. "Environmental regulation and the location of industry: an international perspective." *Columbia Journal of World Business* 15:55–68.

Leonard, William N. and Marvin Weber. 1970. "Automakers and dealers: a study of criminogenic market forces." *Law and Society Review* 4:407–24.

Lim, Linda. 1983. "Are multinationals the problem? No." *Multinational Monitor* 4 (August):15.

Lindblom, Charles. 1977. *Politics and Markets.* New York: Basic Books.

Mattelart, Armand. 1983. *Transnationals and the Third World.* South Hadley, MA: Bergin and Garvey.

Medawar, Charles. 1979. *Insult or Injury.* London: Social Audit.

Michaloswki, Raymond. 1985. *Order, Law, and Crime.* New York: Random House.

Mintz, Morton. 1985. *At Any Cost: Corporate Greed, Women and the Dalkon Shield.* New York: Pantheon.

Multinational Monitor. 1984. "Profits climb; foreign investments fall." *Multinational Monitor* 5 (January):11.

Nash, June. 1979. "Men, women and the international division of labor." Paper presented at the annual meetings of the Latin American Studies Association, Philadelphia.

New York Times. 1978. "Safety panel votes to ban export of Tris sleepwear." *New York Times*, May 7:A26.

O'Connor, David and Chia Siew Wong. 1983. "Are multinationals the problem? Yes." *Multinational Monitor* 4 (August):16.

Ong, A. 1983. "Global industries and Malay peasants in peninsular Malaysia." Pp. 426–39 in June Nash and M. P. Fernandez-Kelly (eds.), *Women, Men and the International Division of Labor*. Albany: State University of New York Press.

Pearson, Charles and Anthony Pryor, 1978. *Environment: North and South*. New York: Wiley Interscience.

Randall, Kenneth. 1977. "Forward." Pp. i-ix in James R. Basche, Jr. (ed.), *Production Costs, Trends and Outlook: A Study of International Business Experience*. New York: Conference Board.

Robinson, John. 1983. *Multinationals and Political Control*. New York: St. Martin's Press.

Schrager, Laura Shill and James F. Short, Jr. 1978. "Toward a sociology of organizational crime." *Social Problems* 25:407–19.

Schneider, Keith. 1986a. "Argentina protests use of live vaccine by scientists of U.S." *New York Times* November 11:A1.

———. 1986b. "Second gene-altered vaccine tested outside the U.S." *New York Times* November 13:A28.

Schwendinger, Herman and Julia Schwendinger. 1970. "Defenders of order or guardians of human rights." *Issues in Criminology* 5:123–57.

Shapiro, Susan. 1983. "The New moral entrepreneurs: corporate crime crusaders." *Contemporary Sociology* 12:304–307.

———. 1984. *Wayward Capitalists*. New Haven, CT: Yale University Press.

Simon, David R. and D. Stanley Eitzen. 1986. *Elite Deviance*, 2nd ed. Boston: Allyn & Bacon.

Strauss, Robert. 1978. Interview. *Environment Reporter* 9 (July):451.

Sunkle, O. 1973. "Transnational capital and national disintegration in Latin America." *Social and Economic Studies* 22:132–71.

Sutherland, Edwin H. 1940. "White collar criminality." *American Sociological Review* 5:1–12.

———. 1961. *White Collar Crime*. New York: Holt, Rinehart and Winston.

Tappan, Paul. 1947. "Who is the criminal?" *American Sociological Review* 12:96–102.

Tift, Larry and Donald Sullivan. 1980. *The Struggle To Be Human: Crime, Criminology, and Anarchism*. Sanday, Orkney U.K.: Cinfuegos Press.

United Nations. 1978. *Transnational Corporations in World Development*. New York: UN Commission on Transnational Corporations.

U.S. Department of Commerce. 1981. *U.S. Direct Investment Abroad*. Washington, DC: U.S. Government Printing Office.

———. 1984. *U.S. Direct Investment Abroad*. Washington, DC: U.S. Government Printing Office.

Vaughn, Diane. 1983. *Controlling Unlawful Organizational Behavior*. Chicago: University of Chicago Press.

Vieira, Anna Da Soledade. 1985. *Environmental Information in Developing Nations: Politics and Policies*. Westport, CT: Greenwood Press.

Wallerstein, Immanuel. 1979. *The Capitalist World-Economy*. New York: Cambridge University Press.

Part VI

EPILOGUE: A MODEL FOR FURTHER INVESTIGATION

CHAPTER 19

The State, the Legal Order, and Social Problems

William J. Chambliss

To unravel the complex relationship between the law and social problems, it is useful to begin by distinguishing between the "state" and the "government." We must approach this territory with caution, however, because of the tendency to reify abstract constructs like the state, society, social order, and law. For all of their importance to the modern world, the twin concepts of "state" and "government" only abstractly depict social reality. Save for the positions, roles, obligations, and actions of people engaged in day-to-day activities, "state" and "government" have no concrete content. This does not imply that an analysis of the role of the state and government in creating and responding to social problems must focus solely on the motivations and decisions of individuals. On the contrary, it is necessary to employ the abstract concepts in order to deal systematically with the social relations and social forces that circumscribe the *constraints and resources that* determine the actions of state and government officials. In that process, we will come to understand that these abstractions are no more or less than useful ways of carving up the world so we can better understand it.

The word "state" should be used to mean the bureaucracies embodying those rules, positions, and statuses that career employees occupy. The "government" should be used to encompass the people whose roles, positions, and statuses have been achieved through election, coercion, or political appointment. Thus, in this vocabulary, the position of attorney general in the U.S. forms part of government (the attorney general is appointed by the president and Congress), but the bureaucracy the Attorney General manages forms part of the state apparatus. Every president from Franklin Roosevelt to George W. Bush has complained about the difficulties a president faces in getting action out of "the bureaucracy." Paradoxically, and dialectically, however, every president and every elected and appointed government official has in many important ways influenced that immovable bureaucracy while at the same time being influenced by it. The state does not constitute an abstract, noncorporeal entity with a life of its own. It consists of living, breathing, and very human people occupying roles. To explain the behavior of the state as a collectivity we must explain how these various role occupants behave and why they behave the way they do.

The Instrumentalist Perspective

In the past, a paradigm that stressed the importance of a "ruling class" was very influential. Harkening back to the works of Marx, Pareto, Michels, Machiavelli, and Weber, social scientists conceived society as an arena within which some few people gained economic and political dominance and became all-powerful. This paradigm is usually referred to as "instrumentalist theory" (Gold, Lo, and Wright 1975).

Applied to law and the legal order the instrumentalist theory sees the state and government as the handmaiden of the ruling class. It takes as its starting point the observation by Karl Marx that "the modern state is but a committee for managing the common affairs of the whole bourgeoisie." The "ruling class" consists primarily of those who own and manage the productive forces (financial and industrial sectors) of the economy.

Following instrumentalist's articulation, a vast array of research conducted in Europe, the United States, Africa, Latin America, and Asia generated findings that seemed to validate it. Throughout the world researchers discovered the existence of cohesive, socially connected elites who communicated with one another and unduly influenced government and state decisions including the law.[1]

Miliband (1974) found that since 1889, the largest single occupational group in the cabinets of the United States consisted of businessmen, and that since 1961 businessmen have accounted for over 60 percent of each cabinet (whether the Republican or Democratic party was in power). Domhoff (1967, 1979) demonstrated empirically how those who sit at the top of the financial and manufacturing sector of the economy attend the same schools, marry into one another's families, vacation at the same resorts, and appoint one another to high-level decision-making positions at all sectors of American life including the media, government, state, business, banking, education, and even "commissions" designed to advise government on long-range internal and foreign policy. But not all the facts fit that theory quite so comfortably. The instrumentalist theory could not account for significant segments of law creation. An entire body of U.S. legislation in the 1930s known as the "New Deal" was strenuously opposed by a large number of powerful capitalists (Mollenkopf 1975). The National Labor Relations Act (1935) stands out as legislation that contradicts instrumentalist theory because the regulations tended to favor workers (Domhoff 1979:119).

INTRA-RULING-CLASS CONFLICT

For the state and government simply to reflect ruling-class interests, then the members of the ruling class must have a high degree of agreement over what their interests demand. Scholars in the structuralist school, particularly Offe (1974) and Poulantzas (1969), offered data demonstrating intra-ruling-class conflict, thus attacking instrumentalist theory. Capitalists' interests do not always mesh. Even Domhoff (1979:119), who convincingly demonstrates the degree to which the capitalist class shares a common consciousness, recognizes a split between "ultraconservatives" and the "moderates."

Theoretical objections to instrumentalist theory also suggest limits to its utility. Poulantzas (1973) points out that instrumentalist theory resembles an empirical generalization rather than an explanation.[2] That a ruling class has influence and control over state and government, even if empirically true, does not give us a very profound explanation of the relationship, why it exists at this historical period in capitalist development, and how it will change. Instrumentalist theory ultimately becomes a static interpretation suggesting a deterministic view of history and society.

Structuralist Theory

The structuralist paradigm retains some of the strengths of the instrumentalist view but attempts to overcome its shortcomings. This "structuralist" perspective argues that a "structural, 'objective relation' between the state and capitalism . . . guarantees that the state, within the limits imposed by inherent contradictions and the class struggle, will operate in the long-term interests of the capitalist class, independent of the direct participation of individual capitalists" (Calavita 1980:37; Whitt 1979; Chambliss 1979).

A state that in the long run perpetuates the interests of the capitalist class has a primary function: the promotion of "capital accumulation" (O'Connor 1973). The state must protect the process of capital accumulation for several reasons: (1) for its survival the state depends, via taxation, on the production of surplus capital, (2) political stability depends on economic stability, and (3) the survival of the state and the interests of the capitalist coincide in that both depend of maintaining the viability of the economy and political stability.

"Capital accumulation" and political stability depend on the promotion of what is variously called "political integration" (Friendland, Piven, and Alford 1978), "social harmony" (O'Connor 1973) and the "cohesion of the social formation" (Poultanzas 1973). These different phrasings all argue that the state and government must legitimize the existing political and economic arrangements in order to provide a stable climate in which capitalist accumulation and production can continue. The system can continue only if it convinces people of its worth, i.e., that it serves their interests. To serve the interests of the ruling class, the state must create the belief among the people that it is serving the interests of everyone. Thus it follows that the law, as the principal mechanism for legitimizing existing social relations, will reflect the needs of *both* capitalist accumulation and predictability (Sumner 1979). In this view, capitalists do not directly control the state and the legal order. On the contrary, the state and the legal order best fulfil their function as legitimizers when they appear to function as value neutral organs fairly and impartially representing the interests of everyone.

Structuralist theory suggests a dynamic relationship that gives a central place to the state's relative autonomy and to attempts to resolve the problems of structure inherent in capitalist democracies. Some problems, however, remain. First, most structuralist theory tends to reify the "state," giving it a life of its own, independent of the people who occupy various positions and make decisions (Cashmore 1978; Piven and Cloward 1977). Second, some structuralists overemphasize the stability of the system.

Althusser, particularly, seems to suggest that the state inevitably handles conflict so as to ensure the survival of capitalism (Althusser 1971; Poultanzas, 1969).[3] Capitalist societies, however, frequently experience rebellions and riots and on occasion, they are overthrown and replaced with a system not at all to the liking of the capitalist class. These facts evidence an underlying tension that the capitalist state has historically been unable to eliminate. Third, other structuralists err in the other direction: O'Connor, for example, stresses the constancy of crisis in the capitalist state. His notion of capitalism's underlying instability seems belied by capitalism's survival for the past three hundred years. As Alan Wolfe points out:

> To accept the cleverness and omnipotence of the rulers as the major explanation of public policy is to ignore the political struggles that went into its creation. Liberal democracy did not, as with some omniscient Zeus, spring full-born out of the forehead of the ruling class. (1977:6)

Nor does the "state" omnisciently respond to maintain "the system" by serving the long-range interests of capitalists.

Finally, structuralist theory distinguishes itself from instrumentalist theory by stressing that the state has "relative" autonomy. That central insight lacks content, however, unless one can specify the mechanisms of ruling-class control over the state and how these mechanisms lead not to complete but to "relative" control and hence to "relative" autonomy of the state.

Neither instrumentalist nor structuralist theory adequately capture the relationship between the state and the legal order on the one hand and society on the other. I propose instead a dialectical theory that resolves the problems with instrumentalist theory as well as the central shortcomings of structuralist theory identified above.

Dialectical Theory

The observed paradox: Instrumentalist theory predicts that the state will respond to the demands of the capitalist class. Structuralist theory agrees that it will do so "in the long run," but that from time to time it will take steps seemingly against those demands—that is the capitalist state has "relative autonomy." The structuralist perspective matches reality in a gross way. As soon as one examines the various ways in which the capitalist state acts inconsistently with the interests of the ruling class, however, it appears that the relative autonomy of the state varies radically in different sectors of the policy and with respect to different issues. For example, if a bank clerk embezzles a hundred thousand dollars, the various minions of the law will act in the capitalist's interests to punish the offender and, if possible, return the money to the bank. If, however, the bank as employer too blatantly discriminates against a black in promotions and pay raises, the same minions may discipline the employer in the interests of her black workers. The same Congress that enacts a budget that favours the rich and powerful (by returning to large corporations billions of dollars in taxes) simultaneously enacts legislation to increase unemployment benefits and provide health insurance for displaced workers. How can this extraordinarily variable "relative autonomy" be explained?

To understand these apparent contradictory acts we should begin not with the instrumentalist and structuralist theory reliance on macro phenomena, but with an analysis of what it means when we say that the state acts with "relative autonomy." To accomplish this we must first define what we mean by "state" and "government."

State and Government

Structuralist theory is inclined to reify the concepts "state" and "government" while also failing to distinguish between them. Treating the state and government as a single entity with its own life and consciousness neglects the interstices of the state and government to discover why it acts autonomously in some instances and consensually in others. Neither "state" nor "government" have clear, unambiguous, universally accepted meanings. These concepts suggest bureaucratic organization, centralization of power, decision making by elected and appointed officials, career public servants who make decisions about public policy regarding what are perceived as "social problems," such things as war making, poverty, discrimination, international affairs, budgeting, social control, law enforcement, and a host more. Earlier I defined the state as the collectivity embodying those rules, positions, and statuses that career employees occupy. The "government" on the other hand consists of the people whose roles, positions, and statuses have been achieved through election, coercion, or political appointment. Neither the state nor the government constitute abstract, noncorporeal entities with lives of their own. They consist, rather, of living, breathing, and very human people occupying roles. To explain the behavior of the state and government as collectivities we must explain how the various role occupants behave and why they behave the way they do.

These definitions also suggest that government and state can and will act in contrary ways. Nowhere does this appear more forcefully than in countries in which a revolutionary government takes office either by way of election or after armed struggle. It appears in the sharp contrast between the motivations and ideologies of members of the government and members of the state. In innumerable instances, South Africa for example with the end of apartheid, a negotiated settlement and subsequent elections brought the revolutionaries into the seats of government power. The civil service bureaucrats, the judges, and the senior police and army officers, however, did not change from the previous regime—so at least initially you have a government dominated by Blacks but controlled by White state officials (bureaucrats) from the previous era.

The contrast between government and state in the circumstances of a country like South Africa appears even more significant if we examine the norms defining the several roles included in the two. Immediately after a revolutionary change in government, the officials of the state continue to follow the norms laid down for their positions. That requires them to enforce the laws, as they then exist. Until the government changes the law, the old laws continue. Thus, the members of the state find themselves enforcing the old laws.

In Zimbabwe, when the revolutionaries took power the new black majority-rule government that replaced the old white minority-rule government espoused a socialist and nonracialist policy to replace the old government's capitalist and racialist policy. The first law of every revolutionary government, however, requires that the old laws continue until changed. Those old laws directed the members of the state—the civil servants, the police, the judges, and so forth—to implement and enforce the property, contract, and even the racialist laws the new government vowed to overthrow. The new revolutionary socialist, non-racialist government found itself presiding over a capitalist, racialist state.

Every decision-making structure has institutions and procedures that prescribe a wide range of potential decisions. A capitalist state has procedures and institutions that make it difficult or impossible to generate decisions appropriate for a socialist polity (and, of course, vice versa). Thus the new socialist, nonracialist government officials of Zimbabwe found themselves in command of a state that not only enforced capitalist, racialist laws, but whose decision-making procedures stubbornly resisted efforts to generate new laws to change the state. Yet until the government radically changes the state's decision-making machinery, and ultimately the legal order itself, the role occupants in the state structure would necessarily continue to act as they had before the revolution-and that would transpire whatever the color of the role occupant's skin. Today, the Zimbabwe government is still struggling to change the laws, especially those governing the ownership of land they inherited when they took power. If by "revolution" one means a change in the government, plainly a change in government does not itself amount to a revolution.

"RELATIVE AUTONOMY"

When the state or the government as a bureaucratic collectivity makes a decision, it appears that the decision emerges from the actions of a few defined actors. A new law emerges from the decisions of a few hundred bureaucrats, congresspeople, their aides, and the president. A court, its clerks, and its sheriffs enforce a contract to collect a debt. A zoning commission gives a steel mill a variance from the zoning laws that will allow the mill to do serious damage to the quality of life of the poor who live in the neighborhood. A lone investigator in the Pure Food and Drug Administration singlehandedly fights a giant drug company to prevent the marketing in Africa of Thalidomide, a drug that produced sadly deformed babies in the rest of the world. In each of these cases, in a sense the government or the state made a decision. In fact, specific actors made the decision in the name of the government or the state.

"State autonomy" therefore means the power of government or state officials to carry out the interests of the state or government as a defined interest group, or to carry out the interests of other classes or strata in society. How, then, do these role occupants behave in light of the structure of social, political, and economic relations in which they are embedded?

Role occupants act by making choices within an arena of *constraints and resources* that includes rules and sanctions of the law. To understand the amount of autonomy that a particular member of the state or government has, we must examine his or her particular arena of choice including, of course, the legal constraints and resources, but also including all of the other factors that we have earlier suggested bear upon the choice.

The Dialectic of the State, the Government, and the Legal Order

The very process of solving one set of social problems gives rise to new conflicts and creates new forces that will create new and equally devastating problems (see Figure 19.1). Some structuralists argue that the capitalist state intervenes in the process of capital accumulation in order to ensure the survival of the capitalist political economy. Even in the short run, that alone does not exhaust the essential function of the capitalist state. Capital accumulation requires maximization of profit. The conditions that provide for and result from the maximization of profit in many cases threatens the stability upon which the political and economic systems depend. For example, one solution to the "falling rate of profits" in capitalist societies is to increase the profits of capital by reducing the cost of labor (Appelbaum 1978). Some U.S. capitalists demand unrestricted immigration in order to create a cheap work force. This policy promotes (1) economic instabilities, such as strikes and high labor force turnover (Calavita 1980), (2) social instabilities, in the form of nativist uprisings and protests (as was the case in 1830s and the white supremacist movements today), and (3) political instabilities, by way of the electoral process and by way of radical political movements.

At any particular time, conflicts arise from the contradiction between some industrialists' need for profit maximization and the need for legitimacy (Silver 2003). For example, during the 1830s, 1840s, and 1850s, some industries demanded an increasing supply of cheaper labor (Calavita 1980). These demands led to riots and protests defined

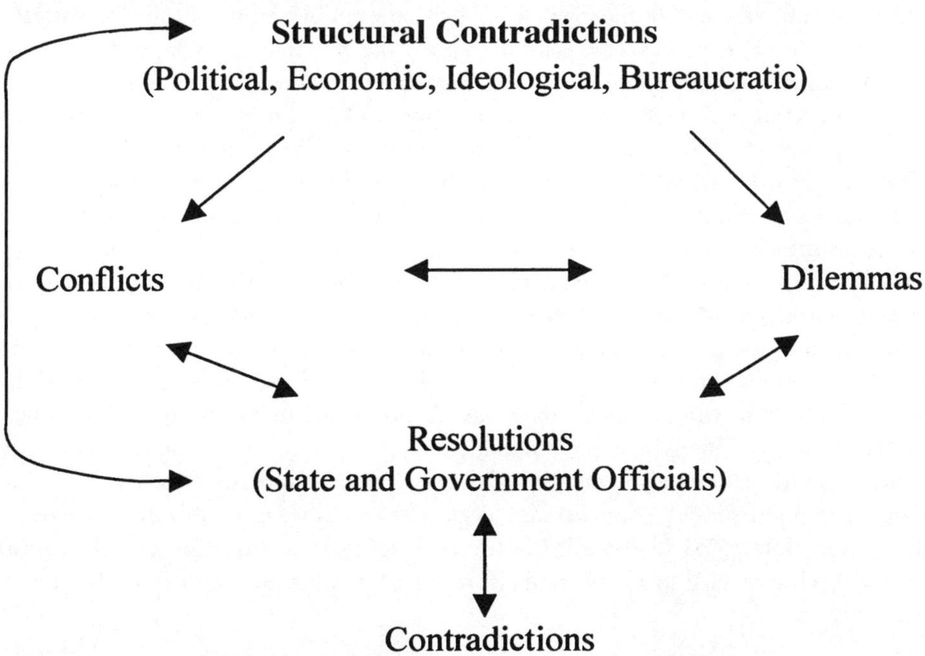

Figure 19.1. Structural Contradictions

by government and state officials as crimes, against the influx of cheap labor (which in the 1850s was primarily Irish Catholic labor). This influx of cheap labor led other capitalists to demand the cutting off of easy immigration, for the riots threatened their capital accumulation.

This suggests the following general proposition: The state's efforts to protect and enhance capital accumulation must lead to protest by the working class; these protests threaten system instability; thus, measures to further capital accumulation for the benefit of one fraction of the capitalist class leads to protest by another fraction of the capitalist class whom the particular measures do not benefit. Organized protest thus sometimes achieves substantial results. To the extent that protesting groups can, until the state satisfies their demands, threaten the normal working of the political economy, they may force significant change. In American history as elsewhere, examples are legion: the women's movement forcing the government to give them the vote, the civil rights movement achieving an end to legal segregation, and the antiwar movement creating an atmosphere conducive to ending the Viet Nam War.

What is often overlooked, however, is the degree to which the government and state officials *anticipate* the potential for riots and rebellions among the lower classes and act to preempt it. The fact that law enforcement agencies in all societies devote the vast majority of their resources to controlling the "dangerous classes" while allocating only a miniscule portion of their resources to the control of white collar crime, corruption, or police malfeasance proves the point.

At times, a delicate balance is struck between allowing some fractions of the lower classes to engage in unruly "mob behavior" and even riots when it serves to oppress other fractions of the lower classes deemed more dangerous. Such was the case in the United States soon after the end of the Civil War when state and government officials, with the support of the white ruling class, institutionalized the lynching of black people.

Between 1882 and 1944, 3,417 black people were lynched throughout the former confederate states (Curriden and Phillips 1999). Their "crimes," sometimes "proved" in court, sometimes not, ranged from murder to insulting a white person. The dialectical nature of lawmaking and the role of the ruling class were apparent from the outset of this "vigilante justice." Slavery was officially abolished in 1863 and the proclamation abolishing it went into effect two years later with the end of the Civil War. The ruling class faced a formidable challenge: if the ideology that legitimized the pursuit of the war by the government (Lincoln and Congress) the ruling class not only would lose slavery as the pillar of its economy, former slaves would quickly move to positions of political power. Blacks made up over one-fourth of the population and in some districts they were a substantial majority. As a result, black legislators were elected in every southern state. From 1870 to 1901, twenty-two African Americans served in the U.S. Congress, while hundreds of others served in state legislatures, on city councils, and as elected and appointed officials throughout the South (Holt 1977). Early political successes sent shock waves through the southern ruling elite and led to a concerted effort to reverse the trend. As a Tennessee newspaper put it:

> Black people may no longer be slaves, but whites must find means to retain control over the coloreds. (Neufeld 2001: 28)

One resolution was found in the response of the white lower classes perceived threat of a free black worker and their willingness to resort to violence to control them:

> The wealthy and powerful, on the one hand, supported and encouraged the mob's desire for speedy "justice." On the other hand, their fear that the lower-class elements that made up the mob would get out of control and threaten larger social stability [i.e., capital accumulation] led them to favor quick execution by the state over lynching as the preferred means of maintaining white supremacy without undermining class rule. (Neufeld 2001: 29)

There were many other ways to control the black population as well including "Jim Crow" laws, poll taxes, literacy requirements to vote, legal discrimination, and segregation, among others. Behind these legal resolutions of the conflicts and dilemmas posed by the threat of black power also was the institutionalization of lynching as a means of social control. The ruling class had to play a delicate balancing act. To assuage their northern conquerors and their overseas clients they could not allow "the mob" to take complete control. On the other hand, winking at lynching enabled them to keep the lower class whites in check by focusing their dissatisfaction on the black population. A criminal court judge in Tennessee captured the dilemma in addressing a lynch mob impatient for retribution:

> I know you want justice and punishment. I do as well. But this is not the way. We have laws we must follow. I have called for a special session of the county grand jury for next Saturday to take up the case. Following an indictment, I will give the criminal trial precedence over all other trials. I hope that before the week's end, the rapist will be convicted, under sentence of death and executed according to law before the setting of Saturday's sun. (Neufeld 2001:30)

The sheriff agreed that allowing the court to settle the case was preferable to a lynching because it gave a greater appearance of legitimacy to the system. Justice is quick enough when it really wants to be. This is not quite so quick as lynching, but it reads better in the statistics. In other words, even truncated, rushed, guilty-until-proven-innocent "justice" provides an element of legitimacy to the system that lynching does not, and is therefore preferable in the eyes of state and government officials.

Legitimacy, Mystification, and Symbolic Law

As Max Weber pointed out, a legal order helps ruling elites to maintain its rule by satisfying the disinherited masses that governance proceeded through general rules, applied equally to everyone without fear or favor. Althusser and his followers argue that the state rules in the interests of the ruling class, but that, paradoxically, it can do so only to the extent that it creates a perception of legitimacy in the eyes of "the people." To manage this, the state must possess some autonomy from the capitalists. In this way Althusser and others account for the disparity between the idea that the "ruling class" controls the state and the empirical fact that the state sometimes passes and enforces laws contrary to ruling-class interests. Althusserian theory argues that even when the state appears to act in ways seemingly incompatible with ruling-class interests, it in fact acts consistently with their interests.

The problem with the Althusserian argument is that it is a tautology. If the state acts to defend capitalist interests, it acts because of capitalist control of the state. If it acts against capital interests, despite appearances, the state still acts in capital interests. A theory that data cannot conceivably contradict, i.e., a nonfalsifiable theory, tells us very little.

In general, the sorts of social control that lead to legal–rational legitimacy, the rule of law, due process, the civilized rationality of judicial process as against the irrationality of rule by a police officer's nightstick govern the lives of the middle class but not the masses. Governments and states use legal–rational legitimacy as a way of disciplining dissident elements of the ruling class, not the working class. For controlling the working class, other methods are more commonplace.

Everywhere, the legal order engages in *mystification*: it shrouds itself in weird rituals, outlandish costumes, and incomprehensible language. Many of these forms arose in other historical contexts for reasons that then seemed valid. Why do they continue to this day? The reason is that many of the forms of mystification serve to persuade both dissident elements of the ruling class and the mass of the population that the law resides so far beyond their understanding that they can only accept it, as E. P. Thompson (1976) showed in his study of eighteenth-century courts and law.

A third technique for persuading both dissident fractions of the ruling class and the mass not to threaten stability lies in the use of *symbolic law*—that is, the enactment of law that seemingly responds to a particular demand, without inducing in its addressees the behavior that it prescribes. For example, despite antitrust law, the United States economy remains largely controlled by monopolistic enterprises. Antitrust law constitutes the symbol, not the actuality, of antitrust laws and respond "We do what we can." Why agitate for a law against monopolies when on already exists? Thus even where corporations are in clear violation of the antitrust laws, as in the recent case of Microsoft, legal sanctions are minimal to nonexistent. Symbolic law concerns law that the government enacts but that role occupants of the state bureaucracies do not enforce. The formal processes of lawmaking take place in full public view. Enforcement decisions—the sorts of decisions that members of the bureaucracy make—take place mainly in their office, behind closed doors. What the public learns about can affect the legitimacy of government and the state. What the public does not learn about cannot affect legitimacy.

The State, the Government, and Crime: The Case of Corruption

In most countries, numerous laws attempt to regulate behavior such as gambling, using certain drugs, prostitution, usury, and money laundering. Despite the laws, business activities profiting from illegal enterprises are ubiquitous. These illegal goods and services thrive as an economic force because of the corruption of state and government officials at all levels. In the U.S. and most other countries, corruption is widespread and institutionalized (Chambliss 2001; Labrousse and Laniel 2001; Klitgaard 1988). Yet at the same time, exposure of corruption and collusion between state and government officials and purveyors of illegal goods and services is quite commonplace. Both the persistence of these crimes and the enforcement of laws against corruption illustrate the utility of the sociological model of law outlined above and its importance for the study of crime (Chambliss 1978).

The constraints and resources embedded in the structure of policing combined with the rush to capital accumulation of members of the ruling class virtually guarantees widespread corruption. The principal source of the corruption is the tens of billions of dollars a year in profits generated by the underground economy in drugs, gambling, loan sharking, money laundering, and prostitution. The combination of these forces leads to a symbiotic relationship between people who provide the goods and services on the street level (what is usually referred to as members of "organized crime"), members of the elite who manage and organize criminal activities at the managerial level, and law enforcement agencies. State officials in the role of law enforcement from street patrol officers to police chiefs as well as members of the prosecuting attorney's office accept payoffs from people who organize illegal gambling, prostitution, and drug sales and they communicate with selected members of the ruling class to solve problems as they arise.

One of the constraints inherent in the political and economic structure, however, is the fact that not all members of the ruling class are part of the network that organizes illegal activities. While they may benefit from the ongoing relationships in the form of a booming economy spurred by tourism and other economic benefits of the underground economy, they are not themselves directly benefiting. Furthermore, exposure of the prevalence of illegal enterprises undermines the legitimacy of the legal system on which the ruling class depends for regulating business activities, enforcing contracts, and controlling the "dangerous classes."

There is, therefore, a built in instability that can be exploited by competitors for control of the profits from illegal business or, more often, by state or government officials who are not part of the ongoing system of corruption. Members of the political party that is out of power often play a deciding role in setting in motion the wheels that expose corruption in the opposition party. Thus, we see the importance of seeing that the "relative autonomy" of officials of the federal government is proportional to the constraints and resources inherent in the structure of their political, economic, and social relations. They possess the resources to investigate, expose, and punish corruption, but they are constrained by political forces that reflect ruling class interests.

Another major source of exposure in the U.S. derives from the division between local and federal government and state officials. Officials of the federal government (the Federal Bureau of Investigation, for example) who are not part of the local corruption investigate, expose, and prosecute state and government officials for corruption in local government. This resource is used to great advantage by the political party in control of the national government against the opposition party's control of local government. When the Republicans are in control of the federal government and therefore have control over the federal law enforcement bureaucracies, there is inevitably an increase in the exposure of corruption in democratically controlled city and state governments. When the Democrats control the federal government the situation is reversed (Chambliss 1978).

How do these findings fit the theory of the relationship between the state, government, and capital? It is clear from the description that the constraints and resources available to the police, politicians, and businessmen who provide and protect criminal activities such as gambling, drug dealing, and money laundering that these relations inevitably become institutionalized. Those responsible for organizing policing learn early and quickly that in order to *maximize rewards and minimize strains* for the organization it is best not to enforce laws against the vices. Suppose, for example, that a police chief in Seattle, Chicago, New Orleans, or Detroit decided to "clean up the city." Suppose to do this, they meet with their police captains, lieutenants, sergeants, and patrol officers and communicate very clearly to them their decision. They could, within the reach of his office, also provide sanctions if they did not enforce vice laws. They could create, in fact, a situation in which anti-vice laws would be enforced. The chief would not be able to stay in office six weeks.

Business people who depended on tourism and large conventions (restaurants, hotels, motels) not to mention those who profit directly from racketeering would organize a campaign against the chief of police. Law enforcement in all other areas—all those areas where informants who sell narcotics or organize the vices provide crucial information—would suddenly come to a standstill. Furthermore, the enforcement of these laws would clearly not be in the interests of many if not most of the police officers and politicians in the city. Campaign contributions for politicians that had formerly come from the profits from illegal businesses in the city would cease coming and pressure from national and state politicians would be brought to bear on the local political party organizations. The chief would simply have to go (Chambliss 1978).

Conclusion

In this essay, I have argued that a dialectical model of state and government decision-making helps solve problems that are inherent in other theories of law. This model avoids the determinism of instrumental and structural theory, for it admits of struggle between different fractions of the ruling class as well as struggles between the ruling class and nonruling elements of the population, including the poor, racial minorities, women, and the working class, within the framework of capitalism. It explains how both relative stability and periodic change become normal for the capitalist state, depending upon the vigor and determination of the state on the one hand and elements of the population on the other.

A theory of the state and government that tautologically argues that the state in capitalist societies exists to legitimize existing social relations is a weak claim at best. It obscures the fact that the state consists of a complex set of bureaucracies and political managers to which, along with the interests of the ruling class, it responds. The state has some autonomy that manifests itself in a tendency toward increasing control of the economy. The state is not independent from the capitalist class or from class struggle, even in countries such as Sweden or Great Britain where the state has a greater role in the economy that it has in the United States or Canada.

People make choices responding to inherent contradictions in the extant political, economic, and social relations that comprise their reality. Those at the top employ all the means at their disposal to maintain their position. Those at the bottom, struggle against oppression. The contrary interests embedded in the structure generate conflicts, in response to which the government and the state promulgate and enforce laws. The relationship between state, legal order and government becomes complex, interactive, and ever changing. In a word, it is dialectical.

Notes

1. For example, C. Wright Mills, *Power Elite*; G. W. Domhoff, *Who Rules America*? (Englewood Cliffs, NJ: Prentice-Hall, 1967; *The Powers That Be* (New York: Random House, 1978); *The Power Elite and the State: How Policy is Made in America* (New York: deGruyter, 1990); *Power Elites and Organizations* (Newbury Park, CA: Sage, 1987); Miliband, *The State in Capitalist Society* (London: Quartet, 1974); G. Kolko, *The Triumph of Conservatism* (New York: Free Press, 1963), and *Railroads and Regulations* (Princeton, NJ: Princeton University Press, 1965).
2. For a good discussion of this general issue, see Göran Therborn, *What Does the Ruling Class Do When It Rules?: State Apparatuses and State Power under Feudalism, Capitalism and Socialism*, London: Verso, pp. 25–27.
3. See also E. P. Thompson's critique of structuralism in *The Poverty of Theory* (London: Merlin, 1978).

References

Althusser, Louis. 1971. "Ideology and Theological State Apparatus," in *Lenin and Philosophy.* New York: Monthly Review Press.

Appelbaum, Richard P. 1978. "Marx's Theory of the Falling Rate of Profits," *American Sociological Review* 43: 67–80.

Calavita, Kitty. 1980. "A Sociological Analysis of U.S. Immigration Policy," Ph.D. Dissertation, University of Delaware.

Cashmore, E. 1978. "The Social Organization of Canadian Immigration Law," *Canadian Journal of Sociology* 364:409–429.

Chambliss, William J. 1979. "On Lawmaking," *British Journal of Law and Society* 6:149–71.

———. 2001. *Power, Politics, and Crime.* Boulder, CO: Westview.

———. 1978. *On the Take: From Petty Crooks to Presidents.* Bloomington: Indiana University Press.

Curriden, Mark and Leroy Phillips Jr. 1999. *Contempt of Court: The Turn-of-the Century Lynching that Launched a Hundred Years of Federalism.* New York: Faber and Faber.

Domhoff, G. William. 1967. *Who Rules America*? Engelwood Cliffs, NJ: Prentice-Hall.

———. 1979. *The Powers that Be*. New York: Vintage Books.

Friendland, R., F. Piven, and R. Alford. 1978. "Political Conflict, Urban and the Fascist Crisis," in Douglas Ashford, ed., *Public Policy: New Approaches and Methods, Yearbook in Political and Public Policy.* Beverly Hills, CA: Sage.

Gold, David A., Clarence Y. H. Lo, and Erik Olin Wright. 1975. "Recent Developments in Marxist Theories of the Capitalist State," *Monthly Review* 27, 6/5(October and November): 29–43; 36–51.

Holt, Thomas. 1977. *Black over White: Negro Political Leadership in South Carolina during Reconstruction.* Urbana:University of Illinois Press.

Klitgaard, Robert. 1988. *Controlling Corruption.* Berkeley: University of California Press.

Labrousse, Alain and Laurent Laniel. 2001. "The World of Geopolitics of Drugs, 1998/1999." *Crime, Law and Social Change* 31.

Miliband, Ralph. 1974. *The State in Capitalist Society*. London, Quartet.

Mollenkopf, J. 1975. "Theories of the State and Power Structure and Research," *Insurgent Sociologist* 5(1975):245–264.

Neufeld, Russell. 2001. "The Rope and the Law," *The Nation* December 10: 29.

O'Connor, James. 1973. *The Fiscal Crisis of the State.* New York: St Martin's Press.

Offe, Claus. 1974. "Political Authority and Class Structure: An Analysis of Late Capitalist Societies," *International Journal of Social Sciences* 2:73–108.

Poulantzas, Nicos. 1969. "The Problem of the Capitalist State," *New Left Review* 58 (1969):67–78.

Piven, Frances Fox and R. Cloward. 1977. *Poor People's Movements: Why They Succeed, How They Fail.* New York: Pantheon Books.

Silver, Beverly. 2003. *Forces of Labor: Worker's Movements and Globalizations since 1870.* New York: Cambridge University Press.

Sumner, C. 1979. *Reading Ideologies.* London: Academic Press.

Thompson, E. P. 1976. *Whigs and Hunters: The Origin of the Black Act.* New York: Pantheon Books.

Wolfe, Alan. 1977. *The Limits of Legitimacy.* New York: Free Press.

Whitt, Alan A. 1979. "Class-Dialectical Model of Power," *American Sociological Review* 44: 81–99.

Index

About the Contributors

Piers Beirne is professor of criminology and legal studies at the University of Southern Maine.

Michael L. Benson is professor of criminal justice at the University of Cincinnati. He is a former department head and full professor of sociology at the University of Tennessee and has published extensively in the areas of white-collar and corporate crime.

Sherry Cable is associate professor of sociology at the University of Tennessee. Her research interests are in environmental conflicts and environmental justice.

Kitty Calavita is professor of criminology, law, and society at the University of California, Irvine.

William J. Chambliss is professor of sociology at George Washington University and codirector of the Institute on Crime, Justice, and Corrections at George Washington University. He was SSSP president in 1992–1993.

Richard A. Dello Buono is associate professor of sociology at Dominican University and was vice-president of SSSP in 2002–2003.

Evelyn Nakano Glenn was 1998–1999 president of the SSSP and is professor of women's studies and ethnic studies and founding director of the Center for Race and Gender at the University of California, Berkeley.

Valerie Jenness is chair and associate professor in the Department of Criminology, Law, and Society at the University of California, Irvine. She was SSSP vice-president in 2003–2004.

Ronald C. Kramer is professor of sociology and director of the Criminal Justice Program at Western Michigan University.

Gregory M. Maney is assistant professor at Hofstra University. His research interests include social movements; peace, war, and social conflict; race and ethnicity; and development and change.

Holly J. McCammon is associate professor of sociology at Vanderbilt University. Her interests include social movements and their strategies and framing efforts. She is currently comparing U.S. women's activism to change married women's property laws in the nineteenth century with women's attempts to win the right to sit on juries in the twentieth century.

Raymond J. Michalowski is professor of criminology at the Criminal Justice Department of Northern Arizona University.

W. Lawrence Neuman is professor of sociology at the University of Wisconsin, Whitewater.

Dorothy Pawluch is associate professor of sociology at McMaster University.

Stephen Pfohl is professor of sociology at Boston College. He was SSSP president in 1991–1992.

Frances Fox Piven is a distinguished professor of political science and sociology at the City University of New York and an internationally renowned authority on poverty and politics. She was president of the SSSP in 1979–1980.

Jill Quadagno is professor of sociology at Florida State University. She is past president of the American Sociological Association and author of *One Nation, Uninsured* (Oxford University Press).

James Ron is an associate professor of sociology and Canada Research Chair in conflict and human rights at McGill University.

A. Kathryn Stout is associate professor of sociology and director of criminology at Dominican University.

Austin T. Turk is professor of sociology at the University of California, Riverside. He is a Fellow and past president of the American Society of Criminology as well as a former trustee of the Law and Society Association.

Steve Valocchi is associate professor of sociology at Trinity College.

Steve Woolgar is director of research and professor of marketing at the Saïd Business School, University of Oxford. He was formerly professor of sociology and head of the Department of Human Sciences and director of CRICT (Centre for Research into Innovation, Culture and Technology) at Brunel University, and director of the Virtual Society?Programme.

About the Editors

William J. Chambliss is professor of sociology at George Washington University and codirector of the Institute on Crime, Justice, and Corrections at the George Washington University. He is a pioneer in the field of critical criminology and former president of the Society for the Study of Social Problems (SSSP) and the American Society of Criminology (ASC). Chambliss has served as Visiting Professor at prestigious universities in various countries, such as Zambia, Austria, United Kingdom, Sweden, and Norway, and is the author of numerous well-known articles and books, including *Power, Politics and Crime* and *On the Take.*

Richard A. Dello Buono is associate professor of sociology at Dominican University and former SSSP vice-president. He was Visiting Professor of political studies and international relations at the National University of Colombia in Bogotá, Fulbright Professor at the University of Panama, and invited Graduate Studies Professor both at the University of Havana, Cuba, and at the Autonomous University of Zacatecas, Mexico. Dello Buono was previously editor of *Social Problems Forum* and is currently an associate editor of *Critical Sociology.* He is author of "State Repression and Popular Resistance: The Criminalization of Puerto Rican Independentistas" and "Nicaragua's Emerging Model of Popular Justice" (with A. Kathryn Stout).

A. Kathryn Stout is associate professor of sociology and director of criminology at Dominican University. She is active in the Society for the Study of Social Problems, the American Society of Criminology, and various scholar-activist organizations. She has been recognized for her pedagogical expertise and curriculum development in community-based, criminology, and social justice programs. Specializing on the intersection of law and social movements, she is author of "Political Prisoners as an Emergent Contradiction of State Repression" (with Richard A. Dello Buono) and *Sanctuary in the 1980s: The Dialectics of Law and Social Movement Development.*